D040822

Bali
& Lombok

Ryan Ver Berkmoes
Adam Skolnick, Marian Carroll

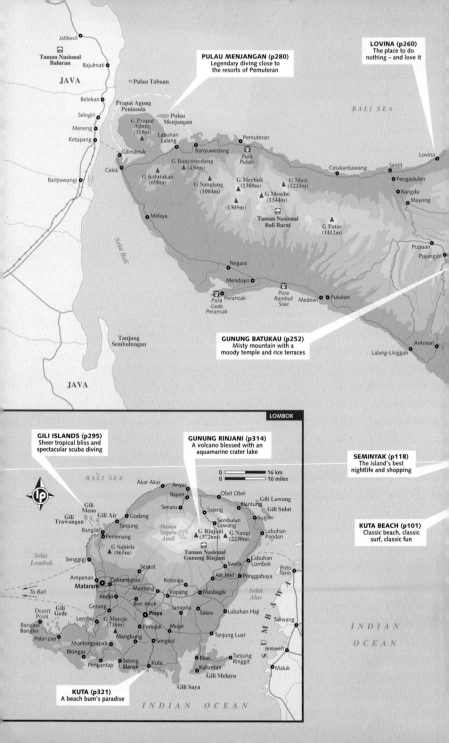

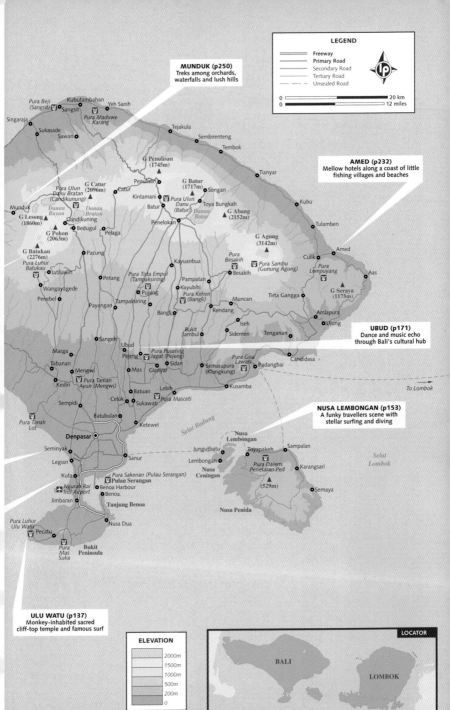

MUNDUK (p250)
Treks among orchards, waterfalls and lush hills

AMED (p232)
Mellow hotels along a coast of little fishing villages and beaches

UBUD (p171)
Dance and music echo through Bali's cultural hub

NUSA LEMBONGAN (p153)
A funky travellers scene with stellar surfing and diving

ULU WATU (p137)
Monkey-inhabited sacred cliff-top temple and famous surf

LEGEND

Freeway
Primary Road
Secondary Road
Tertiary Road
Unsealed Road

0   20 km
0   12 miles

Pura Beji (Sangsit)
Kubutambahan
Yeh Sanih
Sangsit
Pura Maduwe Karang
Singaraja
Sukasade
Sawan
Tejakula
Sembirenteng
Tembok
Tianyar
G Penulisan (1745m)
Penulisan
G Batur (1717m)
Songan
Kubu
G Catur (2096m)
Catur
Kintamani
Pura Ulun Danu Bratan (Candikunung)
Batur
Pura Ulun Danu (Batur)
Toya Bungkah
Tulamben
Munduk
Danau Buyan
Danau Bratan
Candikuning
Penelokan
Danau Batur
G Ahang (2152m)
Amed
G Lesong (1860m)
G Pohon (2063m)
Bedugul
Pelaga
Aas
G Batukau (2276m)
Pacung
Kayuanbua
G Agung (3142m)
Pura Besakih
Culik
Pura Lempuyang
Pura Luhur Batukau
Jatiluwih
Pura Tirta Empul (Tampaksiring)
Besakih
Pura Sambu (Gunung Agung)
G Seraya (1175m)
Petang
Pampatan
Wangayagede
Pujung
Kayubihi
Tirta Gangga
Penebel
Tampaksiring
Pura Kehen (Bangli)
Muncan
Amlapura
Payangan
Bangli
Rendang
Ujung
Sangeh
Bukit Jambul
Iseh
Marga
Ubud
Pura Pusering Jagat (Pejeng)
Sidemen
Tenganan
Candidasa
Tabanan
Peleng
Sidan
Pura Goa Lawah
Mengwi
Mas
Semarapura (Klungkung)
Padangbai
Kediri
Pura Taman Ayun (Mengwi)
Gianyar
Batuan
Lebih
Pura Masceti
Kusamba
Sempidi
Celuk
Sukawati
To Lombok
Batubulan
Ketewel
Selat Badung
Pura Tanah Lot
Denpasar
Nusa Lembongan
Seminyak
Sanur
Jungutbatu
Toyapakeh
Sampalan
Selat Lombok
Legian
Lembongan
Nusa Ceningan
Karangsari
Kuta
Pura Sakenan (Pulau Serangan)
Pura Dalem Penetaran Ped
Ngurah Rai Intl Airport
Pulau Serangan
Benoa Harbour
Semaya
Jimbaran
Benoa
(529m)
Tanjung Benoa
Pura Luhur Ulu Watu
Nusa Dua
Nusa Penida
Pecatu
Pura Mas Suka
Bukit Peninsula

ELEVATION

2000m
1500m
1000m
500m
200m
0

LOCATOR

BALI

LOMBOK

On the Road

RYAN VER BERKMOES
Coordinating Author

When I saw this sign near the market in Gianyar (p208) I thought 'Bone! [Otherwise known as Bona] The centre of basket weaving!' While visions of the beautiful objects you can create with palm leaves danced in my head, I hurried off to the market for some of the famous *babi guling,* the tasty roast pig that's stuffed with lots of garlic and herbs and marinated for hours.

MARIAN CARROLL Entering northern Bali's lush mountains is like visiting another world, with endless views of rice fields rolling into coffee, clove and vanilla plantations. The many treks you can do through this terrain remind you how small you are in the overall scheme of things.

ADAM SKOLNICK After a sensational Astari (p324) breakfast, I buzzed up the coast west of Kuta (p325) in search of white sand and pristine coves, which I found over and over again. This was snapped when the view got so good I just had to stop the bike and take it all in. It kept happening over and over again.

For author biographies, see p384.

BECOMING BALI

White-sand beaches, world-class surf, coral reefs and spas galore – yes, this is a fun-in-the-sun retreat…and oh, so much more. Trek up a volcano and peer down on its crater lake, hike cool valley trails and immerse yourself in natural hot springs, soak in the serenity of a hillside temple and be transfixed by a traditional dance performance – have the full island experience.

The Life Aquatic

When water hits these shores, it creates some of the world's best surfing; no matter what time of year you visit, you'll find legendary surf spots. There's world-class diving too, with extensive coral reefs and abundant marine life.

❶ Kuta, Bali

Surfing novices and those feeling a little rusty will find the tubes around Halfway Kuta (p107) a great place to start; for the more serious stuff, go to the reefs south of the beach breaks – they're about a kilometre out to sea.

❷ Ulu Watu

Paddle out through the cave to catch the most famous surfing break in Bali. Ulu Watu (p137) has about seven different breaks, including the Corner, a fast-breaking hollow left that holds about 6ft.

❸ Pulau Menjangan

Dive or snorkel the rich and pristine waters off West Bali: they offer tropical fish, soft corals, great visibility (usually), caves and a spectacular drop-off. Experienced divers should venture out to the mysterious Anker Wreck (p280).

❹ Desert Point

A legendary, if elusive, wave that was voted the best surf in the world by *Tracks* magazine (p97). Only suitable for very experienced surfers, this left-handed tube can offer a 300m ride.

❺ Kuta, Lombok

The other Kuta (p322) is a barefoot surf paradise, with half a dozen world-class breaks within a 45-minute motorbike ride of town. Think barrels folding and crashing on deserted white-sand beaches, without the overpopulated line-up.

❻ Gili Islands

Renowned for their snorkelling and diving, these three exquisite droplets of white sand, bordered by glistening turquoise waters, are sprinkled with coconut palms and surrounded by coral reefs. All have excellent dive sites, but Gili Trawangan is probably the best of the three (p304).

Relax & Unwind

The resorts of Kuta, Legian, Seminyak and Ubud are teeming with spas offering traditional treatments with which to indulge and pamper yourself. What better way to recuperate after a hard day at the beach…? Elsewhere, low-key resorts positively soothe and relax.

❶ Air Panas Banjar

Hot springs percolating down through a series of pools amid lush tropical plants (p267); soak in the top pools, or get a pummelling massage from the water as it falls into the lower pools.

❷ Nusa Lembongan

What better place to mellow out? Quiet, white-sand beaches; simple rooms right on the beach; incredible sunsets…this is the Bali that many imagine, but rarely find. Find your inner peace amid the serenity (p153).

❸ Lovina

Need an antidote to Kuta? Come to Lovina (p260), a relaxed, low-key, low-rise beach resort that is Kuta's polar opposite. Even the waves are calm… Here, you can get Balinese or Ayurveda treatments in simple, soothing settings.

❹ Senggigi Beach

If the hustle isn't too much hassle, sit back and wait for the local masseurs to find you on Senggigi Beach (p292); it will take some hard bargaining, but you should be able to cut a good deal.

Head Inland

Deep river valleys, luxuriant green rice fields, cool mountain trails, soaring volcanoes and plunging waterfalls. Drag yourself away from the beach and explore Bali's interior for experiences you will remember forever.

❶ Gunung Kawi

On the northern outskirts of Ubud, these ancient rock-cut shrines (p201) tower an awe-inspiring 8m over the lush green river valley; legend has it that they were carved in a single night by the mighty fingernails of Kebo Iwa.

❷ Sidemen Road

Winding its way through paddy fields and along beautiful river valleys, with extraordinary views of Gunung Agung (clouds permitting), the Sidemen Road (p214) gets more popular every year. If you want to know the real definition of verdant, come here.

❸ Jatiluwih Rice Fields

These terraces (p252) have been nominated for Unesco status and you'll soon see why as you follow the twisting 18km road up into them. Follow the water as it runs through channels and bamboo pipes from one plot to the next.

❹ Gunung Rinjani

Lombok's iconic volcano (p314) is Indonesia's second largest and an absolute stunner: rivers and waterfalls gush down its fissured slopes, while its summit sizzles with hot springs and a dazzling crater lake. Climbing it is an unforgettable experience.

❺ Munduk

This simple village (p250) is one of Bali's most appealing mountain retreats. With its cool, misty ambience, set among lush hillsides with jungle, rice, fruit trees and myriad waterfalls tumbling off precipices, you'll find hikes and treks galore…

The Culture

Balinese culture is written on its landscape, from its rice fields to its temples. Its architecture has so captivated the world that we've dedicated a whole section to it (p29). And while galleries and craft shops are filled with paintings and carvings, where should you go to experience real Balinese culture?

❶ Traditional Dance Performances, Ubud

Wherever there's a festival or celebration, you'll find a quality dance performance, but you'll find exceptional performances in Ubud every night of the week. If you can, catch a dance performance at Ubud Palace (p176).

❷ Textile shopping, Denpasar

You can't leave Bali without a sarong or two, and the Pasar Kumbasari in Denpasar (p169) has a multilevel treasure house of vibrant fabrics from which to choose, from casual cottons to elaborate ikat.

❸ Lunch at a warung

There's one of these traditional roadside eateries every few metres in most towns; cheap no-frills hang-outs with well-worn seats, a relaxed atmosphere and good, ridiculously cheap, fresh local food (p70).

❹ Visit the temples, Pura Luhur Batukau

The most spiritual temple you can visit easily in Bali, Pura Luhur Batukau (p252) is surrounded by forest and often shrouded in mist. Listen to the chant of priests backed by birdsong as you sit by the tumbling whitewater stream.

Contents

On the Road	4
Becoming Bali	5
Destination Bali & Lombok	16
Getting Started	19
Itineraries	23
Balinese Architecture	29
History	37
The Culture	46
Food & Drink	70
Environment	80
Bali & Lombok Outdoors	86
Kuta, Legian & Seminyak	99
KUTA & LEGIAN	**101**
History	101
Orientation	101
Information	104
Dangers & Annoyances	105
Sights	106
Activities	106
Tours	109
Festivals & Events	109
Sleeping	109
Eating	112
Entertainment	115
Shopping	116
Getting There & Away	118
Getting Around	118

SEMINYAK	**118**
Orientation	118
Information	119
Sights	119
Activities	120
Sleeping	121
Eating	123
Entertainment	125
Shopping	126
Getting There & Around	128
NORTH OF SEMINYAK	**128**
Kerobokan	128
Berewa	129
Canggu	129
Echo Beach	130
Pererenan Beach	130
South Bali	131
History	133
BUKIT PENINSULA	**133**
Jimbaran	133
Central Bukit	135
Balangan Beach	136
Pecatu Indah	136
Bingin	136
Ulu Watu & Around	137
Nusa Dua	139
Tanjung Benoa	142
SANUR	**145**
History	145
Orientation	145
Information	145
Sights	146
Activities	147
Sleeping	148
Eating	149
Drinking	151
Shopping	151
Getting There & Away	152
Getting Around	152
SOUTH OF SANUR	**152**
Pulau Serangan	152
Mangrove Information Centre	153
Benoa Harbour	153
NUSA LEMBONGAN & ISLANDS	**153**
Nusa Lembongan	153
Nusa Ceningan	159
Nusa Penida	159
DENPASAR	**162**
History	162

14 CONTENTS

Orientation	163
Information	163
Sights	163
Activities	166
Walking Tour	166
Festivals & Events	167
Sleeping	167
Eating	168
Shopping	169
Getting There & Away	169
Getting Around	170

Ubud & Around   171

UBUD	**172**
History	172
Orientation	172
Information	173
Sights	176
Activities	180
Walking Tours	181
Courses	183
Tours	184
Festivals & Events	184
Sleeping	184
Eating	191
Drinking	194
Entertainment	195
Shopping	196
Getting There & Away	197
Getting Around	198
AROUND UBUD	**198**
Bedulu	198
Pejeng	200
Tampaksiring	201
Tegallalang	202
North of Ubud	202
South of Ubud	203

East Bali   206

Coast Road to Kusamba	207
Gianyar	208
Sidan	209
Bangli	209
Semarapura (Klungkung)	210
Around Semarapura	213
Sidemen Road	214
Pura Besakih	215
Gunung Agung	216
Rendang to Amlapura	217
Kusamba to Padangbai	218
Padangbai	219
Padangbai to Candidasa	222
Candidasa	224

Candidasa to Amlapura	228
Amlapura	228
Around Amlapura	230
Tirta Gangga	230
Around Tirta Gangga	231
Amed & the Far East Coast	232
Kubu Region	236
Tulamben	236
Tulamben to Yeh Sanih	237

Central Mountains   239

GUNUNG BATUR AREA	**240**
Trekking Gunung Batur	241
Villages Around Gunung Batur Crater	244
Villages Around Danau Batur	245
DANAU BRATAN AREA	**247**
Bedugul	247
Candikuning	247
Pancasari	250
Danau Buyan & Danau Tamblingan	250
Munduk & Around	250
GUNUNG BATUKAU AREA	**252**
Orientation	252
Sights & Activities	252
Getting There & Away	253

North Bali   254

Yeh Sanih	255
Singaraja	255
Around Singaraja	259
Lovina	260
West of Lovina	266
Pemuteran	267

West Bali   270

Pura Tanah Lot	271
Kapal	271
Pura Taman Ayun	271
Belayu	272
Marga	272
Sangeh	273
Tabanan	273
South of Tabanan	274
North of Tabanan	275
Antosari & Bajera	276
Balian Beach & Lalang-Linggah	276
Jembrana Coast	276
Negara	277
Around Negara	278

Belimbingsari & Palasari	278
Cekik	279
Gilimanuk	279
Taman Nasional Bali Barat	280
Labuhan Lalang	282

Lombok   283

WESTERN LOMBOK	**285**
Mataram	285
Around Mataram	289
Lembar	290
Southwestern Peninsula	290
Senggigi	291
GILI ISLANDS	**295**
Gili Air	297
Gili Meno	300
Gili Trawangan	304
NORTH & CENTRAL LOMBOK	**310**
Bangsal to Bayan	310
Sembalun Valley	313
Sapit	313
Gunung Rinjani	314
Tetebatu	318
South of Tetebatu	319
SOUTH LOMBOK	**320**
Praya	320
Around Praya	320
Kuta	321
East of Kuta	325
West of Kuta	325
EAST LOMBOK	**326**
Labuhan Lombok	326
North of Labuhan Lombok	326
South of Labuhan Lombok	326

Directory   327

Accommodation	327
Activities	330
Business Hours	330
Children	330
Climate Charts	331
Courses	332
Customs	332
Dangers & Annoyances	333
Embassies & Consulates	335
Festivals & Events	335
Food	337
Gay & Lesbian Travellers	337
Holidays	337
Insurance	338
Internet Access	338
Legal Matters	338

Maps	338	Bemo	353	Infectious Diseases	366
Money	339	Bicycle	354	Traveller's Diarrhoea	369
Photography & Video	340	Boat	354	Environmental Hazards	369
Post	340	Bus	355	Women's Health	371
Shopping	340	Car & Motorcycle	355		
Solo Travellers	342	Hitching	359		
Telephone	343	Local Transport	359	**Language**	**373**
Time	344	Tours	361		
Toilets	344			**Glossary**	**380**
Tourist Information	344	**Health**	**363**		
Travellers with Disabilities	344	**BEFORE YOU GO**	**363**	**The Authors**	**384**
Visas	344	Insurance	363		
Volunteering	346	Recommended Vaccinations	363	**Behind the Scenes**	**385**
Women Travellers	347	Required Vaccinations	364		
Work	347	Medical Checklist	364		
		Internet Resources	365	**Index**	**390**
Transport	**349**	Further Reading	365		
GETTING THERE & AWAY	**349**	**IN TRANSIT**	**365**	**GreenDex**	**399**
Entering the Country	349	Deep Vein Thrombosis (DVT)	365		
Air	349	Jet Lag & Motion Sickness	365	**Map Legend**	**400**
Sea	352	**IN BALI & LOMBOK**	**365**		
GETTING AROUND	**353**	Availability & Cost of Health Care	365		
To/From the Airport	353				
Air	353				

Regional Map Contents

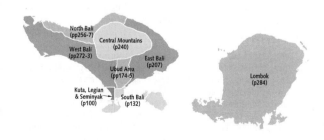

North Bali (pp256-7)

Central Mountains (p240)

West Bali (pp272-3)

East Bali (p207)

Ubud Area (pp174-5)

Kuta, Legian & Seminyak (p100)

South Bali (p132)

Lombok (p284)

Destination Bali & Lombok

It can't be said often enough – Bali is like no other destination in the world. Its rich culture is played out at all levels of life, from the exquisite flower-petal offerings placed seemingly everywhere, to the processions of joyfully-garbed locals, shutting down major roads as they march to one of the myriad temple ceremonies, to the otherworldly traditional music and dance still being performed island-wide by a record number of troupes.

Yes, Bali has beaches, surfing, diving and resorts great and small, but it's the essence of Bali – and the Balinese – that make it so much more than just a fun-in-the-sun retreat. It is possible to take the cliché of the smiling Balinese too far, but in reality, the inhabitants of this small island are indeed a generous, genuinely warm people. There's also a fun, sly sense of humour behind the smiles; upon seeing a bald tourist, many locals exclaim '*bung ujan*' (today's rain is cancelled) – it's their way of saying that the hairless head is like a clear sky.

These very qualities are also cause for the constant hand-wringing and worry that Bali is doomed to choke on its very success. Although concerns that Balinese culture is imperilled by tourism have been heard since the 1920s (when visitors numbered fewer than 1000 a year), the fears may finally be gaining wide traction with visitor numbers passing two million in 2008 – a record. (Lombok is also experiencing boom times, which may mean a new airport and new resorts in now-rural Kuta.)

This could all have contributed to the excitement surrounding the election of a new governor in 2008, notable given that no level of government inspires confidence in Bali (at the scene of an accident, the one thing all sides agreed upon was *not* to call the police). Made Pastika, who took office in August of 2008, is viewed as a genuine hero, the can-do former police chief who was given much credit for helping solve the 2002 Kuta bombings. The danger now though is that too much will be expected of him at a time when Bali faces some real problems, from its place within Islamic Indonesia, to the pressures of too many people trying to use too few resources, to the sheer popularity of a place that has too many people trying to make a buck however they can.

Pastika has also fuelled expectations with his campaign promises: to raise wages by 100%, ensure that Bali is not sold out to unfettered tourism and, all the while, protect Bali's environment. It's an ambitious, daunting and some would say critical agenda for the future.

MODERN CHALLENGES

Pastika's concern about development and the environment reflects the top issue for locals and expats alike. Although it's a problem far from unique to Bali, unconstrained development threatens some of the very qualities that make Bali a wonderful place to visit. The coast is especially vulnerable. In 2000, for example, there were just rice fields north of Seminyak, all the way to Pura Tanah Lot – the hundreds of villas dotting that same landscape now illustrate the scope of the issue. Unfortunately, many of the problems are caused by builders simply ignoring existing rules put in place to combat these very issues.

There are rumblings though that a limit may have been reached. There's a good chance that a 5km zone of exclusion will be enforced around Pura

Ulu Watu in the south; a hotel built shockingly close to the high-tide line in Seminyak was forced to demolish a new and popular rooftop bar that violated the 15m height rule (p123); and locals in North Bali have confronted government officials who allowed villa projects to proceed under dubious circumstances.

As with so much else, there are calls across the island for Governor Pastika to 'get tough' on the issue. With the rice fields of Bali succumbing to development by 700 to 1000 hectares a year, solutions will be needed soon before the villa-spotted fields of Kerobokan and Canggu become the norm. These solutions may pose very hard questions for the Balinese though, with the average youth now preferring a better-paying job in tourism than one working in the back-breaking conditions of the rice fields. Who would work the rice farms that are saved? And who would deny the farmers, who have never had anything, the money their land could bring them?

Balancing these concerns is a challenge going forward. Tourism has brought enormous benefits to the Balinese, evident from the economic and psychological crash that came when people stayed away after the 2002 bombings. And while no one should stay away out of fear for the island's future, it is good to know that there's a recognition that there is a limit to what the island can sustain.

Like a canary in a coal mine, water has served as a valuable warning to the Balinese that their beautiful island doesn't have unlimited resources. The images of rushing streams and gurgling rice fields are as much a part of Bali's

---

BALI

As I mentioned this morning to Charlie
There is far too much music in Bali
And altho' as a place it's entrancing
There is also a thought too much dancing.
It appears that each Balinese native
From the womb to the tomb is creative,
From sunrise till long after sundown,
Without getting nervy or rundown
They sculpt and they paint and they practise their songs,
They run through their dances and bang on their gongs,
Each writhe and each wriggle,
Each glamorous wriggle
Each sinuous action,
Is timed to a fraction.
And altho' the results are quite charming,
If sometimes a trifle alarming!
And altho' all the 'Lovelies' and 'Pretties'
Unblushingly brandish their titties
The whole thing's a little too clever
And there's too much artistic endeavour!

Forgive the above mentioned Charlie,
I had to rhyme something with Bali.

*Noel Coward (he wrote this to his travelling companion Charlie Chaplin
during a visit to Bali in the 1920s).*

image as beaches and dance, but even this seemingly limitless commodity is imperilled by the island's growth.

The Balinese are showing that they will find a way to adapt to this challenge as they have to so many others before. Sewer systems are being installed and water mains are replacing shallow wells that drain the water table. Visitors have also been important in raising awareness by demanding clean water and clean beaches. In fact, everyone visiting the island can have a positive impact just by following some of the tips in this book (see p84) for a green holiday.

Visitors also help preserve this paradise by demanding that businesses act responsibly and by giving their custom to those leading the way. The number of environmentally savvy businesses (such as those listed in the GreenDex, p397) grows daily. Dive shops are teaching locals how to protect reefs and keep beaches clean, while hotels are ensuring that wastes are recycled properly.

A CULTURE THRIVES

The Balinese have always found a way to stay true to themselves, whether it was in the face of invasions from Java, volcanoes blowing their lid or while welcoming two million visitors. Who can question the ingenuity of people who today fly kites both so they can have fun *and* so they can talk to the gods?

In a world where change accelerates exponentially, the Balinese never forsake the very fundamentals of their society. They still ask 'where are you from?' and 'where do you go?' to figure out where you fit into the greater scheme. They still closely adhere to the *banjar* (p43), the uniquely Balinese form of consensus government that was created in the villages centuries ago and continues as strong as ever, even now that villages are linked by mobile phones. And every time you discover a tiny offering – even just an incense stick still smoking outside your hotel room – you're reminded that the Balinese get it. They never underestimate their power to embrace change and flourish from it.

Getting Started

To get started for your adventure to Bali, all you really need is a ticket. (Well, maybe also a visa, p344, a passport, some money…but you get the idea.) The entire island is so well set up for visitors, the Balinese are so welcoming and the climate and weather so agreeable that you really *can* just hop on a plane and go.

Although Lombok isn't quite as easy, it's not too hard to find your way around with a little advance preparation. Simply getting to either place is the biggest hurdle (and it's a low one at that).

And as Bali and Lombok reward the spontaneous traveller, they also reward the traveller who plans. This is especially the case in Bali – you can stay at exquisite places, experience unique aspects of the culture and tailor your trip to a remarkable degree with advance work. If you want to make time for real discoveries or just discover some good bargains, you can reap the rewards of forethought.

Whatever your travel style, you'll find the real obstacles to independent travel in this part of the world are few. The islands are used to travellers of all stripes, English is widely spoken and, even if you forgot something at home, you can get it here.

WHEN TO GO

The best time to visit Bali, in terms of the weather, is during the dry season (April to September). The rest of the year is more humid, cloudier and has more rainstorms, but you can still enjoy a holiday.

There are also distinct tourist seasons that affect the picture. The European, American and Japanese summer holidays bring the biggest crowds – July, August and early September are busy. Accommodation can be very tight in these months and prices are higher. Lots of Australians arrive between Christmas and early January – flights are booked solid. (School holidays are also busy – early April, late June to early July and late September in particular. The resort areas in South Bali such as Legian cater to this sort of package

See climate charts (p331) for more information.

DON'T LEAVE HOME WITHOUT…

- Double-checking the ever-changing visa situation (p344).
- Sunglasses and a hat to deflect the fierce equatorial sun (buy your sunscreen in Bali to avoid airport seizure).
- Ascertaining your country's travel advice for Indonesia (p332).
- A travel insurance policy covering you for any calamity.
- Earplugs for the endless repetitions of 'Jammin'' at beach bars.
- Your favourite brand of wax for your surfboard.
- Comfortable but rugged walking shoes or sandals.
- Flip-flops in *your* size for hanging out by the pool.
- That clichéd extra bag for all the stuff you'll buy.
- That book you've been waiting to read.
- An iPod full of tunes to give your adventures a beat.
- Leaving lots of stuff *at* home (if you need it you can probably buy it in Bali).

TOP PICKS

BEACHES

Beaches ring Bali, but iconic ones with white sand are not as common as you'd think – most are some variation of tan or grey. Surf conditions also range from limp to torrid, depending on whether there is an offshore reef. Almost any beach will have at least one vendor happy to supply a cold Bintang.

Kuta Beach (p101) Cynics aside, this long, curved, wide stretch of sand boasts great surf that swimmers and surfers alike can enjoy. It's a place enjoyed both by locals and visitors – especially at sunset.

Balangan Beach (p136) This curving white-sand beach on the Bukit Peninsula, backed by an impromptu resort, is ramshackle in an endearing way and perfect for a snooze on the beach.

Pasir Putih (p228) A throwback gem east of Candidasa, this crescent of palm-fringed white sand is postcard perfect.

Nusa Lembongan (p153) There's a whole series of light-sand beaches at this relaxed and funky island off East Bali. Surf, dive, drink beer or just hang out.

Gili Island beaches (p295) The beaches on these three islands are uniformly gorgeous, with circles of white sand, great snorkelling and a timeless traveller vibe.

FESTIVALS

As well as the amazing selection of religious events that Bali offers, there is an impressive line-up of festivals to fascinate and transfix you. These events occur throughout the year and are scheduled using a Balinese calendar, very different from Western calendars. See p335 for details. The events below follow an annual schedule and are all worthy reasons to hop on a plane.

Nyale Fishing Festival (p323; February or March; Kuta, Lombok) Thousands of Sasak fishermen build bonfires on the beach at Lombok's Kuta while myriad rituals take place.

Bali Arts Festival (p167; mid-June to mid-July; Denpasar) Denpasar hosts a month of cultural performances by the best groups on the island, who compete for prizes.

Kuta Karnival (p109; late September and early October; Kuta, Bali) The always-near-the-surface zany side of Kuta is let loose

though parades, arts competitions, cultural shows, beach sports tournaments, kite-flying contests and more.

Ubud Writers & Readers Festival (p184; October; Ubud) Top authors from around the world gather in a celebration of writing – especially that which touches on Bali.

Nyepi (p62) The ultimate anti-festival, the entire island truly shuts down for 24 hours – even walking outside is a no-no. Think of it as the ultimate chill-out.

travel.) Many Indonesians visit Bali during some Indonesian holidays, see p337. Outside these times, Bali is quieter – you can find a room in most places and just turn up at your restaurant of choice.

Balinese festivals, holidays and special celebrations occur all the time, and as most of them are not scheduled according to Western calendars, don't worry too much about timing your visit to coincide with local events (see p335).

Just 8 degrees south of the equator, Bali has a tropical climate – the average temperature hovers around 30°C (around 85°F) all year. Direct sun feels incredibly hot, especially in the middle of the day. In the wet season, from

October through March, the humidity can be very high and oppressive. The almost daily tropical downpours come as a relief but then pass quickly.

The dry season (April to September) is nicer, although this shouldn't be an overriding factor in your decision. The days are slightly cooler but it still rains some. You can escape the heat at any time of the year by heading to upland places like Ubud, where cool mountain air makes evenings a pleasure.

On Lombok, the west (where the main town and tourist areas are based) has a climate similar to South Bali but drier. The wet season, from late October to early May, is less extreme, with December, January and February the wettest months. In the dry season, from June to September, temperatures will range from hot to scorching. Travel on the island is slightly less convenient during Ramadan, the Muslim fasting month (the ninth month in the Muslim calendar), especially in the traditional rural areas. In the tourist areas though, there should be little difference in services.

Clouds and mist usually envelop the slopes of the major volcanoes in Bali and Lombok, so those iconic postcard shots might be hard to come by. Also, temps can get chilly up the slopes at night.

COSTS & MONEY

In Bali, you can spend as much or as little as you want – there are fabulous resorts where a room costs US$500 or more a night, where dinner costs more than US$75 per person and you can be reborn in a spa for US$100 an hour. At the other extreme, you can easily find decent budget rooms for US$10 and enjoy a fresh meal from a warung (food stall) for under US$2. In short, Bali is a bargain for budget travellers and offers excellent value for those seeking luxury.

A good comfortable room in a small hotel near the beach in the south or amid the rice fields of Ubud will cost US$60 on average (and often less). Expect it to come with a pool, air-con, fridge, patio and decor that is comfortable if not exactly stylish. You can have an excellent three-course meal for US$7 (including a large bottle of beer) at many tourist restaurants, while US$20 buys you a more creative, memorable meal. See Accommodation (p327) for a full discussion of what kind of bed your money will buy you in Bali and Lombok.

Transport is affordable – remember that Bali and Lombok are small islands. Public buses and bemo (minibuses) are the local form of public transport and they're very cheap – 35,000Rp will get you across the island. A rental motorbike costs around US$4 per day and a small jeep runs about US$12 per day. You can charter a car *and* a driver for around US$35 to US$50 per day.

Nearly every museum, major temple or tourist site has an entry charge of about 6000/3000Rp per adult/child – it's a trifling amount. Galleries, bars and clubs are almost always free and the only place you'll really have to pay a premium is at a few attractions aimed at visitors (such as animal parks) and adventure activities like river-rafting or water sports.

Overall, it's possible to live a simple life for US$15 a day. This gets you a cheap room in Kuta, three fresh, local meals at warung, a few cold beers and all the free surfing you want. Spend more, say US$100 a day, and you'll pretty much be able to eat, drink or do anything you want while enjoying a great midpriced room.

HOW MUCH?

Cost to send an email taunting friends with all the fun you're having: under 500Rp

Simple beachside room with a great view: under US$40

Traditional gamelan music and dance performance: 80,000Rp

Ice-cold Bintang on the beach at sunset: 15,000Rp

Cost of walking the emerald rice fields of Ubud: free

TRAVEL LITERATURE

Books about Bali are common. Visit one of the bookshops on the island and you'll have plenty of choices, with new works of variable quality appearing monthly. Titles dealing with Lombok, however, are a rarity.

Eat, Pray, Love is the publishing sensation that has women of a certain age flocking to Bali to find the answer to life's dreams. For more, see the boxed text, p178. It's certainly the best known of an entire over-subscribed genre

For tips for respecting traditions and acting appropriately while in Bali and Lombok, see the boxed text, p348.

of books written by women who turn up in Bali unsettled, only to find the meaning of life while there.

Diana Darling's *The Painted Alphabet* is based on a Balinese epic poem with all the usual ingredients: good, evil, a quest, baby-swapping and various mystical events. It's a gentle and beguiling way to get your head into Balinese folklore.

A House in Bali by Colin McPhee is the timeless classic about a Canadian who experienced Balinese cultural and village life to the core in the 1930s.

Our Hotel in Bali by Louise Koke is another classic about Westerners in Bali in the 1930s. She and her husband Bob created the first-ever Kuta Beach hotel and had numerous delightful encounters along the way. It's a quick and fun read with lots of photos.

Gecko's Complaint is a morality tale presented as an old Balinese children's fable. The recent Periplus edition is richly illustrated.

The online journal of the irrepressible Made Wijaya, Stranger in Paradise (www.strangerinparadise.com), is filled with insightful and at times hilariously profane takes on local life.

INTERNET RESOURCES

Bali Advertiser (www.baliadvertiser.biz) This online edition of Bali's expat journal is filled with insider tips.

Bali Blog (www.baliblog.com) Essays, news and information about Bali.

Bali Discovery (www.balidiscovery.com) Although run by a tour company, this site is easily the best source for Balinese news and features, week in and week out. Excellent.

Lombok Network (www.lombok-network.com) Very comprehensive, this site brings together huge amounts of current information on the island.

LonelyPlanet.com (www.lonelyplanet.com) Share knowledge and experiences with other travellers; these islands have been Lonely Planet favourites from the start.

Itineraries
CLASSIC ROUTES

TOTAL BALI & LOMBOK
Two Weeks

Start your trip in **Seminyak** (p118), with the best places to go out for a meal, a drink or even a new frock, and allow at least three days to experience the wild charms of **Kuta Beach** (p101). Once you're sated, head west, driving back roads around **Tabanan** (p273) and **Jatiluwih** (p252), where enormous bamboo trees hang over the roads and the rice terraces await a final blessing by Unesco.

Continue west through **Taman Nasional Bali Barat** (West Bali National Park; p280). Stop here, or press on and settle in at **Pemuteran** (p267). From here, you can snorkel or scuba Bali's best dive site at **Pulau Menjangan** (p280). Driving east, stop at **Lovina** (p260) and enjoy its laid-back beach-town vibe and then head up and over the string of volcanoes that are the heart – and soul – of the island.

Carry on through **Kintamani** (p244), where you'll be rewarded with vistas of Bali's big three: **Gunung Batur** (p240), **Gunung Abang** (p242) and the holiest of holies, **Gunung Agung** (p242). Coming back down on the wet side of the island, head straight to **Ubud** (p172), the spiritual centre of Bali. Nights of dance and culture are offset by days of walking through the serene countryside. Head down to funky **Padangbai** (p219) and catch the Perama boat to the beach resorts of **Senggigi** (p291) and then on to the great travellers' scene on the **Gili Islands** (p295).

The best of everything in Bali and Lombok comes together on this two-week trip of tropical and cultural delights. Bask on the best beaches, drown in a sea of green rice paddies, let the aura of amazing temples flow over you like a warm bath and immerse yourself in Bali's incredible culture; it will be an island trip like no other.

TROPICAL PLEASURES   Two Weeks

Don't stray far from the airport, as **Kuta** (p101), in all its party glory, is only 10 minutes away. Hit the bars and clubs after midnight and come back to earth on the beach by day. Be sure to get to the trendy restaurants and clubs of **Seminyak** (p118) before you leave this part of South Bali behind. Maybe you can learn how to surf, or at least brush up on your skills. Eventually, head south to sober up and mellow out. **Bingin** (p136) has groovy cliffside inns overlooking fab surfing. When you're ready and rested, get a boat from **Sanur** (p145) to **Nusa Lembongan** (p153). This little island still has the classic, simple charm of a rural beach town, with a string of hotels – from basic to semi-posh – lining the sands. It's a timeless travellers' scene with a backdrop of excellent surfing and splendid snorkelling and diving.

Return to Bali and press on from Sanur to the beaches along the southeast coast. Try some of wild beaches around **Lebih** (p208), where the surf pounds the grey sand. Stop and test the waters with a little surfing, or grab a meal at one of the warung (food stalls) lining the roads to the beach. When you get to **Padangbai** (p219), stop. This fun little port town is an ideal place to hang out for a couple of days before you hop a boat to Lombok, docking in **Senggigi** (p291), the heart of Lombok's beach scene. The coastline is lovely and as you're gazing back towards Bali, you'll already feel you've made a journey – fewer people visit Lombok than Bali.

Now it's time to push on to the ultimate reward for your island adventure: the **Gili Islands** (p295). Depart from Senggigi and compare the scenes on Gili Trawangan, Gili Meno and Gili Air – then pick your favourite.

Surf and swim by day and party by night. Sleep? That'll happen sometime. Start in timeless Kuta, then sample hidden beaches and great travellers' scenes south of Bali and off its coast. Then it's over to Lombok for more day and night action.

BEST OF BALI
One Week

Start with a large room by the pool, or on the beach at one of the resorts in **Legian** (p101) or **Seminyak** (p118). Sample the **Kuta Beach** (p101) surf and head to Seminyak for world-class **shopping** (p126). Maybe a seafood dinner on **Jimbaran Bay** (p135), or a trendy restaurant in **Seminyak** (p123). Then, hit the edgy clubs in Kuta or the scenester joints in Seminyak.

Consider some day trips. Head down to surfing beaches like **Balangan Beach** (p136) for some sun and fun, then on to the spiritual centre (and monkey home) of **Pura Luhur Ulu Watu** (p137). Bali's ancient rice terraces will exhaust your abilities to describe green. Sample these in a drive up to the misty **Pura Luhur Batukau** (p252), followed by the terraces of **Jatiluwih** (p252).

In the east, take the coast road to wild and unvisited beaches like the one near **Pura Masceti** (p208), followed by the well-mannered royal town of **Semarapura** (p210) with its ruins. Head north up the breathtaking **Sidemen Road** (p214), which combines ribbons of rice terraces with lush river valleys and cloud-shrouded mountains. Pass through **Muncan** (p218) and then go west to **Ubud** (p172), the crowning stop on any itinerary.

Bali's rich culture is most-celebrated and most-accessible in Ubud, as you can easily be enraptured by nightly dance performances. Hike through the surrounding rice fields to river valleys like the **Sungai Ayung** (p182), take a break in **museums** (p176) bursting with paintings in the many styles reflecting Bali, or head north to the imposing thousand-year-old rock monoliths at **Gunung Kawi** (p201).

To spoil yourself, stay in one of the many **hotels** (p184) near the centre with views across rice fields and rivers. Sample the offerings at a **spa** (p180) before you sample one of the myriad great **restaurants** (p191) to choose from.

First-time visitors to Bali as well as old hands love the island for its beaches, shopping, nightlife, culture and simply beautiful scenery. This itinerary gives you the best of all this and more. Start in the hedonistic south and end up in the cultured climes of Ubud. You may need more than a week!

BALI SEA

BALI

Jatiluwih
Pura Luhur Batukau
Gunung Kawi
Muncan
Ubud
Sidemen Rd
Semarapura
Selat Badung
Pura Masceti
Selat Bali
Seminyak
Legian
Kuta Beach
Jimbaran Bay
Balangan Beach
Pura Luhur Ulu Watu
Nusa Penida
Selat Lombok

INDIAN OCEAN

ROADS LESS TRAVELLED

LEAVING THE CROWDS BEHIND   Two Weeks

Escape the day-trippers' trails and explore the central mountains. Tackle **Gunung Agung** (p216), the spiritual centre of the island. Start early to reach the top and take in the views before the daily onslaught of clouds and mist.

Having climbed Bali's most legendary peak, head west to the village of **Munduk** (p250), which looks down to the north coast and the sea beyond. Go for a walk in the area and enjoy waterfalls, truly tiny villages, wild fruit trees and the sinuous bands of rice paddies lining the hills like ribbons. Then head south to the wonderful temple of **Pura Luhur Batukau** (p252), and consider a trek up Bali's second-highest mountain, **Gunung Batukau** (p252).

Next, bounce across the waves to **Nusa Penida** (p159), the island visible from much of the south and east – it's lush, arid and almost unpopulated. Take in the amazing vistas from its cliffs and dive under the waves to check out the marine life.

Head to Lombok, but ignore the resorts in the east. Instead, head south. Well off the beaten path, the south coast near Lombok's **Kuta** (p321) has stunning beaches and surfing to reward the intrepid. The little-driven back roads of the interior will thrill the adventurous and curious, with tiny villages where you can learn about the amazing local handicrafts. Many of these roads lead up the flanks of **Gunung Rinjani** (p314), the volcanic peak that shelters the lush and remote **Sembalun Valley** (p313). Trekking from one village to the next on the rim can take days, but is one of the great walks.

First have fun in Bali's south, then get the heck out! This trip takes you up Bali's stunning and spiritual peaks before sending you hiking lush hillside hideaways and on to mostly undiscovered Nusa Penida. Then it's off to the quietest parts of Lombok.

TAILORED TRIPS

DISCOVER LOMBOK

Just next door, but virtually unknown to most of Bali's millions of tourists and thousands of expats, Lombok is waiting to be discovered. Begin by taking advantage of the islands' proximity and hop one of the fast speedboat services from Bali (see p354) to **Gili Trawangan** (p304). By day, you'll dive into reefs teeming with marine life (p302), and on land you'll love the beaches, dining and nightlife on Gili T.p304 Take a Perama boat (p304) from the Gilis to **Senggigi** (p291), where you can motorbike between deserted fishing beaches, visit the lovely Pura Batu Balong (p291) and take advantage of terrific hotel deals. Hit the market in **Bertais** (p288) to get localised and recover from *bule* overload, then head through the craftsman towns of **Sukarara** (p320) and **Penujak** (p320) to rugged, majestic **Kuta** (p321). Take your time here – swim at **Tanjung Aan** (p325) and **Selong Blanak** (p325), and surf at **Mawan** (p325). Let the rural coastline burn into your brain, because by the time you return it may begin to resemble Nusa Dua. After arid Kuta, you'll dig the rice-paddy walk to Air Terjun Jukut (p318) in lush, fertile **Tetebatu**. After a night or two here, you'll be ready to climb the slopes of **Gunung Rinjani** (p314), dip into her hot springs, and bag her peak. While you're there remember to give thanks to Lombok's mountain gods.

INCREDIBLE DIVES

Everyone can see the surfer on top of Bali's waves, but little do they realise that underwater there's even more action. Follow the coast around Bali and you'll be rewarded with one legendary dive spot after another, all with great dive shops and a place to kick back and relax in nearby towns. Head west to **Pulau Menjangan** (p280), in the Taman Nasional Bali Barat. It's renowned for its coral and sheer wall and has a fine beach ashore. The nearby **Pemuteran** (p267) hotels define relaxation; staying at these wonderfully isolated resorts is yet another reason why this is a good place to hang up your flippers. **Lovina** (p260) is a good diving base. As well as it being a snoozy beach town, from here you can reach many of Bali's best sites by day and still have time for one of the amazing local night dives.

Down the east coast is **Tulamben** (p236), where scores of people explore the shattered hulk of a WWII freighter. A smaller wreck lurks off the shores of **Aas** (p232) near Amed. **Padangbai** (p219) is another good diving base; there are lots of local sites to explore and the marine life encompasses everything from sharks to sunfish.

But wait, the brass ring for your dives might be in the distance, offshore. The islands of **Nusa Penida** (p159) and **Nusa Lembongan** (p153) both have scores of demanding dives to challenge experienced divers. The rewards are deep grottoes, dropoffs, and everything from mantas to turtles.

SPOIL ME

Kilometre for kilometre, Bali has about the greatest density of fabulous resorts and spas you'll find anywhere. From incredible food to hedonistic pampering, you can give yourself every sensation you want and deserve. Massage, spa treatments or just lounging by a pool – you'll find the peace and pampering you want. Two great hotels – the serene **Samaya** (p122), and the understated **Oberoi** (p122) – are just north of Kuta in Seminyak. They set the standards for the clean, tropical look that has come to be known as 'Bali Style'.

Great places circle the Bukit Peninsula like a pearl necklace. The **Four Seasons Jimbaran Bay** (p134) in Jimbaran, with its white sand and blue sea, pushes exclusivity while the **Ritz Carlton** (p134) pushes posh. Across the peninsula, the new **St Regis Bali Resort** (p141) and the **Conrad** (p144) are beacons of luxe in Nusa Dua and Tanjung Benoa. At the Conrad you can plunge off your own patio into the vast pool that encircles the hotel.

Some of the most famous places in Bali can be found in the lush lands around Ubud. Along the Ayung Valley, another **Four Seasons Resort** (p191) blends effortlessly with its verdant surrounds. John Hardy's village fantasy, **Bambu Indah** (p191), and the reborn **Amandari** (p191) both head the A-list going north along the valley.

Along the east coast, with its remote beaches and its views, you can be pampered in two excellent places with sweeping views of Nusa Penida: the environmentally conscious **Bloo Lagoon Village** (p221) on a beautiful beach near Padangbai and, near Manggis, the stunning **Amankila** (p223).

BALI'S SPIRITUAL CENTRE

Start at **Pura Luhur Ulu Watu** (p137) right at the southern tip of Bali. On the Bukit Peninsula, it's one of only nine directional temples on the island, as well as being a sea temple honouring the many gods in the waters right around the island. Head east around the peninsula to **Pura Mas Suka** (p139), with its remote outlook over the Indian Ocean. From here, go north, following the sea temples along the west coast of South Bali – **Pura Petitenget** (p119) in Seminyak is a classic example. Time your visit to **Pura Tanah Lot** (p271), one of the most important and photographed sea temples, for the morning when crowds are few. One glimpse of its perfect location and you'll understand why the hordes descend for sunset.

In **Ubud** (p172), settle in for a few days at one of the amazing hotels and experience Balinese art and culture. It won't take long to see how beauty of the mind and spirit merge so easily here. You will find the best of Balinese culture both here and in the surrounding villages.

Heading east, **Semarapura** (p210), commonly known as Klungkung, was once the centre of Bali's most important kingdom. While here, learn about how the Balinese held out against the Dutch among its fascinating palace ruins. Or, head into the verdant hills and valleys of East Bali to find your own spiritual centre. End your journey in **Amed** (p232), with its dramatic and contemplative ocean overlooks.

Balinese Architecture

The venerated sea temple of Pura Tanah Lot (p271) is a sunset-watcher's favourite

It brings together the living and the dead, pays homage to the gods, and wards off evil spirits, not to mention the torrential rain. As spiritual as it is functional, as mystical as it is beautiful, Balinese architecture has a life force of its own.

On an island bound by deep-rooted religious and cultural rituals, the priority of any design is appeasing the ancestral and village gods. This means reserving the holiest (northeast) location in every land space for the village temple, the same corner in every home for the family temple, and providing a comfortable, pleasing atmosphere to entice the gods back to Bali for ceremonies.

So while it exudes beauty, balance, age-old wisdom and functionality, a Balinese home is not a commodity designed with capital appreciation in mind; even while an increasing number of rice farmers sell their ancestral land to foreigners for villa developments, they're keeping the parcel on which their home stands.

Cliff-top Pura Luhur Ulu Watu (p137)
STEPHANE VICTOR

'For the Balinese, their house where they have the family temple represents the most prestige in their lives,' says renowned architect Popo Danes. 'It's the house of their roots. Selling it would be like selling their ancestors.'

In this context, the design is traditionally done by an *undagi,* a combination architect-priest – it must maintain harmony between god, man and nature under the concept of *Tri Hita Karana.* If it's not quite right, the universe may fall off balance and no end of misfortune and ill health will visit their community. Best to get it spot on then!

HUMAN SCALE

In Balinese architecture, the concept of human scale prescribes a unique measurement system awarding the tallest and best-fed man with the biggest dwelling. The size and proportions of pavilions, walls, shrines and gates are based on the owner's body measurements, which are marked on a bamboo stick used for laying out the complex.

Just as every structure is considered a living being with feet (represented by the stylobate base), body (the building) and head (roof), the family compound is also metaphorically likened to the body. The shrine is the head; sleeping and guest pavilions, the arms; central courtyard, the navel; hearth, the sexual organs; kitchen, the legs and feet; and the refuse pit, what else but the anus.

GOLDEN RULES OF BALINESE DESIGN

The seven cardinal principles of Balinese architecture:

- hierarchy of space;
- cosmological orientation according to the *kaja* (towards the mountains)–*kelod* (towards the sea) axis;
- balanced cosmology;
- human scale and proportion (see the boxed text, left);
- open-air, court concept;
- clarity of structure;
- truth of material.

Magic powers are believed to reside in the holy springs of Tirta Empul (p202)

WIBOWO RUSLI

top five

TEMPLES

- Pura Luhur Ulu Watu (p137), on the Bukit Peninsula, one of Bali's nine directional temples, with a spectacular cliff-top location.
- Pura Tirta Empul (p202) at Tampaksaring, renowned for its beauty and nearby springs and bathing pools.
- Pura Luhur Batukau (p252) on the slopes of Gunung Batukau, with its cool, misty atmosphere.
- Pura Kehen (p210), state temple of the Bangli kingdom and miniature version of Pura Besakih.
- Pura Maduwe Karang (p260), near Kubutambahan, an elaborate seaside temple with some surprising carving.

Heights (mountains) are inhabited by gods and reserved for temples, middle areas are for humans, and low-lying areas, such as the sea, are the abode of demons.

Houses and temples always face the sacred Gunung Agung, with their backs to the 'impure' sea. Only foreigners who put ocean-views above universal harmony defy this tenet, which even affects a Balinese person's sleeping position.

Generally, every temple and home – whether a royal palace or a simple rice-farmer's dwelling – follows a traditional formula; surrounded by a high wall, it looks inwards. Only the materials used, adornments, workmanship and temple size give clues to the village or owner's wealth, status and region.

As many as five generations may live together in a family compound (p50), which comprises several individual *bale* (open-sided pavilions with steep *alang-alang* [thatch] roofs). These open onto a garden and central courtyard: the 'living room' in Bali's mild climate.

More than just a direction, orientation determines each pavilion's function. The hallowed *kaja-kangin* (northeast or mountain-sunrise) corner is for the temple; the 'lowest' southwest location, the kitchen, *lumbung* (rice barn) and animals; the east, the sleeping *bale*; and the west, the guest pavilions.

Lush courtyard at Ubud's Royal Palace (p176)
JOHN KERSHAW/ALAMY

PALACES & TEMPLES

Bali does not have mansions like in the West. Visitors are often surprised by how unimposing a *puri* (palace) is. Although the residence of royalty, a *puri* is never above one storey high because a noble could not possibly be underneath someone else's feet on the floor above. The *puri* ruins and restored buildings at Taman Kertha Gosa (p212) in historic Klungkung, once Bali's most important kingdom, are a stunning showpiece of royal architecture.

Bali's most elaborate buildings are its major temples (for our recommendations, see the boxed text, p31). This stems from the historical function of sculpture and painting, once exclusively reserved for religious purposes (see p58).

Temples consist of an outer and inner courtyard, where several shrines of varying sizes are dedicated to village founders and local deities; a Padma Stone throne for the sun god Surya occupies the *kaja-kangin* corner. There's usually an 11-roofed *meru* (multiroofed shrine) to Sanghyang Widi, the supreme Balinese deity, and a three-roofed *meru* to Gunung Agung.

For tips on respecting traditions and acting appropriately while visiting temples, see the boxed text, p348, and for a directory of important temples, see the boxed text, p51.

THE BIRTH OF BALI STYLE

Tourism has given Balinese architecture unprecedented exposure and it seems that every visitor wants to take a slice of this island back home with them. Burgeoning villa developments have further fuelled demand domestically.

ANCIENT WISDOM

In addition to religious function, Balinese design reflects the climate and seismology, and the availability of technology and local materials.

Instead of walls, columns support *bale,* allowing maximum sunlight and ventilation and minimising earthquake damage. Water gardens are both aesthetically pleasing and efficient passive cooling systems.

As protection against torrential rains, *bale* have high bases and the *alang-alang* roof is pitched at 45 degrees for the most efficient run-off of water. No nails are used to support the roof; instead, pegs made from the heart of coconut wood bind the beams together.

Candi bentar (entrance gates) play a religious and practical role in guarding homes and temples. After passing through the gates, which resemble a mountain or tower split in half, guests come face-to-face with a small wall known as an *aling aling*, requiring them to turn a sharp left or right to access the building proper. This ensures both privacy from passers-by and protection from demons, which the Balinese believe cannot turn corners! Talk about 'hitting the wall'.

Shops along Ngurah Rai Bypass churn out pre-fabricated, knock-down *bale* for shipment to far-flung destinations: the Caribbean, London, Perth and Hong Kong. Furniture workshops in Kerobokan and handicraft villages near Ubud are flat-chat making ornaments for domestic and export markets: wall sculptures, carved doors, statues, and the ubiquitous Buddha images and handicrafts from all over Indonesia that have erroneously become synonymous with Balinese decor.

Local suppliers can't keep up with demand. *Alang-alang* farmers now use fertiliser chemicals to harvest their crop several times a year instead of just once, while many craftsmen import wood and other materials from other provinces.

The craze stems back to the early 1970s, when Australian artist Donald Friend

top five
ARCHITECTURE BOOKS

■ *Architecture of Bali,* by Made Wijaya, contains stunning vintage photographs and illustrations, accompanied by informative personal observations from the Australian-born landscape designer.

■ *Bali Style,* by Rio Helmi and Barbara Walker, details the clean and open-plan design ethos that's attracted a cult following.

■ *Architectural Conservation In Bali,* by Edo Budiharjo, makes the case for preserving Bali's architectural heritage.

■ *Architecture Bali: Birth of the Tropical Boutique Resort,* by Philip Goad, explores the origin and direction of contemporary Balinese design.

■ *A House on Bali,* by Colin McPhee, is the classic account of the intricacies of building a traditional family compound.

The 'Floating Pavilion' at the fascinating Taman Kertha Gosa complex (p211) in Semarapura
RICHARD I'ANSON

ICONS OF MODERN BALI STYLE

- Guest villas based on buildings such as a family compound or *wantilan* (community hall), with single-storey, thatch-roofed pavilions that open onto courtyards, the whole space enclosed by a wall, with a *candi bentar* entrance for maximum privacy.
- Sliding doors enabling pavilions to be open to the elements, or closed for air-conditioning and privacy.
- Western-style outdoor garden bathrooms, based on Muller's innovative adaptation of a local *mandi* bathing space at Oberoi (p122).
- Floating pavilions over infinity-edged pool, pioneered by Muller at Amandari (p191).
- Intimate courtyards between villas, and village-style 'lanes' lined with limestone rubble walls.
- Water gardens featuring landscaped moats and ponds.

Poolside Bali Style is exemplified at the storied Amandari resort (p191)

TONY WHEELER

formed a partnership with Manado-born Wija Waworuntu, who had built the Tandjung Sari (p149) on Sanur beach a decade earlier, the classic prototype for the Balinese boutique beach hotel. With a directive to design traditional, village-style alternatives to the Western multistoreyed hotels, they brought two architects to Bali: Australian Peter Muller and the late Sri Lankan Geoffrey Bawa. Some of the most iconic symbols of modern Balinese architecture are attributed to Bawa and Muller, credited with being the first to capture the spirit of traditional architecture and adapt it to Western standards of luxury.

Muller is best known for his village-style designs of the Oberoi (p122) in the early 1970s and the exclusive Amandari resort (p191) 15 years later – still among the most eulogised resorts in Bali.

Bawa's influence is particularly remarkable considering he designed just one resort, and that was never actually finished – the original Batujimbar Estates in Sanur, inspired by 19th-century palaces at Klungkung and Amlapura. Only two houses and the museum were built before Friend and Waworuntu's partnership dissolved. The remaining 13 plots were sold, and the property, next door to Café Batu Jimbar (p151), features a mesh of architectural styles. However, it brought together artists and celebrities from around Indonesia and the world, and Bawa's overall vision was considered revolutionary; notably, the museum was based on a *bale agung* (assembly hall for the gods), with a raised stylobate base to create another room below the open-air pavilion on top.

Together, the pair's work won international acclaim and their legacy has been sustained at resorts like Four Seasons Jimbaran (p134), Amankila (p223) and Alila Manggis (p223).

Before long, the cult movement known as 'Bali Style' was born. Then, the term reflected Muller and Bawa's sensitive, low-key approach, giving precedence to culture over style, and respect for traditional principles and craftsmen, local renewable materials and age-old techniques. Today, the development of a mass market has inevitably produced a much looser definition.

TRADITIONAL DESIGN IN MODERN TIMES

Although the techniques and materials behind Balinese architecture have been mastered over centuries, specifically for this rice-farming society, architects are constantly being asked how they can be modified for an urban setting like London, or an apartment in India. The answer is: not easily. Bali Style can now often refer more to cosmetic touches – carved gates or an outdoor bathroom – rather than a walled-in compound with pavilions, communal courtyard and water gardens.

'I had a client in Costa Rica ask me to recreate Peter Muller's Amandari design for a multi-million dollar resort there,' said Popo Danes. 'I had to say no – it just wouldn't have worked in that environment. People are crazy about Balinese architecture, but I would love to export the understanding of it, not just our architecture as a commodity.'

OVER THE TREETOPS

As tourism development took off in the 1970s, Bali's government introduced regulations to preserve the low-rise skyline and architecture. One key law prohibited any structure from standing taller than a coconut tree, estimated at 15m.

Consequently, and quite amazingly, there are no skyscrapers in Bali. Most hotels are less than three storeys high; the tallest is the 10-storey Inna Grand Bali Beach in Sanur, opened in 1966 as the first five-star resort.

However, amid rising land prices, many developers have tried to maximise value by building resorts and malls 'up', well above the palms.

Villas, particularly north of Seminyak, in supposed 'greenbelt' rice-growing villages and along the Bukit Peninsula have also triggered complaints that they show scant regard for traditional design. Flat roofs have become more common, metaphorically beheading the structure which by law should have a pitched roof, while orientation and hierarchy of space rarely feature at all.

'Post-1999 monetary crisis, the floodgates opened for a lot of unscrupulous real-estate brokers and tasteless developers,' said Australian-born author and landscape architect Made Wijaya. 'Foreigners, including Jakartans, are building with no respect for the environment, local culture or architecture.'

Architects blame the lack of enforcement of building regulations.

'I know the government is wary of deterring investors,' said Popo Danes, 'but we built our architectural principles over many, many centuries, and we can destroy them in only half a century if we're not careful.'

For the fate of one recent attempt at surpassing the 15m rule, see the boxed text, p123.

Outdoor bathrooms and tropical gardens set the scene for sleeping in style

LEFT: ELIZABETH WHITING & ASSOCIATES/ALAMY; RIGHT: JOHN KERSHAW/ALA

While several recent developments have prompted calls for stricter enforcement of regulations to preserve the island's facade and heritage, all you need to do is venture off the main road and slip down a quiet *gang* (lane) to see that not much has changed in how the Balinese themselves live.

Foreigners may bend traditional principles to suit themselves, but the Balinese still take great pride in their architecture. Ubud is a notable tribute to how traditional design can survive modern development, with few houses deviating from time-honoured form. The home of the late I Gusti Nyoman Lempad, a painter, sculptor and architect, is now a gallery (p179) and remains a good example of a traditional family compound. South of Ubud, you can enjoy an in-depth tour of the Nyoman Suaka Home in Singapadu (p204).

Many small hotels around Bali are set up like family compounds, *puri* or even *lumbung,* providing a unique and charming experience for travellers who may otherwise never get to experience the way a Balinese family lives firsthand. See the boxed text, right, for some good picks.

In more remote areas, many villages remain virtually untouched, such as Munduk (p250) and the ancient Bali Aga hamlet of Tenganan (p224), with neat rows of identical houses and a wall surrounding the whole village, which is closed to motor vehicles.

All over Bali, the architecture remains inextricably tied up in the religious, cultural and social rituals underpinning village life. The gods still get the best seat in the house, and they're not moving for anyone.

top five
UBUD HOMESTAYS

Ubud is still the place to go for a simple room in a traditional family compound – usually for well under US$20. Among the many good choices:

- **Donald Homestay** (p186)
- **Eka's Homestay** (p187)
- **Family Guest House** (p188)
- **Jungut Inn** (p185)
- **Sania's House** (p185)

History

There are few traces of Stone Age people in Bali, although it's certain that the island was populated very early in prehistoric times – fossilised humanoid remains from neighbouring Java have been dated to as early as 250,000 years ago. The earliest human artefacts found in Bali are stone tools and earthenware vessels dug up near Cekik in western Bali, estimated to be 3000 years old. Discoveries continue, and you can see exhibits of bones that are estimated to be 4000 years old at the Museum Situs Purbakala Gilimanuk (p279). Artefacts indicate that the Bronze Age began in Bali before 300 BC.

Little is known of Bali during the period when Indian traders brought Hinduism to the Indonesian archipelago, although it is thought it was embraced on the island by the 7th century AD. The earliest written records are inscriptions on a stone pillar near Sanur, dating from around the 9th century; by that time, Bali had already developed many similarities to the island you find today. Rice, for example, was grown with the help of a complex irrigation system, probably very like the one employed now, and the Balinese had already begun to develop their rich cultural and artistic traditions.

If little is known about the earliest inhabitants of Bali, then even less is known about Lombok until about the 17th century. Early inhabitants are thought to have been Sasaks from a region encompassing today's India and Myanmar.

A Short History of Bali – Indonesia's Hindu Realm, by Robert Pringle, is a thoughtful analysis of Bali's history from the Bronze Age to the present, with excellent sections on the 2002 bombings and ongoing environmental woes caused by tourism and development.

HINDU INFLUENCE

Java began to spread its influence into Bali during the reign of King Airlangga (1019–42), or perhaps even earlier. At the age of 16, when his uncle lost the throne, Airlangga fled into the forests of western Java. He gradually gained support, won back the kingdom once ruled by his uncle and went on to become one of Java's greatest kings. Airlangga's mother had moved to Bali and remarried shortly after his birth, so when he gained the throne, there was an immediate link between Java and Bali. It was at this time that the courtly Javanese language known as Kawi came into use among the royalty of Bali, and the rock-cut memorials seen at Gunung Kawi, near Tampaksiring (p201), provide a clear architectural link between Bali and 11th-century Java.

After Airlangga's death, Bali remained semi-independent until Kertanagara became king of the Singasari dynasty in Java two centuries later. Kertanagara conquered Bali in 1284, but the period of his greatest power lasted a mere eight years, until he was murdered and his kingdom collapsed. However, the great Majapahit dynasty was founded by his son, Vijaya (or Wijaya). With Java in turmoil, Bali regained its autonomy, and the Pejeng dynasty, centred near modern-day Ubud, rose to great power. In 1343 the legendary Majapahit

The 14th-century epic poem, *Sutasoma*, has been given a sparkling new translation by Kate O'Brien. It follows the life of a Javanese prince as he becomes king and defeats the ultimate demon using the mystical beliefs that underpin Balinese faith today.

TIMELINE

50 million BC	2000 BC	7th century
A permanent gap in the Earth's crust forms between what becomes Asia and Australia. Now called the Wallace Line (p83), it keeps Australian species from crossing to Bali until the invention of cheap Bintang specials.	A Balinese gentleman passes away. One of the first known inhabitants of the island, he rests peacefully until his bones are found and placed on display in Gilimanuk (p279).	Indian traders bring Hinduism to Bali. Little is known about what exactly was traded although some speculate that they left with lots of wooden carvings of penises and bootleg *lontar* books (p260).

prime minister, Gajah Mada, defeated the Pejeng king Dalem Bedaulu, and Bali was brought back under Javanese influence.

Although Gajah Mada brought much of the Indonesian archipelago under Majapahit control, this was the furthest extent of their power. The 'capital' of the dynasty was moved to Gelgel, in Bali, near modern Semarapura, around the late 14th century, and this was the base for the 'king of Bali', the Dewa Agung, for the next two centuries. The Gelgel dynasty in Bali, under Dalem Batur Enggong, extended its power eastwards to the neighbouring island of Lombok and even westwards across the strait to Java.

The collapse of the Majapahit dynasty into weak, decadent petty kingdoms opened the door for the spread of Islam from the trading states of the north coast into the heartland of Java. As the Hindu states fell, many of the intelligentsia fled to Bali. Notable among these was the priest Nirartha, who is credited with introducing many of the complexities of Balinese religion to the island, as well as establishing the chain of 'sea temples', which includes Pura Luhur Ulu Watu (p137) and Pura Tanah Lot (p271). Court-supported artisans, artists, dancers, musicians and actors also fled to Bali at this time and the island experienced an explosion of cultural activity. The great exodus to Bali was complete by the 16th century.

> Kuta was never a part of mainstream Bali. During royal times, the region was a place of exile for malcontents and troublemakers. It was too arid for rice fields, the fishing was barely sustainable and the shore was covered with miles of useless sand…

DUTCH DEALINGS

The first Europeans to set foot in Bali itself were Dutch seamen in 1597. Setting a tradition that has prevailed to the present day, they fell in love with the island and when Cornelius de Houtman, the ship's captain, prepared to set sail from the island, two of his crew refused to come with him. At that time, Balinese prosperity and artistic activity, at least among the royalty, was at a peak, and the king who befriended de Houtman had 200 wives and a chariot pulled by two white buffaloes, not to mention a retinue of 50 dwarfs, whose bodies had been bent to resemble the handle of a kris (traditional dagger). By the early 1600s, the Dutch had established trade treaties with Javanese princes and controlled much of the spice trade, but they were interested in profit, not culture, and barely gave Bali a second glance.

> The Balinese rulers of Lombok recognised Dutch sovereignty in 1844, however most of the island's population had other ideas and strife continued for more than 50 years.

In 1710, the 'capital' of the Gelgel kingdom was shifted to nearby Klungkung (now called Semarapura), but local discontent was growing; lesser rulers were breaking away, and the Dutch began to move in, using the old strategy of divide and conquer. In 1846 the Dutch used Balinese salvage claims over shipwrecks as a pretext to land military forces in northern Bali, bringing the kingdoms of Buleleng and Jembrana under their control. Their cause was also aided by the various Balinese princes who had gained ruling interests on Lombok and were distracted from matters at home and also unaware that the wily Dutch would use Lombok against Bali.

9th century	1019	1100
A stone-carver – the first of many! – creates an account in Sanskrit of now-long-forgotten military victories. Bali's oldest dated artefact is proof of early Hindu influence and ends up hidden in Sanur (p147).	A future king, Airlangga, is born in Bali. Setbacks soon force him to live in the jungles of Java until he gains political power and becomes king of the two islands, unifying both cultures.	Give or take a few years, the amazing, incredible and stupendous series of 10 7m-high statues are carved from stone cliffs in a river valley north of Ubud (p201). About 900 years later, Unesco notices…

THE BATTLE FOR LOMBOK

In 1894, the Dutch sent an army to back the Sasak people of eastern Lombok in a rebellion against the Balinese rajah (lord or prince) who controlled Lombok with the support of the western Sasak. The rajah quickly capitulated, but the Balinese crown prince decided to fight on.

The Dutch camp at the Mayura Water Palace was attacked late at night by a combined force of Balinese and western Sasak, forcing the Dutch to take shelter in a temple compound. The Balinese also attacked another Dutch camp further east at Mataram, and soon, the entire Dutch army on Lombok was forced back to Ampenan where, according to one eyewitness, the soldiers 'were so nervous that they fired madly if so much as a leaf fell off a tree'. These battles resulted in enormous losses of men and arms for the Dutch.

Although the Balinese had won the first battles, they had begun to lose the war. They faced a continuing threat from the eastern Sasak, while the Dutch were soon supported with reinforcements from Java.

The Dutch attacked Mataram a month later, fighting street-to-street against Balinese and western Sasak soldiers and civilians. The Balinese crown prince was killed, and the Balinese retreated to Cakranegara (Cakra), where they had well-armed defensive positions. Cakra was attacked by a large combined force of Dutch and eastern Sasak. Rather than surrender, Balinese men, women and children opted for the suicidal *puputan* (a warrior's fight to the death) and were cut down by rifle and artillery fire. Their stronghold, the Mayura Water Palace, was largely destroyed.

The Balinese rajah and a small group of commanders fled to Sasari near Lingsar, and though the rajah surrendered, most of the Balinese held out. In late November 1894, the Dutch attacked Sasari and, again, a large number of Balinese chose the *puputan*. With the downfall of the dynasty, the local population abandoned its struggle against the Dutch. The conquest of Lombok, considered for decades, had taken the Dutch barely three months. The old rajah died in exile in Batavia (now Jakarta) in 1895.

In 1894, the Dutch, the Balinese and the people of Lombok collided in battles that would set the course of history for the next several decades. See the boxed text, above.

With the north of Bali long under Dutch control and the conquest of Lombok successful, the south was never going to last long. Once again, it was disputes over the ransacking of wrecked ships that gave the Dutch an excuse to move in. In 1904, after a Chinese ship was wrecked off Sanur, Dutch demands that the rajah (lord or prince) of Badung pay 3000 silver dollars in damages were rejected and in 1906 Dutch warships appeared at Sanur.

The Dutch forces landed despite Balinese opposition and, four days later, had marched 5km to the outskirts of Denpasar. On 20 September 1906, the Dutch mounted a naval bombardment on Denpasar and began their final assault. The three princes of Badung realised that they were completely outnumbered and outgunned, and that defeat was inevitable. Surrender and exile, however, would have been the worst imaginable outcome, so they

For much of the 19th century, the Dutch earned enormous amounts of money from the Balinese opium trade. Most of the colonial administrative budget went to promoting the opium industry, which was legal until the 1930s.

1292	**1343**	**1520**
Bail gains complete independence from Java with the death of Kertanagara, a powerful king who had ruled the two islands for eight years. Power shifts frequently between the islands: 'If it's Tuesday, we must be Javanese!'	Maybe it was a Tuesday! The legendary Majapahit prime minister, Gajah Mada, brings Bali back under Javanese control. For the next two centuries, the royal court is just south of today's Semarapura (p211).	The last bit of Java is converted to Islam, leaving Bali in isolation as a Hindu island. Priests and artists move to Bali, concentrating and strengthening the island's culture against conversion.

THE TOURIST CLASS

Beginning in the 1920s, the Dutch government realised that Bali's unique culture could be marketed internationally to the growing tourism industry. Relying heavily on images that emphasised the topless habits of Bali's women, Dutch marketing drew wealthy Western adventurers who landed in the north at today's Singaraja and were whisked about the island on rigid three-day itineraries that featured canned cultural shows at a government-run tourist hotel in Denpasar. Accounts from the time are ripe with imagery of supposedly culture-seeking Europeans who really just wanted to see a boob or two. Such desires were often thwarted by Balinese women who covered up when they heard the Dutch jalopies approaching.

But some intrepid travellers arrived independently, often at the behest of the small colony of Western artists such as Walter Spies in Ubud (see p179). Two of these visitors were Robert Koke and Louise Garret, an unmarried American couple who had worked in Hollywood before landing in Bali in 1936 as part of a global adventure. Horrified at the stuffy strictures imposed by the Dutch tourism authorities, the pair (who were later married) built a couple of bungalows out of palm leaves and other local materials on the otherwise deserted beach at Kuta. Having recently been to Hawaii on a film shoot, Bob and Louise knew the possibilities of a good beach, which at that point was home to only a few impoverished fishing families. Robert left another lasting impression by teaching local boys to surf.

Word soon spread, and the Kokes were booked solid. Guests came for days, stayed for weeks and told their friends. At first, the Dutch dismissed the Koke's Kuta Beach Hotel as 'dirty native huts', but soon realised that increased numbers of tourists were good for everyone. Other Westerners built their own thatched hotels, complete with the bungalows that were to become a Balinese cliché in the decades ahead.

WWII wiped out both tourism and the hotels (the Kokes barely escaped ahead of the Japanese), but once people began travelling again after the war, Bali's inherent appeal made its popularity a foregone conclusion. The introduction of jet travel, reasonably affordable tickets and dirt-cheap accommodation on beautiful Kuta Beach gave Bali an endless summer, which began in the 1960s.

In 1987, Louise Koke's long-forgotten story of the Kuta Beach Hotel was published as *Our Hotel in Bali*, illustrated with her incisive sketches and her husband's photographs.

decided to take the honourable path of a suicidal *puputan* (a warrior's fight to the death). First the princes burned their palaces, and then, dressed in their finest jewellery and waving ceremonial golden kris, the rajah led the royalty, priests and courtiers out to face the modern weapons of the Dutch.

The Dutch implored the Balinese to surrender rather than make their hopeless stand, but their pleas went unheeded and wave after wave of the Balinese nobility marched forward to their death, or turned their kris on themselves. In all, nearly 4000 Balinese died. The Dutch then marched northwest towards Tabanan and took the rajah of Tabanan prisoner – he also committed suicide rather than face the disgrace of exile.

1546	1597	1830
The Hindu priest Nirartha arrives in Bali. He transforms religion into what is still practised today and builds temples by the dozen, including Pura Rambut Siwi (p277), Pura Tanah Lot (p271) and Pura Luhur Ulu Watu (p137).	A Dutch expedition arrives off Kuta. Most have died from disease, murder and piracy. A contemporary describes the skipper, Cornelius de Houtman, as a 'braggart and a scoundrel'. If only he'd anchored off Seminyak.	The Balinese slave trade ends. For over two centuries, squabbling Balinese royal houses helped finance their wars by selling some of their most comely subjects, an especially horrific exploitation of classic Balinese beauty.

The kingdoms of Karangasem and Gianyar had already capitulated to the Dutch and were allowed to retain some of their powers, but other kingdoms were defeated and their rulers exiled. Finally, in 1908, the rajah of Semarapura followed the lead of Badung, and once more the Dutch faced a *puputan*. As had happened at Cakranegara on Lombok, the beautiful palace at Semarapura, Taman Kertha Gosa (p212), was largely destroyed.

With this last obstacle disposed of, all of Bali was under Dutch control and became part of the Dutch East Indies. There was little development of an exploitative plantation economy in Bali, and the common people noticed little difference between Dutch rule and rule under the rajahs. On Lombok, conditions were harder as new Dutch taxes took a toll on the populace.

> For a different take on Bali, read Geoffrey Robinson's enlightening revisionist history *Bali, The Dark Side of Paradise*. He explores the iron Balinese will, which is often lost on outsiders who see only rice farmers and artisans.

WWII

In 1942, the Japanese landed unopposed in Bali at Sanur (most Indonesians saw the Japanese, at first, as anticolonial liberators). The Japanese established headquarters in Denpasar and Singaraja, and their occupation became increasingly harsh for the Balinese. When the Japanese left in August 1945 after their defeat in WWII, the island was suffering from extreme poverty. The occupation had fostered several paramilitary, nationalist and anticolonial organisations that were ready to fight the returning Dutch.

INDEPENDENCE

In August 1945, just days after the Japanese surrender, Soekarno, the most prominent member of the coterie of nationalist activists, proclaimed the nation's independence. It took four years to convince the Dutch that they were not going to get their great colony back. In a virtual repeat of the *puputan* nearly 50 years earlier, a Balinese resistance group called Tentara Keamanan Rakyat (People's Security Force) was wiped out by the Dutch in the battle of Marga in western Bali (p272) on 20 November 1946. The Dutch finally recognised Indonesia's independence in 1949 – Indonesians celebrate 17 August 1945 as their Independence Day though.

At first, Bali, Lombok and the rest of Indonesia's eastern islands were grouped together in the unwieldy province of Nusa Tenggara. In 1958 the central government recognised this folly and created three new governmental regions from the one, with Bali getting its own and Lombok becoming part of Nusa Tenggara Barat.

> Bali's airport is named for I Gusti Ngurah Rai, the national hero who died leading the resistance against the Dutch at Marga in 1946. The text of a letter he wrote in response to Dutch demands to surrender ends with 'freedom or death!'

1965 COUP & BACKLASH

Independence was not an easy path for Indonesia to follow. A European-style parliamentary assembly was mired in internecine squabbles, with Soekarno as the beloved figurehead president. When Soekarno assumed more direct control in 1959 after several violent rebellions, he proved to be as inept a peacetime administrator as he was inspirational as a revolutionary

1856	**1908**	**1912**
Mads Lange, a Danish trader, dies mysteriously in Kuta (p101). For 16 years he earned a fortune selling Balinese goods to ships anchored off the beach. His death is put down to poisoning by jealous rivals.	The Balinese royalty go out with colour and flair. Wearing their best dress and armed with 'show' daggers, they march headlong into Dutch gunfire in a suicidal *puputan* or 'warrior's death' in Klungkung (today's Semarapura; p210).	A German, Gregor Krause, photographs many beautiful Balinese woman topless. WWI intervenes, but in 1920 an 'art book' of photographs is published and Dutch steamers docking in Singaraja (p256) now bring tourists.

THE 1963 ERUPTION

The most disastrous volcanic eruption in Bali in 100 years took place in 1963, when Gunung Agung blew its top in no uncertain manner at a time of considerable prophetic and political importance.

Eka Dasa Rudra, the greatest of all Balinese sacrifices and an event that takes place only every 100 years on the Balinese calendar, was to culminate on 8 March 1963. It had been well over 100 Balinese years since the last Eka Dasa Rudra, but there was dispute among the priests as to the correct and most favourable date.

Naturally, Pura Besakih was a focal point for the festival, but Gunung Agung was acting strangely as final preparations were made in late February. Despite some qualms, political pressures forced the ceremonies forward, even as ominous rumblings continued.

On 17 March, Gunung Agung exploded. The catastrophic eruption killed more than 1000 people (some estimate 2000) and destroyed entire villages – 100,000 people lost their homes. Streams of lava and hot volcanic mud poured right down to the sea at several places, completely covering roads and isolating the eastern end of Bali for some time. The entire island was covered in ash.

---

leader. In the early 1960s, as Soekarno faltered, the army, communists, and other groups struggled for supremacy. On 30 September 1965, an attempted coup – blamed on the Partai Komunis Indonesia (PKI, or Communist Party) – led to Soekarno's downfall. General Soeharto (he didn't get the Muhammad moniker until the late '80s) emerged as the leading figure in the armed forces, displaying great military and political skill in suppressing the coup. The PKI was outlawed and a wave of anticommunist reprisals followed, escalating into a wholesale massacre of suspected communists throughout the Indonesian archipelago.

In Bali, the events had an added local significance as the main national political organisations, the Partai Nasional Indonesia (PNI, Nationalist Party) and the PKI, crystallised existing differences between traditionalists, who wanted to maintain the old caste system, and radicals, who saw the caste system as repressive and who were urging land reform. After the failed coup, religious traditionalists in Bali led the witch-hunt for the 'godless communists'. Eventually, the military stepped in to control the anticommunist purge, but no one in Bali was untouched by the killings, estimated at between 50,000 and 100,000 out of a population of about two million, a percentage many times higher than on Java. Many tens of thousands more died on Lombok.

Bali and the Tourist Industry, by David Shavit, is a highly entertaining look at how tourism developed in Bali between the wars with the help of a menagerie of local and Western characters.

SOEHARTO COMES & GOES

Following the failed coup in 1965 and its aftermath, Soeharto established himself as president and took control of the government, while Soekarno was shoved aside, spending his final days under house arrest in the hills above

---

1925	1936	1946
The greatest Balinese dancer of the modern age, Mario, first performs the Kebyar Duduk, his enduring creation. From a stooped position, the dancer moves as if in a trance to the haunting melody of gamelan (traditional Balinese orchestra).	Americans Robert and Louise Koke build a hotel of thatched bungalows on then-deserted Kuta Beach. Gone is stuffy, starched tourism, replaced by fun in the sun followed by a cold beer.	Freedom fighter Ngurah Rai dies with the rest of his men at Marga (p272) but takes a lot of the Dutch army with him. This *puputan* slays the colonial spirit and soon, Indonesia is independent.

Jakarta. Under Soeharto's 'New Order' government, Indonesia looked to the West for its foreign policy, and Western-educated economists set about balancing budgets, controlling inflation and attracting foreign investment.

Politically, Soeharto ensured that Golkar (not officially a political party), with strong support from the army, became the dominant political force. Other political parties were banned or crippled by the disqualification of candidates and the disenfranchisement of voters. Regular elections maintained the appearance of a national democracy, but until 1999, Golkar won every election hands down. This period was also marked by great economic development in Bali and later on Lombok as social stability and maintenance of a favourable investment climate took precedence over democracy.

In early 1997, Southeast Asia began to suffer a severe economic crisis, and within the year, the Indonesian currency (the rupiah) had all but collapsed and the economy was on the brink of bankruptcy. To help deal with the continuing economic crisis, Soeharto agreed to the International Monetary Fund's (IMF) demand to increase the government-subsidised price of electricity and petrol, resulting in immediate increases in the cost of public transport, rice and other food staples. Riots broke out across Indonesia and although Bali and Lombok were spared most of the violence, their tourism-dependent economies were battered.

Unable to cope with the escalating crisis, Soeharto resigned in 1998, after 32 years in power. His protégé, Dr Bacharuddin Jusuf Habibie, became president. Though initially dismissed as a Soeharto crony, he made the first notable steps towards opening the door to real democracy, such as freeing the press from government supervision. However, he failed to tackle most of the critical issues dogging Indonesia such as corruption, and poorly handled East Timor's rocky path towards independence.

In Praise of Kuta, by Hugh Mabbett, recounts Kuta's early history and its frenetic modern development. Written in the 1980s, it recalls a time when Kuta was reviled as a hippie hang-out.

LOCAL RULE BALI STYLE

Within Bali's government, the most important body is also the most local. More than 3500 neighbourhood organisations called *banjar* wield enormous power. Comprising the married men of a given area (somewhere between 50 and 500), a *banjar* controls most community activities, whether it's planning for a temple ceremony or making important land-use decisions. Decisions are reached by consensus and woe to a member who shirks his duties. The penalty can be fines or worse: banishment from the *banjar*.

Although women and even children can belong to the *banjar*, only men attend the meetings where important decisions are taken. Women, who often own the businesses in tourist areas, have to communicate through their husband to exert their influence. One thing that outsiders in a neighbourhood quickly learn is that one does not cross the *banjar*. Entire streets of restaurants and bars have been closed by order of the *banjar* after it was determined that neighbourhood concerns over matters such as noise were not being addressed.

1963	1965	1970
The sacred volcano Gunung Agung erupts, taking out a fair bit of East Bali, killing a thousand or more and leaving 100,000 homeless. The disastrous effects still echo decades later (opposite).	Indonesia's long-running and bitter rivalry between communists and conservatives erupts after a supposed coup-attempt by the former. The latter triumphs and in the ensuing purges, tens of thousands are killed in Bali.	A girl ekes out a living selling candy on a path to the beach in Kuta. Surfers offer advice, she posts a menu, then she builds a hut and calls it Made's Warung. She prospers (p113).

TERRORISTS & RECOVERY

In 1999 Indonesia's parliament met to elect a new president. The frontrunner was Megawati Sukarnoputri, whose party received the largest number of votes at the election. Megawati was enormously popular in Bali, partly because of family connections (her paternal grandmother was Balinese) and partly because her party was essentially secular (the mostly Hindu Balinese are very concerned about any growth in Muslim fundamentalism). However, the newly empowered Islamist parties helped to shift the balance of power. By astutely playing both the Islam card and using his long-standing relationship with Golkar leaders, Abdurrahman Wahid, the moderate, intellectual head of Indonesia's largest Muslim organisation, emerged as president.

Outraged supporters of Megawati took to the streets of Java and Bali. In Bali, the demonstrations were typically more disruptive than violent – trees were felled to block the main Nusa Dua road, and government buildings were damaged in Denpasar and Singaraja. The election of Megawati as vice-president quickly defused the situation.

On Lombok, however, religious and political tensions spilled over in early 2000 when a sudden wave of attacks starting in Mataram burned Chinese and Christian businesses and homes across the island. The impact on tourism was immediate and severe, and the island is only now emerging from this shameful episode.

As with his predecessor Soekarno, Wahid's moral stature and vast intellect did not translate into administrative competence. His open contempt towards squabbling parliamentarians did little to garner him much-needed support. After 21 months of growing ethnic, religious and regional conflicts, parliament had enough ammunition to recall Wahid's mandate and hand the presidency to Megawati.

Indonesia's cultural wars continued and certainly played a role in the October 2002 bombings in Kuta. More than 200 tourists and Balinese were killed, and hundreds more were injured. Besides the obvious enormous monetary loss (tourism immediately fell by more than half), the blasts fuelled the ever-present suspicions the Hindu Balinese hold regarding Muslims (that the Muslim Javanese are trying to muscle in on the profitable Bali scene, and the Muslims from Indonesia are, in general, looking to show prejudice against non-Muslim Balinese) and shattered the myth of isolation enjoyed by many locals. See the boxed text, opposite.

Still, tourism numbers had almost recovered by October 2005 when three suicide bombers killed 20 people. Again, tourism numbers suffered and the entire island's economy took a hit.

On the national front, the elections of 2004 managed to dispel fears and were remarkably peaceful. Susilo Bambang Yudhoyono (popularly known as 'SBY') beat incumbent Megawati Sukarnoputri. A former general and government minister, SBY promised strong and enlightened leadership. He has been

Bali Blues, by Jeremy Allan, tells of the struggle by locals to survive in Kuta during the year following the 2002 terrorist attacks. Using composite characters, it explores a side of Bali rarely seen by tourists.

With staff reviews, hard-to-find titles and stellar recommendations, *the* place for books about Bali is Ganesha Books in Ubud (p173). The website (www.ganeshabooksbali .com) offers a vast selection and the shop does mail orders.

1979	1998	2000
Australian Kim Bradley, impressed by the gnarly surfing style of locals, encourages them to start a club. Sixty do just that (good on an island where people fear the water). Today, competitions attract thousands (p107).	Soeharto, who always had close ties to Bali, resigns as president after 32 years. His family retains control of several Bali resorts, including the thirsty Pecatu Indah resort (p136).	Rioting elsewhere in Indonesia spreads to Lombok and hundreds of homes and businesses belonging to Chinese, Christians and Balinese are looted and burned. The worst begins after a Muslim-sponsored rally to decry violence turns ugly.

THE BALI BOMBINGS

On Saturday, 12 October 2002, two bombs exploded on Kuta's bustling Jl Legian. The first blew out the front of Paddy's Bar. A few seconds later, a far more powerful bomb obliterated the Sari Club. The blast and fireballs that followed destroyed or damaged neighbouring clubs, pubs, shops and houses.

Close to midnight on the busiest night of the week, the area was packed. More than 300 people from at least 23 countries were injured. The number dead, including those unaccounted for, reached over 200, although the exact number will probably never be known. Many injured Balinese made their way back to their villages, where, for lack of decent medical treatment, they died.

Indonesian authorities eventually laid the blame for the blasts on Jemaah Islamiyah, an Islamic terrorist group. Dozens were arrested and many were sentenced to jail, including three who received the death penalty (which was carried out in November 2008 after many delays). But most received relatively light terms, including Abu Bakar Bashir, a radical cleric who many thought was behind the explosions. His convictions on charges relating to the bombings were overturned by the Indonesian supreme court in 2006, enraging many in Bali and Australia.

On 1 October 2005, three suicide bombers blew themselves up: one in a restaurant on Kuta Sq and two more at beachfront seafood cafés in Jimbaran. It was again the work of Jemaah Islamiyah, and although documents found later stated that the attacks were targeted at tourists, 15 of the 20 who died were Balinese and Javanese employees of the places bombed.

---

put to the test numerous times since, with the tsunami that devastated Aceh in 2004, the spread of bird flu and the volcano eruption and tsunami that hit Java in 2006. Navigating the many competing interests in such a vast nation has proved challenging. Recently, he has bowed to hardliners who want to pass a pornography bill that many fear would crush Balinese culture.

By 2007, Bali was back in the tourism business big-time. The backbone of the local economy recovered, scores of new resorts were under construction and visitors numbers looked set to hit record numbers.

2002	**2005**	**2008**
Bombs in Kuta on October 22 kill more than 200, many at the Sari Club. Bali's economy is crushed as tourists stay away and there is economic devastation across the island. The memory remains raw for many.	Schapelle Corby is convicted of drug smuggling and sentenced to 20 years in Kerobokan prison (p128). A public sensation, the waves of tawdry admissions snuff out public support and enrich Australian media conglomerates.	A decade's troubles forgotten, Bali coasts to a record 2 million visitors for the year. The old formula proves as popular as ever: fun in the sun followed by a cold beer.

The Culture

REGIONAL IDENTITY
Bali

Ask any traveller what they love about Bali and, most times, 'culture' – sometimes expressed as 'the people' – will top their list. Since the 1920s, when the Dutch used images of bare-breasted Balinese maidens to lure tourists and A-list celebrities like Charlie Chaplin, Noel Coward and anthropologist Margaret Mead, Bali has embodied the mystique and glamour of an exotic paradise. Countless books, films and poems, including Coward's famous but somewhat cynical verse (see p17), have eulogised the traditions and rituals rooted in this Hindu rice-farming culture.

For all the romanticism, there is a harsher reality. For most Balinese, as for Lombok's Sasaks, life remains a hand-to-mouth existence and the idea of culture can sometimes seem misplaced as overzealous touts on streets and beaches test your patience. See p333 for suggestions on responding to these offers.

But for all the romanticism, there's also some truth to this idea. There is no other place in the world like Bali, not even in Indonesia. Being the only surviving Hindu island in the world's largest Muslim country, its distinctive culture is worn like a badge of honour by a fiercely proud people. After all, it's only a hundred years ago that 4000 Balinese royalty, dressed in their finest, walked into the gunfire of the Dutch army rather than surrender and become colonial subjects (p38).

True, development has changed the landscape and prompted endless debates about the impact of the displacement of an agricultural society by a tourism services industry. There are nightclubs that feature stuntmen bungy jumping on motorcycles (p116), and the upmarket spas, clubs, boutiques and restaurants in Seminyak might have you mistaking hedonism for the local religion, not Hinduism. But scratch the surface and you'll find that Bali's soul remains unchanged.

The island's creative heritage is everywhere you look, and the harmonious dedication to religion permeates every aspect of society, underpinning the strong sense of community. There are temples in every house, office and village, on mountains and beaches, in rice fields, trees, caves, cemeteries, lakes and rivers. Yet religious activity is not limited to places of worship. It can occur anywhere, sometimes smack-bang in the middle of peak-hour traffic.

No matter where you stay, you'll witness women making daily offerings around their family temple and their home, hotels, shops and other public places. You're also sure to see vibrant ceremonies in full swing, where whole villages turn out in ceremonial dress and police close the roads for a spectacular procession that can stretch for hundreds of metres – men play the gamelan (traditional Balinese orchestra) while women elegantly balance magnificent tall offerings of fruit and cakes on their heads.

There's nothing manufactured about what you see. Dance and musical performances at hotels are among the few events 'staged' for tourists, but they do actually mirror the way in which Balinese traditionally welcome visitors, whom they refer to as *tamu* (guests). Otherwise, it's just the Balinese going about their daily life as they would without spectators. In fact, it would no doubt be more enjoyable without the gawking and happy snaps by anonymous foreigners.

Luckily, the Balinese are famously tolerant and hospitable towards other cultures, though they rarely travel themselves, such is the importance of

While Bali's tourism arrivals slumped some 60% after the 2002 terrorist attack, they're now back to record levels.

Island of Bali, by Miguel Covarrubias, written in the 1930s, is still a fantastic introduction to the romance and seduction of the island and its culture.

their village and family ties, not to mention the financial cost. If anything, they're bemused by all the attention, which reinforces their pride; the general sense is, whatever we're doing, it must be right to entice millions of people to leave their homes for ours.

They're unfailingly friendly, love a chat and can get quite personal (see below). English is widely spoken (less so on Lombok) but they love to hear tourists attempt Bahasa Indonesia, or, better still, throw in a Balinese phrase like *sing ken ken* (no worries) and you'll make a friend for life. They have a fantastic sense of humour and their easygoing nature is hard to ruffle. They generally find displays of temper distasteful and laugh at 'emotional' foreigners who are quick to anger. They are always willing to help and will fall over themselves to get to your kids, making Bali an extremely family-friendly destination. You do have to wonder what they must think of their guests sometimes though, when they feel the need to put up signs declaring 'Sorry, No Nude Shopping' at a big new hypermarket in Kuta. Clearly even Balinese tolerance has its limits!

For tips on respecting traditions and acting appropriately while in Bali and Lombok, see the boxed text, p348.

Lombok

While Lombok's culture and language is often likened to Bali, this does neither island justice. True, Lombok's language, animist rituals and music and dance are reminiscent of the Hindu and Buddhist kingdoms that once ruled Indonesia, and of its time under Balinese rule in the 18th century. But the majority of Lombok's Sasak tribes are Muslim – they have very distinct traditions, dress, food and architecture, and have fought hard to keep them. While the Sasak peasants in western Lombok lived relatively harmoniously under Balinese feudal control, the aristocracy in the east remained hostile and led the rebellion with the Dutch that finally ousted their Balinese lords in the late 1800s. To this day, the Sasaks take great joy in competing in heroic trials of strength, such as the stick-fighting matches held every August near Tetebatu (p318).

Bali is Indonesia's number one tourist destination, accounting for around one-third of the national market.

Lombok remains much poorer and less developed than Bali, and is generally more conservative. Its Sasak culture may not be as prominently displayed as Bali's Hinduism, but that can be its own reward as you peel away the layers.

SMALL TALK *Marion Carroll*

'Where do you stay?' 'Where do you come from?' 'Where are you going?' You'll hear these questions over and over from your super-friendly Balinese hosts. While Westerners can find it intrusive, it's just Balinese small talk and a reflection of their communal culture; they want to see where you fit in and change your status from stranger to friend.

Saying you're staying 'over there' or in a general area is fine, but expect follow-ups to get increasingly personal. 'Are you married?' Even if you're not, it's easiest to say you are. Next will be 'Do you have children?' The best answer is affirmative. Never say you don't want any. *'Belum'* (not yet) is also an appropriate response, which will likely spark a giggle and an 'Ah, still trying!'.

On Lombok, Sasak language does not have greetings such as 'good morning' or 'good afternoon'. Instead, they often greet each other with 'How's your family?'. Don't be surprised if a complete stranger asks about yours!

When I first moved to Indonesia, I quickly realised that honesty was over-rated. People had difficulty understanding that a single woman could enjoy living alone in a strange country, and I found it much easier to be married with two children, the 'perfect' family unit. But be warned: somewhere along the line, my lies became a reality. The Balinese concept of karma has a lot to answer for!

RELIGION
Hinduism

Bali's official religion is Hindu, but it's far too animistic to be considered
in the same vein as Indian Hinduism. The Balinese worship the trinity
of Brahma, Shiva and Vishnu, three aspects of the one (invisible) god,
Sanghyang Widi, as well as the *dewa* (ancestral gods) and village founders;
gods of the earth, fire, water and mountains; gods of fertility, rice, technology
and books; and demons who inhabit the world underneath the ocean. They
share the Indian belief in karma and reincarnation, but much less emphasis
is attached to other Indian customs. There is no 'untouchable caste', arranged
marriages are very rare, and there are no child marriages.

Bali's unusual version of Hinduism was formed after the great Majapahit
Hindu kingdom that once ruled Indonesia evacuated to Bali as Islam spread
across the archipelago. While the Bali Aga retreated to the hills to escape this
new influence, the rest of the population simply adapted it for themselves,
overlaying the Majapahit faith on their animist beliefs incorporated with
Buddhist influences.

The most sacred site on the island is Gunung Agung (p216), home to
Pura Besakih and frequent ceremonies involving anywhere from hundreds
to sometimes thousands of people. Smaller ceremonies are held across the
island every day to appease the gods and placate the demons to ensure balance between good *(dharma)* and evil *(adharma)* forces. See p53 for more
on how ceremonies shape everyday life in Bali.

Islam

Islam is a minority religion in Bali; most followers are Javanese immigrants
or descendants of seafaring people from Sulawesi.

The majority of Lombok's Sasak people practise a moderate version of
Islam, as in other parts of Indonesia. It was brought to the island by Gujarati
merchants via the Celebes (now Sulawesi) and Java in the 13th century. The
Sasaks follow the Five Pillars of Islam; the pillars decree that there is no god
but Allah and Mohammad is His prophet, and that believers should pray
five times a day, give alms to the poor, fast during the month of Ramadan
and make the pilgrimage to Mecca at least once in their lifetime. However,
in contrast to other Islamic countries, Muslim women are not segregated,
head coverings are not compulsory, and polygamy is rare. In addition, many
Sasaks still practise ancestor and spirit worship; a stricter version of Islam is
beginning to emerge in east Lombok.

Wektu Telu

Believed to have originated in Bayan, north Lombok, Wektu Telu is an indigenous religion unique to Lombok. Now followed by a minority of Sasaks,
it was the majority religion in northern Lombok until as recently as 1965,
when Indonesia's incoming president Soeharto decreed that all Indonesians
must follow an official religion. Indigenous beliefs such as Wektu Telu were
not recognised. Many followers thus state their official religion as Muslim,
while practising Wektu traditions and rituals. Bayan remains a stronghold
of Wektu Telu; you can spot believers by their *sapu puteq* (white headbands)
and white flowing robes.

Wektu means 'result' in Sasak and telu means 'three', and it probably
signifies the complex mix of Balinese Hinduism, Islam and animism that
the religion is. The tenet is that all important aspects of life are under-
pinned by a trinity. Like orthodox Muslims, they believe in Allah and that
Muhammad is Allah's prophet – they pray three times a day and honour
just three days of fasting for Ramadan. Followers of Wektu Telu bury their

---

The ancient Hindu swas-
tika seen all over Bali
is a symbol of harmony
with the universe. The
German Nazis used a
version where the arms
were always bent in a
clockwise direction.

Most villages have three
temples: *pura desa* (civil
temple) for main celebra-
tions, *pura puseh* (temple
of 'origin') dedicated to
the village founder, and
pura dalem (temple of the
dead) in the cemetery.

EARLY WAKEUP

Sleep in and you'll miss it. Bali, that is. At least, that's the opinion of one of the island's most renowned art collectors and cultural ambassadors, the self-made Anak Agung Rai. Clawing his way up from a humble childhood working in his father's rice fields, he founded the Agung Rai Museum of Art and attached cultural resort in Ubud (see p177).

'Can you imagine, the best beauty of Bali is missed by most visitors, who wake at 9am? That's too late,' Rai laments. 'The first light and mist represent the aura of Bali, the healing.'

While Rai is alarmed by the disappearance of rice fields for relentless villa development, particularly in South Bali, he entices visitors to venture beyond the main towns to experience village life much as it was before tourism displaced the agricultural economy.

'You don't have to go far. Just get out of bed at daybreak and *jalan jalan* (stroll) through the village as people go about their lives, and you will feel it. It makes your hair stand on end. It's still like when I was 10-years-old,' he says.

Rai, who stopped attending school at 14 to help his father, began collecting art as a teenager. Ubud was much more isolated then and he would walk 9km every day to catch the bus to Denpasar to sell paintings to backpackers, and then walk back again every evening. He astutely invested his income to gradually build his collection, and he now boasts one of the island's most esteemed museums and galleries. Rai still remains proud of his roots and welcomes visitors to join what he calls his free 'Golden Hour' tour every morning. The early walk always follows a different route through quaint villages near Ubud, providing an unmatched glimpse of the rituals, architecture and hypnotic beauty of Bali's rice-farming heritage. Snapshots of what you may see:

- palm-lined dirt tracks winding through a dazzling green landscape of terraced fields, whose impact is doubled by their stunning reflections in the paddies;
- wiry, tanned farmers riding ancient bicycles to their fields, or leading their ducks on foot, scythes in hand;
- farmers sauntering home during a downpour, using enormous banana leaves as umbrellas;
- young women making offerings around their village, tending to babies and cooking;
- old women trudging up and down steep roads with baskets or sacks balanced on their heads, perhaps heading to market or taking snacks to their husbands in the fields;
- children walking or cycling to school, or helping with chores in the village;
- people bathing by the side of the road, uninhibited, as they believe they are invisible whilst doing so;
- the biggest smiles from everyone you meet.

For some, setting the alarm for the crack of dawn while on holiday may sound criminal, but if you can drag yourself out of bed, you won't regret it. You can always rely on Bali's strong coffee to get you through the day. Better still, take a nanna nap in the afternoon, like the Balinese do, while other tourists head out in the hot sun.

dead with their heads facing Mecca and all public buildings have a prayer corner facing Mecca, but they do not make pilgrimages there. Similarly to Balinese Hinduism, they believe the spiritual world is firmly linked to the natural – Gunung Rinjani (p314) is the most revered site.

RICE FARMING

Rice cultivation is the backbone of Bali's strict communal society. Traditionally, each family makes just enough to satisfy their own needs and offers to the gods, and perhaps a little to sell at market. The island's most popular deity is Dewi Sri, goddess of agriculture, fertility and success, and every stage of cultivation encompasses rituals to intone gratitude and prevent a poor crop, bad weather, pollution or theft by mice and birds.

The complexities of tilling and irrigating terraces in mountainous terrain requires that all villagers share the work and responsibility. Under a centuries-old system, the four mountain lakes and criss-crossing rivers irrigate fields via a network of canals, dams, bamboo pipes and tunnels honed through rock. More than 1200 *subak* associations oversee this democratic supply of water, and every farmer must belong to his local *subak*, which in turn is the foundation of the powerful *banjar* of each village. The Balinese also introduced the *subak* system into western Lombok in the 1700s. For more on the life of rice farmers, see the boxed text, p275.

Although Bali's civil make-up has changed with tourism from a mostly homogenous island of farmers to a heterogenous population with diverse activities and lifestyles, the collective responsibility rooted in rice farming continues to dictate the moral code behind daily life, even in the urban centres. Every married male belongs to their *banjar*, a local division of a village, which oversees religious, political and economic decisions, and neighbours gladly work together on tasks such as house renovations. For more on *banjar*, see the boxed text, p43.

Bali's government has called for all nations to embrace a Global Day of Silence inspired by the island's own annual Nyepi tradition (see the boxed text, p62), in a bid to reduce greenhouse gas emissions. Visit www .worldsilentday.org for more information.

LIFESTYLE

The pace of life in Bali is gloriously sloooow. So slow that before international time standards were adopted, the longest measure of time was *akejepan barong*, literally 'Barong's wink'. Since a Barong mask never winks, this is akin to saying 'don't hold your breath'. A common maxim in both Bali and Lombok is *jam karet* (rubber time), which you may associate with tailors and craftsmen when you go to collect your goods, or restaurants as you wait for your meal. Rushing them is futile, so you may as well sit back and enjoy the break.

Nothing, not even monetary gain, takes priority over community and religion. The Balinese don't work long hours, but neither do they have much time off. You may see them just hanging around a lot, but their whole lives centre on their village temple and their household, within the framework of their complex Hindu calendar (see the boxed text, p66).

As they're usually preparing for or taking part in one ceremony or another, the idea of travelling to a resort island for sun, surf, shopping and spa treatments is quite foreign to Balinese. All this responsibility may seem daunting, but to the them, it's the unifying centre of their life and a source of much entertainment, socialisation and festivity. The vibrant rituals are also a major factor behind what makes the island such a captivating destination – something to remember next time you're stuck in traffic and have to detour around a ceremony!

Take Me to Paradise, by Jan Cornall, is a witty account of a divorced mother's quest to find meaning and enlighten-ment in Ubud. It's a light read with humor-ous monologues and colourful depictions of travelling in Bali.

Family Ties

Through their family temple, Balinese have an intense spiritual connection to their home. And if you thought your mother-in-law was too close at a distance of 800km, consider this: as many as five generations share a Balinese home, in-laws and all. Grandparents, cousins, aunties, uncles and various distant relatives all live together. When the sons marry, they don't move out, their wives move in. Similarly, when daughters marry, they live with their in-laws, assuming household and child-bearing duties. Because of this, Balinese consider a son more valuable than a daughter. Not only will his family look after them in their old age, but he will inherit the home and perform the necessary rites after they die to free their souls for reincarnation, so they do not become wandering ghosts.

Men play a big role in village affairs and helping to care for children, and only men plant and tend to the rice fields. Women are the real workhorses

MAJOR TEMPLES

Bali has thousands of temples, but some of the most important are listed here, and shown on the colour highlights map, pp2–3. Attending ceremonies at these temples is a major obligation for Balinese and a core part of their lifestyle.

Directional Temples

Some temples are so important they are deemed to belong to the whole island rather than particular communities. There are nine *kahyangan jagat,* or directional temples, in Bali.

- **Pura Besakih** (p215) Besakih, East Bali
- **Pura Goa Lawah** (p219) Near Padangbai, East Bali
- **Pura Lempuyang** (p232) Near Tirta Gangga, East Bali
- **Pura Luhur Batukau** (p252) Gunung Batukau, Central Mountains
- **Pura Luhur Ulu Watu** (p137) Ulu Watu, South Bali
- **Pura Masceti** (p208) Near Gianyar, East Bali
- **Pura Sambu** (p216) Gunung Agung, East Bali
- **Pura Ulun Danu Batur** (p246) Batur, Central Mountains
- **Pura Ulun Danu Bratan** (p248) Candikuning (Danau Bratan), Central Mountains

Most of these are well known and accessible, but some are rarely seen by visitors to Bali. Pura Masceti, on the coast east of Sanur, for example, is easily reached on the coast road but seldom visited, and it's an ambitious walk to remote Pura Lempuyang.

Sea Temples

The 16th-century Majapahit priest Nirartha founded a chain of temples to honour the sea gods. Each was intended to be within sight of the next, and several have dramatic locations on the south coast. From the west, they include the following:

- **Pura Gede Perancak** (p278) Where Nirartha first landed
- **Pura Rambut Siwi** (p277) On a wild stretch of the west coast
- **Pura Tanah Lot** (p271) The very popular island temple
- **Pura Luhur Ulu Watu** (p137) A spectacular cliff-top position (also one of the nine directional temples)
- **Pura Mas Suka** (p139) At the very south of the Bukit Peninsula
- **Pura Sakenan** (p152) Pulau Serangan, in southern Bali
- **Pura Pulaki** (p267) Near Pemuteran, in northern Bali

Other Important Temples

Some other temples have particular importance because of their location, spiritual function or architecture. They include the following:

- **Pura Beji** (p259) In Sangsit, northern Bali, this temple is dedicated to the goddess Dewi Sri, who looks after irrigated rice fields.
- **Pura Dalem Penetaran Ped** (p161) On Nusa Penida, this temple is dedicated to the demon Jero Gede Macaling, and is a place of pilgrimage for those seeking protection from evil.
- **Pura Kehen** (p210) This fine hillside temple is in Bangli, eastern Bali
- **Pura Maduwe Karang** (p260) An agricultural temple on the north coast, this temple is famous for its spirited bas-relief, including one of a bicycle rider.
- **Pura Pusering Jagat** (p200) One of the famous temples at Pejeng, near Ubud, this temple has an enormous bronze drum.
- **Pura Taman Ayun** (p271) This large and imposing state temple is at Mengwi, northwest of Denpasar.
- **Pura Tirta Empul** (p202) The beautiful temple at Tampaksiring, with springs and bathing pools at the source of Sungai Pakerisan (Pakerisan River), is north of Ubud.

in Bali, from manual labour jobs (you'll see them carrying baskets of wet cement or bricks on their heads) to market stalls and almost every job in tourism. In fact, their traditional role of caring for people and preparing food means that women have established many successful shops and cafés. In between all of these tasks, women also prepare daily offerings for the family temple and house, and often extra offerings for upcoming ceremonies; their hands are never idle.

Busy tourist areas in Bali feature the same hassles as large towns anywhere – traffic, noise, pollution and various social ills. Gambling on cockfights is a major problem and the main jail is overcrowded with convicted drug traffickers and dealers, including Australians and other foreigners. However, the village lifestyle remains strong in rural areas; even in urban centres, the sense of tradition is evident, albeit with modern variations.

Dagang (mobile traders) still carry baskets of snacks and drinks around town, but these days they mostly use motorbikes rather than go by foot. Motorbikes are an invaluable mode of transport in other ways too: they carry everything from floor mats and children's toys, to towers of bananas and rice sacks headed to the market, from whole families in full ceremonial dress going to the temple to bare-chested surfers. The Balinese relaxed manner extends to their driving. Seemingly oblivious to trucks, buses and cars roaring past, they will simultaneously chat on their phones or exchange pleasantries with a friend meandering alongside.

Black magic is still a potent force and spiritual healers known as *balian* are consulted in times of illness and strife. There are plenty of stories floating around about the power of this magic. The last thing a shopkeeper in Denpasar remembers before being robbed is being put under a spell which he was powerless to resist. Disputes between relatives or neighbours are also often blamed on curses, as are tragic deaths. In once case, a Gianyar man who lost his second wife and new baby during childbirth blames their deaths on a curse from his first wife; shortly before she died, he had promised he would never remarry. In a bid to overcome this curse, he commissioned a priest to perform *ngulapin* (cleansing) rituals (see opposite).

> Bali's airport, main highway and a university are named after revered national resistance leader I Gusti Ngurah Rai, who died in a *puputan* (fight to the death) against the Dutch at Marga in 1946.

OFFERINGS

Tourists in Bali may be welcomed as honoured guests, but the real VIPs are the gods, ancestors, spirits and demons. They are presented with offerings throughout each day to show respect and gratitude, or perhaps to bribe a demon into being less mischievous.

A gift to a higher being must look attractive, so each offering is a work of art. The most common offering is a palm-leaf tray little bigger than a saucer, topped with flowers, food (especially rice, and modern touches such as Ritz crackers or individually-wrapped lollies) and small change, crowned with a *saiban* (temple/shrine offering). More important shrines and occasions call for more elaborate offerings, which can include colourful towers of fruits and cakes, and even entire animals cooked and ready to eat, as in Bali's famous *babi guling* (suckling pig; see p72).

Once presented to the gods an offering cannot be used again, so new ones are made again and again, each day, usually by women. You'll see easy-to-assemble offerings for sale in markets, much as you'd find quick dinner items in Western supermarkets.

Offerings to the gods are placed on high levels and to the demons on the ground. Don't worry about stepping on these; given their ubiquity, it's almost impossible not to (just don't try to). In fact, at Bemo Corner in Kuta (p101), offerings are left at the shrine in the middle of the road and are quickly flattened by cars. Across the island, dogs with a taste for crackers hover around fresh offerings. Given the belief that gods or demons instantly derive the essence of an offering, the critters are really just getting leftovers.

Name is the first indicator of where a Balinese person belongs in their family and society, revealing birth order and caste (see the boxed text, p54). Although the Balinese are easygoing and generally egalitarian, they still observe some rules of engagement defined by the ancient caste system. Those from the Sudra caste, which comprises over 90% of Balinese, use the highest form of the Balinese language when speaking to anyone from the three highest castes composed of royalty, generals and priests. Lombok's Sasaks also observe a caste system, in contrast to Muslims elsewhere. In both Bali and Lombok, women are not allowed to marry a man from a lower caste; those that defy this usually elope. To maintain caste status, marriage between cousins is quite common, especially in rural areas and among the nobility.

A great resource on Balinese culture and life is www.murnis.com. Click through to Culture to find explanations on everything from kids' names to what one wears to a ceremony and the weaving of the garments.

Lombok

On Lombok, *adat* (tradition, customs and manners) underpins all aspects of daily life, especially regarding courtship, marriage and circumcision. Friday afternoon is the official time for worship, and government offices and many businesses close. Many, but not all, women wear headscarfs, very few wear the veil, and large numbers work in tourism. Middle-class Muslim girls are often able to choose their own partners. Circumcision of Sasak boys normally occurs between the ages of six and 11 and calls for much celebration following a parade through their village.

The significant Balinese population on Lombok means you can often glimpse a Hindu ceremony while there; the minority Wektu Telu, Chinese and Buginese communities add to the diversity.

Ceremonies & Rituals

Between the family temple, village temple and district temple, a Balinese person takes part in dozens of ceremonies every year, on top of their daily rituals. Most employers in large towns are ultra-flexible in allowing staff to return to their villages for these obligations, which consume a vast chunk of income and time. For tourists, this means there are ample opportunities to witness ceremonial traditions.

Each ceremony is carried out on an auspicious date determined by a priest and often involves banquets, dance, drama and musical perform-ances to entice the gods to continue their protection against evil forces. The most important ceremonies are Nyepi (see the boxed text, p62), which includes a rare day of complete rest, and Galungan (p335), a 10-day reun-ion with ancestral spirits to celebrate the victory of good over evil.

Under their karmic beliefs, the Balinese hold themselves responsible for any misfortune, which is attributed to an overload of *adharma*. This calls for a *ngulapin* ritual to seek forgiveness and recover spiritual protection. A *ngulapin* requires an animal sacrifice and often involves a cockfight, satisfying the demons' thirst for blood.

The biggest *ngulapin* was a dramatic island-wide event following the 2002 terrorist attack, but other smaller purifications are performed every day. You may notice a priest performing one on site after a traffic acci-dent, or a mother rubbing her hair against her child's sore spot or injury after a fall.

Ceremonies are also held to overcome black magic and to cleanse a *sebel* (ritually unclean) spirit after childbirth, bereavement, during men-struation or illness.

On top of all of these ceremonies, there are 13 major rites of passage throughout every person's life. The most extravagant and expensive is the last – cremation.

WHAT'S IN A NAME?

Far from being straightforward, Balinese names are as fluid as the tides. Everyone has a traditional name, but their other names often reflect events in a person's life. They also help distinguish between people of the same name, which is perhaps nowhere more necessary than in Bali.

Under traditional naming customs, Wayan is commonly given to a first-born child, followed by Made for second-born, Nyoman for third-born and Ketut for fourth-born. Subsequent children re-use the same set, but as many families now settle for just two children, you'll meet many Wayans and Mades. For those from the Sudra caste, these names are preceded by the title 'I' for a boy or 'Ni' for a girl. Upper-caste titles are Ida Bagus for a male and Ida Ayu for a female, followed by Cokorda, Anak Agung, Dewa or Gusti.

Traditional names are followed by another given name. This is where parents can get creative. Some names reflect hopes for their child, as in I Nyoman Darma Putra, who's supposed to be 'dutiful' or 'good' (*dharma*). Others reflect modern influences, such as I Wayan Radio who was born in the 1970s, and Ni Made Atom who said her parents just liked the sound of this scientific term that also had a bomb named after it. Tourists have inspired names like Eddie and David, and celebrity tags such as Jagger (after the rocker who married in Bali).

Some monikers honour the child's birth. I Wayan Kamar (room) was born at home, but his brother I Made Meja (table) isn't sure how he got his name. Ni Kadek Novi was named after her birth month November.

There is little attachment to these names and many Balinese adopt others as they go through life. Some herald their own deeds, such as Wayan Subamia who's better known as Wayan Kecak for his dancing prowess. Some allude to parents' misdeeds, as in I Wayan Parwa Darmaja, who's known as Wayan Sangkur, after a rooster with no tail, to reflect his father's pastime of gambling on cockfighting. Apparently fortunes had changed by the time Wayan's brother arrived: I Made Godeg was named after a rooster with a long tail.

Many are tagged for their appearance and luckily don't take offence. Nyoman Darma is often called Nyoman Kopi (coffee) for the darkness of his skin compared to his siblings. I Wayan Rama, named after the *Ramayana* epic, is called Wayan Gemuk (fat) to differentiate his physique from his slighter friend Wayan Kecil (small).

Then there are monikers that come from abbreviating formal names. Wayan Kecil's son Putu Gede is called Tude, after the second half of each name. And because parents assume their first child's name, Wayan Kecil also goes by Pak Tude (literally, Father of Tude).

The Dutch colonialists were so confused by the constant name-changing that they insisted that each person stick to just one. The Balinese obliged, officially, but their naming customs remain an expression of their cultural identity. Today, most Balinese use formal names at school, work and when meeting strangers, and nicknames around their house and village.

Note: All names mentioned here are real!

BIRTH & CHILDHOOD

The Balinese believe babies are the reincarnation of ancestors, and honour them as such. Offerings are made during pregnancy to ensure the mini-deity's wellbeing, and after birth, the placenta, umbilical cord, blood and afterbirth water – representing the child's four 'spirit' guardian brothers – are buried in the family compound.

Balinese men traditionally do not cut their hair during their wives' pregnancies. This supposedly gives the baby good hair, while making the husband less comfortable and handsome in empathy with his wife's discomfort.

Newborns are literally carried everywhere for the first three months, as they're not allowed to touch the 'impure' ground until after a purification ceremony. At 210 days (the first Balinese year), the baby is blessed in the ancestral temple and there is a huge feast. Later in life, birthdays lose their significance and many Balinese couldn't tell you their age. Today, many parents also hold much smaller, simpler celebrations to mark their child's birthday according to the Gregorian calendar.

A rite of passage to adulthood – and a pre-requisite to marriage – is the tooth-filing ceremony at around 16- to 18-years-old, when a priest files a small part of the upper canines and upper incisors to flatten the teeth. Pointy fangs are, after all, distinguishing features of dogs and demons – just check out a Rangda mask! Balinese claim the procedure doesn't hurt, likening the sensation to eating very cold ice: slightly uncomfortable, but not painful.

Another important occasion for girls is their first menstruation, which calls for a purification ceremony.

MARRIAGE

Marriage defines a person's social status in Bali – for men, it makes them automatic members of the *banjar* – and Balinese believe it's their duty when they come of age to marry and have children, including at least one son. Divorce is rare as a divorced woman is cut off from her children.

The respectable way to marry, known as *mapadik,* is when the man's family visits the woman's family and proposes. But the Balinese like their fun and some prefer marriage by *ngrorod* (elopement or 'kidnapping'). After the couple returns to their village, the marriage is officially recognised and everybody has a grand celebration.

DEATH & CREMATION

The body is considered little more than a shell for the soul, and upon death it is cremated in an elaborate ceremony befitting the ancestral spirit. It usually involves the whole community and for important people such as royalty, can be a spectacular event involving thousands of people.

Because of the burdensome cost of even a modest cremation (estimated at around 5,000,000Rp), as well as the need to wait for an auspicious date, the deceased is often buried, sometimes for years, and disinterred for a mass cremation. Brahmanas (high priests), however, must be cremated immediately.

The body is carried in a tall, incredibly artistic, multi-tiered pyre made of bamboo, paper, tinsel, silk, cloth, mirrors, flowers and anything else colourful, on the shoulders of a group of men. The tower's size depends on the deceased's importance. A rajah or high priest's funeral may require hundreds of men to tote the 11-tiered structure.

Along the way, the group sets out to confuse the corpse so it cannot find its way back home; the corpse is considered an unclean link to the material world, and the soul must be liberated for its evolution to a higher state. The men shake the tower, run it around in circles, simulate war battles, hurl water at it and generally rough-handle it, making the trip anything but a stately funeral crawl. Meanwhile, the priest halfway up the tower hangs on grimly, doing his best to soak bystanders with holy water. A gamelan sprints behind, providing an exciting musical accompaniment.

At the cremation ground, the body is transferred to a funeral sarcophagus reflecting the deceased's caste – a black bull for a Brahmana, white bull for priests, winged lion for a Ksatriyasa, and elephant-fish for a Sudra. Finally, it all goes up in flames and the ashes are scattered in the ocean. The soul is then free to ascend to heaven and wait for the next incarnation, usually in the form of a grandchild, while further ceremonies are performed to consecrate the soul and give it a place in the family temple.

ECONOMY

Bali's traditional agriculture-driven economy has been supplanted by the cold hard cash of tourism. Economists estimate that agriculture now contributes only around 20% of local GDP and a small share of the exports through coffee, copra, seaweed and cattle. Tourism-related revenue and investment

---

The Balinese tooth-filing ceremony closes with the recipient being given a delicious jamu (herbal tonic), made from freshly pressed turmeric, betel-leaf juice, lime juice and honey.

Balinese culture keeps intimacy behind doors. Holding hands is not customary for couples in Bali, and is generally reserved for small children; however, linking arms for adults is the norm, as is affection between heterosexual men.

Although exact numbers are hard to come by, it's generally agreed that Bali has Indonesia's highest literacy rate.

is the real economic pillar of the region, contributing 50 to 80% of GDP. This gap is widening further as foreign demand drives land prices as high as 500,000,000Rp per *are* (100 sq metres) in prime locations, prompting many farmers to sell or lease rice fields for villa developments.

Economists now fear Bali has become too dependent on tourism. The imbalance was starkly evident after the 2002 and 2005 bombings that prompted mass cancellations by travellers. Thousands of Balinese went out of business or lost their jobs, poverty levels rose sharply and GDP growth slowed to around 3% from 8% previously. Other crises from Avian bird flu to SARS have also hit Bali hard in recent years.

Luckily, visitor numbers have since recovered to record highs. In 2008, foreign tourist numbers were forecast to top 2.1 million compared with almost 1.7 million in 2007, led by Japanese and Australians and emerging markets like Russia and China.

The money these visitors spend at hotels, restaurants, shops and service providers, on top of revenue from investments and exports (dominated by handicrafts), means that Bali is relatively well-off compared with other provinces in Indonesia. Per-capita income is among the top 10 in Indonesia and life expectancy and literacy levels are high. So too is immigration, as Indonesians from poorer islands come seeking work, creating a large informal workforce.

Foreign tourists spend an average of US$100 per day in Bali. In comparison, locals in Denpasar spend less than US$2 per day.

However, the spoils are not evenly distributed. Some 95% of tourism revenue is divided between just three southern districts: Denpasar, Badung (including Kuta, Seminyak and Nusa Dua) and Gianyar (including Ubud). And the tourist and expat markets have created something of a dual economy: you can eat for less than US$1 at a warung (food stall), or you can indulge in champagne, caviar and imported delicacies at fine-dining restaurants for well over US$100 per person, while annual school fees range from 3,000,000Rp at local high schools, to up to US$10,000 at international schools.

Lombok's tourism industry, though much smaller, has suffered several lean years since rioting provoked by religious and cultural tensions affected Senggigi in 2000. It's also suffered as a by-product of the Bali bombings. While visitor numbers remain depressed in many areas, the Gili Islands, particularly Trawangan, have made a strong comeback. In addition, promises of a long-awaited international airport have attracted investment in tourism developments.

In both Bali and Lombok, the basic cost of living has skyrocketed. The national government continues to cut fuel subsidies and the petrol price alone rose by one-third in 2008, while the price of other basics such as rice and

STOPPING CHILD-SEX TOURISM IN BALI

Unfortunately, Indonesia has become a destination for foreigners seeking to sexually exploit local children. A range of socioeconomic factors renders many children and young people vulnerable to such abuse and some individuals prey upon this vulnerability. The sexual abuse and exploitation of children has serious, life-long and even life-threatening consequences for the victims. Strong laws exist in Indonesia to prosecute offenders and many countries also have extraterritorial legislation which allows nationals to be prosecuted in their own country for these intolerable crimes.

For more information, contact the following organisations:

Child Wise (☎ 0361-226783 ext 127; www.childwise.net) This is the Australian member of ECPAT.

ECPAT (End Child Prostitution & Trafficking; www.ecpat.org) A global network working on these issues, with over 70 affiliate organisations around the world.

PKPA (Center for Study & Child Protection; ☎ 061-663 7821 in Medan, Sumatra) An organisation committed to the protection of Indonesia's children and the prevention of child-sex tourism.

cooking oil have also risen, with no corresponding increase in the minimum wage. The average Balinese earns around US$100 a month and the disposable income of a family of four is about 40,000Rp a day. Many impoverished parents – from Bali, Lombok and other islands such as Sumba – send their children to orphanages in Bali to guarantee them an education. Food for thought when considering whether or not to leave a tip.

POPULATION & MULTICULTURALISM

The Balinese are predominantly descendents of the Malays, who travelled southeast from China around 3000 BC. Before that, ethnic strands have been traced to the Australian Aborigine, India, Polynesia and Melanesia, and a diverse range of physical features from these groups can be seen in Bali's people.

Bali is densely populated. Although tourism work has attracted many young people to urban centres in the south, most people still live in rural villages and many commute long distances to work in Denpasar. Tourism opportunities have also attracted immigrants: Indonesians from Java, Sumatra and Nusa Tenggara; Chinese, Indian and Arab merchants; and thousands of Western expats. Ethnic minorities also include the Bali Aga of the central highlands, whose Hindu traditions predate the arrival of the Majapahit court in the 15th century.

Like anywhere with high immigration, social problems such as theft, prostitution and begging are often blamed on immigrants, in this case the Javanese. However, Bali is a model of tolerance and the many different cultures and religions all coexist remarkably harmoniously. There are Chinese temples, a Buddhist monastery, Indian Ashram, Christian villages and churches, and substantial Muslim communities around Denpasar and the ports of Gilimanuk, Singaraja, Benoa and Padangbai.

On Lombok, the majority of people live in and around the principal centres of Mataram, Praya and Selong. Almost 90% are Sasak Muslims, 10% Balinese, and a small number are Chinese, Buginese, Javanese and Arab. The Sasaks are assumed to have come from northwestern India or Myanmar (Burma), and the clothing the women wear today – long black sarongs called *lambung* held by long scarves trimmed with brightly coloured stripes, and short-sleeved blouses with V-necks – is very similar to attire from those areas.

The Balinese of Lombok are a legacy of the era when Bali controlled its neighbouring island in the 1700s, and they have retained many of their traditions and customs. They contributed to the emergence of the Wektu Telu religion, and Balinese temples, ceremonies and processions remain a colourful part of western Lombok's cultural life. Among the other minority groups, the Buginese were mostly fishing families who came from south Sulawesi in the late 19th century to settle in coastal areas. The Chinese were brought over to serve as coolies in the rice paddies in the 18th century; many went on to set up their own businesses, which were singled out in the riots of 2000.

MEDIA

Following the end of Soeharto's authoritarian rule in 1998, the press enjoyed an unprecedented freedom that gave rise to many new publications and broadcasters. Although self-censorship has been a concern in light of defamation suits against editors and reporters that were based on the Criminal Code instead of the Press Law, corruption cases and human rights abuses by high-profile politicians and businessmen regularly feature in news reports. Scandalous reports based on unnamed sources are also regular features of national newspapers, along with gruesome photos and footage from disasters and crime scenes.

The magazine/comic *Bog Bog*, by a Balinese cartoonist, is a satirical and humorous insight into the contrast between modern and traditional worlds in Bali. It's available in bookshops and supermarkets and is highly recommended.

Long before the gorilla appears (!), you know *Road to Bali* is one of the lesser 'road' movies of Bob Hope and Bing Crosby. Few last long enough to see the pair vie for the affections of 'Balinese princess' Dorothy Lamour.

The tourist and expat markets in Bali and Lombok have given rise to many tourist magazines in various languages: English, Japanese, Italian, French and more. Some are very high quality and distributed internationally. See p328 and p344 for details and availability of publications and broadcast media.

ARTS

Bali's vibrant arts scene makes the island so much more than just a tropical destination. In the paintings, sculpture, dance and music, you will see the natural artistic talent inherent in every Balinese, a legacy of their Majapahit heritage. The artistry displayed here will stay with you long after you've moved on from the island.

The Sweat of Pearls: Short Stories About Women of Bali, by Putu Oka Sukanta, is a small collection of engaging stories about village life. Try to find a copy in one of the many used-book stalls you'll find across Bali.

But it is telling that there is no Balinese equivalent for the words 'art' or 'artist'. Until the tourist invasion, artistic expression was exclusively for religious and ritual purposes, and almost exclusively done by men. Paintings and carvings were purely to decorate temples and shrines, while music, dance and theatrical performances were put on to entertain the gods who returned to Bali for important ceremonies. Artists did not strive to be different or individual as many in the West; their work reflected a traditional style or a new idea, but not their own personality.

That changed in the late 1920s when foreign artists began to settle in Ubud; they went to learn from the Balinese and to share their knowledge, and helped to establish art as a commercial enterprise. Today, it's big business. Women are getting in on the act and there's more individual expression, although the term copyright has little meaning here and you will find new ideas quickly replicated. Ubud remains the undisputed artistic centre of the island and artists still come from near and far to draw on its inspiration, from Japanese glass-blowers to European photographers and Javanese painters.

Galleries and craft shops are all over the island; the paintings, stone- and woodcarvings are stacked up on floors and will trip you up if you're not careful. Much of it is churned out quickly, and some images are just plain vulgar – corkscrews in the form of life-sized male appendages, for instance – but you will still find a great deal of beautiful work. And even if it looks ordinary among its clones in Bali, it adds an exotic touch to your wall or shelf back home.

There are excellent crafts available on Lombok as well, including pottery in villages such as Banyumulek (p290). There are also many good shops and galleries in Mataram (p288) and Senggigi (p295).

Richly illustrated, The Art & Culture of Bali, by Urs Ramseyer, is a comprehensive work on the foundations of Bali's complex and colourful artistic and cultural heritage.

Dance

BALI

There are more than a dozen different dances in Bali, each with rigid choreography, requiring high levels of discipline. Most performers are not professionals, but have learned through painstaking practice with an expert. No visit is complete without enjoying this purely Balinese art form.

You can catch a quality dance performance anywhere there's a festival or celebration, and you'll find exceptional performances in and around Ubud (see p195). Performances are typically at night and can last several hours. Absorb the hypnotic music and the alluring moves of the performers and the time will, er, dance past. Admission is generally around 50,000Rp. Music, theatre and dance courses are also available in Ubud (see p183).

With the short attention spans of tourists in mind, many hotels offer a smorgasbord of dances – a little Kecak, a taste of Barong and some Legong to round it off. These can be pretty abbreviated, with just a few musicians and a couple of dancers.

On your travels, you may also notice women bringing offerings to a temple while dancing the Pendet, their eyes, heads and hands moving in spectacularly controlled and coordinated movements. This is a typical trait of Balinese dance; every flick of the wrist, hand and fingers is charged with meaning, and facial expressions are carefully choreographed to convey the character's mood. It also tends to be precise, jerky, shifting and jumpy, much like Balinese music, with its abrupt changes of tempo and dramatic contrasts between silence and crashing noise. This comic blend of seriousness and slapstick is also on show.

Dancing Out of Bali, by John Coast, tells of a ground-breaking international tour by a Balinese dance troupe in the 1950s.

Kecak

Probably the best-known dance for its spell-binding, hair-raising atmosphere, the Kecak features a 'choir' of men and boys who sit in concentric circles and slip into a trance as they chant and sing the 'chak-a-chak-a-chak', imitating a troupe of monkeys. Sometimes called the 'vocal gamelan', this is the only music to accompany the dance re-enactment from the Hindu epic *Ramayana*, the familiar love story about Prince Rama and his Princess Sita.

The tourist version of Kecak was developed in the 1960s. This spectacular performance is easily found in Ubud and also at the Pura Luhur Ulu Watu (p137).

Barong & Rangda

This rivals the Kecak as Bali's most popular dance for tourists. Again, it's a battle between good (the Barong) and bad (the Rangda). The Barong is a good but mischievous and fun-loving shaggy dog-lion, while the widow-witch Rangda is bad through and through.

The story features a duel between Rangda and Barong, whose supporters draw their kris (traditional dagger) and rush in to help. The long-tongued, sharp-fanged Rangda throws them into a trance though, making them stab themselves. It's quite a spectacle. Thankfully, the Barong casts a spell that neutralises the kris power so it cannot harm them.

Playing around with all that powerful magic, good and bad, requires the presence of a *pemangku* (priest for temple rituals), who must end the dancers' trance and make a blood sacrifice using a chicken to propitiate the evil spirits.

Kuta And Kuta, Sanur: The Birthplace of Bali Style and *Ubud is a Mood* comprise a trilogy published by Yayasan Bali Purnati that provides a fascinating insight into Bali's vibrant culture and tourism development, with essays and photographs by local and expat contributors.

Legong

Characterised by flashing eyes and quivering hands, this most graceful of Balinese dances is performed by young girls. Their talent is so revered that in old age, a classic dancer will be remembered as a 'great Legong'.

Peliatan's famous dance troupe, often seen in Ubud, is particularly noted for its Legong Keraton (Legong of the Palace). The very stylised and symbolic story involves two Legong dancing in mirror image. They are elaborately made up and dressed in gold brocade, relating a story about a king who takes a maiden captive and consequently starts a war, in which he dies. There's a message in that somewhere.

Sanghyang

These dances were developed to drive out evil spirits from a village – Sanghyang is a divine spirit who temporarily inhabits an entranced dancer. The Sanghyang Dedari is performed by two young girls who dance a dream-like version of the Legong in perfect symmetry while their eyes are firmly shut. Male and female choirs provide a background chant until the dancers slump to the ground. A *pemangku* blesses them with holy water and brings them out of the trance. The modern Kecak dance developed from the Sanghyang.

In the Sanghyang Jaran, a boy in a trance dances around and through a fire of coconut husks, riding a coconut palm 'hobby horse'. Variations of this are called the Kecak Fire Dance (or Fire and Trance Dance for tourists) and are performed in Ubud almost daily.

Other Dances

The warrior dance, the Baris, is a male equivalent of the Legong – grace and femininity give way to an energetic and warlike spirit. The highly-skilled Baris dancer must convey the thoughts and emotions of a warrior first preparing for action, and then meeting the enemy: chivalry, pride, anger, prowess and, finally, regret are illustrated.

In the Topeng, which means 'pressed against the face', as with a mask, the dancers imitate the character represented by the mask. This requires great expertise because the dancer cannot convey thoughts and meanings through facial expressions – the dance must tell all. The Topeng Tua is a classic solo dance using the mask of an old man. A full collection of Topeng masks numbers up to 40.

One of the most popular comic dances is the Cupak, which tells of a greedy coward (Cupak) and his brave but hard-done-by younger brother, and their adventures while rescuing a beautiful princess.

Dance in Bali is not a static art form. The Oleg Tambulilingan for example, developed in the 1950s, was originally a solo female dance. Later, a male part was added and the dance now mimics the flirtations of two *tambulilingan* (bumblebees).

LOMBOK

Lombok also has its own unique dances, but they are not widely marketed. Performances are staged in some luxury hotels and in Lenek village, known for its dance traditions. If you're in Senggigi in July, there are also dance and *gendang beleq* (big drum) performances (p321). The *gendang beleq*, a dramatic war dance also called the Oncer, is performed by men and boys who play a variety of unusual musical instruments for *adat* festivals in central and eastern Lombok.

The music, lyrics and costumes of Rudat performances reveal a mixture of both Muslim and Sasak cultures. The Rudat is danced by pairs of men in black caps and jackets and black-and-white chequered sarongs, backed by singers, tambourines and *jidur* (large cylindrical drums).

The Cupak Gerantang is based on one of the Panji stories, an extensive cycle of written and oral stories originating on Java in the 15th century. It's often performed at traditional celebrations. Another version of a Panji story is the Kayak Sando in central and eastern Lombok, but here the dancers wear masks.

The Tandak Gerok combines dance with music played on bamboo flutes and the *rebab* (bowed lute), as well as singers imitating the sound of gamelan instruments. It is usually performed after harvesting or other hard labour.

Music

BALI

Balinese music is based around an ensemble known as a gamelan, also called a *gong*. A *gong gede* (large orchestra) is the traditional form, with 35 to 40 musicians. The more ancient gamelan *selunding* is still occasionally played in Bali Aga villages like Tenganan.

The modern, popular form of a *gong gede* is *gong kebyar*, with up to 25 instruments. This melodic, sometimes upbeat and sometimes haunting

Canadian musician Colin McPhee played a key role in introducing Balinese music to the West and supporting gamelan tours overseas. McPhee's *A House in Bali* is one of the best written accounts of the island, packed with humorous anecdotes of music and building.

percussion that often accompanies traditional dance is one of the most lasting impressions for tourists to Bali.

The prevalent voice in Balinese music is from the xylophone-like *gangsa,* which the player hits with a hammer, dampening the sound just after it's struck. The tempo and nature of the music is controlled by two *kendang* drums – one male and one female. Other instruments are the deep *trompong* drums, small *kempli* gong and *cengceng* cymbals used in faster pieces. Not all instruments require great skill, making music a common village activity.

The pieces are learned by heart and passed down from father to son. (Music was traditionally a male occupation, although nowadays there's an all-women *gong kebyar.*) There's little musical notation, although CDs are widely available in music shops and department stores. Walter Spies, as good a musician as he was painter, was the first to record Balinese music.

Many shops in South Bali and Ubud (p196) sell the distinctive gongs, flutes, bamboo xylophones and bamboo chimes.

Balinese Music, by Michael Tenzer, features photographs, a sonography and a guide to all types of gamelan, each with its own tradition, repertoire and social or religious context.

LOMBOK

The *genggong,* a performance seen on Lombok, uses a simple set of instruments, including a bamboo flute, a *rebab* and knockers. Seven musicians accompany their music with dance movements and stylised hand gestures.

Theatre

Drama is closely related to music and dance in Bali, with the sound effects and puppets' movements an important part of *wayang kulit* (leather shadow puppet) performances. The *arja,* a dance-drama, is comparable to Western opera.

WAYANG KULIT

Much more than sheer entertainment, *wayang kulit* has been Bali's candle-lit cinema for centuries, embodying the sacred seriousness of classical Greek drama. (The word drama comes from the Greek *dromenon,* a religious ritual.) The performances are long and intense – lasting six hours or more and often not finishing before sun-up – and while many tourists become bored after a short time, every movement has symbolic meaning for the Balinese.

Originally used to bring ancestors back to this world, the show features painted buffalo-hide puppets believed to have great spiritual power, and the *dalang* (puppet master and storyteller) is an almost mystical figure. A person of considerable skill and even greater endurance, he sits behind a screen and manipulates the puppets while telling the story, conducting the *gender wayang* (small gamelan orchestra) and beating time with his chanting. Having run out of hands, he does this with a horn held by his toes!

The *dalang* is also a linguist; the standard set of traditional characters includes nobles who speak the high Javanese language Kawi, and common clowns who use everyday Balinese, as well as the national language, Bahasa Indonesia.

Balinese Dance, Drama And Music, A Guide to the Performing Arts of Bali, by I Wayan Dibia and Rucina Ballinger, is a lavishly illustrated in-depth guide to Bali's cultural performances.

Stories are chiefly derived from the great Hindu epics, the *Ramayana* and, to a lesser extent, the *Mahabharata.*

For performances in Ubud, see p195.

ARJA

An *arja* drama is not unlike *wayang kulit* in its melodramatic plots, its offstage sound effects and its cast of easily identifiable goodies (the refined *alus*) and baddies (the unrefined *kras*). It's performed outside, often with a curtain as a backdrop. A small house is sometimes built on stage and set on fire at the climax of the story!

BALI CALLS ON THE WORLD TO 'PLAY DEAD'

If you're ever in Bali for the Hindu New Year, you will be asked to play dead. Nyepi, which falls around March or April according to the Çaka calendar, is Bali's biggest purification festival designed to clean out all the bad spirits and begin the year anew. Starting at sunrise, the whole island literally shuts down for 24 hours. No planes may land or take off, no vehicles of any description may be operated, and no power sources may be used. That means no fire, lights, TV or iPods. All businesses must shut, except for hotels and hospitals. Everyone, including tourists, must stay off the streets.

For the Balinese, it's a day for meditation and introspection. For foreigners, the rules are more relaxed, so long as you respect the 'Day of Silence' by not leaving your residence or hotel and keeping noise to a minimum. If you do sneak out, you will quickly be escorted back to your hotel by a stern village police officer *(pecalang)*.

The cultural reasoning behind Nyepi is to fool evil spirits into thinking Bali has been abandoned so they will go elsewhere. The Balinese government is also promoting Nyepi as an innovative model of tackling climate change, and has called on the world to embrace a Global Day of Silence. This may seem far-fetched and impractical, but the government believes that forbidding all energy consumption for just one day would reduce pollution and encourage behavioural change. Is it likely to happen? No. But surely it's worth a try!

As daunting as it sounds, Nyepi is actually a fantastic time to be in Bali. Firstly, there's the inspired concept of being forced to do nothing, which even for resort-goers can be a complete change of scene. Catch up on some sleep, or if you must, read, sunbathe, write postcards, play board games…just don't do anything to tempt the demons! Secondly, there are the colourful festivals either side of Nyepi, which are a sight to behold.

On Nyepi Eve, you will see large ceremonies across the island with the most beautiful offerings to lure out the demons. Their rendezvous point is believed to be the main crossroads of each village, and this is where the priests perform exorcisms. Then the whole island erupts in mock 'anarchy', with people banging on *kulkuls,* drums and tins, letting off firecrackers and yelling *'megedi megedi!'* (get out!) to expel the demons. This accompanies a lively street parade of *ogoh-ogoh* (huge papier-mâché monster dolls with menacing fingers and frightening faces), whose artistic creation involves many weeks and many hands. They all go up in flames in a spectacular finale. Any demons that survive this wild partying are believed to evacuate when confronted with the boring silence on the morrow.

The day after Nyepi is known as *Ngembak Geni* (relighting the fires) and is marked by a public kissing 'war' on Jl Raya Sesetan in Banjar Kaja, Denpasar. This is the only community that still practises this unique *med-medan* (tug-of-war without rope) tradition. A referee officiates as young boys and girls pull each other to kiss on the cheek while spectators throw water all over them, apparently to deter them! Great spectator sport.

For much more on the Balinese calendar, see p335.

Future Dates of Nyepi

2009	26 Mar
2010	16 Mar
2011	4 Apr
2012	23 Mar

As the story is told by clown characters who describe and explain the actions of the nobles, the dialogue uses both high and low Balinese. The plot is often just a small part of a longer story well known to the Balinese audience but very difficult for a foreigner to understand or appreciate.

Painting

Balinese painting is probably the art form most influenced by Western ideas and demand. There is a relatively small number of creative original painters in Bali, and an enormous number of imitators. Shops are packed full of paintings in whatever style is popular at the time – some are quite good and a few are really excellent. It's rare to see anything totally unique though.

Museums in Ubud (p176) such as the Neka Art Museum, Agung Rai Museum of Art and Museum Puri Lukisan showcase the best of Balinese art and some of the European influences that have shaped it. Commercial galleries like Neka Gallery (p177) and Agung Rai Gallery (p178) offer high-quality work for sale. If you buy a painting, consider buying a frame as well. These are often elaborately carved works of art in themselves.

Traditional paintings, faithfully depicting religious and mythological subjects, were for temple and palace decoration, and the set colours were made from soot, clay and pigs' bones. In the 1930s, Western artists introduced the concept of paintings as artistic creations that could also be sold for money. To target the tourist market, they encouraged deviance to scenes from everyday life. They introduced acrylics and oils and a wider range of colours, ready-made paintbrushes and fine-woven canvas, as well as the use of perspective. The range of themes, techniques, styles and materials expanded enormously, and women painters emerged for the first time. Their work is now on show at Ubud's Seniwati Gallery (p177).

A loose classification of styles is: classical, or Kamasan, named for the village of Kamasan near Semarapura; Ubud style, developed in the 1930s under the influence of the Pita Maha; Batuan, which started at the same time in a nearby village; Young Artists, begun post-war in the 1960s, and influenced by Dutch artist Arie Smit; and finally, modern or academic, free in its creative topics, yet strongly and distinctively Balinese.

Perceptions of Paradise: Images of Bali in the Arts, by Garret Kam, is not only a detailed guide to Ubud's Neka Art Museum (p176) but also a beautiful primer on Balinese art in general.

CLASSICAL PAINTING

There are three basic types of classical painting – *langse, iders-iders* and calendars. *Langse* are large decorative hangings for palaces or temples which display *wayang* figures, rich floral designs and flame-and-mountain motifs. *Iders-iders* are scroll paintings hung along temple eaves. Calendars are, much as they were before, used to set dates for rituals and predict the future.

Langse paintings helped impart *adat* to the ordinary people in the same way that traditional dance and *wayang kulit* puppetry do. The stylised human figures depicted good and evil, with romantic heroes like Ramayana and Arjuna always painted with small, narrow eyes and fine features, while devils and warriors were prescribed round eyes, coarse features and facial hair. The paintings tell a story in a series of panels, rather like a comic strip, and often depict scenes from the *Ramayana* and *Mahabharata*. Other themes are the Kakawins poems, and demonic spirits from indigenous Balinese folklore – see the ceilings of the Kertha Gosa (Hall of Justice; p211) in Semarapura for an example.

A good place to see classical painting in a modern context is at the Nyoman Gunarsa Museum near Semarapura (p213), which was established to preserve and promote classical techniques.

Artists on Bali, by Ruud Spruit, is a well-illustrated description of the work of Nieu-wenkamp, Bonnet, Spies, Hofker, Le Mayeur and Smit, who studied and documented the culture and natural beauty of the island.

THE PITA MAHA

In the 1930s, with few commissions from temples, painting was virtually dying out. European artists Rudolf Bonnet and Walter Spies, with their patron Cokorda Gede Agung Surapati, formed the Pita Maha (literally, Great Vitality) to take painting from a ritual-based activity to a commercial one. The cooperative had more than 100 members at its peak in the 1930s and led to the establishment of Museum Puri Lukisan in Ubud, the first museum dedicated to Balinese art. Although Pita Maha has dissolved, its legacy is the never-ending trail of handicraft and souvenir shops around South Bali.

The changes Bonnet and Spies inspired were revolutionary. Balinese artists such as the late I Gusti Nyoman Lempad started exploring their own styles. Narrative tales were replaced by single scenes, and romantic legends by daily life: the harvest, markets, cockfights, offerings at a temple or a cremation. These paintings were known as Ubud style.

Meanwhile, painters from Batuan retained many features of classical painting. They depicted daily life, but across many scenes – a market, dance and rice harvest would all appear in a single work. This Batuan style is also noted for its inclusion of some very modern elements, such as sea scenes with the odd windsurfer.

Treasures of Bali, by Richard Mann, is a beautifully illustrated guide to Bali's museums, big and small.

The painting techniques also changed. Modern paint and materials were used and stiff formal poses gave way to realistic 3-D representations. More importantly, pictures were not just painted to fit a space in a palace or a temple.

In one way, however, the style remained unchanged – Balinese paintings are packed with detail. A painted Balinese forest, for example, has branches, leaves and a whole zoo of creatures reaching out to fill every tiny space.

This new artistic enthusiasm was interrupted by WWII and Indonesia's independence struggle, and stayed that way until the development of the Young Artists' style.

THE YOUNG ARTISTS

Dutch painter Arie Smit was in Penestanan, just outside Ubud, in 1956, when he noticed an 11-year-old boy drawing in the dirt and wondered what he could produce if he had the proper equipment. As the legend goes, the boy's father would not allow him to take up painting until Smit offered to pay somebody else to watch the family's ducks.

Other 'young artists' soon joined that first pupil, I Nyoman Cakra, but Smit did not actively teach them. He simply provided the equipment and encouragement, and unleashed what was clearly a strong natural talent. Today, this style of rural scenes painted in brilliant technicolour is a staple of Balinese tourist art.

I Nyoman Cakra still lives in Penestanan, still paints, and cheerfully admits that he owes it all to Smit. Other 'young artists' include I Ketut Tagen, I Nyoman Tjarka and I Nyoman Mujung.

OTHER STYLES

There are some other variants to the main Ubud and Young Artists' painting styles. The depiction of forests, flowers, butterflies, birds and other naturalistic themes, for example, sometimes called Pengosekan style, became popular in the 1960s. It can probably be traced back to Henri Rousseau, who was a significant influence on Walter Spies. An interesting development in this particular style is the depiction of underwater scenes, with colourful fish, coral gardens and sea creatures. Somewhere between the Pengosekan and Ubud styles sit the miniature landscape paintings that are popular commercially.

The non-profit Lontar Foundation (www.lontar .org) works to get Indonesian books translated into English so that universities around the world can offer courses in Indonesian literature.

The new techniques also resulted in radically new versions of Rangda, Barong, Hanuman and other figures from Balinese and Hindu mythology. Scenes from folk tales and stories appeared, featuring dancers, nymphs and love stories, with an understated erotic appeal.

Literature

The Balinese language has several forms, but the only written kind is 'high Balinese', a form of Sanskrit used for religious purposes and to recount epics such as the *Ramayana* and the *Mahabharata*. Illustrated versions of these epics, inscribed on *lontar* (specially prepared palm leaves), are Bali's earliest books. The poems and stories of the early Balinese courts, from the 11th to the 19th centuries, were written in Old Javanese or Middle Javanese, and were meant to be sung or recited rather than read. Even the most elaborate drama and dance performances had no real written scripts or choreography, at least not until Westerners like Colin McPhee started to produce them in the 1930s.

In the colonial period, some Indonesians began writing in Dutch, while Dutch scholars began documenting Balinese language and literature. Later, the use of Indo-Malay (called Bahasa Indonesia) became more widespread. One of the first Balinese writers to be published in that language was Anak Agung Pandji Tisna, from Singaraja. His second novel, *The Rape of Sukreni* (1936), adapted all of the features of traditional Balinese drama: the conflict between good and evil, and the inevitability of karma. It was a popular and critical success; an English translation is available in bookshops in Bali.

Most modern Balinese literature has been written in Bahasa Indonesia, although the annual Ubud Writers and Readers Festival aims to market Balinese and other Indonesian authors internationally to help them get their work translated into English. Short stories and poems are frequently published in anthologies, newspapers and magazines. An important theme is tradition versus change and modernisation, often depicted as a tragic love story involving couples of different castes. Politics, money, tourism and relations with foreigners are also explored. There are several anthologies translated into English, some by renowned author Putu Oka Sukanta. Other writers of note include Oka Rusmini, whose book *Tarian Bumi* follows the lives of generations of Balinese women; poet and novelist Pranita Dewi; and author Gusti Putu Bawa Samar Gantang.

It's striking how much has been published about Bali internationally, and (until recently) how little of it has been penned by Balinese – it says much about the Western fascination with the island.

Crafts

Bali is a showroom for crafts from around Indonesia. A nicer tourist shop will sell puppets and batiks from Java, ikat garments from Sumba, Sumbawa and Flores, and textiles and woodcarvings from Bali, Lombok and Kalimantan. The kris, so important to a Balinese family, will often have been made in Java.

On Lombok, where there's never been much money, traditional handicrafts are practical items, but are still skilfully made and beautifully finished. The finer examples of Lombok weaving, basketware and pottery are highly valued by collectors. Some traditional crafts have developed into small-scale industries and villages now specialise in them: textiles from Sukarara, batik paintings from Sade and Rembitan, and pottery from Penujak. Shops in Ampenan, Cakranegara and Senggigi have a good range of Lombok's finest arts and crafts, as do local markets.

OFFERINGS & EPHEMERA

Traditionally, many of Bali's most elaborate crafts have been ceremonial offerings not intended to last: *baten tegeh* (decorated pyramids of fruit, rice cakes and flowers); rice-flour cookies modelled into entire scenes with a deep symbolic significance and tiny sculptures; *lamak* (long, woven palm-leaf strips used as decorations in festivals and celebrations); stylised female figures known as *cili*, which are representations of Dewi Sri (the rice goddess); or intricately carved coconut-shell wall hangings. Marvel at the care and energy that goes into constructing huge funeral towers and exotic sarcophagi, all of which will go up in flames.

Menagerie 4, edited by John McGlynn and I Nyoman Darma Putra, features short stories, essays and poems by Balinese and other Indonesian writers, exploring modern issues surrounding this mystical island's age-old beliefs and traditions.

Bali Behind the Seen: Recent Fiction from Bali, translated by Vern Cork and written by Balinese authors, conveys much of the tension between deeply rooted traditions and the irresistible pressure of modernisation.

KEEPING TRACK OF TIME

Wondering what day of the week it is? You may have to consult a priest. The Balinese calendar is such a complex, intricate document that it only became publicly available some 60 years ago. Even today, most Balinese need a priest or *adat* leader to interpret it in order to determine the most auspicious day for any undertaking. 'In Bali, the calendar is not just to be glanced at once a day, but a document of daunting sophistication requiring extensive study to understand,' said I Nyoman Darma Putra, lecturer at Udayana University's Faculty of Letters.

The calendar defines daily life. Whether it's building a new house, planting rice, having your teeth filed, getting married or cremated, no event has any chance of success if it does not occur on the proper date. Legend has it that Bali's most esteemed artist, I Gusti Nyoman Lempad, chose the most auspicious date for his departure from the world, aged at least 116, when he simply closed his eyes and never awoke.

The calendar incorporates three systems: the 365-day Gregorian calendar, the 210-day Pawukon calendar, and the 12-month Saka lunar calendar which begins with Nyepi every March or April. The Saka calendar began 78 years after the Gregorian, so this Saka year is 1931. 'For any given date, there are several distinct names based on an interlocking cycle reflecting the 10 'weeks' *(wewaran)* consisting of between one and 10 days each, the 30 'weeks' *(wuku)* of the Pawukon calendar consisting of seven days each, and the 12 months of the Saka calendar,' said Putra. 'Auspicious days are assigned to specific combinations of these days.'

Confused yet? That's not the half of it. Certain weeks are dedicated to humans, others to animals and bamboo, and the calendar also lists forbidden activities for each week, such as getting married, and cutting wood or bamboo.

Besides the date, each box on a calendar page contains the lunar month, the names of each of the 10 week 'days', attributes of a person born on that day according to Balinese astrology, and a symbol of either a full or new moon. Along the bottom of each month is a list of propitious days for specific activities, as well as the dates of *odalan* temple anniversaries – colourful festivals that visitors are welcome to attend.

In the old days, a priest consulted a *tika* – a piece of painted cloth or carved wood displaying the Pawukon cycle – with auspicious days represented by tiny geometric symbols. Today, many people have their own calendars, but it's no wonder the priests are still in business! See the boxed text, p336, for more on the popular commercial version of the calendar.

For more on Balinese religious days and festivals, see p335.

TEXTILES & WEAVING
Bali

Textiles in Bali and Lombok are woven by women for daily wear and ceremonies, as well as for gifts. They are often part of marriage dowries and cremations, where they join the deceased's soul as it passes to the afterlife.

The most common thread in Bali is the sarong, which can be used as an article of clothing, a sheet or a towel, among other things. The cheap cottons, either plain or printed, are for everyday use, and popular with tourists for beachwear.

For special occasions such as a temple ceremony, Balinese men and women use a *kamben*, a length of *songket* wrapped around the chest. The *songket* is silver- or gold-threaded cloth, hand woven using a floating weft technique, while another variety is the *endek* (like *songket,* but with pre-dyed weft threads).

The men pair the *kamben* with a shirt and the women pair it with a *kebaya* (long-sleeved lace blouse). A separate slim strip of cloth known as a *kain* (known as *prada* when decorated with a gold leaf pattern) is wound tightly around the hips and over the sarong like a belt to complete the outfit.

Traditional batik sarongs, which fall somewhere between a cotton sarong and *kamben* for formality, are handmade in central Java. The dyeing process has been adapted by the Balinese to produce brightly coloured and patterned

The Bali Arts Festival showcases the work of thousands of Balinese each June and July in Denpasar. See p335 for details.

fabrics. Watch out for 'batik' that's been screenprinted. The colours will be washed out and the pattern is often only on one side (the dye in proper batik should colour both sides to reflect the belief that the body should feel what the eye sees).

Ikat involves dyeing either the warp threads (those stretched on the loom) or weft threads (those woven across the warp) before the material is woven. The resulting pattern is geometric and slightly wavy. The colouring typically follows a similar tone – blues and greens; reds and browns; or yellows, reds and oranges. Gianyar, in East Bali, has a few factories where you can watch ikat sarongs being woven on a hand-and-foot-powered loom. A complete sarong takes about six hours to make.

Unique to the Bali Aga village of Tenganan, in eastern Bali, *gringsing* is a complex and time-consuming double ikat process in which both warp and weft threads are pre-dyed. Typical colours are red, brown, yellow and deep purple made from natural dyes, some of which can take years to mix and age. The dyes also weaken the cotton fabric, so old examples of *gringsing* are extremely rare.

Any market, especially in Denpasar (p169), will have a good range of textiles as does Jl Arjuna in Legian (p116). Threads of Life (p177) in Ubud is a Fair Trade–certified textiles gallery that preserves traditional Balinese and Indonesian hand-weaving skills.

Balinese Textiles, by Hauser, Nabholz-Kartaschoff & Ramseyer, is a large and lavishly illustrated guide detailing weaving styles and their significance.

Lombok

Lombok is renowned for traditional weaving on backstrap looms, the techniques handed down from mother to daughter. Abstract flower and animal motifs such as buffalo, dragons, crocodiles and snakes sometimes decorate this exquisite cloth. Several villages specialise in weaving cloth, while others concentrate on fine baskets and mats woven from rattan or grass. You can visit factories around Cakranegara and Mataram that produce weft ikat on old hand-and-foot-operated looms.

Sukarara and Pringgasela are centres for traditional ikat and *songket* weaving. Sarongs, Sasak belts and clothing edged with brightly coloured embroidery are sold in small shops.

WOODCARVING

Woodcarving in Bali has evolved from its traditional use for doors and columns, religious figures and the theatrical masks to modern forms encompassing a wide range of styles. While Tegallalang and Jati, on the road north from Ubud, are noted woodcarving centres, along with the route from Mas through Peliatan, you can find pieces in any souvenir store.

The common style of a slender, elongated figure reportedly first appeared after Walter Spies gave a woodcarver a long piece of wood and commissioned him to carve two sculptures from it. The carver couldn't bring himself to cut it in half, instead making a single figure of a tall, slim dancer.

Other typical works include classical religious figures, animal caricatures, life-size human skeletons, picture frames, and whole tree trunks carved into ghostly 'totem poles'. In Kuta, there are various objects targeting beer drinkers: dildo beer-openers and signs to sit above your bar (perhaps next to the skeleton) bearing made-to-order slogans like Billy's Bar or Last Drink For 300km. You can also find life-sized American Indians, and enough species of animals to create your own replica zoo!

Almost all carving is of local woods including *belalu,* a quick-growing light wood, and the stronger fruit timbers such as jackfruit wood. Ebony from Sulawesi is also used. Sandalwood, with its delightful fragrance, is expensive and soft and is used for some small, very detailed pieces.

The website www .lombok-network.com gives details of customs on Lombok, and the arts and crafts of various areas.

On Lombok, carving usually decorates functional items such as containers for tobacco and spices, and the handles of betel-nut crushers and knives. Materials include wood, horn and bone, and you'll see these used in the recent trend: primitive-style elongated masks. Cakranegara, Sindu, Labuapi and Senanti are centres for carving on the island.

Wooden articles lose moisture when moved to a drier environment. Avoid possible shrinkage by placing the carving in a plastic bag at home, and letting some air in for about one week every month for four months.

Mask Carving

Masks used in theatre and dance performances such as the Topeng require a specialised form of woodcarving. The mask master – always a man – must know the movements each performer uses so the character can be accurately depicted in the mask. These masks are believed to possess magical qualities and can even have the ability to stare down bad spirits.

Other masks, such as the Barong and Rangda, are brightly painted and decorated with real hair, enormous teeth and bulging eyes.

Mas is the centre of mask carving and the Museum Negeri Propinsi Bali in Denpasar (p163) has an extensive mask collection so you can get acquainted with different styles before buying.

> Belgian artist Adrien Jean Le Mayeur married renowned Legong (classic Balinese dance) dancer Ni Polok when he was 55 and she was 15. His house of antique carvings became a museum (see p146).

STONE CARVING

Traditionally for temple adornment, stone sculptures now make popular souvenirs ranging from frangipani reliefs to quirky ornaments that display the Balinese sense of humour: a frog clutching a leaf as an umbrella, or a weird demon on the side of a bell clasping his hands over his ears in mock offence.

At temples, you will see stone carving in set places. Door guardians are usually a protective personality such as Arjuna. Above the main entrance, Kala's monstrous face often peers out, his hands reaching out to catch evil spirits. The side walls of a *pura dalem* (temple of the dead) might feature sculpted panels showing the horrors awaiting evildoers in the afterlife.

Among Bali's most ancient stone carvings are the scenes of people fleeing a great monster at Goa Gadja, the so-called 'Elephant Cave' (p198), believed to date to the 11th century. Inside the cave, a statue of Ganesha, the elephant-like god, gives the rock its name. Compare this to modern sculptures like the McDonald's characters outside its Kuta restaurant for a taste of the clash between new and old in Bali.

> A carefully selected list of books about art, culture and Balinese writers, dancers and musicians can be found at www .ganeshabooksbali. com/bookstore.html.

Much of the local work is made in Batubulan from grey volcanic stone called *paras*, so soft it can be scratched with a fingernail (which, according to legend, is how the giant Kebo Iwa created the Elephant Cave). Because the stone is light, it's possible to take a friendly stone demon home in your luggage, but be wary of careless handling.

KRIS

Usually adorned with an ornate, jewel-studded handle and a sinister-looking wavy blade, the kris is Bali's traditional, ceremonial dagger, dating back to the Majapahit era. A kris is often the most important of family heirlooms, a symbol of prestige and honour and a work of high-end art. Made by a master craftsman, it's believed to have great spiritual power, sending out magical energy waves and thus requiring great care in its handling and use.

OTHER CRAFTS

To see potters at work, visit Ubung and Kapal, north and west of Denpasar respectively. Nearly all local pottery is made from low-fired terracotta and is very ornate, as are functional items such as vases, flasks, ashtrays and lamp bases. Pejaten (p274), near Tabanan, also has a number of workshops producing ceramic figures and glazed ornamental roof tiles. Stunning collections of designer, contemporary glazed ceramics are produced at Jenggala Keramik in Jimbaran (p135), which also hosts exhibitions of various Indonesian art and antiques.

Earthenware pots have been produced on Lombok for centuries. They're shaped by hand, coated with a slurry of clay or ash to enhance the finish, and fired in a simple kiln filled with burning rice stalks. Pots are often finished with a covering of woven cane for decoration and extra strength. Newer designs feature bright colours and elaborate decorations. Penujak, Banyumulek and Masbagik are some of the main pottery villages, or head towards Mataram to visit the Lombok Pottery Centre (p288).

Lombok is also noted for its spiral-woven rattan basketware; bags made of *lontar* or split bamboo; small boxes made of woven grass; plaited rattan mats; and decorative boxes of palm leaves shaped like rice barns and decorated with shells. Kotaraja and Loyok (p319) are noted for fine basketware, while Rungkang, near Loyok, combines pottery and basketware. Sayang is known for palm-leaf boxes.

Architecture

BALI

Bali's architecture plays such a key role in religious, cultural and social customs that it gets its own colour section (see p29).

LOMBOK

Similarly to Bali, Lombok's architecture is governed by traditional laws and practices. Construction must begin on a propitious day, always with an odd-numbered date, and the building's frame must be completed on that same day.

A traditional Sasak village layout is a walled enclosure. There are three types of buildings – the *beruga* (open-sided pavilion), the *bale tani* (family house) and the *lumbung* (rice barn). The *beruga* and *bale tani* are both rectangular, with low walls and a steeply pitched thatched roof, although, of course, the *beruga* is much larger. A *bale tani* is made of bamboo on a base of compacted mud. It usually has no windows and the arrangement of rooms is very standardised. There is a *serambi* (open verandah) at the front and two rooms on two different levels inside – one for cooking and entertaining guests, the other for sleeping and storage. There are some picturesque traditional Sasak villages in Rembitan and Sade (p320) near Kuta.

Following its period under Balinese control in the 18th and 19th centuries, Lombok also features some fine examples of ancient Balinese architecture like the Mayura water palace (see p285) and Pura Meru (see p287). The magnificent temple compound, Pura Lingsar (p289), is the holiest on Lombok and contains both a Balinese Hindu and a Wektu Telu temple, representing the relationship between the two religions.

Australian artist Donald Friend found the freedom to pursue his provocative art and lifestyle in Bali in the 1960s. Living in Sanur, he created the Tanjung Sari Hotel, the island's first boutique hotel, and helped launch modern interpretations of Balinese architecture (see p29).

All temples and homes in Bali face the sacred Gunung Agung to pay homage to the source of irrigation for rice fields, and the site of Bali's mother temple, Pura Besakih (p215).

WARUNG = FOOD STALL

Food & Drink

Food, glorious food. Or should that be food, laborious food? Balinese cooking is a time-consuming activity, but no effort at all is required to enjoy it. That part is easy, and it's one of the best things about travelling around Bali: the sheer variety and quality of the local cuisine will have your taste buds dancing all the way to the next warung (food stall). You'll be hard-pressed to have a bad meal. Quite the opposite, you'll probably find the biggest problem is making room in your tummy and limiting yourself to three meals a day!

The fragrant aroma of Balinese cooking will taunt you wherever you go. Even in your average village compound, the finest food is prepared fresh every day. Women go to their local marketplace first thing in the morning to buy whatever produce has been brought from the farms overnight. They cook enough to last all day, diligently roasting the coconut until the smoky sweetness kisses your nose, painstakingly grinding the spices to form the perfect paste *(base)* and perhaps even making fresh fragrant coconut oil for frying. The dishes are covered on a table or stored in a glass cabinet for family members to help themselves to throughout the day.

A traditional Balinese kitchen has a wood-fired oven fuelled by bamboo or sometimes even coffee wood that creates a smoky sweetness and wonderful earthy flavour. While modern gas-powered stoves are now common, the freshness of ingredients and particular blend of spices remain defining characteristics of Balinese cuisine.

Compared with other Indonesian islands, Balinese food is more pungent and lively, with a multitude of layers that make the complete dish. A meal will contain the six flavours (sweet, sour, spicy, salty, bitter and astringent), which promote health and vitality and stimulate the senses.

There's a predominance of ginger, chilli and coconut flavours, as well as the beloved candlenut, often mistaken for the macadamia native to Australia. The biting combination of fresh galangal and turmeric is matched by the heat of raw chillies, the complex sweetness of palm sugar, tamarind and shrimp paste, and the clean fresh flavours of lemongrass, musk lime, kaffir lime leaves and coriander seeds.

Lonely Planet's *World Food Indonesia* by Patrick Witton has the low-down on Balinese high feasts as well as details of the cuisine for which the islands are known.

MARKET LIFE

There's no better place to get acquainted with Balinese cuisine than the local market. But it's not for late sleepers. The best time to go is around 6am to 7am. If you're any later than 10am, the best selections have been snapped up and what's left has begun to rot in the tropical climate.

Markets offer a glimpse of the variety and freshness of Balinese produce, often brought from the mountains within a day or two of being harvested, sometimes sooner. The atmosphere is lively and colourful with baskets loaded with fresh fruits, vegetables, flowers, spices, and varieties of red, black and white rice. There are trays of live chickens, dead chickens, freshly slaughtered pigs, sardines, eggs, colourful cakes, ready-made offerings and *base* (spice paste), and stalls selling *es cendol* (colourful iced coconut drink), *bubur* (rice porridge) or *nasi campur* (mixed rice) for breakfast. There are small packets of coffee, noodles and cleaning detergents, and cooking utensils made from natural materials, such as a stone spice grinder, coconut-wooden spoons, coconut-shell ladles and bamboo steaming pots. There's no refrigeration, so things come in small packages and what you see is for immediate sale. Bargaining is expected.

Good markets include Pasar Badung (p169) in Denpasar; the village market (p133) in Jimbaran; Bemo Corner (p101) in Kuta; Pasar Bedugal (a stone's throw from the farms); and the produce market (p196) on Ubud's Jl Raya Ubud. Market tours are usually included in cooking courses (p77).

dian, Malaysian and Chinese flavours, stem-
on and trading with seafaring pioneers. Many
uced; the humble chilli was brought by the
itous snake bean and bok choy by the Chinese,
a, by the Dutch. In true Balinese style, village
ost durable new ingredients and adapted them
yles.

a tourist resort, Bali has become the clichéd
around Indonesia and the world. Once famous
for standard backpacker fare like jaffles, banana pancakes and black-rice
pudding, Bali now offers the best of French, Moroccan, Italian, Chinese,
Japanese, Indian and even Russian cuisine. Lombok's tourist spots, especially
Senggigi and the Gili Islands, also boast a variety of food from around the
world. In fact, the diversity is so great in Bali and Lombok that it's easy to
eat Western or other Asian cuisine every meal, if that's your preference, but
it will also be your loss! See p75 for our top picks.

STAPLES & SPECIALITIES

Rice is the staple dish in Bali and Lombok and is revered as a gift of life from
God (see p49). It is served generously for every meal – anything not served
with rice is considered *jaja* (a snack). It acts as the medium for the various
fragrant, spiced foods that accompany it, almost like condiments, with many
dishes chopped finely to complement the dry, fluffy grains and for ease of
eating with the hand. In Bali, this dish of steamed rice with mixed goodies
is known as *nasi campur*. It's the island's undisputed 'signature' dish, eaten
for breakfast, lunch and dinner.

There are as many variations of *nasi campur* as there are warung. Just like
a sandwich in the West can combine any number of fillings, each warung
serves its own version according to budget, taste and whatever ingredients
are fresh at the market. There are typically four or five different dishes that
make up a single serving, including a small portion of pork or chicken (small
because meat is expensive), fish, tofu and/or tempe (fermented soy-bean
cake), egg, various vegetable dishes and crunchy *krupuk* (flavoured rice
crackers). Beef rarely features, as the Balinese believe cows are sacred. These
'side dishes' are arrayed around the centrepiece of rice and accompanied
by the warung's signature sambal (paste made from chillies, garlic or shallots, and salt). The food is not usually served hot, as it has been prepared
in the morning.

Heinz von Holzen, the chef-owner of Bumbu Bali (p144) restaurant and
author of numerous books on Balinese cuisine, says many people mistakenly
believe Balinese food is spicy. 'The food itself is not normally spicy, the
sambal is', Heinz says. That said, the Balinese certainly like some heat, and
relish a dollop of fiery sambal with every meal; you may want to taste it to
gauge the temperature before ploughing in. If you can't tolerate spicy food,
request *tanpa sambal* (without chilli paste), but make sure your pronunciation is not confused with *tamba* (more) *sambal!*

Bali's multicultural population means many warung serve pan-
Indonesian and Asian cuisine, offering a taste of different foods from
across the archipelago. Common menu items are often confused with
being Balinese, such as *nasi goreng* (fried rice), *mie goreng* (fried noodles),
the ever-popular *gado-gado*, which is actually from Java, and *rendang sapi*
(beef curry), which is from Sumatra. There are many Padang restaurants
(see p76) in main tourist areas of Bali and Lombok, and Chinese food
is especially common on Lombok. See the boxed text, p72, for some of
Lombok's famous dishes.

Janet de Neefe's *Fragrant Rice* is part memoir, part cookbook and part cultural guide. It's a warm and informative telling of her deepening immersion into Balinese life, framed around traditional food and the rich rituals and customs that surround it.

The Food of Bali by Heinz von Holzen and Lother Arsana brings to life everything from *cram cam* (clear chicken soup with shallots) to *bubuh injin* (black-rice pudding). Von Holzen's books also include a forthcoming one on Balinese markets.

SPICY SASAK FLAVOURS

Lombok's Sasak people are predominantly Muslim, so Bali's porky plethora does not feature in their diet of fish, chicken, vegetables and rice. The fact that *lombok* means chilli in Indonesian makes sense, as Sasaks like their food spicy; *ayam taliwang* (whole split chicken roasted over coconut husks served with a peanut, tomato-chilli-lime dip) is one example.

Ares is a dish made with chilli, coconut juice and banana-palm pith; sometimes it's mixed with chicken or meat. *Sate pusut* is a delicious combination of minced fish, chicken or beef flavoured with coconut milk, garlic, chilli and other spices and wrapped around a lemongrass stick and grilled. Three vegetarian dishes are *kelor* (hot soup with vegetables), *serebuk* (vegetables mixed with grated coconut) and *timun urap* (sliced cucumber with grated coconut, onion and garlic).

Breakfast

Many Balinese save their appetite for lunch. They might kick-start the day with a cup of rich, sweet black coffee and a few sweet *jaja* at the market: colourful temple cakes, glutinous rice cakes, boiled bananas in their peels, fried banana fritters and *kelopon* (sweet-centred rice balls). Popular fresh fruits include snake fruit, named after its scaly skin, and jackfruit, which is also delicious stewed with vegetables.

The famous *bubur injin* (black-rice pudding with palm sugar, grated coconut and coconut milk), which most tourists find on restaurant dessert menus, is actually a breakfast dish and a fine way to start the day. Another variation available at the morning market is the nutty *bubur kacang hijau* (green mung-bean pudding) fragrantly enriched by ginger and *pandan* leaf and served warm with coconut milk. It's popular with pregnant women, as it's believed to bestow a good head of hair to the baby.

If the Balinese feel like a bigger breakfast, *nasi campur* is the standard fare they'll opt for. They may eat leftovers from the previous day while they await the fresh offerings at lunch, or grab a fresh *nasi bungkus* (takeaway meal wrapped in banana leaves or grease-proof paper) at a market stall or street cart.

Lunch & Dinner

The household or warung cook usually finishes preparing the day's dishes midmorning, so lunchtime is around 11am when the food is freshest. This is the main meal of the day. Leftovers are eaten for dinner, or by tourists who awake late and do not get around to lunch until well and truly after everyone else has had their fill! Dessert is a rarity; for special occasions, it consists of fresh fruit and gelati-style coconut ice cream.

The secret to a good *nasi campur* is often in the cook's own *base*, which flavours the pork, chicken or fish, and sambal, and which may add just the right amount of heat to the meal at one place, or set your mouth ablaze at another. The range of dishes is endless. Some local favourites include *babi kecap* (pork stewed in sweet soy sauce), *ayam goreng* (fried chicken), *urap* (steamed vegetables with coconut), *lawar* (see the boxed text, opposite), fried tofu or tempe in a sweet soy or chilli sauce, fried peanuts, salty fish or eggs, *perkodel* (fried corn cakes) and various satay made from chunks of goat meat, chicken, pork or even turtle, although there are laws against illegal turtle slaughter.

Ceremonial dishes (see p74) are widely available at warung and restaurants, and a meal of *babi guling* (suckling pig) is the quintessential Bali experience. The whole pig is stuffed with chilli, turmeric, ginger, galangal, shallots, garlic, coriander seeds and aromatic leaves, basted in turmeric and coconut oil

If you really enjoy spicy food, you can ask the staff in any restaurant to serve a fresh sambal of chopped chilli drowned in *kecap manis* (sweet soy sauce).

and skewered on a wooden spit over an open fire. Men perform the sweaty and no doubt mouth-watering job of turning it for hours and hours until it's cooked to perfection, the meat taking on the flavour of the spices inside the animal's stomach, and the fire-pit giving a rustic smoky flavour to the crispy crackling.

Short of being invited to a ceremonial feast (for which you should acquire appropriate dress!), you can enjoy *babi guling* at the famous Warung Ibu Oka (p193) near Ubud's royal palace. Another highly recommended *babi guling* specialist that's yet to be 'discovered' is Warung Dobil on Jl Srikandi in Nusa Dua.

Bebek or *ayam betutu* (smoked duck or chicken) is another ceremonial favourite. The bird is stuffed with spices, wrapped in coconut bark and banana leaves, and cooked all day over smouldering rice husks and coconut husks. Ubud is the best place to enjoy smoked duck – head to Bebek Bengil (p193). *Ayam betutu* is more prevalent in Denpasar. Often served at marriage ceremonies, *jukut ares* is a light, fragrant broth made from banana stem and usually containing chopped chicken or pork. The satay for special occasions, *sate lilit,* is a fragrant combination of good-quality minced fish, chicken or pork with lemongrass, galangal, shallots, chilli, palm sugar, kaffir lime and coconut milk. This is wrapped onto skewers and grilled. Big ceremonies will call for hundreds of *sate lilit,* which is becoming more common on restaurant menus. Snap it up if you see it!

White pepper is the preferred pepper in Asia, so don't be surprised if it's hard to find black pepper in restaurants.

DRINKS

Beer drinkers are well catered for in Bali thanks to Indonesia's national brew, Bintang, and locally produced Storm microbrews, which are excellent if somewhat uncommon. Wine connoisseurs, however, had better have a fat wallet. The abundance of high-end eateries and hotels has made fine *vino* from the world's best regions widely available but it is whacked with a hefty luxury tax. There are two local producers. The finest is Wine of the Gods, which overcomes the import duties by bringing freshly crushed grapes from Western Australia and processing and bottling the wine in Denpasar. Hatten Wine, based in North Bali, has gained quite a following for its glowing pink rosé. While alcohol is not as prolific on Lombok, liquors and beer are available in touristy areas like Senggigi.

At large social gatherings, Balinese men might indulge in *arak* (fermented rice wine that tourists may associate with rocket fuel in Kuta bars),

WE DARE YOU *Janet de Neefe*

Horrifying to most tourists, *daluman* is a wobbly green drink full of natural chlorophyll and a bunch of health-giving nutrients. You could be forgiven for thinking it's green slime or something scooped out of a Balinese river, but when served with palm-sugar syrup and a swirl of roasted coconut milk, it is sublime! It cools down a hot tummy and is said to help prevent stomach cancer.

Eels are an islandwide favourite and there's nothing tastier than deep-fried seasoned eel or even eel chopped and steamed in banana leaves, with freshly ground spices and a touch of delicate torch ginger.

Lawar is another popular dish not for the faint-hearted: a mix of vegetables including long beans, young jackfruit, young papaya, star fruit leaves and wild fern tips are hand-mixed with chopped fried liver, fried entrails, a dollop of congealed pig's blood, and flavoured with fragrant coconut milk broth, roasted shredded coconut and sambal.

For a refreshing treat, try *es campur*. It is a mountainous mix of crushed ice, fresh fruits, fermented yam, seaweed jelly and lashings of sweetened condensed milk and iridescent pink syrup.

TOP FIVE TOP-END RESTAURANTS

- Bumbu Bali (p144) – Hands-down the best Balinese food on the island in a traditional house set-up. Gorge on the *rijsttafel*.

- Kafe Warisan (p125) – Lauded as Bali's best restaurant for its classic French fare with (receding) rice-paddy views. Save room for dessert.

- La Lucciola (p124) – Magical beachfront setting, delightful Mediterranean food. Don't miss brunch.

- Lombok Lounge (p324) in Kuta, Lombok – Scintillating chilli crab and mouth-smacking Sasak favourites like *sate pusut*.

- Mozaic (p194) – Modern French food with a Balinese twist. Indulge in the tasting menu.

---

but generally they are not big drinkers, and Lombok's majority Muslim population frowns upon alcohol consumption. Local non-alcoholic refreshments available from markets, street vendors and some warung are colourful, tasty and even a little psychedelic without the hangover! One of Bali's most popular is *cendol,* an interesting mix of palm sugar, fresh coconut milk, crushed ice and various other random flavourings and floaties. Another adventurous concoction is *daluman* (see the boxed text, p73), while a creamy treat is *es teler,* a mix of avocado, young coconut and sago. Fresh coconut juice is enjoyed straight out of the shell through a straw at many tourist sites.

Many Western eateries sell imported coffees and teas alongside local brands, some of which are very good, but by far the most expensive – and arguably the world's rarest – is Indonesia's peculiar *kopi luwak,* aka 'cat-poo coffee'. Around 200,000Rp a cup, this coffee is named after the cat-like civet *(luwak)* indigenous to Sulawesi, Sumatra and Java that feasts on ripe coffee cherries. Entrepreneurs with a nose for a gimmick collect the intact beans found in the civet's droppings and process them to produce an extra-bitter, strong brew. Anyone keen for a cup of – quite literally – shit coffee can find it at Bali@Cyber Café (p105) in Kuta.

CELEBRATIONS & CEREMONIES

Food is not just about enjoyment and sustenance. Like everything in Balinese life, it is an intrinsic part of the daily rituals and a major part of ceremonies to honour the gods. The menu varies according to the importance of the occasion. By far the most revered dish is *babi guling* (see p72), presented during rites-of-passage ceremonies such as a baby's three-month blessing, an adolescent's tooth filing, or a wedding. This will be accompanied by towers of *sate* (satay), plaques of *sarad* (colourful rice cakes) and *nasi kuning* (pyramids of yellow rice flavoured with saffron, turmeric and ginger). A small home ceremony might include *bebek betutu* (see p73) and *jukut ares* (see p73).

While women cook the daily food, only men are allowed to be ceremonial chefs, becoming 'spice Gods' for the occasion. The action begins in the early hours of the morning, when pigs, ducks or chickens are slaughtered and then prepared for a banquet of dishes that will be used as offerings to God and to feed all those who have helped in the preparations. It's community work at its best, sometimes with hundreds of men pounding meat and grinding kilos of spices, chopping and slicing vegetables, boiling coconut milk, frying entrails and making hundreds of satays. Once blessed, the cooked food is shared and eaten by the family and their guests.

Balinese ceremonies are determined by the phases of the sun, the moon and the stars, and you only have to glance at a Balinese calendar to see how many religious celebrations are held annually. For more information on the Balinese calendar, check out www.indo.com/culture/calendar.html.

WHERE TO EAT & DRINK

The most common place for dining out in Bali and Lombok is a warung, the traditional roadside eatery. There's one every few metres in major towns, and several even in small villages. They are cheap, no-frills hang-outs with a couple of well-worn bench seats and a relaxed atmosphere; you may find yourself sharing a table with strangers as you watch the world go by. The food is fresh and different at each, and usually displayed in a glass cabinet at the entrance where you can create your own *nasi campur* or just order the house standard.

A warung *lesehan* (resting place) is often found hugging the coastline or out in the villages. These simple above-ground wooden pavilions are furnished with low tables and bamboo mats on which diners sit.

Rumah makan or *restoran* is a step above a warung in terms of atmosphere, although the food is often similar. For fine dining, there are many more upmarket and expensive restaurants particularly in Seminyak (home to Jl Laksmana) and Ubud, and in exclusive hotels. These are often run by chefs who serve excellent world-class cuisine, some of it inspired by Balinese flavours or techniques. See opposite for our top picks.

Quick Eats

As many Balinese can't afford fine food and surrounds, the most authentic food is found at street level. Even high-rollers know this, and businessmen, politicians and judges gather alongside taxi drivers and construction workers around simple food stalls in markets and on village streets, wave down *dagang* (mobile traders) who ferry sweet and savoury snacks around by bicycle or motorcycle, and queue for *sate* or *bakso* (Chinese meatballs in a light soup) at the *kaki-lima* carts. *Kaki-lima* translates as something five-legged and refers to the three legs of the cart and the two of the vendor, who is usually Javanese. You can see the carts winding through village streets and scurrying out of the way of buses and trucks on busy highways. See p76 for hygiene considerations regarding street food.

Every town of any size in Bali and Lombok will have a *pasar malam* (night market). You can sample a vast range of fresh offerings from warung and carts after dark.

VEGETARIANS

Bali is a dream come true for vegetarians. Protein-rich tofu and tempe are part of the staple diet, and many local dishes that just happen to be vegetarian are so tasty they almost convert carnivores. Try *nasi saur* (rice flavoured by toasted coconut and accompanied by tofu, tempe, vegetables and sometimes egg), *urap* (a delightful blend of steamed vegetables mixed with grated coconut and spices), *gado-gado* (tofu and tempe mixed with steamed vegetables, boiled egg and peanut sauce), and *sayur hijau* (leafy green vegetables, usually *kangkung* – water spinach – flavoured with a tomato-chilli sauce). See the boxed text on p72 for Sasak-style vegetarian food on Lombok.

TOP FIVE WARUNG

- Ayam Goreng Kalasan (p168) – Amazing chicken that's been marinated in a plethora of spices.
- Cak Asm (p168) – Spotless place serving truly amazing fare, especially seafood.
- Nasi Ayam Kedewatan (p194) – The place for *sate lilit* in a simple open-front dining room on the edge of Ubud.
- Warung Kolega (p125) – With an extension range of delicious dishes from across the archipelago, this warung offers an authentic alternative to the touristy places along Seminyak's 'Eat Street' (Jl Oberoi).
- Warung Nikmat (p112) – Great fare in an area (Tuban) better known for humdrum offerings.

FOOD FOR THOUGHT

The dreaded Bali Belly is not nearly as common as it once was and that old rule of avoiding raw foods in Bali no longer applies. Most warung and restaurants take great care with hygiene, particularly in tourist areas, and wash vegetables and fruits in bottled or at least boiled water.

However, if you want to sample the street food, keep in mind that meat products that sit in a glass cabinet in tropical heat require a major dose of preservatives such as formaldehyde and probably lashings of MSG. Known as 'ajina moto', MSG is also used as a flavouring in many warung. Those that don't use it will often advertise this to attract the tourist crowd.

Padang restaurants are especially risky hygiene-wise. While delicious when cooked fresh, Padang fare (which originates from Sumatra) takes the idea of 'sharing a meal' to a new level. The dishes are displayed in a glass cabinet and the waiter brings a portion of each to your table. You're free to sample as few or as many as you like: a spoonful of this, a spoonful of that. What a great way to try so many different dishes and flavours. But, here's the kicker: what you don't eat (and similarly what the person before you didn't eat) is mixed back into the big pots, ready for the next table. Waste not, want not!

In addition, the way *nasi campur* is served means it's easy to request no meat, instead enjoying an array of fresh stir-fries, salads and tofu and tempe. When ordering curries and stir-fries such as *cap cay* in both Bali and Lombok, diners can usually choose either meat, seafood or vegetarian.

Western-style vegetarian pasta and salads abound in most restaurants and many purely vegetarian eateries cater for vegans. Famous for their gourmet organic fare are Zula Vegetarian Paradise (p123) in Seminyak, Bali, and the vegetarian-with-a-view, Astari (p324) in Kuta, Lombok.

For 'aquatarians' (vegetarians who eat seafood), nearly all menus feature several seafood options. In Bali the string of seafood warung (p135) along Jimbaran beach are famous for their whole fish barbecued over coconut husks and served with Balinese condiments at your table on the sand as the sun goes down. If you're heading up the east coast, stop at any of the numerous warung *lesehan* along the main road to Karangasem, after the Keramas surf break, which are renowned for serving delicious minced seafood three ways: grilled inside banana leaves *(ikan pepes)*, rolled over a wooden skewer *(sate lilit)*, or rounded into balls and served with soup *(bakso)*. On Lombok, delicious fresh grilled fish can be found at Warung Manega (p295) in Senggigi, and Juku (p309) on Gili Trawangan.

For an exhaustive run-down of eating options in Bali, check out www .balieats.com. The listings are encyclopaedic, although you may wish it were a bit more critical.

EATING WITH KIDS

Eating out as a family is one of the joys of travelling around Bali and Lombok. Highchairs are not common but children are treated like deities by doting staff who will clamour to grab yours (especially young babies) while Mum and Dad enjoy some quiet time together. Try not to be too uptight about strangers getting up close and personal with your little 'uns. Indonesians just cannot help themselves, so sit back, relax and enjoy the opportunity!

Obviously, if your children don't like spicy foods, show caution in offering them local cuisine. Many warung will serve food without sauces upon request, such as plain white rice, fried tempe or tofu, chicken, boiled vegetables and boiled egg. Most restaurants serve old favourites like spaghetti, chips, eggs on toast, and ice cream.

Commercial baby foods and milk formula are available in supermarkets.

HABITS & CUSTOMS

Eating is a solitary exercise in Bali and conversation is limited. Families rarely eat together; everyone makes up their own plate whenever they're hungry.

The Balinese eat with their right hand, which is used to give and receive all good things. The left hand deals with unpleasant sinister elements (such as ablutions). It's customary to wash your hands before eating, even if you use a spoon and fork; local restaurants always have a sink outside the restrooms. If you choose to eat the local way, use the bowl of water provided at the table to wash your hands after the meal, as licking your fingers is not appreciated.

The easygoing Balinese do not complain in restaurants, but if there's something you don't like about a meal, you will get a better response if you let the waiter know in a polite, almost apologetic way.

Balinese are formal about behaviour and clothing, and it isn't polite to enter a restaurant or eat a meal half-naked, no matter how many sit-ups you've been doing or new piercings and tattoos you've acquired. And while it's OK to chomp on your food, blowing your nose at the table is quite offensive.

If you wish to eat in front of a Balinese, it's polite to invite them to join you, even if you know they will say 'No', or you don't have anything to offer. If you're invited to a Balinese home for a meal, your hosts will no doubt insist you eat more, but you may always politely pass on second helpings or refuse food you don't find appealing.

Despite its name, mangosteen is not related to the mango. It is, however, a popular tropical fruit for the peach-like flavour and texture of its white centre, and is often called 'queen of fruit'.

COOKING COURSES

Preparing your own Balinese banquet is a fantastic, hands-on way to get acquainted with the ingredients, flavours and techniques of Balinese cooking, and the habits and rituals associated with food. Even if you do not fancy yourself as a cook, you will savour every bite all the more for appreciating the work that went into it. There are several half- and full-day cooking courses in South Bali, which usually start with an early-morning market tour to introduce you to the freshness and variety of produce, and the vibrancy of market life. Look for cooking classes in Tanjung Benoa (p143), Seminyak (p121) and Ubud (see p183).

EAT YOUR WORDS

Although you won't find language much of a barrier, see the Language chapter (p373) for pronunciation guidelines.

You must not speak harshly of anything that lives in the rice fields, including ducks, eels, frogs and rats. Rice is the sacred grain and any creature that lives in these verdant fields must be treated with respect.

Useful Phrases

Here are some handy phrases that will help you enjoy a meal in Bali and Lombok.

Where's a...?	*... di mana?*
food stall	*warung*
night market	*pasar malam*
restaurant	*rumah makan*
Can I see the menu, please?	*Minta daftar makanan?*
Do you have a menu in English?	*Apaka ada daftar makanan dalam baasa Inggeris?*
I'm hungry.	*Saya lapar.*
I'll try what they're having.	*Saya mau masakan seperti yang mereka pesan.*
Not too spicy, please.	*Kurang pedas.*
I like it hot and spicy.	*Saya suka masakan pedas.*

I don't eat...	*Saya tidak mau makan...*
chicken	*ayam*
fish	*ikan*
meat	*daging*
milk & cheese	*susu dan keju*
pork	*daging babi*
poultry	*ayam*
seafood	*makanan laut*

A bowl of cooked *kangkung* (water spinach) for dinner is guaranteed to give you a good night's sleep, as it is full of natural tryptophan.

Thank you, that was delicious.	*Enak sekali, terima kasee.*
The bill, please.	*Minta bon.*
Do you accept credit cards?	*Bisa bayar dengan kartu kredit?*

| **Do you have a highchair for the baby?** | *Ada kursi khusus untuk bayi?* |

I'm a vegetarian/I eat only vegetables.	*Saya hanya makan sayuran.*
Do you have any vegetarian dishes?	*Apakah ada makanan nabati?*
Does this dish have meat?	*Apakah masakan ini ada dagingnya?*
Can I get this without the meat?	*Bisa minta masakan ini tanpa daging?*

| **What's that?** | *Apa itu?* |

Can you please bring me (some/more)...?	*Bisa minta... (lagi)?*
chilli sauce/relish	*sambal*
beer	*bir*
a napkin	*tisu*
pepper	*lada*
soy sauce	*kecap*
a spoon	*sendok*
coffee	*kopi*
tea (with sugar)	*teh manis*
tea (without sugar)	*teh pahit*
water	*air minum*

Food & Drink Glossary

Green coconut juice is the perfect traditional remedy for heatstroke, Bali belly and fever.

Almost every restaurant in Bali – from humble to fabled – will have a few of these classic dishes on the menu. Some can be found throughout Indonesia, others are unique to Bali and/or Lombok.

air botol, aqua – bottled water

air minum – drinking water

arak – spirits distilled from palm sap

ayam – chicken

ayam taliwang – whole split chicken roasted over coconut husks served with a tomato-chilli-lime dip (Lombok)

babi – pig

babi guling – spit-roast pig stuffed with a Balinese spice paste (Bali)

bakmi/mie goreng – rice-flour noodles fried with vegetables, and often meat and sauces

bakso ayam – light chicken soup with glass noodles and meatballs; a street-stall standard

bebek betutu – duck stuffed with Balinese spice paste, wrapped in coconut bark and banana leaves and cooked all day over smouldering rice husks and coconut husks (Bali)

beef rendang – beef cooked until very tender with coconut and spices

brem – a type of rice wine, distilled from white and black rice (Bali)

bubur injin – black-rice pudding made from black sticky rice and served with coconut milk (Bali)

cap cai – stir-fried vegetables (Chinese)
cendol – coconut-milk drink mixed with palm sugar and crushed ice
daging sapi – beef
dingin – cold
es campur – a mixture of sliced fresh fruit, coconut fruits, seaweed jelly and fermented cassava served with shaved ice and sweet syrup
fu yung hai – a Chinese-style omelette with a sweet-and-sour sauce
gado-gado – steamed or salad vegetables tossed in a spicy peanut sauce
goreng – fried
isen – galangal, a gingerlike spice; also called *laos* and *lengkuas*
ikan – fish
jambu – guava
jeruk manis – orange
kacang – peanut
kari – curry
kelor – hot soup with vegetables (Lombok)
kentang – potatoes
kepiting – crab
kerupuk – rice crackers; also called *krupuk*
kodok – frog
kopi – coffee
krupuk udang – prawn crackers
lawar – a salad of chopped coconut, spices, meat (pork, chicken or liver) and sometimes blood
mangga – mango
mie kuah – noodle soup
nanas – pineapple
nangka – jackfruit
nasi campur – steamed rice served with a selection of meat and vegetable side dishes
nasi goreng – fried rice that includes Chinese greens and often meat; often served with satay and a fried egg
nasi putih – plain white steamed rice
pahit – 'bitter'; word meaning 'no sugar' in tea or coffee
panas – hot (temperature)
pepesan ikan – spiced fish wrapped in banana leaves and steamed or grilled
pisang goreng – fried banana fritters; a popular streetside snack
rambutan – red fruit covered in hairy spines, containing sweet white flesh
rendang – beef coconut curry
rijsttafel – literally, rice table; a Dutch adaptation of an Indonesian banquet encompassing a wide variety of dishes
sambal – chilli sauce or paste; contains chillies, garlic or shallots, and salt
sares – chilli, coconut juice and banana-palm pith; sometimes mixed with chicken or meat (Lombok)
sate – grilled meat on skewers with peanut sauce; also spelled satay
sayur – vegetable
serebuk – vegetables mixed with grated coconut (Lombok)
serombotan – spicy salad of chilli, water spinach, bean sprouts, long beans, coconut milk and peanuts
soto ayam – light chicken soup
susu – milk
teh – tea
tempe – Indonesian soy-bean cake
timun urap – sliced cucumber with grated coconut, onion and garlic (Lombok)
tom – pounded duck, pork, chicken or their livers, with spices and steamed in a banana leaves (Bali)
tuak – palm beer/wine
urap – greens with grated coconut, chilli, shallots and garlic

Before sharing cooked food among themselves, the Balinese offer a little to the gods, in gratitude for the gift of life that food represents.

If you happen to be drinking coffee with a Balinese person, don't be surprised if they tip the top layer of their coffee on the ground. This is an age-old protection against evil spirits.

Environment

THE LAND

Bali is a small island, midway along the string of islands that makes up the Indonesian archipelago. It's adjacent to the most heavily populated island of Java, and immediately west of the chain of smaller islands comprising Nusa Tenggara, which includes Lombok.

The island is visually dramatic – a mountainous chain with a string of active volcanoes, it includes several peaks around 2000m. Gunung Agung, the 'Mother Mountain', is over 3000m high. The agricultural lands in Bali are south and north of the central mountains. The southern region is a wide, gently sloping area, where most of the country's abundant rice crop is grown. The northern coastal strip is narrower, rising rapidly into the foothills of the central range. It receives less rain, but coffee, copra, rice and cattle are farmed there.

Bali also has some arid, less-populated regions. These include the western mountain region, and the eastern and northeastern slopes of Gunung Agung. The Nusa Penida islands are dry, and cannot support intensive rice agriculture. The Bukit Peninsula is similarly dry, but with the growth of tourism and other industries, it's becoming more populous.

Bali is volcanically active and extremely fertile. The two go hand-in-hand as eruptions contribute to the land's exceptional fertility, and high mountains provide the dependable rainfall that irrigates Bali's complex and amazingly beautiful patchwork of rice terraces. Of course, the volcanoes are a hazard as well – Bali has endured disastrous eruptions in the past and no doubt will again in the future. Apart from the volcanic central range, there are the limestone plateaus that form the Bukit Peninsula, in the extreme south of Bali, and the island of Nusa Penida.

As with Bali, Lombok's traditional economy has driven intensive rice cultivation. The wooded slopes of Gunung Rinjani have provided timber, as have the coconut palms that also provide fibre and food. The land use has been environmentally sustainable for many years, and the island retains a natural beauty largely unspoiled by industry, overcrowding or overdevelopment.

WILDLIFE

The island is geologically young, and while most of its living things have migrated from elsewhere, true native wild animals are rare. This is not hard to imagine in the heavily populated and extravagantly fertile south of Bali, where the orderly rice terraces are so intensively cultivated they look more like a work of sculpture than a natural landscape.

In fact, rice fields cover only about 20% of the island's surface area, and there is a great variety of other environmental zones: the dry scrub of the northwest, the extreme northeast and the southern peninsula; patches of dense jungle in the river valleys; forests of bamboo; and harsh volcanic regions that are barren rock and volcanic tuff at higher altitudes. Lombok is similar in all these respects.

Animals

Bali has lots and lots of lizards, and they come in all shapes and sizes. The small ones (onomatopoeically called *cecak*) that hang around light fittings in the evening, waiting for an unwary insect, are a familiar sight. Geckos are fairly large lizards, often heard but less often seen. The loud and regularly repeated two-part cry 'geck-oh' is a nightly background noise that visitors

Each day Bali produces 150 tons of waste, at least 30% of which is non-biodegradable and most of which is generated directly or indirectly by tourism. That is everything from plastic water bottles to your empty container of sunblock.

Balinese Flora & Fauna, published by Periplus, is a concise and beautifully illustrated guide to the animals and plants you'll see in your travels. The feature on the ecology of a rice field is excellent.

RICE

Rice cultivation has shaped the social landscape in Bali – the intricate organisation necessary for growing rice is a large factor in the strength of community life. Rice cultivation has also changed the environmental landscape – terraced rice fields trip down hillsides like steps for a giant, in shades of gold, brown and green, green and more green.

The elaborate irrigation system used to grow rice makes careful use of all the surface water. The fields are a complete ecological system, home for much more than just rice. In the early morning you'll often see the duck herders leading their flocks out for a day's paddle around a flooded rice field; the ducks eat various pests and leave fertiliser in their wake.

There are three words for rice – *padi* is the growing rice plant (hence paddy fields); *beras* is the uncooked grain; and *nasi* is cooked rice, as in *nasi goreng* (fried rice) and *nasi putih* (plain rice). A rice field is called a *sawah*.

A harvested field with its leftover burnt rice stalks is soaked with water and repeatedly ploughed, often by two bullocks pulling a wooden plough. Once the field is muddy enough, a small corner is walled off and seedling rice is planted there. When it is a reasonable size, it's replanted, shoot by shoot, in the larger field. While the rice matures, there is time to practise the gamelan (traditional Balinese orchestral music), watch the dancers or do a little woodcarving. Finally, the whole village turns out for the harvest – a period of solid hard work. While it's strictly men-only planting the rice, everybody takes part in harvesting it.

In 1969, new high-yield rice varieties were introduced. These can be harvested a month sooner than the traditional variety and are resistant to many diseases. However, the new varieties also have greater needs for fertiliser and irrigation water, which strains the imperilled water supplies. More pesticides are also needed, causing the depletion of the frog and eel populations that depend on the insects for survival.

Although everyone agrees that the new rice doesn't taste as good as *padi* Bali, the new strains now account for more than 90% of rice. Small areas of *padi* Bali are still planted and harvested in traditional ways to placate the rice goddess, Dewi Sri. Temples and offerings to her dot every rice field. One place you can still enjoy traditional rice is at Warung Beras Bali in Denpasar (p168).

To learn more, see the boxed text p275.

soon become accustomed to – it's considered lucky if you hear the lizard call seven times.

Bats are also quite common, and the little chipmunk-like Balinese squirrels are occasionally seen in the wild, although more often in cages.

Bali has more than 300 species of birds, but the one that is truly native to the island, the Bali starling, is probably extinct in the wild (thousands can be found in cages). Much more common are colourful birds like the orange-banded thrush, numerous species of egrets, kingfishers, parrots, owls and many more.

Bali's only wilderness area, Taman Nasional Bali Barat (West Bali National Park, p280), has a number of wild species, including grey and black monkeys (which you will also see in the mountains and East Bali), *muncak* (mouse deer), squirrels and iguanas. Bali used to have tigers and, although there are periodic rumours of sightings in the remote northwest of the island, nobody has proof of seeing one for a long time. Mostly though, Bali and Lombok aren't places to visit if you want to marvel at wildlife in nature.

There is a rich variety of coral, seaweed, fish and other marine life in the coastal waters of the islands. Much of it can be appreciated by snorkellers, but you're only likely to see the larger marine animals while diving. The huge, placid sunfish found off Nusa Penida lure divers from around the world.

Dolphins can be found right around the island and have unfortunately been made into an attraction off Lovina.

Keeping birds has been a part of Indonesian culture for centuries. It's common to see caged songbirds and they are sold in most markets.

SEA TURTLES

Both the green sea and hawksbill turtles inhabit the waters around Bali and Lombok, and the species are supposedly protected by international laws that prohibit trade in anything made from sea turtles.

In Bali, however, green sea turtle meat is a traditional and very popular delicacy, particularly for Balinese feasts. Bali is the site of the most intensive slaughter of green sea turtles in the world – no reliable figures are available, although in 1999 it was estimated that more than 30,000 are killed annually. It's easy to find the trade on the backstreets of waterside towns such as Benoa. Ironically, tourism money helps more people afford turtle meat both for consumption and for religious rituals and offerings.

Still, some progress is being made. 'People in Kuta used to eat turtles, now they save them,' says Wayan Wiradnyana, head of ProFauna in Bali, a group that works to protect animals across Indonesia. In Bali, the group has spurred police to enforce a 1999 ban on turtle killing and it has helped release turtles seized from poachers. But its biggest achievement has been in public education. 'In Kuta,' he says, '30 turtles a year lay eggs on the beach. The community now helps us guard them and make certain the babies hatch and get to the water.'

Many other individuals and organisations are involved in protecting the species, including Heinz von Holzen, the owner of Bumbu Bali restaurant in Tanjung Benoa (p144), and the Reef Seen Turtle Project at Reef Seen Aquatics in Pemuteran (p268). Bali's Hindu Dharma, the body overseeing religious practice, has also contributed, decreeing that turtle meat is essential in only very vital ceremonies.

A broad coalition of divers and journalists supports the SOS Sea Turtles campaign (www .sos-seaturtles.ch), which spotlights turtle abuse in Bali. It has been instrumental in exposing the illegal poaching of turtles at Wakatobi National Park in Sulawesi for sale in Bali. This illegal trade is widespread and, like the drug trade, hard to prevent. The best way to stop it is to eliminate the market for poached turtles in Bali.

Turtle hatcheries open to the public such as the sanctuary on – fittingly – Turtle Island (p153) and another on Gili Meno (p301). They do a good job of educating locals about the need to protect turtles and think of them as living creatures as opposed to satay, but many environmentalists are still against them for keeping captive turtles.

INTRODUCED SPECIES

Bali is thick with domestic animals, including ones that wake you up in the morning and others that bark throughout the night. Chickens and roosters are kept both for food purposes and as domestic pets. Cockfighting is a hugely popular male activity, and a man's fighting bird is his prized possession (if you see a thicket of cars and motorbikes by the side of the road in rural Bali but don't see any people, they may all be at a cockfight 'hidden' behind a building – like in *Casablanca*, the cops will be betting too).

Dogs (when not pampered pets) have hard lives – they're far down the social ladder, mostly ignored and thought by some to be friendly with evil spirits (thus the constant barking). But some people are trying to improve the lives of feral mutts; see the boxed text, p184.

Balinese pigs are related to the wild boar, and look really gross, with their sway backs and sagging stomachs. They inhabit the family compound, cleaning up all the garbage and eventually end up spit-roasted at a feast – they taste a lot better than they look!

Balinese cattle, by contrast, are delicate and graceful animals that seem more akin to deer than cows. Although the Balinese are Hindus, they do not generally treat cattle as holy animals, yet cows are seldom eaten or milked. They are, however, used to plough rice paddies and fields, and there is a major export market for Balinese cattle to Hong Kong and other parts of Asia.

One hawksbill sea turtle that visited Bali was tracked for the following year. His destinations: Java, Kalimantan, Australia (Perth and much of Queensland) and then back to Bali.

Ducks are another everyday Balinese domestic animal and a regular dish at feasts. Ducks are kept in the family compound, and are put out to a convenient pond or flooded rice field to feed during the day. They follow a stick with a small flag tied to the end, and the stick is left planted in the field. As sunset approaches, the ducks gather around the stick and wait to be led home again. The morning and evening duck parades are one of Bali's small delights.

Plants
TREES

Almost all of the island is cultivated, and only in the Taman Nasional Bali Barat are there traces of Bali's earliest plant life. As with most things in Bali, trees have a spiritual and religious significance, and you'll often see them decorated with scarves and black-and-white chequered cloths. The *waringin* (banyan) is the holiest Balinese tree and no important temple is complete without a stately one growing within its precincts. The banyan is an extensive, shady tree with an exotic feature: creepers that drop from its branches take root to propagate a new tree. Thus the banyan is said to be 'never-dying', since new offshoots can always take root. *Jepun* (frangipani or plumeria trees), with their beautiful and sweet-smelling white flowers, are also common in temples and family compounds.

Bali has monsoonal rather than tropical rainforests, so it lacks the valuable rainforest hardwoods that require rain year-round. The forestry department is experimenting with new varieties in plantations around Taman Nasional Bali Barat, but at the moment, nearly all the wood used for carving is imported from Sumatra and Kalimantan.

A number of plants have great practical and economic significance. *Tiing* (bamboo) is grown in several varieties and is used for everything from satay sticks and string to rafters and gamelan resonators. The various types of palm provide coconuts, sugar, fuel and fibre.

FLOWERS & GARDENS

Balinese gardens are a delight. The soil and climate can support a huge range of plants, and the Balinese love of beauty and the abundance of cheap labour means that every space can be landscaped. The style is generally informal, with

Bali's forests cover 127,000 hectares, ranging from virgin land to tree farms to densely forested mountain villages. The total is constantly under threat from wood-poaching for carved souvenirs and cooking fuel, and from development.

THE WALLACE LINE

The 19th-century naturalist Sir Alfred Wallace (1822–1913) observed great differences in fauna between Bali and Lombok – as great as the differences between Africa and South America. In particular, there were no large mammals (elephants, rhinos, tigers etc) east of Bali, and very few carnivores. He postulated that during the ice ages, when sea levels were lower, animals could have moved by land from what is now mainland Asia all the way to Bali, but the deep Lombok Strait would always have been a barrier. He drew a line between Bali and Lombok, which he believed marked the biological division between Asia and Australia.

Plant life does not display such a sharp division, but there is a gradual transition from predominantly Asian rainforest species to mostly Australian plants such as eucalypts and acacias, which are better suited to long dry periods. This is associated with the lower rainfall as one moves east of Java. Environmental differences – including those in the natural vegetation – are now thought to provide a better explanation of the distribution of animal species than Wallace's theory about limits to their original migrations.

Modern biologists do recognise a distinction between Asian and Australian fauna, but the boundary between the regions is regarded as much fuzzier than Wallace's line. Nevertheless, this transitional zone between Asia and Australia is still called 'Walacea'.

RESPONSIBLE TRAVEL

The best way to responsibly visit Bali and Lombok is to try to be as least-invasive as possible. This is of course easier than it sounds but consider the following tips:

- **Watch your use of water.** Travel into the rice-growing regions of Bali and you'll think the island is coursing with water, but demand outstrips supply. Take up your hotel on its offer to save itself big money, er, no, to save lots of water, by not washing your sheets and towels every day. Cynicism aside, this will save water. You can also forgo your own private plunge pool at the high end, or a pool altogether – although this is almost impossible at any price level.

- **Don't hit the bottle.** Those bottles of Aqua (the top local brand of bottled water, owned by Danone) are convenient but they add up. The zillions of such bottles tossed away each year are a major blight. Still, you're wise not to refill from the tap, so what do you do? Ask your hotel if you can refill from their huge containers of drinking water. And, if your hotel doesn't give you in-room drinking water in reusable glass containers, tell them you noticed and tell them you care. In Ubud, stop by the Pondok Pecak Library & Learning Centre (p173) – it will refill your water bottle and tell you which other businesses offer this service. In restaurants, ask for '*air putih*', which will get you a glass of water from the Aqua jug out back, saving yet more plastic bottles.

- **Don't play golf.** The resorts will hate this, but tough. Having two golf courses on the arid Bukit Peninsula is environmentally unsustainable.

- **Support environmentally aware businesses.** The number of businesses committed to good environmental practices is growing fast in Bali and Lombok. Check out the GreenDex (p397) in this book for a list.

- **Conserve power.** Sure you want to save your own energy on a sweltering afternoon, but using air-con strains an already overloaded system. Much of the electricity in Bali comes from Java and the rest is produced at the roaring and smoking plant near Benoa Harbour. Open the windows at night in Ubud for cool mountain breezes and the symphony of sounds off the rice fields.

- **Don't drive yourself crazy.** The traffic is already bad – why add another vehicle to it? Can you take a tourist bus instead of a chartered or rental car? Would a walk, trek or hike be more enjoyable than a road journey to an over-visited tourist spot (Pura Tanah Lot comes to mind)? The beach is a fast and fun way to get around Kuta, Legian and Seminyak quickly (often faster than a taxi in traffic). Cycling is more popular than ever, and you can hire a bike for US$3 per day or less.

For organisations that have more info on the local environment and may be able to use your help in protecting it, see p346.

---

curved paths, a rich variety of plants and usually a water feature. Who can't be enchanted by a frangipani tree dropping a carpet of fragrant blossoms?

You can find almost every type of flower in Bali, but some are seasonal and others are restricted to the cooler mountain areas. Many of the flowers will be familiar to visitors – hibiscus, bougainvillea, poinsettia, oleander, jasmine, water lily and aster are commonly seen in the southern tourist areas, while roses, begonias and hydrangeas are found mainly in the mountains. Less-familiar flowers include: Javanese *ixora (soka, angsoka)*, with round clusters of bright red-orange flowers; *champak (cempaka)*, a very fragrant member of the magnolia family; flamboyant, the flower of the royal poinciana flame tree; *manori (maduri)*, which has a number of traditional uses; and water convolvulus *(kangkung)*, the leaves of which are commonly used as a green vegetable. There are literally thousands of species of orchid.

Flowers of Bali and *Fruits of Bali*, by Fred and Margaret Wiseman, are nicely illustrated books that will tell you what you're admiring or eating.

Flowers can be seen everywhere – in gardens or just by the roadside. Flower fanciers should make a trip to the Danau Bratan area in the central mountains to see the Bali Botanical Gardens (p247), the Botanic Garden Ubud (p179), or visit the plant nurseries along the road between Denpasar and Sanur.

NATIONAL PARKS

The only national park in Bali is Taman Nasional Bali Barat, p280. It covers 19,000 hectares at the western tip of Bali, plus a substantial area of coastal mangrove and the adjacent marine area, including the excellent dive site at Menjangan.

The Taman Nasional Gunung Rinjani (Gunung Rinjani National Park) on Lombok covers 41,330 hectares and is the water-collector for most of the island. At 3726m, Gunung Rinjani is the second-highest volcanic peak in Indonesia and is very popular for trekking (see p314).

ENVIRONMENTAL ISSUES

A fast-growing population in Bali has put pressure on limited resources. The tourist industry has attracted new residents, and there is a rapid growth in urban areas and of resorts and villas that encroach onto agricultural land.

Water use is a major concern. Typical top-end hotels use more than 500L of water a day per room, and the growing number of golf courses – the new one on the arid Bukit Peninsula in the Pecatu Indah development for example – suck an already stressed resource. Water pollution is another problem both from deforestation brought on by firewood-collecting in the mountains, and lack of proper treatment for the waste produced by the Balinese population. The vast mangroves along the south coast near Benoa Harbour are losing their ability to filter the water that drains here from much of the island (the Mangrove Information Centre near Sanur has more on this, see p153).

Air pollution is another problem, as anyone stuck behind a smoke-belching truck or bus on one of the main roads knows. And it's not just all those plastic bags and water bottles but just the sheer volume of waste produced by the ever-growing population that is another problem – what to do with it?

Just growing Bali's sacred grain rice has become fraught with environmental concerns. (See the boxed text, p81 for details.)

On the upside, there is a nascent effort to grow rice and other foods organically, reducing the amount of pesticide and fertiliser run-off into water supplies. Things may finally be moving forward on starting a sewage treatment program in the south (but it will take years and the money is not there) and proposals to expand the airport's runways have inspired efforts to protect the nearby mangroves.

The Indonesian Ecotourism Centre (www.indecon.or.id) is devoted to highlighting responsible tourism. It lists places in Bali and Lombok that have made a commitment to the local environment and culture.

Bali's businesses can get their trash taken away by recyclers for under US$10 per month – it may seem like a good deal until you consider that a small Kuta warung may barely make that as profit in a week.

Bali & Lombok Outdoors

Bali offers so much more than a beach holiday with an overlay of amazing culture – it is an incredible places to get outside and play. Sure you may have to actually get up off the sand to do this, but the rewards are many.

In waters around the island you'll find world-class diving that ranges from reefs to shipwrecks to huge, rare critters. When that water hits shore, it creates some of the world's best surfing. No matter what time of year you visit, you'll find legendary surf spots. Away from the waves, plenty of aquatic-fun companies offer everything from parasailing to banana-boat racing.

On land, hikes abound through the luxuriant green of the rice fields and deep into the river valleys. In the cool mountains, trails lead past a profusion of waterfalls, lakes and lush forest. If you want to head high, you can climb any of the island's three main active volcanoes for views, vent holes and visions of a lunar landscape.

Or, you can just whiz through the beautiful scenery on a bike. Cycling has become hugely popular in Bali and much of the island is good for riding. For riding of a different kind, beach rides on horseback are both thrilling and relaxing.

Lombok doesn't have the same level of organisation but it has fine diving, surfing (often in remote locations), hiking, and a famous volcano trek.

Supporting a new guidebook, *Bali by Bike*, www.balibybike.com is a website covering routes hither and yon across the island with tips for beginners and veteran riders.

CYCLING

Cyclists are discovering Bali in a big way. The back roads of the island more than make up for the traffic-clogged streets of the south.

The main advantage of touring Bali by bike is the quality of the experience. By bicycle, you can be totally immersed in the environment – you can hear the wind rustling in the rice paddies or the sound of a gamelan (traditional Balinese orchestra) practising, and catch the scent of the flowers. Even at the height of the tourist season, cycle tourers on the back roads experience the friendliness that seems all but lost on the usual tourist circuit. Once you get away from the congested south, the roads are more relaxed and the experience sublime.

Lombok is also good for touring by bicycle. In the populated areas the roads are flat, and the traffic across the island is less dangerous than in Bali.

Some people are put off cycling by tropical heat, heavy traffic, frequent showers and high mountains. But, when you're riding on level or downhill, the breeze really moderates the heat.

Multigear mountain bikes make it possible to get up the higher mountains in Bali or on Lombok, but with a bit of negotiating and patience you can get a bemo (minibus) to take you and your bike up the steepest sections.

For details on the practicalities of riding bikes on the islands, including where to rent as well as get repairs, see p354.

Bali being Bali, many of the growing legion of long-distance cyclists are charmed to find warm and cheery welcomes, even when they stumble into a hotel lobby hot, sweaty and covered in road grime.

Where to Ride

It's really easier to tell you where *not* to ride in Bali. Denpasar, south through Sanur in the east, and Seminyak to Kuta in the west suffer from lots of traffic and narrow roads.

BUKIT PENINSULA

Past the airport, the Bukit Peninsula is less congested than Kuta and Denpasar. You can have an excellent day-ride by going counter-clockwise from Jimbaran south, past the surf breaks and temple at Ulu Watu, then across the bottom of the island on small village roads before pausing in Nusa Dua. You can explore the mangroves around Tanjung Benoa before returning north on the one bit of nasty road past the airport.

NUSA LEMBONGAN & NUSA PENIDA

The islands, Nusa Lembongan and Nusa Penida, are nearly traffic-free and offer remote vistas of the sea, sheer cliffs, white beaches and lush jungle. You can make short work of Lembongan in a day – it's a popular cycling destination. Penida is for the serious cyclist and you need to arrive with a bike.

UBUD

Ubud has always been popular with cyclists and many tour companies based there lead tours. Explore the many narrow mountain roads that head upwards from Ubud for ancient monuments and the kind of jaw-dropping rice-terrace views that will have you lost in a sea of green.

EAST BALI

In the east, the coast road is busy but wide, and every small lane heading south will take you to another nearly deserted beach. North of the coast, it's like the west, uncrowded and serene: East Bali is your oyster. You might focus on the popular and gorgeous Sidemen Road, which has the advantage of passing many cool lodges popular with trekkers and cyclists.

CENTRAL MOUNTAINS

Bali's peaks reward ambitious riders, especially in the Danau Bratan area. Heading downhill to the north coast from Munduk is popular, as is heading south on small roads from the heights of Candikuning.

NORTH BALI

The north is wide open. A journey around the north from Amlapura takes you past isolated villages such as Tembok. A good day's ride would take you from, say, Padangbai to the northeast, where scattered resorts see their share of long-distance riders. Elsewhere in the north, pretty much any road off the main coast road will offer serenity and discoveries. Base yourself at Lovina and you can have your pick of day trips to remote waterfalls and temples.

WEST BALI

West of Denpasar, the island is riding heaven. If you're into hills, take the beautiful trip up to Pura Luhur Batukau and explore the rice terraces around Jatiluwih. Otherwise, just cut loose and explore. The rice fields and dense jungle drives in and around Tabanan, Kerambitan and Bajera are simply gorgeous. Further west you'll find little traffic off the main road to Gilimanuk, but you will find rushing mountain streams, deserted beaches and hidden temples.

LOMBOK

Lombok rewards cyclists with the exhilaration of exploration.

East of Mataram there are several attractions that would make a good day trip – south to Banyumulek via Gunung Pengsong and then back to Mataram would be one such jaunt. Some of the coastal roads have hills and curves like a roller coaster – try going north from Mataram, via Senggigi, to Pemenang, and then (if you feel energetic) return via the steep climb over the Pusuk Pass.

The Gilis are good for riding as well, even if you have to do laps to build up any mileage.

Bali has an excellent bike shop in Denpasar: Planet Bike Bali (☎ 0361-746 2858; Jl Gunung Agung 148). Call for directions and hours. It stocks Giant, Trek, Shimano and other brands.

Bali's first cyclist is commemorated on a stone carving at a temple in Kubutambahan – look for the lotus blossom used as a rear wheel (p260).

Cycling Tours

Popular tours start high up in the central mountains at places such as Kintamani or Bedugal. The tour company takes you to the top and then you ride down relatively quiet mountain roads soaking up the lush scenery, village culture and tropical scents. Rides in and around Ubud are also common. The costs with bicycle, gear and lunch is US$25 to US$40.

Some operators include transport to/from South Bali hotels as part of the price.

Archipelago Adventure (☎ 0361-844 4624; www.archipelago-adventure.com) Offers a range of tours, including ones on Java. In Bali, there are rides around Jatiluwih, Danau Buyan and mountain biking on trails from Kintamani.

Bali Bintang (☎ 0361-746 2290; bintangtours@hotmail.com) Two hours of downhill riding north of Ubud at Pejang. A one-hour trek through rice fields follows.

Bali Eco & Educational Cycling Tours (☎ 0361-975557, 0813 3742 0420) Tours start at Kintamani and take small roads through lush scenery south to Ubud.

Bali Fun & Action (☎ 0361-790 0741; balifunandaction@yahoo.com) The choice for people who like descriptive names; this Ubud-based operator starts in Kintamani, passes some of the ancient sites north of Ubud and ends with a village tour and an optional rice-field trek.

Bike-Baik Bali Countryside Tours (☎ 0361-978052, 0813 3867 3852; www.balibike.com) Tours run downhill from Kintamani; the emphasis is on cultural immersion and there are frequent stops in tiny villages and rice farms.

On Lombok, you can find tours out of Senggigi (p292).

DIVING & SNORKELLING

With its warm water, extensive coral reefs and abundant marine life, Bali offers excellent diving and snorkelling possibilities. Reliable dive schools and operators all around Bali's coast can train complete beginners or arrange challenging trips that will satisfy the most experienced divers. The best sites can all be accessed in a day trip from the south of Bali, although the more distant ones will involve several hours of travelling time. Lombok is close behind Bali for diving. It has good sites, especially around its northwest coast.

Snorkelling gear is available near all the most accessible spots, but if you're keen, it's definitely worthwhile bringing your own, and checking out some of the less-visited parts of the coasts.

Dive Costs

For a local trip, count on US$45 to US$90 per person for two dives, which includes all equipment. Many operators offer open-water diving certification for US$350 to US$400. Note that it is becoming common to price in euros.

Dive Courses

If you're not a qualified diver, and you want to try some scuba diving in Bali, you have three options.

First, nearly all operators offer an 'introductory', 'orientation' or 'initial' dive for beginners, usually after classroom training and shallow-water practice. Courses are reasonably cheap (from around US$60 for one dive), but it is essential to stick to one of the recommended dive operators (see p90) for safety's sake.

Second, some of the larger hotels and diving agencies offer four- or five-day courses that certify you for basic dives in the location where you do the course. A resort course will give you a better standard of training than just an introductory dive, but it doesn't make you a qualified diver. These courses cost about US$300.

Sportdiver magazine on Bali's best dive site at Pulau Menjangan: 'Nothing prepares me for just how vibrant the coral is down the length of the sheer walls here. Dozens of species of hard and soft corals overrun each other in a glorious abundance of shades and textures that continually bewitch the eye.'

Huge sunfish, up to 2.5m in length and twice as high, are a much-treasured sight for divers. They can usually be found around Nusa Lembongan, Nusa Penida and at times off Tulamben. These gentle giants feed on jellyfish and plankton.

SINK OR SWIM: DIVING SAFELY

Diving is justifiably popular in Bali and on Lombok. But like all diving destinations, it is important to stay safe in and out of the water. Here are some tips to make your trip the best possible.

Choosing a Dive Operator

In general, diving in Bali and on Lombok is safe, with a good standard of staff training and equipment maintenance. However, as with anywhere in the world, some operations are more professional than others, and it is often difficult, especially for inexperienced or beginner divers, to select the best operation for their needs. Here are a few tips to help you select a well-set-up and safety-conscious dive shop.

- Are its staff fully trained and qualified? Ask to see certificates or certification cards – no reputable shop will be offended by this request. Guides must reach 'full instructor' level (the minimum certification level) to be able to teach any diving course. To guide certified divers on a reef dive, guides must hold at least 'rescue diver' or preferably 'dive master' qualifications. Note that a dive master cannot teach – only fully qualified instructors can do that.

- Do they have safety equipment on the boat? At a minimum, a dive boat should carry oxygen and a first-aid kit. A radio or mobile phone is also important.

- Is the boat's equipment OK and its air clean? This is often the hardest thing for a new diver to judge. A few guidelines are:

    1. Smell the air – open a tank valve a small way and breathe in. Smelling dry or slightly rubbery air is OK. If it smells of oil or car exhaust, that tells you the operator doesn't filter the air correctly.

    2. When the equipment is put together, are there any big air leaks? All dive centres get some small leaks at some time, however, if you get a *big* hiss of air coming out of any piece of equipment, ask to have it replaced.

- Is it conservation-oriented? Most good dive shops explain that you should not touch corals or take shells from the reef. It's also common for the better places to work with local fishermen to ensure that certain areas are protected. Some even clean beaches!

Safety Guidelines for Diving

Before embarking on a scuba diving or snorkelling trip, carefully consider the following points to ensure a safe and enjoyable experience:

- Possess a current diving certification card from a recognised scuba diving instructional agency (if scuba diving).

- Be sure you are healthy and feel comfortable diving.

- Obtain reliable information about physical and environmental conditions at the dive site (eg from a reputable local dive operation). Conditions vary greatly between dive sites around Bali and the islands. Seasonal changes can significantly alter any site and dive conditions.

- Be aware of local customs and etiquette about marine life and the environment.

- Dive only at sites within your realm of experience; if available, engage the services of a competent, professionally trained dive instructor or dive master.

Finally, if you're serious about diving, the best option is to enrol in a full open-water diving course, which gives you an internationally recognised qualification. A four-day open-water course, to PADI standards, with a qualified instructor, manual, dive table and certification, will cost about US$300 to US$400. Experienced divers can also upgrade their skills with advanced open-water courses in night, wreck and deep diving etc, from around US$200 for a three-day course.

RESPONSIBLE DIVING

Please bear in mind the following tips when diving and help preserve the ecology and beauty of reefs:

- Never use anchors on the reef, and take care not to run boats aground on coral.

- Avoid touching or standing on living marine organisms or dragging equipment across the reef.

- Be conscious of the effect from your fins. Even without contact, the surge from fin strokes near the reef can damage delicate organisms. Also, take care not to kick up clouds of sand, which can smother organisms.

- Practise and maintain proper buoyancy control. Major damage can be done by divers descending too fast and colliding with the reef.

- Do not collect or buy corals or shells or loot marine archaeological sites (mainly shipwrecks).

- Ensure that you take home all your rubbish and any other litter you may find as well. Plastics in particular are a serious threat to marine life.

- Do not feed the fish.

- Minimise your involvement with marine animals. Do not *ever* ride on the backs of turtles and learn as much as you can about the animals' natural habitat.

Dive Operators

Major dive operators in tourist areas can arrange trips to the main dive sites all around the island. Distances can be long though, so it's better to stay relatively close to your destination.

For tips on choosing a dive shop, see the boxed text, p89. Places with good dive shops in Bali include Sanur (p147), Padangbai (p220), Candidasa (p225), Amed (p232), Lovina (p261), Pemuteran (p268) and Nusa Lembongan (p155).

On Lombok, look for dive operators in Senggigi (p292), Gili Air (p298), Gili Meno (p301) and Gili Trawangan (p304). Kuta (p323) has dive shops that specialise in sites with hammerhead sharks.

Diving & Snorkelling Sites

BALI

The Sanur-based environmental group PPLH Bali (see p145) has several programs devoted to protecting Bali's reefs and educating people about their value.

Bali's main diving and snorkelling sites include the places we've listed above with good dive centres. For details, see those sections of the book. In addition, Nusa Penida (p159) and Pulau Menjangan (p280) in Taman Nasional Bali Barat (West Bali National Park) are renowned for their diving.

LOMBOK

There is some very good scuba diving and snorkelling off the Gili Islands (see the boxed text, p302), especially Gili Trawangan (p306), though some of the coral has been damaged by dynamite fishing. There are also some good reefs near Senggigi (p292).

Equipment

All the equipment you need is available in Bali and on Lombok, but you may not be able to get exactly what you want in the size you need. The quality is variable – some operators use equipment right to the end of its service life. Most dive operators in Bali include the cost of equipment in the cost of the dive, but if you have your own equipment (excluding mask, snorkel and fins), you'll receive a discounted rate. Tanks and weight belt – as well as lunch, drinking water, transport, guides and insurance – are generally included in dive trips.

The most essential basic equipment to bring is a mask, snorkel and fins – they're not too difficult to carry and that way you know they'll fit. Anywhere with coral and tourists, you'll be able to rent snorkelling gear for around 30,000Rp per day – make sure that you check the condition of the equipment carefully before you take it away.

Also worth bringing, if you plan to do a lot of diving, is a thin, full-length wetsuit, which is important for protection against stinging animals and possible coral abrasions. A thicker one (3mm) would be preferable if you plan frequent diving, deep dives or a night dive – the water can be cold, especially deeper down.

Some small, easy-to-carry things to bring from home include protective gloves, spare straps, silicone lubricant and extra globes for your torch (flashlight). Most dive operators can rent good-quality regulators (about US$10 per day) and BCVs (aka BCDs or Buoyancy Control Devices; about US$5), but if you bring your own, you'll save money. It's a good idea especially if you're planning to dive in more remote and secluded locations than Bali, where the rental equipment may not be as good.

> That dog barking at you as you walk just needs a little love! See p184 for details on two groups that are working to brighten the future for Bali's pooches.

HIKING & TREKKING

You could wander Bali and Lombok for a year and still not see all the islands have to offer. But their small size means that you can nibble off a bit at a time – day-hikes and treks are easily arranged. Guides can help you surmount volcanoes, while tour companies will take you to remote regions and emerald-green valleys of rice terraces and flowing water.

Bali

Bali is a pretty darn walkable place. No matter where you're staying, you can ask for recommendations and set off for discoveries and adventure. Even from Kuta or Seminyak, you just head out to the beach, turn right and walk north as far as you wish along the amazing surf while civilisation seems to evaporate.

Bali does not offer remote 'wilderness treks' as it's simply too densely populated. For the most part, you'll make day trips from the closest village, often leaving before dawn to avoid the clouds and mist that usually blanket the peaks by mid-morning – for most treks you'll go on you won't need camping gear.

Treks up the sides of the iconic volcanoes are a memorable adventure and there's a good coterie of guides ready to show you the way. Hassles aside, the otherworldly scenery of Gunung Batur (p240) is like none other. Gunung Batukau (p252) offers misty climbs amid the clouds with few crowds, while Gunung Agung (p216) is renowned for its sunrises and isolated temples.

There are numerous primitive treks – you'll need a guide – within Taman Nasional Bali Barat (p281), the remote national park in the far west.

Hiking is a good way to explore the wilds of Bali – you can trek from village to village on small tracks and between the rice paddies. Munduk (p250) is a very popular place to hike, thanks to its lack of hassles and lush, waterfall-riven landscape.

> The Balinese have made walking an art. Here's what Miguel Covarrubias said in the classic 1937 *Island of Bali*: 'From childhood the women walk for miles carrying heavy loads on their heads.'

You can easily go on short hikes, without guides, around Danau Buyan and Danau Tamblingan (p250), Tirta Gangga (p230) and the Sidemen Road area (p214).

Ubud has long been a centre for explorations on foot (p181), from relaxed hour-long rice-field wanders to all-day escapades covering river-valley jungles and ancient monuments.

Several agencies offer organised walking and trekking trips around Bali. In addition, some small operations organise walks around Ubud (p184).

SAFETY GUIDELINES FOR TREKKING

Before embarking on a trekking trip, consider the following points to ensure a safe and enjoyable experience:

- Pay any fees and possess any permits required by local authorities; often, these will be rolled into the guide's fee, meaning that it's all negotiable.
- Be sure you are healthy and feel comfortable walking for a sustained period.
- Obtain reliable information about physical and environmental conditions along your intended route, eg the weather can get quite wet and cold in the upper reaches of the volcanoes.
- Confirm with your guide that you will only go on walks/treks within your realm of experience.
- Carry the proper equipment. Depending on the trek and time of year this can mean rain gear or extra water. Carry a torch (flashlight); don't assume the guide will have one.

Recommended agencies include:

Bali Culture Tours (☎ 0813 3827 2777; murjana70@hotmail.com) Offers highly customisable programs around Ubud and East Bali, including the slopes of Gunung Agung and artists' homes.

Bali Nature Walk (☎ 0817 973 5914; dadeputra@hotmail.com) Walks in isolated areas in the Ubud region. Routes are customisable depending on your desires.

Bali Sunrise Trekking and Tours (☎ 0818 552 669; www.balisunrisetours.com) Leads treks throughout the central mountains.

Lombok

On Lombok, the Gunung Rinjani area (p314) is superb for trekking. People climb the 3726m summit to then drop down into a crater where there's a sacred lake and hot springs. The entire mountain is a national park.

You can organise explorations of Gunung Rinjani at the Rinjani Trek Centre (p312) in Senaru or Senggigi (p292). Another good place is the Rinjani Information Centre (p313) in Sembalun Lawang. You can find outfitters in Senaru (p311). Note that expert advice is crucial on Gunung Rinjani as people die on its slopes every year.

The slopes of Rinjani are also good for hiking. There are good trails through the garlic-scented Sembalun Valley (p313) and the fertile agricultural lands of Tetebatu (p318).

If scaling a volcano isn't your style, there are waterfalls such as Air Terjun Sindang Gila near Senaru (p311). Perhaps the ultimate in beach-bum adventure can be had circumnavigating any of the Gilis. Maybe you'll find a message in a bottle.

Lombok's trekking favourite, Gunung Rinjani, is an active volcano and the second-largest in Indonesia. It rises to 3726m (12,224ft) and erupted as recently as 2004.

KAYAKING & CANOEING

You can canoe across the reflections of volcanoes on Danau Batur (p245). Otherwise, the water-sports centres in Sanur (see p148) and Tanjung Benoa (p143) are catching on to kayaking. The boats may not be pristine, but they take to the placid, reef-protected waters just fine.

Sobek and Bali Adventure Tours (below) offer white-water kayaking along with their rafting trips.

On Gili Trawangan, you can rent kayaks from Karma Kayak (p306) and circumnavigate the amazingly teal-shaded waters and dazzling white beaches.

RAFTING

Rafting is very popular, usually as a day trip from either South Bali or Ubud. Operators pick you up from your hotel, take you to the put-in point, provide all the equipment and guides, and return you to your hotel at the end of the day. The best time is during the wet season (October to March), or just after;

by the middle of the dry season (April to September), the best river rapids may be better called 'dribbles'.

Some operators use the Sungai Ayung (Ayung River; see p180), near Ubud, where there are between 19 and 25 Class II to III rapids (ie potentially exciting but not perilous). As you float along, you can admire the stunning gorges and rice paddies from the boat. The Sungai Telagawaja (Telagawaja River) near Muncan in East Bali (p214) is also popular. It's more rugged than the Ayung and the scenery is more wild.

Dress to get wet and bring something dry for afterwards. Companies will pick you up at your hotel in South Bali and Ubud.

Advertised prices run from US$50 to US$90; discounts are common.

Consider the following:

Bahama Adventure (☎ 0361-270811; bali_bahama@yahoo.com) Sungai Ayung.

Bali Adventure Tours (☎ 0361-721480; www.baliadventuretours.com) Sungai Ayung; some of the company's profits go to environmental projects.

Bali View Rafting (☎ 0361-281443) Sungai Telagawaja.

Sobek (☎ 0361-287059; www.balisobek.com) Trips on both the Sungai Ayung and Sungai Telagawaja.

RIDING HORSES

You see them trotting along the beach in Seminyak and further north, happy people astride trusty steeds. Riding a horse along the sand and through the waves is thrilling and certainly a green way to have some fun.

You can ride horses in Bali from stables in Kerobokan (p128), just up the coast at Yeh Gangga (p275) and in the north at Pemuteran (p268).

A variety of rides are on offer depending on your experience and desires. Away from the shore, rides through rice fields and lush river valleys are popular.

On Lombok you can saddle up on Gili Trawangan (p306).

SURFING

In recent years, the number of surfers in Bali has increased enormously, and good breaks can get very crowded. Many Balinese have taken to surfing, and the grace of traditional dancing is said to influence their style. The surfing competitions in Bali are a major local event. Facilities for surfers have improved, and surf shops in Kuta will sell just about everything you need.

Equipment

A small board is usually adequate for the smaller breaks, but a few extra inches on your usual board length won't go astray. For the bigger waves – 8ft and upwards – you'll need a gun. For a surfer of average height and build, a board around the 7ft mark is perfect.

If you try to bring more than two or three boards into the country, you may have problem with customs officials.

There are surf shops in Kuta (p107) and elsewhere in South Bali. You can rent boards of varying quality and get supplies at most popular surf breaks. If you need repairs, ask around, there are lots of places.

Other recommended equipment:

- Solid luggage for rugged airline travel
- Board-strap for carrying
- Tough shoes for walking down rocky cliffs
- Your favourite wax if you're picky
- Wetsuit or reef booties
- Wetsuit vest or other protective cover from the sun, cloudy days, reefs and rocks
- Surfing helmet for rugged conditions (and riding a rented motorbike)

Not quite a thoroughbred, Bali has its own indigenous breed of pony, the – surprise! – Bali pony. You'll find it in stables, pulling carts and otherwise working for its living as the breed has done on the island for at least a thousand years.

Bungy jump at 3am and then hit one of Bali's hottest clubs, Double Six, which is right below. (Just don't literally hit it.) See p108. Go nuts and take the plunge with a dirt bike.

Where to Surf

BALI

Swells come from the Indian Ocean, so the surf is on the southern side of the island and, strangely, on the northwest coast of Nusa Lembongan, where the swell funnels into the strait between there and the Bali coast.

In the dry season (around April to September), the west coast has the best breaks, with the trade winds coming in from the southeast; this is also when Nusa Lembongan works best. In the wet season, surf the eastern side of the island, from Nusa Dua around to Padangbai. If there's a north wind – or no wind at all – there are also a couple of breaks on the south coast of the Bukit Peninsula.

Balangan

Go through the growing Pecatu Indah resort and follow the road around to the right past Dreamland to reach the Balangan warung (food stall). Balangan (p136) is a fast left over a shallow reef, unsurfable at low tide, good at mid-tide with anything over a 4ft swell; with an 8ft swell, this can be one of the classic waves.

Balian

There are a few peaks near the mouth of Sungai Balian (Balian River, p276) in western Bali. The best break here is an enjoyable and consistent left-hander that works well at mid- to high tide if there's no wind. Lots of inns are springing up here.

Bingin

North of Padang and accessible by road, this spot (p137) can now get crowded. It's best at mid-tide with a 6ft swell, when it manufactures short but perfect left-hand barrels. The cliffs backing the beach are lined with funky accommodation.

Canggu

North of Seminyak, on the northern extremity of the bay, Canggu (p129) has a nice white beach and many surfers. An optimum size for Canggu is 5ft to 6ft. There's a good right-hander that you can really hook into, which works at high tide.

Dreamland

You have to go through Pecatu Indah resort and past the water-sucking golf course to reach this spot (p136), which can also get crowded. At a low 5ft swell, this solid peak offers a short, sharp right and a longer, more tubular left.

Impossibles

Just north of Padang Padang, this outside reef break (p137) has three shifting peaks with fast left-hand tube sections that can join up if the conditions are perfect.

Ketewel & Lebih

These two beaches (p208) are northeast of Sanur. They're both right-hand beach breaks, and are dodgy at low tide and close out over 6ft.

Kuta Area

For your first plunge into the warm Indian Ocean, try the beach breaks at the beach at Kuta (p107); on full tide, go out near the life-saving club at the southern end of the beach road. At low tide, try the tubes around Halfway

---

Bali-based Surf Travel Online (☎ 0361-750550; www.surftravelonline.com) has information on surf camps, boat charters and package deals for surf trips to remote Indonesian locations, as well as Nusa Lembongan.

www.indosurf.com.au has web links and surfing info; it is also the home site of *Indo Surf,* a best-selling guidebook to breaks across the archipelago.

www.wannasurf.com has surf reports and a message board not just from Bali but the entire world. The World Surf Atlas feature is the thing dreams are made from.

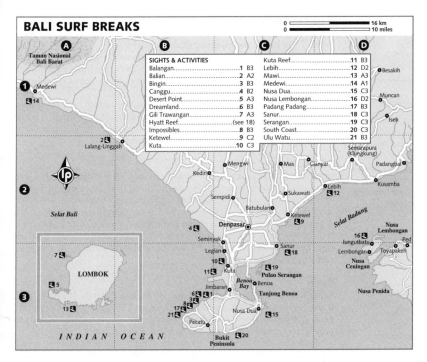

BALI SURF BREAKS

SIGHTS & ACTIVITIES		
Balangan	1	B3
Balian	2	A2
Bingin	3	B3
Canggu	4	B2
Desert Point	5	A3
Dreamland	6	B3
Gili Trawangan	7	A3
Hyatt Reef	(see 18)	
Impossibles	8	B3
Ketewel	9	C2
Kuta	10	C3
Kuta Reef	11	B3
Lebih	12	D2
Mawi	13	A3
Medewi	14	A1
Nusa Dua	15	C3
Nusa Lembongan	16	D2
Padang Padang	17	B3
Sanur	18	C3
Serangan	19	C3
South Coast	20	C3
Ulu Watu	21	B3

Kuta, probably the best place in Bali for beginners to practise. Start at the beach breaks if you are a bit rusty, but treat even these breaks with respect.

Further north, the breaks at Legian Beach can be pretty powerful, with lefts and rights on the sandbars off Jl Melasti and Jl Padma. For a local perspective, see 'Legian's Surfing Legend', p107.

For more serious stuff, go to the reefs south of the beach breaks, about a kilometre out to sea. **Kuta Reef**, a vast stretch of coral, provides a variety of waves. You can paddle out in around 20 minutes, but the easiest way is by boat, for a fee. The main break is a classic left-hander, best at mid- to high tide, with a 5ft to 6ft swell, when it peels across the reef and has a beautiful inside tube section.

As elsewhere, when in doubt here, ask locals.

Medewi

Further along the south coast of western Bali is a softer left called Medewi (p276) – it's a point break that can give a long ride right into the river mouth. This wave has a big drop, which fills up, then runs into a workable inside section. There's accommodation nearby.

Nusa Dua

During the wet season, you should surf on the east side of the island, where there are some very fine reef breaks. The reef off Nusa Dua (p139) has very consistent swells. The main break is 1km off the beach to the south of Nusa Dua – go past the golf course and look for the whole row of warung and some boats to take you out. There are lefts and rights that work well on a small swell at low to mid-tide. Further north, in front of the Club Med, there is a fast, barrelling right reef break called Sri Lanka, which works best at mid-tide.

www.surftravel.com.au is an Australian tour company with camps, yacht charters and a website with destination information, surfer reviews and more. It has trips to more unusual parts of Indonesia.

Nusa Lembongan

In the Nusa Penida group, this island (p155) is separated from the southeast coast of Bali by the Selat Badung (Badung Strait).

The strait is very deep and generates huge swells that break over the reefs off the northwest coast of Lembongan. Shipwreck, clearly visible from the beach, is the most popular break, a longish right that gets a good barrel at mid-tide with a 5ft swell.

A bit to the south, Lacerations is a very fast, hollow right breaking over a very shallow reef – hence the name. Still further south is a smaller, more user-friendly left-hander called Playground. Remember that Lembongan is best with an easterly wind, so it's dry-season surfing.

Surfing Indonesia, by Leonard and Lorca Lueras, has about 80 pages on Bali. It has great photos, a comprehensive coverage of the waves, and some good surfing background.

Padang Padang

Just Padang (p137) for short, this super-shallow, left-hand reef break is just north of Ulu Watu towards Kuta. Again, check this place carefully before venturing out. It's a very demanding break that only works over about 6ft from mid- to high tide – it's a great place to watch from the clifftop.

If you can't surf tubes, backhand or forehand, don't go out: Padang is a tube. After a ledgey take-off, you power along the bottom before pulling up into the barrel. Not a wave for the faint-hearted and definitely not a wave to surf when there's a crowd.

Sanur

Sanur Reef (p147) has a hollow wave with excellent barrels. It's fickle, and doesn't even start until you get a 6ft swell, but anything over 8ft will be world-class, and anything over 10ft will be brown board-shorts material. There are other reefs further offshore and most of them are surfable.

Hyatt Reef, over 2km from shore, has a shifty right peak that can give a great ride at full tide. Closer in, opposite the Sanur Beach Market, Tanjung Sari gives long left rides at low tide with a big swell, while Tanjung Right can be a very speedy wall on a big swell. The classic right is off the Grand Bali Beach Hotel.

Serangan

www.surfaidinter national.org is a very well-regarded inter-national surfer-run aid organisation that has done impressive work for the tsunami-ravaged islands off Sumatra.

The destructive development at Pulau Serangan (Turtle Island) has caused huge disruption at the southern and eastern sides of the island, and this has made the surf here much more consistent. The causeway has made the island much more accessible, and several warung face the water, where waves break right and left in anything over a 3ft swell (p152).

South Coast

The extreme south coast (p139), around the end of Bukit Peninsula, can be surfed any time of the year provided there is a northerly wind, or no wind at all – get there very early to avoid onshore winds. The peninsula is fringed with reefs and big swells are produced, but access is a problem. There are a few roads, but the shoreline is all cliff. If you want to explore it, charter a boat on a day with no wind and a small swell.

Ulu Watu

When Kuta Reef is 5ft to 6ft, Ulu Watu (p137), the most famous surfing break in Bali, will be 6ft to 8ft with bigger sets. Kuta and Legian sit on a huge bay – Ulu Watu is way out on the southern extremity of the bay, and consequently picks up more swell than Kuta.

Teluk Ulu Watu (Ulu Watu Bay) is a great set-up for surfers – local boys will wax your board, get drinks for you and carry the board down into the cave, which is the usual access to the waves. There are warung and there's accommodation for every budget.

Ulu Watu has about seven different breaks. The Corner is straight in front of you to the right. It's a fast-breaking, hollow left that holds about 6ft. The reef shelf under this break is extremely shallow, so try to avoid falling headfirst. At high tide, the Peak starts to work. This is good from 5ft to 8ft, with bigger waves occasionally right on the Peak itself. You can take off from this inside part or further down the line. It's a great wave.

Another left runs off the cliff that forms the southern flank of the bay. It breaks outside this in bigger swells, and once it's 7ft, a left-hander pitches right out in front of a temple on the southern extremity. Out behind the Peak, when it's big, is a bombora (submerged reef) appropriately called the Bommie. This is another big left-hander and it doesn't start operating until the swell is about 10ft. On a normal 5ft to 8ft day, there are also breaks south of the Peak.

Observe where other surfers paddle out and follow them. If you are in doubt, ask someone. It is better having some knowledge than none at all. Climb down into the cave and paddle out from there. When the swell is bigger you will be swept to your right. Don't panic – it is an easy matter to paddle around the white water from down along the cliff. Coming back in you have to aim for the cave. When the swell is bigger, come from the southern side of the cave as the current runs to the north.

LOMBOK
Lombok has some good surfing and the dearth of tourists means that breaks are uncrowded.

Desert Point
Located in an extremely remote part of Lombok, Desert Point (p290) is a legendary if elusive wave that was voted the 'best wave in the world' by *Tracks* magazine. Only suitable for very experienced surfers, on its day this left-handed tube can offer a 300m ride, growing in size from take-off to close-out (which is over razor-sharp coral). Desert Point only really performs when there's a serious ground swell and can be flat for days and days – May to September offers the best chance of the right conditions. The nearest accommodation is about 12km away in Pelangan, down a rough dirt track, so many surfers either camp next to the shoreline, or cruise in on surf safaris from Bali.

Gili Trawangan
Much better known as a diving mecca, Trawangan (p304) also boasts a little-known surf spot off the island's southwestern tip, offshore from the Vila Ombak hotel. It's a quick right-hander that breaks in two sections, one offering a steeper profile, and breaks over rounded coral. It can be surfed all year long but is best at high tide.

Mawi
About 18km west of Kuta (Lombok), the stunning bay of Mawi (p321) has a fine barrelling left with a late take-off and a final tube. It's best in the dry season from May to October with easterly offshore winds and a southwest swell. As there are sharp rocks and coral underwater, and the riptide is very fierce, take great care. Unfortunately, thefts have been reported from the beach, so leave nothing of any value behind and tip the locals to look after your vehicle.

Look for the free newspaper *Magic Wave* – distributed around Kuta, it has full coverage of the Bali surfing scene.

Indo Surf & Lingo (www .indosurf.com.au), by Peter Neely, tells surfers where and when to find good waves around Bali and other Indonesian islands. The book also has a language guide with Indonesian translations of useful words. It's available at surf shops in the Kuta region.

If you've already worked your way around Bali and Lombok and are ready for far-flung adventure, www.surftravelonline .com has information on remote Indonesian locations.

ACTIVITIES FOR KIDS

There's lots of outdoors adventure for kids in Bali. Of the activities in this chapter, some hikes and walks are short and well within short attention spans. The promise of rice fields filled with ducks, frogs and other fun critters only adds to the appeal. Older children can find adventures snorkelling, riding horses and rafting.

The water-sports centres have activities geared to kids and for those that are ready to surf, with most surf schools offering programs aimed at youngsters.

There are also family-friendly attractions that have little to do with Bali or its culture but which are simply fun. Colourful kites are sold in shops and market stalls; get some string at a super-market. Water play is also always fun – you can often use hotel pools, even if you're not staying there; with a mask and snorkel, there is a lot of fun to be had on the beaches, too. Waterbom Park in Tuban (p107) is usually a big hit with most kids.

Other activities popular with kids include visiting Bali Bird Park and Rimba Reptil Park near Ubud (p203), and river rafting (p92).

The long-running Elephant Safari Park north of Ubud (p202) charms anyone with a penchant for pachyderms while the new Bali Safari and Marine Park (p208) is a veritable open-air festival of wildlife.

WATER SPORTS

The east coast of South Bali is popular for water sports. The close-in reefs off Sanur and Tanjung Benoa (Benoa Headland) mean that the water is usually calm enough for a lot of aquatic fun. Parasailing, jet-skiing, waterskiing and banana-boat rides are just some of the choices. In Sanur (see p148) there are activity huts along the beach. In Tanjung Benoa (p143), several large water-sports centres are located on the beach. Most fetch and return patrons from all over the south. Costs for the various mechanised marvels can quickly add up to US$20 an hour or more. Just swimming off the beach is free.

For watery adventures with an island voyage, try one of the party boats making daily excursions to Nusa Lembongan (p153) and Nusa Penida p158). There, you have a full range of water sports based aboard a barge that often looks like something from the Kevin Costner dud *Waterworld*. It's all organised frolic and the most basic activities like snorkelling the interesting reefs are included in the package cost (per person US$60 to US$90). Note that with pick-up and drop-off at your South Bali hotel, plus the boat ride to/from the barge, it can be a very long day.

Kuta, Legian & Seminyak

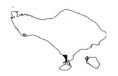

The more things change… Kuta has always been a rebel. For centuries, it was where the Balinese nobility sent their black sheep. The farming and fishing were marginal, so people had to get by on their wiles. The community – such as it was – stretched from today's Kuta and Tuban north through Legian and Seminyak. It was the first part of Bali to make a profit from foreigners and the lesson stuck.

While little of the pastoral coconut-palm-shaded land remains, what does remain is the beach: it's the unifier of the communities and the great engine that drives life from Kuta to Seminyak. This seemingly endless, curving swath of golden sand is where tourism began in Bali in the 1930s and where it continues to thrive today. Washed by perfectly surfable waves that arrive with the regularity of streetcars, the beach is the ribbon of pleasure that easily makes one forget the area's ever-more-breathless lucre. From a surfer extending her stay for yet another week in a US$10 Kuta room, to a lounger summoning yet more pleasure from his beachside repose at a Seminyak resort, the beach is ever democratic in its joys.

Renowned shopping, all-night clubs, fabulous restaurants, cheap beer and relentless hustle and bustle are all part of the experience. But just when you wonder what any of this has to do with Bali – the island supposedly all about spirituality and serenity – a religious procession appears and shuts everything down. And then you know the answer.

HIGHLIGHTS

- Losing your day on **Kuta Beach** (p106)
- Losing your night in **Seminyak** (p125)
- Losing your resolve shopping in **Seminyak** (p126)
- Losing your tension at a spa in **Legian** (p108) or **Seminyak** (p120)
- Losing the crowds at **Echo Beach** (p130), north of Seminyak

★ Echo Beach

★ Seminyak

★ Legian

Kuta Beach ★

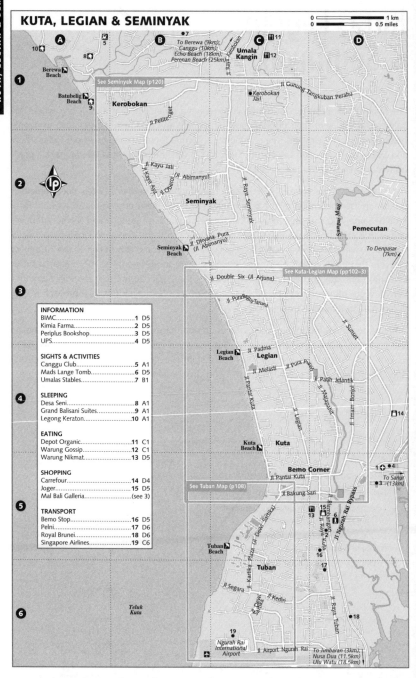

KUTA, LEGIAN & SEMINYAK

0 — 1 km
0 — 0.5 miles

INFORMATION
BIMC.....................................1 D5
Kimia Farma.........................2 D5
Periplus Bookshop.................3 D5
UPS......................................4 D5

SIGHTS & ACTIVITIES
Canggu Club..........................5 A1
Mads Lange Tomb.................6 D5
Umalas Stables......................7 B1

SLEEPING
Desa Seni..............................8 A1
Grand Balisani Suites.............9 A1
Legong Keraton...................10 A1

EATING
Depot Organic......................11 C1
Warung Gossip.....................12 C1
Warung Nikmat....................13 D5

SHOPPING
Carrefour.............................14 D4
Joger...................................15 D5
Mal Bali Galleria...........(see 3)

TRANSPORT
Bemo Stop............................16 D5
Pelni....................................17 D6
Royal Brunei........................18 D6
Singapore Airlines................19 C6

See Seminyak Map (p120)

See Kuta-Legian Map (pp102–3)

See Tuban Map (p108)

To Berewa (9km);
Canggu (10km);
Echo Beach (18km);
Perenan Beach (25km)

Berewa
Beach

Batubelig
Beach

Kerobokan

Umala
Kangin

Kerobokan
Jail

Jl Gunung Tangkuban Perahu

Jl Petitenget

Jl Kayu Jati

Jl Kaya Aya

Jl Oberoi

(Jl Abimanyu)

Jl Raya Seminyak

Seminyak

Pemecutan

Sungai Mati

Seminyak
Beach

Jl Dhyana Pura
(Jl Abimanyu)

To Denpasar
(7km)

Jl Double Six (Jl Arjuna)

Jl Purabagu Taruna

Jl Sunset

Legian
Beach

Jl Padma

Jl Pura Puseh

Legian

Jl Melasti

Jl Patih Jelantik

Jl Pantai Kuta

Jl Majapahit

Jl Legian

Jl Imam Bonjol

Kuta
Beach

Kuta

Bemo Corner

Jl Pantai Kuta

Jl Bakung Sari

To Sanur
(13km)

Jl Ngurah Rai Bypass

Jl Raya Kuta

Bambaran

Tuban
Beach

Jl Kartika Plaza (Jl Dewi Sartika)

Tuban

Jl Segara

Jl Kediri

Jl Dewi Sartika

Jl Raya Tuban

Teluk
Kuta

Ngurah Rai
International
Airport

Jl Airport Ngurah Rai

To Jimbaran (3km);
Nusa Dua (11.5km);
Ulu Watu (18.5km)

KUTA & LEGIAN

☎ 0361

Only 20 years ago, Kuta hotels still tacked their signs up to palm trees. Today, amidst the wall-to-wall commercialism in Kuta and its symbiotic neighbour to the north, Legian, such an image seems as foreign as the thought that the area was once rice fields. Loud, frenetic and brash are just some of the descriptions commonly used for the centre of mass tourism in Bali.

Hate 'em or love 'em, Kuta and Legian (and to a lesser extent their snoozy southern neighbour Tuban) inspire strong opinions. Kuta has narrow lanes, jammed with cheap cafés, surf shops and myriad traveller services. Its main streets have Bali's most raucous clubs, and you can still find a decent, albeit simple, room for US$10 in its dozens of hotels. Legian appeals to a slightly older crowd (wags say it's where fans of Kuta go after they're married). It has a long row of family-friendly hotels close to the waves.

And those waves! They break on the beach that put Kuta on the map. The strand of sand stretching for kilometres from Tuban north to Kuta, Legian and beyond to Seminyak is always a scene of surfing, playing, massaging, chilling, imbibing and more. You're never more than 10 minutes away from the sand here.

HISTORY

Mads Lange, a Danish copra trader and 19th-century adventurer, set up a successful trading enterprise near modern-day Kuta in 1839. He mediated profitably between local rajahs (lords or princes) and the Dutch, who were encroaching from the north. His business soured in the 1850s and he died suddenly, just as he was about to return to Denmark. It's thought that his death may have been the result of poisoning by locals jealous of his wealth. His restored **tomb** (Map p100; Jl Tuan Langa) is on his homesite in a quiet, tree-shaded area by the river.

Much to the annoyance of the Dutch Resident, Bob and Louise Koke's Kuta Beach Hotel thrived in the 1930s. The guests, mostly from Europe and the US, were housed in thatched bungalows built in an idealised Balinese style (the Resident called them 'filthy native huts'). After WWII, Westerners and Balinese continued the trend, building their own hotels along the beach, although most visitors at that point were still wealthy travellers who arrived from abroad on ocean liners.

Kuta really began to change in the late 1960s when it became a stop on the hippie trail between Australia and Europe. At first, most visitors stayed in Denpasar and made day trips to Kuta. But as more accommodation opened, by the early 1970s Kuta had relaxed losmen (basic accommodation) in pretty gardens, friendly places to eat and a delightfully laid-back atmosphere. Surfers also arrived, enjoying the waves at Kuta and using it as a base to explore the rest of Bali's coastline. Enterprising Indonesians seized the opportunity to profit from the tourist trade, often in partnership with foreigners seeking a pretext to stay longer.

Legian, the village to the north, sprang up as an alternative to Kuta in the mid-1970s. At first it was a totally separate development, but these days you can't tell where one ends and the other begins.

ORIENTATION

The Kuta region is disorienting. It's flat, with few landmarks or signs, and streets and alleys that are crooked and often walled on one or both sides so it feels like a maze. Traffic is terrible and walking is often the quickest way to get around, although scooters speeding down narrow *gang* (alleys) can cause problems.

Busy Jl Legian runs roughly parallel to the beach from Kuta north into Seminyak. At the southern end is Bemo Corner, a small roundabout at the junction with Jl Pantai Kuta (Kuta Beach Rd). This one-way street runs west from Bemo Corner and then north along the beach to Jl Melasti. Together, these are the main roads, although traffic and numerous one-way traffic restrictions will still have you needing a cold one.

Between Jl Legian and the beach there is a tangle of narrow streets, tracks and alleys, with a hodgepodge of hotels, souvenir stalls,

---

GONE TO THE DOGS

Mads Lange was known for the kennel of Dalmatians he imported to Bali from Europe. To this day, there are locals in Kuta who believe that any mutt with a trace of black and white spots carries Lange's spirit and is forever searching for those who poisoned him.

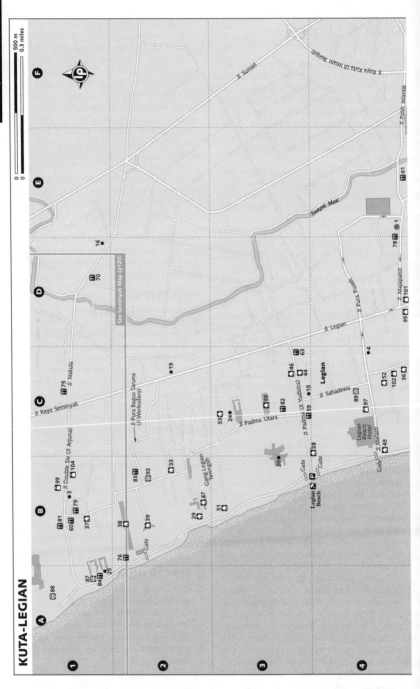

KUTA-LEGIAN

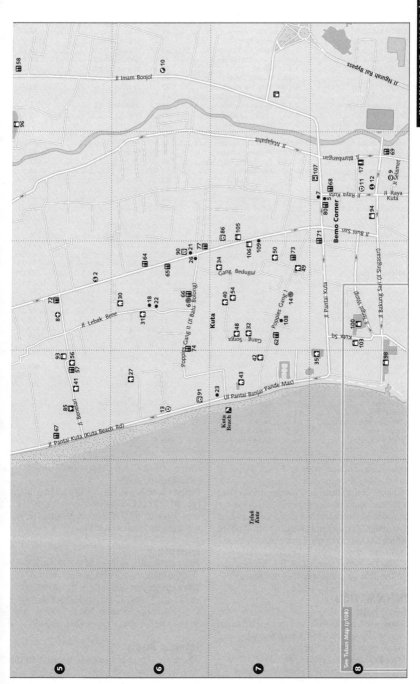

See Tuban Map (p108)

INFORMATION
Bali@Cyber Café.............................1 E4
Bank Commonwealth......................2 D5
Cevin Tour & Travel.......................3 B1
Guardian Melasti............................4 C4
Hanafi...5 E8
Internet Outpost............................6 D6
Kerta Bookshop.............................7 E8
Legian Medical Clinic.....................8 D5
Main Post Office............................9 E8
Netherlands Consulate.............10 F6
Police Station.............................11 E8
Swiss Consular Agent............(see 96)
Tourist Information Centre.......12 E8
Tourist Police Post....................13 C6
VIP Bali Internet.......................14 D7

SIGHTS & ACTIVITIES
AJ Hackett Bungy...................(see 88)
Ambiente Reflexology..............15 C3
Aroma Jepun............................16 D1
Chinese Temple.......................17 E8
G-Land Jungle Surf Camp........18 D6
Hard Rock Hotel Aquatic
    Playground.......................(see 35)
Kudo's.....................................19 C2
Mandara Spa 20 B3
Memorial Wall.........................21 D6
Naruki Surf Shop.....................22 D6
Pro Surf School........................23 C7
Putri Bali................................24 C3
Rip Curl School of Surf.............25 A1
Site of Sari Club.......................26 D6
Spa.......................................(see 29)

SLEEPING
Bali Bungalo............................27 C6
Bali Mandira Hotel...................28 C4
Bali Niksoma Beach Resort........29 B2
Bendesa..................................30 D6
Bene Yasa I..............................31 D6
Berlian Inn..............................32 D7
Bhuwana Beach Cottages.........33 B2
Gemini Star.............................34 D7
Hard Rock Hotel......................35 C8

Hotel Camplung Mas................36 C4
Hotel Kumala...........................37 B1
Hotel Kumala Pantai.................38 B2
Jayakarta Hotel........................39 B2
Kedin's II.................................40 D7
Komala Indah I.........................41 C5
Kuta Puri Bungalows................42 C7
Kuta Seaview Cottages.............43 C7
Legian Beach Bungalow............44 C3
Legian Nirwana.......................45 C4
Lokha Legian...........................46 C3
Maharta Beach Resort..............47 B2
Mimpi Bungalows.................. 48 D7
Poppies Cottages......................49 D7
Puri Agung Homestay...............50 D7
Sari Beach Inn.........................51 B3
Senen Beach Inn......................52 C4
Sri Beach Inn...........................53 C3
Suji Bungalow..........................54 D7
Three Brothers Inn...................55 C3
Un's Hotel...............................56 C5

EATING
Balcony...................................57 C5
Bali Bakery..............................58 F5
Bianco....................................59 C3
Cozy Corner.............................60 B1
Dapur Alam.............................61 E4
Havana Club.............................62 D7
Indo- National..........................63 C3
Ketupat...................................64 D6
Kopi Pot.................................65 D6
Kori Restaurant & Bar...............66 D6
Kuta Food Court.......................67 C5
Kuta Market............................68 E8
Kuta Night Market....................69 E8
Legian Night Market.................70 D1
Made's Warung........................71 E8
Mama's...................................72 D5
Poppies Restaurant..................73 D7
Rainbow Cafe...........................74 D6
Saleko....................................75 C1
Seaside...................................76 B2
Sky Garden Lounge..................77 D6
Swiss Restaurant.................(see 96)

Take.......................................78 E4
Warung Asia............................79 B1
Warung Hanafi.........................80 E8
Warung Murah.........................81 B1
Warung Yogya.........................82 C3
Yut'z......................................83 B2
Zanzibar..................................84 A1

DRINKING
Bed...85 C5

ENTERTAINMENT
Apache Reggae Bar................(see 86)
Bounty....................................86 E7
De Ja Vu.................................87 A1
Double Six Club........................88 A1
Legend....................................89 C4
Mbargo...................................90 D6
Ocean Beach Club....................91 C6
Ye Olde Foo-Kin Pub................92 B2

SHOPPING
Black Sands Surfboard Bags......93 C5
Bouchra...............................(see 104)
Busana Agung.....................(see 104)
Capt Black Bikers Fashion Shop.94 E8
IO & CO..................................95 D4
Istana Kuta Galleria..................96 F5
Jl Melasti Art Market................97 C4
Jonathan Gallery.................(see 64)
Kuta Sq Art Market...................98 C8
Lavender Bali..........................99 B1
Matahari.................................100 D8
Ming......................................101 D4
Puri Naga Studio......................102 C4
Rip Curl..................................103 D8
Sriwijaya.................................104 B1
Surfer Girl...............................105 E7
Uluwatu.................................106 C3

TRANSPORT
Bemos to Tegal, Jimbaran,
    Uluwatu & Nusa Dua..........107 E8
Gili Paradise Shop....................108 D7
Perama...................................109 D7

cafés, construction sites and cars trying to drive where they shouldn't.

North of Jl Melasti, Kuta merges into Legian, which is mostly distinguished by slightly wider roads. Somewhere south of Bemo Corner along Jl Kartika Plaza, Kuta merges with Tuban, which has beach resorts, a huge beachside mall and a fair amount of low-key life.

See the boxed text, p119, for information on the changing street names in the region.

INFORMATION
Bookshops
Small used-book stalls and book exchanges can be found scattered along the *gang* and roads, especially the Poppies.

Kerta Bookshop (Map pp102-3; ☎ 758047; Jl Pantai Kuta 6B) A book exchange with a better-than-average

selection of books. Many break the Patterson–Brown–Cornwall schlock mould.

Periplus Bookshop Discovery Shopping Mall (Map p108; ☎ 769757; Jl Kartika Plaza, Tuban); Bali Galleria shopping centre (Map p100; ☎ 752670; Ngurah Rai Bypass) Has the largest selection of new books in Bali.

Emergency
Police station (Map pp102-3; ☎ 751598; Jl Raya Kuta; ☺ 24hr) Next to the Tourist Information Centre.
Tourist police post (Map pp102-3; ☎ 7845988; Jl Pantai Kuta; ☺ 24hr) This is a branch of the main police station in Denpasar. Right across from the beach, the officers have a gig that is sort of like a Balinese Baywatch.

Internet Access
There are scores of places to connect to the internet. Most have poky connections and

charge about 300Rp a minute. The following places have fast broadband connections and offer numerous services, including wi-fi, CD burning, digital camera downloads and more. Connection rates average 600Rp per minute.

Bali@Cyber Café (Map pp102-3; ☎ 761326; www.bali cyber.net; Jl Patih Jelantik; meals 20,000-30,000Rp; ⏰ 8am-11pm) Has a full range of computer options, parking and a good menu of snacks, meals and tasty smoothies. Many expats use it as their office.

Internet Outpost (Map pp102-3; ☎ 763392; Poppies Gang II; ⏰ 8am-2am) Has desks, couches and cold drinks.

VIP Bali Internet (Map pp102-3 ☎ 0813 3719 6105; Poppies Gang I; ⏰ 8.30am-midnight) Decent speed, plus wi-fi, scanning, Skype etc.

Laundry

Most hotels, even the top-end ones, offer guests a laundry service for a comparatively low price. Backstreet laundries are only marginally cheaper – about 1500Rp for jeans, 1000Rp for a shirt or shorts, 500Rp for underwear – and you have less recourse if something goes awry.

Medical Services

See p365 for medical clinics serving all of Bali.

Guardian Melasti (Map pp102-3; ☎ 765217; Jl Melasti; ⏰ 8am-10pm) Modern chain pharmacy; a good stop if you need prescription drugs.

Kimia Farma (Map p100; ☎ 757483; Jl Raya Kuta 15; ⏰ 24hr) Part of a local chain of pharmacies, it's well stocked and carries hard-to-find items like that antidote for irksome cocks in the morning: earplugs.

Legian Medical Clinic (Map pp102-3; ☎ 758503; Jl Benesari; ⏰ on call 24hr) Has an ambulance and dental service. It's 400,000Rp for a consultation with an English-speaking Balinese doctor, or 800,000Rp for an emergency visit to your hotel room. It has a well-stocked pharmacy attached to the clinic.

Money

There are banks along Jl Legian and at Kuta Sq. In addition, ATMs abound and can be found everywhere, including in the ubiquitous Circle K and Mini Mart convenience stores.

The numerous 'authorised' moneychangers are faster and efficient, open long hours and may offer better exchange rates. Be cautious, though, especially where the rates are markedly better than average. Extra fees may apply or, judging by the number of readers' letters we continue to receive, they may be adeptly short-changing their customers.

Exchange counters run by international banks are a new phenomenon and should offer reliable service.

Bank Commonwealth Tuban (Map p108; ☎ 750049; Jl Dewi Sartika 8X; ⏰ 11am-7pm); Legian (Map pp102-3; ☎ 758070; Jl Legian; ⏰ 11am-7pm)

Post

Postal agencies that can send but not receive mail are common.

There are several cargo agencies in the Kuta area. If you've bought bulky items, the store will usually have arrangements with shippers to handle things for you. Or, for fast service, you can use one of the expensive international companies.

Main post office (Map pp102-3; Jl Selamet; ⏰ 7am-2pm Mon-Thu, 7-11am Fri, 7am-1pm Sat) On a small road east of Jl Raya Kuta, this small and efficient post office has an easy, sort-it-yourself poste restante service. It's well practised in shipping large packages.

Tourist Information

Places that advertise themselves as 'tourist information centres' are usually commercial travel agents or worse: time-share condo sales operations.

Tourist Information Centre (Map pp102-3; ☎ 766180; Jl Raya Kuta; ⏰ 8am-3pm Mon-Thu, 8am-1pm Fri) Handles the Kuta region and the rest of Bali. Its usefulness is limited, however.

Hanafi (Map pp102-3; ☎ 756454; www.hanafi.net; Jl Pantai Kuta 1E) This gay- and family-friendly tour operator and guide operates from a small veterinary clinic he shares with his sister. He's a valuable source of information, can also organise tours and has a small café.

Travel Agencies

Many travel agents will arrange transport or car and motorcycle rental. They also sell tickets for dance performances, adventure activities and a variety of tours. Most will also change money and many can book airline tickets, although for some discount carriers you're better off at an internet café.

Cevin Tour & Travel (Map pp102-3; ☎ 7437343; marti flightcentrebali@yahoo.com; Jl Arjuna 23) A reputable agent, popular with expats.

DANGERS & ANNOYANCES

The streets and *gang* are usually safe but there are annoyances. Scooter-borne prostitutes (who hassle single men late at night) cruise after dark. Walking along you may hear: 'massage' followed by 'young girl' and

---

GETTING AWAY FROM IT ALL

Dodging cars, motorcycles, touts, dogs and dodgy footpaths can make walking through Kuta and Legian seem like anything but a holiday. It's intense and it can be stressful. You may soon be longing for uncrowded places where you hear little more than the rustling of palm fronds and the call of a bird.

Think you need to book a trip out of town? Well, think again. You can escape to the country without leaving Kuta and Legian. All those teeming streets surround vacant swaths of land and once you poke through the wall of commerce, you can be transported back to a Kuta and Legian of 20 years ago. The secret is to get off the streets and onto the *gang*. In Kuta, this is hard, as even these can be crowded, but take any alley or lane heading east of Jl Legian and you'll be in the quieter neighbourhood where the locals live.

Better still is Legian. Take any of the narrow *gang* into the area bounded by Jl Legian, Jl Padma, Jl Padma Utara and Jl Pura Bagus Taruna. Soon you'll be on narrow paths that go past local houses and the occasional simple warung (food stall) or shop. Wander at random and enjoy the silence accented by, yes, the sound of palm fronds and birds.

---

the ubiquitous 'transport' followed by 'blow'. But your biggest irritation will likely be the ever-worsening traffic.

Hawkers

Crackdowns mean that it's rare to find carts in the Kuta tourist area, but street selling is common, especially on hassle street, Jl Legian, where selling and begging can be aggressive. The beach isn't unbearable, but the upper part has souvenir sellers and masseuses (who may grab hold of you and not let go). Closer to the water you can sunbake on the sand in peace – you'll see where the invisible line is.

Surf

The surf can be very dangerous, with a strong current on some tides, especially up north in Legian. Lifeguards patrol swimming areas of the beaches at Kuta and Legian, indicated by red-and-yellow flags. If they say the water is too rough or unsafe to swim in, they mean it. Red flags with a skull and crossbones mean no swimming allowed.

The lifeguards are very dedicated, as anyone who saw the Bali series of the show *Bondi Rescue* can attest.

Theft

Visitors lose things from unlocked (and some locked) hotel rooms and from the beach. Going into the water and leaving valuables on the beach is simply asking for trouble (in any country). Snatch thefts are rare, but valuable items can be left at your hotel reception.

Water Pollution

The sea water around Kuta is commonly contaminated by run-off from both built-up areas and surrounding farmland, especially after heavy rain. Swim away from streams.

SIGHTS

The real sight here is of course the beach. You can immerse yourself in local life without even getting wet. A new walkway runs south from where Jl Pantai Kuta meets the beach. Stretching almost to the airport, it has fine views of the ocean as well as the efforts to preserve some of Tuban's nearly-vanished beach.

Wanderers, browsers and gawkers will find much to fascinate, delight and irritate amidst the streets, alleys and constant hubbub. You can even discover the odd non-touristy site like an old **Chinese Temple** (Map pp102-3; Jl Blambangan).

Reflecting the international character of the 2002 bombings (see p45) is the **memorial wall** (Map pp102-3; Jl Raya Seminyak), where people from many nationalities pay their respects. Listing the names of the 202 known victims, including 88 Australians and 35 Indonesians, it has an emotional effect on many who view it. Across the street, a vacant lot is all that is left of the Sari Club. Plans to turn the site into a memorial park (www.balipeacepark.com) are proving difficult, and in the meantime it's used for motorbike parking.

ACTIVITIES

From Kuta you can easily go surfing, sailing, diving, fishing or rafting anywhere in the southern part of Bali and still be back for the start of happy hour at sunset.

Many of your activities in Kuta will centre on the superb beach. Hawkers will sell you sodas and beer, snacks and other treats, and you can rent lounge chairs and umbrellas (negotiable at 10,000Rp to 20,000Rp) or just crash on the sand. You'll see everyone from bronzed international youth strutting their stuff, to local families trying to figure out how to get wet *and* preserve their modesty. When the tide is out, the beach seems to stretch forever and you should be tempted for a long stroll. Sunsets are a time of gathering for just about everyone in South Bali. When conditions are right, you can enjoy a fuchsia-streaked spectacle that photos just can't capture properly.

Organised activities on land and sea are almost as frenzied as the efforts to sell you them, see p86 for details.

Surfing

The beach break called Halfway Kuta, offshore near the Hotel Istana Rama, is the best place to learn to surf. More challenging breaks can be found on the shifting sandbars off Legian, around the end of Jl Padma; and at Kuta Reef, 1km out to sea off Tuban Beach (see p93 for details on these surf breaks). Shops large and small sell big-brand surf gear and surfboards (p117). Stalls on the side streets hire out surfboards (for a negotiable 30,000Rp per day) and boogie boards, repair dings and sell new and used boards. Some can also arrange transport to nearby surfing spots. Used boards in good shape average US$200. Check out the free surfing magazines such as *Magic Wave*. Surf schools line the beach.

G-Land Jungle Surf Camp (Map pp102-3; ☎ 763166; www.g-land.com; Poppies Gang II; tours from US$350) is the Kuta office for the surf camp at legendary G-Land on Java. Overnight transfers penetrate the jungle to the simple lodge and spectacular breaks.

Naruki Surf Shop (Map pp102-3; ☎ 765772; Jl Poppies Gang II; ☉ 10am-7pm) is one of dozens of surf shops lining the *gang* of Kuta. The friendly guys here will rent you a board, fix your ding, offer advice or give you lessons.

Pro Surf School (Map pp102-3; ☎ 744 1466; www.pro surfschool.com; Jl Pantai Kuta; lessons from US$45; ☉ classes from 9am) is right across from the classic stretch of Kuta Beach. Facilities here include a swimming pool and semi-private lesson areas where you can first stroke your board.

Rip Curl School of Surf (Map pp102-3; ☎ 735858; www.ripcurlschoolofsurf.com; Jl Arjuna; lessons from US$45; ☉ classes from 8am), run by the high-profile, local surf-wear conglomerate, is a school offering classes for beginners and experts alike. Located right on ever-popular Double Six beach.

Waterbom Park

This popular **theme park** (Map p108; ☎ 755676; www.waterbom.com; Jl Kartika Plaza, Tuban; adult/child US$21/11; ☉ 9am-6pm), south of Kuta, is set on 3.5 hectares of landscaped tropical parks and has assorted water slides, swimming pools, play areas, a supervised park for children under five years old, and a 'superbowl', where you literally go down the drain. Other indulgences include a food court, swim-up bar and a spa. There are lifeguards and it's well supervised.

Swimming Pools

Most hotels will allow non-guests to use their pool for a fee. The most impressive is the Hard Rock Hotel's **aquatic playground**

LEGIAN'S SURFING LEGEND

Tippi Jabrik, 30, is head of the Indonesia Surfing Championships and a longtime surfer who grew up in Legian. He started surfing when he was five years old on the beach near his home in Legian. It's the place where surfing began in Bali, when the American hotel pioneer Robert Koke brought it to the island from Hawaii in the 1930s. As a youngster, Jabrik was one of the few Balinese taking to the waves. And even though locals had by tradition feared the water, he dived into the sport. Why? 'My Dad took me to the beach a lot and I saw other guys doing it and it looked fun. Of course then there were like 50 people surfing, now there are thousands.' He notes that surfing has definitely found its place amongst Bali's youth. 'There are more locals on the beach than tourists.' But he says despite the popularity of the sport, everyone can get along if visitors simply 'show respect for the locals'. His greater fear is for Kuta Beach itself. 'Since they lengthened the runway at the airport a few years ago, the sand has been going away. Look at the breakwaters they are having to build in Tuban.'

KUTA, LEGIAN & SEMINYAK

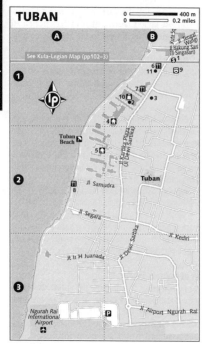

TUBAN

0 ———— 400 m
0 ———— 0.2 miles

See Kuta-Legian Map (pp102-3)

Tuban Beach

Tuban

Jl Samudra

Jl Segara

Jl Kediri

Jl Ir H Juanada

Jl Airport Ngurah Rai

Ngurah Rai International Airport

INFORMATION
Bank Commonwealth..**1** B1
Periplus Bookshop...(see 10)

SIGHTS & ACTIVITIES
Amazone..**2** B1
Waterbom Park..**3** B1

SLEEPING 🛏
Discovery Kartika Plaza Hotel.................................**4** B1
Hotel Santika Beach...**5** A2

EATING 🍴
B Couple Bar n' Grill..**6** B1
Bread Talk..(see 10)
Discovery Shopping Mall ....(see 10)
Food Court..(see 10)
Kafe Batan Waru...**7** B1
Ma Joly...**8** A2

ENTERTAINMENT 🎭
DeeJay Cafe...**9** B1

SHOPPING 🛍
Discovery Shopping Mall.......................................**10** B1

TRANSPORT
Garuda...**11** B1
Qatar Airways...(see 4)

(Map pp102-3; ☎ 761869; Jl Pantai Kuta; adult/child/family 100,000/50,000/250,000Rp; ⏰ 8am-9pm). The vast, sinuous pool features two water slides and a sandy beach island. There are lifeguards, and if you need a snog, you can rent private cabanas for 200,000Rp.

Massages, Spas & Salons

The top-end **Mandara Spa** (Map pp102-3; ☎ 752111; www.mandaraspa.com; Jl Padma 1; massages from US$35; ⏰ 10am-8pm) is in the Hotel Padma Bali. This divine spa is decorated with water features and impressive stone sculptural reliefs.

As stylish as its host hotel, **Spa** (Map pp102-3; ☎ 751946; Bali Niksoma Beach Resort, Jl Padma Utara; traditional massage 300,000Rp; ⏰ 9am-9pm) offers private suites where you can indulge in everything from a pampering Bali coffee scrub to shiatsu.

The delightfully relaxed spa at **Putri Bali** (Map pp102-3; ☎ 755987; Jl Padma Utara; massage from 60,000Rp; ⏰ 10am-9pm) at the Wisata Beach Inn offers a cream bath that has set the hearts of many spa-o-philes a-twitter with delight. Located off the main street, this lovely spa has very competitive prices.

Another local favourite, **Aroma Jepun** (Map pp102-3; ☎ 847 5655; Jl Nakula; massage from 85,000Rp; ⏰ 10am-8pm) has treatments with intriguing names like Aroma Cook Scrub and Cappucino Body Scrub. It also offers massage by two masseuses in order to get you out the door faster, although that seems to run counter to the goal.

Enjoy a 'Foot Frenzy' at **Ambiente Reflexology** (Map pp102-3; ☎ 758174; Jl Sahadewa; sessions from 65,000Rp; ⏰ 10am-7pm). Although the focus is on your lower echelons, your head might also swell with joy after a 'Scalp Seduction', one of a wide range of massages and treatments – which includes 'Ultimate Pleasure'.

Run by stylish hipsters, **Kudo's** (Map pp102-3; ☎ 756030; Jl Legian 456; ⏰ 10am-8pm) is a high-concept salon that is *the* place to go for a cut and blow-dry. It's popular with brides before their big moment.

Bungy Jumping

AJ Hackett Bungy (Map pp102-3; ☎ 731144; Jl Arjuna; from US$79; ⏰ noon-8pm daily, 2-6am Fri & Sat), beside the beach at the Double Six Club (p116) in Legian, has a great view of the coast (you can't see the hideous tower you're standing on – or bouncing from). Late-night hours for boozers give new meaning to 'Look out below!'.

Activities for Children

Except for the traffic, the Kuta area is a pretty good place for kids. With supervision – and sunscreen! – they can cavort on the beach for hours. Almost all the hotels and resorts above the surfer-dude category have pools and the better ones offer kids' programs. See p330 for details on other things kids will enjoy.

Amazone (Map p108; Discovery Shopping Mall, Jl Kartika Plaza, Tuban; ☺ 10am-10pm) has hundreds of screeching arcade games on the top floor of the mall.

TOURS

A vast range of tours all around Bali, from half-day to three-day tours, can be booked through your hotel or the plethora of stands plastered with brochures. These tours are a quick and easy way to see a few sights if your time is limited and you don't want to rent or charter a vehicle. See p361 for more information on the types of tours available.

FESTIVALS & EVENTS

The first **Kuta Karnival** (www.kutakarnival.com) was held in 2003 as a way of celebrating life after the tragedy of 2002. It's become an almost-annual event held in September or October (except when it's in June…). Events include parades, arts competitions, cultural shows, beach-sports tournaments, parades and more. You can try to check the website to find out when the next karnival may (or may not) be on.

There are surfing contests throughout the year.

SLEEPING

Kuta, Legian and Tuban have hundreds of places for you to stay. The top-end hotels are along the beachfront, midrange places are mostly on the bigger roads between Jl Legian and the beach, and the cheapest joints are generally along the smaller lanes in between. Tuban and Legian have mostly mid-range and top-end hotels – the best places to find budget accommodation are Kuta and southern Legian.

With hotel names, be sceptical about words such as 'beach', 'sea view', 'cottage' and 'bungalows'. Places with 'beach' in their name may not be anywhere near the beach, and a featureless, three-storey hotel block may rejoice in the name 'cottages'. Note that hotels on Jl Pantai Kuta are separated from the beach by

a busy main road south of Jl Melasti. North of Jl Melasti in Legian, though, the beach road is protected by gates that exclude almost all vehicle traffic. Hotels here have what is in effect a quiet, paved beachfront promenade.

Any place that is west of Jl Legian won't be more than a 10-minute walk to the beach.

Budget

The best budget accommodation is in a losmen with rooms facing a central garden. Look for a place that is far enough off the main roads to be quiet, but close enough so that getting to the beach, shops and restaurants isn't a problem. Luxuries like air-con and pools have become common, although the cheapest rooms are fan- and cold-water-only.

One street can have lots of places with similar rates but quality can vary markedly: one hotel will have a scrum of three-storey blocks jammed into a small site while next door there's a sunny compound with sunny rooms around a pool. Definitely shop around, especially out of peak season when prices are negotiable.

KUTA

Many of the cheap places in Kuta are along the tiny alleys and lanes between Jl Legian and the beach in central Kuta. This is a good place to base yourself: it's quiet, but only a short walk from the beach, shops and nightlife. A few places on the eastern side of Jl Legian are close to the bars and restaurants, but can be noisy and a hike from the beach. Jl Benesari is a great place to stay, close to the beach and quieter than the Poppies Gangs. Gang Sorga is another top pick, with scores of options.

Puri Agung Homestay (Map p102-3; ☎ 750054; off Poppies Gang I; s/d 30,000/50,000Rp) The budget winner in Kuta. Hungover surfers will appreciate the 12 dark, cold-water rooms at this attractive little place that features a tiny grotto-like garden. Non-vampires can find more light on the top floor.

Komala Indah I (Map pp102-3; ☎ 753185; Jl Benesari; r 50,000-150,000Rp; ⚡) The rooms here are set around a pleasant garden; the cheapest of the 30 rooms have squat toilets, fans and twin beds only. It's part of the Komala empire that dates back to the early days of Kuta tourism.

Berlian Inn (Map pp102-3; ☎ 751501; off Poppies Gang I; r 70,000-225,000Rp; ⚡) A stylish cut above other budget places, the 24 rooms in two-storey buildings here are pleasingly quiet and have ikat bedspreads and an unusual open-air bathroom design. Pricier rooms have air-con and hot water.

Kedin's II (Map pp102-3; ☎ 763554; Gang Sorga; s/d from 80,000/110,000Rp; 🅿 🖵) One of the best budget choices. Here the 16 cold-water rooms (with showers) have hints of style and verandahs with fine views of the gardens and the good-sized pool.

Bene Yasa I (Map pp102-3; ☎ 754180; Poppies Gang II; r 80,000-200,000Rp; 🕸 🅿) The grounds at this 44-room hotel are large and open, with palms providing some shade. Three-storey blocks overlook the pool area, and the plethora of patios encourages a lively social scene (except at midday, when many guests are passed out on loungers). Better rooms have tubs and air-con.

Gemini Star Hotel (Map pp102-3; ☎ 750558; aquarius hotel@yahoo.com; Poppies Gang II; r 90,000-185,000Rp; 🕸 🅿) Only the monosyllabic mutterings of lounging surfers interrupt the peace at this small, quiet hotel on a narrow alley. Two two-storey blocks shelter the sunny and surprisingly large pool area. Cheap rooms have fans and hot water; more money adds air-con and fridges.

Bendesa (Map pp102-3; ☎ 754366; www.bendesaaccomodation.com; off Poppies Gang II; r US$13-30; 🕸 🅿) The 42 rooms here include 10 new ones with air-con. The location is quiet and there's an attractive pool. The cheapest rooms – all clean – have cold water (some with bathtubs) and fan.

Mimpi Bungalows (Map pp102-3; ☎ 751848; kumimpi @yahoo.com.sg; Gang Sorga; r 150,000R-200,000Rp; 🕸 🅿) The cheapest of the 10 bungalow-style rooms here are the best value. The private gardens boast orchids and shade, and the pool is a good size. The owner, Made Supatra, is a tireless promoter of Kuta.

LEGIAN

The streets are wider here and the pace is less frenetic than just south in Kuta. Budget places tend to be larger as well. Wander off the main roads for some quiet gems.

Senen Beach Inn (Map pp102-3; ☎ 755470; Gang Camplung Mas 25; r 50,000-70,000Rp) In a quiet little *gang* near Jl Melasti, this 18-room, cold-water place is run by friendly young guys. Rooms have outdoor bathrooms and are set around a small garden. There are several other family-run cheapies hidden back here.

Sri Beach Inn (Map pp102-3; ☎ 755897; Gang Legian Tewngah; r 60,000Rp) Follow a series of paths into

the heart of old Legian. When you hear the rustle of palms overhead, you're close to this homestay with eight simple, clean rooms. The gardens get lovelier by the year; agree to a monthly rate and watch them grow.

Legian Beach Bungalow (Map pp102-3; ☎ 751087; legianbeachbungalow@yahoo.co.id; Jl Padma; r 70,000-175,000Rp; 🕸 🅿) The cheapest of the 20 rooms at this simple place only have cold water but all have air-con; some have bathtubs. The single- and two-storey blocks hem in the pool.

Bhuwana Beach Cottages (Map pp102-3; ☎ 752234; Jl Padma Utara; r from 150,000Rp) Barebones budget accommodation in the commercial heart of Legian (and when we say commercial, we mean it – you can even buy a date). The eight cold-water rooms have thatched walls and are far from modern. But the proximity to a beach quieter than Kuta's attracts many.

Midrange

The bulk of accommodation in the Kuta area falls into the midrange category, especially in Legian. Quality varies widely, with some places offering quite a bit in terms of location, amenities and service. Leave the rest for hapless groups.

KUTA

These places are handy to the beach.

Suji Bungalow (Map pp102-3; ☎ 765804; www.sujibglw .com; off Poppies Gang I; r US$20-32; 🕸 🅿 🖵 wi-fi) You can have your choice of 47 bungalows and rooms in two-storey blocks set in a spacious, quiet garden around a pool (which has a slide into the kiddie area) at this cheery place. The verandahs and terraces are good for relaxing.

Kuta Puri Bungalows (Map pp102-3; ☎ 751903; www .kutapuri.com; Poppies Gang I; r US$25-35, with air-con & hot water US$35-50; 🕸 🅿 🖵 wi-fi) The 47 bungalow-style rooms here are well maintained and are nestled in verdant, tropical grounds. The pool has a shallow kids' area. Get a room close to reception for the best wi-fi signal.

our pick Un's Hotel (Map pp102-3; ☎ 757409; www.uns hotel.com; Jl Benesari; s/d US$26/36, with air-con US$38/45; 🕸 🅿 🖵 wi-fi) A hidden entrance sets the tone for the secluded feel of Un's. It's a two-storey place with bougainvillea spilling over the pool-facing balconies. The 30 spacious rooms in a facing pair of two-storey blocks (the southern one is quieter) feature antiques, comfy cane loungers and open-air bathrooms.

Bali Bungalo (Map pp102-3; ☎ 755109; www.bali -bungalo.com; off Jl Pantai Kuta; r from 375,000Rp; 🕸 🅿)

Large rooms close to the beach yet away from irritations are a big part of the appeal of this older, 44-room hotel. It's well maintained and there are prancing statues of horses to inspire horseplay in the pool. Rooms are in two-storey buildings and have patios/porches.

Poppies Cottages (Map pp102-3; ☎ 751059; www.poppiesbali.com; Poppies Gang I; r US$75-100; ❄ ⊛ ⬜ wi-fi) This Kuta institution has a lush, green garden setting for its 20 thatch-roofed cottages with outdoor sunken baths. Bed choices include kings and twins. The pool is surrounded by stone sculptures and water fountains in a garden that almost makes you forget you are in the heart of Kuta.

Kuta Seaview Cottages (Map pp102-3; ☎ 751961; www.kutaseaviewhotel.com; Jl Pantai Kuta; r US$80-110; ❄ ⊛ ⬜) The 82 stylishly decorated rooms feature the dark-wood-and-créme-walls minimalist look that's de rigueur right now. Choices include rooms with beach views and cottages set in the lovely gardens. Right across the street from the beach, the pool area has surf views. Nappers should avoid rooms near the bar and its bad sunset rock.

LEGIAN
Further north, many hotels have great locations on the beach. There's a crop of good-value places along Jl Lebak Bene.

Three Brothers Inn (Map pp102-3; ☎ 751566; www.threebrothersbungalows.com; off Jl Padma Utara; r US$20-35, with air-con US$25-45; ❄ ⊛) Twisting banyan trees shade scores of brick bungalows holding 83 rooms in the Brothers' sprawling and garden-like grounds. The fan rooms are the best option, but all rooms are spacious, some with alluring outdoor bathrooms (all have tubs). Top-end rooms have DVD players.

Hotel Camplung Mas (Map pp102-3; ☎ 751461; www.camplungmashotel.com; Jl Lebak Bene; r US$35-60; ❄ ⊛ ⬜) Balinese stone architecture highlights the lush gardens here. Of the 69 rooms, the private bungalows set in walled compounds are appealing. Some of the well-maintained rooms have a whitewashed brick motif. Several other midrange choices are nearby.

Maharta Beach Resort (Map pp102-3; ☎ 757688; maharta@indo.net.id; Jl Padma Utara; r US$45-70; ❄ ⊛) Tucked into a tiny beachfront pocket, the Maharta is a few years old but solidly maintained. Its real advantage is its beachy location. The 34 rooms (with patios/balconies) have typical Balinese wood furnishings, some

with bathtubs and tile floors. Some beds boast an oddly angled overhead mirror that invites contortions by narcissists.

Hotel Kumala Pantai (Map p102-3; ☎ 755500; www.kumalapantai.com; Jl Werkudara; r US$50-70; ❄ ⊛ ⬜ wi-fi) One of the better deals in Legian. The 108 rooms (20 in a new building) are large, with marble bathrooms that have a separate shower and tub. The three-storey blocks are set in nicely landscaped grounds across from popular Double Six beach. The breakfast buffet is bountiful. A cheaper sister property, the Hotel Kumala (☎ 732186; Jl Pura Bagus Taruna), is nearby.

Sari Beach Inn (Map pp102-3; ☎ 751635; sbi@indo.net.id; off Jl Padma Utara; r US$50-90; ❄ ⊛) Follow your ears down a long *gang* to the roar of the surf at this great-value beachside hotel that defines mellow. The 24 rooms have patios and the best have big soaking tubs. The grassy grounds boast many little statues and water features.

Jayakarta Hotel (Map pp102-3; ☎ 751433; www.jayakartahotelsresorts.com; Jl Pura Bagus Taruna; r US$70-150; ❄ ⊛ ⬜ wi-fi) The Jayakarta fronts a long and shady stretch of beach. The palm-shaded grounds, 277 large rooms, several pools and various restaurants make it a favourite with groups and families. Hair-braiders give kids that holiday look by the pool. Wi-fi reception varies by room.

Lokha Legian (Map pp102-3; ☎ 766 7601; www.thelokhalegian.com; Jl Padma; r from US$90; ❄ ⊛ ⬜ wi-fi) This modern and stylish place in Legian sets the midrange standard. The 49 rooms are not huge but neither are the prices. The close-in U-shaped block overlooks a large pool and pals from Perth shout from one terrace to the next. The beach is a five-minute walk.

Top End
A beachfront room is the goal of many. Note that those in Tuban and north in Seminyak (p121) are usually right on the beach – Seminyak's beach is far superior. Beachfront hotels in Kuta front busy Jl Pantai Kuta while most of Legian's top hotels (and some more modest ones) front a fine swath of beach and a road closed to traffic – in effect, a long promenade.

TUBAN
It's quieter here than Kuta but the action is a short walk north along the new oceanfront

walkway (the beach can get mighty small at high tide). This one is on the water.

Hotel Santika Beach (Map p108; ☎ 751267; www .santika.net; Jl Kartika Plaza; r US$90-175; ⚙ ⚡ 💻 wi-fi) A cute frangipani-lined entrance leads into verdant grounds. Bungalows are secluded and have private gardens; the 170 rooms have private balconies (although the cheapest are on a back acre). The design is restrained compared to some of the big group-tour behemoths nearby and the staff are warm and professional.

Discovery Kartika Plaza Hotel (Map p108; ☎ 751067; www.discoverykartikaplaza.com; Jl Kartika Plaza; r US$140-220; ⚙ ⚡ 💻 wi-fi) The 312 spacious rooms in four-storey blocks at this large resort front expansive gardens and a gigantic swimming pool. For a real splurge, rent one of the private villas on the water (units 2 to 7 are best). The business centre has Macs.

KUTA

Top-end hotels in Kuta suffer from being on the wrong side of busy Jl Pantai Kuta.

Hard Rock Hotel (Map pp102-3; ☎ 761869; www.hard rockhotels.com; Jl Pantai Kuta; r from US$120; ⚙ ⚡ 💻 wi-fi) Nothing is understated about the ostentatious 400 rooms which, despite various themes, all feel like a retail opportunity. The pool is more fantasyland than amenity (see p107). The staff are skilful and you never need long to buy a T-shirt in the Megastore.

LEGIAN

Most of the top-end places in Legian are directly opposite the beach on stretches of road closed to traffic. These tend to be relaxed places favoured by families. A vast new condo–hotel, the Legian Nirwana, is set to open in 2009 and may well spark a new building boom.

Bali Mandira Hotel (Map pp102-3; ☎ 751381; www .balimandira.com; Jl Pantai Kuta; r US$110-180, cottage from US$160; ⚙ ⚡ 💻 wi-fi) Gardens filled with bird of paradise flowers set the tone at this 191-room full-service resort. Cottages have modern interiors, and the bathrooms are partly open-air. A dramatic pool at the peak of a stone ziggurat (which houses a spa) offers sweeping ocean views, as does the café. Wi-fi is best near reception.

Bali Niksoma Beach Resort (Map pp102-3; ☎ 751946; www.baliniksoma.com; Jl Padma Utara; r US$125-175, villas from US$600; ⚙ ⚡ 💻 wi-fi) An older beachside hotel, the Niksoma was rebuilt into a chic boutique hotel. One of the two multilevel

pools seems to disappear into the ocean and horizon. The decor is spare while the grounds are spacious. There is a noteworthy spa called, well, Spa (p108).

EATING

There's a profusion of places to eat around Kuta and Legian. Cafés with their cheap menus of Indonesian standards, sandwiches and pizza are ubiquitous. Other forms of Asian fare can be found as well and there are numerous places serving fresh seafood, steaks and pasta. There is also a good range of excellent yet humble Balinese places.

If you're looking for the laid-back scene of a classic travellers café, wander the *gang* and look for the crowds. Often what's busy one night will be quiet the next. For quick snacks and 4am stubbies, Circle K convenience stores are everywhere and are open 24 hours.

Tuban

The beachfront hotels all have restaurants – in most cases, the best features for non-guests are the beachside cafés, good for a tropical snack or a sunset drink.

Discovery Shopping Mall (Map p108; Jl Kartika Plaza; ⚙) Home to many places to eat, including a top-floor food court (meals 5000Rp to 10,000Rp) with scores of vendors selling cheap, fresh Asian food. You can eat outside on a terrace overlooking Kuta Beach. Near the entrance, Bread Talk is a wildly popular bakery where you grab tongs and choose your own goodies. There are also several stylish coffee cafés (and we're not talking about the joint on level 1 that rhymes with 'sucks').

Warung Nikmat (Map p100; ☎ 764678; Jl Banjar Sari; dishes 10,000-25,000Rp) This Javanese favourite in downtown Kuta is known for its array of authentic halal dishes ranging from beef rendang to *perkodel* (fried corn cakes), prawn cakes, spiced shredded chicken and various curries and vegetable dishes. Get there before 2pm or you'll be left with the scraps.

Kafe Batan Waru (Map p108; ☎ 766303; Jl Kartika Plaza; mains 25,000-50,000Rp) The Tuban branch of one of Ubud's best eateries (p192) is a slicked-up version of a warung (foor stall), albeit with excellent and creative Asian and local fare. There's also good coffee, baked goods and magazines.

B Couple Bar n' Grill (Map p108; ☎ 761414; Jl Kartika Plaza; mains from 30,000Rp; ⏰ 24hr) A vibrant mix of upscale local families and a swath of tourists (menus are even in Russian) tuck into Jimbaran-style grilled seafood in this slick operation. Pool tables and live music add to the din while flames flare in the open kitchens.

Ma Joly (Map p108; ☎ 753708; Jl Segara; dishes 60,000-180,000Rp) Having been partially washed away – along with the beach – by high tides in 2008, this smart, open-air restaurant has been rebuilt and still has its snazzy ocean views right on a private bit of beach. The menu is ambitious (with prices to match) – look for complex seafood creations and mains with a French flair.

Kuta

The local **Kuta market** (Map pp102-3; Jl Paya Kuta; ⏰ 6am-4pm) is not big but its popularity ensures constant turnover. Look for some of Bali's unusual fruits here, such as the mangosteen.

Kuta Food Court (Map pp102-3; Jl Pantai Kuta; meals from 7000Rp; ⏰ 5pm-3am) A slick, modern version of a night market, this open-air collection of food stalls is as tidy as they come. Choose from a vast array of local specialities plus seafood from Jimbaran. Dine for as little as 7000Rp with karaoke and cover bands thrown in for free (although some may say this is a cost).

ON THE BEACH

Busy Jl Pantai Kuta keeps beachside businesses to a minimum in Kuta. Beach vendors are pretty much limited to drinks.

CENTRAL KUTA

Kuta night market (Map pp102-3; Jl Blambangan; dishes 5000-15,000Rp; ⏰ 6pm-midnight) This enclave of stalls and plastic chairs bustles with locals and tourism workers chowing down on hot-off-the-wok treats, grilled goods and other fresh foods.

Made's Warung (Map pp102-3; ☎ 755297; Jl Pantai Kuta; dishes 15,000-90,000Rp) Made's was the original tourist warung in Kuta. Through the years, the Westernised Indonesian menu has been much copied. Classic dishes such as *nasi campur* (rice served with side dishes) are served with colour and flair. Although not the hub it once was, Made's is still a pleasant spot.

Warung Hanafi (Map pp102-3; ☎ 765442; Jl Pantai Kuta 1C; mains from 20,000Rp) Run by a longtime guide; the best dish here is straight from Hanafi's mother: *mie goreng* (the secret is day-old rice). Watch the passing traffic chaos while you try a refreshing – and bright-red – tamarillo juice. The drinks menu is booze-free and everything is cooked halal.

Poppies Restaurant (Map pp102-3; ☎ 751059; Poppies Gang I; dishes 30,000-100,000Rp; wi-fi) Right on its namesake *gang*, long-running Poppies is popular for its lush garden setting, which has a timeless romance. The menu combines upscale Western (avocado and shrimp) and Balinese (your own little grill of satay) tastes.

Havana Club (Map pp102-3; ☎ 767448; Poppies Gang I; mains 30,000-100,000Rp) Somewhere between Madrid, Cancun and Kuta in concept and execution, this somewhat posh bodega has steaks and Mexican food that takes a back seat to the pricey pitchers of sangria. Asian standards and pastas are right out of central casting.

ALONG JL LEGIAN

The possibilities of eating choices along Jl Legian seem endless, but avoid tables close to the busy street.

Kopi Pot (Map pp102-3; ☎ 752614; Jl Legian; dishes 25,000-60,000Rp; wi-fi) Shaded by trees, Kopi Pot is a favourite, popular for its coffees, milkshakes and myriad desserts. The multilevel, open-air dining area sits back from noxious Jl Legian.

Ketupat (Map pp102-3; ☎ 754209; Jl Legian; dishes 30,000-120,000Rp) Hidden behind the antique-filled Jonathan Gallery, Ketupat is a calm, serene oasis. Open-air dining pavilions overlook an azure pool. Dishes originate from across Indonesia, including Javanese curries like *nasi hijau harum* (fried rice with greens, shrimps and herbs). This is one of the best places for a fancy local meal in the Kuta area.

Mama's (Map pp102-3; ☎ 761151; Jl Legian; dishes 30,000-120,000Rp; ⏰ 24hr) This German classic serves up schnitzel and other pork-heavy dishes around the clock. Bintang comes by the litre and the open-air bar is a merry place for enjoying various other imported brews and the excellent local Storm microbrew.

ON & NEAR POPPIES GANG II

Rainbow Cafe (Map pp102-3; ☎ 765730; Poppies Gang II; mains from 20,000Rp) Join generations of Kuta denizens quaffing the afternoon away. Deeply shaded, the vibe here is little changed in years. Many current customers are the offspring of backpackers who met at adjoining tables.

Balcony (Map pp102-3; ☎ 757409; Jl Benesari 16; dishes 20,000-80,000Rp) The Balcony has a breezy tropical design and sits above the din of Jl Benesari below. Get ready for the day with a long menu of eggs and pancakes. At night there's something for everyone, although the grilled steak and seafood skewers are a speciality.

Kori Restaurant & Bar (Map pp102-3; ☎ 758605; Poppies Gang II; meals 20,000-110,000Rp) Kori's tables are scattered about a succession of gardens and ponds. Definitely a few cuts above its very casual neighbours, this is the place to linger over a gin and tonic and a steak. Enjoy a secluded rendezvous in the flower-bedecked nooks out back. Some nights there's live acoustic music.

EAST OF KUTA

Dapur Alam (Map pp102-3; ☎ 757506; Jl Patih Jelantik 81; mains from 15,000Rp; ⏰ 5-11pm) A real find (if you can find it). The name of this upscale night market means 'Natural Kitchen'. Spotless tables under two pavilions welcome diners to this shady spot below the road near the river. Various open kitchens serve dishes from across the archipelago. Even standards like the spicy *satay ayam* (chicken satay) are inspired. Kids enjoy a playground.

Bali Bakery (Map pp102-3; ☎ 755149; Jl Imam Bonjol; meals 20,000-60,000Rp; 📶 wi-fi) There are fresh baguettes and much more daily at this classic Western bakery. The chocolates are excellent. It also has a large and popular café with a good menu of salads, sandwiches and pasta.

Swiss Restaurant (Map pp102-3; ☎ 761511; Istana Kuta Galleria, Jl Patih Jelantik; meals 30,000-90,000Rp; 📶) Bali's Swiss consul, Jon Zürcher, plays his violin on Sunday nights and hosts a Balinese banquet and dancers on Thursday nights. On other nights you may enjoy Sumatran singers while you trade volcanoes for the Alps and enjoy *raclette* and fondue.

Take (Map pp102-3; ☎ 759745; Jl Patih Jelantik; meals from 50,000Rp) Flee Bali for Tokyo just by ducking under the traditional fabric shield over the door. Hyper-fresh sushi, sashimi and more are prepared under the fanatical eye of a team of chefs behind a long counter. Dine at low tables or hang out in a booth.

Legian

Some of the beachside hotels have restaurants – often Italian – with nice views. Better still is the clutch of places at the end of Jl Double Six that afford views of sandy action by day, strolling fun-seekers by night and sunsets in between. Along the streets of Legian, the ho-hum mix with the superb, so take your time choosing.

Legian Night Market (Map pp102-3; Jl Nakula; meals from 10,000Rp; ⏰ 5pm-midnight) A classic collection of simple stalls creating fresh Balinese and

Indonesian classics for the noshing masses. See that guy with the glare? That's the cab driver you forgot to trip.

Warung Yogya (Map pp102-3; ☎ 750835; Jl Padma Utara; dishes 10,000-15,000Rp) A real find in the tourist heart of Legian, this basic warung is spotless and serves up hearty portions of Balinese classics. The *gado-gado* comes with a huge bowl of peanut sauce.

Saleko (Map pp102-3; Jl Nakula 4; meals from 10,000Rp) Just off the madness of Jl Legian, this simple storefront draws the discerning for its simple Sumatran fare. Spicy grilled chicken and fish dare you to ladle on the volcanic sambal.

Warung Murah (Map pp102-3; ☎ 732082; Jl Arjuna; meals from 20,000Rp) Lunch goes swimmingly at this authentic warung specialising in seafood. An array of grilled fish awaits; if you prefer fowl over fin, the *satay ayam* is succulent *and* a bargain.

Cozy Corner (Map pp102-3; ☎ 0813 3890 7464; cnr Jl Arjuna & Jl Padma Utara; cones from 5000Rp) Finish off that hot day on the beach with a cool cone of Bali-made gelato at this corner spot. Lounge on the comfy wicker chairs while you get your tongue around any of 10 fresh flavours.

Warung Asia (Map pp102-3; ☎ 742 0202; off Jl Double Six & Jl Pura Bagus Taruna; dishes 10,000-30,000Rp; wi-fi) Look down a couple of little *gang* for this dollhouse of a café. Traditional Thai dishes are paired with an authentic Italian espresso machine; lose your afternoon over the many newspapers.

Indo-National (Map pp102-3; ☎ 759883; Jl Padma 17; mains 20,000-90,000Rp) Kerry and Milton Turner's popular restaurant is a home-away-from-home for legions of fans. Grab a cold one with the crew up front at the bar with a sweeping view of Legian's action. Or head back to a pair of shady and romantic tables. Order the heaping grilled seafood platter and Bali's best garlic bread; the prawn toast is tops. Toss back a few Bintangs and see how many world monuments you can name amidst the sky-blue murals.

Bianco (Map pp102-3; ☎ 760070; Jl Padma; mains from 30,000Rp) Although there's a dash of colonial style at this breezy place, lips here are more likely to be puckered around a cold Bintang than cheroot. Oz satellite sports dominates the screens at the sports bar-cum-restaurant. The menu mixes Indonesian and Italian fare.

Yut'z (Map pp102-3; ☎ 765047; Jl Pura Bagus Taruna 52; dishes 30,000-120,000Rp) An upscale European restaurant, Yut'z overlooks the street and a small garden. The menu is centered on steaks in a variety of cuts and preparations. If your day doesn't start without muesli, you can get your *Frühstück* fix here.

DOUBLE SIX BEACH

These places are right on the popular beach, which is always thronged with locals and visitors alike. The following are good come sunset.

Zanzibar (Map pp102-3; ☎ 733529; Jl Double Six; dishes 30,000-70,000Rp) A flash rehab has added a second level with views over the shade trees. The menu is a typical mix of Indo-pasta-sandwiches and very good thin-crust pizza, but that's not your priority – get a large table with a group and enjoy the beachy views.

Seaside (Map pp102-3; ☎ 737140; Jl Double Six; dishes 30,000-80,000Rp) The curving sweep of seating at this sleek place provides beach views for one and all. Upstairs, there's a vast patio with oodles of picnic tables for counting stars after the sun goes down. Seafood and meat dishes come with a touch of style.

ENTERTAINMENT

Around 6pm every day, sunset on the beach is the big attraction, perhaps while enjoying a drink at a café with a sea view. Later on, even as the temperature diminishes, the action heats up, especially at the raging clubs of Kuta. Many spend their evening at one of the hipster joints in Seminyak (p125) before working their way south to oblivion.

Watching DVDs at a bar with a crowd is a Kuta evening tradition (and much more budget-friendly than a Seminyak club) and you'll find scores of places in and around the Poppies. Look for signs during the day or follow your ears at night. Expect anything with lots of guns and unshaven guys.

Check out the free mag, *The Beat* (www .beatmag.com), for good club listings and other 'what's on' news.

Bars & Clubs

Most bars are free to enter, and often have special drink promotions and 'happy hours' between about 5pm and 8pm. A cover charge is uncommon. Ambience ranges from the low-down vibe of the surfer dives to the high-concept nightclubs with their renowned DJs, long drink menus and hordes of prowling servers.

At the more raucous clubs you'll see plenty of young women (usually from the north or a neighbouring island) looking to make a 'friend' – usually a Western guy who's a multiple of their age.

The high-concept clubs of Seminyak are most popular with gays and lesbians, but in general you can find a mixed crowd pretty much anywhere in Kuta and Legian.

TUBAN

DeeJay Cafe (Map p108; ☎ 758880; 2nd fl, Kuta Centre, off Jl Kartika Plaza 8x; ☺ 9pm-7am) The post-midnight hours see this place rocking in the post-apocalyptic Kuta Centre, the run-down shell of a tourist mall. House DJs play tribal underground, progressive trance and more. Beware of posers who set their alarms for 5am and arrive all fresh.

KUTA

Jl Legian is lined with interchangeable bars with bar stools moulded to the butts of hard-drinking regulars.

Apache Reggae Bar (Map pp102-3; ☎ 761212; Jl Legian 146; ☺ 11pm-4am) One of the rowdier spots in Kuta, Apache jams in locals and visitors, many of whom are on the make. The music is loud, but that pounding you feel the next day is from the free-flowing *arak* (local spirits) served in huge plastic jugs.

Bed (Map pp102-3; ☎ 483978; Jl Benesari; ☺ 8am-1am) Don't expect to get horizontal on a queen-size here despite the name (although there are some mighty seductive loungers). Near the beach, this stylish café-bar has funky music at night and calorie-laden food to combat hangovers by day. The menu climaxes with categories like 'oral pleasures' (sodas, ho-hum).

Bounty (Map pp102-3; ☎ 752529; Jl Legian; ☺ 10pm-6am) Set on a pirate ship amidst a mini-mall of food and drink, the Bounty is a vast open-air disco that humps, thumps and pumps all night. Play seaman and get down on the poop deck to hip-hop, techno, house and anything else the DJs come up with. Watch for a new location nearby.

Mbargo (Map pp102-3; ☎ 756280; Jl Legian; cover from 10,000Rp; ☺ 7pm-4am) Throbs with the Gangsta vibe, enjoyed by well-heeled suburbanites. Hard-edged DJs encourage the sweaty throngs to misbehave.

Ocean Beach Club (Map pp102-3; ☎ 755423; www .escbali.com; Jl Pantai Kuta; ☺ 11am-late) This flash place occupies a swath of prime real estate across from the beach. Lounge on vivid red pillows and watch the sunset, or plunge into the pool – before or after your stint at the pool bar. There's a long menu of bar snacks and meals (salads, sandwiches, pastas etc). Later, it throbs to an open-air club vibe.

Sky Garden Lounge (Map pp102-3; ☎ 756362; www .escbali.com; Jl Legian 61; ☼ 24hr) Part of the ESC empire (which includes the Ocean Beach Club, above), this multilevel palace of flash flirts with height restrictions from its rooftop bar. Look for top DJs, a ground-level café and paparazzi-wannabes.

LEGIAN

Most of Legian's bars are smaller and appeal to a more sedate crowd of visitors than those in Kuta. The very notable exception is the area at the end of Jl Double Six.

Legend (Map pp102-3; ☎ 755376; Jl Sahadewa; ☼ 3-11pm) A popular open-air spot, the Legend draws nightly crowds for karaoke and other nonsense like 'DIY Elvis nights'. Live music spans pop to country.

Ye Olde Foo-Kin Pub (Map pp102-3; ☎ 751802; Jl Werkudara 525; ☼ 3-11pm; ☒) With drinks like Foo-kin Creamy, you get the point. Burgers and more are served in an air-con bar that's probably more fun than the ones the Aussie patrons enjoy at home.

Jl Arjuna/Double Six

The eponymous club is the big destination here.

De Ja Vu (Map pp102-3; ☎ 732777; Jl Double Six; ☼ 5pm-4am; ☒) DJs are on duty from opening every night at this high-concept, glass-fronted club with tables overlooking the beach outside.

Double Six Club (Map pp102-3; ☎ 0812 462 7733; www .doublesixclub.com; Jl Arjuna; ☼ 11pm-6am) Are venerable and trendy mutually exclusive? This legendary club (and namesake for the beach, road and more) continues reinventing itself. The swimming pool is still there and so is the bungy jump (see p108). Top international DJs play a mix of dance tunes in a sleek open-air pavilion. A café up front adds glitz to sunset drinks.

Balinese Dance & Music

The Ubud area (p195) is really the place to go for authentic dance, and you'll see offers from tour operators in many hotels. But note that you won't get back to Kuta until after 10pm with most of these. Local performances are geared for tourists who treat culture like vitamins and are often perfunctory at best.

SHOPPING

Many people spend – literally – a major part of their trip shopping. Kuta has a vast concentration of cheap places, as well as huge, flashy surf-gear emporiums on Kuta Sq and Jl Legian. As you head north along the latter into Legian, the quality of the shops improves and you start finding cute little boutiques, especially past Jl Melasti. Jl Arjuna is lined with wholesale fabric, clothing and craft stores, giving it a bazaar feel. Continue into Seminyak (see p126) for absolutely fabulous shopping.

In Tuban, the Discovery Shopping Mall is popular, but nearby Kuta Sq is a nightmare of people who put their dukes up if you accidentally call them 'bogan'.

Simple stalls with T-shirts, souvenirs and beachwear are everywhere (especially along the Poppies). See p341 for tips on cutting a deal. Many of these stalls are crowded together in 'art markets' like the **Kuta Square Art Market** (Map pp102–3) or the **Jl Melasti Art Market** (Map pp102–3). Here, the 'art' ends with Bintang logos printed on cotton. The top-selling gift for those left at home are penis-shaped bottle openers in a range of colours and sizes. Bargain hard to avoid paying a stiff price.

Arts & Crafts

Shops in Kuta and Legian sell arts and crafts from almost every part of the island, from Mas woodcarvings to Kamasan paintings to Gianyar textiles. There are also many interesting pieces from other parts of Indonesia, some of questionable authenticity and value.

Lavender Bali (Map pp102-3; ☎ 490243; Jl Arjuna 10X) Follow your nose to this aromatherapy emporium, brimming with potions, lotions, unguents and more.

Jonathan Gallery (Map pp102-3; ☎ 754209; Jl Legian 109) A hoard of traditional art and antiques is beautifully displayed in this shop.

Puri Naga Studio (Map pp102-3; ☎ 751334; Jl Lebak Bene; ☼ roughly 10am-6pm) This offbeat place in Legian is run by half a dozen local artists. The paintings of artist Wahyoe Wijaya are on display, as well as all manner of items good, bad and profane.

Beachwear & Surf Shops

A huge range of surf shops sells big-name surf gear – including Mambo, Rip Curl and Billabong – although goods may be only marginally cheaper than overseas. Local names include Surfer Girl and Quicksilver. Most have numerous locations in South Bali.

Black Sands Surfboard Bags (Map pp102-3; ☎ 0813 3847 5849; Jl Benesari) Choose from myriad patterns and colours and then watch your bag (from 250,000Rp) get made on the shop floor in two days or less. There are lots of other family-run surfer shops nearby.

Rip Curl (Map pp102-3; ☎ 765035; Kuta Sq) The brightest store on the square. Come here to replace that minimalist black with something eye-popping. Choose from a huge range of beach clothes, water wear and surfboards.

Surfer Girl (Map pp102-3; ☎ 752693; Jl Legian 138) The sugary-sweet logo says it all about this vast store for girls of all ages. Clothes, undies, gear, bikinis, you name it.

Clothing

The local fashion industry has diversified from beach gear to sportswear and fashion clothing. From the intersection with Jl Padma, go north on Jl Legian to Seminyak for the most interesting women's (and men's) clothing shops.

Capt Black Bikers Fashion Shop (Map pp102-3; ☎ 752735; Jl Bakung Sari 2B) Leather duds for the Harley set are peddled here by a self-professed legend. Get dolled up and then zip off, ahem, on your scooter.

IO & CO (Map pp102-3; ☎ 754093; Jl Legian 361) Gauzy, silky and fashionable women's wear in a sleek multilevel air-con shop. This Bali label also sells housewares in vibrant patterns.

Joger (Map p100; Jl Raya Tuban; ❍ 11am-6pm) Look for the mobs of Indonesian tourists in front of this huge T-shirt shop east of Tuban. The sign out front says *'Pabrik kata-kata'*, which means 'factory of words'. The T-shirts are nationally iconic and bear sayings in Bahasa Indonesia that are wry, funny or simply arch.

Ming (Map pp102-3; ☎ 755426; Jl Legian) An oasis of elegant resortwear amidst the T-shirt tat of Kuta. Named for the designer who has a vision of flowing cotton and linen.

Uluwatu (Map pp102-3; ☎ 751933; Jl Legian) The largest of numerous locations across Bali, this elegant shop showcases the collection of lace-accented linen and cotton clothing. The styles are simple, but there are few tables that wouldn't stand out with a set of Uluwatu table

linens. The items are made in villages around Tabanan in West Bali.

Department Stores & Malls

Carrefour (Map p100; ☎ 847 7222; Jl Sunset; ❍ 9am-10pm) This vast outlet of the French discount chain combines lots of small shops (books, computers, bikinis etc) with one huge hypermarket. It's the place to stock up on staples and there's a large ready-to-eat section and a food court as well. The downside, however, is inescapable: it's a mall.

Discovery Mall (Map p108; ☎ 755522; www.discovery shoppingmall.com; Jl Kartika Plaza; ❍ 9am-9pm) Maybe if they hadn't gone and ruined the shoreline… Anyway, this huge, hulking and popular enclosed Tuban mall is built on the water and is filled with stores of every kind, including the large Centro (☎ 769629) and trendy Sogo (☎ 769555) department stores.

Istana Kuta Galleria (Map pp102-3; Jl Patih Jelantik) An enormous open-air mall that seems like a dud until you find an interesting shop amidst the canyon of glass. There is a hardware store in the rear if your needs run towards spare bulbs or duct tape.

Mal Bali Galleria (Map p100; ☎ 758875; Jl Ngurah Rai) A huge and newly expanded mall that is busy with locals and tourists alike. There are numerous large stores and plenty of well-known international shops. The duty-free emporium is big with the group-tour set.

Matahari (Map pp102-3; ☎ 757588; Kuta Sq; ❍ 9.30am-10pm) This store has the basics – fairly staid clothing, a floor full of souvenirs, jewellery and a supermarket. You can find most things here, including some decent-quality luggage should you need extra bags to haul your wretched excess home.

Fabric

Stroll Jl Double Six in Legian for a festival of open-air wholesalers selling fabrics, clothes and housewares. **Bouchra** (Map pp102-3; ☎ 733594; Jl Arjuna 10) sells fabric with Gauginesque designs that has been hand-painted in Denpasar. **Busana Agung** (Map pp102-3; ☎ 733442; Jl Arjuna) has stacks of vibrant batiks and other fabrics that scream 'sew me!'. **Sriwijaya** (Map pp102-3; ☎ 733581; Jl Arjuna 35) makes batik and other fabrics to order in myriad colours.

Furniture

On Jl Patih Jelantik, between Jl Legian and Jl Pura Puseh, there are scores of furniture shops manufacturing everything from instant 'antiques' to wooden Indians. However, a few of the stores make and sell teak outdoor furniture of very high quality at very low prices. A luxurious deckchair goes for about 200,000Rp to 300,000Rp. Most of the stores work with freight agencies and you can get eight of these chairs sent to Australia for about US$150.

GETTING THERE & AWAY
Bemo
Dark-blue public bemo (minibuses) regularly travel between Kuta and the Tegal terminal in Denpasar – the fare should be 8000Rp. The route goes from a **bemo stop** onto Jl Raya Kuta near Jl Pantai Kuta, looping past the beach and then on Jl Melasti and back past Bemo Corner (Map pp102–3) for the trip back to Denpasar.

Bus
PUBLIC BUS
For public buses to anywhere in Bali, you'll have to go to the appropriate terminal in Denpasar first; see above.

TOURIST SHUTTLE BUS
Perama (Map pp102-3; ☎ 751551; www.peramatour.com; Jl Legian 39; ☯ 7am-10pm) is the main shuttle-bus operation in town, and will sometimes pick you up from your hotel for free (confirm this with them when making arrangements). Perama usually has at least one bus a day to all of its destinations.

Destination	Fare	Duration
Candidasa	60,000Rp	3½hr
Lovina	125,000Rp	4½hr
Padangbai	60,000Rp	3hr
Sanur	25,000Rp	30min
Ubud	50,000Rp	1½hr

GETTING AROUND
The hardest part about getting around the Kuta area is the traffic. It can be awful in the afternoon and evening, and anytime the vital streets like Jl Legian are closed for religious processions or for what seems to be constant construction.

See p353 for more details on getting around. Besides the frequent taxis, you can rent a motorbike, often with a surfboard rack, or a bike – just ask where you're staying. One of the nicest ways to get around the Kuta and Legian area though is by foot, along the beach.

To/From the Airport
An official taxi from the airport costs 30,000Rp to Tuban, 45,000Rp to Kuta and 50,000Rp to Legian. Travelling *to* the airport, get a metered taxi for much less.

Taxi
As always, the distinctive blue taxis of **Bali Taxi** (☯ 701111) are far and away the best bet.

SEMINYAK

Seminyak may be immediately north of Kuta and Legian, but in many respects it feels like it's almost on another island. It's flash, brash, phoney and filled with bony models. It's also the centre of life for hordes of the island's expats, many of whom own boutiques or design clothes, surf, or seem to do nothing at all.

It's also a very dynamic place. It's home to dozens of restaurants and clubs – when a hot new place opens, it's usually in Seminyak. Along Jl Raya Seminyak and Jl Laksmana, and the odd side street, there are a wealth of creative shops and galleries, and world-class hotels line the beach. And what a beach it is, as deep and sandy as Kuta's but less crowded.

A lot of the good and bad about Seminyak seems to be taken from the pages of a glossy magazine, but there are also surprises. Not every beachfront hotel is worldclass or charges world-class prices. All those restaurants and clubs combine to give travellers the greatest choice of style and budget in Bali. And sure there are exclusive boutiques, but there are also workshops where you can purchase it all wholesale. And just when you've tired of trying to cross the street in front of 4WD-steering expats, a religious procession comes through and shuts everything down. That's Seminyak: one surprise after another.

ORIENTATION
The southern border of Seminyak runs north of Jl Arjuna. Jl Raya Seminyak is the continuation of Jl Legian from Kuta and is lined with shops. Jl Abimanyu runs to the beach and passes many bars and restaurants.

Jl Laksmana also heads west to the beach. From here, things get real tricky as the road wanders north through a part of Seminyak

PICK A NAME, ANY NAME

A small lane or alley is known as a *gang,* and most of them in Bali lack signs or even names. Some are referred to by the name of a connecting street, eg Jl Padma Utara is the *gang* going north of Jl Padma.

Meanwhile, some streets in Kuta, Legian and Seminyak have more than one name. Many streets are unofficially named after a well-known temple and/or business place, or according to the direction they head. In recent years there has been an attempt to impose official – and usually more Balinese – names on the streets. But the old, unofficial names are still common.

In this guide, all names are shown on the maps and we give preference in the listings to the street name that is most prevalent, eg Jl Arjuna has now surpassed Jl Double Six in common usage. Conversely Poppies Gang II remains just that. Here are the old (unofficial) and new (official) names, from north to south.

Old/unofficial	New/official
Jl Oberoi	Jl Laksmana
Jl Raya Seminyak	Northern stretch: Jl Raya Basangkasa
Jl Dhyana Pura/Jl Gado Gado	Jl Abimanyu
Jl Double Six	Jl Arjuna
Jl Pura Bagus Taruna/Rum Jungle Rd	Jl Werkudara
Jl Padma	Jl Yudistira
Poppies Gang II	Jl Batu Bolong
Jl Pantai Kuta	Jl Pantai Banjar Pande Mas
Jl Kartika Plaza	Jl Dewi Sartika
Jl Segara	Jl Jenggala
Jl Satria	Jl Kediri

that some people call Petitenget, that's properly called Jl Pantai Kaya Aya, but is also known by its old name: Jl Oberoi. Either way, the road is home to a profusion of restaurants, upscale boutiques and hotels. Meanwhile, as Jl Raya Seminyak continues north it changes to Jl Raya Kerobokan (except where it is known as Jl Petitenget…) and is lined with many craft and furniture showrooms and workshops.

See the boxed text, above, for more information on the confusing street names in the region. You'll find all the sites in this section on the Seminyak map (p120), unless otherwise indicated.

INFORMATION

Seminyak shares many services with Kuta and Legian.

Bookshops

Bintang Supermarket (p125) has a good newsstand.

Periplus Bookshop Made's Warung II (☎ 734843; Jl Raya Seminyak) Bali Deli (☎ 734578; Jl Kunti) The island-wide chain of lavishly-fitted bookshops has enough design books to have you fitting out even your

garage in Bali Style; also stocks best-sellers, magazines and newspapers.

Internet Access

Most hotels have broadband connections for guests, and many cafés offer free wi-fi for patrons as noted in the listings.

Medical Services

Taiga Pharmacy (☎ 732621; Jl Raya Seminyak 19; ⏰ 24hr) Across from Bintang Supermarket, it has a full range of prescription medications.

Money

ATMs can be found along all the main roads.

Post

Postal agency (☎ 761592; Bintang Supermarket, Jl Raya Seminyak 17)

SIGHTS

North of the string of hotels on Jl Pantai Kaya Aya, **Pura Petitenget** is an important temple and the scene of many ceremonies. It is one of a string of sea temples that stretches from Pura Luhur Ulu Watu on the Bukit Peninsula, north to Tanah Lot in western

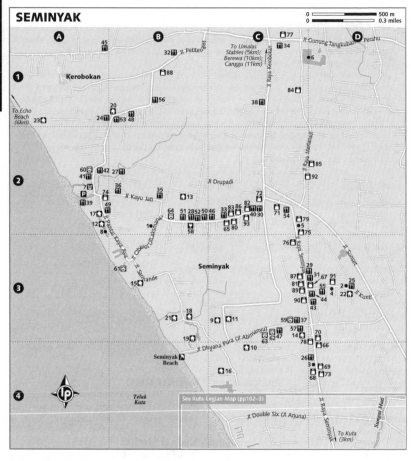

SEMINYAK

0 — 500 m
0 — 0.3 miles

Kerobokan

To Echo Beach (6km)

To Umalas Stables (5km); Berewa (10km); Canggu (11km)

Jl Petitenget

Jl Gunung Tangkuban Perahu

Jl Drupadi

Jl Kayu Jati

Seminyak

Jl Oberoi (Jl Laksmana)

Jl Sarigande

Jl Dhyana Pura (Jl Abimanyu)

Seminyak Beach

Jl Kunti

Jl Sunset

Teluk Kuta

See Kuta-Legian Map (pp102–3)

Jl Double Six (Jl Arjuna)

To Kuta (3km)

Bali. Petitenget loosely translates as 'magic box', a treasured belonging of the legendary 16th-century priest Nirartha, who refined the Balinese religion and visited this site often. Also in the compound, look for **Pura Masceti**, an agricultural temple where farmers pray for relief from rat infestations and savvy builders make offerings of forgiveness before planting yet another villa in the rice fields.

For tips on respecting traditions and acting appropriately while visiting temples, see the boxed text, p348. For a directory of important temples, see the boxed text, p51.

The **beach** here is a good one and is usually not crowded. There's plenty of parking (2000Rp).

ACTIVITIES

Because of the limited road access, the beaches in Seminyak tend to be less crowded than further south in Kuta. This also means that it's less patrolled and the water conditions are less monitored. The odds of encountering dangerous rip tides and other hazards are ever-present, especially as you head north.

Spas

Jari Menari (☎ 736740; Jl Raya Seminyak 47; ⏰ 10am-9pm) has won international acclaim. Its name means 'dancing fingers' and your body will be one happy dance floor. The all-male staff use massage techniques that emphasise rhythm. Fees start at 250,000Rp for 75 minutes.

INFORMATION
Diamond Selular Center..........(see 26)
Exotiq Real Estate........................**1** B2
Periplus...(see 43)
Periplus...**2** D3
Postal Agency...............................(see 26)
Rim Cargo..(see 25)
Taiga Pharmacy..............................**3** D4

SIGHTS & ACTIVITIES
Chill..**4** D3
Jari Menari.......................................**5** C2
Kerobokan Jail...............................**6** D1
Prana..(see 22)
Pura Masceti...................................(see 7)
Pura Petitenget..............................**7** A2
Sate Bali...(see 49)
Spa...**8** A2
Spa Bonita......................................(see 53)

SLEEPING
Bali Agung Village........................**9** C3
Green Room.................................**10** C4
Harmony...**11** C3
Legian...**12** A2
Mutiara Bali **13** B2
Ned's Hide-Away.........................**14** C3
Oberoi..**15** B3
Raja Gardens................................**16** C4
Samaya..**17** A2
Sarinande Beach Inn...................**18** B3
Sofitel Seminyak Bali..................**19** B3
Taman Ayu Cottage.....................**20** B1
Villa Kresna...................................**21** B3
Villas Bali..**22** D3
W Hotel...**23** A1

EATING
Bali Catering Co..........................**24** A1
Bali Deli...**25** D3

Bintang Supermarket.................**26** D4
Blossom...**27** B2
Café Bali...**28** B2
Café Moka.....................................**29** C3
Café Seminyak...........................(see 26)
Corner Store.................................**30** C2
Delicious Onion............................**31** C3
Dodos Café...................................**32** B1
Earth Cafe......................................**33** C2
Fruit Market..................................**34** C1
Grocer & Grind............................**35** B2
Ibu Mangku..................................**36** B2
Jef Burgers....................................**37** C3
Kafe Warisan.................................**38** C1
La Lucciola....................................**39** A2
Lazumba...**40** C2
Le Tebu...**41** A2
Living Room..................................**42** A2
Made's Warung II........................**43** D3
Mannekepis...................................**44** D3
Panoramix......................................**45** A1
Rumours...**46** C2
Santa Fe Bar & Grill....................**47** C3
Sarong...**48** B1
Sate Bali..**49** A2
Trattoria...**50** B2
Tuesday Night Pizza Club..........**51** B2
Ultimo...**52** B2
Waroeng Bonita...........................**53** B1
Warung Ibu Made.......................**54** C2
Warung Italia...............................**55** D3
Warung Kolega............................**56** B1
Zula Vegetarian Paradise..........**57** C3

DRINKING
Metro..**58** B2

ENTERTAINMENT
Bahiana...**59** C3
Hu'u..**60** A2

Ku De Ta..**61** B3
Obsession.......................................**62** C3
Q-Bar..**63** C3
Zappaz..**64** B2

SHOPPING
Ashitaba..(see 67)
Bamboo Blonde............................**65** C2
Bananas Batik..............................(see 87)
Biasa...**66** D4
Biasa Art Space..........................(see 66)
Blue Glue.......................................**67** D3
Body & Soul..................................**68** D4
Body & Soul Outlet.....................**69** D4
Copycat...**70** D3
DeZine Hammocks.......................**71** C2
Divine Diva...................................**72** C2
ET Club...**73** D4
Goris Art Shop..............................**74** A2
Heliconia...**75** C2
Inti..**76** C3
JJ Bali Button................................**77** C1
Joe Joe..**78** D3
Kemarin Hari Ini..........................**79** C2
Lily Jean...**80** C2
Luna Collection.............................**81** C3
Milo's Bazaar................................**82** C2
Morena..**83** C2
Nostalgia Antique........................**84** C1
Nôblis...**85** D2
Paul Ropp......................................**86** C2
Rama Shinta Ki Jay......................**87** C3
Richard Meyer Culture...............**88** B1
Sabbatha..**89** C3
Sacado..**90** C3
Uma and Leopold........................**91** D3
You Like Lamp.............................**92** C2
Zakx..**93** C3

Spa (☎ 730622; Jl Pantai Kaya Aya; ⏰ 10am-9pm) in the Legian hotel is suitably lavish, and gives clients the opportunity to avail themselves of various private spa suites set among gardens.

The name says it all at **Chill** (☎ 734701; ⏰ 10am-10pm). This Zen place embraces reflexology, with treatments starting at 80,000Rp. Its sister property **Prana** (☎ 730840; Jl Kunti) is a palatial Moorish fantasy that is easily the most lavishly decorated spa in Bali. Massages start at 60,000Rp.

Spa Bonita (☎ 731918; www.bonitabali.com; Jl Petitenget 2000x; ⏰ 9am-9pm), part of the delightful Waroeng Bonita (p125), has a range of services in a simply elegant setting. Massages start at 85,000Rp.

Cooking School

Sate Bali (☎ 736734; Jl Laksmana 22; course 350,000Rp; ⏰ 9.30am-1.30pm) runs an excellent Balinese cooking course taught by noted chef Nyoman Sudiyasa. Students learn to prepare Balinese spices and sambals, which are then used to fla-

vour duck, fish and pork. Not up to attending school? The restaurant is delicious (p124).

SLEEPING

Seminyak has a good range of places to stay, from world-class resorts like the Oberoi to more humble hotels hidden away on backstreets. This is also the start of villa-land, which runs north from here through the vanishing rice fields. For details on booking a private villa, see p327. The opening of the new W Hotel on the beach north of the Legian (due to open September 2009) is sure to cause much excitement.

Budget

Ned's Hide-Away (☎ 731270; nedshide@dps.centrim .net.id; Gang Bima 3; r from 100,000Rp) Named after Aussie icon Ned Kelly, this simple, 15-room, two-storey place is popular with those hoping to lie low between bouts of fun. Rooms have hot water and there's a character-filled bar. Look for the sign on Jl Raya Seminyak north of Bintang Supermarket.

Midrange

Many of Seminyak's most pleasant hotels are located on small lanes off major roads such as Jl Abimanyu and Jl Laksmana. They are both quiet and close to the action.

Sarinande Beach Inn (☎ 730383; www.sarinandehotel.com; Jl Sarinande 15; s/d US$30/32; ❄ ⬛ ⬜ wi-fi) An excellent-value place. The 24 rooms are in two-storey blocks around a small pool; the decor is older but everything is well maintained. Amenities include fridges, satellite TV and a café. The beach is three minutes by foot.

Harmony (☎ 737711; www.theharmonybali.com; Jl Drupadi 234; r 300,000-450,000Rp; ❄ ⬛ ⬜) An architecturally distinctive hotel for the minimalist set. The 20 rooms here carry the theme by being minimalist in size, right down to the school-sized plastic chairs by the door. The colour palette is limited to greys with a splash of red; fortunately, the place you'll splash out is in the pool.

Raja Gardens (☎ 730494; jdw@eksadata.com; Jl Abimanyu; r 300,000-500,000Rp; ❄ ⬛ ⬜ wi-fi) Enjoy spacious, grassy grounds in this quiet inn almost on the beach. Rooms are fairly barebones but there are open-air bathrooms and plenty of potted plants. The basic rate gets you cold water and a fan; more money buys hot water, air-con and a fridge.

Green Room (☎ 731412; www.thegreenroombali.com; Jl Abimanyu 63B; r 300,000-550,000Rp; ❄ ⬛) A new-age cheapie, the Green Room evokes Robinson Crusoe from its hammocks to its banana-tree motif. Lounge around the small inkblot-shaped pool or chill in the open *bale* (traditional pavilion) with its media centre. Among the 14 rooms in a two-storey block are ones with jungle themes.

Bali Agung Village (☎ 730367; www.bali-agung.com; off Jl Abimanyu; r US$40-80, villas US$80-150; ❄ ⬛) Off a hidden backstreet, this attractive place has 41 rooms in bungalow-style units that are popular with budget-conscious groups. The grounds are lush and there's a profusion of Balinese wood and stone carvings. Look for the statue of a giraffe as you navigate in along the alleys.

Villa Kresna (☎ 730317; www.villa-kresna.com; Jl Sarinande 19; r US$40-85, villas US$150-220; ❄ ⬛ ⬜ wi-fi) The beach is only 50m from this cute, idiosyncratic property tucked away on a small *gang*. The 10 art-filled units are mostly suites, which have a nice flow-through design with both public and private patios. A small, sinuous pool wanders through the property.

Mutiara Bali (☎ 708888; www.mutiarabali.com; Jl Karang Mas Sejahtera 88; r US$60-90, villas from US$250; ❄ ⬛ ⬜ wi-fi) Although hidden on a small road behind Jl Laksmana, the Mutiara is close to everything: fine dining – two minutes; the beach – five minutes, etc. There are 29 good-sized and nicely furnished rooms in two-storey blocks around a frangipani-draped pool area. Seventeen large private villas occupy one half of the compound.

Taman Ayu Cottage (☎ 730111; www.tamanayucottage.com; Jl Petitenget; r US$50-80; ❄ ⬛ ⬜) In a fast-growing part of the north end of Seminyak. The cottage in the name here is a bit of a misnomer, as most of the rooms are in two-storey blocks around a pool shaded by mature trees. Clutter-phobes will appreciate the barebones decor in the large rooms.

Grand Balisani Suites (Map p100; ☎ 730550; www.balisani.com; Jl Batubelig; r $80-150; ❄ ⬛ ⬜ wi-fi) Straddling the border between midrange and top end, this elaborately carved complex is right on the beach, just a few minutes along the sand north of Seminyak. The 97 rooms are large and have amenities such as DVD players and standard teak furniture plus terraces.

Top End

Sofitel Seminyak Bali (☎ 730730; www.sofitel.com; Jl Dhyana Pura; r from US$180, villas from US$400; ❄ ⬛ ⬜ wi-fi) This hotel's beachside location is good, although the hulking Anantara Resort looms to the south. The rooms are done in a smart contemporary style. What really sets the property apart are the private walled units, which feel like an old Balinese village (try for number 17).

Oberoi (☎ 730361; www.oberoihotels.com; Jl Laksmana; r from US$220, villas from US$500; ❄ ⬛ ⬜ wi-fi) One of the world's top hotels, the beautifully understated Oberoi has been a refined Balinese-style beachside retreat since 1971. All accommodation has private verandahs and as you move up through the food chain, additional features include private villas, ocean views and private, walled pools. From the café overlooking the almost-private sweep of beach, to the numerous luxuries, this is a place to spoil yourself.

Legian (☎ 730622; www.ghmhotels.com; Jl Pantai Kaya Aya; ste from US$300, villas from US$600; ❄ ⬛ ⬜ wi-fi) The Legian is flash and brash, one of the reasons it's a fave with Russian oil oligarchs. All 67 rooms claim to be suites, even if some are just large rooms (called 'studios'). On

TROUBLE BY THE SEA

Opened to much fanfare in 2008, the Anantara Resort (Jl Abimanyu) immediately generated controversy that is a window onto the wider debate about development on the island. Built *very* close to the high tide, the then-17.2m-tall upscale condo-hotel was built in violation of the local height limit of 15m – a rule designed to keep buildings from being taller than a coconut palm.

After months of threats, the local government finally got the popular rooftop bar, health club and other amenities demolished, effectively lopping a storey off the hotel. This enforcement caught many by surprise because government zoning action in Bali is usually limited to hand-wringing. Many wonder if this will mark a new beginning in efforts to rein in developers.

a little bluff, the views are panoramic The design mixes traditional materials with contemporary flair.

Villas Bali (☎ 730840; www.thevillas.net; Jl Kunti 118X; villas from US$300; 🆒 🅿 🖳 wi-fi) Hidden off a Seminyak side street, 50 large one-, two- and three-bedroom villas are clustered in several compounds. All have large pools in private walled gardens. The living space is an open design that blends nature with the classic rattan furniture. Services include breakfast cooked in your unit. The Villas have two spas, including Chill (p120).

ourpick **Samaya** (☎ 731149; www.thesamayabali .com; Jl Pantai Kaya Aya; villas from US$300; 🆒 🅿 🖳 wi-fi) A management shake-up has propelled the beachfront Samaya (until recently a sleeper in Seminyak) to the front ranks. The 24 villas in the beachside compound are attractive, roomy and have small pools. A compound across the road trades location for even larger units. Food, from breakfast onwards, is creative and superb.

EATING

Jl Laksmana is the focus of Seminyak eating but there are interesting choices virtually everywhere. Note that where indicated, some restaurants morph into clubs as the night wears on. Conversely, some of the places listed under Bars & Clubs also do decent food. Think of it as fusion fun.

Jl Abimanyu

Jef Burgers (☎ 0817 473 4311; Jl Dhyana Pura 24; dishes from 13,000Rp; ⏰ 24hr) Munchies central: Jef cooks up highly customisable burgers around the clock, from a small grill out front.

Zula Vegetarian Paradise (☎ 732723; Jl Dhyana Pura 5; dishes 15,000-40,000Rp; ⏰ 8am-4am) It's all vegetarian at this newly enlarged café, where you can get tofu cheese, a tofu spring roll and tofu cheesecake. Or go wild with a brown-rice surprise.

Santa Fe Bar & Grill (☎ 731147; Jl Dhyana Pura 11A; dishes 20,000-60,000Rp; ⏰ 7am-4am) Popular pizza and Southwestern food draw people here at all hours, especially late when there's live music (mostly rock). Many people alternate shots with sushi. Yikes.

Jl Raya Seminyak

Warung Ibu Made (Jl Raya Seminyak; meals 10,000Rp; ⏰ 7am-7pm) The woks roar almost dawn to dusk amidst the constant hubbub on this busy corner of Jl Raya Seminyak. It's one of a few simple stalls. The meals from this warung couldn't be fresher and put to shame some of the Western fakery just down the road.

Café Moka (☎ 731424; Jl Raya Seminyak; meals 18,000-40,000Rp; 🆒) Enjoy French-style baked goods at this popular bakery and café. Many escape the heat and linger here for hours. The bulletin board spills over with notices.

Café Seminyak (☎ 736967; Jl Raya Seminyak 17; meals from 20,000Rp; wi-fi) Right in front of the busy Bintang Supermarket, this cute and casual place has excellent smoothies and croissant sambos.

Delicious Onion (☎ 0813 3789 4243; Jl Raya Seminyak; mains 20,000-25,000Rp) A groovy little café amidst the retail frenzy, the Delicious Onion features a long menu of cheap and cheerful veggie and chicken dishes. There are also cocktails to help you fortify your shopping courage.

Warung Italia (☎ 737437; Jl Kunti 2; meals from 20,000Rp; ⏰ 8am-7pm) The climax in any classic warung happens at lunch, when happy diners walk down the displays and have their plates filled with a wide selection of treats. No matter what they choose, the price is the same (and it's low). Here, warung-style meets Italian as diners select from a range of pastas, salads and more. You can also order off a long menu.

Made's Warung II (☎ 732130; Jl Raya Seminyak; dishes 20,000-90,000Rp) This northern branch of the Kuta standby is set in a sheltered courtyard area. Well-prepared Indonesian food is the speciality here and the presentation is always artful. Even the little bags of Balinese snack crackers are a delight.

Mannekepis (☎ 847 5784; Jl Raya Seminyak 2; mains 35,000-85,000Rp; wi-fi) That little icon of Brussels is permanently peeing out front at this surprisingly good Belgian bistro. Tear your eyes away from the fish swimming in the ceiling tank to peruse a selection of excellent steaks, all served with top-notch *frites*. There is live jazz and blues many nights.

Jl Laksmana

Saddled by some with the unimaginative name 'Eat Street', this restaurant row has scores of choices. Stroll the strip and see what sparks a craving. Prices are uniformly popular.

Ibu Mangku (☎ 780 1824; Jl Kayu Jati; meals 15,000Rp) Look for the cabs in front of this bamboo place that serves superb minced-chicken satay redolent with lemongrass and other spices.

Lazumba (☎ 731899; Jl Oberoi; dishes 15,000-40,000Rp; wi-fi) More pavilion than restaurant, this coffee bar has good hot and cold drinks (fine smoothies) and a short menu of Indonesian standards. Opt for the sublime chocolate-chip cookies.

Earth Cafe (☎ 736645; Jl Laksmana 99; mains from 20,000Rp) The good vibes are organic at this vegetarian café and store amidst the upscale retail squalor of Seminyak. Sweet potato and garbanzo bean soup is a fine lead-in to the creative salads or whole-grain goodies. A retail section sells potions and lotions. While perusing the bookshelves, don't get ahead of yourself in the colonic irrigation section.

Grocer & Grind (☎ 0817 354 104; Jl Kayu Jati 3X; mains 20,000-60,000Rp; wi-fi) Keep your vistas limited and you might think you're at just another sleek Sydney café, but look around and you're unmistakably in Bali, albeit one of the trendiest bits. Classic sandwiches, salads and big breakfasts issue forth from the open kitchen. Eat in the open-air or choose air-con tables in the deli area.

Corner Store (☎ 730276; Jl Laksmana 10A; dishes 30,000-60,000Rp; ⊙ 7am-5pm) Seminyak's fashionistas gather here most mornings (aka Tuck Shop to the expats) to dish the gossip and breakfast on upscale, healthy fare like organic muesli. Tell everyone you're a 'cushion designer' and look bored under the beautiful frangipani tree.

Café Bali (☎ 736484; Jl Laksmana; mains 30,000-60,000Rp) The smoothly curved bar feels right out of colonial times here, as does the light and airy wood interior with fans gently moving the air. But this popular café is really just a fantasy come true. It's a recent addition to 'Eat Street'. Diners enjoy a varied menu that fuses Asian and Italian influences with a fresh vibe. The dessert list is long.

Tuesday Night Pizza Club (☎ 730614; www.tuesday nightpizzaclub.com; Jl Oberoi; pizza 30,000-130,000Rp; ⊙ 6pm-midnight) Pizzas come in five sizes at this brightly lit joint and have a range of pop culture names like Hawaii Five-O (ham and pineapple). There are but a few tables – many folks opt for the fast and efficient delivery to hotels and villas alike.

Rumours (☎ 738720; Jl Oberoi 100; mains 30,000-125,000Rp; ⊙ 6pm-midnight) Italian and Indonesian standards are mere supporting cast members for the real menu stars: steaks. There's a range of cuts and preparations, topping out at the 500g T-bone. Terrace tables (t-tables?) are tops.

Ultimo (☎ 738720; Jl Laksmana 104; mains 30,000-100,000Rp) *Uno*: find a table overlooking the street action or out back in one of the gardens. *Due*: choose from the surprisingly authentic Italian menu. *Tre*: marvel at the efficient service from the army of servers. *Quattro*: smile at the reasonable bill.

Trattoria (☎ 737082; Jl Oberoi; mains 35,000-90,000Rp; ⊙ 6pm-midnight) Enjoy authentic Italian cuisine at tables inside or out. The menu changes often but always features fresh pasta, grilled meats and seafood. Even the breadsticks – as plentiful as the lines of waiting patrons – score.

Sate Bali (☎ 736734; Jl Oberoi 22; mains from 40,000Rp; ⊙ 11am-10pm) Some very fine traditional Balinese dishes are served at this small café run by chef Nyoman Sudiyasa. The multicourse *rijsttafel* (200,000Rp) is a symphony of tastes including the addictive *babi kecap* (pork in a soy sauce) and *tum bebek* (minced duck in banana leaf).

La Lucciola (☎ 730838; Jl Pantai Kaya Aya; dishes 80,000-160,000Rp) This beachside restaurant is near the temple and secluded on all sides but the one that counts: the ocean. Stylish sunset-watchers enjoy good views from the 2nd floor across a lovely lawn to the surf. The menu is a creative fusion of international fare; the bar inventive.

Northern Seminyak

Some of Bali's most interesting restaurants are found amidst the curving roads and villas here.

Warung Kolega (☎ 0852 3794 9778; Jl Petitenget; meal 15,000Rp ☺ 11am-3pm) A Javanese classic: choose your rice (we prefer the fragrant yellow), then choose from a delectable array that includes tempe in sweet chilli sauce, *sambal terung* (spicy eggplant), *ikan sambal* (spicy grilled fish) and other daily specials.

Bali Catering Co (☎ 732115; Jl Petitenget 45; snacks from 20,000Rp; ☒) Like a gem store of treats, this upscale deli-bakery is owned by top-end fave Kafe Warisan (right). Many spend all day battling the temptation of the mango ice cream, others succumb to the croissants.

Le Tebu (☎ 847 8152; Jl Petitenget 40x; mains 25,000-55,000Rp; wi-fi) Seminyak always surprises with its cultural fusion and this little corner café is a perfect example. Think Left Bank meets Bali and you've got the concept. Lovely wicker chairs surround shady tables within incense-sniffing distance of Pura Petitenget. The menu features coq au vin, *croque monsieur* and healthy breakfasts and salads. But just when you're ready for some attitude, the smiling service reminds you you're in Bali.

our pick **Waroeng Bonita** (☎ 731918; www.bonita bali.com; Jl Petitenget 2000x; dishes 30,000-70,000Rp) Balinese dishes such as *ikan rica-rica* (fresh fish in a spicy green chilli sauce) and the classic, spicy beef rendang are the specialities here. Nab a table under the trees, unless it's Baliwood night when the staff are dragooned into performing with drag queens in an unmissable and flamboyant spectacle.

Dodos Café (☎ 732392; Jl Petitenget 125; mains US$3-10; ☺ 8am-4pm) Ladies who lunch (and men too) sit primly on delicate French chairs here and gaze out at Seminyak's number-one endangered species: rice terraces. Although there are a few breakfast items on the menu, Dodos is all about long, Italian-accented lunches. A salad bar, plenty of sandwiches and a kids' menu round out the offerings.

Living Room (☎ 735735; www.livingroombali.com; Jl Petitenget; mains 80,000-100,000Rp; ☺ noon-late) At night, hundreds of candles twinkle on and about the scores of outdoor tables at this fusion of Balinese thatching with colonial posh. The fusion menu combines French classics with Asian flair – think Saigon before things went pear-shaped. The famous soundtrack? Fusion of course (house, jazz and trance).

Sarong (☎ 737809; www.sarongbali.com; Jl Petitenget 19X; mains US$5-10; ☺ noon-10pm) The food is almost as magical as the setting at this top-end, high-concept restaurant. Largely open to the evening breezes, the dining room has plush furniture and gleaming place-settings that twinkle in the candlelight. Opt for tables out back where you can let the stars do the twinkling. The food spans the globe – small plates are popular for an evening spent enjoying the commodious bar.

Kafe Warisan (☎ 731175; www.kafewarisan.com; Jl Raya Kerobokan; set dinner menus US$25-40; ☺ noon-2pm Mon-Sat, 5-10pm daily) Chef Nicolas Tourneville gives fine French cooking a Mediterranean flair in a deceptively simple setting overlooking rice fields. The changing menu reflects what's in season locally, but it always features signature dishes such as duck confit tartare. Set menus allow the kitchen to show its expertise. Desserts include sublime house-made ice creams.

Blossom (☎ 735552; www.balisentosa.com; Sentosa Private Villas & Spa, Jl Pura Telaga Waja; meals from US$30) Arguably Bali's finest restaurant, Blossom is certainly one of the most captivating. Occupying much of the ground level of the ultra-posh Sentosa Villas, the restaurant has widely spaced tables in an elegant open-air space overlooking smoothly-flowing water features. Pretty much everything else here flows smoothly, including the drinks from the long bar and dishes from the vaunted kitchen. The menu changes often but is always global in outlook and creative in execution.

Self-Catering

Bali Deli (☎ 738686; Jl Kunti 117X; ☐ wi-fi) The lavish deli counter at this upscale market is loaded with imported cheese, meats and baked goods. This is the place to start a special meal. The breezy café also has a good, fresh menu.

Bintang Supermarket (☎ 730552; Jl Raya Seminyak 17) Always busy, this large supermarket is the stock-up favourite among expats (although Carrefour is tough competition).

ENTERTAINMENT
Bars & Clubs

Like your vision at 2am, the division between restaurant, bar and club blurs in Seminyak. For instance, Living Room and Sarong (left) have large and inviting bars that fill with people who never take a crack at a menu. Meanwhile, Ku De Ta and Hu'u (p126) serve good food to the partying masses. Although Seminyak lacks any real hardcore clubs where you can greet the dawn (or vice versa), stalwarts can head south to the rough edges of Kuta in the wee hours.

JL ABIMANYU

Numerous bars line Jl Abimanyu (aka Dhyana Pura), although noise-sensitive locals complain if things get too raucous.

Bahiana (☎ 738662; Jl Abimanyu 4; ⏱ 5pm-late) Rum flows almost as freely as the moves on the dance floor at this salsa-themed club. Live music alternates with DJs; there are salsa lessons many nights.

Obsession (☎ 730269; Jl Abimanyu; ⏱ 6pm-2am) Fear not, the 'global music' at this rather intimate venue isn't reggae. Latin, blues, soul and more get feet tapping through the night.

Q-Bar (☎ 762361; Jl Abimanyu; ⏱ 8pm-3am) This bright and always-popular bar caters to gay clubbers. The music of choice is house. There are good views of the action – inside and out – from the upper floor.

JL LAKSMANA

Hu'u (☎ 736443; www.huubali.com; Jl Pantai Kaya Aya; ⏱ 4pm-late) There's a menu someplace, but really, this spot is all about air-kissing, seeing and making the scene, an enchanting outdoor garden and pavilion. Action peaks around midnight before the club exodus begins.

Ku De Ta (☎ 736969; www.kudeta.net; Jl Laksmana; ⏱ 7am-1am) Ka Lee Shay? Hardly an article gets written about Bali that doesn't mention this beachside lounge, heaving with Bali's beautiful and their attendant scenesters. Perfect your 'bored' look over drinks, although the gorgeous sunsets shine through many a sneer.

Metro (☎ 736280; Jl Laksmana 52; ⏱ 11am-11pm) The only designer wear you'll find here has a swoosh or three stripes, and it's on the big-screen TVs. On a street that often seems ready to choke on its own style, this genial sports bar has a full line-up of Aussie sports nabbed off satellites by a set-up worthy of Parkes tracking station.

Zappaz (☎ 7425534; Jl Laksmana; ⏱ 11am-midnight) Brit Norman Findlay tickles the ivories nightly at this popular piano bar (although critics might call that tickle an attack). The most enjoyable part of this performance is his enthusiastic patter with the crowd.

SHOPPING

Seminyak shops could occupy days of your holiday. Designer boutiques (Bali has a thriving fashion industry), funky stores, slick galleries, wholesale emporiums and family-run workshops are just some of the choices.

The action picks up in the south from Kuta and Legian (p116) and heads north along Jl Legian and Jl Raya Seminyak (there's no exact demarcation between the two and some people call parts of the latter Jl Raya Basangkasa…). The retail strip branches off into the prime real estate of Jl Laksmana while continuing north on Jl Raya Kerobokan into Kerobokan itself (p128). Of course, this being Bali, try not to get too overwhelmed by the glitz or you'll step into one of the yawning pavement caverns.

If you need help navigating this retail paradise, check out the Retail Therapy column in the *Bali Advertiser* (www.baliadvertiser .biz). It's written by the singularly named Marilyn (retailtherapym@yahoo.com.au) who brings a veteran retailer's keen eye to the local scene. For advanced studies, she's available for consultations.

Accessories

Sabbatha (☎ 731756; Jl Raya Seminyak 97) Megabling! The glitter, glam and gold here are almost blinding and that's just what customers want. Opulent handbags and other sun-reflecting accessories are displayed like so much king's ransom.

Zakx (☎ 736653; Jl Laksmana 49) Zakx is a shoefetishist's fantasy from the bottom of the stiletto heels to the tips of the leather laces.

Beachwear

Blue Glue (☎ 844 5956; Jl Raya Seminyak) Has a collection of Bali-made bathing suits from teensy to trendy.

Body & Soul (☎ 733564; Jl Raya Seminyak) The flagship store in Bali for the Australian chain of beachy, cottony clothes. Many of the items here are Bali-made. Across the street, an outlet store (☎ 733011; Jl Raya Seminyak 16C) has hot deals on cool clothes.

Clothing

Bamboo Blonde (☎ 780 5919; Jl Laksmana 61) Frilly, sporty or sexy frocks and more formal wear tempt from this cheery designer boutique.

Bananas Batik (☎ 730938; www.bananasbatik.com; Jl Raya Seminyak) Flouncy clothes for women that you don't have to travel to the source for – the exquisite duds are made at Pondok Pisang (p222), a small inn on the ocean near

Candidasa. The batik is very finely made and the muted colours keep everything classy.

Biasa (☎ 730308; www.biasabali.com; Jl Raya Seminyak 36) This is Bali-based designer Susanna Perini's premier store. Her line of tropical wear for men and women combines cottons, silks and embroidery. Ex-husband Paul Ropp has a small shop across the street.

Copycat (☎ 0812 385 0480; Jl Raya Seminyak 40) As the name implies, these breezy linen clothes are knock-offs of pricier designs. The spunky attitude extends to its best-selling T-shirt: 'Who the fuck is Prada?'.

Divine Diva (☎ 731903; Jl Oberoi 1A) Bali-made breezy styles for fuller female figures. A friend calls it: 'the essense of agelessness'.

ET Club (☎ 730902; Jl Raya Seminyak 14A) Out-of-this-world prices on designer knock-offs and bohemian bags, belts, shoes and clothes.

Inti (☎ 733664; Jl Raya Seminyak 11) Shoppers tired of pawing through racks of size 2 clothes will sigh with relief at this shop filled with resortwear aimed at mature women who have something to show for their years of good living.

Joe Joe (☎ 732678; Jl Raya Seminyak 43) Sequin-encrusted bags and purses glitter in the lights here. Styles range from vintage to far-out. In one word: bling!

Lily Jean (☎ 734864; Jl Oberoi 102X) Saucy knickers underpin sexy women's clothing that both dares and flirts; most is Bali-made.

Milo's Bazaar (☎ 735551; www.milos-bali.com; Jl Laksmana 38) The legendary local designer of silk finery has followed the hordes to designer row. Look for batik bearing eye-popping orchid patterns.

Morena (☎ 745 3531; Jl Oberoi 69) Puerto Rican-born Wilma sells her line of sexy, flouncy, comfy and colourful women's clothes here.

Paul Ropp (☎ 734208; www.paulropp.com; Jl Oberoi) Elegant main store for one of Bali's premier high-end fashion designers. Rich silks and cottons, vivid to the point of gaudy, effervesce with hints of the tie-dyed '60s.

Sacado (☎ 730605; Jl Raya Seminyak) Your crazy kid will be a cool kid with the bright and cheery duds from this designer boutique.

Uma and Leopold (☎ 733670; www.umaandleopold.com; Jl Kunti 8x) Luxe clothes and little frilly things to put on before slipping off…

Galleries

Biasa Art Space (☎ 744 2902; www.biasaart.com; Jl Raya Seminyak 34) This large, airy and chilly gallery is owned by Biasa designer Susanna Perini. Changing exhibits highlight bold works.

Kemarin Hari Ini (☎ 735262; Jl Raya Basangkasa) Glass objects created with laminated Japanese paper sparkle in the light at this airy gallery. Primitive works mix with the starkly modern.

Richard Meyer Culture (☎ 744 5179; Jl Petitenget 200X) This gallery sells photos and artworks by renowned contemporary Bali artists. It's been lauded for its conservation and historical collection.

Housewares

our pick **Ashitaba** (☎ 737054; Jl Raya Seminyak 6) Tenganan, the Aga village of East Bali (p224), produces the intricate and beautiful rattan items sold here. Containers, bowls, purses and more (from US$5) display the very fine weaving.

DeZine Hammocks (☎ 742 2379; Jl Raya Seminyak) Talk about a gift that keeps on giving, let alone swaying. Choose from a rainbow of in-stock hammocks in a multitude of sizes. Or have one custom-made to your exact size using the fabric of your dreams (trust us, you'll be dreaming once you hop aboard). Total cost for the one-day service: about US$20.

Goris Art Shop (☎ 0859 3507 8570; Jl Laksmana) Acacia wood is carved into primitive creations at this shop that looks like something in a jungle clearing. A throne worthy of a royal caveman goes for 2.5 million rupiah.

Heliconia (☎ 732700; Jl Raya Seminyak) Stunning and exotic floral arrangements out of a Mapplethorpe album – who knew you could do that with a baby pineapple?

Nôblis (☎ 0815 5800 2815; Jl Raya Mertanadi 54) Feel like royalty here with everything from knock-offs of items from the various French Louis's, to regal bits of decor from around the globe.

Nostalgia Antique (☎ 735192; Jl Mertanadi 60) Wander off the road to this dusty and atmospheric collection of primitive creations from the island of Madura off the coast of Java.

Rama Shinta Ki Jay (☎ 0812 360 6979; Jl Raya Seminyak 70) Dedicated to all things incense, this shop is a party for your nose. Sniff out the fun in the sandalwood section.

You Like Lamp (☎ 733755; Jl Raya Mertanadi) Why yes, we do. All manner of endearing little paper lamps – many good for tea lights – are sold here cheap by the bag full. Don't see what you want? The staff working away on the floor will rustle it up immediately.

Jewellery

Luna Collection (☎ 0811 398 909; Jl Raya Seminyak) Handmade sterling silver jewellery in a range of designs. The local craftsmen are quite creative and the mother-of-pearl works are museum quality.

GETTING THERE & AROUND

Most transport information is the same as for Kuta (p118). Metered taxis are easily hailed. A trip from the airport in an official airport taxi costs 60,000Rp, to the airport about half that. A taxi to the heart of Kuta will be about 15,000Rp. You can beat the traffic, save the ozone and have a good stroll by walking south down the beach. Legian is about 15 minutes away.

NORTH OF SEMINYAK

☎ 0361

Growth is marching north and west along the coast, much of it anchored by the endless swath of beach. Kerobokan is morphing into Seminyak; cloistered villas here lure the well-heeled who whisk past stooped rice farmers in their air-con comfort. Traffic may be the ultimate commoner's revenge: road-building is a decade or two behind settlement.

Small roads lead off the main clogged artery that runs to Pura Tanah Lot. Use these to reach beaches at Berewa, Canggu, Echo Beach (Batu Mejan) and Pererenan Beach. These are uncrowded and wild, with pounding surf, perilous swimming and sweeping views to the south. An ever-growing number of tiny lanes thread through the rice fields and villas allowing you to link up the beaches without venturing to the Tanah Lot road. Along the grey-sand beach, it is only 4.5km from Pura Petitenget to Echo Beach, although a couple of rivers may impede your stroll.

Getting to most of the places below is only convenient with your own transport or by taxi. Think 25,000Rp or more from Kuta, 15,000Rp from Seminyak.

KEROBOKAN

The next area north of Seminyak is seamlessly blending with the south. There's a lot of upscale development here – villas jut from the ground like pustules on an adolescent. At times the mix of commerce and rice fields can be jarring. One notable landmark is the

Kerobokan jail, home to Schapelle Corby and other prisoners both notable and humble.

Activities

Umalas Stables (Map p100; ☎ 731402; www.balionhorse .com; Jl Lestari 9X), 5km north of Seminyak, has a stable of 30 horses and ponies and offers 30-minute rice-field rides for US$20, and very popular two-/three-hour beach rides for US$60/85. Lessons in beginner to advanced equestrian events such as dressage and show-jumping can also be arranged.

Sleeping

Sorting through the myriad villa options is best done with the help of an agent; see p329 for details.

Eating

Kerabokan is still spread out enough that there's no real strip of places to eat. But you'll find some worthy choices scattered about. At the corner of Jl Raya Kerobokan and Jl Gunung Tangkuban Perahu, there's a scrumptious little **fruit market** (Map p120) where you can do your lab work in Bali fruits and veg 101.

Depot Organic (Map p100; Jl Pengubengan Kauh; lunch 10,000Rp; ✆ 11am-3pm) In a compound of offices for local environmental groups, this warung is as unadorned as the leaves of its lettuce. Enjoy simple foods prepared with high-quality and sustainable coconut oil at benches under a palm tree.

Warung Gossip (Map p100; ☎ 0817 970 3209; Jl Pengubengan Kauh; meals from 20,000Rp; ✆ noon-4pm) Always popular thanks to its Westernised versions of Balinese warung staples. Get a plate, tell the staff what you'd like and you'll soon be enjoying a fine lunch at one of the shady tables. There's also a café area for more formal dining. It is about 1km north of the jail.

Panoramix (Map p120; ☎ 788 4140; Jl Batu Belig 2; ✆ 5-11pm) Feast on hearty country French fare like roast pig or various steaks and chops. Or go for local seafood accented with classic sauces like a flaming cognac. The kitchen never stops surprising and the food may actually draw your eyes away from the splendid rice-terrace views. Although preparations are just so, everything else at this rustic spot is *tres* casual.

Shopping

Buy 'em by the kilo at **JJ Bali Button** (Map p120; ☎ 730001; Jl Gunung Tangkuban Perahu). Zillions of beads and buttons made from shells,

---

SO YOU WANT TO LIVE IN BALI?

Numbers are fuzzy, but it's estimated that anywhere from 7000 to 30,000 people from other countries live more-or-less full-time in Bali. They come for the same reasons as many visitors (sun, surf, sex) or for more tangible reasons (culture, love, job) or just because it's really cheap ('A gardener, maid and driver for US$200 a month? Where's my ticket?!?').

You see them all over the south and Ubud and even scattered about the east, the north and the west; deeply tanned expats going – or not going – about their business every day. There's simply no way to generalise what they do, although the image of the Westerner idling away afternoons with US$1 Bintangs is common.

'You work?!?' That's the number one reaction Nicoline Dolman gets when she meets people and tells them she not only lives in Bali but also works there (as director of sales for the Villas resort in Seminyak). 'People think I must be lounging by the pool all the time,' says Dolman, who came to Bali on a tourism internship, fell in love with the place and never left.

'I get paid in local wages, so you bet I work.'

Ashley Bickerton, the renowned American artist, has discovered rare qualities in Bali. 'There are places on this planet that have kinetic electricity and there are those that don't. Bali has it in spades. Like the great oceanic washes of opposing currents and upswellings that create nutrient-rich banks, Bali is ablaze with conflicting currents; edge is everywhere.'

Both Bickerton and Dolman, however, are not universal in their regard for all things expat. 'The rampant greed and short-sightedness running amok in Bali today threatens to strangle the very things that drew people here in the first place,' says Bickerton, while Dolman says she gets tired of idlers with attitudes out of tune with the local vibe. 'You meet someone and they say with a smirk, "I'm a fashion designer, you?"'

Still, neither would leave their life in Bali. 'Every time a long-term expat starts grumbling about moving on, they are invariably stumped by the same question: "Where?",' says Bickerton, or as Dolman says, 'Other qualities aside, you've got a glass of beer, you're in the sun by that pool, why leave?'

---

plastic, metal and more are displayed in what first looks like a candy store (and it *is* for creative types).

BEREWA

The greyish beach, secluded among rice fields and villas, is about 2km up the sand from Seminyak and about 10km by roundabout lanes. There are a couple of surfer cafés by the pounding surf. The grey, volcanic sand here slopes steeply into the foaming waters.

Bali's monied elite shuttlecock themselves silly at the **Canggu Club** (Map p100; ☎ 844 6385; www.cangguclub.com; Jl Pantai Berawa; daypass adult/family US$30/65), a new-age version of something you'd expect to find during the Raj. The vast, perfectly virescent lawn is manicured for croquet. Get sweaty with tennis, squash, polo, cricket, the spa or the 25m pool.

At the well-run 40-room **Legong Keraton** (Map p100; ☎ 730280; www.legongkeratonhotel.com; Berewa Beach; r US$60-140; ❄ ⚤ ☐), right on the deserted sands of Berewa, the meeting rooms are the perfect place for a secret corporate retreat to work out the next redundancy scheme.

The grounds are shaded by palms and the pool borders the beach. The best rooms are in bungalow units facing the surf.

One person described **Desa Seni** (Map p100; ☎ 844 6392; www.desaseni.com; Jl Kayu Putih 13; r US$150-300; ❄ ⚤ ☐ wi-fi) as like a 'hippie Four Seasons', and that's not far off. Desa Deni bills itself as a 'village resort' and what a village it is. Classic wooden homes have been brought to the site from across Indonesia and turned into luxurious quarters (LCD TVs, DVD players etc). Guests enjoy a menu of organic and healthy cuisine while pondering which yoga class, spa session or cultural event to sign up for.

CANGGU

A popular surf spot, Canggu draws a lot of locals and expat residents at weekends. Access to the paved parking area costs 2000Rp and there are cafés and warung for those who work up an appetite in the water or watching others in the water.

Right at Canggu Beach, **Hotel Tugu Bali** (Map p132; ☎ 731701; www.tuguhotels.com; Jl Pantai Batu

Bolong, Desa Canggu; r US$200-500; 🔀 🔊 🖳 wi-fi) is an exquisite hotel surrounded by rice fields and beach. It blurs the boundaries between a museum and gallery, especially the Walter Spies and Le Mayeur Pavilions, where memorabilia from the artists' lives decorates the rooms. The stunning collection of antiques and artwork begins in the lobby and extends throughout the hotel. There's a spa and numerous customised dining options. Even by day, candles twinkle amidst the flowing fabrics in the breezy public areas.

To get to Canggu, go west at Kerobokan and south at Kayutulang. Taxis from Kuta will cost 40,000Rp or more.

ECHO BEACH

Just 500m northwest of Canggu Beach is Echo Beach, or Batu Mejan. It has reached critical mass in popularity and has become its own scene. Shops are moving in and the burgeoning number of cafés includes **Mandira Cafe** (Map p132; Jl Pura Batu Mejan; dishes 8000-15,000Rp), which has a timeless menu of jaffles, banana pancakes, club sandwiches and smoothies.

Slicker yet, the **Beach House** (Map p132; ☎ 738471; Jl Pura Batu Mejan; dishes 30,000-80,000Rp; wi-fi) faces the waves and draws stylish loungers. It has a variety of couches and picnic tables where you can hang out, watch the waves and enjoy the menu of breakfasts, salads, grilled fare and ambitious dishes such as calamari with aioli.

On Sunday afternoons Echo Beach literally rocks with local musicians jamming to one big party.

PERERENAN BEACH

Yet to be found by the right developer, this is the beach if you want your sand windswept and your waves unridden. It's 300m further on from Echo Beach by sand, over 1km by road.

Once you've found it, why leave? The friendly guys at **Pondok Wisata Nyoman** (Map p132; ☎ 0812 390 6900; Jl Raya Pantai Pererenan; r 120,000Rp) have four simple rooms (although the bathrooms have a certain colourful flair) just behind the beach. There's a tiny café nearby and that's it.

South Bali

You could spend your entire trip in South Bali and still not see everything. Ignoring the massive tourism hub of Kuta and Seminyak, this vast region is both the home of most Balinese and the place where most visitors spend at least some of their time.

The ocean is never far away, especially on the Bukit Peninsula, which hangs below the island like a silky cocoon. In Jimbaran several luxurious hotels are a counterpoint to wildly popular beachside seafood grills. Some of the world's best surf breaks are found along the coast leading to Ulu Watu. This idiosyncratic area has a delightful collection of cliffside places to stay. Across the peninsula, the gated development of Nusa Dua attracts well-heeled package tourists to its cloistered calm. Just north, Tanjung Benoa offers watery frolics on the reef-protected seas.

Sanur is the genteel place where tourism in Bali began. It has an alluring beachfront walkway with fine views across Selat Badung (Badung Strait) to the islands, which include Nusa Lembongan. Many journey out to this small island to find a Bali locked in a simpler time, and to enjoy great diving, fine surfing or simply doing nothing at all. Nearby Nusa Penida proves that you can still have a remote tropical adventure even in ever-more-popular Bali.

Denpasar, the capital, has museums, parks and intriguing markets. But its real highlights are the many warung (food stalls), cafés and restaurants found along its streets and alleys, many serving some of the best local food on the island.

SOUTH BALI

HIGHLIGHTS

- Picking a lobster for the grill at a seafood joint in **Jimbaran** (p135)
- Watching from **Sanur** (p145) as a full moon climbs over Nusa Penida
- Staying at a characterful inn while watching the surf breaks in and around **Ulu Watu** (p137)
- Finding your own inner peace amid the serenity of **Nusa Lembongan** (p153)
- Savouring in **Denpasar** (p168) the best US$1 meal you've ever had

SOUTH BALI

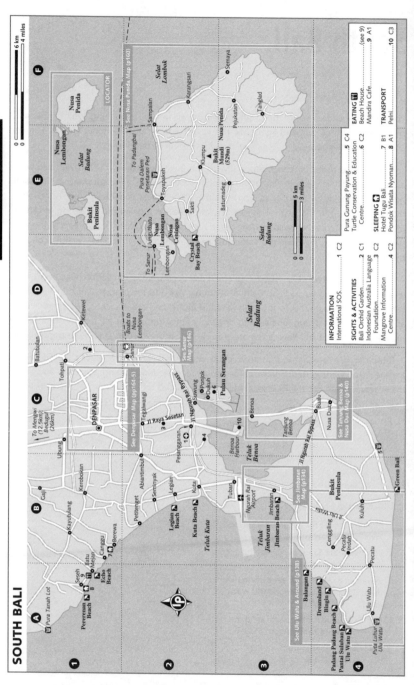

SOUTH BALI

LOCATOR

Nusa Penida

INFORMATION
International SOS.....................................1 C2

SIGHTS & ACTIVITIES
Bali Orchid Garden................................2 C1
Indonesian Australia Language
  Foundation......................................3 C2
Mangrove Information
  Centre..4 C2

Pura Gunung Payung.............................5 C4
Turtle Conservation & Education
  Centre..6 C2

SLEEPING 🛏
Hotel Tugu Bali....................................7 B1
Pondok Wisata Nyoman........................8 A1

EATING 🍴
Beach House...9 A1
Mandira Cafe....................................(see 9)

TRANSPORT 🚗
Pehn...10 C3

HISTORY

Following the bloody defeat of the three princes of the kingdom of Badung in 1906, the Dutch administration was relatively benign, and southern Bali was little affected until a fateful day in 1936 when Californians Bob and Louise Koke opened their idea of a little tropical resort on then-deserted Kuta Beach.

Mass tourism took off – or landed – in 1969 when Ngurah Rai international airport opened. The first planned tourist resort was conceived in the early 1970s by 'experts' working for the UN and the World Bank. As luxury hotels were built at Nusa Dua, unplanned development raced ahead from Kuta to Legian. People made the most of their opportunities, and small-scale, low-budget businesses were set up with limited local resources.

At first, tourism development was confined only to designated areas such as Kuta, Sanur and Nusa Dua, but the boom of the 1990s saw it spreading north and south of Kuta, extending beyond Jimbaran Bay and north of Nusa Dua to Tanjung Benoa. All the while, real-estate speculators grabbed prime coastal spots around the Bukit Peninsula and north along the beach from Seminyak.

The annual cycle of more visitors bringing more money was disrupted in the new millennium by the seemingly never-ending series of terrorist attacks, natural disasters elsewhere in Indonesia, various economic crises and other unsettling events that persuaded many visitors to stay home.

Pain was felt throughout tourist-dependent South Bali; slowly but surely, though, visitors returned, development continued on parts of the Bukit Peninsula and Nusa Lembongan, and somehow the traffic – which never got better – got worse.

BUKIT PENINSULA

☎ 0361

Hot and arid, the southern peninsula is known as Bukit (*bukit* means 'hill' in Bahasa Indonesia). It's the centre of much tourism in Bali, from booming Jimbaran to the cloistered climes of Nusa Dua. The rugged west coast running down to the important temple of Ulu Watu fronts some of the best surfing in the world. Little coves anchor an increasing number of hotels at places such as Balangan and Bingin.

JIMBARAN

Just south of Kuta and the airport, Teluk Jimbaran (Jimbaran Bay) is an alluring crescent of white sand and blue sea, fronted by a long string of seafood warung (food stalls) and ending at the southern end in a bushy headland, home to the Four Seasons Jimbaran Bay. Despite its many charms (eg great markets), it has always been a snoozy sort of place. And that is perfectly fine for many visitors, who enjoy the proximity to the bright lights of Kuta and Seminyak but savour the calm here.

But that's changing. Jimbaran is on the map, as it were. Long-running budget hotels by the water have vanished and fences are going up around construction sites for glam condos and villas. Whether this means a more frenetic future remains to be seen. Maybe Jimbaran will get its first real bar?

Facilities are limited. Jl Raya Ulu Watu has some small markets and Jl Ulu Watu II has ATMs and mini-markets. For most things head to Kuta. Expect to pay 2000Rp for vehicles to reach the beach.

Sights & Activities

The temple **Pura Ulun Siwi** (Map p134) dates from the 18th century. It is different from other Balinese temples in that it faces east, rather than north to Gunung Agung. It's thought this is because the site dates back to the 11th century when Java's Mt Semeru was still the focus of local piety. Look for farmers collecting water here to bless their fields: it's thought the anti-rodent powers are especially strong.

Across from the temple, the **produce market** (Map p134; Jl Ulu Watu; ✆ 5am-2pm) is small but has one of Bali's best selections of fruit and veg. Many savvy top-end chefs do their shopping here, and farmers from across the island know to bring their best or most unusual items here.

Another highlight is the smelly, lively and frenetic open-air **fish market** (Map p134). Boats land with their haul and the deal-making, selling and transporting is manic. Watch out for porters carting impossible loads barefoot through the muck. The earlier you arrive at both markets, the better.

Out on the water, Jimbaran is a good place to access the surf breaks off the airport.

The **Ganeesha Gallery** (Map p134) at the Four Seasons Jimbaran Bay (p134) has exhibitions by international artists and is worth a visit – walk south along the beach.

Sleeping

Some of South Bali's most luxurious resorts are found in and around Jimbaran, as well as a few midrange places off the beach. Most offer some form of shuttle through the day to Kuta and beyond. Watch for offers from new beachside resorts.

MIDRANGE

Hotel Puri Bambu (Map p134; ☎ 701377; www.puri bambu.com; r US$35-90; 🐕 🈁 🖳) A mere 200m from the beach, the flash-free Puri Bambu is an older but well-run and good-value option. The 48 standard rooms (some with tubs) are in three-storey blocks around a large pool.

Udayana Eco Lodge (Map p134; ☎ 7474204; www .ecolodgesindonesia.com; r 550,000-800,000Rp; 🐕 🈁 🖳 wi-fi) Inland near Udayana University, this lodge has grand views over South Bali from its perch on a knoll in 70 hectares of bushland. The 10 rooms are comfortable and there is an inviting common area with an excellent library. Much effort has been made to preserve and reuse water.

Puri Kosala (Map p134; ☎ 701673; www.purikosala .com; Jl Yoga Perkanti 2; villas US$90-200; 🐕 🈁 🖳) This secluded property makes for a good getaway. The six cottages have elaborate traditional Balinese details and simple bathrooms with tubs. Although it's close to the beach and has a large pool and manicured gardens, it does not have a top-end level of service, so get a deal.

TOP END

At this price level, check for special offers during slack periods.

Jimbaran Puri Bali (Map p134; ☎ 701605; www .jimbaranpuribali.com; Jl Yoga Perkanti; cottages US$150-400; 🐕 🈁 🖳) Reborn under the tutelage of Orient-Express Resorts, this beachside resort is set in nice grounds complete with a maze-like pool that looks onto open ocean. The 41 cottages have private gardens, large terraces and stylish room design with sunken tubs.

Hotel Intercontinental Bali (Map p134; ☎ 701888; www.bali.intercontinental.com; Jl Ulu Watu; r from US$200; 🐕 🈁 🖳 wi-fi) With 419 rooms, the Intercontinental is really a little city on the beach. Decorated with Balinese arts and handicrafts, it tries to meld local style to a huge resort. The plethora of pools feed each other and meander through the grounds. There is a good kids' club and the crescent of beach is fine.

Ritz Carlton (Map p132; ☎ 702222; www.ritzcarlton .com; r US$300-450, villas US$500-950; 🐕 🈁 🖳 wi-fi)

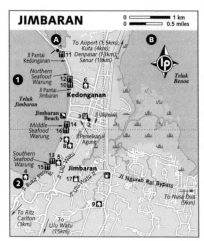

SIGHTS & ACTIVITIES
Fish Market...1 A1
Ganeesha Gallery..................................(see 4)
Produce Market.......................................2 A1
Pura Ulun Siwi...3 A1

SLEEPING 🏠
Four Seasons Jimbaran Bay....................4 A2
Hotel Intercontinental Bali.....................5 A2
Hotel Puri Bambu....................................6 A1
Jimbaran Puri Bali...................................7 A2
Puri Kosala...8 A2
Udayana Eco Lodge.................................9 A2

EATING 🍴
Fortuin Café...10 A1
Ganesha Pudak Cafe.............................11 A1
New Langsam Café................................12 A1
Roma..13 A2
Roman Café..14 A1
Teba Cafe...15 A2
Warung Bamboo....................................16 A1

SHOPPING 🛍
Jenggala Keramik Bali...........................17 A2

Hidden in vast private grounds 3km southwest of Jimbaran, the Ritz-Carlton surveys the sea from its isolated cliff-top spot. The 290 rooms are spacious and set in large blocks. Villas offer the ultimate for people who want a grand resort experience. Nearby, the Ritz jealously guards its own gem of a beach. Note that legal issues may cause the Ritz to change its name and management.

Four Seasons Jimbaran Bay (Map p134; ☎ 701010; www.fourseasons.com; villas from US$700; 🐕 🈁 🖳 wi-fi) The 147 villas here are designed in a traditional Balinese manner complete with a carved entranceway, which opens onto an open-air dining pavilion overlooking a water-sucking plunge pool. The spa is guests-only, which maintains the very exclusive air. The site is a hillside overlooking Jimbaran Beach, which is a very short walk away.

Eating

The warung are the destination of tourists across the south. Jimbaran's three groups of seafood warung do fresh barbecued seafood every evening (and lunch at many). The open-sided affairs are right by the beach and perfect for enjoying sea breezes and sunsets. Tables and chairs are set up on the sand almost to the water's edge.

The usual deal is to select your seafood fresh from iced displays or tanks, and to pay according to weight. Expect to pay around 40,000Rp per 100g for live lobster, 15,000Rp to 25,000Rp for prawns, and 9000Rp for fish, squid and clams. Prices are open to negotiation and the accuracy of the scales is a joke among locals. Agree to a price before ordering. Some places simplify things with fixed menu prices.

The best kitchens marinate the fish in garlic and lime, then douse it with chilli and oil while grilling over coconut husks. Thick clouds of smoke from the coals are part of the atmosphere, as are roaming bands, who perform tunes from the 'Macarena' playlist. Many people actually join in.

NORTHERN SEAFOOD WARUNG

The longest row of warung is at the northern seafood warung, south of the fish market. This is the area you will be taken to by a taxi if you don't specify otherwise. Most of these places are restaurant-like with tables inside and out on the immaculate raked sand. Call for free transport to/from much of the south. Recommendations:

Fortuin Café (Map p134; Jl Pantai Kedonganan) How fortuitous, the name means 'the chosen'.

Ganesha Pudak Cafe (Map p134; ☎ 0813 3855 3800; Jl Pantai Kedonganan) Many fish displays.

Roman Café (Map p134; Jl Pantai Kedonganan) Takes credit cards.

MIDDLE SEAFOOD WARUNG

The middle seafood warung are in a compact group just south of Jl Pantai Jimbaran and Jl Pemelisan Agung. These seafood warung are the simplest affairs, with old-fashioned thatched roofs and wide-open sides. The

beach is a little less manicured, with the fishing boats resting up on the sand. Don't plan on getting any public transport out here. Warung recommendations:

New Langsam Café (Map p134; ☎ 703170; Jl Pantai Jimbaran)

Warung Bamboo (Map p134; ☎ 702188; off Jl Pantai Jimbaran)

SOUTHERN SEAFOOD WARUNG

The southern seafood warung are just north of the Four Seasons Jimbaran Bay. In many ways the warung are like the Three Bears: this group – not as formal as the northern group, not as rickety as the middle group – is just right. There's a parking area off Jl Bukit Permai and the places are right in a row. The beach here is well groomed with nice trees. Call for transport. Recommendations:

Roma (Map p134; ☎ 702387; off Jl Bukit Permai) Redolent with garlic.

Teba Cafe (Map p134; ☎ 0817 346 068; off Jl Bukit Permai) Lots of special platters and a local fave.

Right on the beaches the luxury hotels have cafés and restaurants, which afford beautiful views of the surf, sea and sunset.

Shopping

Jenggala Keramik Bali (Map p134; ☎ 703310; www.jenggala-bali.com; Jl Ulu Watu II; ⏰ 9am-6pm) A modern air-con showroom displays beautiful ceramic homewares. It has a viewing area where you can watch production, and a café. Ceramic courses are available for adults and children (US$10/50 for one/six sessions). The outlet store for Jenggala is Gudang Keramik in Sanur (p152).

Getting There & Away

Public bemo (small minibuses) from Tegal terminal in Denpasar go via Kuta to Jimbaran (12,000Rp), and continue to Nusa Dua. They don't run after about 4pm, but plenty of taxis wait around the beachfront warung in the evening to take diners home (about 35,000Rp to Kuta). Some of the seafood warung provide free transport if you call first.

CENTRAL BUKIT

Jl Ulu Watu goes south of Jimbaran, climbing 200m up the peninsula's namesake hill, affording views over southern Bali.

Garuda Wisnu Kencana Cultural Park (GWK; Map p132; ☎ 703603; admission 15,000Rp, parking 5000Rp;

8am-6pm) is the yet-to-be-completed huge cultural park that is meant to be home to a 66m-high statue of Garuda. This Brobdingnagian dream is supposed to be erected on top of a shopping and gallery complex, for a total height of 146m. Touted as the biggest and highest statue in the world, it is to be surrounded by performance spaces, art galleries, a food court and an adventure playground.

Well, that's the plan. So far the only completed part of the statue is the large bronze head. The buildings that do exist are mostly empty. However, besides the perverse fascination with big things gone bad, there's another good reason to visit the site: the views. From a small café off the parking lot there are sweeping views across all of South Bali. And if it's clear enough to see the volcanoes, then GWK is worth a detour.

BALANGAN BEACH

First of a string of small beaches backed by cliffs that run along the west coast of the Bukit Peninsula south to Ulu Watu, Balangan Beach is a real find. A long and low area at the base of the cliffs is covered with palm trees and is fronted by a ribbon of near-white sand. At the north end there is a small temple, **Pura Dalem Balangan** (Map p138); at the south end, a few surfer shacks cluster, renting out loungers and serving drinks.

For details on the fast left surf break here, see p94.

Back on the bluff above the water are what are likely to be the first of many places to stay; both have cafés. The beach is a five-minute walk.

Run by the same family who had the now-demolished Robby & the Kids Warung at Dreamland Beach (right), **Balangan Sea View Bungalows** (Map p138; ☎ 0812 376 1954; robbyandrosita@hotmail.com; r from 250,000Rp; ⊠) is a cluster of thatched bungalows surrounding a small pool in an attractive compound.

At **Flower Bud Bungalows** (Map p138; ☎ 0828 367 2772; www.flowerbudbalangan.com; r 250,000-375,000Rp), the raised thatched bungalows are well spaced around simple gardens. There's a certain Crusoe-esque motif, and fans and sprightly pillows are among the 'luxuries'. It is directly across from Balangan Sea View Bungalows.

Balangan Beach is 6km off the main Ulu Watu road via Cenggiling. The turn is 1.5km past GWK. When you near the bluff, take

---

NIGHTMARE LAND

On a typical day, scores of people sat on loungers on the too-white sand enjoying the cinematic surfing action, pausing once and a while for a drink or a snack from one of the family-run, thatched losmen (basic accommodation). Then the bulldozers arrived. As part of the vast Pecatu Indah project, the beach named Dreamland was effectively privatised for upscale development. Most of the warung moved north to Balangan; the surfers scattered like sand crabs.

---

the dirt road to the left that goes past the bungalows and ends at a parking area close to the beach.

Taxis from the Kuta area cost at least 40,000Rp per hour for the round-trip and waiting time.

PECATU INDAH

This 400-hectare **resort complex** (Map p138; www.balipecatu.com) rises between central Bukit Peninsula and the coast. The land is arid but that hasn't stopped the developers from building a huge hotel, condos, houses and, worst of all, a water-sucking 18-hole golf course. Follow the grand boulevards and you can see that the course doesn't benefit from any water-conserving measures such as shade. You do see a lot of water trucks hauling water all the way in from Denpasar. It's meant to be an international resort community but the environmental cost is obvious. Less obvious to newbies was the destruction of a sweet little beach named Dreamland for the construction of a Ku De Ta–type bar.

BINGIN

A fast-evolving scene, Bingin comprises several funky places to stay scattered across cliffs and one strip of white sand down below. A 1km dirt road turns off the paved road (look for the thicket of accommodation signs), which in turn branches off the main Ulu Watu road at the small village of Pecatu.

An elderly resident collects 3000Rp at a T-junction, which is near parking for the trail down to the **beach**. The surf here is often savage but the sands are calm and the roaring breakers mesmerising. For details on the renowned left break, see p94.

The scenery here is simply superb, with virescent cliffs dropping down to a row of houses and the foaming edge of the azure sea. Several places to stay enjoy the views while more modest places are set back. All have at least simple cafés, although for nightlife – like the rest of this coast – you'll be heading north to Kuta (unless your idea of nightlife is more intimate). Plans for upscale villas and hotels are constantly rumoured.

Sleeping

Bingin Garden (Map p138; ☎ 0816 472 2002; tommy barrell76@yahoo.com; r from 150,000Rp) Four basic and new bungalows are set around tidy grounds back from the cliffs and 300m north of the toll gate. Each unit sleeps two and has cold water and a fan.

Micks Place (Map p138; ☎ 0812 391 3337; micksplace bali@yahoo.com.au; r from US$60, villas US$200; 🖥) The turquoise water in the postage-stamp infinity pool matches the turquoise sea below. Funky is an understatement for this highly personable place with six artful round huts set in lush grounds. Most have no power or hot water but do have the sound of the surf. A walled villa does have power and its own pool.

Mu (Map p138; ☎ 847 0976; www.mu-bali.com; r €55-185; 🖥 🖥 🖥 wi-fi) Turn left after the toll gate for the most stylish option in Bingin. Seven very individual bungalows with round, pointed thatched roofs are scattered about a compound dominated by a cliffside infinity pool. All have open-air living spaces; some have air-con bedrooms and hot tubs with a view.

ULU WATU & AROUND

Ulu Watu has become the generic name for the southwestern tip of the Bukit Peninsula. It includes the much-revered temple and the fabled surf breaks at Padang Padang, Suluban and Ulu Watu. Surfers are most common in these parts, although a spate of villa-building is changing that. (In fact, authorities are waging war against new construction within about 2km of the temple.)

Sights & Activities

PURA LUHUR ULU WATU

This **temple** (Map p138; admission incl sarong & sash rental 3000Rp, parking 1000Rp; ☉ 8am-7pm) is one of several important temples to the spirits of the sea along the south coast of Bali. In the 11th century the Javanese priest Empu Kuturan first established a temple here. The temple

was added to by Nirartha, another Javanese priest who is known for the seafront temples at Tanah Lot (p271), Rambut Siwi (p277) and Pura Sakenan (p152). Nirartha retreated to Ulu Watu for his final days when he attained *moksa* (freedom from earthly desires).

The temple is perched precipitously on the southwestern tip of the peninsula, atop sheer cliffs that drop straight into the pounding surf. You enter through an unusual arched gateway flanked by statues of Ganesha. Inside, the walls of coral bricks are topped with intricate carvings of Bali's mythological menagerie. Only Hindu worshippers can enter the small inner temple that is built onto the jutting tip of land. However, the views of the endless swells of the Indian Ocean from the cliffs are almost spiritual. At sunset, walk around the clifftop to the left (south) of the temple to lose some of the crowd.

For tips on respecting traditions and acting appropriately while visiting temples, see p348. For a directory of important temples, see p51.

An enchanting and popular **Kecak dance** is held in the temple grounds at sunset; tickets cost 40,000Rp. Although the performance caters for tourists, the gorgeous setting makes it one of the more delightful on the island.

SURFING

From the paved road that goes northwest from Pecatu village (turn right at the small temple), it's easy to access the breaks at Bingin (opposite). **Impossibles** is nearby and **Padang Padang** is about 1km on. There is parking just north of a bridge.

Ulu Watu (Ulu's) is a storied surf spot – the stuff of dreams and nightmares. It's about 1km south of Padang Padang and its legend is matched closely by nearby **Pantai Suluban**. Since the early 1970s these breaks have drawn surfers from around the world. The left breaks seem to go on forever. The area boasts numerous small inns and warung that sell and rent

---

DAMN MONKEYS

The temple is home to scores of grey monkeys. Greedy little buggers, when they're not energetically fornicating, they snatch sunglasses, handbags, hats and anything else within reach. Of course if you want to start a riot, show them your banana…

surfboards, and provide food, drink, ding repairs or a massage – whatever you need most. Pantai Suluban is the best place to swim in the area. From its bluff, you get a good view of all the area surf breaks.

See p93 for more on the area's surf breaks.

Sleeping

If you're not picky you can count on being able to find accommodation of some sort near the surf break of your choice. Expect to pay at least 80,000Rp for a room with cold water, a fan and a shared bathroom. Many surfers choose to stay in Kuta and make the commute of less than an hour. More luxurious accommodation is also on offer, with more planned.

Padang Padang Inn (Map p138; ☎ 0812 391 3617; Jl Melasti 432; r from 80,000Rp) A better-than-average budget place, Padang Padang has 24 tidy rooms with private cold-water bathrooms and a little café. It can arrange all manner of surfing services like lessons, trips etc.

Gong (Map p138; ☎ 769976; thegongacc@yahoo.com; Jl Pantai Suluban; r from US$12) Few stay away long from the Gong. Eight tidy rooms with good

ventilation and hot water face a small compound and have distant ocean views. There's also a café.

Rocky Bungalows (Map p138; ☎ 0817 346 209; off Jl Ulu Watu; r 400,000-500,000Rp; ✴ ▣) This ever-expanding hotel is just west of the Padang Padang surf break. It has 14 rooms with views out to sea from the balconies and pool and is a five-minute walk to the water. The best rooms have air-con and DVD players.

Eating

Most of the places to stay have cafés and any beach where there are surfers will have a few warung selling necessities like beer.

Yeye's Warung (Map p138; Jl Labuan Sait; mains 18,000-30,000Rp) A gathering point away from the cliffs, Yeye's has an easygoing ambience, cheapish beers and tasty Western, Indonesian and vegetarian food. But pizza is the perennial number-one attraction.

Jiwa Juice (Map p138; ☎ 7424196; Jl Melasti; mains 20,000-30,000Rp; ✴ ▣) Jiwa means 'soul', and the juices and fresh, light food here are good for the same. This popular stop has internet access, a rarity in these parts.

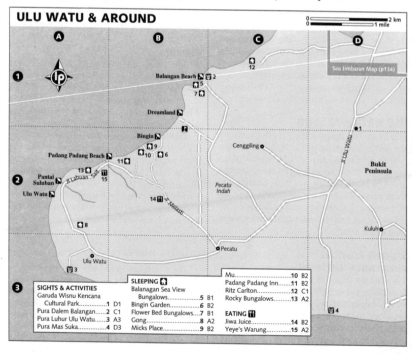

ULU WATU & AROUND

0   2 km
0   1 mile

See Jimbaran Map (p134)

Balangan Beach 🏖 2
5
7

Dreamland 🏖

Bingin 🏖
9
10 6

Padang Padang Beach 🏖
13
11

Pantai Suluban 🏖
Jl Labuan Sait
15

Ulu Watu 🏖

14 Jl Melasti

8

Ulu Watu
3

Cengggiling

Pecatu Indah

Bukit Peninsula

Kuluh

Pecatu

12

1

Jl Ulu Watu

4

SIGHTS & ACTIVITIES		
Garuda Wisnu Kencana		
Cultural Park	1	D1
Pura Dalem Balangan	2	C1
Pura Luhur Ulu Watu	3	A3
Pura Mas Suka	4	D3

SLEEPING 🛌		
Balanagan Sea View		
Bungalows	5	B1
Bingin Garden	6	B2
Flower Bed Bungalows	7	B1
Gong	8	A2
Micks Place	9	B2

Mu	10	B2
Padang Padang Inn	11	B2
Ritz Carlton	12	C1
Rocky Bungalows	13	A2

EATING 🍴		
Jiwa Juice	14	A2
Yeye's Warung	15	A2

SOUTH BALI

DETOUR: THE SOUTH COAST

The south coast of the Bukit Peninsula has high wind-blown cliffs and big swells. Development choked off after the 1990s and, as you gaze out to the whitecaps of the Indian Ocean, you feel on the edge of the world.

Lots of little tracks lead to the cliffs from the southern roads linking Nusa Dua with Pecatu via Kuluh. Try exploring some. From the west, look for a steep track down to the beach and the **Green Ball** (Map p132) surf break about 4km from the little village of Ulu Watu. Other roads lead down to the coast to small beaches and sea temples such as **Pura Gunung Payung** (Map p132), which is near the invasive Nikko Bali Resort, a Soeharto-era leftover. Diminutive **Pura Mas Suka** (Map p132) is reached by a twisting narrow road through a barren red-rock landscape, but the views are divine. See p94 for details of the area's surf breaks.

Getting There & Away

The best way to see the west coast is with your own vehicle or by chartering a taxi. Note that the cops often set up traps near Pecatu Indah for motorcycle-riding Westerners. While you pay a fine for a 'loose' chin strap, helmet-less locals whiz by laughing.

Drivers' note: coming from the east to Pantai Suluban you will first encounter a gated parking area (car/motorcycle 3000/2000Rp), which is about a 400m walk from the water. Continuing over a bridge, there is an older parking area (car/motorcycle 2000/1000Rp) that is a hilly 200m from the water. Watch out for 'gate-keepers' looking for bonuses.

Public bemo to Ulu Watu are infrequent and stop running by mid-afternoon. Some from Kuta serve Jimbaran and Ulu Watu – it's best to catch one west of Tuban (on Jl Raya Kuta, outside the Supernova shopping centre) or in Jimbaran (on Jl Ulu Watu).

NUSA DUA

Nusa Dua translates literally as Two Islands – although they are actually small raised headlands, each with a little temple. But Nusa Dua is much better known as Bali's gated compound of resort hotels. It's a vast and manicured place where you leave the rest of the island behind as you pass the guard. Gone are the street vendors, hustle, bustle and engaging chaos of the rest of the island. Here you even talk more quietly.

Built in the 1970s, Nusa Dua was designed to compete with international beach resorts the world over. The goal was to attract free-spending holidaymakers while keeping them isolated from the rest of the island. Balinese 'culture' in the form of attenuated dances and other performances are literally trucked in for the masses nightly.

With thousands of hotel rooms Nusa Dua can live up to some of its promise when it's full, but during slack times it's rather desolate. Certainly it is closer in atmosphere to a generic international beach resort than to anything Balinese – although some of the hotels try to apply a patina of Bali style, an effort akin to putting lipstick on a, er, you guessed it.

Orientation & Information

Nusa Dua is very spread out. You enter the enclave through one of the guarded gateways; inside there are expansive lawns, manicured gardens and sweeping driveways leading to the lobbies of large resort hotels. It can be surprisingly confusing to walk or drive anywhere as streets curve this way and that.

In the middle of the resort, the Bali Collection shopping centre (p142) has some chain stores and ATMs. For most supplies, try the huge new Hardy's superstore (p142) outside the gates in Bualu. A **post office** (Map p140; Jl Ngurah Rai) is nearby.

Sights
PASIFIKA MUSEUM

This grand new **museum** (Map p140; ☎ 774559; Bali Collection, Block P, Nusa Dua; admission 50,000Rp; ☺ 10am-6pm) suffers from the same visitor neglect as the rest of the Bali Collection (p142). Good! You'll likely have the place to yourself. Several centuries of art from cultures around the Pacific Ocean are displayed (the tikis are cool). The influential wave of European artists that thrived in Bali in the early 20th century is well represented. Look for works by Arie Smit, Adrien Jean Le Mayeur and Theo Meier. Staff will follow you from one wing to the next turning lights on and off. This museum is reason enough to visit Nusa Dua.

SOUTH BALI

TANJUNG BENOA & NUSA DUA

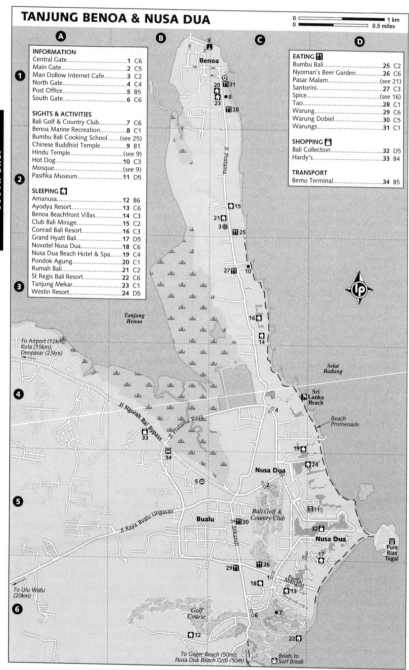

INFORMATION
Central Gate	**1** C6
Main Gate	**2** C5
Man Dollow Internet Cafe	**3** C2
North Gate	**4** C4
Post Office	**5** B5
South Gate	**6** C6

SIGHTS & ACTIVITIES
Bali Golf & Country Club	**7** C6
Benoa Marine Recreation	**8** C1
Bumbu Bali Cooking School	(see 25)
Chinese Buddhist Temple	**9** B1
Hindu Temple	(see 9)
Hot Dog	**10** C3
Mosque	(see 9)
Pasifika Museum	**11** D5

SLEEPING
Amanusa	**12** B6
Ayodya Resort	**13** C6
Benoa Beachfront Villas	**14** C3
Club Bali Mirage	**15** C2
Conrad Bali Resort	**16** C3
Grand Hyatt Bali	**17** D5
Novotel Nusa Dua	**18** C6
Nusa Dua Beach Hotel & Spa	**19** C4
Pondok Agung	**20** C1
Rumah Bali	**21** C2
St Regis Bali Resort	**22** C6
Tanjung Mekar	**23** C1
Westin Resort	**24** D5

EATING
Bumbu Bali	**25** C2
Nyoman's Beer Garden	**26** C6
Pasar Malam	(see 21)
Santorini	**27** C3
Spice	(see 16)
Tao	**28** C1
Warung	**29** C6
Warung Dobiel	**30** C5
Warungs	**31** C1

SHOPPING
Bali Collection	**32** D5
Hardy's	**33** B4

TRANSPORT
Bemo Terminal	**34** B5

Activities

BEACH PROMENADE

One of the nicest features of Nusa Dua is the 5km-long beach promenade that stretches the length of the resort and continues north along much of the beach in Tanjung Benoa. Not only is it a good stroll at any time but it also makes it easy to sample the pleasures of the other beachside resorts. The walk is paved for most of its length.

SURFING & BEACHES

The reef-protected beach at Nusa Dua is shallow at low tide, and the wave action is pretty limp. The surf breaks at Nusa Dua are way out on reefs to the north and south of the two 'islands'. They work best with a big swell during the wet season. **Sri Lanka** is a right-hander in front of Club Med. The so-called **Nusa Dua** breaks are peaks, reached by boat from the beach south of the Ayodya Resort – go past the golf course and turn left on a dirt road. Nonsurfers from all over southern Bali also flock to this pretty beach just north of Geger Beach, which now has a dozen warung.

The beach between the two peaks behind Bali Collection is also nice and has a large, shady and paved parking area that makes it a good stop for day-trippers, especially families, who will enjoy the calm atmosphere.

GOLF

The **Bali Golf & Country Club** (Map p140; ☎ 771791; www.baligolfandcountryclub.com; green fees US$150) is an 18-hole course with all the amenities one would expect from a course at a major resort. Its popularity has sparked condo development along the fairways and new resorts have begun opening nearby. It uses a lot of scarce water.

SPAS

All the resort hotels have pricey spas that provide a broad range of therapies, treatments and just plain, simple relaxation. The most lauded of the spas are at the Amanusa, Westin and Grand Hyatt in Nusa Dua (see below) and at the Conrad (p144) in Tanjung Benoa. All are open to non-guests.

Sleeping

The Nusa Dua hotels are similar in several ways: they are all big (some are just plain huge) and they have long beachfronts. Each has several restaurants and bars, as well as various pools and other resort amenities. But what's most important is in the detail, as that's where the real differences lie. Some hotels, such as the Westin and Grand Hyatt, have invested heavily in property, adding loads of amenities (such as the elaborate pools and day camps for kids) demanded by travellers today. Other hotels seem little changed from when they were built during the heyday of the Soeharto era in the 1970s.

If you're considering a stay at Nusa Dua, prowl the internet looking for deals. During the off-season you can get excellent deals that bring nightly rates down by up to half.

Novotel Nusa Dua (Map p140; ☎ 848 0555; www.novotelnusaduabali.com; r from US$150; ✹ ✹ ▭ wi-fi) The closest sand to this 188-unit resort are the bunkers on the golf course that surrounds the complex. Large apartments here come with one to three bedrooms and are excellent for families. The beach is a 10-minute walk away.

Grand Hyatt Bali (Map p140; ☎ 771234; www.bali.grand.hyatt.com; r from US$250; ✹ ✹ ▭ wi-fi) A little city, of sorts, the 648-room Hyatt has directional signs that have up to 21 arrows. Like any city, some neighbourhoods are better than others. Some rooms in the West Village (there are four; the East and South Villages are best located) face the taxi parking lot. The riverfront pool (one of six) is huge and has a fun slide. The children's club will keep 'em busy for days.

Westin Resort (Map p140; ☎ 771906; www.westin.com/bali; r from US$250; ✹ ✹ ▭ wi-fi) Attached to a large convention centre, the Westin has an air-conditioned lobby (a rarity) and vast public spaces. Guests in the 355 rooms enjoy the best pools in Nusa. There are waterfalls and more in this aquatic playground. The Kids Club has extensive activities and facilities. The landmark 2007 meetings on climate change were held here.

St Regis Bali Resort (Map p140; ☎ 847 8111; www.starwoodhotels.com; ste from US$500; ✹ ✹ ▭ wi-fi) The newest Nusa Dua resort leaves most of the others in the sand. Every conceivable luxury from the electronics to the furnishings to the marble is provided. Pools abound and units are huge. Golf course and the beach adjoin.

Amanusa (Map p140; ☎ 772333; www.amanresorts.com; villas from US$850; ✹ ✹ ▭ wi-fi) Overlooking the golf course and beyond across Selat Badung, the Amanusa is one of Bali's best hotels. The elegant, understated architecture, rich decorations, superb service and brilliant views are the province of just 35 individual villas. Guests enjoy a private beach.

Other notable Nusa Dua resorts:

Nusa Dua Beach Hotel & Spa (Map p140; ☎ 771210; www.nusaduahotel.com; r from US$150; 🔀 🖭 🖵 wi-fi) The design of many of the 381 plush rooms has a curious preponderance of walls where there could be windows. This is a good place to score a cheap package.

Ayodya Resort (Map p140; ☎ 771102; www.ayodya resortbali.com; r from US$160; 🔀 🖭 🖵 wi-fi) An enormous place with 537 rooms (although it actually feels bigger) in six-storey blocks, the Ayodya dropped the Hilton name in 2006. Lagoons covering the grounds are all for show – for swimming use the OK pool.

Eating

Restaurants can be found by the dozen in the huge resorts. Prices are high even by top-end Bali standards. For people not staying at the hotels, the best reason to venture in is if you want a bounteous Sunday brunch at one of the international chains.

South of Nusa Dua, the various warung at the surfers' beach serve some very good and typically fresh local standards. Other good warung (Map p140) cluster at the corner of Jl Srikandi and Jl Pantai Mengiat. Also along the latter street, just outside the central gate, there are a string of open-air eateries offering an unpretentious alternative to Nusa Dua dining. None will win any culinary awards; most will provide transport.

Warung Dobiel (Jl Srikandi; meals from 15,000Rp; 🕑 8am-3pm) It's all about pork at this beloved open-front warung. Pork satay, pork soup, and green beans with shredded pork are among the favourites. The sautéed jackfruit will make you a convert; the green sambal is redolent with spices. Seating is on stools at long tables.

Nyoman's Beer Garden (Map p140; ☎ 775746; Jl Pantai Mengiat; dishes 25,000-50,000Rp) Best of the bunch just outside the gates. There's a party atmosphere at the tables inside and out. The menu cuts a broad swath: Asian, pasta, pizza, burgers and, yes, schnitzel. Order the lobster in advance and it comes with the owner's secret – and tasty – sauce.

Nusa Dua Beach Grill (Map p140; ☎ 743 4779; Jl Pura Geger; mains 30,000-60,000Rp) A hidden gem, this warm-hued café is the star of Geger beach, itself a hidden gem south of Nusa Dua. Reef-protected sands lure expat families; on weekends you could be in Nice, it's so continental. Fresh grilled seafood is another lure. To get here, head south through Nusa Dua to the Bale Hotel, where a small road runs down to the beach and the temple, Pura Geger.

Entertainment

Most of the hotels offer Kecak and Legong dances on one or more nights. Hotel lounges also often have live music, from crooners to mellow rock bands.

Shopping

Bali Collection (Map p140; ☎ 771662) This shopping centre has had numerous name changes. The latest incarnation is mostly empty except for the dozens of assistants in the small Sogo Department Store. A few other souls try to make merry on their Bali holiday at the deserted Starbucks. Good luck. Although its problems can be traced to the rigorous security and closed nature of Nusa Dua, the isolation means that the boom other local malls are enjoying is a bust here.

Hardy's (Map p140; Jl Ngurah Rai Bypass, Bualu; 🕑 8am-9pm) Huge new store by the local chain of supermarkets. Besides groceries it has most other supplies you can think of, plus ATMs.

Getting There & Away

The fixed taxi fare from the airport is 85,000Rp; a metered taxi *to* the airport will be less. Taxis to/from Seminyak average 70,000Rp.

Public bemo travel between Denpasar's Tegal terminal and the terminal at Bualu (12,000Rp). From Bualu, it's at least 1km to the hotels – not that anyone paying US$250 per night has ever taken a bemo to Nusa Dua.

Getting Around

Find out what shuttle-bus services your hotel provides before you start hailing taxis. A free **shuttle bus** (☎ 771662; 🕑 9am-10pm) connects all Nusa Dua and Tanjung Benoa resort hotels with the Bali Collection shopping centre about every hour. Better: use the delightful beach promenade.

TANJUNG BENOA

The peninsula of Tanjung Benoa extends about 4km north from Nusa Dua to Benoa village. It's flat and lined with family-friendly resort hotels, most of midrange calibre. By day the waters buzz with the roar of dozens of motorised water-sports craft. Group tours arrive by the busload for a day's excitement straddling a banana boat and other thrills.

Like beaches at Sanur and Nusa Dua, those here are protected from waves by an offshore reef. That has allowed a local beach-activities industry to flourish in the placid waters.

Overall, Tanjung Benoa is a fairly sedate place, especially at night when the pleasures of Kuta and Seminyak are a bit of a hike (although there's one restaurant that draws people *to* Tanjung Benoa).

Orientation & Information

Restaurants and hotels are strung out all along Jl Pratama, which runs the length of the peninsula. It may be one of the most perilous streets in South Bali for a stroll. From the Nusa Dua north gate north to the Conrad Hotel, there are no footpaths and in many places nowhere to walk but on the narrow road, which also has blind curves. Fortunately, the beach promenade is a wonderful alternative.

The police station is easy to find. There's middling internet access at **Man Dollow Internet Cafe** (Map p140; ☎ 748 3887; Jl Pratama). Other services can be found south in the Nusa Dua area.

Sights

Benoa is one of Bali's multidenominational corners, with an interesting **Chinese Buddhist temple** (Map p140), a **mosque** (Map p140) and a **Hindu temple** (Map p140) within 100m of each other. It's a fascinating little fishing town that makes for a good stroll. On the dark side, however, it is also the centre of Bali's illegal trade in turtles (p82).

Activities

Quite a few water-sports centres along Jl Pratama offer daytime diving, cruises, windsurfing and waterskiing. Check equipment and credentials before you sign up, as a few tourists have been killed frolicking here. Most centres have a thatched-roof bar and restaurant attached to their premises where prospective customers are given the hard sell. Each morning convoys of buses arrive from all over South Bali bringing day-trippers, and by 10am parasailers float over the water like goony birds looking for a place to crash.

Among the established water-sports operators are **Benoa Marine Recreation** (BMR; Map p140; ☎ 771757; www.bmrbali.com; Jl Pratama 99) and **Hot Dog** (Map p140; ☎ 778090; Jl Pratama). As if by magic, all operators have similar prices.

Water sports include the following:

Banana-boat rides (per 15 minutes US$30) Wild rides for two as you try to maintain your grasp on the inflatable fruit over the waves.

Diving With the operators mentioned, diving costs US$80/95 for one/two dives around Tanjung Benoa, including equipment rental; US$120 for two dives in Tulamben; and about US$400 for a three-day PADI open-water course. A minimum of two people is required for most dive trips and courses.

Glass-bottomed boat trips (60-minute tour with snack US$25) The non-wet way to see the denizens of the shallows.

Jet-skiing (per 15 minutes US$25) Big with people who like to go fast and belch smoke.

Parasailing (per round US$25) Popular; you float above the water while towed by a speedboat.

Snorkelling (per hour per person US$25) These trips include equipment and a boat ride to a reef (minimum two people).

COOKING SCHOOL

Bumbu Bali Cooking School (Map p140; ☎ 774502; Jl Pratama; classes US$75; ☺ 6am-3pm, Mon, Wed & Fri) Heinz von Holzen, who has done much to raise Bali's culinary profile to the greater world, runs a very popular cooking school. It starts with a 6am visit to Jimbaran's fascinating fish and village markets to buy goods, and finishes with lunch. Von Holzen shares his unique perspectives on life, food and more as the class progresses. It's almost a floor show.

Sleeping

The Conrad Resort is the notable high-end and high-profile hotel amid what are mostly midrange places aimed at groups. There's a dearth of small independent places with character. On the plus side, most of the beachside places are very family friendly and offer kids' programs.

BUDGET

Two places close to Benoa village offer no-frills accommodation across from the beach.

Tanjung Mekar (Map p140; ☎ 0812 363 1374; Jl Pratama; r 120,000-150,000Rp; ☒) Set in a little garden back from the street, this small family-run guesthouse has four simple, pleasant rooms, some with air-con.

Pondok Agung (Map p140; ☎ 771143; roland@eksa data.com; Jl Pratama; r 150,000-250,000Rp; ☒) The eight airy rooms (most with tubs) in a large houselike building are good value. Higher-priced rooms come with air-con and TV. The gardens are attractive and the staff are savvy.

MIDRANGE

Club Bali Mirage (Map p140; ☎ 772147; www.clubbali mirage.com; Jl Pratama 72; r from US$70; ☒ ☒) This compact, J-shaped resort has a good-sized freeform swimming pool. Palms shade the grounds and the beach is right out front. Rooms feature bold colours, the better to jolt you out of your jet lag – or hangover. All 98 rooms have balconies or terraces. All-inclusive plans are available.

Benoa Beachfront Villas (Map p140; ☎ 771634; www.thebenoavillas.com; Jl Pratama 15B; r US$90-140; 🔀 🍴 🖳) The 18 bungalow-style rooms of the Puri Benoa have been reborn as the Benoa Beachfront Villas. Rooms now sport a cream-and-dark-wood motif that you'd find in a Bali Style book. The outdoor bathrooms are airy. Given the rates, it's worth going for an oceanfront room.

Rumah Bali (Map p140; ☎ 771256; www.balifoods.com; Jl Pratama; r US$100-125, villas from US$250; 🔀 🍴 🖳 wi-fi) Rumah Bali is a luxurious interpretation of a Balinese village by Heinz von Holzen of Bumbu Bali fame (right). Guests have large family rooms or individual villas (some with three bedrooms) with their own plunge pools. There's a 'village centre' with a tasty warung, Pasar Malam (below). Besides a large communal pool, there's also a tennis court. The beach is a short walk away.

TOP END

Some top-end resorts are really time-share properties renting out rooms, while others are used almost exclusively by people on package tours.

Conrad Bali Resort (Map p140; ☎ 778788; www.conradhotels.com; Jl Pratama; r from US$200; 🔀 🍴 🖳 wi-fi) Tanjung Benoa's best hotel is from the luxury branch of the Hilton chain. It combines a Bali modern look with a refreshing, casual style. The 298 rooms are large and thoughtfully designed. Some units have patios with steps right down into the 33m pool, easing the morning dip. Bungalows have their own private lagoon and there is a large kids' club. Travellers regularly name the Conrad their favourite hotel in polls.

Eating & Drinking

Each hotel has several restaurants. There are also several tourist restaurants in or near Tanjung Benoa. On the border with Nusa Dua, some warung cater to hotel guests and offer good value for money, while several busy local warung are clustered around the police station in Benoa.

Pasar Malam (Map p140; ☎ 771256; Jl Pratama; dishes 20,000-70,000Rp) Inside Rumah Bali (above), this warung fulfils the role of the village market

eatery. There are local coffees, and exhibits and dishes celebrate the many forms of Balinese rice. The food is of the same high standard as that at Bumbu Bali.

Santorini (Map p140; ☎ 777942; Jl Pratama; meals 30,000-60,000Rp) A vision of white, this taverna brings the Greek Islands to the island of Bali. One of the more fun places on this street. The food is authentic – the wine too (not that that retsina is a plus…).

Tao (Map p140; ☎ 772902; Jl Pratama 96; mains 40,000-90,000Rp) You'd never know this airy beachfront club was part of the nearby Ramada Resort (except maybe when you see prices). The menu is mostly Thai – although that menu stalwart, the club sandwich, is there at the bottom. The preparation is inventive. Best of all, for the mere price of a drink you can use Tao's pool, beach loungers and other facilities.

our pick Bumbu Bali (Map p140; ☎ 774502; Jl Pratama; dishes 45,000-90,000Rp; ⏰ noon-9pm) One of the finest restaurants on the island, Bumbu Bali serves the best Balinese food you'll have during your visit. Long-time resident and cookbook author Heinz von Holzen, his wife Puji and enthusiastic staff serve exquisitely flavoured dishes. Many diners opt for one of several set menus (210,000Rp). The *rijsttafel* (selection of spiced rice dishes) shows the range of cooking in the kitchen, from satays served on their own little coconut-husk grill to the tender *be celeng base manis* (pork in sweet soy sauce) to the amazingly tasty and different *jaja batun bedil* (sticky dumpling rice in palm sugar), with a dozen more courses in between. Tables are set under the stars and in small pavilions. The sound of frogs can be heard from the fish ponds. There's complimentary transport in the area. It's wise to book.

Spice (Map p140; ☎ 778788; Conrad Resort, Jl Pratama; dishes 80,000-200,000Rp; ⏰ dinner) Has a grand setting atop the hotel with tables inside and out. Nusa Lembongan twinkles in the distance. Service is excellent; the wine list voluminous. Chef Richard Millar's menu is a kaleidoscope of tastes from Asia, India and beyond.

Getting There & Around

Taxis from the airport cost 100,000Rp. Take a bemo to Bualu, then take one of the infrequent green bemo that shuttle up and down Jl Pratama (3000Rp) – after about 3pm bemo become really scarce on both routes. A metered taxi will be much easier and quicker. Or stroll the beach promenade.

SANUR

☎ 0361

Maybe Sanur is the Bali beachfront version of the youngest of the Three Bears, the one that's not too frantic (like Kuta) or too snoozy (like Nusa Dua). Many do indeed consider Sanur 'just right' (and don't befall the fate of Goldilocks), as it lacks most of the hassles found to the west while it has a good mix of restaurants and bars that aren't all owned by a hotel.

The beach, while thin, is protected by a reef and breakwaters, so families appreciate the limpid waves. Sanur has a good range of places to stay and it's well placed for day trips around the south, and north to Ubud. Really, it doesn't at all deserve its local moniker, 'Snore'.

HISTORY

Inscriptions on a stone pillar found near modern Sanur tell of King Sri Kesari Varma, who came to Bali to teach Buddhism in AD 913.

Sanur was one of the places favoured by Westerners during their pre-WWII discovery of Bali. Artists Miguel Covarrubias, Adrien Jean Le Mayeur and Walter Spies, anthropologist Jane Belo and choreographer Katharane Mershon all spent time here. The first simple tourist bungalows appeared in Sanur in the 1940s and 1950s, and more artists, including Australian Donald Friend (whose antics earned him the nickname Lord Devil Donald), made their homes in Sanur. This early popularity made Sanur a likely locale for Bali's first big tourist hotel, the Soekarno-era Grand Bali Beach Hotel.

During this period, Sanur was ruled by insightful priests and scholars, who recognised both the opportunities and the threats presented by the expanding tourism. Properly horrified at the high-rise Grand Bali Beach Hotel, they imposed the famous rule that no building could be higher than a coconut palm. They also established village cooperatives that owned land and ran tourist businesses, ensuring that a good share of the economic benefits remained in the community.

The priestly influence remains strong, and Sanur is one of the few communities still ruled by members of the Brahmana caste. It is known as a home of sorcerers and healers, and a centre for both black and white magic. The black-and-white chequered cloth known

as *kain poleng*, which symbolises the balance of good and evil, is emblematic of Sanur.

ORIENTATION

Sanur stretches for about 5km along an east-facing coastline, with the lush and green landscaped grounds of resorts fronting right onto the sandy beach. West of the beachfront hotels is the busy main drag, Jl Danau Tamblingan, with hotel entrances and oodles of tourist shops, restaurants and cafés.

Noxious Jl Ngurah Rai, commonly called Bypass Rd, skirts the western side of the resort area, and is the main link to Kuta and the airport.

INFORMATION
Bookshops
Periplus (☎ 282790; Hardy's Supermarket, Jl Danau Tamblingan 136) Good selection of glossy books, bestsellers and periodicals.

Emergency
Police station (☎ 288597; Jl Ngurah Rai)

Internet Access
Most hotels have some form of internet access. Many cafés and bars listed in this section have wi-fi.

Medical Services
Guardian Pharmacy (☎ 284343; Jl Danau Tamblingan 134) The chain pharmacy has a doctor on call.

Money
Moneychangers here have a dubious reputation. There are numerous ATMs along Jl Danau Tamblingan and several banks.

Post
Post office (☎ 754012; Jl Danau Buyan; 🕑 8am-7pm Mon-Sat) Located west of Jl Ngurah Rai.

SANUR'S ENVIRONMENTAL HUB

PPLH Bali (Pusat Pendidikan Lingkungan Hidup; ☎ 288221; www.pplhbali.or.id; Jl Hang Tuah 24) organises a broad range of environmental and educational programs and has a library and resource centre. Among the current programs is a 'green school' initiative to teach schoolchildren about the need to protect Bali's environment. Visitors are welcome.

SOUTH BALI

SIGHTS

Sanur's **beachfront walk** was the first in Bali and from day one has been delighting locals and visitors alike. Over 4km long, it follows the sand south as it curves to the west. Oodles of cafés with tables in the sand will give you plenty of reason to pause. Look for ferries crossing Selat Badung between Sanur and mysterious Nusa Penida. Offshore you'll see gnarled fishermen in woven bamboo hats standing in the shallows rod-fishing for a living. At the northern end of the beach, elderly men gather at sunrise for *meditasi* – swimming and baking in the black volcanic sand found only at that end of the beach.

A few highlights: just north of the Bali Hyatt are the kind of lavish villas you wished your friends owned. This was the centre of expat life when Donald Friend ruled the roost (p145). Just south of the Hyatt is a long area where multihued **fishing boats** are pulled ashore and repaired under the trees. And look for surprises like a cow grazing next to a luxury resort or a bored beach-activities tout carving beautifully elaborate designs in the sand.

In keeping with the local demeanour, the white-sand **beach** is sheltered by a reef and the surf is sedate. At low tide the beach is wide, but the water is shallow and you have to pick your way out over rocks and coral through knee-deep water. At high tide the swimming is fine, but the beach is narrow and almost nonexistent in places. The hulking Inna Grand Bali Beach Hotel, located at the northern end of the strip, fronts the best stretch of beach.

Just south of Jl Kesumasari there are simple warung, which rent loungers for 10,000Rp and battered kayaks for 20,000Rp.

Museum Le Mayeur

The Belgian artist Adrien Jean Le Mayeur de Merpes (1880–1958) arrived in Bali in 1932. Three years later, he met and married the beautiful Legong dancer Ni Polok when she was just 15. They lived in this compound, which houses the museum, when Sanur was still a quiet fishing village. The main house must have been delightful – a peaceful and elegant home filled with art and antiques right by the tranquil beach. After the artist's death, Ni Polok lived in the house until she died in 1985. The house is an interesting example of Balinese-style architecture – notice the beautifully carved window shutters that recount the story of Rama and Sita from the *Ramayana*.

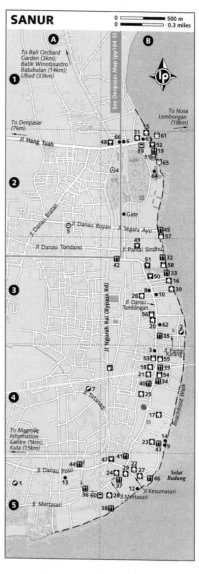

Despite security (some Le Mayeur paintings have sold for US$150,000) and conservation problems, almost 90 Le Mayeur paintings are displayed inside the **museum** (☎ 286201; adult/child 2000/1000Rp; ☺ 7.30am-3.30pm) in a naturalistic Balinese interior of woven fibres. Some of Le Mayeur's early works are Impressionist paintings from his travels in

INFORMATION		
French Consulate	1	A5
German Consulate	2	B3
Guardian Pharmacy	3	B4
Periplus	(see 39)	
Police Station	4	B2
Post Office	5	A2
PPLH Bali	6	B2
UK Consulate	7	A4

SIGHTS & ACTIVITIES		
Cheeky Monkeys	8	B3
Crystal Divers	(see 18)	
Fishing Boat Area	9	B4
Jamu Traditional Spa	10	B3
Museum Le Mayeur	11	B2
Simple Warung	12	B5
Stone Pillar	13	A5
Surya Water Sports	14	B4

SLEEPING		
Ananda Beach Hotel	15	B2
Anjani	16	B3
Bali Hyatt	17	B4
Crystal Santai Hotel	18	B4
Diwangkara Beach Hotel	19	B2
Flashbacks	20	B3
Hotel Bali Rita	21	B4
Hotel Palm Garden	22	B5

Hotel Segara Agung	23	B4
Jade Villas	24	B5
Jati Homestay	25	B4
Keke Homestay	26	B3
Kesumasari	27	B5
Puri Santrian	28	B5
Stana Puri Gopa Hotel	29	B5
Tandjung Sari	30	B3
Watering Hole I	31	B2

EATING		
Beach Café	32	B3
Bonsai Cafe	33	B3
Café Batu Jimbar	34	B4
Café Smorgås	35	B3
Cat & Fiddle	36	A5
Char Ming	37	B5
Denata Minang	(see 47)	
Donald's Beach Café	38	B5
Hardy's Supermarket	39	B4
Lumut	40	B4
Massimo	41	B5
Organic Market	(see 54)	
Pasar Sindhu Night Market	42	B3
Porch Café	(see 20)	
Sanur Bay	43	B4
Sari Bundo	44	A5
Spirit Café	45	B2
Stiff Chili	46	B5

DRINKING		
Café Billiard	47	B5
Jazz Bar & Grille	48	B2
Kalimantan	49	B3
Piccadilly	50	B3
Street Cafe	51	B3
Sunrise Bar & Grill	52	B2

SHOPPING		
Body Talk	53	B4
Gudang Keramic	54	B4
Hardy's Supermarket	(see 39)	
Hug A Bug	55	B4
Nogo	56	B3
Pasar Sindhu Art Market	(see 42)	
Sanur Beach Market	57	B2
Shindu Beach Market	58	B3

TRANSPORT		
Bemo Stop	59	B2
Bemo Stop	60	A5
Boats to Nusa Lembongan & Nusa Penida	61	B2
Gilicat Office	62	B3
Perama Office	63	B2
Qantas	64	B2
Scoot Departures	65	B2
Scoot Office	66	B2
Thai Airways	(see 64)	

SOUTH BALI

Africa, India, the Mediterranean and the South Pacific. Paintings from his early period in Bali are romantic depictions of daily life and beautiful Balinese women – often Ni Polok. The works from the 1950s are in much better condition and show fewer signs of wear and tear, displaying the vibrant colours that later became popular with young Balinese artists. Look for the haunting black-and-white photos of Ni Polok.

Bali Orchid Garden

Given Bali's warm weather and rich volcanic soil, no one should be surprised that orchids thrive in abundance here. At this **garden** (Map p132; ☎ 466010; Coast Rd; admission 50,000Rp; ◷ 8am-6pm) you can see thousands of orchids in a variety of settings. It's 3km north of Sanur along Jl Ngurah Rai, just past the major intersection with the coast road.

Stone Pillar

The pillar, down a narrow lane to the left as you face Pura Belangjong, is Bali's oldest dated artefact and has ancient inscriptions recounting military victories of more than a thousand years ago. These inscriptions are in Sanskrit and are evidence of Hindu influence 300 years before the arrival of the Majapahit court.

ACTIVITIES

Much activity is centred on or near the beach, where families frolic. However if you're ready to take a holiday from the little ones, **Cheeky Monkeys** (☎ 282420; www.cheekymonkeysbali.com; Jl Danau Tamblingan 82; ◷ 8.30am-4pm) offers day care, babysitting, playgroups, art lessons and more for junior travellers-in-training age six and under. Sessions cost from 35,000Rp.

Surfing

Sanur's fickle breaks (tide conditions often don't produce waves) are offshore along the reef. The best area is called **Sanur Reef**, a right break in front of the Inna Grand Bali Beach Hotel. Another good spot is known as the **Hyatt Reef**, in front of, you guessed it, the Bali Hyatt. You can get a fishing boat out to the breaks for 200,000Rp per hour. See p96 for more details on these surf breaks.

Diving

The diving near Sanur is not great, but the reef has a good variety of fish and offers quite good snorkelling. Sanur is a good departure point for dive trips to Nusa Lembongan.

Among several good options, **Crystal Divers** (☎ 286737; www.crystal-divers.com; Jl Danau Tamblingan 168; intro dives from US$25) is a slick diving operation and has its own hotel, Crystal Santai Hotel (p148), and a large diving pool right outside the office. Recommended for beginners, the shop offers a long list of courses, including PADI open-water for US$425.

Water Sports

Various water sports are offered at kiosks along the beach: close to Museum Le Mayeur; near Sanur Beach Market; and at **Surya Water Sports** (☎ 287956; www.suryadive.com; Jl Duyung 10), which is the largest. You can go parasailing (US$20 per go), snorkelling by boat (US$30, two hours), windsurfing (US$30, one hour), or enjoy a two-tank dive at the nearby reef (US$50).

Spas

Most of the large beachside hotels have spas. **Jamu Traditional Spa** (☎ 286595; www.jamutraditional spa.com; Jl Danau Tamblingan 41; massage from US$45) has a beautifully carved teak-and-stone entry that sets the mood. This gracious spa offers a range of treatments including a popular Earth Essence Bust Treatment and a Kemiri Nut Scrub.

SLEEPING

Usually the best places to stay are right on the beach; however, beware of properties that have been coasting for decades. Modest budgets will find comfort on the nonbeach side of Jl Danau Tamblingan.

If you find yourself at the mercy of a travel agent, don't let them book you into the Inna Grand Bali Beach Hotel, which is past its prime.

Budget

Keke Homestay (☎ 287282; Jl Danau Tamblingan 96; r 60,000-135,000Rp; 😊) Set 150m down a *gang* (alley) from the noisy road, Keke welcomes backpackers into its genial family. The seven quiet, clean rooms vary from fan-only to air-con cool.

Watering Hole I (☎ 288289; www.wateringholesanur bali.com; Jl Hang Tuah 37; r 60,000-150,000Rp; 😊 🖥) In the northern part of Sanur, the Hole is a busy, friendly place close to the Nusa Lembongan boats. It has 20 pleasant, clean rooms; the cheapest having fan cooling and cold water. There's a sister Watering Hole at the south end of Jl Tamblingan.

Ananda Beach Hotel (☎ 288327; Jl Hang Tuah 143; r US$15-35; 😊 🖥) Built around a large shrine and right on the beach, the Ananda has slightly dark rooms that are a jumble of old furniture. Deluxe room number 7 has a nice balcony with sea views; some of the 16 others are fan-only.

GETTING HIGH OVER SANUR

Travelling South Bali you can't help but notice scores of kites overhead much of the year. These creations are often huge (10m or more in length, with tails stretching another 100m) and fly at altitudes that worry pilots. Many have noisemakers that make eerie humming and buzzing noises. Like much in Bali there are spiritual roots: the kites are meant to figuratively whisper into the ears of the gods suggestions that abundant harvests might be nice. But for many Balinese, these high-fliers are simply a really fun hobby.

Each July, hundreds of Balinese and international teams descend – as it were – on Sanur for the **Bali Kite Festival**. They compete for an array of honours in such categories as original design and flight endurance.

Kesumasari (☎ 287824; Jl Kesumasari 6; r fan/air-con 175,000/250,000Rp; 😊) The only thing between you and the beach is a small shrine. Beyond the lounging porches, the multihued carved Balinese doors don't prepare you for the riot of colour inside the 11 idiosyncratic rooms.

Crystal Santai Hotel (☎ 286737; www.crystal -divers.com; Jl Danau Tamblingan 168; r fan/air-con US$20/30; 😊 🖥 🖵) HQ for Crystal Dive (p147). A two-storey building forms an L around the pool where divers literally get their feet wet. The 18 rooms are large and clean.

Jati Homestay (☎ 281730; www.hoteljatiandhome stay.com; Jl Danau Tamblingan 168; r 200,000Rp; 🖵) Jati means 'genuine' and you will feel right at home at this attractive inn. The 15 bungalow-style rooms are situated in pretty grounds; some of the units have small kitchens.

Hotel Bali Rita (☎ 282630; balirita@hotmail.com; Jl Danau Tamblingan 174; r 250,000Rp; 😊) Lovely Rita is tailor-made for those who want a traditional-style bungalow room in a nice garden. The 12 rooms here are large, with big fridges and tubs in open-air bathrooms. You've nothing to fear from meter maids at this secluded compound well off busy Jl Danau Tamblingan. The beach is 10 minutes east.

Midrange

our pick **Flashbacks** (☎ 281682; www.flashbacks-chb .com; Jl Danau Tamblingan 106; s/d 145,000/165,000Rp, bungalows 335,000/360,000Rp; 😊 🖵) This welcoming place has nine rooms that vary greatly in size. The better ones are bungalows or suites while more modest rooms share bathrooms and have cold water. The lovely design takes a lot of cues from traditional Balinese style. Porch Café (p150) is out front.

Hotel Segara Agung (☎ 288446; www.segaraagung .com; Jl Duyung 43; r US$25-50; 🆒 🕹 🖳) Down a quiet, sandy lane lined with villas, the hotel is only a three-minute walk from the beach. The 16 rooms are clean though spartan; the cheapest are fan and cold-water only. The big swimming pool is private.

Hotel Palm Garden (Taman Palem; ☎ 287041; www .palmgarden-bali.com; Jl Kesumasari 3; r from 275,000Rp; 🆒 🕹) Everything is low-key here, from the 17 large rooms (with satellite TVs and fridges) to the relaxed service and pretty grounds. It's one minute to the beach; there is a nice medium-sized pool with a small waterfall.

Anjani (☎ 289567; alit_suarta@hotmail.com; Jl Danau Tamblingan 31; r 350,000Rp; 🆒) Nearly lost amid larger beachside hotels (and its own overgrown grounds), the Anjani has six basic bungalow-style rooms on a narrow plot right on the beach. The units are barebones but do have basic kitchens and padded headboards for headbangers.

Stana Puri Gopa Hotel (☎ 289948; www.puri gopabali.com; Jl Kesumasari 4; r US$35-55; 🆒 🕹) This 24-room hotel has traditional Balinese architecture, large bathrooms (some with large tubs), solid teak furniture and a small pool. It's a two-minute walk from the beach, which you can see from a few rooms.

Diwangkara Beach Hotel (☎ 288577; www.holiday villahotelbali.com; Jl Hang Tuah 54; r US$65, villas US$90-180; 🆒 🕹 🖳 wi-fi) Facing the beach near the end of Jl Hang Tuah, this 38-unit hotel has traditional Balinese architecture and richly decorated rooms. You can smell the thatching. Pool villas have their own plunge pool right off a wooden terrace.

Top End

Puri Santrian (☎ 288009; www.santrian.com; Jl Mertasari; r from US$110, bungalows from US$150; 🆒 🕹 🖳) Lush gardens, three large pools with fountains, a tennis court and beach frontage, as well as 184 comfortable, well-equipped rooms make this a popular choice. Many rooms are in older-style bungalows, others in two- and three-storey blocks. Floating *bale* (traditional pavilions) in the ocean provide breezy relief from midday heat.

Bali Hyatt (☎ 281234; www.bali.resort.hyatt.com; Jl Danau Tamblingan; r US$160-400; 🆒 🕹 🖳 wi-fi) The Made Wijaya–designed gardens are an attraction themselves at this 390-room beachfront resort. Hibiscus, wild ginger, lotus and more than 600 species of plants and animals can be found here. Rooms are comfortable; note that balconies shrink on higher floors. Regency Club rooms come with free drinks and food in a serene pavilion. The two pools are vast, and one has a waterfall-shrouded snogging cave.

Tandjung Sari (☎ 288441; www.tandjungsari.com; Jl Danau Tamblingan 29; bungalows US$170-270; 🆒 🕹 🖳 wi-fi) The mature trees along the shaded driveway set the gracious tone at this Sanur veteran, which was one of the first Balinese boutique hotels. Like a good tree, it has flourished since its start in 1967 and continues to be lauded for its artful design. The 26 traditional-style bungalows are superbly decorated with crafts and antiques. At night, lights in the trees above the pool are magical. The gracious staff are a delight. Balinese dance classes are taught by one of Bali's best dancers (see p150).

Jade Villas (☎ 284069; www.balijadevillas.com; Jl Danau Tamblingan; villas US$180-300; 🆒 🕹 🖳) This low-key condo development at the south end of Sanur is a five-minute walk from the beach. The nine units are large, private and have their own pools. The decor is basic and comfortable; there's broadband internet in each. If you decide to linger, you can buy your unit starting at US$200,000.

EATING

Dine on the beach in a traditional open-air pavilion or in a genial bar – the choice is yours in Sanur. Although there are plenty of uninspired choices on Jl Danau Tamblingan, there are also some gems. Many of the places listed under Drinking (p151) also do food.

For groceries and personal items, there's a large **Hardy's Supermarket** (☎ 285806; Jl Danau Tamblingan 136). Nearby is the gourmet market of Café Batu Jimbar (p151).

On Sundays, there's an **organic market** (Jl Danau Tamblingan; ☷ 10am-2pm) in Gudang Keramik parking lot.

The **Pasar Sindhu night market** (off Jl Danau Tamblingan; ☷ 6am-midnight) sells fresh vegetables, dried fish, pungent spices and various household goods.

SOUTH BALI

A CLASSIC BALINESE DANCER

Since 1970 Nyoman Supadmi has taught thousands of women the precise moves and elaborate choreography demanded by classic Balinese dances such as Legong. And the key word is classic, as she has become a major force against the dilution of the island's great dances by what she dismisses as 'modernity'.

And just what is this aberration that brings such a frown to her otherwise serene face? Well, she demonstrates. 'The basic moves of classic dance require enormous discipline,' she says as she slips into the rigid pose with splayed arms and wide eyes that is immediately recognisable to anyone who has seen a performance.

Continuing, she says, 'Modern is like this,' and slumps into a slouch that would do any slacker proud. Still, she understands the allure of the modern. 'It's much easier to learn and people have so many distractions that they can't find the time to learn the old ways.'

'My teachers emphasised the basics,' says Nyoman, whose dancer mother provided her with a private tutor. 'Your hand went here and your bottom here,' a statement backed up by a seemingly simple shift of position in her chair that leaves no doubt of her meaning.

'Today people just approximate the position.'

Should you want to assume the proper position, Nyoman Supadmi offers dance lessons through the Tandjung Sari (p149).

Beach

The beach path offers restaurants, warung and bars where you can catch a meal, a drink or a sea breeze. There are usually places near the end of each road that leads to the beach. Sunset drink specials are common (though the beach faces east, so you'll need to enjoy the reflected glow off Nusa Penida).

Donald's Beach Café (☎ 287637; Beachfront Walk; mains 20,000-50,000Rp) If this were owned by Donald Trump, the site would no doubt be condo-ised in a New York minute. And that would be a shame, as the mature trees here shade tables with great views out to sea. The timeless (timeworn?) menu comprises Indo standards, pizza and burgers.

Stiff Chili (☎ 288371; Jl Kesumasari; mains 20,000-60,000Rp) Besides the evocative name, this beachside café has fine views. Pizza and pasta head the surprisingly ambitious menu.

Spirit Café (☎ 285908; Paradise Plaza; dishes 20,000-60,000Rp) This vaguely new-agey place has wide beach views. Smoothies, juices and veggie sandwiches highlight the small but creative menu. Try the carrot cake.

Bonsai Cafe (☎ 282908; Jl Danau Tamblingan 27; dishes 20,000-60,000Rp) Order from a long list of beach-café standards while chilling in comfy and shady wicker chairs. Then wander inland for a surprise: hundreds of the café's namesake plants growing small in a rather sensational formal garden.

Beach Café (☎ 282875; Beachfront Walk; mains 25,000-50,000Rp; wi-fi) Brings a bit of Med style to the Sanur beach cliché of palm fronds and plastic chairs. Zone out on wicker sofas or hang on a low cushion on the sand. Enjoy salads and seafood.

Sanur Bay (☎ 288153; Jl Duyung; 25,000-50,000Rp) You can hear the surf and see the moonlight reflecting on the water at this classic beachside seafood grill, set on the sand amid fishing boats.

Jl Danau Tamblingan

Porch Café (☎ 281682; Jl Danau Tamblingan; mains from 20,000Rp) Fronting Flashbacks, a charmer of a small hotel, this newish café is housed in a traditional wooden building replete with the namesake porch. Snuggle up to a table out front or shut it all out in the air-con inside. The menu is a tasty mix of comfort food like burgers and freshly baked goods. There's a long list of fresh juices. It's popular for breakfast.

Café Smorgås (☎ 289361; Jl Danau Tamblingan; mains from 20,000Rp) Set back from traffic, this sprightly eatery has nice wicker chairs outside and cool air-con inside. The menu has a healthy bent: try a detox drink (the opposite of fun for many…) and then live it up with quiche or carrot cake.

Lumut (☎ 270009; Jl Danau Tamblingan; dishes 25,000-80,000Rp; ✆ 10am-10pm) This gracious 2nd-floor open-air café is set back from the road. The emphasis is on fresh seafood and Indonesian fare. Service is stylish and should be: part of the complex is a high-end housewares store.

Café Batu Jimbar (☎ 287374; Jl Danau Tamblingan 152; dishes 30,000-60,000Rp) This popular top-end café has a large wooden patio out front and an airy dining room. The baked goods on display compete for attention with the ice-cream case. Besides the best banana smoothie in Bali, the menu has Indonesian classics as well as smattering of other items.

Massimo (☎ 288942; Jl Danau Tamblingan 206; dishes 30,000-125,000Rp) The interior at this authentic Italian restaurant is like an open-air Milan café while the outside is a Balinese garden. The lengthy menu includes wood-fired pizzas. The scent of garlic pours out onto the street, where you can stop and get a gelato from a window.

our pick Char Ming (☎ 288029; www.charming -bali.com; Jl Danau Tamblingan 97; mains 40,000-100,000Rp; ☽ noon-10pm) Barbecue with a French accent. A daily menu-board lists the fresh seafood available for grilling. Other dishes include plenty of pork and beef. The highly stylised location features lush plantings and carved-wood details and antiques inside and out. Much of the structure was built from wood reclaimed from old boats and structures.

South Sanur

Sari Bundo (☎ 281389; Jl Danau Poso; dishes 5,000-10,000Rp; ☽ 24hr) This spotless and simple Padang-style joint serves the best curry chicken in Sanur.

Denata Minang (Jl Danau Poso; meals 10,000Rp) One of the better Padang-style warung, it's located just west of Café Billiard. Like its brethren, it has fab *ayam* (chicken) in myriad spicy forms – only better.

Cat & Fiddle (☎ 282218; Jl Cemara 36; dishes 30,000-80,000Rp) Look for Brit standards like proper breakfasts and pork pies on the menu at this open-air pub that's – not surprisingly – popular with expats. Surprises include the 'Blarnyschnitzel', which is made with chicken.

DRINKING

Many of Sanur's drinking establishments cater to retired expats and are, thankfully for them, air-conditioned. This is not a place where things go late. Note that many places to eat are good for drinks and vice versa.

Note that Sanur is known as a haven for prostitution. You won't find any in the public bars – except for a couple of dubious ones near Jl Segara Ayu – but along Jl Danau Poso there are numerous huge and discreet brothels that are given away only by the constant traffic.

Café Billiard (☎ 281215; Jl Danau Poso; ☽ noon-1am) It's expat heaven! Play billiards and toss down cheap draughts of Heineken until your pension cheque is gone! It's a merry place where you lose your hat on the way home and wake up wishing to be asleep.

Jazz Bar & Grille (☎ 285892; Kompleks Sanur 15, Jl Ngurah Rai; ☽ 10am-2am; ☒) Offers live jazz and/or pop most nights and even a couple of tables out front. The menu features Mexican and Mediterranean dishes (30,000Rp to 80,000Rp).

Kalimantan (☎ 289291; Jl Pantai Sindhu 11) AKA Borneo Bob's, this veteran boozer is one of many casual joints on this street. Enjoy cheap drinks under the palms or squint at live American football on the satellite TV. You can have a bite to eat too (dishes 15,000Rp to 55,000Rp).

Piccadilly (☎ 289138; Jl Danau Tamblingan 27; ☽ 9am-midnight; wi-fi) Like Kuta's notorious Paddy's bar only without the spectre of something communicable. Cheery expats enjoy pints of draught Bintang while pondering satellite sports channels. Totally open to street life; passersby can enjoy the '70s rock. Or not.

Street Cafe (☎ 289259; Jl Danau Tamblingan 21; wi-fi) A street bar that verges on stylish, with a modern, airy vibe and a choice of loungers, stools or tables. Instead of sports on TV, groove to the live piano music here most nights. Sink your teeth into a menu of steaks (average 65,000Rp).

Sunrise Bar & Grill (☎ 0813 3809 0486; Beachfront Walk) This aptly named beachside bar has tables and chairs on the sand, which will cushion your fall should your over-indulge on the signature – and potent – *arak* drinks. Of course, hearing Bob Marley here – one more time! – may drive you to drink.

SHOPPING

Sanur is no Seminyak (p126) in the shopping department, although a few designers from there are opening branches here. You can kill an afternoon browsing the length of Jl Danau Tamblingan.

Body Talk (☎ 270046; Jl Danau Tamblingan 156) Ultra-comfortable women's wear in cotton and other relaxing fibres. Everything stretches right with you. The custom tailoring has fans not just in Bali but among expats across the archipelago.

Gudang Keramik (☎ 289363; Jl Danau Tamblingan) The outlet store for Jenggala Keramik Bali in Jimbaran (p135) has amazing prices on the firm's gorgeous tableware and decorator items. What's called 'seconds' here would be firsts everywhere else.

Hug A Bug (☎ 288445; Jl Danau Tamblingan 71) This ant-sized shop is as cute as the little buggers who drag their mums here. Clothes, hand-made toys, doll's houses, puppets and more. There's not an insipid DVD or numbskull video game in sight.

Nogo (☎ 288765; Jl Danau Tamblingan 100) Look for the wooden loom out front of this classy store, which bills itself as the 'Bali Ikat Centre'. The goods are gorgeous and easy to savour in the air-con comfort.

Souvenirs

For souvenirs, try the numerous shops on the main street, or one of the various 'art markets'. **Sanur Beach Market** (off Jl Segara Ayu) has a wide selection. **Pasar Sindhu Art Market** (off Jl Danau Tamblingan) and the mazelike **Shindu Beach Market** (south of Jl Pantai Sindhu) have numerous stalls selling T-shirts, sarongs, woodcarvings and other tatty items.

Hardy's Supermarket (☎ 285806; Jl Danau Tamblingan 136) has a range of goods on its 2nd floor at very good prices.

GETTING THERE & AWAY
Bemo

The public bemo stops are at the southern end of Sanur on Jl Mertasari, and just outside the main entrance to the Inna Grand Bali Beach Hotel on Jl Hang Tuah. You can hail a bemo anywhere along Jl Danau Tamblingan and Jl Danau Poso – although drivers will first try to hail you.

Green bemo go along Jl Hang Tuah to the Kereneng terminal in Denpasar (7000Rp).

Boat

Public boats and the Perama boat (p158) to Nusa Lembongan leave from the beach at the end of Jl Hang Tuah. The fast Scoot boat has an **office** (☎ 285522; Jl Hang Tuah) in Sanur; boats depart from a nearby portion of beach. See p158 for details on the trips. None of these services uses a dock – be prepared to wade to the boat.

Gilicat (☎ 271680; www.gilicat.com; Jl Danau Tamblingan 51) has a Sanur office for its departures to Lombok. See p355 for details.

Tourist Shuttle Bus

The **Perama office** (☎ 285592; Jl Hang Tuah 39; ⏲ 7am-10pm) is at Warung Pojok at the northern end of town. It runs shuttles to the following destinations, most only once daily.

Destination	Fare	Duration
Candidasa	60,000Rp	2¾hr
Kuta	25,000Rp	15min
Lovina	125,000Rp	4hr
Padangbai	60,000Rp	2½hr
Ubud	40,000Rp	1hr

GETTING AROUND

Bemo go up and down Jl Danau Tamblingan and Jl Danau Poso for 4000Rp. Metered taxis can be flagged down in the street, or call **Bali Taxi** (☎ 701111).

SOUTH OF SANUR

PULAU SERANGAN

Otherwise known as Turtle Island, Pulau Serangan is an example of all that can go wrong with Bali's environment. Originally it was a small 100-hectare island offshore of the mangroves to the south of Sanur. However, in the 1990s it was selected by Soeharto's infamous son Tommy as a site for new development. Soon heavy machinery appeared and much of the original island was obliterated while a new landfill area over 300 hectares in size was grafted on. A new causeway was built to the mainland and plans were drawn for hotels, condos etc. The Asian economic crisis pulled the plug on the scheme until recently, when the heavy equipment began moving again. Exactly what form the new development will take is unclear, but it's big.

Meanwhile on the original part of the island the two small and poor fishing villages, Ponjok and Dukuh, are still there, as is one of Bali's holiest temples, **Pura Sakenan**, just east of the causeway. Architecturally it is insignificant, but major festivals attract huge crowds of devotees, especially during the Kuningan festival (see p336).

You can visit the irregular **surf break** (see p96 for details on the surfing) at the southern end of the landfill area, but you have to check in at a construction gate and then drive across a crushed limestone wasteland that looks like a war zone. A few warung supply drinks to the hardy.

Perhaps the best reason to visit is the **Turtle Conservation and Education Centre** (Map p132; ☎ 0813 3841 2716; donation requested; ☟ 9am-5pm). Follow the signs to what was once a beach and you'll find a small complex where turtle eggs are hatched for return to the sea while injured adult turtles are kept in tanks to heal. See p82 for more on the controversies surrounding Bali's turtles.

MANGROVE INFORMATION CENTRE

Southwest of Sanur you'll find vast mangroves covering 600 hectares and stretching almost to Kuta. Learn about this vital yet abused resource at the **Mangrove Information Centre** (Map p132; ☎ 0361-726969; admission 50,000Rp, parking 50,000Rp; ☟ 8am-4pm Mon-Fri). The Japanese-funded centre studies ways to preserve the health of mangroves, which are vital to filtering much of the island's ever-growing run-off, even as they choke on the volume of pollution.

Start your visit at the visitor centre, which has tanks filled with various species of mangrove critters – although the most common one, the plastic bag, is missing. Next follow a 1.5km signposted boardwalk to a beach. Finally, stop off and help plant a mangrove tree.

Look for the centre's signs 5km west of Sanur. It's 1.5km south of Jl Ngurah Rai Bypass.

BENOA HARBOUR

Bali's main port is at the entrance of Teluk Benoa (Benoa Bay), the wide but shallow body east of the airport runway. Benoa Harbour (Map p132) is on the northern side of the bay – a square of docks and port buildings on reclaimed land, linked to mainland Bali by a 2km causeway. It's referred to as Benoa port or Benoa Harbour to distinguish it from Benoa village, on the south side of the bay.

Benoa Harbour is the port for tourist day-trip boats to Nusa Lembongan and for Pelni ships to other parts of Indonesia; however, its shallow depth prevents cruise ships from calling.

Public bemo (7000Rp) leave from Sanglah terminal in Denpasar. A taxi from Kuta or Sanur should cost around 35,000Rp one way, plus the toll.

For more information on cruises to Nusa Lembongan from Benoa Harbour, see p156.

NUSA LEMBONGAN & ISLANDS

Look towards the open ocean southeast of Bali and the hazy bulk of Nusa Penida dominates the view. But for many visitors the real focus is Nusa Lembongan, which lurks in the shadow of its vastly larger neighbour. Here there's great surfing, quiet white beaches and the kind of funky vibe travellers cherish. It's a popular destination and justly so – it's the one excursion you should make while in Bali.

Nusa Penida is seldom visited, which means that its dramatic vistas and unchanged village life are yours to explore. Tiny Nusa Ceningan huddles between the larger islands. It is an interesting quick jaunt from Lembongan.

The islands have been a poor region for many years. Thin soils and a lack of fresh water do not permit the cultivation of rice, but other crops such as maize, cassava and beans are staples grown here. The main cash crop, however, is seaweed (p155).

NUSA LEMBONGAN
☎ 0366

It's the Bali many imagine but never find: simple rooms on the beach, cheap beers with incredible sunsets, days spent surfing and diving, and nights spent riffling through a favourite book or hanging with new friends.

Nusa Lembongan grows in popularity each year, but even as rooms for travellers proliferate, it remains a very mellow place. The 7000 hard-working locals welcome the extra money brought by visitors and time is marked by the crow of a rooster and the fall of a coconut.

Orientation

Most surfers, divers and budget travellers stay at Jungutbatu Beach in the island's northwest, while more upmarket accommodation is further south towards Mushroom Bay, where many of the day-trip cruise boats stop.

About 4km southwest along the sealed road from Jungutbatu is Lembongan village, the island's other town. Leaving Jungutbatu, when heading towards Lembongan village, you climb up a steep knoll that offers a wonderful view back over the beach.

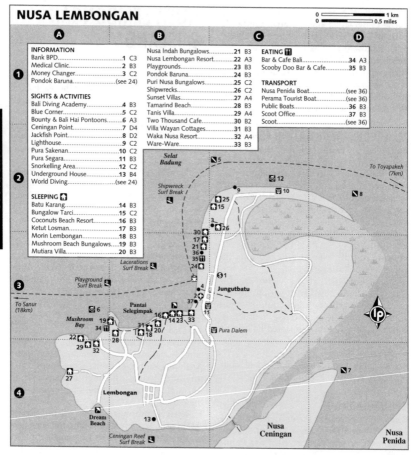

NUSA LEMBONGAN

INFORMATION
Bank BPD.................................**1** C3
Medical Clinic...........................**2** B3
Money Changer.......................**3** C2
Pondok Baruna....................(see 24)

SIGHTS & ACTIVITIES
Bali Diving Academy.................**4** B3
Blue Corner.............................**5** C2
Bounty & Bali Hai Pontoons.....**6** A3
Ceningan Point........................**7** D4
Jackfish Point..........................**8** D2
Lighthouse..............................**9** C2
Pura Sakenan.........................**10** C2
Pura Segara...........................**11** B3
Snorkelling Area......................**12** C2
Underground House.................**13** B4
World Diving......................(see 24)

SLEEPING
Batu Karang...........................**14** B3
Bungalow Tarci.......................**15** C2
Coconuts Beach Resort...........**16** B3
Ketut Losman.........................**17** B3
Morin Lembongan...................**18** B3
Mushroom Beach Bungalows....**19** B3
Mutiara Villa..........................**20** B3

Nusa Indah Bungalows............**21** B3
Nusa Lembongan Resort..........**22** A3
Playgrounds...........................**23** B3
Pondok Baruna.......................**24** B3
Puri Nusa Bungalows...............**25** C2
Shipwrecks.............................**26** C2
Sunset Villas..........................**27** A4
Tamarind Beach......................**28** B3
Tanis Villa..............................**29** A4
Two Thousand Cafe.................**30** B2
Villa Wayan Cottages...............**31** B3
Waka Nusa Resort..................**32** A4
Ware-Ware.............................**33** B3

EATING
Bar & Cafe Bali......................**34** A3
Scooby Doo Bar & Cafe..........**35** B3

TRANSPORT
Nusa Penida Boat...............(see 36)
Perama Tourist Boat............(see 36)
Public Boats...........................**36** B3
Scoot Office...........................**37** B3
Scoot.................................(see 36)

Information

It's vital that you bring sufficient cash for your stay, as there's no ATM. **Bank BPD** (☉ 8am-3pm Mon-Thu, 8am-1pm Fri) can exchange travellers cheques and cash but the rates are bad.

If the name **Money Changer** (☉ 8am-9pm) provokes images of the usurious being chased from the temple, you'd be right. Cash advances here on credit cards incur an 8% service charge. Still, for those exclaiming 'Dude, there's no ATM?!?' this service is a fiscal lifeline.

Pondok Baruna (☎ 0812 390 0686) has public internet terminals. Wi-fi is being installed at many places.

Small markets can be found near the bank, but unless you're on a diet of bottled water and Ritz crackers, the selection is small.

The medical clinic in the village is well versed in minor surfing injuries and ear ailments.

Sights
JUNGUTBATU

The beach here, a mostly lovely arc of white sand with clear blue water, has views across to Gunung Agung in Bali. The village itself is mellow, with quiet lanes, no cars and lots of seaweed production. **Pura Segara** and its enormous banyan tree are the site of frequent ceremonies.

At the north end of town is a rickety metal **lighthouse**. Follow the road around east to **Pura Sakenan**.

PANTAI SELEGIMPAK
A long, straight strip of sand is usually lapped by small waves at this remote-feeling beach with a couple of places to stay. About 200m east up and over a knoll is a minute cove with a nub of sand and a tiny warung. It's cute.

MUSHROOM BAY
This beautiful little bay, unofficially named for the mushroom corals offshore, has a crescent of bright white sand. During the day, the tranquillity may be disturbed by banana-boat rides or parasailing. At other hours, this can be a beach of dreams.

The most interesting way to get here from Jungutbatu is to walk along the trail that starts from the southern end of the main beach and follows the coastline for a kilometre or so (see Hiking Lembongan, p156). Alternatively, get a boat from Jungutbatu for about 25,000Rp.

DREAM BEACH
Down a little track, on the south side of the island, this 150m crescent of white sand has pounding surf and a warung for sunset beers.

LEMBONGAN
The other main town on the island looks across the seaweed-farm-filled channel to Nusa Ceningan. It's a beautiful scene of clear water and green hills. You may get some hype for the **underground house**. Ignore it; it's a diversion for day-trippers and amounts to little more than somebody's hole in the ground.

Activities
Most places rent gear for aquatic fun. Well-used surfboards go for 50,000Rp per day.

SURFING
Surfing here is best in the dry season (April to September), when the winds come from the southeast. It's definitely not for beginners, and can be dangerous even for experts. There are three main breaks on the reef, all aptly named. From north to south are **Shipwreck**, **Lacerations** and **Playground**. Depending on where you are staying, you can paddle directly out to whichever of the three is closest; for others it's better to hire a boat. Prices are negotiable – from about 20,000Rp for a one-way trip. You tell the owner when to return. A fourth break – **Racecourses** – sometimes emerges south of Shipwreck.

The surf can be crowded here even when the island isn't – charter boats from Bali sometimes bring groups of surfers for day trips from the mainland for a minimum of 800,000Rp.

For more on surfing here, see p96.

DIVING
World Diving (☎ 0812 390 0686; www.world-diving.com), based at Pondok Baruna (p156) on Jungutbatu Beach, is well regarded. It offers

see p156; see p96

SEAWEED SUNDAE
The next time you enjoy some creamy ice cream, you might thank the seaweed growers of Nusa Lembongan and Nusa Penida. Carrageenan is an emulsifying agent that is used to thicken ice cream as well as cheese and many other products. It is also used as a fat substitute in 'diet' foods (just look for it on the endless ingredients label). In nature it turns seawater into a gel that gives seaweed its structure.

On Lembongan 85% of the population work at farming seaweed for carrageenan (as opposed to 5% in tourism). It's the island's major industry. Although returns are OK, the work is very intensive and time-consuming. Women are the main labourers.

As you walk around the villages, you'll see – and smell – vast areas used for drying seaweed. Looking down into the water, you'll see the patchwork of cultivated seaweed plots. Small pieces of a marine algae (*Eucheuma*) are attached to strings that are stretched between bamboo poles – these underwater fences can be seen off many of the beaches, and especially in the shallows between Lembongan and Ceningan and at low tide. Growth is so fast that new shoots can be harvested every 45 days. This region is especially good for production, as the waters are shallow and rich in nutrients. The dried red and green seaweed is exported around the world for final processing.

a complete range of courses, including five-day PADI open-water courses for US$375, and dive trips from US$27 to US$40 per dive to sites around all three islands. Other dive operations include the long-running **Bali Diving Academy** (☎ 0361-270252; www.scubali.com), which has an office at Bungalow Number 7.

See Diving the Islands, p159 for details on the area's dive sites.

SNORKELLING
Good snorkelling can be had just off the Mushroom Bay and Bounty pontoons off Jungutbatu Beach, as well as in areas off the north coast of the island. You can charter a boat from 200,000Rp per hour, depending on demand, distance and the number of passengers. A trip to the challenging waters of Nusa Penida costs 400,000Rp. Snorkelling gear can be rented for 20,000Rp to 30,000Rp per day. World Diving allows snorkellers to join dive trips and charges 150,000Rp for a four-hour trip.

There's good drift snorkelling along the mangrove-filled channel west of Cenigan Point between Lembongan and Ceningan.

CRUISES
A number of cruise boats offer day trips to Nusa Lembongan from Benoa Harbour (Map p132) in South Bali. Trips include hotel transfer from South Bali, basic water sports, snorkelling, banana-boat rides, island tours and a buffet lunch. Note that with hotel transfers, the following day trips can make for a long day.

Bali Hai (☎ 0361-720331; www.balihaicruises.com; reef cruises adult/child US$85/42.50; catamaran cruises adult/child US$85/42.50) Cruises use an unsightly offshore pontoon for snorkelling and water play.

Bounty Cruises (☎ 0361-726666; www.balibounty cruises.com; cruises adult/child US$95/47.50) Boats dock at a garish offshore pontoon with water slides and other amusements.

Island Explorer Cruises (☎ 0361-728088; www.bali -activities.com; per adult/child US$80/40) This has three ways to get to Lembongan, which all get you back to Bali around 5pm: relaxing and slow-sailing yacht, party boat, and fast wave-bouncing boat. These trips include use of the outfit's Coconuts Beach Resort pool.

Sleeping & Eating
With exceptions, rooms and amenities become increasingly posh as you head south and west along the water to Mushroom Bay. Almost every property has a café serving – unless noted – basic Indonesian and Western dishes for under 25,000Rp.

JUNGUTBATU
Lodgings in Jungutbatu are mostly basic. However as a group they are undergoing the typical Bali development cycle: each year more rooms are added and old ones are spruced up. Unless noted otherwise, amenities are limited to cold water and fans.

Puri Nusa Bungalows (☎ 24482; r 70,000-200,000Rp; ⌘) The 17 rooms here are clean and comfortable (some with hot water and air-con); the two upstairs in front have excellent views and there's a good café. There are nice loungers under trees.

Pondok Baruna (☎ 0812 3900 686; www.world -diving.com; r 75,000-100,000Rp; ⌨ ⌘) Associated with World Diving, this simple place has eight rooms with terraces facing the ocean. The restaurant serves excellent meals. Staff, led by the manager Putu, are charmers.

HIKING/BIKING LEMBONGAN
You can walk around the entire island in a day, or less on a bike. It's a fascinating journey into remote and rural Balinese life. Start along the hillside trail from **Jungutbatu** past the Mutiara Villa and move on to **Pantai Selegimpak**. Here it becomes a little tricky to reach **Mushroom Bay**, but with a little Tarzan spirit, you can stay with the faint trail and be rewarded by refreshments (this is the one segment you can't do by bike, use the roads inland).

From Mushroom Bay, head over to dreamy **Dream Beach**.

Next go to **Lembongan** village and optionally take the suspension bridge to Nusa Ceningan. From Lembongan village you can take a gentle uphill walk along the sealed road to the killer hill that leads *down* to Jungutbatu, which cuts the circuit to about half a day.

To explore the rest of the island, stick to the paved road that follows the channel with Nusa Ceningan and then curves north along the mangroves all the way to the lighthouse. Note that motorbikes won't be able to navigate the trails.

Two Thousand Cafe (☎ 0812 381 2775; r 100,000-300,000Rp; ☒) Eight rooms in two-storey blocks offer decent comfort; some have hot water and air-con. There's a fun café-bar right on the sand.

Bungalow Tarci (☎ 24494; r from 120,000Rp) The front units upstairs at this two-level place have excellent views of the water. It's got a popular bar and café. At this end of the beach the water laps right at the foundations at high tide.

Ketut Losman (☎ 0361-747 4638, 0813 3784 6555; r 125,000-300,000Rp; ☒) Six two-storey bungalow-style units perch on sandy soil here. Each has two rooms, some with hot water and air-con, others with fans and cold water; the two upstairs units in the front pair of bungalows have fine beach views. Rocking chairs await on terraces to occupy the antsy.

Nusa Indah Bungalows (☎ 0811 398 553; purna maindah@hotmail.com; r with fan/air-con 150,000/250,000Rp; ☒) Five classic thatched cottages on a sizeable beach front this friendly place with a popular café. There are five rooms out back in a two-storey block.

Shipwrecks (☎ 0813 3803 2900; www.nusalembongan .com.au; r from 330,000Rp ☒) This beautiful property is set back from the beach in a coconut-shaded garden. There are three rooms in the compound, which is constructed in old Balinese style with natural wood. The beds are king-sized and the bathrooms open-air. An open common area is good for lounging or watching movies on DVD.

Scooby Doo Bar & Cafe No doubt hoping to lure shaggy surfers, Scooby's serves up a long list of snacks and drinks right on the sand to a big crowd every night. Surf videos compete with the views for limited attention spans.

HILLSIDE

The steep hillside just south of Jungutbatu offers great views and an ever-increasing number of more luxurious rooms.

Ware-Ware (☎ 0812 397 0572; r 200,000-400,000Rp; ☒ ☒) The units at this hillside place are a mix of traditional square and groovy circular numbers with thatched roofs. The 10 rooms (some fan-only) are large and have rattan couches and big bathrooms. The café scores with a spectacular, breezy cliffside location. Dishes (20,000Rp to 50,000Rp) include fresh seafood.

Playgrounds (☎ 24524; www.playgroundslembon gan.com; r 450,000-600,000Rp; ☒ ☒ ☐ wi-fi) On the hillside, Playgrounds' rooms have good views,

satellite TV and fridges. The cheaper rooms are fan-cooled but do have better views from their long porch.

Coconuts Beach Resort (☎ 0361-728088; www.bali -activities.com; r US$50-100; ☒ ☒ ☐) Coconuts has podlike, spacious bungalows (some fan-only) staggered up the hillside overlooking a large pool and the sea. It's part of Island Explorer Cruises (opposite), so look for package deals.

Batu Karang (☎ 24880; www.batukaranglembon gan.com; r from US$150; ☒ ☒ ☐) A precursor to Lembongan's future, this upscale resort has a large infinity pool perched on a terraced hillside with 23 luxury units. Some have multiple rooms, plunge pools and sweeping views. All have open bathrooms and wooden terraces.

PANTAI SELEGIMPAK

Leaving Jungutbatu, the island gets less tamed as you go west. With backpacks, you may want to avail yourself of the boat-greeting luggage carriers for the walk here along the hillside trail. It's a 15-minute up-and-down scenic walk from the boat-landing area.

Tamarind Beach (☎ 0812 398 4234; www.balitama rind.com; r 150,000-250,000Rp) Trance music plays in the simple common area at this wild tropical setting right on the beach. The six rooms are simple, with cold-water tubs for getting clean and cooling off. The tiny café couldn't be closer to the water. Ring ahead for a pick-up by outrigger from the boat-landing area on Jungutbatu Beach.

Villa Wayan Cottages (☎ 745527, 0361-271212; r US$25-40) Villa Wayan Cottages has seven varied and unusually decorated rooms; some are suitable for families or groups. Trees give the hillside grounds a remote tropical feel.

Morin Lembongan (☎ 0812 385 8396; wayman40@ hotmail.com; r US$30-45; ☐) More lushly planted than many of the hillside places, Morin has four woodsy rooms with views over the water from their verandahs. It's cold-water and fan-only; be sure to bargain.

Mutiara Villa (☎ 0361-745 3857; www.mutiara-villa .com; r US$50-120; ☒ ☒) Mutiara means 'mother-of-pearl' and you might just spot one at the groovy water cave reached by a stairway. Ever-expanding, there are 10 modern hillside rooms in circular wood-and-brick buildings. Dine high on the hill or down in the cave.

MUSHROOM BAY

It's your own treasure island. This shallow bay has a nice beach and plenty of

SOUTH BALI

overhanging trees. It offers the nicest lodging on Lembongan. Get here from Jungutbatu by road (10,000Rp) or boat (25,000Rp).

Mushroom Beach Bungalows (☎ 24515; www .mushroom-lembongan.com; r US$45-80; 🖾 🖳) Perched on a tiny knoll at the east end of Mushroom Bay, this family-run place has 11 rooms, some fan-only. There are good-sized bathtubs and a popular cliffside café for viewing sunsets.

Tanis Villa (☎ 0361-743 2344, 0819 1626 8871; www .tanisvillas.com; villas with fan/air-con US$55/70; 🖾 🖳) Tucked into a corner of the beach, the 11 villas here are simple and have pretty bathrooms with large tubs. It's a short hop across the white sand from the large pool to the big sea.

Waka Nusa Resort (☎ 0361-723629; www.wakaexpe rience.com; bungalows from US$120; 🖾 🖳) A primitive motif blends with creature comforts at this low-key resort run by the Waka group. Ten thatch-roofed bungalows are set on sandy grounds at the shore. The beachside restaurant and bar is shaded by coconut palms. Transfers from Bali are aboard a catamaran.

Nusa Lembongan Resort (☎ 0361-725864; www .nusa-lembongan.com; villas from US$185; 🖾 🖳) Twelve well-appointed and stylish villas overlooking the picture-perfect bay are the draw here. Flowering shrubs and trees highlight the lavish gardens. The resort has a creative terrace restaurant (meals US$10 to US$25) with views over the bay.

Bar & Cafe Bali (☎ 0828 367 1119, 24536; dishes 20,000-50,000Rp) Follow the chicken tracks in the sand to tiered tables right near the high-tide mark. Enjoy pizza, pasta, seafood and the Indo-usuals. The bar is lively and you can arrange for transport from Jungutbatu.

ELSEWHERE

Sunset Villas (☎ 0813 3859 5776, 0812 395 7616; r 175,000Rp) A real getaway, especially after you've bounced along the dirt track to get to this isolated west-coast location. Just a few minutes' walk from a little beach in a cove, the four 'villas' here are really just simple buildings with cold water and fans. The common area is comfy and the views live up to the name. Bring a pile of books and lose yourself for a bit.

Getting There & Away

Getting to or from Nusa Lembongan offers numerous choices. In descending order of speed are the fast boats like Scoot, the Perama

boat and the public boats. Boats anchor offshore, so be prepared to get your feet wet. And travel light – wheeled bags are comically inappropriate in the water and on the beach and dirt tracks. Porters will shoulder your steamer trunk for 10,000Rp (and don't be like some lowlifes we've seen and stiff them for their service).

SANUR

Public boats to Nusa Lembongan leave from the northern end of Sanur beach at 7.45am (45,000Rp, 1¾ to two hours). This is the boat used for supplies, so you may have to share space with a melon. A faster public boat (150,000Rp, one hour) makes the run in under an hour: 3pm from Lembongan, 4pm from Sanur.

The Perama tourist boat leaves Sanur at 10.15am (100,000Rp, 1¾ hours). The Lembongan office is near the Mandara Beach Bungalows.

The speed champ is **Scoot** (☎ 0361-780 2255; one way/return US$18/30), a fast service (30 to 40 minutes) that flies over and through the waves. There are at least two returns daily; check schedules when you book. Note: anyone with money for a speedboat is getting into the fast-boat act; be wary of fly-by-night operators with fly-by-night safety.

For details on the Sanur end of the services, see p152.

BENOA HARBOUR

The day-tripping cruise boats to Nusa Lembongan from Benoa Harbour (p156) will usually take passengers only for about US$30 round-trip. Call to confirm. Alternatively, if you go on the full day trip and then decide you want to stay, you can return on a boat another day.

NUSA PENIDA

Boats take locals between Jungutbatu and Toyapakeh (one hour) between 5.30am and 6am for 30,000Rp. Otherwise, charter a boat for 250,000Rp one way.

Getting Around

The island is fairly small and you can easily walk most places. There are no cars (yeah!); bicycles (30,000Rp per day) and small motorbikes (25,000Rp per hour) are widely available for hire. One-way rides on motorbikes or trucks cost 5000Rp.

DIVING THE ISLANDS

There are great diving possibilities around the islands, from shallow and sheltered reefs, mainly on the northern side of Lembongan and Penida, to very demanding drift dives in the channel between Penida and the other two islands. Vigilant locals have protected their waters from dynamite bombing by renegade fishing boats, so the reefs are relatively intact. And a side benefit of seaweed farming is that locals no longer rely so much on fishing.

There are dive shops on Nusa Lembongan (p155) and Nusa Penida (p161).

If you arrange a dive trip from Padangbai or South Bali, stick with the most reputable operators, as conditions here can be tricky and local knowledge is essential. A particular attraction are the large marine animals, including turtles, sharks and manta rays. The large (3m fin-to-fin) and unusual *mola mola* (sunfish) is sometimes seen around the islands between mid-July and October, while manta rays are often seen south of Nusa Penida.

The best dive sites include **Blue Corner** (Map p154) and **Jackfish Point** (Map p154) off Nusa Lembongan and **Ceningan Point** (Map p154) at the tip of that island. The channel between Ceningan and Penida is renowned for drift diving, but it is essential you have a good operator who can judge fast-changing currents and other conditions. Upswells can bring cold water from the open ocean to sites such as **Ceningan Wall** (Map p160). This is one of the world's deepest natural channels and attracts all manner and sizes of fish.

Sites close to Nusa Penida include **Big Rock**, **Crystal Bay**, **SD**, **Pura Ped**, **Manta Point** (Map p160) and **Batu Aba** (p161). Of these, Crystal Bay, SD and Pura Ped are suitable for novice divers and are good for snorkelling. For more on diving in Bali, see p88.

NUSA CENINGAN

There is a narrow suspension bridge crossing the lagoon between Nusa Lembongan and Nusa Ceningan, which makes it quite easy to explore the network of tracks on foot or by bicycle. The lagoon is filled with frames for seaweed farming and there are also several small agricultural plots and a fishing village. The island is quite hilly, and if you're up for it, you'll get glimpses of great scenery as you wander or cycle around the rough tracks.

To really savour Nusa Ceningan, take an overnight tour of the island with **JED** (Village Ecotourism Network; ☎ 0361-737447; www.jed.or.id; per person US$120), the cultural organisation that gives people an in-depth look at village and cultural life. Trips include family accommodation in a village, local meals, a fascinating tour with seaweed workers and transport to/from Bali.

There's a **surf break** at Ceningan reef, but it's very exposed and it is only surfable when the other breaks are too small.

NUSA PENIDA
☎ 0366

Largely overlooked by tourists, Nusa Penida awaits discovery. It's an untrammelled place that answers the question: what would Bali be like if tourists never came? There are not a lot of formal activities or sights; rather you go to Nusa Penida to explore and relax, to adapt to the slow rhythm of life here, and to learn to enjoy subtle pleasures such as the changing colour of the clouds and the sea. Life is simple; you'll still see topless older women carrying huge loads on their heads.

The island is a limestone plateau with white-sand beaches on its north coast, and views over the water to the volcanoes in Bali. The beaches are not great for swimming, as most of the shallows are filled with bamboo frames used for seaweed farming. The south coast has 300m-high limestone cliffs dropping straight down to the sea and a row of offshore islets – it's rugged and spectacular scenery. The interior is hilly, with sparse-looking crops and old-fashioned villages. Rainfall is low and parts of the island are arid.

The population of around 50,000 is predominantly Hindu, although there is a Muslim community in Toyapakeh. The culture is distinct from that of Bali: the language is an old form of Balinese no longer heard on the mainland. Dance, architecture and crafts are also unique, including a type of red ikat weaving (cloth in which the pattern is produced by dyeing individual threads before weaving). Nusa Penida was once used as a place of banishment for criminals and other undesirables from the kingdom of Klungkung, and still has a somewhat sinister reputation.

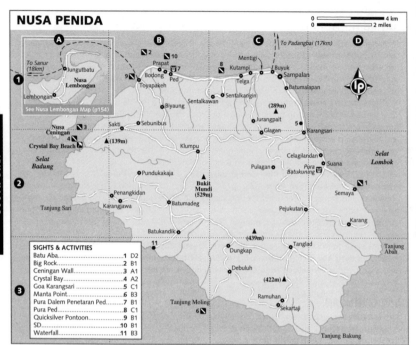

NUSA PENIDA

SIGHTS & ACTIVITIES
Batu Aba	1	D2
Big Rock	2	B1
Ceningan Wall	3	A1
Crystal Bay	4	A2
Goa Karangsari	5	C1
Manta Point	6	B3
Pura Dalem Penetaran Ped	7	B1
Pura Ped	8	C1
Quicksilver Pontoon	9	B1
SD	10	B1
Waterfall	11	B3

Services are limited to small shops in the main towns. Bring cash and anything else you'll need.

Activities

Nusa Penida has world-class **diving**; see Diving the Islands, p159. There's a dive shop in Toyapakeh; see opposite. Alternatively, make arrangements through a dive shop on Nusa Lembongan. If you plan to go **snorkelling**, bring your own gear or rent it from the dive shop in Toyapakeh.

Between Toyapakeh and Sampalan there is excellent **cycling** on the beautiful, flat coast road. The hitch is you need to bring a *good* bike with you to Penida. If you really want to explore, bring a mountain bike and camping equipment from the mainland (but remember, Nusa Penida is hilly). Alternatively, plan to do some serious **hiking**, but come well prepared.

Sampalan

Sampalan, the main town on Penida, is quiet and pleasant, with a market, schools and shops strung out along the curving coast road. The **market area**, where the bemo congregate,

is in the middle of town. It's a good place to absorb village life.

SLEEPING & EATING

Not many people stay here, although there are plenty of rooms, so just show up. For meals you'll need to try one of the small warung in town – no more than 10 minutes by foot from any of the inns.

Made's Homestay (☎ 0828 368 6709; r 100,000Rp) Four small, clean rooms in a pleasant garden. Breakfast is included. A small side road between the market and the harbour leads here.

Nusa Garden Bungalows (☎ 0813 3812 0660; s/d 100,000/160,000Rp) Crushed-coral pathways running between animal statuary link the 10 rooms here. Rates include a small breakfast. Turn on Jl Nusa Indah just east of the centre.

Bungalow Pemda (☎ 0813 3871 0981; r 120,000Rp) Opposite the police station, 200m east of the market, is this run-down government resthouse. Four rooms are OK but lack mosquito nets. Major renovations planned for 2009 could take advantage of the great sea views.

Toyapakeh

If you come by boat from Lembongan, you'll probably be dropped at the beach at Toyapakeh, a pretty village with lots of shady trees. The beach has clean white sand, clear blue water, a neat line of boats, and Gunung Agung as a backdrop. Step up from the beach and you're at the road where bemo can take you to Ped or Sampalan (5000Rp).

Offshore, the big grey thing that looks like a tuna-processing plant is the **Quicksilver pontoon** (☎ 0361-7425161; www.quicksilver-bali.com). There are day trips (adult/child US$85/42.50) from Benoa Harbour which include a buffet lunch, snorkelling, banana-boat rides and an excursion ashore to an extremely unattractive 'tourist village' of souvenir sellers. Two new **bungalows** (150,000Rp; ✷) here, however, are attractive and perfect for those hoping to meditate at night.

Toyapakeh is ripe for some groovy tourist accommodation, although it's been ripe for a long time. Still, Quicksilver's rooms may help to bring just enough attention here so that some intrepid bungalow-builder starts the process of turning it into the next Nusa Lembongan. In the meantime you could be the intrepid traveler and see if rooms have appeared, knowing that you can always go to nearby Sampalan (p160) for a simple room.

Around the Island

A trip around the island, following the north and east coasts, and crossing the hilly interior, can be completed in half a day by motorcycle or in a day by bike if you're in shape. You could spend much longer, lingering at the temples and the small villages, and walking to less accessible areas, but there's no accommodation outside the two main towns. The following description goes clockwise from Sampalan.

The coastal road from Sampalan curves and dips past bays with rows of fishing boats and offshore seaweed gardens. After about 6km, just before the village of Karangsari, steps go up on the right side of the road to the narrow entrance of **Goa Karangsari** caves. There are usually people who can provide a lantern and guide you through the cave for a small negotiable fee of around 20,000Rp each. The limestone cave is over 15m tall in some sections. It extends more than 200m through the hill and emerges on the other side to overlook a verdant valley.

Continue south past a naval station and several temples to **Suana**. Here the main road swings inland and climbs up into the hills, while a very rough side track goes southeast, past more interesting temples to **Semaya**, a fishing village with a sheltered beach and one of Bali's best dive sites offshore, **Batu Aba**.

About 9km southwest of Suana, **Tanglad** is a very old-fashioned village and a centre for traditional weaving. Rough roads south and east lead to isolated parts of the coast.

A scenic ridge-top road goes northwest from Tanglad. At Batukandik, a rough road and 1.5km track leads to a spectacular **waterfall** (*air terjun*) that crashes onto a small beach. Get a guide (20,000Rp) in Tanglad.

Limestone cliffs drop hundreds of feet into the sea, surrounded by crashing surf. At their base, underground streams discharge fresh water into the sea – a pipeline was made to bring the water up to the top. Look for the remains of the rickety old wooden scaffolding women used to clamber down, returning with large pots of water on their heads.

Back on the main road, continue to Batumadeg, past **Bukit Mundi** (the highest point on the island at 529m; on a clear day you can see Lombok), through Klumpu to Sakti, which has traditional stone buildings. Return to the north coast at Toyapakeh, about one hour after Bukit Mundi.

The important temple of **Pura Dalem Penetaran Ped** is near the beach at Ped, a few kilometres east of Toyapakeh. It houses a shrine for the demon Jero Gede Macaling

PENIDA'S DEMON

Nusa Penida is the legendary home of Jero Gede Macaling, the demon who inspired the Barong Landung dance. Many Balinese believe the island is a place of enchantment and *angker* (evil power) – paradoxically, this is an attraction. Although few foreigners visit, thousands of Balinese come every year for religious observances aimed at placating the evil spirits.

The island has a number of interesting temples dedicated to Jero Gede Macaling, including Pura Dalem Penetaran Ped, near Toyapakeh. It houses a shrine, which is a source of power for practitioners of black magic, and a place of pilgrimage for those seeking protection from sickness and evil.

SOUTH BALI

SOUTH BALI

YOUR OWN PERFECT BEACH

South of Toyapakeh, a 10km road through the village of Sakti leads to idyllic **Crystal Bay Beach**, which fronts the popular dive spot. The sand here is the whitest around Bali and you'll likely have it to yourself. Should you somehow have the gear, this would be a fine place to camp.

(see p161). The temple structure is sprawling and you will see many people making offerings for safe sea voyages from Nusa Penida; you may wish to join them.

Across from the temple, the spotless and simple **Depot Anda** (meals 5000-10,000Rp; 6am-9pm) is the eating choice on the island, with tasty local standards. Have a banana juice at **Warung Ibu Nur** (dishes from 3000Rp).

The road between Sampalan and Toyapakeh follows the craggy and lush coast.

Getting There & Away

The strait between Nusa Penida and southern Bali is deep and subject to heavy swells – if there is a strong tide, boats often have to wait. You may also have to wait a while for the public boat to fill up with passengers. Boats to and from Kusamba are not recommended.

PADANGBAI

On the beach just east of the car park in Padangbai, you'll find the twin-engine fibreglass boats that run across the strait to Buyuk, 1km west of Sampalan on Nusa Penida (30,000Rp, 45 minutes, four daily). The boats run between 7am and noon. A large and new car ferry has been built for the route but its operation is spotty, owing to insufficient government funding.

NUSA LEMBONGAN

Boats runs between Toyapakeh and Jungutbatu (30,000Rp, one hour) between 5.30am and 6am. Enjoy the mangrove views on the way. Otherwise, charter a boat for 250,000Rp.

Getting Around

Bemo regularly travel along the sealed road between Toyapakeh and Sampalan, and sometimes on to Suana and up to Klumpu, but beyond these areas the roads are rough and transport is limited. You should be able to charter your own bemo or private vehicle with driver for about 30,000Rp per hour or rent a motorbike for 70,000Rp per day.

You may also be able to negotiate an *ojek* (motorcycle that takes passengers) for about 30,000Rp per hour.

DENPASAR

☎ 0361

Sprawling, hectic and ever-growing, Bali's capital has been the focus of a lot of the island's growth and wealth over the last five decades. It can seem a daunting and chaotic place but spend a little time on its tree-lined streets in the relatively affluent government and business district of Renon and you'll discover a more genteel side.

Denpasar might not be a tropical paradise, but it's as much a part of 'the real Bali' as the rice paddies and cliff-top temples. This is the hub of the island for locals and here you will find their shopping malls and parks. Most enticing, however, is the growing range of fabulous restaurants and cafés aimed at the burgeoning middle class. You'll also want to sample Denpasar's markets, its excellent museum and its purely modern Balinese vibe. Most visitors stay in the tourist towns of the south and visit Denpasar as a day trip. Others may pass through while changing bemo or catching a bus to Java.

HISTORY

Denpasar, which means 'next to the market', was an important trading centre and the seat of local rajahs (lords or princes) before the colonial period. The Dutch gained control of northern Bali in the mid-19th century, but their takeover of the south didn't start until 1906. After the three Balinese princes destroyed their own palaces in Denpasar and made a suicidal last stand – a ritual *puputan* – the Dutch made Denpasar an important colonial centre. And as Bali's tourism industry expanded in the 1930s, most visitors stayed at one or two government hotels in the city of Denpasar.

The northern town of Singaraja remained the Dutch administrative capital, but a new airport was built in the south. This made Denpasar a strategic asset in WWII, and when the Japanese invaded, they used it as a springboard to attack Java. After the war the Dutch moved their headquarters to Denpasar, and in 1958, some years after Indonesian independence, the city became the official capital of the province of Bali. Denpasar is a self-governing municipality that includes Sanur and Benoa Harbour.

Many of Denpasar's residents are descended from immigrant groups such as Bugis mercenaries and Chinese, Arab and Indian traders. Recent immigrants, including civil servants, artisans, business people and labourers, have come from Java and all over Indonesia, attracted by opportunities in schools, factories and businesses in the growing Balinese capital. Much of the business infrastructure that supports Balinese tourism is based here.

Although non-Balinese tend to live in detached houses or small apartments, Balinese communities still maintain their traditions and family compounds, even as their villages are engulfed by growth. In fact, Denpasar's edges have merged with Sanur, Kuta and Seminyak.

ORIENTATION

The main road, Jl Gunung Agung, starts at the western side of town. It changes first to Jl Gajah Mada, then Jl Surapati and finally Jl Hayam Wuruk. This name-changing is common in Denpasar, and can be confusing.

In contrast to the rest of Denpasar, the Renon area, southeast of the town centre, is laid out on a grand scale, with wide streets, large car parks and huge tracts of landscaped space. You'll find the government offices here, many of which are impressive structures displaying an ersatz Balinese style.

INFORMATION
Emergency
Police office (☎ 424346; Jl Pattimura) The place for any general problems.
Tourist Police (☎ 224111)

Medical Services
Rumah Sakit Umum Propinsi Sanglah (Sanglah Hospital; ☎ 227911; Sanglah; ☯ 24hr) The city's general hospital has English-speaking staff and an ER. It's the best hospital on the island.

Money
All major Indonesian banks have offices and ATMs in Denpasar. Several are on Jl Gajah Mada, near the corner of Jl Arjuna, and there are also plenty of ATMs in the shopping malls.

Post
Main post office (☎ 223565; Jl Panjaitan; ☯ 8am-8pm) Has poste restante service; in Renon.

Tourist Information
Denpasar tourist office (☎ 234569; Jl Surapati 7; ☯ 7.30am-3.30pm Mon-Thu, 8am-1pm Fri) Deals with tourism in the Denpasar municipality (including Sanur), but also has some information about the rest of Bali. It's not worth a special trip, but may have the useful *Calendar of Events* booklet.
Ubung tourist office (☯ 8am-2pm Mon-Thu, 8am-noon Fri) This useful office is located at the Ubung bus and bemo terminal and offers transport advice.

SIGHTS
Museum Negeri Propinsi Bali
This **museum** (☎ 222680; adult/child 2000/1000Rp; ☯ 8am-12.30pm Mon-Fri, 8am-3pm Sun) was originally established in 1910 by a Dutch resident who was concerned by the export of culturally significant artefacts from the island. Destroyed in a 1917 earthquake, it was rebuilt in the 1920s, but used mainly for storage until 1932. At that time, German artist Walter Spies and some Dutch officials revived the idea of collecting and preserving Balinese antiquities and cultural objects, and creating an ethnographic museum. Today the museum is well organised and most displays are labelled in English. You can climb one of the towers inside the grounds for a better view of the whole complex.

The museum comprises several buildings and pavilions, including many examples of Balinese architecture. See p29 for details. The main building, to the back as you enter, has a collection of prehistoric pieces downstairs, including stone sarcophagi and stone and bronze implements. Upstairs are examples of traditional artefacts, including items still in everyday use. Look for the intricate wood-and-cane carrying cases for transporting fighting cocks, and tiny carrying cases for fighting crickets.

The **northern pavilion**, in the style of a Tabanan palace, houses dance costumes and masks, including a sinister Rangda (widow-witch), a healthy-looking Barong (mythical lion-dog creature) and a towering Barong Landung (tall Barong) figure. See p59 for more about these mythical figures.

The **central pavilion**, with its spacious verandah, is like the palace pavilions of the Karangasem kingdom (based in Amlapura), where rajahs held audiences. The exhibits

DENPASAR

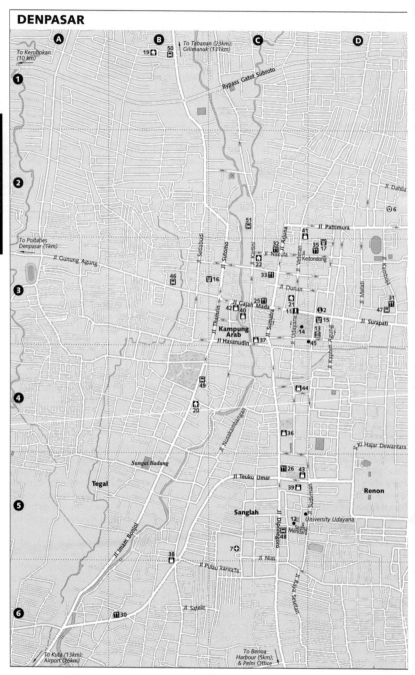

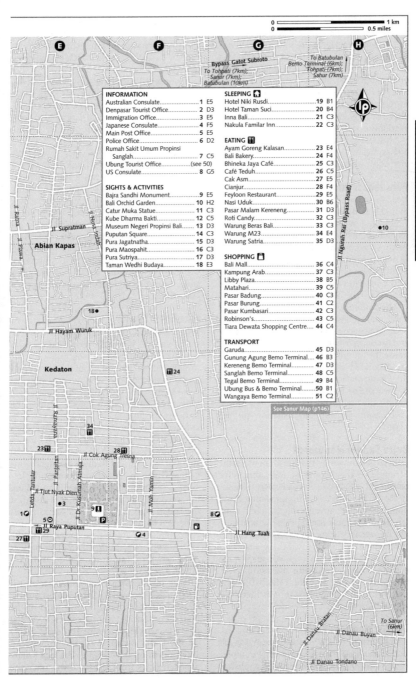

INFORMATION
Australian Consulate.........................**1** E5
Denpasar Tourist Office....................**2** D3
Immigration Office...........................**3** E5
Japanese Consulate..........................**4** F5
Main Post Office..............................**5** E5
Police Office.....................................**6** D2
Rumah Sakit Umum Propinsi
    Sanglah......................................**7** C5
Ubung Tourist Office..................(see 50)
US Consulate....................................**8** G5

SIGHTS & ACTIVITIES
Bajra Sandhi Monument....................**9** E5
Bali Orchid Garden.........................**10** H2
Catur Muka Statue..........................**11** C3
Kube Dharma Bakti.........................**12** C5
Museum Negeri Propinsi Bali.........**13** D3
Puputan Square...............................**14** C3
Pura Jagatnatha..............................**15** D3
Pura Maospahit...............................**16** C3
Pura Sutriya...................................**17** D3
Taman Wedhi Budaya.....................**18** E3

SLEEPING 🏠
Hotel Niki Rusdi..............................**19** B1
Hotel Taman Suci.............................**20** B4
Inna Bali...**21** C3
Nakula Familar Inn..........................**22** C3

EATING 🍴
Ayam Goreng Kalasan.....................**23** E4
Bali Bakery.....................................**24** F4
Bhineka Jaya Café............................**25** C3
Café Teduh.....................................**26** C5
Cak Asm...**27** E5
Cianjur...**28** F4
Feyloon Restaurant..........................**29** E5
Nasi Uduk.......................................**30** B6
Pasar Malam Kereneng.....................**31** D3
Roti Candy......................................**32** C3
Warung Beras Bali...........................**33** C3
Warung M23....................................**34** E4
Warung Satria..................................**35** D3

SHOPPING 🛍
Bali Mall...**36** C4
Kampung Arab.................................**37** C3
Libby Plaza.....................................**38** B5
Matahari...**39** C5
Pasar Badung..................................**40** C3
Pasar Burung..................................**41** C2
Pasar Kumbasari..............................**42** C3
Robinson's......................................**43** C5
Tiara Dewata Shopping Centre........**44** C4

TRANSPORT
Garuda...**45** D3
Gunung Agung Bemo Terminal.......**46** B3
Kereneng Bemo Terminal.................**47** D3
Sanglah Bemo Terminal...................**48** C5
Tegal Bemo Terminal.......................**49** B4
Ubung Bus & Bemo Terminal...........**50** B1
Wangaya Bemo Terminal..................**51** C2

SOUTH BALI

are related to Balinese religion, and include ceremonial objects, calendars and priests' clothing.

The **southern pavilion** (Gedung Buleleng) has a varied collection of textiles, including *endek* (a Balinese method of weaving with pre-dyed threads), double ikat, *songket* (silver- and gold-threaded cloth, hand-woven using a floating weft technique) and *prada* (the application of gold leaf or gold or silver thread in traditional Balinese clothes).

Museum staff often play music on a bamboo gamelan to magical effect. Visit in the afternoon when it's uncrowded.

Pura Jagatnatha

Next to the museum, the **state temple**, built in 1953, is dedicated to the supreme god, Sanghyang Widi. Part of its significance is its statement of monotheism. Although Balinese recognise many gods, the belief in one supreme god (who can have many manifestations) brings Balinese Hinduism into conformity with the first principle of Pancasila – the 'Belief in One God'.

The *padmasana* (shrine) is made of white coral, and consists of an empty throne (symbolic of heaven) on top of the cosmic turtle and two *naga* (mythical serpents), which symbolise the foundation of the world. The walls are decorated with carvings of scenes from the *Ramayana* and *Mahabharata*.

Two major festivals are held here every month, during the full moon and new moon, and feature *wayang kulit* (shadow-puppet plays).

Bajra Sandhi Monument

Otherwise known as the Monument to the Struggle of the People of Bali, this huge **monument** (☎ 264517; Jl Raya Puputan; admission 2000Rp; ⌚ 9am-5.30pm) is as big as its name and dominates what's already a big park in Renon. Inside this vaguely Borobodur-like structure are dioramas tracing Bali's history. Taking the name as a cue, you won't be surprised that they have a certain jingoistic soap-opera quality. But they're a fun diversion. Note that in the portrayal of the 1906 battle with the Dutch, the King of Badung is literally a sitting target.

Taman Wedhi Budaya

This **arts centre** (☎ 222776; admission free; ⌚ 8am-3pm Mon-Thu, 8am-1pm Fri-Sun) is a sprawling complex in the eastern part of Denpasar. Established

in 1973 as an academy and showplace for Balinese culture, its lavish architecture houses an art gallery with an interesting collection, but few performances or much else most of the year.

From mid-June to mid-July, however, the centre comes alive for the Bali Arts Festival (see opposite), with dances, music and craft displays from all over Bali. You may need to book tickets at the centre for more popular events.

ACTIVITIES

Many Balinese wouldn't think of having a massage from anyone but a blind person. Government-sponsored schools offer lengthy courses to certify blind people in reflexology, shiatsu massage, anatomy and much more. Usually graduates work together in group locations such as **Kube Dharma Bakti** (☎ 749 9440; Jl Serma Mendara 3; massage per hr 30,000Rp; ⌚ 9am-9pm). In this airy building redolent with liniments, you can choose from a range of therapies and contribute to a very good cause at the same time.

WALKING TOUR

While Denpasar can seem formidable and traffic-choked, it actually rewards those who mount an exploration on foot.

This walk includes most of the attractions in the middle of town and a few vestiges of when Denpasar – and Bali – moved at a much slower pace. Allow extra time for visiting the museum or shopping.

Start the walk at **Museum Negeri Propinsi Bali** (**1**; p163). Opposite is **Puputan Square (2)**, a park that commemorates the heroic but suicidal stand of the rajahs of Badung against the invading Dutch in 1906. A monument depicts a Balinese family in heroic pose, brandishing the weapons that were so ineffective against the Dutch guns. The woman also has jewels in her left hand, as the women of the Badung court reputedly flung their jewellery at the Dutch soldiers to taunt them. The park is popular with locals at lunchtime and with families near sunset.

Back on the corner of Jl Surapati and Jl Veteran is the towering **Catur Muka statue (3)**, which represents Batara Guru, Lord of the Four Directions. The four-faced, eight-armed figure keeps a close eye (or is it eight eyes?) on the traffic swirling around him. Head 100m north on Jl Veteran to the **Inna Bali (4**; p168). It dates from 1927 and was once the

DENPASAR WALKING TOUR

WALK FACTS

Start Museum Negeri Propinsi Bali
Finish Jl Gajah Mada
Distance 2.5km
Duration Two hours

main tourist hotel on the island. It was a favourite of Soekarno – listen for the echoes of his schemes.

Return to the Catur Muka statue and head west on Jl Gajah Mada (named after the 14th-century Majapahit prime minister). Go past banks, shops and a café towards the bridge over the grubby Sungai Badung (Badung River). Just before the bridge, on the left, is the renovated **Pasar Badung** (**5**; p169), the main produce market. This is one of the better places to see the fertile fruit of Bali. On the left, just after the bridge, **Pasar Kumbasari** (**6**; p169) is a handicraft and textiles market.

At the next main intersection, detour north up Jl Sutomo, and turn left along a small *gang* (alley) leading to the **Pura Maospahit (7)** temple. Established in the 14th century, at the time the Majapahit arrived from Java, the temple was damaged in a 1917 earthquake and has been heavily restored since. The oldest structures are at the back of the temple, but the most interesting features are the large statues of Garuda and the giant Batara Bayu.

Turn back, and continue south along Jl Thamrin to the junction of Jl Hasanudin. On this corner is the **Puri Pemecutan (8)**, a

palace destroyed during the 1906 invasion. It's long since been rebuilt and you can look inside the compound but don't expect anything palatial.

Go east on Jl Hasanudin, then north onto Jl Sulawesi, and you'll be in the area of the gold shops, known as Kampung Arab for the many people there of Middle Eastern or Indian descent. Continue north past Pasar Badung market to return to Jl Gajah Mada.

FESTIVALS & EVENTS

The annual **Bali Arts Festival** (www.baliartsfestival.com), based at the Taman Wedhi Budaya arts centre (opposite), lasts for about a month starting in mid-June. It's a great time to visit Bali, and the festival is an easy way to see a wide variety of traditional dance, music and crafts from the island. The productions of the *Ramayana* and *Mahabharata* ballets are grand, and the opening ceremony and parade in Denpasar are spectacles.

The festival is the main event of the year for scores of village dance and musical groups. Competition is fierce with local pride on the line at each performance. To do well here sets a village on a good course for the year. Some events are held in a 6000-seat amphitheatre, a venue that allows you to realise the mass appeal of traditional Balinese culture. Tickets are usually available before performances, and schedules are available throughout South Bali, Ubud and at the Denpasar tourist office (p163).

SLEEPING

Denpasar has several hotels, but it's hard to think of a compelling reason to stay here unless you want to be close to the bus stations or have some other business here. Otherwise the myriad choices in Sanur and Seminyak are close by.

Hotel Niki Rusdi (☎ 416397; Jl Pidada XIV; r 60,000-200,000Rp; 🕸) Located right behind the Ubung bus terminal, the 26 rooms here are a good choice if you have an early or late bus. Rooms are clean, the cheapest fan-only. There are other options nearby if this hotel is full.

Nakula Familar Inn (☎ 226446; nakula_familiar_inn @yahoo.com; Jl Nakula 4; r 70,000-120,000Rp; 🕸) The eight rooms at this sprightly family-run place are clean (cold-water showers only, some with air-con) and have small balconies. The traffic noise isn't too bad and there is a nice little courtyard in the middle. Tegal–Kereneng bemo go along Jl Nakula.

SOUTH BALI

Hotel Taman Suci (☎ 484445; www.tamansuci.com; Jl Imam Bonjol 45; r from 225,000-275,000Rp; 🅿 🖳) A good choice for business travellers, this modern, multifloor 45-room hotel insulates you from the hubbub outside from the minute you enter its air-con lobby.

Inna Bali (☎ 225681; www.innabali.com; Jl Veteran 3; r from 375,000-460,000Rp; 🅿 🅰 🖳) The Inna Bali has simple gardens, a huge banyan tree and a certain nostalgic charm from its early days as a Dutch hostelry in 1927. Room interiors are standard, but many have deeply-shaded verandahs. The hotel is a good base for the *Ngrupuk* parades that take place the day before Nyepi (see the boxed text, p62), as they pass by the front of the hotel. Get the veteran employees talking; they have many stories.

EATING

Denpasar has the island's best range of Indonesian and Balinese food. Savvy locals and expats each have their own favourite warung and restaurants. At the Pasar Malam Kereneng (Kereneng Night Market) dozens of vendors dish up food till dawn. A number of places along Jl Teuku Umar and in Renon cater to more affluent locals while all the shopping malls have food-court options.

Roti Candy (☎ 238409; Jl Nakula 31; treats 3000Rp) Have a *pia*, a sweet-filled bun, or choose from a variety of other sweets and cakes, plus rolls filled with cheesy goodness.

Bhineka Jaya Café (☎ 224016; Jl Gajah Mada 80; coffee 3000Rp; ⏱ 9am-4pm) Home to Bali's Coffee Co, this storefront sells locally grown beans and makes a mean espresso, which you can enjoy at the two tiny tables while watching the bustle of Denpasar's old main drag.

Warung Satria (Jl Kedondong; dishes 4000-10,000Rp; ⏱ 11am-3pm) A long-running warung on a quiet street; try the wonderful seafood satay served with a shallot sambal. Otherwise, choose from the immaculate displays of what's fresh, but don't wait too long after lunch or it's all gone.

Bali Bakery (☎ 243147; Jl Hayam Wuruk; dishes 5000-30,000Rp; 🅿 🖳 wi-fi) Small branch of the Kuta café known for good Western baked goods.

Nasi Uduk (Jl Teuku Umar; 6000-12,000Rp) Open to the street, this spotless little stall has a few chairs and serves up Javanese treats such as *nasi uduk* (sweetly scented coconut rice with fresh peanut sauce) and *lalapan* (a simple salad of fresh lemon basil leaves).

Warung Beras Bali (☎ 247443; Jl Sahedawa 26; mains 7000-15,000Rp) Organic rice underpins organic vegetables and various Chinese dishes at this appropriately green-hued open-front café. A long list of fresh juices adds to the healthy patina. Try the unusual – and organic vegetarian – *saté sambal plecina*, which is a tasty skewer of grilled spinach and tomato. Or buy a bag of rice.

Renon

The slightly gentrified air here is redolent with the smells of good food.

Café Teduh (☎ 221631; off Jl Diponegoro; dishes from 7000-40,000Rp; wi-fi) Amid the big shopping malls, this little oasis is hidden down a tiny lane. Hanging orchids, trees, flowers and ponds with fountains create a bucolic feel. There's a menu of meaty mains such as *ayam bakar rica* (barbecued chicken with ratatouille) but the real treats are just that, treats. Try the *es cakalele*, a refreshing sundae of lychee and coconut milk.

Cianjur (☎ 230015; Jl Cok Agung Tresna; dishes 8000-30,000Rp; 🅿) Big, airy and cool, this shiny upmarket restaurant has Balinese seafood in an array of preparations (crispy, grilled, steamed or wrapped in a banana leaf). It's hugely popular with families and groups of government workers.

Ayam Goreng Kalasan (☎ 0812 380 9934; Jl Cok Agung Trisna 6; mains from 10,000Rp) The name here says it all. Fried Chicken (Ayam Goreng) named for a Javanese temple (Kalasan) in a region renowned for its fiery, crispy chicken. The version here falls off the bone on the way to the table; the meat is redolent with lemongrass from a long marinade prior to the plunge into boiling oil. There are several other excellent little warung in this strip.

our pick Cak Asm (☎ 798 9388; Jl Tukad Gangga; mains 10,000-30,000Rp) No, the name isn't the sound you make after eating here. If that were the case, this simple café would be named 'yum'. Join government workers and students from the nearby university for superb dishes at rock-bottom prices. Order the *cumi cumi* (calamari) with *telor asin* sauce (a heavenly mixture of eggs and garlic). The resulting buttery, crispy goodness may be the best dish you have in Bali. And it's under US$1.

Warung M23 (Jl Drupadi 24B; mains from 10,000Rp) Run by a lovely older couple. Tables here are hard to come by at night when locals pack in for classically spicy Lombok-style chicken. It also specialises in seafood and has a good range of vegetarian meals. Bamboo screens the open dining area from street noise.

Feyloon Restaurant (☎ 265733; Jl Raya Puputan; mains 15,000-120,000Rp; ✖) Take a trip to a slick Hong Kong seafood restaurant without leaving the Island of the Gods. Feyloon is festooned with fish tanks filled with doomed but tasty critters. The long menus (don't just settle for the 'beginner's' one with pics) have choices that range from steamed whole fish to all manner of shellfish.

SHOPPING
Local goods can be found in the markets and at the large shopping malls south of the centre.

Markets
A must-see destination: shoppers browse and bargain at the **Pasar Badung** morning to night. It's a retail adventure and you'll find produce and food from all over the island as well as easy-to-assemble temple offerings that are popular with working women. Deals include a half-kilo of saffron for 250,000Rp. Ignore guides who may offer their services.

Across the river, the renovated **Pasar Kumbasari** has handicrafts, a plethora of vibrant fabrics, and costumes decorated with gold. It's a modern, multilevel building of shops and stalls and you should just plunge at random into the canyons of colour.

Kampung Arab has jewellery and precious-metal stores. North on Jl Veteran, **Pasar Burung** is a bird market with hundreds of caged birds and small animals, such as guinea pigs, rabbits and monkeys, for sale. There are also gaudy birdcages. Stories abound about endangered species traded behind the scenes.

An impromptu dog market also operates directly opposite the bird market. While you're here, have a look at the elaborate **Pura Sutriya**, just east of the market.

Shopping Malls
Western-style shopping malls show that Western consumer culture has arrived in Bali. They're jammed on Sundays with locals shopping and teens flirting; the brand-name goods are genuine.

Most malls have a food court with stalls serving fresh Asian fare, as well as fast-food joints (which have pleased more than one homesick tourist tot).

Bali Mall (Jl Dipenegoro) Has the top-end Ramayana Department Store and an A&W restaurant.

Libby Plaza (Jl Teuku Umar) Has a huge Hero Supermarket.

Matahari (Jl Teuku Umar) Main branch of the department store, with numerous other stores and a Swenson's Ice Cream café.

Robinson's (Jl Teuku Umar or Jl Sudirman) The arch-competitor of Matahari has a large selection of midrange goods.

Tiara Dewata Shopping Centre (Jl Udayana) Low-rise place with a good food court and a Dunkin' Donuts.

GETTING THERE & AWAY
Denpasar is the hub of public transport in Bali – you'll find buses and minibuses bound for all corners of the island.

Air
Sometimes called 'Denpasar' in airline schedules, Bali's Ngurah Rai international airport is 12km south past Kuta. See p349 for details.

Bemo
The city has several bemo terminals – if you're travelling independently around Bali you'll often have to go via Denpasar, and transfer from one terminal to another. The terminals for transport around Bali are Ubung, Batubulan and Tegal, while the Gunung Agung, Kereneng and Sanglah terminals serve destinations in and around Denpasar. Each terminal has regular bemo connections to the other terminals in Denpasar for 7000Rp. See p353 for a full discussion of Bali's sputtering bemo network.

UBUNG
Well north of the town, on the road to Gilimanuk, Ubung is the terminal for northern and western Bali and most long-distance bus services. In the complex, there is a **tourist office** (☎ 427172) that provides help with fares and schedules. Arriving here by taxi guarantees a reception by baggage and ticket touts.

Destination	Fare
Gilimanuk (for the ferry to Java)	25,000Rp
Kediri (for Tanah Lot)	7000Rp
Mengwi	7000Rp
Munduk	22,000Rp
Negara	20,000Rp
Pancasari (for Danau Bratan)	18,000Rp
Singaraja (via Pupuan or Bedugul)	30,000Rp
Tabanan	7000Rp

SOUTH BALI

SOUTH BALI

BATUBULAN

Located a very inconvenient 6km northeast of Denpasar on a road to Ubud, this terminal is for destinations in eastern and central Bali.

Destination	Fare
Amlapura	20,000Rp
Bangli	12,000Rp
Gianyar	10,000Rp
Kintamani (via Tampaksiring)	18,000Rp
Padangbai (for the Lombok ferry)	18,000Rp
Sanur	6000Rp
Semarapura	18,000Rp
Singaraja (via Kintamani)	30,000Rp
Singaraja (via Semarapura & Amlapura)	30,000Rp
Ubud	8000Rp

TEGAL

On the western side of town on Jl Iman Bonjol, Tegal is the terminal for Kuta and the Bukit Peninsula.

Destination	Fare
Airport	10,000Rp
Jimbaran	12,000Rp
Kuta	8000Rp
Legian	8000Rp
Nusa Dua	12,000Rp
Ulu Watu	15,000Rp

GUNUNG AGUNG

This terminal, at the northwestern corner of town (look for orange bemo), is on Jl Gunung Agung, and has bemo to Kerobokan and Canggu (7000Rp).

KERENENG

East of the town centre, Kereneng has bemo to Sanur (7000Rp).

SANGLAH

On Jl Diponegoro, near the general hospital in the south of the city, Sanglah has bemo to Suwung and Benoa Harbour (7000Rp).

WANGAYA

Near the centre of town, this small terminal is the departure point for bemo services to northern Denpasar and the outlying Ubung bus terminal (6000Rp).

Bus

The usual route to Java is a bus (get one with air-con) from Denpasar's Ubung terminal to Surabaya (120,000Rp, 10 hours), which includes the short ferry trip across the Bali Strait. Other buses go as far as Yogyakarta (210,000Rp, 16 hours) and Jakarta (305,000Rp, 24 hours), usually travelling overnight.

Book directly at offices in the Ubung terminal, 3km north of the city centre. To Surabaya or even Jakarta, you may get on a bus within an hour of arriving at Ubung, but at busy times you should buy your ticket at least one day ahead.

GETTING AROUND
Bemo

Bemo take various circuitous routes from and between Denpasar's many bus/bemo terminals. They line up for various destinations at each terminal, or you can try and hail them from anywhere along the main roads – look for the destination sign above the driver's window. The Tegal–Nusa Dua bemo (dark blue in colour) is handy for Renon; and the Kereneng–Ubung bemo (turquoise) travels along Jl Gajah Mada, past the museum.

Taxi

If you're looking for a taxi, you're in luck – you'll find them prowling the streets of Denpasar looking for fares. As always, the distinctive blue cabs of **Bali Taxi** (☎ 701111) are the most reliable choice.

Ubud & Around

A dancer moves her arm just so and 300 pairs of entranced eyes follow the exact movement. A gamelan player hits a melodic riff and 300 pairs of feet tap along with it. The Legong goes into its second hour as the bumblebee dance unfolds with its sprightly flair and 300 butts forget they're still stuck in rickety plastic chairs.

So another dance performance works its magic on a crowd in Ubud, the town where all that is magical about Bali is combined in one easy-to-love package. From nightly cultural performances on stages humble and grand to museums filled with works by artists whose creativity flowered here and to the unbelievably green rice fields that spill down myriad hillsides to rushing rivers below, Ubud is a feast for the soul.

Somehow as its popularity has grown, Ubud has stayed true to itself. Lavish hotels, stylish cafés and smart boutiques may jostle for room on its streets but it still stays humble. Generations of enchanted travellers treading its lanes still make friends with the locals they meet and many end up staying in one of the countless homestays, becoming part of the rhythm of family life as offerings are made and ceremonies planned.

Ubud, which today is really a collection of villages, runs like rivulets up and down the hills of this part of Bali. Explore the region and you'll find artisans, ancient monuments and a chance to find your own inner Bali.

UBUD & AROUND

HIGHLIGHTS

- Feeling the vibe of a traditional **dance performance** (p195)
- Making new friends and whiling away the hours at a **funky Ubud café** (p191)
- Exploring the green jungle and white water of the **Sungai Ayung valley** (p182)
- Discovering your own hidden talents through an **art or cooking course** (p183)
- Making like Indiana Jones at the towering ancient wonders at **Gunung Kawi** (p201)

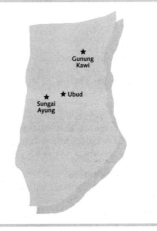

UBUD

☎ 0361

Ubud is culture, yes. It's also home to good restaurants, cafés and streets of shops, many selling goods from the region's artisans. There's somewhere to stay for every budget, and no matter what the price you can enjoy lodgings that reflect the local Zeitgeist: artful, creative and serene.

The weather is slightly cooler but much wetter than the south; expect it to rain at any time. At night mountain breezes make air-con unnecessary and let you hear the symphony of frogs, bugs and distant gamelan practices echoing over the rice fields.

Spend a few days in Ubud to appreciate it properly. It's one of those places where days can become weeks and weeks become months, as the noticeable expat community demonstrates.

For details on routes and sights to Ubud from South Bali, see the section South of Ubud, p203.

HISTORY

Late in the 19th century, Cokorda Gede Agung Sukawati established a branch of the Sukawati royal family in Ubud and began a series of alliances and confrontations with neighbouring kingdoms. In 1900, with the kingdom of Gianyar, Ubud became (at its own request) a Dutch protectorate and was able to concentrate on its religious and cultural life.

The Cokorda's descendants encouraged Western artists and intellectuals to visit the area in the 1930s, most notably Walter Spies, Colin McPhee and Rudolf Bonnet. They provided an enormous stimulus to local art, introduced new ideas and techniques, and began a process of displaying and promoting Balinese culture worldwide. As mass tourism arrived in Bali, Ubud became an attraction not for beaches or bars, but for the arts.

In 2008 Ubud showed off both its considerable artistic and monetary prowess with a royal cremation ceremony that was the largest seen on the island for decades. It drew 100,000 spectators and included a funeral tower almost 30m tall.

ORIENTATION

The once small village of Ubud has expanded to encompass its neighbours – Campuan, Penestanan, Padangtegal, Peliatan and Pengosekan are all part of what we see as Ubud today. The centre of town is the junction of Monkey Forest Rd and Jl Raya Ubud, where the bustling market and bemo (small minibus) stops are found, as well as Ubud Palace and the main temple, Pura Desa Ubud. Monkey Forest Rd (officially Jl Wanara Wana, but always known by its unofficial name) runs south to Sacred Monkey Forest Sanctuary and is lined with shops, hotels and restaurants.

Jl Raya Ubud ('Ubud Main Rd' – often Jl Raya for short) is the main east–west road. In the east, a mix of cheap accommodation, idiosyncratic shops and little cafés gives Jl

---

UBUD IN...

One Day
Stroll the streets of Ubud, enjoying the galleries and sampling the fine cuisine. Try to get out on one of the short nearby walks through the verdant rice fields. Go to an evening dance performance at the **Ubud Palace** (p176).

Three Days
Take longer walks in the countryside, especially the **Campuan Ridge** (p181) and **Sayan Valley** (p182). Visit the **Museum Puri Lukisan** (p176), **Neka Art Museum** (p176) and **ARMA** (Agung Rai Museum of Art; p177). Attend **dance performances** (p195) not just in Ubud, but also in the nearby villages. Indulge at a local **spa** (p180). Drop by the **market** (p196) in the morning.

One Week or More
Do everything we've listed but take time to simply chill out. Get in tune with Ubud's rhythm. Take naps, read books, wander about. Think about a **course** (p183) in Balinese culture. Compare and choose your favourite café, get out to craft villages and ancient sites.

Goutama a feel of Ubud 25 years ago. West of Ubud, the road drops steeply down to the ravine at Campuan, where an old suspension bridge, next to the new one, hangs over Sungai Wos (Wos River). West of Campuan, the pretty village of Penestanan is famous for its painters and bead-work. East and south of Ubud proper, the 'villages' of Peliatan, Nyuhkuning and Pengosekan are known variously for painting, woodcarving and traditional dance. The latter has been the focus of recent development, with rice paddies giving way to new hotels. The area north of Ubud is less densely settled, with picturesque paddies interspersed with small villages, many of which specialise in a local craft.

Maps

The maps in this guidebook will be sufficient for most visitors, but if you want to explore the surrounding villages on foot or by bicycle, the locally sold *Bali Pathfinder* map is useful. (Most other local maps are simply no good.)

INFORMATION

Visitors will find every service they need and then some along Ubud's main roads. Bulletin boards at Bali Buddha (p193) and Kafe (p193) have info on housing, jobs, classes and much more.

Ubud is home to many non-profit and volunteer groups; see p346 for details.

Bookshops

Ubud is the best place in Bali for book shopping. Selections are wide and varied especially for tomes on Balinese art and culture. Many carry titles by small and obscure publishers. Shops typically carry newspapers such as the *International Herald Tribune*.

Agung Rai Museum of Art (ARMA; Map pp174-5; ☎ 976659; www.armamuseum.com; Jl Raya Pengosekan; ☼ 9am-6pm) Large selection of cultural titles.

Ary's Bookshop (Map p186; ☎ 978203; Jl Raya Ubud) Good for art books and maps.

Cinta Bookshop (Map p186; ☎ 973295; Jl Dewi Sita) Nice assortment of used novels and vintage books about Bali.

Ganesha Bookshop (Map pp174-5; ☎ 970320; www.ganeshabooksbali.com; Jl Raya Ubud) Bali's best bookshop has an amazing amount of stock jammed into a small space. Excellent selection of titles on Indonesian studies, travel, arts, music and fiction (including used titles). Good recommendations and mail-order service.

Neka Art Museum (Map pp174-5; ☎ 975074; www.museumneka.com; Jl Raya Sanggingan; ☼ 9am-5pm) Good range of art books.

Periplus Monkey Forest Rd (Map p186; ☎ 975178); Jl Raya Campuan (Map pp174-5; ☎ 976149; Bintang Centre) The branch on Monkey Forest Rd is typically glossy; the Campuan branch is a large store with a small café.

Pondok Pecak Library & Learning Centre (Map p186; ☎ 976194; Monkey Forest Rd; ☼ 9am-5pm Mon-Sat, 1-5pm Sun) Regularly thins its collection and has some excellent fiction for sale. Located on the far side of the football field.

Rendezvousdoux (Map p186; ☎ 747 0163; Jl Raya Ubud 14; ☼) Good selection of books, many French, German and English titles.

Emergency

Police station (Map pp174-5; ☎ 975316; Jl Raya Andong; ☼ 24hr) Located east, at Andong.

Internet Access

The following two neighbouring places are a cut above average with fast broadband connections and large screens. Many of Ubud's cafés offer wi-fi as noted in the listings.

@Highway (Map pp174-5; ☎ 972107; Jl Raya Ubud; per min 500Rp; ☼ 24hr; ☼) Full-service and very fast.

Bali 3000 (Map pp174-5; ☎ 978538; Jl Raya Ubud; per hr 20,000Rp; ☼ 8am-11pm; ☼) Sleek internet café with a full range of computing services and good sandwiches, coffees and juices.

Libraries

Pondok Pecak Library & Learning Centre (Map p186; ☎ 976194; Monkey Forest Rd; ☼ 9am-5pm Mon-Sat, 1-5pm Sun) On the far side of the football field, this relaxed place has a children's book section. Charges membership fees for library use. Small café and a pleasant reading area. See p183 for information on cultural courses.

Medical Services

See Health (p365) for details on international clinics and hospitals in Bali.

Mua Pharmacy (Map p186; ☎ 974674; Monkey Forest Rd; ☼ 8am-9pm)

UBUD AREA

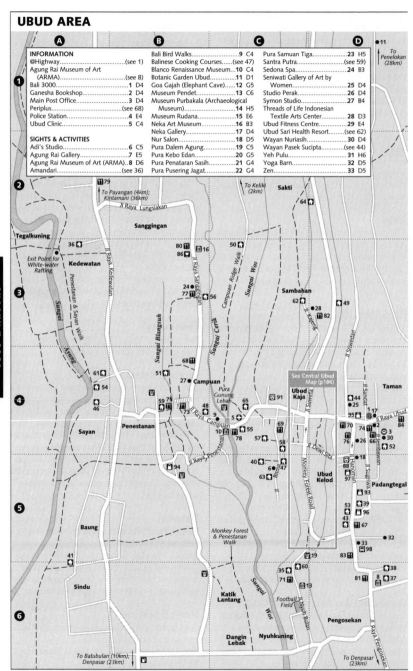

INFORMATION
@Highway..........................(see 1)
Agung Rai Museum of Art
   (ARMA).........................(see 8)
Bali 3000...............................**1** D4
Ganesha Bookshop...............**2** D4
Main Post Office...................**3** D4
Periplus..............................(see 68)
Police Station........................**4** E4
Ubud Clinic...........................**5** C4

SIGHTS & ACTIVITIES
Adi's Studio...........................**6** C5
Agung Rai Gallery.................**7** E5
Agung Rai Museum of Art (ARMA)..**8** D6
Amandari............................(see 36)

Bali Bird Walks......................**9** C4
Balinese Cooking Courses......(see 47)
Blanco Renaissance Museum...**10** C4
Botanic Garden Ubud.............**11** D1
Goa Gajah (Elephant Cave).....**12** G5
Museum Pendet......................**13** C6
Museum Purbakala (Archaeological
   Museum).............................**14** H5
Museum Rudana....................**15** E6
Neka Art Museum..................**16** B3
Neka Gallery..........................**17** D4
Nur Salon...............................**18** D5
Pura Dalem Agung.................**19** C5
Pura Kebo Edan......................**20** G5
Pura Penataran Sasih..............**21** G4
Pura Pusering Jagat...............**22** G4

Pura Samuan Tiga...................**23** H5
Santra Putra...........................(see 59)
Sedona Spa............................**24** B3
Seniwati Gallery of Art by
   Women..............................**25** D4
Studio Perak..........................**26** D4
Symon Studio.........................**27** B4
Threads of Life Indonesian
   Textile Arts Center..............**28** D3
Ubud Fitness Centre...............**29** E4
Ubud Sari Health Resort........(see 62)
Wayan Nuriasih......................**30** D4
Wayan Pasek Sucipta..............(see 44)
Yeh Pulu...............................**31** H6
Yoga Barn.............................**32** D5
Zen......................................**33** D5

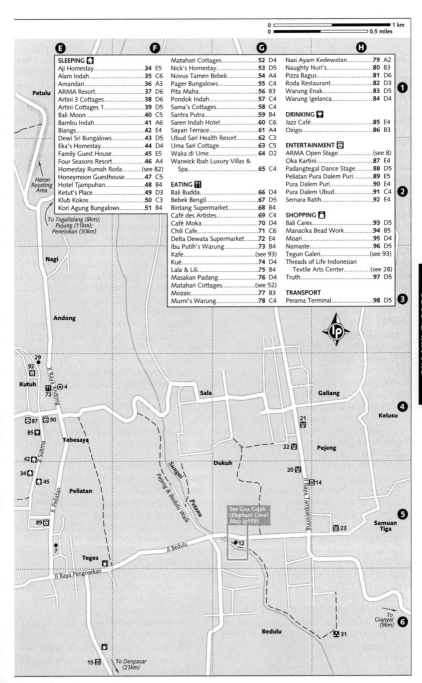

SLEEPING

Aji Homestay	**34** E5
Alam Indah	**35** C6
Amandari	**36** A3
ARMA Resort	**37** D6
Artini 3 Cottages	**38** D6
Artini Cottages 1	**39** D5
Bali Moon	**40** C5
Bambu Indah	**41** A6
Biangs	**42** E4
Dewi Sri Bungalows	**43** D5
Eka's Homestay	**44** D4
Family Guest House	**45** E5
Four Seasons Resort	**46** A4
Homestay Rumah Roda	(see 82)
Honeymoon Guesthouse	**47** C5
Hotel Tjampuhan	**48** B4
Ketut's Place	**49** D3
Klub Kokos	**50** C3
Kori Agung Bungalows	**51** B4
Matahari Cottages	**52** D4
Nick's Homestay	**53** D5
Novus Tamen Bebek	**54** A4
Pager Bungalows	**55** C4
Pita Maha	**56** B3
Pondok Indah	**57** C4
Sama's Cottages	**58** C4
Santra Putra	**59** B4
Saren Indah Hotel	**60** C6
Sayan Terrace	**61** A4
Ubud Sari Health Resort	**62** C3
Uma Sari Cottage	**63** C5
Waka di Ume	**64** D2
Warwick Ibah Luxury Villas & Spa	**65** C4

EATING

Bali Budda	**66** D4
Bebek Bengil	**67** D5
Bintang Supermarket	**68** B4
Café des Artistes	**69** C4
Café Moka	**70** D4
Chili Cafe	**71** C6
Delta Dewata Supermarket	**72** E4
Ibu Putih's Warung	**73** B4
Kafe	(see 93)
Kué	**74** D4
Lala & Lili	**75** B4
Masakan Padang	**76** D4
Matahari Cottages	(see 52)
Mozaic	**77** B3
Murni's Warung	**78** C4

Nasi Ayam Kedewatan	**79** A2
Naughty Nuri's	**80** B3
Pizza Bagus	**81** D6
Roda Restaurant	**82** D3
Warung Enak	**83** D5
Warung Igelanca	**84** D4

DRINKING

Jazz Café	**85** E4
Ozigo	**86** B3

ENTERTAINMENT

ARMA Open Stage	(see 8)
Oka Kartini	**87** E4
Padangtegal Dance Stage	**88** D5
Peliatan Pura Dalem Puri	**89** E5
Pura Dalem Puri	**90** E4
Pura Dalem Ubud	**91** C4
Semara Ratih	**92** E4

SHOPPING

Bali Cares	**93** D5
Manacika Bead Work	**94** B5
Moari	**95** D4
Namaste	**96** D5
Tegun Galeri	(see 93)
Threads of Life Indonesian Textile Arts Center	(see 28)
Truth	**97** D5

TRANSPORT

Perama Terminal	**98** D5

Ubud Clinic (Map pp174-5; ☎ 974911; www.ubudclinic .com; Jl Raya Campuan 36; ❧ 24hr) Best medical centre in Ubud. Charges begin at 200,000Rp for a clinical consultation.

Money

Ubud has numerous banks, ATMs and money-changers along Jl Raya Ubud and Monkey Forest Rd.

Post

Main post office (Map pp174-5; Jl Jembawan; ❧ 8am-5pm) Has a sort-it-yourself poste restante system – address poste restante mail to Kantor Pos, Ubud 80571, Bali, Indonesia.

Tourist Information

Ubud Tourist Information (Yaysan Bina Wisata; Map p186; ☎ 973285; Jl Raya Ubud; ❧ 8am-8pm) The one really useful tourist office in Bali. It has a good range of information and a noticeboard listing current happenings and activities. The staff can answer most regional questions and have up-to-date information on ceremonies and traditional dances held in the area; dance tickets are sold here.

SIGHTS

Palaces & Temples

Ubud Palace and **Puri Saren Agung** (Map p186; cnr Jl Raya Ubud & Jl Suweta) share space in the heart of Ubud. The compound has many ornate corners and was mostly built after the 1917 earthquake. The local royal family still lives here and you can wander around most of the large compound exploring the many traditional and not excessively ornate buildings. If you really like it, you can stay the night (p188). Take time to appreciate the stone carvings, many by noted local artists like I Gusti Nyoman Lempad.

Just north, **Pura Marajan Agung** (Map p186; Jl Suweta) has one of the finest gates you'll find and is the private temple for Ubud's royal family.

Pura Desa Ubud (Map p186; Jl Raya Ubud) is the main temple for the Ubud community. Just a bit west is the very picturesque **Pura Taman Saraswati** (Ubud Water Palace; Map p186; Jl Raya Ubud). Waters from the temple at the rear of the site feed the pond in the front, which overflows with pretty lotus blossoms. There are carvings that honour Dewi Saraswati, the goddess of wisdom and the arts, who has clearly given her blessing to Ubud. There are weekly dance performances by night; by day painters set up easels.

Museums

MUSEUM PURI LUKISAN

The **Museum of Fine Arts** (Map p186; ☎ 975136; www .mpl-ubud.com; off Jl Raya Ubud; admission 20,000Rp; ❧ 9am-5pm) displays fine examples of all schools of Balinese art. Just look at the lush composition of *Balinese Market* by Anak Agung Gde Sobrat to see the vibrancy of local painting.

It was in Ubud that the modern Balinese art movement started, when artists first began to abandon purely religious themes and court subjects for scenes of everyday life. Rudolf Bonnet was part of the Pita Maha artists' cooperative, and together with Cokorda Gede Agung Sukawati (a prince of Ubud's royal family) they helped to establish a permanent collection.

The **first pavilion** straight ahead as you enter has a collection of early works from Ubud and the surrounding villages. These include examples of classical *wayang*-style paintings, fine ink drawings by I Gusti Nyoman Lempad and paintings by Pita Maha artists. Notice the level of detail in Lempad's *The Dream of Dharmawangsa*.

The **second pavilion** on the left has some colourful examples of the 'Young Artist' style of painting and a good selection of 'modern traditional' works.

The **third pavilion** on the right has classical and traditional paintings and is used for special exhibitions.

The museum's collection is well curated and labelled in English, and some of the artwork is often for sale. The museum has a good bookshop and a café.

NEKA ART MUSEUM

Quite distinct from Neka Gallery (p177), the **Neka Art Museum** (Map pp174-5; ☎ 975074; www.museum neka.com; Jl Raya Sanggingan; adult/child 40,000Rp/free; ❧ 9am-5pm) is the creation of Suteja Neka, a private collector and dealer in Balinese art. It has an excellent and diverse collection and is the best place to learn about the development of painting in Bali.

You can get an overview of the myriad local painting styles in the **Balinese Painting Hall**. Look for the *wayang* works, which are influenced by shadow puppetry.

The **Arie Smit Pavilion** features Smit's works on the upper level, and examples of the Young Artist school, which he inspired, on the lower level. Look for the Bruegel-like *The Wedding Ceremony* by I Nyoman Tjarka.

The **Lempad Pavilion** houses Bali's largest collection of works by I Gusti Nyoman Lempad.

The **Contemporary Indonesian Art Hall** has paintings by artists from other parts of Indonesia, many of whom have worked in Bali. The upper floor of the **East-West Art Annexe** is devoted to the work of foreign artists, such as Louise Koke, Miguel Covarrubias, Rudolf Bonnet, Han Snel, the Australian Donald Friend and Antonio Blanco.

The temporary exhibition hall has changing displays, while the **Photography Archive Centre** features black-and-white photography of Bali in the early 1930s and 1940s. The bookstore is noteworthy and there's a café.

AGUNG RAI MUSEUM OF ART (ARMA)

Founded by Agung Rai as a **museum, gallery and cultural centre** (Map pp174-5; ☎ 976659; www .armamuseum.com; Jl Raya Pengosekan; admission 25,000Rp; 🕑 9am-6pm), the impressive ARMA is the only place in Bali to see haunting works by the influential German artist Walter Spies.

The museum is housed in several traditional buildings set in gardens with water coursing through channels. It features work by 19th-century Javanese artist Raden Saleh. It exhibits classical Kamasan paintings, Batuan-style work from the 1930s and '40s, and works by Lempad, Affandi, Sadali, Hofker, Bonnet and Le Mayeur. The collection is well labelled in English.

Look for the enigmatic *Portrait of a Javanese Nobleman and his Wife* by Raden Saleh, which predates the similar *American Gothic* by decades. For an interview with founder, Anak Agung Rai, see 'Early Wakeup', p49.

It's interesting to visit ARMA when local children practise **Balinese dancing** (🕑 3-5pm Mon-Fri, 10.30am-noon Sun) and during **gamelan practice** (🕑 hours vary). See p195 for details on regular Legong and Kecak (types of classic Balinese dance) performances. See p183 for details on the myriad cultural courses offered here.

You can enter the museum grounds from the southern end of Jl Raya Pengosekan (there's parking near Kafe ARMA) or around the corner on Jl Pengosekan at the Kafe ARMA.

THREADS OF LIFE INDONESIAN TEXTILE ARTS CENTER

This small, professional **textile gallery and educational studio** (Map pp174-5; ☎ 972187; www .threadsoflife.com; Jl Kajeng 24; 🕑 10am-6pm Mon-Sat) sponsors the production of naturally dyed, handmade ritual textiles, helping to recover skills in danger of being lost to modern dyeing and weaving methods. Commissioned pieces are displayed in the gallery, which has good explanatory material. It also runs regular textile appreciation courses (see p183) and has a good shop.

MUSEUM RUDANA

This large, imposing **museum** (Map pp174-5; ☎ 975779; www.museumrudana.com; admission 20,000Rp; 🕑 9am-5pm) is the creation of local politician and art-lover Nyoman Rudana and his wife Ni Wayan Olasthini. The three floors contain over 400 traditional paintings, including a calendar dated to the 1840s, some Lempad drawings, and more modern pieces. The museum is beside the Rudana Gallery, which has a large selection of paintings for sale.

BLANCO RENAISSANCE MUSEUM

The picture of Antonio Blanco mugging with Michael Jackson says it all. His namesake **Blanco Renaissance Museum** (Map pp174-5; ☎ 975502; Jl Raya Campuan; admission 50,000Rp; 🕑 9am-5pm) captures the artist's theatrical spirit. Blanco came to Bali from Spain via the Philippines. He specialised in erotic art, illustrated poetry and playing the role of an eccentric artist à la Dali. He died in Bali in 1999, and his flamboyant home is now this museum. More prosaically: enjoy the waterfall on the way in and good views over the river.

Galleries

Ubud is dotted with galleries – every street and lane seems to have a place exhibiting artwork for sale. They vary enormously in the choice and quality of items on display.

Often you will find local artists in the most unusual places, including your place to stay. A good example is **Nyoman Sudiarsa**, a painter who has a studio in the grounds of his family's Padma Accommodation (see p186).

NEKA GALLERY

Operated by Suteja Neka, the **Neka Gallery** (Map pp174-5; ☎ 975034; Jl Raya Ubud; 🕑 9am-5pm) is a separate entity from the Neka Art Museum. It has an extensive selection from all the schools of Balinese art, as well as works by European residents such as the renowned Arie Smit.

SENIWATI GALLERY OF ART BY WOMEN

This **gallery** (Map pp174-5; 🕑 975485; www.seniwatigal lery.com; Jl Sriwedari 2B; 🕑 9am-5pm Tue-Sun) exhibits works by more than 70 Balinese, Indonesian

THAT DAMN BOOK

You see them everywhere these days in Ubud: women of a certain age strolling the streets with that *look*. A mixture of self-satisfaction, entitlement and too much yoga, with maybe just a hint of desperation that they haven't yet found their Felipe. You know, a rich Brazilian who can bed you silly for an entire month. Yes, it's the readers of *Eat, Pray, Love*, the best-selling Elizabeth Gilbert book that chronicles the author's search for self-fulfilment (and fulfilment of a book contract) across Italy, India and, yes, Ubud. 'That Damn Book' was the immediate reaction of a long-time Ubud resident when we asked her about it. And it was the same phrase used by another Ubud friend – we detected a trend.

Much as *A Year in Provence* and *Under the Tuscan Sun* caused hordes of acolytes to traipse across those places trying to recreate those books, the same has happened to Ubud. For the café owners, spa workers and back rubbers who've profited from the influx, it's 'That Wonderful Book'. But others are sorry the book doesn't paint a more complete picture of Ubud's locals, dance, art, expats and walks, warts and all. Of course, by the time Gilbert is waxing poetic about surf spots on the North Coast (there are none), you suspect things might have been ginned up a bit for the plot.

Still, there are real people in the book. Wayan Nuriasih, her elixir-mixing buddy, has a store-front (p180). If you want to find Ketut Liyer, the genial and inspirational friend she abandons once she has Felipe, ask around and you'll be directed. Although his porch is sagging from all the book's readers who turn up.

and resident foreign women artists. The information on many of the artists makes for fascinating reading. Works span all media and this small gallery is an excellent example of the kind of cultural and artistic organisation that can thrive in Ubud.

SYMON STUDIO
Danger! Art! screams the sign in Campuan. With this you know you've found the **gallery/studio** (Map pp174-5; ☎ 974721; www.symonbali .com; Jl Raya Campuan; ◷ 9am-6pm) of the irrepressible American artist Symon. The gallery is a spacious and airy place full of huge, colourful and exotic portraits. The work ranges from the sublime to the profane. (Symon, however, is most often found in his gallery in North Bali; see p255.)

KOMANEKA ART GALLERY
Exhibiting works from established Balinese artists, this **gallery** (Map p186; ☎ 976090; Monkey Forest Rd; ◷ 8am-8pm) is a good place to see high-profile art. The space is large and lofty, making a good place for viewing.

AGUNG RAI GALLERY
This **gallery** (Map pp174-5; ☎ 975449; Jl Peliatan; ◷ 9am-6pm) is in a pretty compound and its collection covers the full range of Balinese styles. It works as a cooperative, with the work priced by the artist and the gallery adding a percentage.

RIO HELMI GALLERY
Noted photographer and Ubud resident Rio Helmi has a small **gallery** (Map p186; ☎ 972304; www.riohelmi.com; Jl Suweta 5; ◷ 10am-8pm) where you can see examples of journalistic and artistic work. Photos change often and offer beautiful insight into Helmi's travels worldwide and across Bali.

ADI'S STUDIO
'Look at this!' cry the signs around town plugging this interesting **gallery** (Map pp174-5; ☎ 977104; Jl Bisma 102; ◷ 10am-5pm), and you should. Many of the better local artists display their works here, including Wayan Pasti, whose carvings give new meaning to 'pork'. It hosts occasional special events like live music.

PHO
You never know what you'll find at idiosyncratic **Pho** (Map p186; ☎ 0813 3866 9382; Jl Goutama), an enigmatic and enthusiastic open-air gallery right beside the road.

KETUT RUDI GALLERY
These sprawling **galleries** (Map p201; ☎ 974122; Pengosekan) showcase the works of more than 50 Ubud artists with techniques as varied as primitive and new realism. The gallery's namesake is on display as well; he favours an entertaining style best described as 'comical realism'.

MUSEUM PENDET
A small **gallery** (Map pp174-5; ☎ 0817 972 5835; Jl Nyuh Bulan; admission 20,000Rp; ✆ 9am-5pm) with carvings and paintings by better local artists. Not worth a special trip but worth a pause on a walk past.

Artists' Homes

The **'Spies house'**, home of German artist Walter Spies, is now part of Hotel Tjampuhan (p190). Aficionados can stay if they book well in advance. Spies played an important part in promoting Bali's artistic culture in 1930s.

Dutch-born artist Han Snel lived in Ubud from the 1950s until his death in 1999, and his family runs his namesake bungalows on Jl Kajeng (p189).

Lempad's House (Map p186; Jl Raya Ubud; admission free; ✆ daylight), the home of I Gusti Nyoman Lempad, is open to the public, but it's mainly used as a gallery for a group of artists, which includes Lempad's grandchildren. There are only a few of Lempad's own paintings and drawings here. The Puri Lukisan (p176) and Neka (p176) museums have more extensive collections of Lempad's drawings. The family compound itself is a good example of traditional Balinese architecture and layout – Lempad was also an architect and sculptor (see his work at the Ubud Palace, p176).

Music scholar Colin McPhee is well known thanks to his perennial favourite *A House in Bali*. Although the actual 1930s house is long gone, you can visit the riverside site (which shows up in photographs in the book) at the Sayan Terrace (p190). The hotel's Wayan Ruma, whose mother was McPhee's cook, is good for a few stories.

Arie Smit (1916–) is the best-known and longest-surviving Western artist in Ubud. He worked in the Dutch colonial administration in the 1930s, was imprisoned during WWII, and came to Bali in 1956. In the 1960s, his influence sparked the Young Artists school of painting in Penestanan, earning him an enduring place in the history of Balinese art. His home is not open to the public.

Sacred Monkey Forest Sanctuary

This cool and dense swath of jungle, officially called **Mandala Wisata Wanara Wana** (Map p186; ☎ 971304; www.monkeyforestubud.com; Monkey Forest Rd; adult/child 15,000/7500Rp; ✆ 8am-6pm), houses three holy temples. The sanctuary is inhabited by a band of grey-haired and greedy long-tailed Balinese macaques who are nothing like the innocent-looking doe-eyed monkeys on the brochures. They are ever vigilant for passing tourists who just might have peanuts and ripe bananas available for a quick hand-out. Don't hand food directly to these creatures.

The interesting **Pura Dalem Agung** (Temple of the Dead) is in the forest and has a real Indiana Jones feel to it. Look for the Rangda figures devouring children at the entrance to the inner temple.

You can enter through one of the three gates: the main one at the southern end of Monkey Forest Rd; 100m further east, near the car park; or from the southern side, on the lane from Nyuhkuning. The forest has recently benefited from an infusion of money. Useful brochures about the forest, macaques and temples are available. Across from the main entrance, the forest's **office** (Map p186) accepts donations for a scheme to offset the carbon you created getting to Bali. Get a tree planted for 150,000Rp.

Botanic Garden Ubud

Discover the stories behind the many plants that make Bali green at **Botanic Garden Ubud** (Map pp174-5; ☎ 970951; www.botanicgardenbali.com; admission 50,000Rp; ✆ 8am-6pm). Spread over more than 6 hectares, the many gardens are devoted to various themes such as orchids (in greenhouses), Bali-grown plants like cinnamon and vanilla, flowering butterfly-friendly gardens, an enormous lotus pond and much more. The work of Stefan Reisner, the gardens are a good counterpoint to art-filled museums. Get lost in the maze and when you finally escape, take comfort from Bali's medicinal plants. The exhibit about the cacti of East Bali is worth the cost of admission alone.

Petulu

Every evening at around 6pm, thousands of big **herons** and **egrets** fly in to Petulu (Map pp174–5), squabbling over the prime perching places before settling into the trees beside the road, and becoming a tourist attraction. The herons, mainly the striped Java pond species, started their visits to Petulu in 1965 for no apparent reason. Villagers believe they bring good luck (as well as tourists), despite the smell and the mess. A few warung (food stalls) have been set up in the paddy fields, where you can have a drink while enjoying the spectacle. Walk quickly under the trees if the herons are already roosting.

A bemo from Ubud to Pujung will drop you off at the turn-off just south of Petulu (the trip should take about 10 to 15 minutes), but it's more convenient with your own transport. It would make a pleasant walk or bicycle ride on any of several routes north of Ubud, but if you stay for the birds you'll be heading back in the dark.

ACTIVITIES
Massage, Spas & Salons

Ubud brims with salons and spas where you can pamper yourself. In fact, visiting a spa is at the top of many a visitor's itinerary. For more on the joys of Bali spas, see p330. Most higher-end hotels have (often lavish) spas.

For a workout, Ubud has a gym, **Ubud Fitness Centre** (Map pp174-5; ☎ 974804; Jl Jero Gading; day/week 50,000/140,000Rp; ☙ 7am-9pm), which offers weight training, aerobics and a boxing studio.

Eve Spa (Map p186; ☎ 747 0910; Monkey Forest Rd; 1hr massage 75,000Rp; ☙ 9am-9pm) will cleanse you of toxins from eating an apple or other dubious substances. The menu is straightforward and affordable, and you can go on something of a spa orgy: an all-day festival of treatments is 325,000Rp.

After a day trekking the beautiful Ubud countryside and listening to all those barking dogs, your own dogs may also be barking. Sessions at **Kenko Reflexology** (Map p186; ☎ 975293; Monkey Forest Rd; foot massage 40,000Rp; ☙ 8am-8pm) start with gentle foot cleansing and only get better.

Milano Salon (Map p186; ☎ 973448; Monkey Forest Rd; 1hr massage 70,000Rp; ☙ 9am-8pm) offers facials and massages in a simple setting, plus hair-cutting (50,000Rp), styling and colouring.

Nur Salon (Map pp174-5; ☎ 975352; Jl Hanoman 28; 1hr massage 105,000Rp; ☙ 9am-8pm) is in a traditional Balinese compound filled with labelled medicinal plants. It offers a long menu of straightforward spa and salon services, including a Javanese massage that takes two hours and starts with a body scrub (275,000Rp).

Ubud Sari Health Resort (Map pp174-5; ☎ 974393; Jl Kajeng; 1hr massage US$30; ☙ 8am-8pm) is a spa and hotel in one. It is a serious place with extensive treatments bearing names such as 'total tissue cleansing' (treatments use organic and other natural materials). Besides a long list of one-day spa and salon services, there are packages that include stays at the hotel (see p189).

Sedona Spa (Map pp174-5; ☎ 975770; Jl Raya Campuan; 1hr massage 70,000Rp; ☙ 10am-9pm) is a very attrac-

tive, purpose-built spa. Art adds to the serene air in the many individual treatment rooms. Baths sound like a breakfast menu: milk, honey, green tea, fruit etc. Call for free pickup or to arrange an outcall to your hotel.

Wayan Nuriasih (Map pp174-5; ☎ 742 6189; balihealer @hotmail.com; Jl Jembawan 5; ☙ 9am-5pm), one of the stars of *Eat, Pray, Love* (p178), can work wonders with medicinal plants – many are for sale out front – as well as massage and other treatments. The 'vitamin lunch' is the antidote for a Bintang dinner.

Yoga Barn (Map pp174-5; ☎ 070992; www.balispirit .com; off Jl Pengosekan; classes from 90,000Rp; ☙ 7am-8pm) sits in its own lotus position amid trees back near a river valley. The name exactly describes what you'll find – although this barn never needs shovelling. A huge range of classes in yoga and life-affirming offshoots are held through the week.

Zen (Map pp174-5; ☎ 970976; Jl Hanoman; 1hr massage 100,000Rp; ☙ 9am-8pm) has a good reputation. It offers body scrubs, 90-minute *mandi lulur* (Javanese body scrub) and a spice bath (160,000Rp).

Cycling

Many shops and hotels in central Ubud display mountain bikes for hire. The price is usually a negotiable 35,000Rp per day. If in doubt where to rent, ask at your hotel and someone with a bike is soon likely to appear.

In general, the land is dissected by rivers running south, so any east–west route will involve a lot of ups and downs as you cross the river valleys. North–south routes run between the rivers, and are much easier going, but can have heavy traffic. Most of the sites in Ubud are reachable by bike.

Riding a bike is an excellent way to visit the many museums and cultural sites described in the Around Ubud section (p198), although you'll need to consider your comfort level with traffic south of Ubud.

See p88 for companies offering cycling tours, many in or near Ubud.

Rafting

The nearby Sungai Ayung (Ayung River) is the most popular river in Bali for white-water rafting, so Ubud is a convenient base for rafting trips. You start north of Ubud and end near the Amandari hotel in the west. Note that depending on rainfall the run can range from sedate to thrilling. See p92 for names of operators.

WALKING TOURS

For information on guided walks see p184. The growth of Ubud has engulfed a number of nearby villages, although they have still managed to retain distinct identities. There are lots of interesting walks in the area to surrounding villages or through the paddy fields. You'll frequently see artists at work in open rooms and on verandahs, and the timeless tasks of rice cultivation continue alongside luxury villas.

In most places there are plenty of warung or small shops selling snack foods and drinks, but bring your own water. Also bring a good hat, decent shoes and wet-weather gear for the afternoon showers; long trousers are better for walking through thick vegetation.

It's good to start walks at daybreak, before it gets too hot. In the walks below, distances are approximate and are measured with the Ubud Palace as the start and end point. Walking times do not include any stops, so you need to factor in your own eating, shopping and rest stops.

Some entrepreneurial rice farmers have erected little toll gates across their fields. You can a) simply detour around them, or b) pay a fee (never, ever accede to more than 10,000Rp).

Monkey Forest & Penestanan

This walk features a good range of rice paddies and rural Ubud scenery.

Take your time strolling through the Sacred Monkey Forest Sanctuary at the bottom of Monkey Forest Rd, then take the sealed road at the southwestern corner of the forest near the temple. Continue south on the lane to the village of **Nyuhkuning**, and turn west along the south end of the football field, then turn south down the narrow road. At the southern end of the village, turn right and follow the paved road across the bridge over Sungai Wos to Dangin Lebak (this busy road is the most unpleasant part of the trip but should only take around 15 minutes). Take the track to the right just after the large Bale Banjar Dangin Lebak (Dangin Lebak Community Hall). From here follow paths due north through the paddy fields, and veer left, westwards, through the rice paddies to a paved road to reach **Katik Lantang**, where a paved road continues north to **Penestanan**. Many artists live here, and you can stop at their homes/studios/galleries at places like I Wayan Karja's Santra Putra gallery and lodging (see p183). Follow the rice-field paths north to reach these places, then descend the steep concrete stairs to Campuan and on to Ubud.

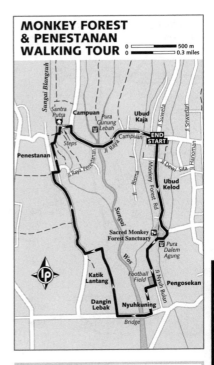

MONKEY FOREST & PENESTANAN WALKING TOUR

0 — 500 m
0 — 0.3 miles

WALK FACTS

Start/Finish Ubud Palace
Distance 8km
Duration Three hours

Campuan Ridge

This walk passes over the lush river valley of Sungai Wos, offering views of Gunung Agung and glimpses of small village communities and rice fields.

At the confluence of Sungai Wos and Sungai Cerik (Cerik River) is **Campuan**, which means 'Where Two Rivers Meet'. The walk leaves Jl Raya Campuan here at the Ibah Luxury Villas. Enter the hotel driveway and take the path to the left, where a walkway crosses the river to Pura Gunung Lebah. From there follow the concrete path north, climbing up onto the ridge between the two rivers. Fields of elephant grass, traditionally used for thatched roofs, slope away on either side.

Continuing north along the Campuan ridge past the Klub Kokos lodging (p189), the road improves as it passes through paddy fields

UBUD & AROUND

UBUD & AROUND

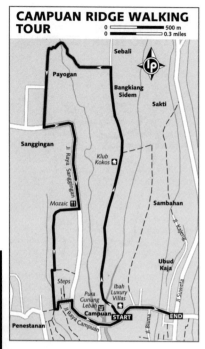

CAMPUAN RIDGE WALKING TOUR

WALK FACTS

Start/Finish Ubud Palace
Distance 8.5km
Duration 3½ hours

and the village of **Bangkiang Sidem**. On the outskirts of the village, an unsigned road heads west, winding down to Sungai Cerik (the west branch of Sungai Wos), then climbing steeply up to **Payogan**. From here you can walk south to the main road, and continue along Jl Raya Sanggingan to the restaurant Mozaic (p194). Here, veer to the west onto trails that stay level with the rice fields as the main road drops away. It's a fantasyland of coursing waterways and good views among the rice and villas. When you come to the steep concrete steps, take them down to Campuan and back to Ubud.

Penestanan & Sayan

The wonders of Sungai Ayung (Ayung River) are the focus of this outing, where you will walk below the luxury hotels built to take advantage of this lush, tropical river valley.

Just west of the Campuan bridge, past the Blanco Renaissance Museum, a steep uphill road, Jl Raya Penestanan, bends left and winds across the forested gully of Sungai Blangsuh (Blangsuh River) to the artists' village of Penestanan. West of Penestanan, head north on the small road north (it's before the busy main road) that curves around to **Sayan**. The Sayan Terrace hotel was Colin McPhee's home in the 1930s, as chronicled in his book *A House in Bali*. The views over the valley of the magnificent **Sungai Ayung** are superb. The best place to get to the riverside is just north of Sayan Terrace hotel (p190) – follow the increasingly narrow tracks down. (This part can be tricky but there are locals who'll show you for a tip of about 2000Rp.)

Following the rough trails north, along the eastern side of the Ayung, you traverse steep slopes, cross paddy fields and pass irrigation canals and tunnels. But for many people, it's a highlight of their walk, as we're talking about serious tropical jungle here. After about 1.5km you'll reach the finishing point for many white-water rafting trips – a good but steep trail goes from there up to the main road at **Kedewatan**, where you can walk back to Ubud. Alternatively, cross the

PENESTANAN & SAYAN WALKING TOUR

WALK FACTS

Start/Finish Ubud Palace
Distance 6.5km
Duration Four hours

river on the nearby bridge and climb up to the very untouristy village of **Tegalkuning** on the other side. There and back will add about 1km to your walk.

COURSES

Ubud is the perfect place to develop your artistic or language skills, or learn about Balinese culture and cuisine. The range of courses offered could keep you busy for a year.

Arts & Crafts

ARMA (Map pp174-5; ☎ 976659; www.armamuseum.com; Jl Raya Pengosekan; 🕑 9am-6pm) A cultural powerhouse offering classes in painting, woodcarving and batik. Other courses include Balinese history, Hinduism and architecture. Classes cost US$25 to US$50.

Kite Workshop (☎ 0813 3876 4495) Kites are a colourful part of Balinese culture. Programs are flexible and geared to families; classes are held in a village near Ubud and include materials and packing for getting the creations home.

Nirvana Batik Course (Map p186; ☎ 975415; www.nirvanaku.com; Nirvana Pension & Gallery, Jl Goutama 10; 🕑 classes 10am-3pm Mon-Sat) Nyoman Suradnya teaches the highly regarded batik courses. Classes cost US$40 to US$150 depending on duration (one to five days).

Pondok Pecak Library & Learning Centre (Map p186; ☎ 976194; Monkey Forest Rd, on the far side of the football field; 🕑 9am-5pm Mon-Sat, 1-5pm Sun) Painting and mask-carving classes. Sessions cost from 75,000Rp for one hour. Good resource centre for other courses offered locally.

Santra Putra (Map pp174-5; ☎ 977810; Penestan; classes per hr 100,000Rp) Intensive painting and drawing classes are run by abstract artist I Wayan Karja, whose studio is on site. Accommodation is also available; see p188.

Studio Perak (Map pp174-5; ☎ 974244; www.studioperak.com; Jl Hanoman) Specialises in Balinese-style silversmithing courses. A three-hour lesson, where you'll make a finished piece, costs 175,000Rp.

Taman Harum Cottages (Map p201; ☎ 975567; www.tamanharumcottages.com; Mas; lessons per hr from US$7) In the centre of Bali's woodcarving district, this place offers carving and painting courses. You can also learn how to make the temple offerings found just about everywhere. See p205 for details on accommodation.

Threads of Life Indonesian Textile Arts Center (Map pp174-5; ☎ 972187; www.threadsoflife.com; Jl Kajeng 24) Textile appreciation courses in the gallery and educational studio last from one day to eight days. Some classes involve extensive travel around Bali and should be considered graduate level.

Cooking

Amandari (Map pp174-5; ☎ 975333; www.amanresorts.com; Kedewatan) Classes begin early at the produce market then move on to a village where you learn how to cook in an actual Balinese home. Instruction is one-on-one and costs US$135, or US$200 for a couple.

Balinese Cooking Courses (Map pp174-5; ☎ 973283; www.casalunabali.com; Honeymoon Guesthouse, Jl Bisma) Janet de Neefe and her team run regular cooking courses at Honeymoon Guesthouse. Half-day courses (250,000Rp) are held six days per week and cover ingredients, cooking techniques and the cultural background of the Balinese kitchen. Sunday tours cover sea-salt and palm-sugar production (300,000Rp).

Bumbu Bali Restaurant (Map p186; ☎ 976698; Monkey Forest Rd) Balinese cooking course (175,000Rp) starts at the produce market and ends with lunch.

Language

Pondok Pecak Library & Learning Centre (see left) offers inexpensive courses. Its noticeboard has ads for the private tutors and teachers who provide courses on an ad hoc basis in both Bahasa Indonesia and the Balinese language.

See p332 for other language options.

Meditation & Spiritual Interests

ARMA (Map pp174-5; ☎ 976659; www.armamuseum.com; Jl Raya Pengosekan; 🕑 9am-6pm) Has classes in Hindu and Balinese astrology.

Ubud Sari Health Resort (Map pp174-5; ☎ 974393; Jl Kajeng; 🕑 8am-8pm) Offers meditation and yoga classes.

Music & Dance

Look for private teachers who advertise instruction in various Balinese/Indonesian instruments. A well-recommended Balinese music teacher is **Wayan Pasek Sucipta** (Map pp174-5; ☎ 970550; Eka's Homestay, Jl Sriwedari 8), who charges 80,000Rp for one hour, or lower rates for longer lessons.

Noted gamelan musician **Nyoman Warsa** (Map p186; ☎ 974807; Pondok Bamboo Music Shop, Monkey Forest Rd) offers courses in that most basic of Balinese instruments. Simple mastery can take six months or more. Those with less time can try a flute lesson (per hour 50,000Rp).

The musical family that runs **Aji Homestay** (Map pp174-5; ☎ 973255; Jl Sukma) offers lessons in Balinese dance and gamelan by several generations of the family. If you stay with them (p188), the cost is small.

Other options include ARMA, Pondok Pecak Library & Learning Centre and Taman Harum Cottages, which all offer courses in Balinese dance and music.

SAVING BALI'S DOGS, ONE POOCH AT A TIME

Mangy curs. That's the only label you can apply to many of Bali's dogs. As you travel the island – especially by foot – you can't help but notice dogs that are sick, ill-tempered, uncared for and victim to a litany of other maladies.

How can such a seemingly gentle island have Asia's worst dog population (and which had its first reported cases of rabies in 2008)? The answers are complex, but benign neglect has a lot to do with it. Dogs are at the bottom of the social strata: few have owners and local interest in them is nil.

Linda Buller first came to Bali 20 years ago. She was moved by the plight of the dogs. When she asked locals about it, she recalls, 'They said, "I am so wrapped up in my own spirituality that I have no time for a dog."'

For a long time she did what she could, adopting as many strays as she could care for. Finally in 2006 she got a chance to turn an abandoned gallery south of Ubud into a shelter. Today her non-profit group, **Bali Adoption Rehab Centre** (Map p201; BARC; ☎ 7904579; www.freewebs.com/balidogs; Jl Raya Pengosekan) cares for almost 100 dogs, places strays with sponsors and operates a mobile clinic for sterilisation.

The group is always looking for support, says Buller. 'I help people because dogs love people. What would the world be like without dogs?'

Note: **Yudisthira, the Bali Street Dog Foundation** (☎ 7424048; www.balistreetdogs.com) is another group that helps Bali's dogs. In 2007 it cared for over 12,000, and like BARC is always looking for donations and support.

TOURS

Specialised tours in Ubud include thematic walks and cultural adventures. Spending a few hours exploring the area with a local expert is a highlight for many.

See also p361 for tours of the Ubud area by companies operating across the Bali.

Bali Bird Walks (Map pp174-5; ☎ 975009; www.bali birdwalk.com; Jl Raya Campuan; walks US$33; ☑ Tue & Fri-Sun 9am-12.30pm) For the keen birdwatcher, this tour started by Victor Mason is still going strong. A gentle morning's walk (from the former Beggar's Bush Bar) will give you the opportunity to see maybe 30 of the 100 or so local species.

Banyan Tree Cycling (☎ 805 1620, 0813 3879 8516; www.banyantree.wikispaces.com) Has day-long tours of remote villages in the hills above Ubud. It's locally owned, and the tours (from 360,000Rp) emphasise interaction with villagers.

Herb Walks (☎ 975051; walks US$18; ☑ 8.30am Mon-Thu) Four-hour walks through lush Bali landscape; medicinal and cooking herbs and plants are identified and explained in their natural environment. Includes herbal drinks. A great deal.

Nomad's Organic Farming (☎ 977169; ☑ 9am Wed & Sun) All the produce used at Nomad (p191) comes from the owner's organic farm in a village some 40km from Ubud. Learn about his extensive recycling efforts and the island's food.

Ubud Tourist Information (Yaysan Bina Wisata; Map p186; ☎ 973285; Jl Raya Ubud; tours 125,000-200,000Rp; ☑ 8am-8pm) Runs interesting and affordable half- and full-day trips to a huge range of places, not to mention Ulu Watu, Mengwi, Alas Kedaton and Tanah Lot, or Goa Gajah, Pejeng, Gunung Kawi and Kintamani.

FESTIVALS & EVENTS

One of the best places to see the many religious and cultural events celebrated in Bali each year is the Ubud area. See p335 for details of the events. The tourist office (p176) is unmatched for its comprehensive information on events each week.

The **Ubud Writers & Readers Festival** (www.ubud writersfestival.com) brings together scores of writers and readers from around the world in a celebration of writing – especially writing that touches on Bali. It is usually held in October.

SLEEPING

Ubud has hundreds of places to stay. Choices range from simple homestays to luxurious retreats that are world-class. Choices can be bewildering, so give some thought to your aim. Do you want to be in the centre or the quiet countryside? Have a rice-field view or enjoy a room with stylish design?

Generally, Ubud offers good value for money at any price level. A simple, clean room within a family home compound is the least expensive option and you can do well for under US$20 a night. Ubud enjoys cool mountain air at night, so air-con isn't necessary, and with your windows open, you'll hear the symphony of sounds off the rice fields and river valleys.

Midrange hotels generally offer swimming pools and other amenities, while the top-end hotels are often perched on the edges of the deep river valleys, with superb views and service (although even some budget places have amazing views).

Addresses in Ubud can be imprecise – but signage at the end of a road will often list the names of all the places to stay. Away from the main roads there are no streetlights and it can be challenging to find your way after dark. If walking, you'll want a torch (flashlight).

Rentals

There are many houses you can rent or share in the Ubud area. For information about options, check the noticeboards at Pondok Pecak Library (p173), Ubud Tourist Information (p176) and Bali Buddha (p193). Also look in the free *Bali Advertiser* (www.baliadvertiser.biz) newspaper.

Budget

Inexpensive family lodgings are very small, often with just two, three or four rooms. They tend to operate in clusters, so you can easily look at a few before making your choice.

CENTRAL UBUD

This was the first place developed for tourists in Ubud and there are many good-value homestays.

Monkey Forest Rd

Jungut Inn (Map p186; ☎ 978237; Jl Arjuna; r 40,000-60,000Rp) A barebones choice on thriftseeker-friendly Jl Arjuna just off Monkey Forest Rd, Jungut's three rooms are cold-water-only and cheap. Ask the family if they need help making offerings.

Frog Pond Inn (Map p186; Monkey Forest Rd; r 80,000-120,000Rp) It's quiet, ultra-basic, friendly and has eight rooms with open-air bathrooms and cold water. Enjoy the breakfast that has charmed generations of backpackers across Asia: banana pancakes.

Pramesti (Map p186; ☎ 970843; uni_pramesti@hotmail.com; Monkey Forest Rd; s/d 100,000/120,000Rp) Down a classic dark alley, the sunny garden here is a true oasis. Gaze upon same from the porches of the bungalow-style rooms (all of which have hot water).

Mandia Bungalows (Map p186; ☎ 970965; Monkey Forest Rd; r 100,000-130,000Rp) It's heliconia heaven in the lush gardens. The four bungalow-style rooms are shaded by coconut palms and cooled by ceiling fans. Porches have comfy loungers.

Puri Muwa Bungalows (Map p186; ☎ 976441; Monkey Forest Rd; r from 100,000Rp) Near the top of Monkey Forest Rd in a thicket of basic places is this quiet homestay in a rambling compound. The cheapest of the nine rooms are cold-water-only.

Loka House (Map p186; ☎ 973326; off Monkey Forest Rd; r 100,000-150,000Rp) The lush entrance sets the mood at this peaceful place, where the two-storey main building overlooks a small carp pond in the garden. The three rooms (one with a tub) have hot water and fans.

Ubud Terrace Bungalows (Map p186; ☎ 975690; ubud_terrace@yahoo.com; Monkey Forest Rd; r 120,000-250,000Rp; ❄ 🛋) All 18 rooms have hot water and some have tubs; the costliest have air-con. The two-storey blocks bracket the pool and are convenient to the centre.

Warsa's Garden Bungalows (Map p186; ☎ 971548; Monkey Forest Rd; r 150,000-200,000Rp; ❄ 🛋) A good-sized pool with fountains enlivens this comfy but simple place in the heart of Monkey Forest action. The 10 rooms are reached through a traditional family-compound entrance. Some have tubs; some are fan-only.

Ibunda Inn (Map p186; ☎ 973252; Monkey Forest Rd; r 150,000-250,000Rp; ❄ 🛋) Three two-storey buildings each with four rooms cluster in a nicely shaded compound. The cheapest rooms are fan- and shower-only. All have the traditional porch for chilling at the end of the day and chatting up the neighbours.

East of Monkey Forest Rd

Small streets east of Monkey Forest Rd, including Jl Karna and Jl Maruti, have numerous, family-style homestays, which are secluded but close to the market and Jl Raya Ubud.

Gandra House (Map p186; ☎ 976529; Jl Karna; r from 100,000Rp) Modern bathrooms and spacious gardens are the highlights of this cold-water 10-room homestay. It's one of several family-run places on this street, so compare.

Sania's House (Map p186; ☎ 975535; sania_house @yahoo.com; Jl Karna 7; r 150,000-250,000Rp; 🛋 🖥) Pets wander about this family-run place, where the large, clear pool, huge terrace and spacious rooms will have you howling at the moon. The 21 rooms are basic but clean.

Jl Goutama

This charming street has several cheap, quiet and accessible places to stay.

Donald Homestay (Map p186; ☎ 977156; Jl Goutama; r 50,000-80,000Rp) The four rooms – some with hot water – are in a nice back corner of the family compound. Like many family-compound places, the chickens running around have a date with a bamboo skewer (although the multigenerational family says the rabbit are purely pets).

Agung Cottages (Map p186; ☎ 975414; Jl Goutama; r 150,000-250,000Rp, villas 300,000Rp; 🌊) Follow a short path to reach this slightly rural-feeling family compound. The six huge, spotless rooms (some fan-only) are set in gardens tended by a lovely family. It's well off the already quiet road.

Nirvana Pension & Gallery (Map p186; ☎ 975415; www.nirvanaku.com; Jl Goutama 10; s/d 200,000/250,000Rp) There are *alang alang* (woven thatch) roofs, a plethora of paintings, ornate doorways and six rooms with modern bathrooms in a secluded locale next to large family temple. Batik courses are also held (p183).

North of Jl Raya Ubud

Both Jl Kajeng and Jl Suweta, leading north from Jl Raya, offer an excellent choice of budget lodgings, some quite close to the centre of town. It's a timeless tableau with kids playing in the streets and women bringing home – balanced on their heads – produce from the market.

Shanti Home Stay (Map p186; ☎ 975421; Jl Kajeng 5; r 60,000-120,000Rp) This is a classic Ubud homestay: you join four generations of the family – plus numerous cute pooches – in a compound with six rooms in bungalow-style units. Rooms are clean and some have hot water. The porches are spacious.

Padma Accommodation (Map p186; ☎ 977247; aswatama@hotmail.com; Jl Kajeng 13; r 120,000Rp) There are but two adjoining, very private bungalows in a tropical garden here. Rooms are decorated with local crafts and the modern outdoor bathrooms have hot water. Nyoman Sudiarsa, a painter and family member, has a studio here and often shares his knowledge with guests.

Mumbul Inn (Map p186; ☎ 975995; Jl Raya Ubud; r US$20-25; 🌊) An Ubud veteran, family-run Mumbul is right in the centre but has classic views across a river gorge. Ponder the tranquil scene from the terrace of the clean, bungalow-style units. Air-con rooms are the best value.

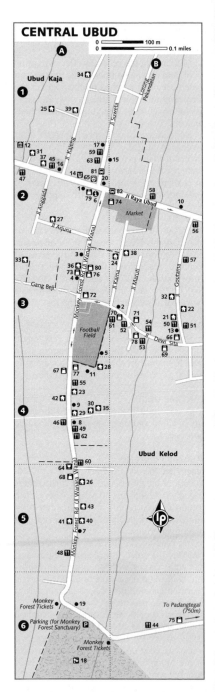

INFORMATION
Ary's Bookshop...........................**1** A2
Cinta Bookshop.........................**2** B3
Mua Pharmacy...........................**3** A3
Periplus.....................................**4** A3
Pondok Pecak Library &
   Learning Centre.....................**5** A3
Puri Saren Agung...................(see 20)
Rendezvousdoux...................(see 58)
Ubud Tourist
   Information............................**6** A2

SIGHTS & ACTIVITIES
Eve Spa.....................................**7** A5
Kenko Reflexology......................**8** A4
Komaneka Art Gallery..................**9** A4
Lempad's House........................**10** B2
Milano Salon.............................**11** A4
Museum Puri Lukisan.................**12** A2
Nirvana Batik Course..............(see 32)
Nyoman Warsa.......................(see 75)
Pho...**13** B3
Pondok Pecak Library &
   Learning Centre...................(see 5)
Pura Desa Ubud.......................**14** A2
Pura Marajan Agung..................**15** B2
Pura Taman Saraswati...............**16** A2
Rio Helmi Gallery......................**17** A2
Sacred Monkey Forest
   Sanctuary............................**18** A6
Sacred Monkey Forest
   Sanctuary Office..................**19** A6
Ubud Palace.............................**20** A2

SLEEPING
Agung Cottages........................**21** B3
Donald Homestay.....................**22** B3
Frog Pond Inn..........................**23** A4

Gandra House...........................**24** B3
Han Snel Bungalow..................**25** A1
Ibunda Inn................................**26** A5
Jungut Inn **27** A2
Loka House...............................**28** A4
Lumbung Sari............................**29** A4
Mandia Bungalows....................**30** A4
Mumbul Inn..............................**31** A2
Nirvana Pension & Gallery........**32** B3
Oka Wati Hotel.........................**33** A3
Padma Accommodation.............**34** A1
Pramesti...................................**35** A4
Puri Muwa Bungalows...............**36** A3
Puri Saraswati Bungalows.........**37** A2
Puri Saren Agung....................(see 20)
Sania's House............................**38** B3
Shanti Home Stay.....................**39** A1
Ubud Inn..................................**40** A5
Ubud Terrace Bungalows...........**41** A5
Ubud Village Hotel...................**42** A4
Warsa's Garden
   Bungalows...........................**43** A5

EATING
Aji's Kites.................................**44** B6
Bumbu Bali Restaurant...........(see 55)
Café Lotus................................**45** A2
Café Wayan & Bakery...............**46** A4
Casa Luna.................................**47** A2
Coffee & Silver.........................**48** A5
Delta Mart................................**49** A4
Devilicious................................**50** B3
Dewa Warung............................**51** B3
Dragonfly.................................**52** B3
Juice Ja Café.............................**53** B3
Kafe Batan Waru.......................**54** B3
Lamak.......................................**55** A4
Nomad......................................**56** B2

Pignou di Penyu.......................**57** B3
Rendezvousdoux.......................**58** B2
Terazo.......................................**59** A2
Three Monkeys.........................**60** A4
Tutmak Café.............................**61** B3
Waroeng...................................**62** A4
Warung Ibu Oka........................**63** A2

DRINKING
Lebong Café............................(see 77)
Napi Orti...................................**64** A5

ENTERTAINMENT
Nyoman Warsa.......................(see 75)
Pura Taman Saraswati.............(see 16)
Ubud Palace...........................(see 20)
Ubud Wantilan..........................**65** A2

SHOPPING
Alamkara..................................**66** B3
Alamkara..................................**67** A4
Ashitaba...................................**68** A5
Helena 'n Kidz...........................**69** B3
Kertas Lingsir............................**70** B3
Kou...**71** B3
Kou Cuisine..............................**72** A3
Macan Tidur..............................**73** A3
Pasar Seni (Art Market)............**74** B2
Pondok Bamboo Music Shop....**75** B6
Pusaka......................................**76** A3
Rum Batik.................................**77** A4
Thebb.......................................**78** B3
Toko East..................................**79** A2
Zarong......................................**80** A3

TRANSPORT
Bemo Stop................................**81** A2
Bemo Stop................................**82** B2

UBUD & AROUND

NORTH OF THE CENTRE

Things get quiet as you head up the gentle slope from Jl Raya Ubud; note that some places are a kilometre or more to the north.

Homestay Rumah Roda (Map pp174–5; ☎ 975487; rumahroda@indo.net.id; Jl Kajeng 24; r 70,000-90,000Rp) Next door to the Threads of Life gallery on peaceful Jl Kajeng, Rumah Roda is a typically mellow homestay. The five bungalows have hot water and there's a good breakfast from the popular Roda Restaurant (see p193). The inn is dedicated to sound ecological principles and you can refill your water bottles here.

EAST OF THE CENTRE

You can get to the heart of Ubud in less than 15 minutes by foot from this low-key part of town.

Jl Sriwedari

Eka's Homestay (Map pp174–5; ☎ 970550; Jl Sriwedari 8; r 70,000Rp) Follow your ears to this nice little family compound with six basic cold-water rooms. Eka's is the home of Wayan Pasek Sucipta, a teacher of Balinese music (see p183). It's in a nice sunny spot on a quiet road (well, except during practice).

Jl Hanoman

East of central Ubud, but still conveniently located, this area has several budget lodgings along Jl Hanoman.

Artini Cottages 1 (Map pp174–5; ☎ 975348; www.artini cottage.com; Jl Hanoman; bungalows 150,000Rp) The Artini family runs a small empire of good-value guesthouses on Jl Hanoman. This, the original, is in an ornate family compound with many flowers. The three bungalows have hot water and large bathtubs. The more up-scale number 2, with rice-field views and a pool, is opposite.

Nick's Homestay (Map pp174–5; ☎ 975526; www.nicks hotels-ubud.com; Jl Hanoman 57; US$15) Nick has a minor empire of three Ubud budget hotels. This, his simplest, is the best. Beds in the six bungalow-style rooms are made from bamboo logs. Watch family life from the copious porches.

Dewi Sri Bungalows (Map pp174-5; ☎ 975300; Jl Hanoman 69; r with fan/air-con 150,000/200,000; 🔀 🖭) The best value here are the split-level fan-only rooms, which have cute, open-air bath-rooms below and a terrace with glimpses of rice above. The air-con rooms are daggy and strictly for those who think they need cool air – in Ubud nature supplies it at night.

Tebesaya

A little further east, this quiet village com-prises little more than its main street, Jl Sukma, which runs between two streams.

Biangs (Map pp174-5; ☎ 976520; Jl Sukma 28; r 50,000-100,000Rp) In a little garden, Biangs – mean-ing 'mama' – has six well-maintained rooms, with hot water. The best rooms have views of a small valley. Should you need a Japanese novel, the book exchange is loaded.

Aji Homestay (Map pp174-5; ☎ 973255; Jl Sukma; r 70,000-150,000Rp) The site tumbles down a small hill into a thicket of bamboo. The nine simple rooms have tubs and some have views. This end of Ubud is always quiet: you can hear water flowing through the fields and doves calling. Plunge into Balinese culture here with dance lessons; see p183.

Family Guest House (Map pp174-5; ☎ 974054; family house@telkom.net; Jl Sukma; r 100,000-300,000Rp) There's a bit of bustle from the busy family at this charming homestay. Healthy breakfasts fea-turing brown bread from Café Wayan are served. The nine rooms are cold-water-only at the low end of the price range; as you reach the middle range, rooms also include tubs; and at the top, they have a balcony with a valley view.

WEST OF THE CENTRE
Jl Bisma

Paved with cement blocks inscribed by residents and donors, Jl Bisma runs into a plateau of rice fields. New places are pop-ping up all the time and many sit amid the paddies.

Pondok Indah (Map pp174-5; ☎ 966323; off Jl Bisma; s/d 150,000/200,000Rp) Follow the swift-flowing waterways for 150m along a path hopping with frogs to this peaceful place where the top-floor terraces look over the fields. All five rooms have hot water.

Bali Moon (Map pp174-5; ☎ 978293; off Jl Bisma; r from 170,000Rp) Watch the moon rise over Gunung Batukau from this simple inn set with a few others down narrow paths between the

rice fields. The four rooms are simple but have ambitions of style with open-air bath-rooms with tubs. One 2nd-floor room is the view-lovers' choice.

Campuan & Penestanan

West of Ubud, but still within walking dis-tance, simple rooms and bungalows in the rice fields are pitched at those seeking low-priced, longer-term lodgings. Most will offer discounted monthly rates (US$200 is aver-age), and some larger bungalows are quite economical if you can share with a group of people. Stroll the narrow paths and you'll find many options – although the owners often find you first.

Note that these places are a steep climb up a set of concrete stairs off Jl Raya Campuan. (You can avoid this by approaching from the west.)

Santra Putra (Map pp174-5; ☎ 977810; karjabali@yahoo .com; off Jl Raya Campuan; r US$12-15) Run by inter-nationally exhibited abstract artist I Wayan Karja (whose studio/gallery is also on site), this place has five big, open airy rooms with hot water. Enjoy paddy-field views from all vantage points. Painting and drawing classes are offered by the artist; see p183.

Kori Agung Bungalows (Map pp174-5; ☎ 975166; off Jl Raya Campuan; r from 150,000Rp) On the terrace with other basic inns above Campuan. Rooms are basic but the location is ideal for those looking for leafy views and solitude. The only noise at night is water coursing through the rice fields.

Midrange

Choices are many in this price range. Expect a pool, hot water, decent service and other fea-tures such as river views, satellite TV, fridge, air-con and often breakfast.

CENTRAL UBUD
Jl Raya Ubud

Don't settle for a room with road noise along Ubud's main drag.

Puri Saren Agung (Map p186; ☎ 975057; fax 975137; Jl Raya Ubud; r US$50-70; 🔀) Part of the Ubud royal family's historic palace (see p176). Rooms are tucked behind the courtyard where the dance performances are held. Accommodation is in traditional Balinese pavilions, with big veran-dahs, four-poster beds, antique furnishings and hot water. Give a royal wave to wandering tourists from your patio.

Puri Saraswati Bungalows (Map p186; ☎ 975164; www.purisaraswati.com; Jl Raya Ubud; r US$60-90; ✳ ☒) Very central and pleasant with lovely gardens that open onto the Ubud Water Palace. The 18 rooms are well back from Jl Raya Ubud, so it's quiet. Some rooms are fan-only; interiors are simply furnished but have richly carved details.

Monkey Forest Rd

Ubud Inn (Map p186; ☎ 975071; www.ubudinn.com; Monkey Forest Rd; r US$25-80; ✳ ☒) Lush loses its meaning in Ubud, but this place takes it to a new level. The 30 rooms span several budgets: basic are fan-only; the rest are large, nicely furnished and have fridges. The L-shaped pool has a children's area.

Oka Wati Hotel (Map p186; ☎ 973386; www.okawati hotel.com; off Monkey Forest Rd; r US$30-60; ☒) Oki Wati (the owner) is a lovely lady who grew up near the Ubud Palace. The 19 rooms have large verandahs where the delightful staff will deliver your choice of breakfast. The decor features vintage details like four-poster beds; some rooms view a small rice field.

Lumbung Sari (Map p186; ☎ 976396; www.lumbung sari.com; Monkey Forest Rd; r US$45-90; ✳ ☒) Artwork decorates the walls at the stylish Sari, which has a nice breakfast *bale* (traditional pavilion) by the pool. The eight rooms (some fan-only) have tubs in elegant bathrooms finished with terrazzo.

North of Jl Raya Ubud

Han Snel Bungalow (Map p186; ☎ 975699; www .hansnelbungalow.com; Jl Kajeng 3; bungalows US$20-50; ✳ ☒) Owned by the family of the late Han Snel, a well-known Ubud painter, this quiet compound has eight bungalows with suitably artful stone designs. Some rooms are perched right on the edge of the river gorge and have excellent views; the small pool is part-way down.

NORTH OF THE CENTRE

Ketut's Place (Map pp174-5; ☎ 975304; www.ketutsplace .com; Jl Suweta 40; r US$21-46; ✳ ☒) The nine rooms here range from basic with fans to deluxe versions with air-con and bathtub. All have artful accents and enjoy a dramatic pool shimmering down the hillside and river-valley views. On some nights, an impressive Balinese feast is served by Ketut, a local luminary.

Ubud Sari Health Resort (Map pp174-5; ☎ 974393; www.ubudsari.com; Jl Kajeng; r US$35-60; ✳ ☒) Like

your colon after a week of treatments here, this 10-room health resort has been spiffed up. See p180 for details on the spa. The plants in the gardens are labelled for their medicinal qualities and the café serves organic, vegetarian fare. Guests can use the health facilities, including the sauna and whirlpool.

Klub Kokos (Map pp174-5; ☎ 978270; www.klubkokos .com; r US$48-100; ✳ ☒) A beautiful 1.5km walk north along the Campuan ridge (see p181 for details), Klub Kokos is a ridge-top hideaway with a big pool and seven spotless bungalow-style rooms. It's reachable by car from the north; call for directions. Rates include breakfast and snacks and there's a café.

EAST OF THE CENTRE

Matahari Cottages (Map pp174-5; ☎ 975459; www .matahariubud.com; Jl Jembawan; r US$35-60; ✳) This delightful place has six flamboyant, themed rooms, including the 'Batavia Princess' and the 'Indian Pasha'. The library is a vision out of a 1920s fantasy. It also boasts a self-proclaimed 'jungle Jacuzzi' and a multicourse breakfast and high tea elaborately served on silver (free for guests). And in a nod to the modern day, the hotel fully recycles.

SOUTH OF THE CENTRE

Artini 3 Cottages (Map pp174-5; ☎ 974147; www.artini ubudhotel.com; Jl Raya Pengosekan; r US$35-45; ✳ ☒) The top choice of the Artini empire, the 16 rooms here are in attractive stone buildings arrayed around a spectacular pool area down by a stream. Get a room facing east for the best views through the palms. Room decor is comfortable but standard.

Saren Indah Hotel (Map pp174-5; ☎ 971471; www .sarenhotel.com; Jl Nyuh Bulan, Nyuhkuning; r US$40-90; ✳ ☒) South of the Monkey Forest, this 15-room hotel sits in the middle of rice fields – be sure to get a 2nd-floor room to enjoy the views. Rooms are spotless; better ones have TVs, fridges and baths with stylish tubs. Be sure to negotiate for rates at the lower end of the scale.

our pick **Alam Indah** (Map pp174-5; ☎ 974629; www .alamindahbali.com; Jl Nyuh Bulan; r US$50-95; ✳ ☒) Just south of the Monkey Forest in Nyuhkuning, this isolated and spacious resort has 10 rooms that are beautifully finished in natural materials to traditional designs. The Wos Valley views are entrancing, especially from the multilevel pool area. The walk in at night follows a driveway lined with tea candles.

WEST OF THE CENTRE
Jl Bisma
Close to town, this area retains rural charm while moving upmarket.

Uma Sari Cottage (Map pp174-5; ☎ 981538; www.uma sari.com; Jl Bisma; r $30-40; ❄ ☑ ☐) While ducks patrol the rice in the surrounding fields looking for bugs, you can waggle your tail in the jade-green pool. Most of the eight large rooms are fan-only; go for the upper floor, as the verandahs have the best views of the ducks in action. All have tubs.

Sama's Cottages (Map pp174-5; ☎ 973481; samas cottages@indo.com; Jl Bisma; s/d US$33/39; ☑) This lovely little hideaway is terraced down a hill. The bungalow-like rooms have lashings of Balinese style layered on absolute simplicity. The oval pool feels like a jungle oasis. Ask for low-season discounts.

Honeymoon Guesthouse (Map pp174-5; ☎ 973282; www.casalunabali.com; Jl Bisma; r 350,000-600,000Rp; ❄ ☑ ☐) Run by the Casa Luna (p192) clan, the 19 rooms here have terraces and tubs; some have air-con. There's a play area for kids. Avoid the dark rooms; some rooms have air-con and those near reception have wi-fi. See p183 for details about the cooking classes held here.

Campuan & Penestanan
Just west of the Campuan bridge, steep Jl Raya Penestanan branches off to the left, and climbs up and around to Penestanan.

Pager Bungalows (Map pp174-5; ☎ 975433; Jl Raya Campuan; r 150,000-300,000Rp, villas 500,000Rp) Run by painter Nyoman Pageh and his family, this cute homestay hugs a verdant hillside location that feels like you're lost in the bottom of the spinach bowl on a salad bar. Two large bungalows face the compound; five more rooms are comfortable and have views. The family villa is a fully appointed apartment.

Hotel Tjampuhan (Map pp174-5; ☎ 975368; www .pitamaharesorts-bali.com; Jl Raya Campuan; r US$65-120; ❄ ☑) This venerable place overlooks the confluence of Sungai Wos and Campuan. The influential German artist Walter Spies lived here in the 1930s, and his former home, which sleeps four people (US$220), is now part of the hotel. Bungalow-style units spill down the hill and enjoy mesmerising valley views.

Sayan & Ayung Valley
Sayan Terrace (Map pp174-5; ☎ 974384; www.sayanterrace resort.com; Jl Raya Sayan; r US$80-160; ❄ ☑ ☐ wi-fi)

Gaze into the Sayan Valley from this venerable hotel and you'll understand why this was the site of Colin McPhee's namesake *A House in Bali*; see p179 for details. Stay here while your neighbours – distant neighbours it should be said – are housed in luxury resorts paying far more. Here the 11 rooms are simply decorated but are large and have *that* view. Rates include afternoon tea.

Top End
At this price range you have your choice of prime properties in the area. The big decision: close to town or not? Look for views, expansive pools, striking architectural features such as marble and/or outdoor bathrooms, and a full range of amenities. Most resorts provide shuttle service around the Ubud area.

CENTRAL UBUD
Ubud Village Hotel (Map p186; ☎ 975571; www.theubud village.com; Monkey Forest Rd; r US$70-160; ❄ ☑ ☐) Mainstream comfort is the order of the day at this centrally located 28-room hotel. Rooms have elegant traditional Balinese decor with plenty of teak and ikat, and the pool area is large. The owners have a luxe villa resort with the same name in Pengosekan.

NORTH OF THE CENTRE
Waka di Ume (Map pp174-5; ☎ 973178; www.wakadi umeubud.com; Jl Suweta; r US$150, villas from US$300; ❄ ☑ ☐ wi-fi) Located a gentle 1.5km uphill from the centre, this elegant compound enjoys engrossing virescent views across rice fields. New and old styles mix in the large units; go for a villa with a view. Service is superb yet relaxed. Listening to gamelan practice echoing across the fields at night is quite magic.

SOUTH OF THE CENTRE
ARMA Resort (Map pp174-5; ☎ 976659; www.armaresort .com; Jl Raya Pengosekan; r US$80-180, villas from US$375; ❄ ☐ ☑) Get full Balinese cultural immersion at the hotel enclave of the ARMA compound (see p177 for details about the excellent museum and p183 for details on the range of courses offered). The expansive property has a large library and elegant gardens. Villas come with private pools.

WEST OF THE CENTRE
Properties generally go from posh to posher as you near the fabled Ayung Valley.

Campuan
Warwick Ibah Luxury Villas & Spa (Map pp174-5; ☎ 974466; www.warwickibah.com; off Jl Raya Campuan; ste US$200-530; ✕ ⚐ 🖳 wi-fi) Overlooking the rushing waters of the Wos Valley, the Ibah offers refined luxury in 15 spacious, stylish individual suites and villas, which combine ancient and modern details. The swimming pool is set into the hillside amid gardens and lavish stone carvings.

Pita Maha (Map pp174-5; ☎ 974330; www.pitamaha resorts-bali.com; Jl Raya Sanggingan; villas US$275-400; ✕ ⚐ 🖳 wi-fi) Broad, open views across a valley to the rice fields beyond are the highlight of this understated but luxurious hotel. The traditional-style villas are large and built with real attention to detail. More money gets you good views and a private plunge pool – although the main curving infinity pool may seduce you.

Sayan & Ayung Valley
Two kilometres west of Ubud, the fast-flowing Sungai Ayung has carved out a deep valley, its sides sculpted into terraced paddy fields or draped in thick rainforest. Overlooking this verdant valley are some of Bali's best hotels.

Novus Tamen Bebek (Map pp174-5; ☎ 975385; www .baliwww.com/tamanbebek; Jl Raya Sayan; r US$180-300; ✕ ⚐) A spectacular location overlooking the Sayan Valley may keep you glued to your terrace throughout the day. Five large villas are almost lost amid the plethora of green. All have mannered, classic Balinese wood-and-thatch architecture. Reception shares a parking area with the Sayan Terrace.

Bambu Indah (Map pp174-5; ☎ 975124; www.bambu indah.com; Baung; house US$200-500; ⚐ 🖳 wi-fi) Famed expat entrepreneur John Hardy sold his namesake jewellery company in 2007 and became a hotelier. On a ridge near Sayan and his beloved Sungai Ayung, he's assembled a compound of four 100-year-old royal Javanese houses. Several outbuildings create a timeless village with underpinnings of luxury. The entire compound is run to a very 'green' standard.

Four Seasons Resort (Map pp174-5; ☎ 977577; www .fourseasons.com; Sayan; ste from US$550, villas from US$700; ✕ ⚐ 🖳 wi-fi) Set below the valley rim, the curved open-air reception area looks like a Cinerama screen of Ubud beauty. Many villas have private pools and all share the same amazing views and striking modern design. At night you hear just the water rushing below. The service wins rave reviews.

Amandari (Map pp174-5; ☎ 975333; www.amanresorts .com; Kedewatan; ste from US$700; ✕ ⚐ 🖳 wi-fi) In Kedewatan village, the storied Amandari does everything with charm and grace – sort of like a classical Balinese dancer. Superb views over the jungle and down to the river – the 30m green-tiled swimming pool seems to drop right over the edge – are just some of the inducements. The 30 private pavilions have been given a rather lavish makeover that has magazine photographers drooling.

EATING
Ubud's cafés and restaurants are some of the best in Bali. It's a good place to try authentic Balinese dishes, as well as Asian and other international cuisine.

Many eateries make beautiful use of natural design elements and some offer serene settings with views out over the rice fields. Cafés where you can sip an excellent coffee or juice are common – some people never seem to leave. There are also many inexpensive warung serving fresh and tasty authentic Indonesian dishes. Note: Ubud's nightlife fades fast after the last note of gamelan music; don't wait past 9pm to eat or you won't. Better restaurants will provide transport to and from; call to arrange.

For organic foods, try Bali Buddha (p193). Good **organic farmers markets** are held each week, at Pizza Bagus (p194) every Saturday from 8am to 1pm and at Dragonfly (p192) every Wednesday from 3pm to 6pm.

On Monkey Forest Rd there's a centrally located branch of **Delta Mart** (Map p186; Monkey Forest Rd; ☽ 24hr), a local chain of convenience stores that's useful for snacks and sundries. **Delta Dewata Supermarket** (Map pp174-5; ☎ 973049; Jl Raya Andong) has a huge selection of goods. **Bintang Supermarket** (Map pp174-5; Bintang Centre, Jl Raya Campuan) is well located and has a large range of food and other essentials.

Central Ubud
JL RAYA UBUD
There are busy and tasty choices on Ubud's main street.

Nomad (Map p186; ☎ 977169; Jl Raya Ubud; dishes 15,000-60,000Rp) Offers a daily barbecue, often with a gamelan player providing the soundtrack. Balinese food is served in tapas-sized portions. Assume the position – lotus that is – at low Japanese-style tables. The owners offer tours of their organic farm (p184).

Casa Luna (Map p186; ☎ 977409; Jl Raya Ubud; dishes 15,000-60,000Rp) Renaissance woman Janet de Neefe of cooking school (p183) and writers festival (p184) fame runs this ever-popular Indonesian-focused restaurant, which has a delicious range of bread, pastries, cakes and more from its well-known bakery.

Rendezvousdoux (Map p186; ☎ 747 0163; Jl Raya Ubud 14; dishes 20,000-35,000Rp; ⊠) How to define it? A fusion of French-accented forms: café, library and bookshop, Rendezvousdoux is the most creative spot on the street. Bonuses include global music (at times live) and historic films about Ubud on loop.

Café Lotus (Map p186; ☎ 975357; Jl Raya Ubud; dishes 25,000-60,000Rp) A meal at this Ubud veteran, overlooking the lotus pond at Pura Taman Saraswati, is a relaxing treat for many when they first arrive in Ubud. The menu features well-prepared Western and Indonesian fare. For 50,000Rp you can book front-row seats for dance performances at Pura Taman Saraswati (p176).

MONKEY FOREST RD

Waroeng (Map p186; ☎ 970928; Monkey Forest Rd; dishes from 15,000Rp; wi-fi) Not your Made's Warung but rather a casual café with good Indonesian food aimed at the discriminating Western palate. Get a table at a bench in front and enjoy the passing Monkey Forest parade. The same owners operate the popular Jazz Café (p194).

Bumbu Bali (Map p186; ☎ 976698; Monkey Forest Rd; dishes 15,000-50,000Rp) A good place for Balinese food in the heart of Ubud. The menu features dishes such as *lawar* (green bean salad), *ayam pelalah* (spicy shredded chicken salad) and *sambal goreng udang* (prawns in a tangy coconut-milk sauce). Like your food? Learn to cook it (p183).

Three Monkeys (Map p186; ☎ 974830; Monkey Forest Rd; mains 20,000-50,000Rp) Mellow music and artworks set a cultured mood. The tables overlooking the rice field out back make it magic. By day there are sandwiches, salads and gelato. At night there's a fusion menu of Asian classics, including addictive Vietnamese summer prawn rolls.

Coffee & Silver (Map p186; ☎ 975354; Monkey Forest Rd; dishes 20,000-70,000Rp; ⊠ 10am-midnight; wi-fi) Tapas and more substantial items make up the menu at this comfortable café with seating inside and out. Vintage photos of Ubud line the walls. Many linger over the good coffee and other drinks for hours.

Lamak (Map p186; ☎ 974668; Monkey Forest Rd; dishes 40,000-160,000Rp; ⊠ 11am-midnight) The large open kitchen has a creative take on Indonesian food and each day there are specials highlighting dishes you seldom see. The main menu is top-end fusion. Long wine list.

EAST OF MONKEY FOREST RD

Juice Ja Café (Map p186; ☎ 971056; Jl Dewi Sita; snacks from 15,000Rp) Glass of spirulina? Dash of wheatgrass with your papaya juice? Organic fruits and vegetables go into the food at this funky bakery-café. Little brochures explain the provenance of items like the organic cashew nuts.

Tutmak Café (Map p186; ☎ 975754; Jl Dewi Sita; dishes 15,000-35,000Rp; wi-fi) The breezy multilevel location here, facing both Jl Dewi Sita and the football field, is a popular place for a refreshing drink or a meal. Local comers on the make huddle around their laptops plotting their next move.

Dragonfly (Map p186; ☎ 972973; Jl Dewi Sita; dishes 20,000-60,000Rp; wi-fi) Once a brash newcomer but now an established fave, Dragonfly has a popular menu for mostly organic breakfasts, and salads, sandwiches, and Indo and Italian fare other times. Listen to live jazz Friday and Saturday nights from tables inside and out.

Kafe Batan Waru (Map p186; ☎ 977528; Jl Dewi Sita; dishes 20,000-70,000Rp) This ever-popular café has an expanded outdoor terrace. It serves consistently excellent Indonesian food, which is presented with a dash of colour and flair. The *mie goreng* noodles are made fresh daily – a noteworthy detail given the number of places that substitute pot noodles. Western dishes include sandwiches and salads.

JL GOUTAMA

Choose from several simple and funky eateries on this nearly traffic-free lane.

Dewa Warung (Map p186; Jl Goutama; dishes 5000-20,000Rp) When it rains, the tin roof sounds like a tap-dance convention and the bare lightbulbs sway in the breeze. A little garden surrounds tables a few steps above the road where diners tuck into plates of sizzling fresh Indo fare.

Devilicious (Map p186; ☎ 745972; Jl Goutama; mains from 20,000Rp) Jl Goutama is a delightful street for a stroll and this café is one of the reasons why. Just wandering the narrow lane is like stepping back 30 years in Ubud, and creative little places like this café seem to appear like mushrooms after the rain. Look for theme nights like Cajun Fridays and Italian Tuesdays.

Pignou di Penyu (Map p186; ☎ 972577; Jl Goutama 5; mains 25,000-85,000Rp) It looks like a cute Indonesian café (open front above the road, screened by flowers) but the menu speaks French. Daily specials can include rack of lamb with lima beans or a vegetable platter right out of Provence. And where else in Bali could you tuck into the creamy cheesy goodness of *gratin dauphinois*?

NORTH OF JL RAYA UBUD

ourpick Warung Ibu Oka (Map p186; Jl Suweta; dishes 7000-10,000Rp; ⏲ 11am-3pm) Join the lunchtime lines opposite Ubud Palace waiting for one thing: the eponymous Balinese-style roast suckling pig. Locals and expats in the know travel far for meat they say is the most tender and tasty on the island. Order a *spesial* to get the best cut.

Terazo (Map p186; ☎ 978941; Jl Suweta; dishes 30,000-80,000Rp) A popular restaurant serving creative Balinese fusion cuisine. The wine list is decent and features French, Italian and Australian choices. The spare interior is accented by evocative vintage travel posters and furnished with plush cane chairs. The beautiful framed print for tonic tells you what you need to know about the bar.

North of the Centre

Roda Restaurant (Map pp174-5; ☎ 975487; Jl Kajeng 24; dishes 7000-18,000Rp) Above Threads of Life (p177), Roda (which also rents rooms; p187), serves astonishingly cheap Balinese dishes with a wonderful overlay of local culture. The extended Roda family lives here and prepares dishes handed down for generations. You can order a feast in advance for a mere 30,000Rp per person. (Note: the family is the subject of the cult favourite *A Little Bit One O'clock*, by William Ingram.)

East of the Centre

Warung Igelanca (Map pp174-5; ☎ 974153; Jl Raya Ubud; dishes 8000-15,000Rp) Little bigger than a macaroni, this streetside diner is a temple for noodle lovers. Get 'em in dishes that range from Jakarta chicken noodle soup to North Sumatra fried rice noodles.

Kué (Map pp174-5; ☎ 9767040; Jl Raya Ubud; treats from 10,000Rp; ⏲ 8am-8pm; ✺) A top-end bakery and chocolate shop with a couple of stools

and plenty of luscious, drool-worthy treats. We like the mocha tiramisu and the candied ginger chocolates.

Bali Buddha (Map pp174-5; ☎ 976324; Jl Jembawan 1; dishes 15,000-40,000Rp) A local institution, Bali Buddha has a veggie café with a long list of healthy foods upstairs and a health-food store and bakery downstairs (the blueberry muffins, 6000Rp, are mighty fine). Raw foodists, vegans and just those in search of tasty food and drink will find much to like here. The bulletin board out front is a community resource.

Café Moka (Map pp174-5; ☎ 972881; Jl Raya Ubud; mains 20,000-40,000Rp; ✺) Slick outpost for the Bali chain of coffee shops and bakeries, Café Moka has a front terrace well back from the busy road. Inside, you can cool off with a juice or rev up with an array of coffee drinks.

Matahari Cottages (Map pp174-5; ☎ 975459; Jl Jembawan; high tea 60,000Rp; ⏲ 2-5pm certain days) 'Never do anything by half' is the motto at this almost-goofy over-the-top inn (p189), which serves extravagant high tea in open-air pavilions. Call to confirm.

JL HANOMAN

Masakan Padang (Map pp174-5; Jl Hanoman; dishes 6000-15,000Rp; ⏲ noon-1am) The bright-orange exterior at this Padang-style eatery – where you choose from the plates on display – hints at the fresh and spicy food within.

Kafe (Map pp174-5; ☎ 970992; www.balispirit.com; Jl Hanoman 44; dishes 15,000-40,000Rp) Part of Bali Spirit, an umbrella organisation for a number of Ubud-based NGOs (see p346), Kafe has an organic menu great for veggie grazing or just having a coffee, juice or house-made natural soda. Special Monday-night dinners feature movies.

Bebek Bengil (Map pp174-5; Dirty Duck Diner; ☎ 975489; Jl Hanoman; dishes 20,000-50,000Rp; ⏲ 11am-10pm) This pretty, rambling place is popular for one reason: its crispy Balinese duck, which is marinated for 36 hours in spices and then fried up hot. The few surviving rice fields outside the windows seem as endangered as their ducks.

South of Ubud

Many highly regarded restaurants are found along the curves of Jl Raya Pengosekan. It's always worth seeing what's new.

Warung Enak (Map pp174-5; ☎ 972911; Jl Raya Pengosekan; dishes 15,000-150,000Rp) A breezy two-level restaurant with a winsome logo, Enak specialises in Indonesian food. The *rijsttafel* is justifiably popular or you can go modest by choosing from the long menu of satays and variations on *mie goreng*.

Pizza Bagus (Map pp174-5; ☎ 978520; www.pizzabagus .com; Jl Raya Pengosekan; dishes 18,000-40,000Rp; 🖥 wi-fi) Ubud's best pizza bakes up with a crispy thin crust here. Besides the long list of pizza options, there's pasta and sandwiches – all mostly organic. Tables are in and out, there's a play area and delivery.

Chili Cafe (Map pp174-5; ☎ 978629; Jl Nyuh Bulan; mains 20,000Rp) Great place to stop on a walk south of the Monkey Forest and beyond. A small fish pond is out front and there are gardens out back. The menu is standard Indo-Western; the fruit juices are a refreshing touch.

West of Ubud

The restaurants and cafés west of the centre are dotted among rice fields, lanes and roads.

JL BISMA

Café des Artistes (Map pp174-5; ☎ 972706; Jl Bisma 9X; dishes 22,000-90,000Rp; 🕙 10am-midnight) In a quiet perch up off Jl Raya Ubud, the popular Café des Artistes serves elaborate Belgian-accented food, superb steaks and daily specials. Local art is on display and the bar is refreshingly cultured. Enjoy the enveloping wicker seating inside or in front in a small garden. Book.

CAMPUAN

Murni's Warung (Map pp174-5; ☎ 975233; Jl Raya Campuan; dishes 16,000-50,000Rp) Since 1977, Murni's has traded off its spectacular riverside setting. The four-level dining room and bar overlooks the lush valley, and you can hear the water below. The menu features Indo and Western classics; the large giftshop lies in wait.

SANGGINGAN

our pick **Nasi Ayam Kedewatan** (Map pp174-5; ☎ 742 7168; Jl Raya Kedewatan, Kedewatan; mains under 10,000Rp; 🕙 9am-6pm) Few locals making the trek up the hill pass this open-air place without stopping. The star is *satay lilit* (minced chicken satay), which here reaches heights that belie the common name. Chicken is minced, combined with a array of spices including lemongrass, then moulded onto bamboo skewers and grilled. Simply amazing, as are the traditional Balinese road snacks: fried chips imbued with nuts and spices.

Naughty Nuri's (Map pp174-5; ☎ 977547; Jl Raya Sanggingan; dishes 15,000-60,000Rp) This legendary expat hang-out packs punters in for grilled steaks, tender ribs and burgers. Thursday-night grilled-tuna specials are wildly popular and something of a scene. This is a raw-boned joint where the stiff martinis make up for occasional lapses in the kitchen (which is mostly a barbecue out front).

Mozaic (Map pp174-5; ☎ 975768; www.mozaic-bali .com; Jl Raya Sanggingan; meals 150,000-300,000Rp; 🕙 6-10pm Tue-Sun) Chef Chris Salans oversees this much-lauded top-end restaurant. Fine French fusion cuisine is featured on a constantly changing seasonal menu. Dine in an elegant garden or ornate pavilion. Most people leave the driving to Salans and order a tasting menu (500,000Rp with wine pairings).

PENESTANAN

Ibu Putih's Warung (Map pp174-5; ☎ 976146; off Jl Raya Campuan; dishes 6000-20,000Rp) This shady place along the K2-like cement stairs leading from Campuan to Penestanan serves simple and tasty dishes. There are always a few tuckered folks building courage through drink after the ascent. Expats in nearby monthly rentals hang out for hours.

Lala & Lili (Map pp174-5; ☎ 0812 398 8037; off Jl Raya Campuan, Penestanan; mains 15,000-40,000Rp) Fields of rice stretch away like waves of green from this simple café set on a path on a plateau. The menu is a simple mix of Indo and sandwiches. Many local expat artists hang out here; we overheard this spoken to prospective clients: 'I take my inspiration from mankind.'

DRINKING

Ubud. Bacchanalia. Mutually exclusive. No one comes to Ubud for wild nightlife. A few bars get lively around sunset and later in the night, but the venues certainly don't aspire to the extremes of beer-swilling debauchery and club partying found in Kuta and Seminyak.

Bars close early in Ubud, often by 11pm. Many eating places listed above are also good just for a drink, including Dragonfly, Nomad, Terazo and Naughty Nuri's.

Jazz Café (Map pp174-5; ☎ 976594; www.jazz cafebali.com; Jl Sukma 2; 🕙 5pm-midnight) Always popular, Jazz Café has a relaxed vibe in a garden of coconut palms and ferns. It offers good Asian fusion food (mains 35,000Rp to 60,000Rp) and live jazz in various forms, blues and more, Tuesday to Saturday from 7.30pm. The cocktail list is long. It provides transport around Ubud.

Lebong Café (Map p186; ☎ 971342; Monkey Forest Rd) Get up, stand up, stand up for your… reggae. Ubud's nightly sidewalk roll-up stays in abeyance here at least until midnight. It has live reggae most nights and frequent beer specials. During the day you can watch shoppers walking past wondering if the Polo stores are legit or not.

Napi Orti (Map p186; ☎ 970982; Monkey Forest Rd; ☾ noon-late) This upstairs place is your best bet for a late-night drink. Get boozy under the hazy gaze of Jim Morrison and God himself, Bob Marley.

Ozigo (Map pp174-5; ☎ 0812 367 9736; Jl Raya Sanggingan; ☾ 9pm-2am) Ubud's late-night action – such as it is – is right here at this small and friendly club up by Naughty Nuri's. DJs are in residence nightly with edgy mixes plus lots of dance competitions and prizes. Call for pick-up – as it were.

ENTERTAINMENT

Few travel experiences can be more magical than experiencing a Balinese dance performance, especially in Ubud. Cultural entertainment keeps people returning and sets Bali apart from other tropical destinations. Ubud is a good base for the nightly array of performances and for accessing events in surrounding villages.

Dance

If you're in the right place at the right time, you may see dances performed in temple ceremonies for an essentially local audience. These dances are often quite long and not as accessible to the uninitiated.

Dances performed for visitors are usually adapted and abbreviated to some extent to make them more enjoyable, but usually have appreciative locals in the audience (or peering around the screen!). It's also common to combine the features of more than one traditional dance in a single performance.

In a week in Ubud, you can see Kecak, Legong and Barong dances, *Mahabharata* and *Ramayana* ballets, *wayang kulit* puppets and gamelan orchestras. For details on these classic Balinese arts, see p58.

VENUES

Venues will usually host a variety of performances by various troupes through the week and aren't tied to a particular group.

ARMA Open Stage (Map pp174-5; ☎ 976659; Jl Raya Pengosekan) See also p177; has among the best troupes.

Padangtegal Dance Stage (Map pp174-5; Jl Hanoman) Simple, open venue.

Peliatan Pura Dalem Puri (Map pp174-5; Jl Peliatan) Simple venue.

Pura Dalem Puri (Map pp174-5; Jl Raya Ubud) Opposite Ubud's main cremation grounds.

Pura Dalem Ubud (Map pp174-5; Jl Raya Ubud) Good for the fire dance.

Pura Taman Saraswati (Water Palace; Map p186; Jl Raya Ubud) A beautiful location; see p176.

UBUD & AROUND

DANCE TROUPES: GOOD & BAD

All dance groups on Ubud's stages are not created equal. You've got true artists with international reputations and then you've got some that really shouldn't quit their day jobs. If you're a Balinese dance novice, you shouldn't worry too much about this, just pick a venue and go.

But after a few performances, you'll start to appreciate the differences in talent, and that's part of the enjoyment. Clue: if the costumes are dirty, the orchestra seems particularly uninterested and you find yourself watching a dancer and saying 'I could do that', then the group is B-level. For more perspective on the good and bad of Balinese dancers, see p150.

Most troupes you'll see in Ubud, however, are very good. Here's a few to watch for:

- Cak Rina – Often performs the Kecak at ARMA.
- Gunung Sari – Legong dance.
- Sadha Budaya – Legong dance.
- Sekaa Gong Wanita Mekar Sari – An all-woman Legong troupe from Peliatan.
- Semara Madya – Kekac dance.
- Tirta Sari – Legong dance.

Semara Ratih (Map pp174-5; Kutuh) Stage with a name that means 'Spirit of Bali'; usually one performance per week.
Ubud Palace (Map p186; Jl Raya Ubud) Near-nightly performances in a royal setting; see p176.
Ubud Wantilan (Map p186; Jl Raya Ubud) Unadorned meeting *bale* (pavilion) across from Ubud Palace.

Other performances can be found in nearby towns like Batuan, Mawang and Kutuh.

Ubud Tourist Information (p176) has performance information and sells tickets (usually 80,000Rp). For performances outside Ubud, transport is often included in the price. Tickets are also sold at many hotels, at the venues and by street vendors who hang around outside Ubud Palace – all charge the same price.

Vendors sell drinks at the performances, which typically last about one to 1½ hours. Before the show, you might notice the musicians checking out the size of the crowd – ticket sales fund the troupes. Also watch for potential members of the next generation of performers: local children avidly watch from under the screens, behind stage and from a musician's lap or two.

One note about your mobile phone: nobody wants to hear it.

Shadow Puppets

You can also find shadow-puppet shows – although these are greatly attenuated from traditional performances that often last the entire night. Regular performances are held at **Oka Kartini** (Map pp174-5; 975193; Jl Raya Ubud; tickets 50,000Rp), which has bungalows and a gallery.

Musician **Nyoman Warsa** (Map p186; 974807; Pondok Bamboo Music Shop, Monkey Forest Rd) orchestrates highly recommended puppet shows (50,000Rp) on certain evenings.

SHOPPING

Ubud has myriad art shops, boutiques and galleries. Many offer clever and unique items made in and around the area. You can use Ubud as a base to explore craft and antique shops in villages as far afield as Batubulan (p203).

The euphemistically named **Pasar Seni** (Art Market; Map p186) is a touristy two-storey place that sells a wide range of clothing, sarongs, footwear and souvenirs of highly variable quality at negotiable prices. Decent items *may* include leather goods, batiks, baskets, textiles such as bedspreads, and silverware.

Much more interesting is Ubud's bountiful **produce market**, which operates to a greater or

lesser extent every day and is buried within Pasar Seni. It starts early in the morning and winds up by lunch.

You can spend days in and around Ubud shopping. Jl Raya Ubud, Monkey Forest Rd, Jl Hanoman and Jl Dewi Sita should be your starting points.

Arts & Crafts

You'll find paintings for sale everywhere. Check the gallery listings (p177) for recommendations. Prices range from cheap to collector-level, depending on the artist. Prices often are lower if you buy direct from the artist's workshop.

Surrounding villages are also hotbeds for arts and crafts – as you'll have noticed on your drive to Ubud.

Bali Cares (Map pp174-5; 981504; www.idepfoundation.org; Jl Hanoman 44) This inspired shop sells goods to benefit several local charities including IDEP (see p346). Items range from woodcarvings made from sustainable woods to paintings, handicrafts and other items produced by local people. It adjoins Kafe (p193).

Manacika Bead Work (Map pp174-5; 979131; Jl Raya Penestanan, Penestanan) There's a kaleidoscope for the eyes at this gallery-shop filled with intricate bead creations, from shoes to handbags to containers.

Moari (Map pp174-5; 977367; Jl Raya Ubud) New and restored Balinese musical instruments are sold here.

Pondok Bamboo Music Shop (Map p186; 974807; Monkey Forest Rd) Hear the music of a thousand bamboo wind chimes at this store owned by noted gamelan musician Nyoman Warsa, who offers music lessons (p183) and stages shadow-puppet shows (left).

Tegun Galeri (Map pp174-5; 973361; Jl Hanoman 44) Everything the souvenir stores are not; beautiful handmade items from around the island. Next to Bali Cares.

Threads of Life Indonesian Textile Arts Center (Map pp174-5; 972187; Jl Kajeng 24) The small store here stocks exquisite handmade traditional fabrics. See p183 for information about the courses in weaving.

Clothes

For fashion and fabrics, the most interesting shops are found on Monkey Forest Rd, Jl Dewi Sita and Jl Hanoman. Many will make or alter to order.

Helenea 'n Kidz (Map p186; ☎ 0812 388 2622; Jl Dewi Sita) Danish-born designer Helenea lets loose on the whole family here. Kids can enjoy stylish clothes with a pirate flair while mum can hoover up jewellery, housewares and her own duds.

Pusaka (Map p186; ☎ 978619; Monkey Forest Rd 71) 'Modern ethnic clothing' is the motto here, which translates into cool, comfy yet stylish cottons. Need a gift for somebody small (or not so small)? Adorable house-made plush toys are 50,000Rp.

Zarong (Map p186; ☎ 977601; Monkey Forest Rd) An offbeat, hippie-chic fashion store that brings a patchouli of elegance. There are lots of cool cottons here that will be at home in any Balinese situation.

Housewares

Ashitaba (Map p186; ☎ 464922; Monkey Forest Rd) Tenganan, the Aga village of East Bali (p224), produces the intricate and beautiful rattan items sold here (and in Seminyak, p127). Containers, bowls, purses and more (from US$5) display the fine and intricate weaving.

Macan Tidur (Map p186; ☎ 977121; Monkey Forest Rd) Amid a string of trashy places, this elegant store stands out like Audrey Hepburn amid the Spice Girls. Silks, art, antiques and more are beautifully displayed.

Thebb (Map p186; ☎ 975880; Jl Dewi Sita) Smart and hip housewares in distinctive designs made in Bali.

Toko East (Map p186; ☎ 978306; Jl Raya Ubud) High-end Balinese-made housewares and handicrafts; they're quite stylish, and some, like the exquisite small picture frames, might just fit into your already-full luggage.

Jewellery

Alamkara Monkey Forest Rd (Map p186; ☎ 972213); Jl Dewi Sita (Map p186; ☎ 971004) One of the best jewellery galleries in Ubud. On display are unusual but very wearable designs in gold and silver, featuring black pearls and gems, some made locally.

Other Items

Shops with DVDs of dubious origin have proliferated. Most also have large selections of CDs both legitimate and pirated.

Aji's Kites (Map p186; ☎ 971870; Monkey Forest Rd) You can join Bali's long tradition of kite flying with a ready-made or custom number

from this colourful shop near the Monkey Forest that just screams 'fun!'. Go fly one over a rice field.

Kou (Map p186; ☎ 971905; Jl Dewi Sita) Luxurious handmade organic soaps made locally. Put one in your undies drawer and smell fine for weeks.

Kou Cuisine (Map p186; ☎ 972319; Monkey Forest Rd) Give the gift of exquisite little containers of jams made with Balinese fruit or containers of sea salt made along Bali's shores. Afterwards, clean up with their soap.

Kertas Lingsir (Map p186; ☎ 973030; Jl Dewi Sita) Specialises in interesting paper handmade from banana, pineapple and taro plants. If you're a real fan, ask about factory visits.

Namaste (Map pp174-5; ☎ 796 9178; Jl Hanoman 64) Just the place to buy a crystal to get your spiritual house in order, Namaste is gem of a little store with a top range of new-age supplies. Incense, yoga mats, moody instrumental music, it's all here.

Rum Batik (Map p186; ☎ 971354; Monkey Forest Rd) A refined selection of silks and batiks draws you in; the air-con keeps you in.

Truth (Map pp174-5; ☎ 798 3119; Jl Hanoman 35) Think of this as a gallery of soap. All the bars are handmade amid the rice fields of Tabanan from natural ingredients like palm and coconut oils. Bars are individually polished and then aged until they reach a peak of, er, soapiness.

GETTING THERE & AWAY

Many people get to Ubud from other parts of Bali via a car and driver arranged with a hotel at either end of the trip. The cost can vary between 200,000Rp and 500,000Rp, depending on whether you're making a day of it (or simply cut a bad deal). Given all the outlying points of interest around Ubud, making a day of it can be enjoyable indeed.

Bemo

Ubud is on two bemo routes. Orange bemo travel from Gianyar to Ubud (8000Rp) and larger brown bemo from Batubulan terminal in Denpasar to Ubud (8000Rp), and then head to Kintamani via Payangan. Ubud doesn't have a bemo terminal; bemo stops (Map p186) are in front of the market in the centre of town.

Tourist Shuttle Bus

Perama (Map pp174-5; ☎ 973316; Jl Hanoman; ☺ 9am-9pm) is the major tourist-shuttle operator, but its terminal is inconveniently located in Padangtegal; to get to your final destination in Ubud will cost another 10,000Rp.

Destination	Fare	Duration
Candidasa	50,000Rp	1¾hr
Kuta	50,000Rp	1¼hr
Lovina	125,000Rp	3hr
Padangbai	50,000Rp	1¼hr
Sanur	40,000Rp	1hr

GETTING AROUND

Many better restaurants and hotels offer free local transport for guests and customers. Ask.

To/From the Airport

Official taxis from the airport to Ubud cost 175,000Rp. A taxi or car with driver *to* the airport will cost about half.

Bemo

Bemo don't directly link Ubud with nearby villages; you'll have to catch one going to Denpasar, Gianyar, Pujung or Kintamani and get off where you need to. Bemo to Gianyar travel along eastern Jl Raya Ubud, down Jl Peliatan and east to Bedulu. To Pujung, bemo head east along Jl Raya Ubud and then north through Andong and past the turn-off to Petulu.

To Payangan, bemo travel west along Jl Raya Ubud, go up past the many places on Jl Raya Campuan and Jl Raya Sanggingan and turn north at the junction after Sanggingan. Larger brown-coloured bemo to Batubulan terminal go east along Jl Raya and down Jl Hanoman.

The fare for a ride within the Ubud area shouldn't be more than 5000Rp.

Bicycle

Shops renting bikes have their cycles on display along the main roads; your accommodation can always arrange bike hire. For more info, see p180.

Car & Motorcycle

With numerous nearby attractions, many of which are difficult to reach by bemo, renting a vehicle is sensible. Ask at your accommodation or hire a car and driver. See p355 for details.

Taxi

There are very few taxis in Ubud – those that honk their horns at you have usually dropped off passengers from southern Bali in Ubud and are hoping for a fare back. Instead, use one of the drivers with private vehicles hanging around on the street corners hectoring passersby. From central Ubud to, say, Sanggingan should cost about 15,000Rp to 20,000Rp – rather steep actually.

AROUND UBUD

☎ 0361

The region east and north of Ubud has many of the most ancient monuments and relics in Bali. Some of them predate the Majapahit era and raise as-yet-unanswered questions about Bali's history. Others are more recent, and in other instances, newer structures have been built on and around the ancient remains. They're interesting to history and archaeology buffs, but not that spectacular to look at – with the exception of Bali's own bit of Angkor at Gunung Kawi. Perhaps the best approach is to plan a whole day walking or cycling around the area, stopping at the places that interest you, but not treating any one as a destination in itself.

The area is thick with excursion possibilities. Besides the Elephant Cave, there's the Crazy Buffalo Temple. Heading north you find Bali's most important ancient site at Tampaksiring, and a nearly forgotten shrine nearby, Pura Mengening, that rewards the adventurous.

BEDULU

Bedulu was once the capital of a great kingdom. The legendary Dalem Bedaulu (p200) ruled the Pejeng dynasty from here, and was the last Balinese king to withstand the onslaught of the powerful Majapahit from Java. He was defeated by Gajah Mada in 1343. The capital shifted several times after this, to Gelgel and then later to Semarapura (Klungkung).

Sights
GOA GAJAH

There were never any elephants in Bali; **Goa Gajah** (Elephant Cave; Map pp174-5; adult/child 6000/3000Rp, parking 2000Rp; ☺ 8am-6pm) probably takes its name from the nearby Sungai Petanu, which at one time was known as Elephant

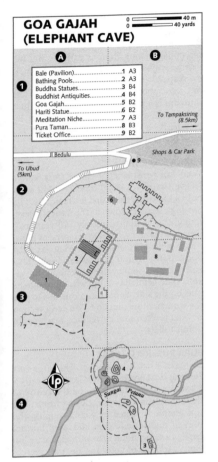

GOA GAJAH (ELEPHANT CAVE)

Bale (Pavilion)....................1 A3	
Bathing Pools....................2 A3	
Buddha Statues.................3 B4	
Buddhist Antiquities..........4 B4	
Goa Gajah.........................5 B2	
Hariti Statue......................6 B2	
Meditation Niche...............7 A3	
Pura Taman.......................8 B3	
Ticket Office......................9 B2	

the face of the demon push back a riotous jungle of surrounding stone carvings.

Inside the T-shaped cave you can see fragmentary remains of the *lingam,* the phallic symbol of the Hindu god Shiva, and its female counterpart the *yoni,* plus a statue of Shiva's son, the elephant-headed god Ganesha. In the courtyard in front of the cave are two square bathing pools with water trickling into them from waterspouts held by six female figures.

From Goa Gajah you can clamber down through the rice paddies to Sungai Petanu (Petanu River), where there are crumbling **rock carvings** of stupas (domes for housing Buddhist relics) on a cliff face, and a small **cave**.

Try to get here before 10am, when the big tourist buses begin lumbering in like, well, modern elephants.

YEH PULU

A man having his hand munched by a boar is one of the scenes on the 25m-long **carved cliff face** (Map pp174–5; adult/child 6000/3000Rp) known as Yeh Pulu, believed to be a hermitage from the late 14th century. Apart from the figure of Ganesha, the elephant-headed son of Shiva, most of the scenes deal with everyday life, although the position and movement of the figures suggests that it could be read from left to right as a story. One theory is that they are events from the life of Krishna, the Hindu god.

One of the first recognisable images is of a man carrying a shoulder pole with two jugs, possibly full of *tuak* (palm wine). He is following a woman whose jewellery suggests wealth and power. There's a whimsical figure peering round a doorway, who seems to have armour on his front and a weapon on his back.

The hunting scene starts with a horseman and a man throwing a spear, while a frog takes on a snake with a club. Above the frog, two figures kneel over a pot, while to the right, two men carry off a slain animal on a pole.

The Ganesha figures of Yeh Pulu and Goa Gajah are quite similar, indicating a close relationship between them. You can walk between the sites, following small paths through the paddy fields, but you might need to pay a local to guide you. By car or bicycle, look for the signs to 'Relief Yeh Pulu' or 'Villa Yeh Pulu', east of Goa Gajah.

Even if your interest in carved Hindu art is minor, this site is quite lovely and rarely will you have much company. From the entrance, it's a 300m lush, tropical walk to Yeh Pulu.

River, or perhaps because the face over the cave entrance might resemble an elephant. Some 2km southeast of Ubud on the road to Bedulu, a large car park with clamorous souvenir shops indicates that you've reached a big tourist attraction.

The origins of the cave are uncertain – one tale relates that it was created by the fingernail of the legendary giant Kebo Iwa. It probably dates to the 11th century, and was certainly in existence during the Majapahit takeover of Bali. The cave was rediscovered by Dutch archaeologists in 1923, but the fountains and pool were not found until 1954.

The cave is carved into a rock face and you enter through the cavernous mouth of a demon. The gigantic fingertips pressed beside

UBUD & AROUND

UBUD & AROUND

THE LEGEND OF DALEM BEDAULU

A legend relates how Dalem Bedaulu possessed magical powers that allowed him to have his head chopped off and then replaced. Performing this unique party trick one day, the servant entrusted with lopping off his head and then replacing it unfortunately dropped it in a river and, to his horror, watched it float away. Looking around in panic for a replacement, he grabbed a pig, cut off its head and popped it upon the king's shoulders. Thereafter, the king was forced to sit on a high throne and forbade his subjects to look up at him; Bedaulu means 'he who changed heads'.

PURA SAMUAN TIGA

The majestic **Pura Samuan Tiga** (Temple of the Meeting of the Three; Map pp174–5) is about 200m east of the Bedulu junction. The name is possibly a reference to the Hindu trinity, or it may refer to meetings held here in the early 11th century. Despite these early associations, all the temple buildings have been rebuilt since the 1917 earthquake. The imposing main gate was designed and built by I Gusti Nyoman Lempad (p179), one of Bali's renowned artists and a native of Bedulu.

Getting There & Away

About 3km east of Teges, the road from Ubud reaches a junction where you can turn south to Gianyar or north to Pejeng, Tampaksiring and Penelokan. The Ubud–Gianyar bemo will drop you off at this junction, from where you can walk to the sights. The road from Ubud is reasonably flat, so coming by bicycle is a good option.

PEJENG

Continuing up the road towards Tampaksiring you soon come to Pejeng and its famous temples. Like Bedulu, this was once an important seat of power, as it was the capital of the Pejeng kingdom, which fell to the Majapahit invaders in 1343.

Sights

MUSEUM PURBAKALA

This archaeological **museum** (Map pp174–5; ☎ 942354; Jl Raya Tampaksiring; admission by donation; ☻ 8am-3pm Mon-Thu, 8am-12.30pm Fri) has a reasonable collection of artefacts from all over Bali,

and most displays are in English. The exhibits in several small buildings include some of Bali's first pottery from near Gilimanuk, and sarcophagi dating from as early as 300 BC – some originating from Bangli are carved in the shape of a turtle, which has important cosmic associations in Balinese mythology. The museum is about 500m north of the Bedulu junction, and easy to reach by bemo or by bicycle. It's a sleepy place and you'll get the most out of it if you come with a guide.

PURA KEBO EDAN

Who can resist a sight called **Crazy Buffalo Temple** (Map p174–5; Jl Raya Tampaksiring)? Although not an imposing structure, it's famous for its 3m-high statue, known as the **Giant of Pejeng**, thought to be approximately 700 years old. Details are sketchy, but it may represent Bima, a hero of the *Mahabharata*, dancing on a dead body, as in a myth related to the Hindu Shiva cult. There is some conjecture about the giant's giant genitalia – it has what appear to be pins on the side. Some claim this was to give the woman more pleasure – an early version of what is often sold by vending machines in public toilets.

PURA PUSERING JAGAT

So that's what it looks like? The large **Pura Pusering Jagat** (Navel of the World Temple; Map pp174-5; Jl Raya Tampaksiring) is said to be the centre of the old Pejeng kingdom. Dating from 1329, this temple is visited by young couples who pray at the stone *lingam* and *yoni*. Further back is a large stone urn, with elaborate but worn carvings of gods and demons searching for the elixir of life in a depiction of the *Mahabharata* tale 'Churning the Sea of Milk'. The temple is on a small track running west of the main road.

PURA PENATARAN SASIH

This was once the state **temple** (Map pp174-5; Jl Raya Tampaksiring) of the Pejeng kingdom. In the inner courtyard, high up in a pavilion and difficult to see, is the huge bronze drum known as the **Fallen Moon of Pejeng**. The hourglass-shaped drum is 186cm long, the largest single-piece cast drum in the world. Estimates of its age vary from 1000 to 2000 years, and it is not certain whether it was made locally or imported – the intricate geometric decorations are said to resemble patterns from places as far apart as Irian Jaya and Vietnam. Even in its inaccessible position, you can make out these patterns and the distinctive heart-shaped face designs.

Balinese legend relates that the drum came to earth as a fallen moon, landing in a tree and shining so brightly that it prevented a band of thieves from going about their unlawful purpose. One of the thieves decided to put the light out by urinating on it, but the moon

exploded and fell to earth as a drum, with a crack across its base as a result of the fall.

Although the big noise here is all about the drum, be sure to notice the **statuary** in the temple courtyard that dates from the 10th to the 12th century.

TAMPAKSIRING

Tampaksiring is a small village about 18km northeast of Ubud with a large and important temple and the most impressive ancient site in Bali, Gunung Kawi. It sits in the Pakerisan Valley, and the entire area has been nominated for Unesco recognition.

Sights

GUNUNG KAWI

On the northern outskirts of town, a sign points east off the main road to Gunung Kawi and its **ancient monuments** (Map p201; adult/child 6000/3000Rp, parking 2000Rp; ☻ 7am-5pm). From the end of the access road, a steep, stone stairway leads down to the river, at one point making a cutting through an embankment of solid rock. There, in the bottom of this lush green river valley, is one of Bali's oldest and largest ancient monuments.

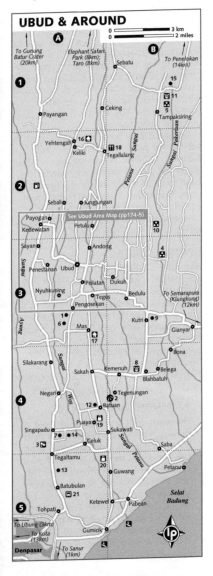

UBUD & AROUND

INFORMATION		
Bali Adoption & Rehab Centre (BARC)	1	A3

SIGHTS & ACTIVITIES		
Air Terjun Tegenungan	2	B4
Bali Bird Park & Rimba Reptil Park	3	A4
Goa Garba	4	B3
Gunung Kawi	5	B1
Ketut Rudi Gallery	6	A3
Nyoman Suaka Home	7	A4
Pura Gaduh	8	B4
Pura Kedarman	9	B3
Pura Krobokan	10	B2
Pura Mengening	11	B1
Pura Puseh & Pura Dasar	12	A4
Pura Puseh Batubulan	13	A5
Singapadu Banyan Tree	14	A4
Tirta Empul	15	B1

SLEEPING ⌂		
Alam Sari Hotel	16	A2
Taman Harum Cottages	17	A3

EATING ☐		
Cafe Kampung	18	B2

SHOPPING ☐		
Mustika Collection	19	A4
Pasar Seni (Craft Market)	20	A5

TRANSPORT		
Batubulan Bus/Bemo Terminal	21	A5

UBUD & AROUND

Gunung Kawi consists of 10 rock-cut *candi* (shrines) – memorials cut out of the rock face in imitation of actual statues. They stand in awe-inspiring 8m-high sheltered niches cut into the sheer cliff face. A solitary *candi* stands about a kilometre further down the valley to the south; this is reached by a trek through the rice paddies on the western side of the rushing river. Be prepared for long climbs up and down.

Each *candi* is believed to be a memorial to a member of the 11th-century Balinese royalty, but little is known for certain. Legends relate that the whole group of memorials was carved out of the rock face in one hard-working night by the mighty fingernails of Kebo Iwa.

The five monuments on the eastern bank are probably dedicated to King Udayana, Queen Mahendradatta, their son Airlangga and his brothers Anak Wungsu and Marakata. While Airlangga ruled eastern Java, Anak Wungsu ruled Bali. The four monuments on the western side are, by this theory, to Anak Wungsu's chief concubines. Another theory is that the whole complex is dedicated to Anak Wungsu, his wives, concubines and, in the case of the remote 10th *candi*, to a royal minister.

TIRTA EMPUL

A well-signposted fork in the road north of Tampaksiring leads to the popular holy springs at **Tirta Empul** (Map p201; adult/child 6000/3000Rp, parking 2000Rp; 8am-6pm), discovered in AD 962 and believed to have magical powers. The springs bubble up into a large, crystal-clear pool within the temple and gush out through waterspouts into a bathing pool – they're the main source of Sungai Pakerisan (Pakerisan River), the river that rushes by Gunung Kawi only 1km or so away. Next to the springs, **Pura Tirta Empul** is one of Bali's most important temples.

Come in the early morning or late afternoon to avoid the tourist buses. You can also use the clean, segregated and free public baths here.

OTHER SITES

There are other groups of *candi* and monks' cells p201 in the area once encompassed by the ancient Pejeng kingdom, notably **Pura Krobokan** (Map p201) and **Goa Garba** (Map p201), but none so grand as Gunung Kawi. Between Gunung Kawi and Tirta Empul, **Pura Mengening** (Map p201) temple has a free-standing *candi*, similar in design to those at Gunung Kawi and much less visited.

TEGALLALANG

There are lots of shops and stalls in this busy market town you're likely to pass through on your visit to the area's temples. Stop for a stroll and you may be rewarded by hearing the practice of one of the local noted game-lan orchestras. Otherwise plenty of carvers stand ready to sell you a carved fertility doll and the like.

You can pause at **Cafe Kampung** (Map p201; 901201; dishes 20,000-50,000Rp), an attractive warung (perfect for lunch) and upscale guesthouse (rooms from US$90) with jaw-dropping rice-terrace views. The design makes great use of natural rock. Nearby, scores of carvers produce works from albesia wood, which is easily turned into simplistic, cartoonish figures. The wood is also a favourite of wind-chime makers.

Go about 3km west of town on a small, very green road to **Keliki**, and you'll pass **Alam Sari** (240308; www.alamsari.com; r from US$60;), a small hotel in a wonderfully isolated location where the bamboo grows like grass. There are 10 luxurious yet rustic rooms, a pool and a great view. The hotel treats its own wastewater, among other environmental initiatives.

NORTH OF UBUD

Abused and abandoned logging elephants from Sumatra have been given refuge in Bali at the **Elephant Safari Park** (Map p201; 721480; www.baliadventuretours.com; adult/child US$16/8; 8am-5pm). Located in the cool, wet highlands of **Taro** (14km north of Ubud), the park is home to almost 30 elephants. Besides a full complement of exhibits about elephants, most people will probably want to *ride* an elephant (adult/child including admission

---

A DIFFERENT WAY TO THE TOP

The usual road from Ubud to Batur is through Tampaksiring, but there are other lesser roads up the gentle mountain slope. One of the most attractive goes north from Peliatan, past Petulu and its birds (see p179), and through the rice terraces between Tegallalang and Ceking, to bring you out on the crater rim between Penelokan and Batur. It's a sealed road all the way and you also pass through **Sebatu**, which is also famous for its dance troupe.

US$53/36). The park has received praise for its conservation efforts; however, be careful you don't end up at one of the rogue parks, designed to divert the unwary to unsanctioned displays of elephants.

The surrounding region produces ochre-coloured paint pigment. The gentle uphill drive from Ubud is a lush attraction itself.

SOUTH OF UBUD

The road between South Bali and Ubud is lined with places making and selling handicrafts. Many visitors shop along the route as they head to Ubud, sometimes by the busload, but much of the craftwork is actually done in small workshops and family compounds on quiet back roads. You may enjoy these places more after visiting Ubud, where you'll see some of the best Balinese arts and develop some appreciation of the styles and themes.

For serious shopping and real flexibility in exploring these villages, it's worth renting or chartering your own transport, so you can explore the back roads and carry your purchases without any hassles. Note that your driver may receive a commission from any place you spend your money – this can add 10% or more to the cost of purchases (think of it as his tip). Also, a driver may try to steer you to workshops or artisans that he favours, rather than those of most interest to you.

From the **Batubulan bus/bemo terminal** (Map p201; see p170), stop at the craft villages along the main road through Negari on your way to Ubud. The following places are presented in the order you'll encounter them on the way to Ubud from the south.

Batubulan

The start of the road from South Bali is lined with outlets for stone sculptures – **stone carving** is the main craft of Batubulan (moonstone). Workshops are found right along the road to Tegaltamu, with another batch further north around Silakarang. Batubulan is the source of the stunning temple-gate guardians seen all over Bali. The stone used for these sculptures is a porous grey volcanic rock called *paras*, which resembles pumice; it's soft and surprisingly light. It also ages quickly, so that 'ancient' work may be years rather than centuries old.

The temples around Batubulan are, naturally, noted for their fine stonework. Just 200m to the east of the busy main road, **Pura Puseh Batubulan** (Map p201) is worth a visit for its moat filled with lotus flowers. Statues draw on ancient Hindu and Buddhist iconography and Balinese mythology; however, they are not old – many are copied from books on archaeology. An attenuated **Barong dance show** (admission 50,000Rp; ☺ 9.30am) about the iconic lion-dog creature is a bus-tour-friendly one-hour long. Note 'Pura Puseh' means 'central temple' – you'll find many around Bali. Some translations have 'Puseh' meaning 'navel', which is apt.

Batubulan is also a centre for making 'antiques', textiles and woodwork, and has numerous craft shops.

Bali Bird Park & Rimba Reptil Park

Just north of Tegaltamu, the **bird park** (Map p201; ☎ 299352; www.bali-bird-park.com; adult/child US$14/7; ☺ 9am-5.30pm) boasts more than a thousand birds from over 250 different species, including rare *cendrawasih* (birds of paradise) from Irian Jaya and the all-but-vanished Bali starlings. Many of these birds are housed in special walk-through aviaries; in one of them you follow a walk at tree-level, or what some with feathers might say is bird-level. The 2 hectares of landscaped gardens feature a fine collection of tropical plants.

Next door, **Rimba Reptil Park** (☎ 299344; adult/child US$10/5; ☺ 9am-5pm) has about 20 species of creatures from Indonesia and Africa, as well as turtles, crocodiles, a python and a solitary Komodo dragon.

Both places are popular with kids. You can buy a combination ticket to both parks (adult/child US$20/10). Allow at least two hours for the bird park alone.

Many tours stop at the parks, or you can take a Batubulan–Ubud bemo, get off at the junction at Tegaltamu, and follow the signs north for about 600m. There is a large parking lot.

Singapadu

The centre of Singapadu is dominated by a huge **banyan tree**. In the past, these were community meeting places. Even today the local meeting hall is just across the road. The surrounding village has a traditional appearance, with walled family compounds and shady trees. You can visit the **Nyoman Suaka**

Home (Map p201; requested donation 10,000Rp; ☼ 9am-5pm), which is 50m off the main road, just south of the big tree. Pass through the old carved entrance to the walled family compound and you'll discover a classic Balinese home. While you snoop about, the family goes about its business. Many pestles are in use in the kitchen producing spices and some of the roofs are still made from thatch on bamboo frames.

Singapadu's dancers now perform mostly at large venues in tourist areas – there are no regular public performances. There are not many obvious places in the town to buy locally produced crafts, as most of the better products are sold directly to dance troupes or quality art shops.

Celuk

Celuk is the **silver** and **gold** centre of Bali. The bigger showrooms are on the main road, and have marked prices that are quite high, although you can always bargain.

Hundreds of silversmiths and goldsmiths work in their homes on the backstreets north and east of the main road. Most of these artisans are from *pande* families, members of a sub-caste of blacksmiths whose knowledge of fire and metal has traditionally put them outside the usual caste hierarchy. Their small workshops are interesting to visit, and have the lowest prices, but they don't keep a large stock of finished work. They will make something to order if you bring a sample or sketch.

Sukawati & Puaya

Once a royal capital, Sukawati is now known for its specialised artisans, who busily work in small shops along the roads. One group, the *tukang prada,* make temple umbrellas, beautifully decorated with stencilled gold paint, which can be seen in their shops. The *tukang wadah* make cremation towers, which you're less likely to see. Other craft products include intricate patterned *lontar* (specially prepared palm leaves) baskets and wind chimes. Look for some fine examples of all these crafts along the road just south of Sukawati proper.

Sukawati is also renowned for its traditional dances, *wayang kulit* (shadow puppet) performances, the *gong gede* (large orchestra) gamelan, the older but smaller *gong saron* gamelan and the Barong dance. Local artisans specialise in producing **masks** for Topeng and Barong dances.

In the town centre is the always-bustling **produce market**, which also sells sarongs and temple ceremony paraphernalia. Pause here for an hour and check out some of the stalls, which sell some of the better crafts from the area. Should you get inspired, there are ATMs at the ready.

About 2km south of town, the much-hyped and very touristy **Pasar Seni** (Art Market; Map p201) is a two-storey market where every type of knick-knack and trinket is on sale. Unless you're on a bus and have no choice, skip it.

Puaya, about 1km northwest of Sukawati, specialises in high-quality **leather shadow puppets** and masks. On the main street, look for a small sign that reads **Mustika Collection** (Map p201; ☎ 299479; Kubu Dauh 62), or ask anyone. Inside the family compound you'll find a workshop for masks and puppets where you can see how cow hide is transformed into these works of art.

Batuan

Batuan's recorded history goes back 1000 years, and in the 17th century its royal family controlled most of southern Bali. The decline of its power is attributed to a priest's curse, which scattered the royal family to different parts of the island.

Just west of the centre, the twin temples of **Pura Puseh** and **Pura Dasar** (admission 10,000Rp) are accessible studies in classic Balinese temple architecture. The carvings are elaborate and visitors are given the use of vermilion sarongs, which look good in photos.

In the 1930s two local artists began experimenting with a new style of **painting** using black ink on white paper. Their dynamic drawings featured all sorts of scenes from daily life – markets, paddy fields, animals and people crowded onto each painting – while the black-and-white technique evoked the Balinese view of the supernatural.

Today, this distinct Batuan style of painting is noted for its inclusion of modern elements. Sea scenes often include a windsurfer, while tourists with gadgets or riding motorcycles pop up in the otherwise traditional Balinese scenery. There are good examples in galleries along, or just off, the main road in Batuan, and in Ubud's Museum Puri Lukisan (p176).

Batuan is also noted for its traditional dance, and is a centre for carved wooden relief panels and screens. The ancient Gambuh dance is performed in the Pura Puseh every full moon. (The carvers also keep busy making all manner of stylish teak furnishings.)

Mas

Mas means 'gold' in Bahasa Indonesia, but **woodcarving** is the principal craft in this village. The great Majapahit priest Nirartha once lived here, and **Pura Taman Pule** is said to be built on the site of his home. During the three-day Kuningan festival (see p335), a performance of *wayang wong* (an older version of the *Ramayana* ballet) is held in the temple's courtyard.

Carving was a traditional art of the priestly Brahmana caste, and the skills are said to have been a gift of the gods. Historically, carving was limited to temple decorations, dance masks and musical instruments, but in the 1930s carvers began to depict people and animals in a naturalistic way. Today it's hard to resist the oodles of winsome creatures produced here.

This is the place to come if you want something custom-made in sandalwood – just be prepared to pay well. Mas is also part of Bali's booming furniture industry, producing chairs, tables and reproduction antiques, mainly from teak imported from other Indonesian islands.

Along the main road in Mas are the **Taman Harum Cottages** (Map p201; ☎ 975567; www .tamanharumcottages.com; r from US$35, villas US$50-75; ✷ ⊠ ☐). There are 17 rooms and villas – some quite large. By all means get one overlooking the rice fields. It's behind a gallery, which is also a venue for a huge range of art and cultural courses (see p183). Ubud shuttles are free.

North of Mas, woodcarving shops make way for the art galleries, cafés, hotels and lights of Ubud.

Alternative Routes

From Sakah, along the road between Batuan and Ubud, you can continue east for a few kilometres to the turn-off to Blahbatuh and continue to Ubud via Kutri and Bedulu.

In Blahbatuh, **Pura Gaduh** (Map p201) has a 1m-high stone head, believed to be a portrait of Kebo Iwa, the legendary strongman and minister to the last king of the Bedulu kingdom. Gajah Mada – the Majapahit strongman – realised that it wouldn't be possible to conquer Bedulu (Bali's strongest kingdom) while Kebo Iwa was there. So Gajah Mada lured him away to Java (with promises of women and song) and had him murdered. The stone head possibly predates the Javanese influence in Bali, but the temple is simply a reconstruction of an earlier one destroyed in the earthquake of 1917.

About 2km southwest of Blahbatuh, along Sungai Petanu (Petanu River), is **Air Terjun Tegenungan** (Tegenungan Waterfall; also known as Srog Srogan; Map p201). Follow the signs from Kemenuh village for the best view of the falls, from the west side of the river.

KUTRI

Heading north from Blahbatuh, Kutri has the interesting **Pura Kedarman** (aka Pura Bukit Dharma; Map p201). If you climb up Bukit Dharma behind the temple, there's a great panoramic view and a **hilltop shrine**, with a stone statue of the six-armed goddess of death and destruction, Durga, killing a demon-possessed water buffalo.

BONA & BELEGA

On the back road between Blahbatuh and Gianyar, Bona is a **basket-weaving** centre and features many articles made from *lontar* leaves. It is also known for fire dances. (Note: most road signs in the area read 'Bone' instead of Bona, so if you get lost, you'll have to ask: 'Do you know the way to Bone?') Nearby, the village of Belega is a centre for bamboo furniture production.

East Bali

Wandering the roads of East Bali is one of Bali's great pleasures. Rice terraces spill down hillsides under swaying palms, wild volcanic beaches are washed by pounding surf, and age-old villages soldier on with barely a trace of modernity.

Watching over it all is Gunung Agung, the 3142m volcano known as the 'navel of the world' and 'Mother Mountain', which has a perfect conical shape when revealed by its curtain of clouds. Trekkers witness sunrises that stretch to Java.

You can find Bali's past amid evocative ruins in the former royal city of Semarapura. Follow the rivers coursing down the slopes on the Sidemen Road to find vistas and valleys that could have inspired Shangri La. Down at the coast, Padangbai is a funky and lively port town with a good travellers' scene, while Candidasa caters to those who want a quieter time contemplating the ever-shifting Lombok Channel.

Resorts and hidden beaches dot the entire length of the coast and await your discovery. The Amed area has a collection of highly characterful inns, many geared for self-exploration and contemplation. Just up the coast, Tulamben is all about external exploration: the entire town is geared for diving.

And once you are off the roads, your wandering can continue. Start at the aquatic fantasyland of Tirta Gangga and see where the paths take you among fields of rice that ripple up and down the hills. Green, surprising and tinged with the smell of the sea, that's East Bali.

EAST BALI

HIGHLIGHTS

- Marvelling at the combination of the sacred and the sublime at **Pura Masceti Beach** (p208)

- Feeling the past at Semarapura's **Kertha Gosa** (p212)

- Trekking the picture-perfect valley at **Sidemen** (p214)

- Chilling with new friends at **Padangbai** (p219)

- Choosing your ideal inn perched along the **Amed Coast** (p232)

Amed Coast ★

★ Sidemen

Kertha Gosa ★   ★ Padangbai

★ Pura Masceti Beach

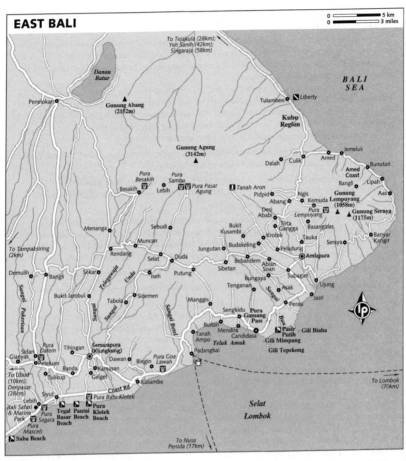

EAST BALI

COAST ROAD TO KUSAMBA

☎ 0361

Bali's coast road running from just north of Sanur east to a junction past Kusamba has been a hit since it opened in 2006. In fact at times it gets choked with traffic and slows to a crawl just like the old route, which meandered through towns far inland such as Gianyar and Semarapura.

Its real impact is still being sorted out. For now it has sparked the construction of scores of warung (food stalls) and trucker cafés along its length. And it has made numerous formerly inaccessible beaches accessible (see p208). Tourism development hasn't yet caught up, but as you drive the road you'll see plenty of new residential villas aimed at foreigners and even more land for sale (signs promising 'beachfront freeholds' are as common as tyre-repair shops).

The coast road (formally named Prof Dr Ida Bagus Mantra Bypass – named for a popular 1980s Balinese governor who did much to promote culture) has brought Padangbai, Candidasa and points east one to two hours closer by road to South Bali. Much of the region is now an easy day trip.

The shoreline the new road follows is striking, with black-sand beaches and pounding waves. The entire coast has great religious significance and there are many temples. At the many small coastal-village beaches, cremation formalities reach their conclusion when the ashes are consigned to the sea.

COAST ROAD BEACHES

The coast road from Sanur heads east past long stretches of shore that until recently were reached only by long and narrow lanes from roads well inland. Development has yet to catch on here – excepting villas – so take advantage of the easy access to enjoy the beaches and the many important temples near the sand.

Don't expect white sand or even tan sand – the grains here are volcanic shades of grey. **Ketewel** (Map p132) and **Lebih** are good spots for surfing; see p94 for details. Swimming in the often pounding surf is dangerous. You'll need your own transport to reach these beaches. Except where noted, services are few, so bring your own drinking water and towels.

From west to east, recommended beaches include the following:

- **Saba Beach** has a small temple, covered shelters, a shady parking area and a short, junglelike drive from the coast road; it's about 12km east of Sanur.
- **Pura Masceti Beach**, 15km east of Sanur, has a few drink vendors. **Pura Masceti** is one of Bali's nine directional temples (see p51). It is right on the beach and is both architecturally significant and enlivened with gaudy statuary.
- **Lebih** has sand composed of mica that sparkles with a billion points of light. There are a couple of cafés. The large Sungai Pakerisan (Pakerisan River), which starts near Tampaksiring, reaches the sea near here. The impressive **Pura Segara** looks across the strait to Nusa Penida, home of Jero Gede Macaling (p161) – the temple helps protect Bali from his evil influence.
- **Tegal Basar Beach** is a turtle sanctuary with no shade but with a good view of Nusa Lembongan.
- **Pantai Beach** is tautological (*pantai* means beach). You'll find a tiny café and a long row of dunes at this picture-perfect spot.
- **Pura Klotek Beach** has very fine black sand. The quiet at **Pura Batu Klotek** belies its great significance. Sacred statues are brought here from Pura Besakih (p215) for ritual cleansing.

Ritual purification ceremonies for temple artefacts are also held on these beaches.

Kids love **Bali Safari and Marine Park** (☎ 950000; Prof Dr Ida Bagus Mantra Bypass; admission from US$25; ◷ 9am-5pm) and their parents are happy they love *someplace*. This big-ticket animal theme park is filled with critters whose species never set foot in Bali until their cage door opened. Displays are large and naturalistic. A huge menu of extra-cost options includes camel and elephant rides. The park is north of Lebih Beach.

GIANYAR

☎ 0361

This is the affluent administrative capital and main market town of the Gianyar district, which also includes Ubud. The town has a number of factories producing batik and ikat fabrics, and a compact centre with some excellent food.

Sights

Although dating from 1771, **Puri Gianyar** (Jl Ngurah Rai) was destroyed in a conflict with the neighbouring kingdom of Klungkung in the mid-1880s and rebuilt. Under threat from its aggressive neighbours, the Gianyar kingdom requested Dutch protection. A 1900 agreement let the ruling family retain its status and its palace, though it lost all political power. The *puri* (palace) was damaged in a 1917 earthquake, but was restored soon after and appears little changed from the time the Dutch arrived. It's a fine example of traditional palace architecture. While tourists are not usually allowed inside, if you report to the guard, you may be given a quick look around, which makes it a bit of illicit fun. The huge banyan tree across from the compound is considered sacred and is a royal symbol.

Eating

People come to Gianyar to sample the market food, like *babi guling* (spit-roast pig stuffed with chilli, turmeric, garlic and ginger – delicious), for which the town is noted. The descriptively named **Gianyar Babi Guleng** (Jl Jata; meals 5000-8000Rp; ◷ 7am-4pm) is favoured by locals among many competitors. (There are lots of cops and bemo (small minibus) drivers here – they know.) It's in a tiny side street at the west end of the centre behind the bemo parking area.

Nearby are numerous stands selling fresh food, including delectable *piseng goreng* (fried banana). Also worth sampling for *babi guling* and other local treats are the food stalls in the **food market** (⊗ 11am-2pm) and the busy **night market** (⊗ 6-11pm). All of these places line both sides of the main section of Jl Ngurah Rai.

Shopping

At the western end of town on the main Ubud road are textile factories, including **Tenun Ikat Setia Cili** (☎ 943409; Jl Astina Utara; ⊗ 9am-5pm) and **Cap Togog** (☎ 943046; Jl Astina Utara 11; ⊗ 8am-5pm). Connoisseurs of hand-woven fabrics will need drool cups. These places have showrooms where you can buy material by the metre, or have it tailored. You can at times see weavers at work and see how the thread is dyed before weaving to produce the vibrantly patterned weft ikat, which is called *endek* in Bali. Prices are 50,000Rp to 75,000Rp per metre for handwoven ikat, depending on how fine the weaving is – costs will rise if it contains silk. You can get a batik sarong for 50,000Rp. Note that the industry is struggling from competition with machine-made Javanese fabric, so your arrival will be welcomed.

Getting There & Away

There are regular bemo between Batubulan terminal near Denpasar and Gianyar's main terminal (10,000Rp), which is behind the main market. Bemo from Gianyar's main terminal also serve Semarapura (8000Rp) and Amlapura (16,000Rp). Bemo to and from Ubud (8000Rp) use the bemo stop across the road from the main market.

SIDAN

When driving east from Gianyar you come to the turn-off to Bangli about 2km out of Peteluan. Follow this road for about 1km until you reach a sharp bend, where you'll find Sidan's **Pura Dalem**. This good example of a temple of the dead has very fine carvings. In particular, note the sculptures of Durga with children by the gate and the separate enclosure in one corner of the temple – this is dedicated to Merajapati, the guardian spirit of the dead.

BANGLI

☎ 0366

Halfway up the slope to Penelokan, Bangli, once the capital of a kingdom, is a humble market town noteworthy for its sprawling temple, Pura Kehen, which is on a beautiful jungle road that runs east past rice terraces and connects at Sekar with roads to Rendang and Sidemen.

INFORMATION	
Bank BRI	1 B2
Hospital	2 A2
Police Station	3 B2
Post Office	4 B2

SIGHTS & ACTIVITIES	
Market	5 B2
Pura Dalem Penunggekan	6 B3
Pura Kehen	7 B1
Sasana Budaya Giri Kusuma	8 B1
Tirta Buana	9 A2

SLEEPING ⌂	
Bangli Inn	10 B2

EATING	
Pasar Malam (Night Market)	11 B2

TRANSPORT	
Bemo Terminal	12 B2

History

Bangli dates from the early 13th century. In the Majapahit era it broke away from Gelgel to become a separate kingdom, even though it was landlocked, poor and involved in long-running conflicts with neighbouring states.

In 1849 Bangli made a treaty with the Dutch. The treaty gave Bangli control over the defeated north-coast kingdom of Buleleng, but Buleleng then rebelled and the Dutch imposed direct rule there. In 1909 the rajah (lord or prince) of Bangli chose to become a Dutch protectorate rather than face suicidal *puputan* (a warrior's fight to the death) or complete conquest by the neighbouring kingdoms or the colonial power.

Information

The compact centre has a **Bank BRI** (Jl Kutai) with international ATM, and there is a nearby hospital. There's a police station and a post office. The shambolic market makes a diverting stroll; watch where you step.

Sights & Activities
PURA KEHEN

The state temple of the Bangli kingdom, **Pura Kehen** (adult/child 6000/3000Rp; 9am-5pm) is one of the finest temples in eastern Bali – it's a miniature version of Pura Besakih (p215). It is terraced up the hillside, with a flight of steps leading to the beautifully decorated entrance. The first courtyard has a huge banyan tree with a *kulkul* (hollow tree-trunk warning drum) entwined in its branches. The Chinese porcelain plates were set into the walls as decoration, but most of the originals have been damaged or lost. The inner courtyard has an 11-roof *meru* (multiroofed shrine), and there are other shrines with thrones for the Hindu trinity – Brahma, Shiva and Vishnu. The carvings are particularly intricate. See if you can count all 43 altars.

There's a counter opposite the temple entrance where you pay your admission.

PURA DALEM PENUNGGEKAN

The exterior wall of this fascinating 'temple of the dead' features vivid relief carvings of wrong-doers getting their just desserts in the afterlife. One panel addresses the lurid fate of adulterers (men in particular may find the viewing uncomfortable). Other panels portray sinners as monkeys, while another is a good representation of evil-doers begging to be spared the fires of hell. It's to the south of the centre.

SASANA BUDAYA GIRI KUSUMA

Supposedly a showplace for Balinese dance, drama, gamelan and the visual arts, this large arts centre seldom has anything on. But it's well maintained, so it's always worth asking if something *will* be on.

BUKIT DEMULIH

Three kilometres west of Bangli is the village of Demulih, and a hill called Bukit Demulih. If you can't find the sign pointing to it, ask local children to direct you. After a short climb to the top, you'll see a small temple and good views over South Bali.

On the way to Bukit Demulih, a steep side road leads down to Tirta Buana, a **public swimming pool** in a lovely location deep in the valley, visible through the trees from the road above. You can take a vehicle most of the way down, but the track peters out and you'll need to walk the last 100m or so.

Sleeping & Eating

Bangli Inn (91419; Jl Rambutan 1; r 120,000Rp) Somewhat modern and popular with locals, the 10 cold-water rooms are clean and include breakfast. You'd only stay here if you wanted to hang at the night market for the evening.

A *pasar malam* (night market), on the street beside the bemo terminal, has some good warung, and you'll also find some in the market area during the day.

Getting There & Away

Bangli is located on the main road between Denpasar's Batubulan terminal (12,000Rp) and Gunung Batur, via Penelokan.

SEMARAPURA (KLUNGKUNG)
 0366

A tidy regional capital, Semarapura should be on your itinerary for its fascinating Kertha Gosa complex, a relic of Bali from the time before the Dutch. Once the centre of Bali's most important kingdom, Semarapura is still commonly called by its old name, Klungkung.

It's a good place to stroll and get a feel for modern Balinese life. The markets are large, the shops many and the streets calmer now that the coast road has diverted a lot of the traffic that used to clog Semarapura's streets.

History

Successors to the Majapahit conquerors of Bali established themselves at Gelgel (just south of modern Semarapura) around 1400, the Gelgel dynasty strengthening the growing Majapahit presence on the island. During the 17th century the successors of the Gelgel line established separate kingdoms, and the dominance of the Gelgel court was lost. The court moved to Klungkung in 1710, but never regained a pre-eminent position.

In 1849 the rulers of Klungkung and Gianyar defeated a Dutch invasion force at Kusamba. Before the Dutch could launch a counter-attack, a force from Tabanan arrived and the trader Mads Lange was able to broker a peace settlement.

For the next 50 years, the South Bali kingdoms squabbled, until the rajah of Gianyar petitioned the Dutch for support. When the Dutch finally invaded the south, the king of Klungkung had a choice between a suicidal *puputan*, like the rajah of Denpasar, or an ignominious surrender, as Tabanan's rajah had done. He chose the former. In April 1908, as the Dutch surrounded his palace, the Dewa Agung and hundreds of his relatives and followers marched out to certain death from Dutch gunfire or the blades of their own kris (traditional dagger). It was the last Balinese kingdom to succumb and the sacrifice is commemorated in the large **Puputan Monument**.

Information

Jl Nakula and the main street, Jl Diponegoro, have several banks with international ATMs.

District tourist office (☎ 21448; ⏰ 8am-2pm Mon-Fri) This small office is in the Museum Semarajaya building of Taman Kertha Gosa. It means well.

Police station (☎ 21115)

Sights

TAMAN KERTHA GOSA

When the Dewa Agung dynasty moved here in 1710, the Semara Pura was established. The palace was laid out as a large square, believed to be in the form of a mandala, with courtyards, gardens, pavilions and moats. The complex is sometimes referred to as Taman Gili (Island Garden). Most of the original palace and grounds were destroyed

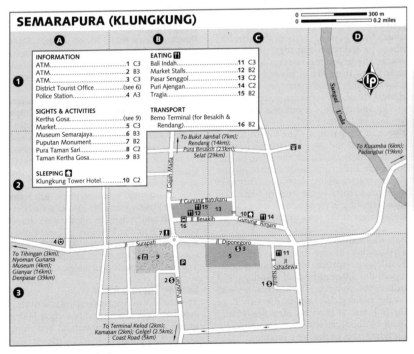

SEMARAPURA (KLUNGKUNG)

0   300 m
0   0.2 miles

INFORMATION	
ATM	1 C3
ATM	2 B3
ATM	3 C3
District Tourist Office	(see 6)
Police Station	4 A3

SIGHTS & ACTIVITIES	
Kertha Gosa	(see 9)
Market	5 C3
Museum Semarajaya	6 B3
Puputan Monument	7 B2
Pura Taman Sari	8 C2
Taman Kertha Gosa	9 B3

SLEEPING	
Klungkung Tower Hotel	10 C2

EATING	
Bali Indah	11 C3
Market Stalls	12 B2
Pasar Senggol	13 C2
Puri Ajengan	14 C2
Tragia	15 B2

TRANSPORT	
Bemo Terminal (for Besakih & Rendang)	16 B2

To Bukit Jambal (7km); Rendang (14km); Pura Besakih (23km); Selat (29km)

To Kusamba (6km); Padangbai (19km)

Sungai Unda

Jl Gajah Mada

Jl Gunung Batukaru

Jl Besakih

Gunung Rinjani

Surapati

Jl Diponegoro

Jl Sahadewa

Jl Puputan

To Tihingan (3km);
Nyoman Gunarsa Museum (4km);
Gianyar (16km);
Denpasar (39km)

To Terminal Kelod (2km);
Kamasan (2km); Gelgel (2.5km);
Coast Road (5km)

EAST BALI

by Dutch attacks in 1908 – the Pemedal Agung, the gateway on the south side of the square, is all that remains of the palace itself (but it's worth a close look to see the carvings). Two important buildings are preserved in a restored section of the grounds, and, with a museum, they comprise the **Taman Kertha Gosa complex** (adult/child 6000/3000Rp, parking 1000Rp; ☺ 7am-6pm). Parking is easy; vendors are persistent.

Kertha Gosa

In the northeastern corner of the complex, the 'Hall of Justice' was effectively the supreme court of the Klungkung kingdom, where disputes and cases that could not be settled at the village level were eventually brought. This open-sided pavilion is a superb example of Klungkung architecture. The ceiling is completely covered with fine paintings in the Klungkung style. The paintings, done on asbestos sheeting, were installed in the 1940s, replacing cloth paintings, which had deteriorated.

The rows of ceiling panels depict several themes. The lowest level illustrates five tales from Bali's answer to the *Arabian Nights,* where a girl called Tantri spins a different yarn every night. The next two rows are scenes from Bima's travels in the afterlife, where he witnesses the torment of evildoers. The gruesome tortures are shown clearly, but there are different interpretations of which punishment goes with what crime. (There's an authoritative explanation in *The Epic of Life – A Balinese Journey of the Soul* by Idanna Pucci, available for reference in the pavilion.) The fourth row of panels depicts the story of Garuda's (mythical man-bird) search for the elixir of life, while the fifth row shows events on the Balinese astrological calendar. The next three rows return to the story of Bima, this time travelling in heaven, with doves and a lotus flower at the apex of the ceiling.

Bale Kambang

The ceiling of the beautiful 'Floating Pavilion' is painted in Klungkung style. Again, the different rows of paintings deal with various subjects. The first row is based on the astrological calendar, the second on the folk tale of Pan and Men Brayut and their 18 children, and the upper rows on the adventures of the hero Sutasona.

Museum Semarajaya

This diverting museum has an interesting collection of archaeological and other pieces. There are exhibits of *songket* (silver- or gold-threaded cloth) weaving and palm toddy (palm wine) and palm-sugar extraction. Don't miss the moving display about the 1908 *puputan,* along with some interesting old photos of the royal court. The exhibit on salt-making gives you a good idea of the hard work involved (see the boxed text, p218).

MARKET

Semarapura's sprawling market is one of the best in East Bali. It's a vibrant hub of commerce and a meeting place for people of the region. You can easily spend an hour wandering about the warren of stalls as well as shops on nearby streets. Mornings are the best time to visit.

PURA TAMAN SARI

The quiet lawns and ponds around this temple make it a relaxing stop and live up to the translation of its name: Flower Garden Temple. The towering 11-roofed *meru* indicates that this was a temple built for royalty.

Sleeping & Eating

Klungkung Tower Hotel (☎ 25637; Jl Gunung Rinjani 18; r 225,000-375,000Rp; ⚒) is a new hotel aimed at business travellers; the 20 rooms here are fairly slick and include satellite TV. Bathrooms have walk-in showers.

The best bet for food locally are the **market stalls** with all manner of lunch items. **Tragia** (☎ 21997; Jl Gunung Batukaru) is a modern supermarket with a large choice of groceries and sundries, while **Pasar Senggol** (☺ 5pm-midnight) is a night market and is by far the best spot to eat if you're in town late. It's the usual flurry of woks, customers and noise.

A decades-old Chinese place, **Bali Indah** (☎ 21056; Jl Nakula 1; dishes 10,000-20,000Rp) serves simple meals and fresh juices. Sumba Rosa almost next door is similar. Klungkung Tower Hotel's restaurant, **Puri Ajengan** (mains 5000-15000Rp), has a good menu of Indonesian and Balinese fare. The bar has popular pool tables.

Getting There & Away

The best way to visit Semarapura is with your own transport and as part of a circle taking in other sites up the mountains and along the coast.

Bemo from Denpasar (Batubulan terminal) pass through Semarapura (18,000Rp) on the way to points further east. They can be hailed from near the Puputan Monument.

Bemo heading north to Besakih (10,000Rp) leave from the centre of Semarapura, a block northeast of Kertha Gosa. Most of the other bemo leave from the inconvenient Terminal Kelod, about 2km south of the city centre.

AROUND SEMARAPURA

East of Semarapura, the main road crosses Sungai Unda (Unda River), then swings south towards Kusamba and the sea. Lava from the 1963 eruption of Gunung Agung destroyed villages and cut the road here, but the lava flows are now overgrown.

Tihingan

Several workshops in Tihingan are dedicated to producing gamelan instruments. Small foundries make the resonating bronze bars and bowl-shaped gongs, which are then carefully filed and polished until they produce the correct tone. Some pieces are on sale, but most of the instruments are produced for musical groups all over Bali. It's not really set up for tourists, but the workshops with signs out the front will receive visitors (albeit sometimes grudgingly); the work is usually done very early in the morning when it's cool. From Semarapura, head west along Jl Diponegoro and look for the signs.

Gunarsa Museum

Dedicated to classical and contemporary Balinese painting, this beautiful **museum complex** (☎ 22256; www.gunarsa.com; adult/child 25,000Rp/free; ☒ 9am-5pm Mon-Sat) was established by Nyoman Gunarsa, one of the most respected and successful modern artists in Indonesia. A vast three-storey building exhibits an impressive variety of well-displayed older pieces, including stone carvings and woodcarvings, architectural antiques, masks, ceramics and textiles.

Many of the classical paintings are on bark paper and are some of the oldest surviving examples. Check out the many old puppets, still seemingly animated even in retirement. The top floor is devoted to Gunarsa's own bold, expressionistic depictions of traditional life. Look for *Offering*.

There's a large performance space nearby with regular performances – check for times.

Enjoy some fine examples of traditional architecture in the compound, a serene place where visitors are always outnumbered by flocks of songbirds.

The museum is about 4km west from Semarapura, near a bend on the Gianyar road – look for the dummy policemen at the base of a large statue nearby.

Kamasan

This quiet, traditional village is the place where the classical Kamasan painting style originated, and several artists still practise this art. You can see their workshops and small showrooms along the main street. The work is often a family affair, with one person inking the outlines while another mixes the paints and yet another applies the colours. The paintings depict traditional stories or Balinese calendars, and although they are sold in souvenir shops all over Bali, the quality is better here. Look for smooth and distinct line-work, evenly applied colours and balance in the overall composition. The village is also home to families of *bokor* artisans, who produce the silver bowls used in traditional ceremonies.

To reach Kamasan, go about 2km south of Semarapura and look for the turn-off to the east.

Gelgel

Situated about 2.5km south of Semarapura on the way to the coast road, Gelgel was once the seat of Bali's most powerful dynasty. The town's decline started in 1710, when the court moved to present-day Semarapura, and finished when the Dutch bombarded the place in 1908.

Today the wide streets and the surviving temples are only faintly evocative of past grandeur. The **Pura Dasar** is not particularly attractive, but its vast courtyards are a real clue to its former importance, and festivals here attract large numbers of people from all over Bali.

A little to the east, the **Masjid Gelgel** is Bali's oldest mosque. It was established in the late 16th century for the benefit of Muslim missionaries from Java, who were unwilling to return home after failing to make any converts.

Bukit Jambal

The road north of Semarapura climbs steeply into the hills via Bukit Jambal, which is understandably popular for its magnificent views.

EAST BALI

There are several restaurants here that provide buffet lunches for tour groups. This road continues to Rendang and Pura Besakih.

Sungai Unda & Sungai Telagawaja

East of Semarapura, the main road crosses the dammed-up Sungai Unda. Further upstream, Sungai Telagawaja (Telagawaja River) is used for white-water rafting trips (see p92).

SIDEMEN ROAD

☎ 0366

Winding through one of Bali's most beautiful river valleys, the Sidemen Road offers marvellous paddy-field scenery, a delightful rural character and extraordinary views of Gunung Agung (when the clouds permit). It's getting more popular every year as a verdant escape, where a walk in any direction is a communion with nature.

German artist Walter Spies lived in Iseh for some time from 1932 in order to escape the perpetual party of his own making in Ubud. Later the Swiss painter, Theo Meier, nearly as famous as Spies for his influence on Balinese art, lived in the same house.

The village of Sidemen has a spectacular location and is a centre for culture and arts, particularly *endek* (ikat) cloth and *songket*, which is woven with threads of silver and gold. **Pelangi Weaving** (☎ 23012; Jl Soka 67; ◷ 8am-6pm) has 25 employees busily creating downstairs, while upstairs you can relax with the Sidemen views from comfy chairs outside its showroom.

There are many **walks** through the rice fields and streams in the multihued green valley. One involves a climb up to **Pura Bukit Tageh**, a small temple with big views. No matter where you stay, you'll be able to arrange guides for in-depth trekking (about 25,000Rp per hour), or just set out on your own exploration.

Sleeping & Eating

Views throughout the area are sweeping, from terraced green hills to Gunung Agung. Most inns have restaurants; it can get cool and misty at night.

Near the centre of Sidemen, a small road heads west for 500m to a fork and a signpost with the names of several places to stay.

Pondok Wisata Lihat Sawah (☎ 24183; www.lihat sawah.com; r 250,000-450,000Rp) Take the right fork in the road to this ever-expanding place with lavish gardens. All 11 rooms have views of the valley and mountain (the best have hot water and tubs, nice after an early-morning hike). The surrounding rice fields course with water. The café shares the views and has a Thai and Indo menu (dishes 12,500Rp to 30,000Rp).

Tanto Villa (☎ 0812 395 0271; r US$25-45) Views of the Luwah Valley are the appeal at this modern house, which has four large and comfortable rooms with hot water. Two upstairs rooms have the best views of the surrounding chilli, bean and peanut fields.

Subak Tabola Inn (☎ 23015; r US$25-60; ⊠) Set in an impossibly green amphitheatre of rice terraces, the 11 rooms here have a bit of style and open-air bathrooms. Verandahs have mesmerising views down the valley to the ocean. The grounds are spacious and there's a cool pool with frog fountains. It's nearly 2km from the hotel signpost.

Nirarta (Centre for Living Awareness; ☎ 24122; www.awareness-bali.com; Br Tabola; r US$25-60) Guests here partake in serious programs for personal and spiritual development, including meditation intensives and yoga. The 11 comfortable rooms are split among several bungalows, some right on the babbling river.

Kubu Tani (☎ 24183; Jl Tebola; r 350,000Rp) There are two apartments at this two-storey house in a quiet location well away from other buildings. Open-plan living rooms have good views of the rice fields and mountains as well as large porches with loungers. Kitchens allow for cooking; there's no café close.

Patal Kikian (☎ /fax 23005; villas US$55-60; ⊠) Two kilometres north of Sidemen look for a steep driveway on the eastern side of the road. This retreat has three spacious villas with verandahs overlooking terraced hillsides; one of the best views in East Bali. Rooms have hot water, simple furnishings and tubs; there is a soaking pool. One bungalow has a huge table and seating outside around another large table.

Sacred Mountain Sanctuary (☎ 24330; villas US$90-140; ⊠ ◫) Close to the river, this remote and somewhat faded resort has a huge spring-fed swimming pool. The bamboo villas are out of *Gilligan's Island* and have open-air bathrooms. The restaurant (mains 20,000Rp to 35,000Rp) features Thai and vegetarian cuisine. The road is paved as far as the river, but then is quite rough to the inn.

Getting There & Away

Sidemen Road can be a beautiful part of any day trip from South Bali or Ubud. It connects in the north with the Rendang–Amlapura road just west of Duda. The road is in good shape and regular bemo shuttle up and down from Semarapura. A less-travelled route to Pura Besakih goes northeast from Semarapura, via Sidemen and Iseh, to the Rendang–Amlapura road – another scenic treat.

PURA BESAKIH

Perched nearly 1000m up the side of Gunung Agung is Bali's most important temple, Pura Besakih. In fact, it is an extensive complex of 23 separate-but-related temples, with the largest and most important being Pura Penataran Agung. Unfortunately, many people find it a disappointing (and dispiriting) experience due to the avarice of various local characters. See the boxed text, p216, for the details, which may help you decide whether to skip it.

The multitude of hassles aside, the complex comes alive during frequent ceremonies.

History

The precise origins of Pura Besakih are not totally clear, but it almost certainly dates from prehistoric times. The stone bases of Pura Penataran Agung and several other temples resemble megalithic stepped pyramids, which date back at least 2000 years. It was certainly used as a Hindu place of worship from 1284, when the first Javanese conquerors settled in Bali. By the 15th century, Besakih had become a state temple of the Gelgel dynasty.

Orientation

The main entrance is 2km south of the complex on the road from Menanga and the south. The fees are as follows: adult/child 7500/6000Rp, still camera 1000Rp, video camera 2500Rp and car park 1000Rp. The fact that you may well be charged for a video camera whether you have one or not gives you a taste of things to come.

About 200m past the ticket office, there is a fork in the road with a sign indicating Besakih to the right and Kintamani to the left. Go left, because going to the right puts you in a large parking lot at the bottom of a hill some 300m from the complex. Going past the road to Kintamani, where there is another ticket office, puts you in the north parking

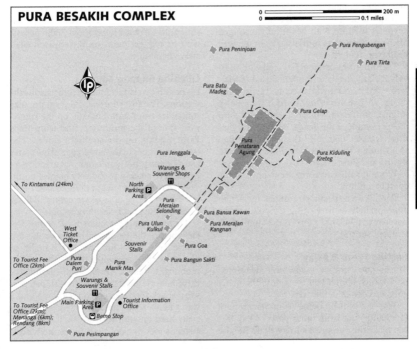

PURA BESAKIH COMPLEX

0 200 m
0 0.1 miles

Pura Peninjoan
Pura Pengubengan
Pura Tirta
Pura Batu Madeg
Pura Gelap
Pura Penataran Agung
Pura Jenggala
Pura Kiduling Kreteg
Warungs & Souvenir Shops
To Kintamani (24km)
North Parking Area
Pura Merajan Selonding
Pura Banua Kawan
Pura Ulun Kulkul
Pura Merajan Kangnan
West Ticket Office
Souvenir Stalls
Pura Goa
To Tourist Fee Office (2km)
Pura Dalem Puri
Pura Manik Mas
Pura Bangun Sakti
Warungs & Souvenir Stalls
To Tourist Fee Office (2km); Menanga (6km); Rendang (8km)
Main Parking Area
Tourist Information Office
Bemo Stop
Pura Pesimpangan

AN UNHOLY EXPERIENCE

So intrusive are the scams and irritations faced by visitors to Besakih that many wish they had skipped the complex altogether. What follows are some of the ploys you should be aware of before a visit.

- Near the main parking area is a building labelled Tourist Information Office. Guides here may emphatically tell you that you need their services. You don't. You may always walk among the temples, and no 'guide' can get you into a closed temple.

- Other 'guides' may foist their services on you throughout your visit. There have been reports of people agreeing to a guide's services only to be hit with a huge fee at the end.

- Once inside the complex, you may receive offers to 'come pray with me'. Visitors who seize on this chance to get into a forbidden temple can face demands of 100,000Rp or more.

---

area only 20m from the complex, and away from scammers at the main entrance.

Sights

The largest and most important temple is **Pura Penataran Agung**. It is built on six levels, terraced up the slope, with the entrance approached from below, up a flight of steps. This entrance is an imposing *candi bentar* (split gateway), and beyond it, the even more impressive *kori agung* is the gateway to the second courtyard. It's most enjoyable during one of the frequent festivals, when hundreds, perhaps thousands, of gorgeously dressed devotees turn up with beautifully arranged offerings. Note that tourists are not allowed inside this temple.

The other Besakih temples – all with individual significance and often closed to visitors – are markedly less scenic. Just as each village in Bali has a *pura puseh* (temple of origin), *pura desa* (village temple) and *pura dalem* (temple of the dead), Pura Besakih has three temples that fulfil these roles for Bali as a whole – Pura Basukian, Pura Penataran Agung and Pura Dalem Puri, respectively.

When it's mist-free, the view down to the coast is sublime.

For tips on respecting traditions and acting appropriately while visiting temples, see the boxed text, p348. For a directory of important temples, see p51.

Getting There & Away

The best way to visit is with your own transport, which allows you to explore the many gorgeous drives in the area.

You can visit by bemo from Semarapura (10,000Rp) but from other parts of Bali this can make the outing an all-day affair. Be sure to ask the driver to take you to the temple entrance, not to the village about 1km from the temple complex. Make certain you leave the temple by 3pm if you want to return to either Semarapura or Denpasar by bemo.

GUNUNG AGUNG

Bali's highest and most revered mountain, Gunung Agung is an imposing peak seen from most of South and East Bali, although it's often obscured by cloud and mist. Many references give its height as 3142m, but some say it lost its head, er summit, in the 1963 eruption and opinion varies as to the real height. The summit is an oval crater, about 700m across, with its highest point on the western edge above Besakih.

Climbing Gunung Agung

It's possible to climb Agung from various directions. The two shortest and most popular routes are from Pura Besakih, on the southwest side of the mountain, and from Pura Pasar Agung, on the southern slopes. The latter route goes to the lower edge of the crater rim (2900m), but you can't make your way from there around to the very highest point. You'll have great views of the south and east, but you won't be able to see central Bali. A similar route goes from Pura Sambu.

To have the best chance of seeing the view before the clouds form, get to the top before 8am. You'll have to start at night, so plan your climb for when there will be some moonlight. Take a strong torch (flashlight), extra batteries, plenty of water (2L per person), snack food, waterproof clothing and a warm jumper (sweater). The descent is especially hard on your feet, so you'll appreciate strong shoes or boots and manicured toes.

You should take a guide for either route. Early in the climb the guide will stop at a shrine to make an offering and say some prayers. This is a holy mountain and you should show respect.

It's best to climb during the dry season (April to September), although July to September are the most reliable months. At other times, the paths can be slippery and dangerous and the views are clouded over (especially true in January and February). Climbing Gunung Agung is not permitted when major religious events are being held at Pura Besakih, which generally includes most of April. No guide will take you up at these times.

GUIDES

Trips with guides on either of the following routes up Gunung Agung generally include breakfast and other meals and a place to stay, but be sure to confirm all details in advance. Guides can also arrange transport.

Most of the places to stay in the region, including those at Selat (p218), along the Sidemen Road (p214) and Tirta Gangga (p230), will recommend guides for Gunung Agung climbs. Expect to pay a negotiable 350,000Rp to 800,000Rp for one or two people for your climb.

Recommended guides include the following:

Gung Bawa Trekking (☎ 0812 387 8168; www.gb -trekking.blogspot.com) Experienced and reliable.

Ketut Uriada (☎ 0812 364 6426; Muncan) This knowledgable guide can arrange transport for an extra fee (look for his small sign on the road east of the village).

Wayan Tegteg (☎ 0813 3852 5677; Selat) Wins reader plaudits.

Yande (☎ 0817 476 0275; Selat) Has many years on the mountain.

FROM PURA PASAR AGUNG

This route involves the least walking, because Pura Pasar Agung (Agung Market Temple) is high on the southern slopes of the mountain (around 1500m) and can be reached by a good road north from Selat. From the temple you can climb to the top in three or four hours, but it's a pretty demanding trek. With or without a guide, you must report to the police station at Selat before you start. If you don't have a guide, the police will strongly encourage you to take one.

It is much better to stay the night near Selat or Sidemen so that you can drive up early in the morning to Pura Pasar Agung. This temple has been greatly enlarged and improved, in part as a monument to the 1963 eruption that devastated this area.

Start climbing from the temple at around 3am. There are numerous trails through the pine forest but after an hour or so you'll climb above the tree line. Then you're climbing on solidified lava, which can be loose and broken in places, but a good guide will keep you on solid ground. At the top, you can gawk into the crater, watch the sun rise over Lombok and see the shadow of Agung in the morning haze over southern Bali.

Allow at least six hours total for this trek. If you don't have a car waiting for you, walk down to Sebudi, from where there are bemo down to Selat.

FROM PURA BESAKIH

This climb is much tougher than the southern approach and is only for the very physically fit. For the best chance of a clear view before the clouds close in, you should start at midnight. Allow at least six hours for the climb, and four to six hours for the descent. The starting point is Pura Pengubengan, northeast of the main temple complex, but it's easy to get lost on the lower trails, so attempting this without a guide would be folly.

RENDANG TO AMLAPURA
☎ 0366

A fascinating road goes around the southern slopes of Gunung Agung from Rendang almost to Amlapura. It runs through some superb countryside, descending more or less gradually as it goes east. Water flows everywhere and there are rice fields, orchards and carvers of stones for temples most of the way.

Cyclists enjoy the route and find going east to be a breezier ride.

You can get to the start of the road in Rendang from Bangli in the west on a very pretty road through rice terraces and thick jungle vegetation. **Rendang** itself is an attractive mountain village; the crossroads are dominated by a huge and historic banyan tree. After going east for about 3km, you'll come into a beautiful small valley of rice terraces. At the bottom is **Sungai Telagawaja**, a popular river for white-water rafting. Some companies (see p92) have their facilities near here.

EAST BALI

The old-fashioned village of **Muncan** has quaint shingle roofs. It's approximately 4km along the winding road. Note the statues at the west entrance to town showing two boys: one a scholar and one showing the naked stupidity of skipping class. Nearby are scores of open-air factories where the soft lava rock is carved into temple decorations.

The road then passes through some of the most attractive rice country in Bali before reaching **Selat**, where you turn north to get to Pura Pasar Agung, a starting point for climbing Gunung Agung. **Puri Agung Inn** (☎ 23037; r 125,000-175,000Rp) has 8 clean and comfortable rooms; the inn has views of rice fields and stone carvers. You can arrange rice-field walks here or climbs up Gunung Agung (p217).

Just before **Duda**, the very scenic Sidemen Road (p214) branches southwest via Sidemen to Semarapura (p210). Further east, a side road (about 800m) leads to **Putung**. This area is superb for hiking: there's an easy-to-follow track from Putung to **Manggis**, about 8km down the hill.

Continuing east, **Sibetan** is famous for growing *salak*, the delicious fruit with a curious 'snakeskin' covering, which you can buy from roadside stalls. This is one of the villages you can visit on tours and homestays organised by **JED** (Village Ecotourism Network; ☎ 0361-735320; www.jed .or.id; tours US$70-100), the non-profit group that organises rural tourism (see p362).

Northeast of Sibetan, a poorly signposted road leads north to Jungutan, with its **Tirta Telaga Tista** – a decorative pool and garden complex built for the water-loving old rajah of Karangasem.

The scenic road finishes at **Bebandem**, which has a cattle market every three days, and plenty of other stuff for sale as well. Bebandem and several nearby villages are home to members of the traditional metal-worker caste, which includes silversmiths as well as blacksmiths.

KUSAMBA TO PADANGBAI

The coast road from Sanur crosses the traditional route to the east at the fishing town of Kusamba before joining the road near Pura Goa Lawah.

Kusamba

A side road leaves the main road and goes south to the fishing and salt-making village of Kusamba, where you will see rows of colourful *prahu* (outrigger fishing boats) lined up all along the beach. The fishing is usually done

---

WORKING IN THE SALT BRINE

For a real day at the beach, try making some salt. You start by carrying, say, 500L of ocean water across the sand to bamboo and wood funnels, which filter the water after it is poured in. Next the water goes into a *palungan* (shallow trough), made of palm-tree trunks split in half and hollowed out, or cement canisters where it evaporates leaving salt behind. And that's just the start, and just what you might see in Kusamba or on the beach in Amed.

In the volcanic areas around the east coast between Sanur and Yeh Sanih in the north, a range of salt-making methods is used. What is universal is that the work is hard, very hard, but is also an essential source of income for many families.

In some places the first step is drying sand that has been saturated with sea water. It's then taken inside a hut, where more sea water is strained through it to wash out the salt. This very salty water is then poured into a *palungan*. Hundreds of these troughs are lined up in rows along the beaches during the salt-making season (the dry season), and as the hot sun evaporates the water, the almost-dry salt is scraped and put in baskets. There are good exhibits on this method at the Museum Semarajaya (p212) in Semarapura.

Most salt produced on the coast of Bali is used for processing dried fish. And that's where Amed has an advantage: although its method of making salt results in a lower yield than that using sand, its salt is prized for its flavour. In fact there is a fast-growing market for this 'artisan salt' worldwide. The grey and cloudy crystals are finding their way into many top-end kitchens.

Visitors to the Amed area can learn all about this fascinating process at the adjoining Hotel Uyah Amed (p234) and Café Garam (p235). Many of the staff here also work in salt production. Tours are offered, and you can buy big bags of the precious stuff (per kilogram 10,000Rp) for a tiny fraction of what it costs once it's gone through many hands and made its way to your local gourmet market.

at night and the 'eyes' on the front of the boats help navigate through the darkness. The fish market in Kusamba is really excellent.

Local boats travel to the islands of Nusa Penida and Nusa Lembongan, which are clearly visible from Kusamba (but you can get faster and safer boats from Padangbai; see p222). Both east and west of Kusamba, there are small salt-making huts lined up in rows along the beach – see the boxed text, opposite.

East of Kusamba and 300m west of Pura Goa Lawah, **Merta Sari** (meals 10,000Rp; ⏰ 10am-3pm) is renowned for its *nasi campur*, which includes juicy, pounded fish satay, a slightly sour, fragrant fish broth, fish steamed in banana leaves, snake beans in a fragrant tomato-peanut sauce and a fire-red sambal. The open-air pavilion is 300m north of the coast road in the village of Bingin. Look for the Merta Sari signs.

Also good is archrival **Sari Baruna** (meals 5000-10,000Rp; ⏰ 10am-6pm), which also grills fish with attitude and authority. It's in a rickety bamboo hut about 200m west of Pura Goa Lawah.

Pura Goa Lawah

Three kilometres east of Kusamba is **Pura Goa Lawah** (Bat Cave Temple; adult/child 6000/3000Rp, car park 2000Rp; ⏰ 8am-6pm), which is one of nine directional temples (see p51) in Bali. The cave in the cliff face is packed, crammed and jammed full of bats, and the complex is equally overcrowded with tour groups, foreign and local. You might exclaim 'Holy Bat Guano, Batman!' when you get a whiff of the odours emanating from the cave. Superficially, the temple is small and unimpressive, but it is very old and of great significance to the Balinese.

Legend says the cave leads all the way to Pura Besakih, some 19km away, but it's unlikely that you'd want to try this route. The bats provide sustenance for the legendary giant snake, the deity Naga Basuki, which is also believed to live in the cave.

PADANGBAI

☎ 0363

There's a real backpacker vibe about this funky little beach town that is also the port for the main public ferry connecting Bali with Lombok.

Padangbai is on the upswing. It sits on a small bay and has a nice little curve of beach. It has a whole compact seaside travellers scene with cheap places to stay and some funky

and fun cafés. A town beautification drive has cleaned up the beach and added a new market area nearby.

The pace is slow, but should ambition strike there's good snorkelling and diving plus some easy walks and a couple of great beaches. Meanwhile you can soak up the languid air punctuated by the occasional arrival and departure of a ferry.

Information

Bank BRI (Jl Pelabuhan) exchanges money and has an international ATM.

You can find slow internet access (per minute 300Rp) at numerous places, including Kerti Bungalows and Made's Homestay (see p221).

Sights

Padangbai is interesting for a stroll. At the west end of town near the post office there's a small **mosque** and a temple, **Pura Desa**. Towards the middle of town, there are two more temples, **Pura Dalem** and **Pura Segara**, and the new **market**, which is home to numerous vendors and cafés.

With its protected bay, Padangbai has a good beach right in front. Others are nearby; walk southwest from the ferry terminal and follow the trail up the hill to the grey sand of **Bias Tugal**, on the exposed coast outside the bay. Be careful in the water, as it is subject to strong currents. There are a couple of daytime warung here.

On a headland at the northeast corner of the bay, a path leads uphill to three temples, including **Pura Silayukti**, where Empu Kuturan – who introduced the caste system to Bali in the 11th century – is said to have lived. It is one of the four oldest in Bali.

EAST BALI

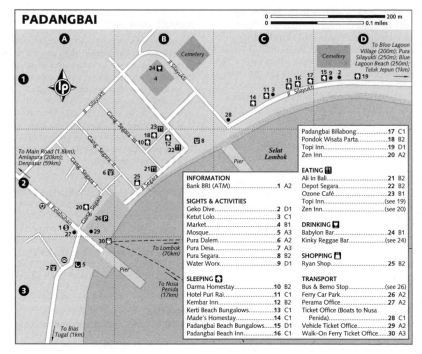

PADANGBAI

INFORMATION	
Bank BRI (ATM)	1 A2

SIGHTS & ACTIVITIES	
Geko Dive	2 D1
Ketut Lolo	3 C1
Market	4 B1
Mosque	5 A3
Pura Dalem	6 A2
Pura Desa	7 A3
Pura Segara	8 B2
Water Worx	9 D1

SLEEPING	
Darma Homestay	10 B2
Hotel Puri Rai	11 C1
Kembar Inn	12 B2
Kerti Beach Bungalows	13 C1
Made's Homestay	14 C1
Padangbai Beach Bungalows	15 D1
Padangbai Beach Inn	16 C1
Padangbai Billabong	17 C1
Pondok Wisata Parta	18 B2
Topi Inn	19 D1
Zen Inn	20 A2

EATING	
Ali In Bali	21 B2
Depot Segara	22 B2
Ozone Café	23 B1
Topi Inn	(see 19)
Zen Inn	(see 20)

DRINKING	
Babylon Bar	24 B1
Kinky Reggae Bar	(see 24)

SHOPPING	
Ryan Shop	25 B2

TRANSPORT	
Bus & Bemo Stop	(see 26)
Ferry Car Park	26 A2
Perama Office	27 A2
Ticket Office (Boats to Nusa Penida)	28 C1
Vehicle Ticket Office	29 A2
Walk-On Ferry Ticket Office	30 A3

About 500m up and over the headland in the east is the small, white-sand **Blue Lagoon Beach**, an idyllic place with a couple of cafés and gentle, family-friendly surf.

Activities

The Topi Inn (opposite) arranges a variety of cultural workshops for guests and non-guests. The fee is 100,000Rp for a course of two to four hours.

DIVING

There's some pretty good diving on the coral reefs around Padangbai, but the water can be a little cold and visibility is not always ideal. The most popular local dives are **Blue Lagoon** and **Teluk Jepun** (Jepun Bay), both in Teluk Amuk, the bay just east of Padangbai. There's a good range of soft and hard corals and varied marine life, including sharks, turtles and wrasse, and a 40m wall at Blue Lagoon.

Several good local outfits offer diving trips in the area, including to Gili Tepekong and Gili Biaha, and on to Tulamben and Nusa Penida. All dive prices are competitive, costing US$40 to US$90 for one or two boat dives,

depending on the site. Dive courses are available. Padangbai is the harbour of choice for departures by many dive operators across East and South Bali.

Recommended operators include the following:

Geko Dive (☎ 41516; www.gekodive.com; Jl Silayukti) The longest-established operator; has a nice café across from the beach.

Water Worx (☎ 41220; www.waterworxbali.com; Jl Silayukti) Another good dive operator; has a diving pool.

SNORKELLING

One of the best and most accessible walk-in snorkel sites is off Blue Lagoon Beach (left). Note that it is subject to strong currents when the tide is out. Other sites such as Teluk Jepun can be reached by local boat (or check with the dive operators to see if they have any room on their dive boats). Snorkel sets cost about 30,000Rp per day.

Local *jukung* (boats) offer snorkelling trips (bring your own snorkelling gear) around Padangbai (50,000Rp per person per hour) and as far away as Nusa Lembongan (350,000Rp) for two passengers. **Ketut Lolo**

(☎ 0819 1623 9123) works in front of the Puri Rai restaurant and arranges trips.

Sleeping

Accommodation in Padangbai – like the town itself – is pretty laid-back. Prices are fairly cheap and it's pleasant enough here that there's no need to hurry through to or from Lombok if you want to hang out on the beach and in cafés with other travellers.

VILLAGE

In the village, there are several tiny places in the alleys, some with a choice of small, cheap downstairs rooms or bigger, brighter upstairs rooms.

Darma Homestay (☎ 41394; Gang Segara III; r 60,000-150,000Rp; ❄) A classic Balinese family homestay. The more expensive of the 12 rooms have hot showers and air-con; go for the private room on the top floor.

Pondok Wisata Parta (☎ 41475, 0817 975 2668; off Gang Segara III; r 70,000-150,000Rp; ❄) The pick of the 10 rooms in this hidden and snoozy spot is the 'honeymoon room', which has a harbour view and good breezes. The most expensive rooms have air-con.

Zen Inn (☎ 41418; www.zeninn.com; Gang Segara; r 75,000-150,000Rp; ❄) Close to the ferry terminal, Zen's four rooms are eclectically decorated with bamboo and rattan interiors and both indoor and outdoor showers. Extra money gets hot water and air-con. The café is faded hip.

Kembar Inn (☎ 41364; kembarinn@hotmail.com; r 100,000-250,000Rp; ❄) There are six rooms at this inn linked by a steep and narrow staircase. The best awaits at the top and has a private terrace with views.

JL SILAYUKTI

On this little strip at the east end of the village, places are close together and right across from the sand.

Made's Homestay (☎ 41441; Jl Silayukti; s/d 50,000/60,000Rp; 🖳) Four basic, clean and simple rooms and internet access are the draws here.

ourpick Topi Inn (☎ 41424; www.topiinn.com; Jl Silayukti; r 50,000-60,000Rp; 🖳 wi-fi) Sitting at the end of the strip in a serene location, Topi has five pleasant rooms, some of which share bathrooms. The enthusiastic owners offer courses in topics as diverse as cooking and gamelan, among other diversions. The café is excellent.

Padangbai Beach Inn (☎ 41439; Jl Silayukti; r 60,000-100,000Rp) The 18 cold-water rooms in cute bungalows are the pick; avoid the rice-barn-style two-storey cottages, which can get hot and stuffy. Breakfast omelettes are a treat.

Kerti Beach Bungalows (☎ 41391; Jl Silayukti; r 70,000-250,000Rp; ❄ 🖳) Go for the 19 rooms in pretty bungalows built in a long narrow strip rather than the rice barns. As you move up the rate ladder here, you gain hot water and air-con.

Padangbai Billabong (☎ 41399; r 75,000Rp) We prefer the bungalows right up front at this scrupulously tidy place, which has 12 rooms set amid immaculate gardens.

Padangbai Beach Bungalows (☎ 41417; Jl Silayukti; r 100,000-400,000Rp; ❄ 🍳) The bungalows are attractive, with open-air bathrooms, and set in a classic Balinese garden setting that now boasts a large pool across from the beach. The top rooms have air-con.

Hotel Puri Rai (☎ 41385; purirai_hotel@yahoo.com; Jl Silayukti 3; r 275,000Rp, with air-con 375,000Rp; ❄ 🍳) The Puri Rai has 30 rooms, some with fans, in a two-storey stone building pleasantly facing the good-sized pool. Other rooms enjoy harbour views or overlook a yucky parking area. Ask to see a couple.

BLUE LAGOON BEACH

Bloo Lagoon Village (☎ 41211; www.bloolagoon.com; r US$75-200; ❄ 🍳 🖳) Perched above Blue Lagoon Beach, the 25 cottages and villas here are all designed in traditional thatched style and the compound is dedicated to sustainable practices. Units come with one, two or three bedrooms and are well-thought-out and stylish.

Eating & Drinking

Beach fare and backpacker staples are what's on offer in Padangbai – lots of fresh seafood, Indonesian classics, pizza and, yes, banana pancakes. Most of the places to stay have a café. You can easily laze away a few hours soaking up the scene at the places along Jl Segara and Jl Silayukti, which have harbour views during the day and cool breezes in the evening.

Depot Segara (☎ 41443; Jl Segara; dishes 10,000-30,000Rp) Fresh seafood such as barracuda, marlin and snapper is prepared in a variety of ways at this popular café. Enjoy harbour views from the slightly elevated terrace.

Ozone Café (☎ 41501; dishes 15,000-35,000Rp) This popular travellers' gathering spot has more character than every other place in East Bali combined. Slogans cover the walls, including this example from a wall of dating advice categorised by astrological sign: 'Capricorn Girls, don't cut the hair of your armpit. It's a good appetizer for your boyfriend.' Ozone has pizza and live music, sometimes by patrons.

Zen Inn (☎ 41418; Gang Segara; dishes 18,000-30,000Rp) Burgers and other meaty mains with a Dutch accent are served in this dark café. If someone remembers, DVDs are sometimes shown at night.

Topi Inn (☎ 41424; Jl Silayukti; mains 18,000-40,000Rp) Juices, shakes and good coffees served up throughout the day. Breakfasts are big, and whatever is landed by the fishing boats outside the front door during the day is grilled by night.

Ali in Bali (☎ 0819 3307 2907; Jl Segara; mains 25,000Rp) A sort of *Arabian Nights* fantasy from the Zen Inn people. The menu has two items: a filling Dutch breakfast (eggs, ham, cheese etc) and doner kebab the rest of the day. There are also good juices.

Babylon Bar (Jl Silayukti) and **Kinky Reggae Bar** (Jl Silayukti) are tiny adjoining bars in the new market area back off the beach. They have a few chairs, tables and pillows scattered about and are perfect places to while away the evening with new friends.

Shopping

Ryan Shop (☎ 41215; Jl Segara 38) Year after year, a name you can trust for quality. It has a fair selection of secondhand paperbacks, some maps and sundries.

Getting There & Away
BEMO
Padangbai is 2km south of the main Semarapura–Amlapura road. Bemo leave from the car park in front of the port; orange bemo go east through Candidasa to Amlapura (8000Rp); blue or white bemo go to Semarapura (8000Rp).

BOAT
Lombok
There are many ways between Bali and Lombok, see p354 for full details.

Public ferries (adult/child 28,000/18,000Rp) travel nonstop between Padangbai and Lembar on Lombok. Motorbikes cost 85,000Rp and cars cost 550,000Rp – go through the weighbridge at the west corner of the Padangbai car park. Passenger tickets are sold near the pier.

Perama has a 40-passenger boat (300,000Rp, six hours), which usually leaves at 9am for Senggigi, where you can connect to the Gilis, although at times it runs there direct. Check details at the shuttle-bus office (below).

Gilicat (☎ 0361-271680; www.gilicat.com; 660,000Rp) serves Gili Trawangan (90 minutes) in a fast, 16-passenger boat. Its local agent is at **Made's Homestay** (Jl Silayukti).

Nusa Penida
On the beach just east of the car park, you'll find the twin-engine fibreglass boats that run across the strait to Buyuk (30,000Rp, 45 minutes, four daily), 1km west of Sampalan on Nusa Penida. The boats run between 7am and noon. A large and new car ferry has been built for the route, but its operation is spotty, owing to sporadic government funding. Ask if it's running, as it's the best way to go.

BUS
To connect with Denpasar, catch a bemo out to the main road and hail a bus to the Batubulan terminal (18,000Rp).

TOURIST SHUTTLE BUS
Perama (☎ 41419; Café Dona, Jl Pelabuhan; ☸ 7am-8pm) has a stop here for its services around the east coast.

Destination	Fare	Duration
Candidasa	25,000Rp	30min
Kuta	60,000Rp	3hr
Lovina	150,000Rp	5hr
Sanur	60,000Rp	2¼hr
Ubud	50,000Rp	1¼hr

PADANGBAI TO CANDIDASA
☎ 0363

It's worth prowling some of the beachside lanes off the main road for little places to stay. It's 11km along the main road from the Padangbai turn-off to the resort town of Candidasa, and there are bemo or buses every few minutes. Between the two towns is an attractive stretch of coast, which has some tourist development, and a large oil-storage depot in Teluk Amuk.

A short way east, a new cruise-ship port at Tanah Ampo could bring a tourism revolution to Bali. Currently cruise ships have no deep-water port in Bali, and the few that call have to shuttle passengers ashore by boat – something the cruise lines and passengers all hate. If the new dock can attract the kinds of megaships common in the Caribbean, it could mean 5000 passengers or more descending on Bali and the east.

Manggis

A pretty village inland from the coast, Manggis is the address used by several luxury resorts hidden along the water.

Two of the island's best hotels are off the main road along here.

One of Bali's best resorts, the **Amankila** (☎ 41333; www.amankila.com; villas from US$650; 🌐 🛋 🖥 wi-fi), is perched along the jutting cliffs. About 5.6km beyond the Padangbai turn-off and 500m past the road to Manggis, a discreetly marked side road leads to the hotel. It features an isolated seaside location with views to Nusa Penida and even Lombok. The renowned architecture features three main swimming pools that step down to the sea in matching shades of blue that actually doesn't seem real. Of the restaurants here, the superb **Terrace** (lunch 80,000-200,000Rp) is the more casual and has a creative and varied menu with global and local influences. Service vies with the view for your plaudits.

About 1km further on from the Amankila, the **Alila Manggis** (☎ 41011; www.alilahotels.com; r US$180-300; 🌐 🛋 🖥 wi-fi) has elegant, white, thatch-roofed buildings in spacious lawn gardens facing a beautiful stretch of secluded beach. The 55 rooms are large with stylish interiors that are heavy on creams with muted wood accents; go for deluxe ones on the upper floor to enjoy the best views. The restaurant, **Seasalt** (mains from US$18), features much-lauded organic fusion and Balinese cuisine. Activities include a kids' camp, a spa and cooking courses.

Mendira & Sengkidu

Coming from the west, there are hotels and losmen (basic accommodation) well off the main road at Mendira and Sengkidu, before you reach Candidasa. Although the beach has all but vanished and unsightly sea walls have been constructed, this area is a good choice for a quiet getaway if you have your own transport. Think views, breezes and a good book.

SLEEPING & EATING

All of the following are on small tracks between the main road and the water; none are far from Candidasa.

The first three places listed here are reached via narrow roads from a single turn off the main road 1km west of Candidasa. Look for a large sign listing places to stay.

Amarta Beach Inn Bungalows (☎ 41230; r 100,000-150,000Rp) In a panoramic seaside setting, the 10 units here are right on the water and are great value. The more expensive ones have hot water and interesting open-air bathrooms. At low tide there is a tiny beach; at other times you can sit and enjoy the views out to Nusas Lembongan and Penida.

Anom Beach Inn (☎ 419024; www.anom-beach .com; r US$22-55; 🌐 🛋) This older resort from a simpler time has 24 rooms in a variety of configurations. The cheapest are fan-only – not a problem given the constant offshore breezes. The best are bungalow-style with air-con and fridges. When we were there, some loyal German customers got so enthused extolling the inn's virtues that they almost missed their airport taxi.

Pondok Pisang (☎ 41065; www.pondokpisang.com; r US$50-65) The name here means 'banana hut', and there's plenty of appeal. The six spacious two-level bungalows face the sea in a large compound. Each has an artful interior, including mosaic-tiled bathrooms. Yoga intensives are held at various times. In a small workshop local ladies sew textiles, which are then sold at the Bananas Batik boutique (p126) in Seminyak.

The following pair are a short walk from Candidasa.

Nirwana Resort (☎ 41136; www.thenirwana.com; r US$45-90; 🌐 🛋 🖥 wi-fi) The builders have been at work: this older resort has been given a massive rehab and is now a stylish place with traditional lashings. A dramatic walk across a lotus pond sets the tone. The 18 units (DVD players and other niceties) are all near the now-standard infinity pool by the ocean.

Lotus Bungalows (☎ 41104; www.lotusbunga lows.com; half-board US$75-110; 🌐 🛋 🖥) Managed by earnest Europeans, the 20 rooms here (some with air-con) are in well-spaced bungalow-style units. Four (numbers 101, 102, 113 and 114) are right on the ocean. The decor is bright and airy, and there is a large and inviting pool area. Half-board is the only option for guests here.

Tenganan

Step back several centuries with a visit to Tenganan, home of the Bali Aga people – the descendants of the original Balinese who inhabited Bali before the Majapahit arrival in the 11th century.

The Bali Aga are reputed to be exceptionally conservative and resistant to change. Well, that's only partially true: TVs and other modern conveniences are hidden away in the traditional houses. But it is fair to say that the village has a much more traditional feel than most other villages in Bali. Cars and motorcycles are forbidden from entering. It should also be noted that this a real village, not a creation for tourists.

The most striking feature of Tenganan is its postcard-like beauty, with the hills providing a photogenic backdrop. The village is surrounded by a wall, and consists basically of two rows of identical houses stretching up the gentle slope of a hill. As you enter the village (5000Rp donation), you'll likely be greeted by a guide who will take you on a tour – and generally lead you back to his family compound to look at textiles and *lontar* (specially prepared palm leaves) strips. Unlike Besakih, however, there's no pressure to buy anything, so you won't need your own armed guards. For more on *lontar* books, see p260.

A peculiar, old-fashioned version of the gamelan known as the *gamelan selunding* is still played here, and girls dance an equally ancient dance known as the Rejang. There are other Bali Aga villages nearby, including Tenganan Dauh Tenkad, 1.5km west off the Tenganan road, with a charming old-fashioned ambience and several weaving workshops. At Asak, southeast of Tenganan, another ancient instrument, the *gamelan gambang*, is still played.

FESTIVALS

Tenganan is full of unusual customs, festivals and practices. At the month-long **Usaba Sambah Festival**, which usually starts in May or June, men fight with sticks wrapped in thorny pandanus leaves. At this same festival, small, hand-powered Ferris wheels are brought out and the village girls are ceremonially twirled around.

TOURS

To really experience the ambience and culture of the village, consider one of the tours offered by **JED** (Village Ecotourism Network; ☎ 0361-735320; www.jed.or.id; tours US$70-100). These highly regarded tours (some overnight) include local guides who explain the culture in detail and show how local goods are produced. Tours include transport from South Bali and Ubud.

SHOPPING

A magical cloth known as *kamben gringsing* is woven here – a person wearing it is said to be protected against black magic. Traditionally this is made using the 'double ikat' technique, in which both the warp and weft threads are 'resist dyed' before being woven. MBAs would be thrilled studying the integrated production of the cloth: everything, from growing the cotton to producing the dyes from local plants to the actual production, is accomplished here. It's very time-consuming, and the exquisite pieces of double ikat available for sale are quite expensive (from about 600,000Rp). You'll see cheaper cloth for sale but it usually comes from elsewhere in Bali.

Many baskets from across the region, made from *ata* palm, are on sale. Another local craft is traditional Balinese calligraphy, with the script inscribed onto *lontar* palm strips in the same way that the ancient *lontar* books were created. Most of these books are Balinese calendars or depictions of the *Ramayana*. They cost 150,000Rp to 300,000Rp, depending on quality.

Tenganan weaving is also sold in Ashitaba shops in Seminyak (p127) and Ubud (p197).

GETTING THERE & AWAY

Tenganan is 3.2km up a side road just west of Candidasa. At the turn-off where bemo stop, motorcycle riders offer *ojek* (motorcycle that carries pillion passengers) rides to the village for about 6000Rp. A nice option is to take an *ojek* up to Tenganan, and enjoy a shady downhill walk back to the main road, which has a Bali rarity: wide footpaths.

CANDIDASA
☎ 0363

Candidasa is a relaxed spot on the route east. It has hotels and some decent restaurants. However, it also has problems stemming from decisions made three decades ago that should serve as cautionary notes to any undiscovered place that suddenly finds itself on the map.

Until the 1970s, Candidasa was just a quiet little fishing village, then beachside losmen and restaurants sprang up and suddenly it was *the* new beach place in Bali. As the facilities developed, the beach eroded – unthinkingly, offshore barrier-reef corals were harvested to produce lime for cement for the orgy of construction that took place – and by the late 1980s Candidasa was a beach resort with no beach.

Mining stopped in 1991, and concrete sea walls and breakwaters (newly beautified in 2008) have limited the erosion and now provide some pockets of sand. The relaxed seaside ambience and sweeping views from the hotels built right on the water appeal to a more mature crowd of visitors. Candidasa is a good base from which to explore the interior of East Bali and the east coast's famous diving and snorkelling sites.

Information

Foto Asri (☎ 41098; Jl Raya Candidasa) sells groceries and sundries. The police station is at the west end of town; the post office the east. **Candi Bookstore** (☎ 41272; Jl Raya Candidasa 45) is a used store run by a cute family. The closest ATMs are in Padangbai and Amlapura.

Sights

Candidasa's temple, **Pura Candidasa** (admission by donation), is on the hillside across from the lagoon at the eastern end of the village strip. It has twin temples devoted to the male-female gods Shiva and Hariti. The fishing village, just east of the lagoon, has colourful *prahu* (outrigger fishing boats) drawn up on what's left of the beach. In the early morning you can watch the boats coasting in after a night's fishing. By day the owners offer snorkelling trips to the reef and the nearby islets.

Apart from the Bali Aga village of Tenganan (opposite), there are several traditional villages inland from Candidasa and attractive countryside for walking.

Ashram Gandhi Chandi (☎ 41108; Jl Raya Candidasa), a lagoon-side Hindu hermitage, follows the pacifist teachings of Mahatma Gandhi. Guests may stay for short or extended periods, but are expected to participate in community life, ie pray to stay. There are simple guest cottages by the ocean and payment is by donation. Early-morning yoga sessions (free) are open to anyone.

Activities

Diving and snorkelling are popular activities in Candidasa. **Gili Tepekong**, which has a series of coral heads at the top of a sheer drop-off, is perhaps the best dive site. It offers the chance to see lots of fish, including some larger marine life. Other features include an underwater canyon, which can be dived in good conditions, but is always potentially hazardous. The currents here are strong and unpredictable, the water is cold and visibility is variable – it's recommended for experienced divers only.

Other dive sites are beside Gili Mimpang, further east at Gili Biaha, and Nusa Penida. A recommended and popular dive operator is **Dive Lite** (☎ 41660; www.divelite.com; Jl Raya Candidasa; dives US$40-105), which dives the local area plus Tulamben and the rest of the island. A four-day PADI open-water course is US$400. Snorkelling trips are US$30.

Hotels and shops along the main road rent snorkel sets for about 20,000Rp per day. For the best snorkelling, take a boat to offshore sites or to Gili Mimpang (a one-hour boat trip should cost about 100,000Rp for up to three people).

On shore, you can catch up on your beauty treatments at **Dewi Spa** (☎ 41042; Jl Raya Candidasa; massage from US$7; ☼ 9am-7pm). Waxing, steaming, rubbing, braiding and more are on offer.

Sleeping

Candidasa's main drag is well supplied with seaside accommodation, as well as restaurants and other tourist facilities. On the small roads branching off Forest Rd east of the lagoon, several places are hidden among the palm trees near the original fishing village. These are nicely relaxed and often have a sliver of beach. You might also consider staying west of town; many places are close.

BUDGET

our pick **Seaside Cottages** (☎ 41629; www.balibeachfront-cottages.com; Jl Raya Candidasa; cottages 40,000-250,000Rp; ▨ ▣) The 15 rooms here are scattered in cottages and span the gamut from cold-water basic to restful units with air-con and tropical bathrooms. The seafront has loungers right along the breakwater. The Temple Café is a mellow place.

Rama Bungalows (☎ 41778; r 60,000-70,000Rp) On a little road near the lagoon and ocean, the eight rooms are split between a two-storey stone

CANDIDASA

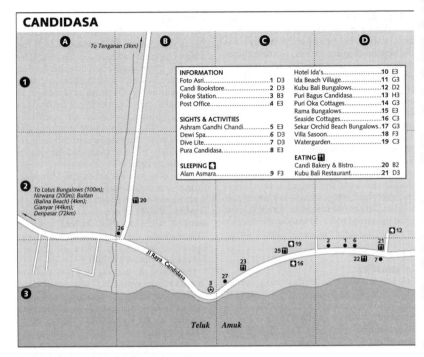

INFORMATION		Hotel Ida's....................................10 E3
Foto Asri....................................1 D3		Ida Beach Village.....................11 G3
Candi Bookstore.........................2 D3		Kubu Bali Bungalows................12 D2
Police Station............................3 B3		Puri Bagus Candidasa..............13 H3
Post Office.................................4 E3		Puri Oka Cottages....................14 G3
		Rama Bungalows.....................15 E3
SIGHTS & ACTIVITIES		Seaside Cottages.....................16 C3
Ashram Gandhi Chandi...............5 E3		Sekar Orchid Beach Bungalows..17 G3
Dewi Spa...................................6 D3		Villa Sasoon.............................18 F3
Dive Lite....................................7 D3		Watergarden............................19 C3
Pura Candidasa..........................8 E3		
		EATING
SLEEPING		Candi Bakery & Bistro...............20 B2
Alam Asmara..............................9 F3		Kubu Bali Restaurant................21 D3

To Tenganan (3km)

To Lotus Bungalows (100m);
Nirwana (200m); Buitan
(Balina Beach) (4km);
Gianyar (44km);
Denpasar (72km)

Jl Raya Candidasa

Teluk Amuk

---

structure and bungalows. Upstairs rooms have views of the lagoon and its birdlife.

Puri Oka Cottages (☎ 41092; puri_oka@hotmail.com; Jl Pantai Indah; r 125,000-500,000Rp;) Hidden by a banana grove east of town. The cheapest of the 19 rooms here are fan-cooled and small, while the better ones have water views and extras like DVD players. The beachside pool is small and is next to a new café; at low tide there's a small beach out front.

Hotel Ida's (☎ 41096; jsidas1@aol.com; Jl Raya Candidasa; bungalows 140,000-250,000Rp) Set in a rambling seaside grove of coconut trees, Ida's has five thatched bungalows with open-air bathrooms. Rustic balcony furniture, including a daybed, gets you to thinking just what you'd choose for 'Desert Island Discs'.

Sekar Orchid Beach Bungalows (☎ 41086; www.sekar-orchid.com; Jl Pantai Indah 26; bungalows 200,000-300,000Rp) The grounds here live up to the name with orchids and bromeliads growing in profusion. There's a small beach and the six large rooms (with hot water and fans) are good value with nice views from the 2nd floor. The site feels isolated but is only a short walk from the centre.

MIDRANGE

Ida Beach Village (☎ 41118; Jl Pantai Indah; r US$35-60;) The 17 units range from Balinese rice-barn-style bungalows with private gardens to more modest cottages (some with tubs). The seaside swimming pool is a good reason to stay here. The quiet location is a good combination of isolation and proximity to town.

Kubu Bali Bungalows (☎ 41532; www.kububali.com; r US$50-75;) Behind Kubu Bali restaurant (p228) and up a lane, this garden spot has streams, ponds and a swimming pool landscaped into a valley in the hillside. The 20 units have views over palm trees, the coast and the sea. Large porches have daybeds and the marble bathrooms have tubs.

Alam Asmara (☎ 41929; www.alamasamara.com; r US$55-95;) Walk on paths lined with little waterways at this private compound. The pool is on the ocean; the 12 rooms have a traditional yet stylish design with lots of room and details such as stone tubs and satellite TV. Ask about diving packages.

Puri Bagus Candidasa (☎ 41131; www.bagus-discovery.com; Jl Pantai Indah; r US$65-150;) At the

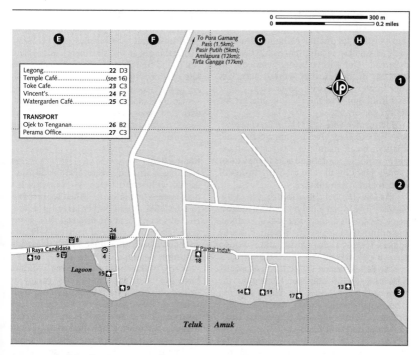

Legong.................................**22** D3
Temple Café.........................(see 16)
Toke Cafe............................**23** C3
Vincent's.............................**24** F2
Watergarden Café.................**25** C3

TRANSPORT
Ojek to Tenganan................**26** B2
Perama Office......................**27** C3

To Pura Gamang
Pass (1.5km);
Pasir Putih (5km);
Amlapura (12km);
Tirta Gangga (17km)

Jl Raya Candidasa

Lagoon

Jl Pantai Indah

Teluk Amuk

eastern end of the shore near an outcropping of outriggers, this mainstream resort is hidden away in the palm trees. The large pool and restaurant have good sea views; the beach is illusory. The 46 rooms have open-air bathrooms; look for deals.

Watergarden (☎ 41540; www.watergardenhotel .com; Jl Raya Candidasa; r from US$100; 🅿 🅡 🖳) The Watergarden lives up to its name with a swimming pool and fish-filled ponds that wind around the buildings. The gardens are lush and worth exploring. Each of the 14 rooms has a verandah projecting over the lily ponds, which are fresher than the somewhat dated interiors. The café is tops (p228).

TOP END
Villa Sasoon (☎ 0818 0567 1467; www.villasasoon.com; Jl Pantasi Indah; villas from US$250; 🅿 🅡 🖳) Four large private villas are in a quiet spot about a two-minute walk from the rocky shore. Each unit is a small compound with large open living areas (you can arrange for a chef) plus smaller bedroom units. All are set around small pools behind walls, so your frolics stay private.

Eating
Some of the hotels have seafront restaurants and cafés that are good for views at lunch and great for sea breezes and moonlight at night.

The places to eat along Jl Raya Candidasa are mostly simple and family-run; beware of traffic noise, although it abates after dark. Where noted, many of these places are also good for a drink. If you're out of town, the better places will provide transport; call.

Candi Bakery & Bistro (☎ 41883; Jl Tenganan; dishes 10,000-65,000Rp) About 100m up from the Tenganan turn-off west of town, this smart café is worth the slight detour. The bakery specialises in delicious pastries, cakes and croissants. You can enjoy a menu of local and German meals plus steaks out on the tree-shaded verandah. Or just savour a Bavarian beer.

Temple Café (☎ 41629; Seaside Cottages, Jl Raya Candidasa; dishes 15,000-35,000Rp) Global citizens can get a taste of home at this café attached to the Seaside Cottages. It has a few menu items from the owner's native Oz, such as Vegemite. The popular bar has a long drink list.

EAST BALI

Legong (☎ 41052; Jl Raya Candidasa; mains 15,000-55,000Rp) This is the kind of family-run joint that you fall for thanks to homey touches such as vaguely incomprehensible banners that read: 'Don't leave before you come.' If it swims in the sea, they serve it here. Get your lobster grilled with garlic. Happy hour lasts until 8pm and there's slow internet for 300Rp per minute.

Watergarden Café (☎ 41540; Jl Raya Candidasa; dishes 15,000-60,000Rp) Overlooking a carp pond, this stylish café maintains a peaceful atmosphere amid the zooming trucks thanks to an artfully placed wall. The food is a fusion of French and Asian touches.

Toke Café (☎ 41991; Jl Raya Candidasa; dishes 20,000-60,000Rp) The open kitchen at this mellow place turns out some good grilled seafood, including *ikan pepes* (fish with Balinese spices). It's got a nice old bar and is a good place for a cocktail.

Kubu Bali Restaurant (☎ 41532; Jl Raya Candidasa; dishes 20,000-60,000Rp) The open kitchen out the front at this airy, open-air dining pavilion (the roaring woks drown out the trucks) prepares Indonesian and Chinese dishes – including excellent seafood.

Vincent's (☎ 41368; Jl Raya Candidasa; dishes 25,000-80,000Rp) Candi's best is a deep and open place with several distinct rooms and a lovely rear garden with rattan lounge furniture. The bar is an oasis of jazz. The menu combines excellent Balinese, fresh seafood and European dishes.

Getting There & Away

Candidasa is on the main road between Amlapura and South Bali, but there's no terminal, so hail bemo (buses probably won't stop). You'll need to change in either Padangbai or Semarapura.

You can charter a ride to Amed in the far east for about 120,000Rp, and Kuta and the airport for 250,000Rp. Ask at your accommodation about vehicle and bicycle rental.

Perama (☎ 41114; Jl Raya Candidasa; ☺ 7am-7pm) is at the western end of the strip.

Destination	Fare	Duration
Kuta	60,000Rp	3½hr
Lovina	150,000Rp	5¼hr
Padangbai	25,000Rp	30min
Sanur	60,000Rp	2¾hr
Ubud	50,000Rp	1¾hr

CANDIDASA TO AMLAPURA

The main road east of Candidasa curves up to **Pura Gamang Pass** (*gamang* means 'to get dizzy' – something of an overstatement), from where you'll find fine views down to the coast and lots of greedy-faced monkeys. If you walk along the coastline from Candidasa towards Amlapura, a trail climbs up over the headland, with fine views over the rocky islets off the coast. Beyond this headland there's a long sweep of wide, exposed black-sand beach.

Pasir Putih

No longer anyone's secret, **Pasir Putih** is an idyllic white-sand beach whose name indeed means 'white sand'. When we first visited in 2004, it was empty, save for a long row of fishing boats at one end. Just a few years later it has well and truly been discovered and is sort of an ongoing lab in seaside economic development.

A row of thatched beach **warung** and **cafés** have appeared. You can get *nasi goreng* or grilled fish for little money. Bintang is of course on ice and loungers await bikini-clad bottoms. The beach itself is truly lovely: a long crescent of white sand backed by coconut trees. At one end cliffs provide shade. The surf is often mellow; bring your own snorkelling gear to explore the waters.

The one thing saving Pasir Putih from being swamped is the access, which is difficult. Look for crude signs with either 'Virgin Beach Club' or 'Jl Pasir Putih' near the village of Perasi. Turn off the main road (about 5km east of Candidasa) and follow a pretty paved track for about 1.5km to a temple where locals will collect a fee (5000Rp). You can park here and walk the gentle hill down or drive a further 600m directly to the beach on a perilous road that barely qualifies as such.

As for any qualms you might have about furthering the commercialisation of this beach, here's what the locals told us: 'The money you pay us for a ticket we spend on our school and medicine.'

AMLAPURA

☎ 0363

Amlapura is the capital of Karangasem district, and the main town and transport junction in eastern Bali. The smallest of Bali's district capitals, it's a multicultural place with Chinese shophouses, several mosques and confusing one-way streets (which are the tidiest in Bali).

It's worth a stop to see the royal palaces but a lack of options means you'll want to spend the night elsewhere, such as Tirta Gangga.

Information

The friendly staff at the **tourist office** (☎ 21196; www.karangasemtourism.com; Jl Diponegoro; ☎ 7am-3pm Mon-Thu, 7am-noon Fri) offer the booklet *Agung Info*, which is filled with useful detail as is the website.

Bank BRI (Jl Gajah Mada) will change money. It has an international ATM as does **Hardy's** (☎ 22363; Jl Diponegoro). There is a **pharmacy** (Apotik; Jl Ngurah Rai 47) and a small hospital across the street.

Sights

Amlapura's three palaces, on Jl Teuku Umar, are decaying reminders of Karangasem's period as a kingdom at its most important when supported by Dutch colonial power in the late 19th and early 20th centuries.

Outside the orderly **Puri Agung Karangasem** (Jl Teuku Umar; admission 10,000Rp; ☎ 8am-5pm), there are beautifully sculpted panels and an impressive three-tiered entry gate. After you pass through the entry courtyard, a left turn takes you to the main building, known as the Maskerdam (Amsterdam), because it was the Karangasem kingdom's acquiescence to Dutch rule that allowed it to hang on long after the demise of the other Balinese kingdoms. Inside you'll be able to see several rooms, including the royal bedroom and a living room with furniture that was a gift from the Dutch royal family. The Maskerdam faces the ornately decorated Bale Pemandesan, which was used for the royal tooth-filing ceremonies. Beyond this, surrounded by a pond, is the Bale Kambang, still used for family meetings and for dance practice.

Across the street, **Puri Gede** (Jl Teuku Umar; donation requested; ☎ 8am-6pm) is still used by the royal family and is surrounded by long walls. The palace grounds feature many brick buildings dating from the Dutch colonial period. Look for stone carving and woodcarvings from the 19th century. The Rangki, the main palace building, has been returned to its glory and is surrounded by fish ponds. Catch the stern portrait of the late king AA Gede Putu.

The other royal palace building, **Puri Kertasura**, is not open to visitors.

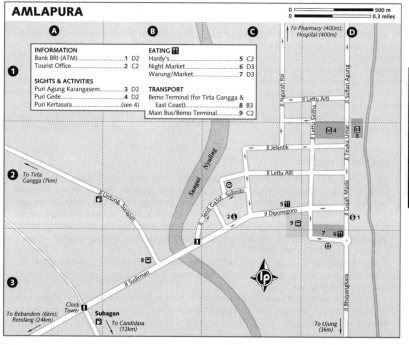

AMLAPURA

0 — 500 m
0 — 0.3 miles

INFORMATION	
Bank BRI (ATM)	1 D2
Tourist Office	2 C2

SIGHTS & ACTIVITIES	
Puri Agung Karangasem	3 D2
Puri Gede	4 D2
Puri Kertasura	(see 4)

EATING	
Hardy's	5 C2
Night Market	6 D3
Warung/Market	7 D3

TRANSPORT	
Bemo Terminal (for Tirta Gangga & East Coast)	8 B3
Main Bus/Bemo Terminal	9 C2

To Pharmacy (400m); Hospital (400m)

Jl Ngurah Rai

Jl Lettu Arti

Jl Lettu Sintha

Jl Teuku Umar

Sultan Agung

Jl Lettu Arti

Jl Jelantik

Jl Lettu Alit

Sungai Nyuling

Jl Gatot Subroto

Jl Diponegoro

Jl Gajah Mada

To Tirta Gangga (7km)

Jl Untung Surapati

Jl Sudirman

Clock Tower

To Bebandem (6km); Rendang (24km)

Subagan

To Candidasa (12km)

To Ujung (3km)

Jl Bhayangkara

EAST BALI

Eating & Shopping

Options are few in Amlapura; there are various **warung** around the market and the main bus/bemo terminal as well as a good **night market** (☼ 5pm-midnight). A vast **Hardy's** (☎ 22363; Jl Diponegoro) supermarket has groceries and lots of sundries. It has the best range of supplies, like sunscreen, east of Semarapura and south of Singaraja. In the parking lot there are numerous stalls serving up lots of cheap and fresh Asian foods (5000Rp to 10,000Rp).

Getting There & Away

Amlapura is a major transport hub. Buses and bemo regularly ply the main road to Denpasar's Batubulan terminal (20,000Rp; roughly three hours) via Candidasa, Padangbai and Gianyar. Plenty of buses also go around the north coast to Singaraja (about 16,000Rp) via Tirta Gangga, Amed and Tulamben.

AROUND AMLAPURA

Five kilometres south of Amlapura, **Taman Ujung** is a major complex that may leave you slack-jawed – and not necessarily with wonder. In 1921 the last king of Karangasem completed the construction of a grand water palace here, which was extensively damaged by an earthquake in 1979. A tiny vestige of the old palace is surrounded by vast modern ponds and terraces built for untold billions of rupiah. Today, the windswept grounds are seldom trod by visitors. It's a bit sad really and you can see all that you'd want to from the road. Just a bit further on is the interesting fishing village of **Ujung** (Edge) and the alternative road to Amed.

TIRTA GANGGA
☎ 0363

Tirta Gangga (Water of the Ganges) is the site of a holy temple, some great water features and some of the best views of rice fields and the sea beyond in East Bali. High on a ridge, it is a relaxing place to stop for an hour or a longer period, which will allow for some treks in the surrounding terraced countryside, which ripples with coursing water.

Sights

Amlapura's water-loving rajah, after completing his lost masterpiece at Ujung, had another go at building the water palace of his dreams. He succeeded at **Taman Tirta Gangga** (adult/child 5000/3000Rp, parking 2000Rp; ☼ site 24hr, ticket office 6am-6pm), which has a stunning crescent of rice terrace–lined hills for a backdrop.

Originally built in 1948, the water palace was damaged in the 1963 eruption of Gunung Agung and again during the political events that rocked Indonesia two years later. Today it is an aquatic fantasy with several swimming pools and ornamental ponds, which serve as a fascinating reminder of the old days of the Balinese rajahs. 'Pool A' (adult/child 6000/4000Rp) is the cleanest and is in the top part of the complex. 'Pool B' is pond-like. Look for the 11-tiered fountain and plop down under the huge old banyans.

Hiking in the surrounding hills is recommended. The rice terraces around Tirta Gangga are some of the most beautiful in Bali. Back roads and walking paths take you to many picturesque traditional villages. Or you can ascend the side of Gunung Agung. Guides are a good idea. Ask at any of the

---

DETOUR TO AMED

Typically travellers bound for the coast of **Amed** (p232) travel the inland route through Tirta Gangga. However, there is a longer, twistier and more adventurous road much less travelled that runs from **Ujung** right around the coast to the Amed area. The road climbs up the side of Gunung Seraya, and the views out to sea are breathtaking. Along the way it passes through numerous small villages where people are carving fishing boats, bathing in streams or simply standing a bit slack-jawed at the appearance of *tamu* (foreigner). Don't be surprised to see a pig, goat or boulder on the road.

Near **Seraya** (which has a cute market) look for weavers and cotton-fabric-makers. For lots of the time, you'll just be in the middle of fruit-filled orchards and jungle. About 4km south of **Aas** there's a lighthouse.

The road is narrow but paved, and covering the 35km to Aas will take about one hour without stops. Combine this with the inland road through Tirta Gangga for a good circular visit to Amed from the west.

accommodation we've listed, especially Homestay Rijasa where the owner I Ketut Sarjana is an experienced guide. Another local guide who comes with good marks is **Komang Gede Sutama** (☎ 0813 3877 0893).

Among the possible treks is a six-hour loop to Tenganan village, plus shorter ones across the local hills, which include visits to remote temples and all the stunning vistas you can handle. Rates average about 50,000Rp per hour for one or two people.

Sleeping & Eating

Most places to stay have cafés with mains under 20,000Rp and there's another cluster by the sedate shops near the entrance. A small valley of rice terraces runs up the hill behind the parking area. It is a majestic vision of emerald steps receding into the distance.

With the exception of Tirta Ayu Hotel and Tirta Gangga Villas, most of the places to stay are cold-water-only and basic. Hot water is not a universal option.

Dhangin Taman (Friendly Hotel; ☎ 22059; r 50,000-100,000Rp) Adjacent to the water palace, this characterful place features elaborate tiled artworks in a garden. It has a range of 14 cold-water rooms – the cheapest ones facing the rice paddies are the best – and a simple café with tables overlooking the palace. You leave your breakfast order hanging on the door, just like at the Hyatt.

Pondok Lembah Dukah (r 50,000-100,000Rp) Down the path to the right of Good Karma, follow the signs for 300m along the rice field and then up a steep set of steps. Three basic bungalows are clean and have fans plus sweeping views over bougainvillea from their porches. Warning: you may go all the way and find no one.

Puri Prima (☎ 21316; r 70,000-120,000Rp) About 1km north of Tirta Gangga along the main road, these nine rooms have outstanding views and vary only in size. It's a snoozy place and you may find a cat asleep on your bed.

Homestay Rijasa (☎ 21873; r 80,000-150,000Rp) With elaborately planted grounds, this well-run place is a recommended choice opposite the water palace entrance. Better rooms have hot water, good for the large soaking tubs. The owner is an experienced trekking guide.

Good Karma (☎ 22445; r 100,000-120,000Rp) A classic homestay, Good Karma has four very clean and simple bungalows and a good vibe derived

from the surrounding pastoral rice field. The good café is close to the parking lot.

Puri Sawah Bungalows (☎ 21847; r 150,000-200,000Rp) Just up the road from the palace, Puri Sawah has four comfortable and spacious rooms and family bungalows that sleep six (with hot water). Besides Indo classics, the restaurant has some interesting sandwiches like 'avocado delight'.

Tirta Ayu Hotel (☎ 22503; www.hoteltirtagangga .com; v US$50-100; ☒) Right in the palace compound, this has four pleasant villas that are clean and have basic, modern decor in the limited palette of creams and coffees that's ubiquitous right now. Flop about like a fish in the hotel's private pool or use the vast palace facilities. The restaurant is a tad upscale (mains from 50,000Rp) and serves creative takes on local classics.

Tirta Gangga Villas (☎ 21383; www.tirtagangga -villas.com; villas US$120-400; ☒) Built on the same terrace as the Tirta Ayu Hotel, the villas are parts of the old royal palace. Thoroughly updated – they have that classic Bali style motif – the villas look out over the water palace from large shady porches. Private cooks are available and you can arrange to rent the entire complex and preside over your own court.

Genta Bali (☎ 22436; dishes 10,000-20,000Rp) Across the road from the parking area, you can find a fine yoghurt drink here, as well as pasta and Indonesian food. It has an impressive list of puddings, including ones with banana, jackfruit and taro. Try out the black-rice wine.

Getting There & Away

Bemo and minibuses making the east-coast haul between Amlapura and Singaraja stop at Tirta Gangga, right outside the water palace or any hotel further north. The fare to Amlapura should be 5000Rp.

AROUND TIRTA GANGGA

The main road running from Amlapura through Tirta Gangga and on to Amed and the coast doesn't do the local attractions justice – although it is an attractive road. To appreciate things, you need to get off the main road or go hiking.

Throughout the area the *rontal* palms all look like new arrivals at army boot camp, as they are shorn of their leaves as fast as they grow them in order to meet the demand for inscribed *lontar* books (see p260).

EAST BALI

Pura Lempuyang

One of Bali's nine directional temples, Pura Lempuyang is perched on a hilltop at 768m. To get here, turn south off the Amlapura–Tulamben road to Ngis (2km), a palm-sugar and coffee-growing area, and follow the signs another 2km to Kemuda (ask for directions if the signs confuse you). From Kemuda, climb 1700 steps to Pura Lempuyang (allow at least two hours, one way). If you want to continue to the peaks of Lempuyang (1058m) or Seraya (1175m), you should take a guide.

Bukit Kusambi

This small hill has a big view – at sunrise Lombok's Gunung Rinjani throws a shadow on Gunung Agung. Bukit Kusambi is easy to reach from Abian Soan – look for the obvious large hill to the northwest, and follow the tiny canals through the rice fields. On the western side of the hill, a set of steps leads to the top.

Budakeling & Krotok

Budakeling, home to several Buddhist communities, is on the back road to Bebandem, a few kilometres southeast of Tirta Gangga. It's a short drive, or a pleasant three-hour walk through rice fields, via Krotok, home of traditional blacksmiths and silversmiths.

Tanah Aron

This imposing monument to the post-WWII Dutch resistance is gloriously situated on the southeastern slopes of Gunung Agung. The road is quite good, or you can walk up and back in about six hours from Tirta Gangga.

AMED & THE FAR EAST COAST
☎ 0363

Stretching from Amed to Bali's far eastern tip, this once-remote stretch of semi-arid coast draws visitors to a succession of small, scalloped, black-sand beaches, a relaxed atmosphere and excellent diving and snorkelling.

The coast here is often called simply 'Amed' but this is a misnomer, as the coast is a series of seaside *dusun* (small villages) that start with the actual Amed in the north and then run southeast to Aas. If you're looking to get away from crowds, this is the place to come and try some yoga. Everything is spread out, so you never feel like you're in the middle of anything much except maybe one of the small fishing villages.

Traditionally this area has been quite poor, with thin soils, low rainfall and very limited infrastructure. Salt production is still carried out on the beach at Amed; see the boxed text, p218. Villages further east rely on fishing, and colourful *jukung* (traditional boats) line up on every available piece of beach. Inland, the steep hillsides are generally too dry for rice – corn, peanuts and vegetables are the main crops.

Orientation

As noted, this entire 10km stretch of coast is often called 'Amed' by both tourists and marketing-minded locals. Most development at first was around two bays: Jemeluk, which has cafés and a few shops, and Lipah, which has warung, shops and a few services. 'Progress' has marched onwards through Lehan, Selang and Aas. To really appreciate the coast, stop at the viewpoint at Jemeluk; besides the sweep of land, you can see fishing boats lined up like a riot of multihued sardines on the beach.

Besides the main road via Tirta Gangga, you can also approach the Amed area from the south; see p230 for details.

Information

You may be charged a tourist tax. Enforcement of a 5000Rp per-person fee at a tollbooth on the outskirts of Amed is sporadic. When collected, the funds go in part to develop the infrastructure at the beaches.

Telephone services have not kept pace with development and land lines have been strung only as far as Lehan. **Aurora Internet & Wartel** (☎ 23519; Lipah; ⏰ 8am-9pm) has dial-up internet service as does Apa Kabar in Jemeluk. Both charge 500Rp per minute. **Pondok Kebun Wayan** (☎ 23473; east of Amed) changes US-dollar travellers cheques and has a small market with groceries and a few sundries.

There are moneychangers in Lipah but the closest ATMs and banks are in Amlapura. Few places take credit cards and many prices are in euros.

Activities
DIVING & SNORKELLING

Snorkelling is excellent at several places along the coast. Jemeluk is a protected area where you can admire live coral and plentiful fish within 100m of the beach. There's a wreck of a Japanese fishing boat near Aas – just offshore

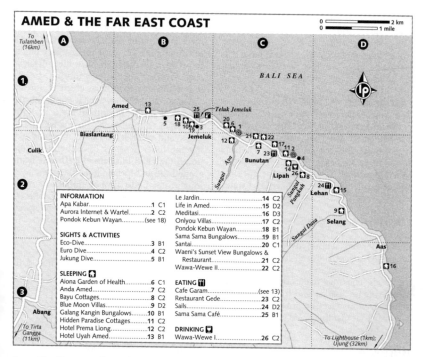

AMED & THE FAR EAST COAST

INFORMATION	
Apa Kabar	1 C1
Aurora Internet & Wartel	2 C2
Pondok Kebun Wayan	(see 18)

SIGHTS & ACTIVITIES	
Eco-Dive	3 B1
Euro Dive	4 C2
Jukung Dive	5 B1

SLEEPING	
Aiona Garden of Health	6 C1
Anda Amed	7 C2
Bayu Cottages	8 C2
Blue Moon Villas	9 D2
Galang Kangin Bungalows	10 B1
Hidden Paradise Cottages	11 C2
Hotel Prema Liong	12 C2
Hotel Uyah Amed	13 B1
Le Jardin	14 C2
Life in Amed	15 D2
Meditasi	16 D3
Onlyou Villas	17 C2
Pondok Kebun Wayan	18 B1
Sama Sama Bungalows	19 B1
Santai	20 C1
Waeni's Sunset View Bungalows & Restaurant	21 C2
Wawa-Wewe II	22 C2

EATING	
Cafe Garam	(see 13)
Restaurant Gede	23 C2
Sails	24 D2
Sama Sama Café	25 B1

DRINKING	
Wawa-Wewe I	26 C2

from Eka Purnama bungalows – and coral gardens and colourful marine life at Selang. Almost every hotel rents snorkelling equipment for about 30,000Rp per day.

Scuba diving is also excellent, with dive sites off Jemeluk, Lipah and Selang featuring coral slopes and drop-offs with soft and hard corals, and abundant fish. Some are accessible from the beach, while others require a short boat ride. The *Liberty* wreck (p236) at Tulamben is only a 20-minute drive away.

Three good dive operators have shown a commitment to the communities by organising regular beach clean-ups and educating locals on the need for conservation. All have similar prices for a long list of offerings (eg local dives from about US$50, open-water dive course about US$350).

Eco-dive (☎ 0363 23482; www.ecodivebali.com; Jemeluk) Full-service shop with simple accommodation for clients. Has led the way on environmental issues.

Euro Dive (☎ 23605; www.eurodivebali.com; Lipah) Has a new facility and offers packages with hotels.

Jukung Dive (☎ 23469; www.jukungdivebali.com; Amed) Relative newcomer pushes eco-credentials and has a dive pool.

TREKKING

Quite a few trails go inland from the coast, up the slopes of Gunung Seraya (1175m) and to some little-visited villages. The countryside is sparsely vegetated and most trails are well defined, so you won't need a guide for shorter walks – if you get lost, just follow a ridge-top back down to the coast road. Allow a good three hours to get to the top of Seraya, starting from the rocky ridge just east of Jemeluk Bay, near Prem Liong Art Bungalows. To reach the top for sunrise, you'll need to start in the dark, so a guide is probably a good idea – ask at your hotel.

Sleeping

The entire area is very spread out, so take this into consideration when choosing accommodation. If you want to venture to restaurants beyond your hotel's own, for example, you'll have to walk or find transport.

You will also need to choose between staying in the little beachside villages or on the sunny and dry headlands connecting the inlets. The former puts you right on the sand and offers a small amount of community life

EAST BALI

while the latter gives you broad, sweeping vistas and isolation.

Accommodation can be found in every price category; almost every place has a restaurant or café. Places with noteworthy dining are indicated in the listings.

EAST OF AMED VILLAGE

Both of these hotels are on or near the ocean.

Pondok Kebun Wayan (☎ 23473; www.amedcafe .com; r €10-50; 🏖 🛢) This Amed empire features a range of 25 rooms mostly on a hillside across from the beach. The most expensive rooms have views, terraces and amenities like air-con while the cheapest have cold water and showers. The café has a good grilled seafood menu.

Hotel Uyah Amed (☎ 23462; hoteluyah@naturebali .com; r €27-40; 🏖 🛢) This cute place features four-poster beds set in stylish, conical interiors bathed in light. From all eight rooms (two with air-con) you can see the saltworks on the beach. The hotel makes the most of this by offering fascinating and free salt-making demonstrations (see the boxed text, p218). The tasty Café Garam (p235) is appropriately named for salt.

JEMELUK

Sama Sama Bungalows (☎ 0813 3738 2945; r 70,000-150,000Rp) There are two simple cold-water rooms in bungalows here (and a good seafood café) across from the beach. The family that runs things is often busy making kites.

Galang Kangin Bungalows (☎ 23480; bali_amed _gk@yahoo.co.jp; r 100,000Rp-300,000Rp; 🏖) Set on the hill side of the road amid a nice garden, the four rooms here mix and match fans, cold water, hot water and air-con. The beach is right over the pavement, as is the café.

Hotel Prema Liong (☎ 23486; www.bali-amed.com; bungalows 180,000-350,000Rp) Large Javanese-style two-storey bungalows are terraced up the hillside and have a new-age ethos. The cold-water, open-air bathrooms (showers only) are lush and feel like extensions of the garden, while the balconies have daybeds for snoozing away the afternoons.

Aiona Garden of Health (☎ 0813 3816 1730; www .aionabali.com; bungalows €18-30) This eccentric place has enough signs outside that it qualifies as a genuine roadside attraction. The simple bungalows are shaded by mango trees and the natural food served seems to have fallen right out of the trees. Stays are a two-night minimum and you can partake of organic potions and lotions, classes in yoga, meditation, tarot reading etc. If you don't get a natural high, your inner peace might improve with the high-fibre diet. A small shell museum (open 2pm to 4pm) boasts that no bivalves died in its creation.

Santai (☎ 23487; www.santaibali.com; r US$50-120; 🏖 🛢) This lovely option is on a slight hill down to the beach. The name means 'relax' and you'll have a hard time not taking the hint. A series of authentic traditional thatched bungalows gathered from around the archipelago hold 10 rooms with four-poster beds, timber floors, open-air bathrooms and big comfy balcony sofas. A swimming pool, fringed by purple bougainvillea, snakes through the property.

BUNUTAN

These places are on a sun-drenched, arid stretch of highland.

Wawa-Wewe II (☎ 23521; wawawewevillas @yahoo.com; r 200,000-250,000Rp; 🏖 🛢) From the headlands, this nice and peaceful place has 10 bungalow-style rooms on lush grounds that shamble down to the water's edge. The natural-stone infinity pool is shaped like a Buddha and is near the water, as are two rooms with ocean views.

Waeni's Sunset View Bungalows (☎ 23515; madesani @hotmail.com; r 250,000-350,000Rp; 🏖) Waeni's is a hillside place with unusual rustic stone cottages that have gorgeous views of the mountains behind and the bay below. The eight rooms have a flash of creative style plus hot water. The café is a good place for a sunset drink.

Onlyou Villas (☎ 23595; www.onlyou-bali.com; villas €50-75; 🏖 🛢) You could go nuts trying to find the missing y in the name of this three-villa complex. Happily it is such a good deal that you'll go 'y not!'. Villas are large and have many amenities such as DVD players, multiple beds, luxurious teak furniture and best of all: private pools.

Anda Amed (☎ 23498; www.andaamedresort.com; villas €50-90; 🏖 🛢) This whitewashed hillside place feels like it could be in Mykonos. The infinity pool has a waterfall and sweeping views of the sea from well above the road. The four villas are a good deal; each has one or two bedrooms and lots of posh details like deep soaking tubs and fridges.

LIPAH

This village is just large enough for you to go wandering.

Le Jardin (☎ 0813 5321 5753; limamarie@yahoo.fr; r €12-25; ❄) Four rooms (some fan-only) are housed in shady thatched bungalows at this French-accented B&B. Open baths have garden decor and you can avail yourself of yoga, meditation etc. The beach on the cove is just steps away.

Bayu Cottages (☎ 23495; www.bayucottages.com; r €25-50; ❄ ⚑) Bayu has six large, comfortable rooms with balconies overlooking the coast from the hillside above the road. There's a small pool and many amenities including open-air marble bathrooms and satellite TV.

Hidden Paradise Cottages (☎ 23514; www.hidden paradise-bali.com; r US$35-75; ❄ ⚑) The 16 simply decorated bungalow-style rooms at this older beachside resort have large patios and open-air bathrooms. The pool is the classic kidney shape in a natural garden setting. Many dive packages are on offer.

LEHAN

Life in Amed (☎ 23152, 0813 3850 1555; www.lifebali .com; r US$60-90, villas US$90-150; ❄ ⚑) If you're the kind of person who wishes this place were in Aas so that there would be a name-change, you probably won't fit in. Life here is posh. The six bungalow-style units are in a slightly cramped compound along with two villas directly on the beach. The café concentrates on seafood and showy local dishes (mains 30,000Rp to 70,000Rp).

SELANG

Blue Moon Villas (☎ 0817 4738 100; www.bluemoon villa.com; r from US$50-130; ❄ ⚑) On the hillside across the road from the cliffs, Blue Moon is a small and upmarket place, complete with a cute pool. The five rooms set in three villas have open-air stone bathrooms. Eco-initiatives include solar hot water and recycling. The restaurant serves good Balinese classics and grilled seafood.

AAS

The butt end of the Amed coast is sparsely developed.

our pick **Meditasi** (fax 22166; r 200,000-250,000Rp) There's nothing like chilled Aas for a respite from the pressures of life. Meditation and yoga help you relax, and the four rooms are close

to good swimming and snorkelling. Open-air baths allow you to count the colours of the bougainvillea and frangipani that grow in profusion. The owners are lovely.

Eating & Drinking

As already noted, most places to stay have cafés. Ones that are worth seeking out are listed here.

our pick **Café Garam** (☎ 23462; Hotel Uyah Amed, east of Amed; dishes 14,000-40,000Rp) There's a relaxed feel here with pool tables and Balinese food plus the lyrical and haunting melodies of live Genjek music at 8pm on Wednesday and Saturday. *Garam* means salt and the café honours the local salt-making industry. Try the *salada ayam*, an addictive mix of cabbage, grilled chicken, shallots and tiny peppers.

Sama Sama Café (☎ 0813 3738 2945; Jemeluk; dishes 15,000-35,000Rp) Super-fresh prawns, barracuda, mackerel and other fish almost jump from the boats onto the grill at this five-table beachside joint right on the sand on this pint-sized bay.

Restaurant Gede (☎ 23517; Bunutan; dishes 16,000-38,000Rp) The huge menu is typical of those found in Chinese restaurants everywhere: long. Views are good from this spot halfway up the hill from the cove. Artwork by the owner decorates the walls.

Sails (☎ 22006; Lehan; mains 30,000-60,000Rp) A high-concept restaurant with high standards for food, Sails is one big terrace with 180-degree views from its cliffside perch. Settle back in the chic blonde furniture and enjoy fusion hits like lamb medallions, spare ribs and grilled fillets of fresh fish with Balinese accents.

Wawa-Wewe I (☎ 23506; Lipah) Spend the evening here and you won't know your wawas from your wewes. This is the coast's most raucous bar – which by local standards means that sometimes it gets sorta loud. A vast CD collection is augmented by local bands on many nights. You can also eat here (mains from 15,000Rp).

Getting There & Around

Most people drive here via the main highway from Amlapura and Culik. The spectacular road going all the way around the headlands from Aas to Ujung is in good shape; it's possible to do the journey as a circle. See p230 for details.

EAST BALI

All the places east of Culik are difficult to reach by public transport. Minibuses and bemo from Singaraja and Amlapura pass through Culik, the turn-off for Amed. Infrequent public bemo go from Culik to Amed (3.5km), and some continue to Seraya until 1pm. A public bemo should cost around 8000Rp from Culik to Lipah.

You can also charter transport from Culik for a negotiable 45,000Rp (by *ojek* is less than half). Be careful to specify which hotel you wish to go to – if you agree on a price to 'Amed', you may be taken only to Amed village, far short of your destination.

Perama offers charter tourist-bus services from Candidasa (see p228); the cost is 125,000Rp each for a minimum of two people. This is similar to the cost of hiring a car and driver.

Many hotels rent bicycles for about 35,000Rp per day.

KUBU REGION

Driving along the main road you will pass through vast old lava flows from Gunung Agung down to the sea. The landscape is strewn with a moonscape of boulders, and is nothing like the lush rice paddies elsewhere.

TULAMBEN

☎ 0363

The big attraction here sunk over 60 years ago. The wreck of the US cargo ship *Liberty* is among the best and most popular dive sites in Bali and this has given rise to an entire town based on scuba diving. Other great dive sites are nearby and even snorkellers can easily swim out and enjoy the wreck and the coral.

But if you don't plan to explore the briny waves, don't expect to hang out on the beach either. The shore is made up of rather beautiful, large washed stones, the kind that cost a fortune at a DIY store.

Orientation & Information

Tulamben is a quiet place, and is essentially built around the wreck – the hotels, all with cafés and many with dive shops, are spread along a 3km stretch either side of the main road.

You can change cash at a few signposted places at the eastern end of the main road; otherwise services are sparse. For dial-up internet access, try **Tulamben Wreck Divers Resort** (per min 500Rp).

Activities

DIVING & SNORKELLING

The *Liberty* is about 50m directly offshore from Puri Madha Bungalows (there's also a shady car park here; 2000Rp); look for the schools of black snorkels. Swim straight out and you'll see the stern rearing up from the depths, heavily encrusted with coral and swarming with dozens of species of colourful fish – and with scuba divers most of the day. The ship is more than 100m long, but the hull is broken into sections and it's easy for divers to get inside. The bow is in quite good shape, the midships region is badly mangled and the stern is almost intact – the best parts are between 15m and 30m deep. You will want at least two dives to really explore the wreck.

Many divers commute to Tulamben from Candidasa or Lovina, and in busy times it can get quite crowded between 11am and 4pm, with up to 50 divers at a time around the wreck. Stay the night in Tulamben or in nearby Amed and get an early start.

Most hotels have their own diving centre, and some will give a discount on accommodation if you dive with their centre. If you are an inexperienced diver, see p89 for tips on choosing a dive operation.

Among the many dive operators, **Tauch Terminal** is one of the longest-established operators in Bali. A four-day PADI open-water certificate course costs about €350. Expect to pay about €30/50 for one/two dives at Tulamben, and a little more for a night dive or dives around Amed.

Snorkelling gear is rented everywhere for 30,000Rp.

Sleeping & Eating

At high tide even the rocky shore vanishes but places situated on the water always have great

---

THE WRECK OF THE LIBERTY

In January 1942 the US Navy cargo ship USAT *Liberty* was torpedoed by a Japanese submarine near Lombok. Taken in tow, it was beached at Tulamben so that its cargo of rubber and railway parts could be saved. The Japanese invasion prevented this and the ship sat on the beach until the 1963 eruption of Gunung Agung broke it in two and left it just off the shoreline, much to the delight of scores of divers.

views of the surf. All the following places to stay are on the hill side of the main road or off it towards the water. All have decent cafés or restaurants.

Ocean Sun (☎ 22912; www.ocean-sun.com; r 60,000-70,000Rp) The budget choice of Tulamben, Ocean Sun has four bungalow-style rooms in a small garden on the hill side of the road. Units are clean and basic. Feel like some head-bangin'? The beds have thickly cushioned headboards.

Puri Madha Bungalows (☎ 22921; r 70,000-300,000Rp; ☒) Refurbished bungalow-style units are directly opposite the wreck on shore. Of the 12 rooms, the best have air-con and hot water. The spacious grounds feel like a public park.

Bali Coral Bungalows (☎ 22909; r 120,000Rp, with air-con 200,000Rp; ☒) Ten basic, clean bungalows with modern bathrooms are built back from the shore near Tauch Terminal. The café has views of the ocean.

Tulamben Wreck Divers Resort (☎ 23400; www.tulambenwreckdivers.com; r 200,000-400,000Rp; ☒ ☒ ☒) There are seven rooms at this comfy two-storey complex on the hill side of the road. At the top end of the rate card, rooms have DVD players, air-con and fridges. All have hot water. The pool is used by the in-house dive operation.

Deep Blue Studio (☎ 22919; www.diving-bali.com; r €30; ☒) Owned by Czechs, this dive operation has eight rooms in two-storey buildings on the hill side of the road. Rooms have fans and balconies plus DVD players. The restaurant is large, and if you're *really* on a budget (or blew your wad diving), you can bunk down in the lounge for €5.

Tauch Terminal Resort (☎ 0361-774504, 22911; www.tauch-terminal.com; r US$50-100; ☒ ☒) Down a side road at the shore, this sprawling hotel has 27 rooms in several categories. Many of the rooms are newly rebuilt and all are comfortable in a modern, motel-style way. Expect all amenities like satellite TV and fridges. Of the two waterfront pools, one is reserved for swimming only (no grubby divers practising…).

Mimpi Resort (☎ 21642; www.mimpi.com; r US$65-95, cottage US$120-200; ☒ ☒ ☒) The choice for a traditional resort experience, Mimpi has a lavish spa, room service, loungers by the shore, a refined restaurant and more. The 13 rooms open onto lush gardens as do 12 large cottages. Four more are on the water. The pounding waves should pound the jet lag right out of your head.

Getting There & Away

Plenty of buses and bemo travel between Amlapura and Singaraja and will stop anywhere along the Tulamben road, but they're infrequent after 2pm. Expect to pay 8000Rp to either town.

Perama offers charter tourist-bus services from Candidasa; the cost is 125,000Rp each for a minimum of two people. This is similar to the cost of hiring a car and driver.

If you are driving to Lovina for the night, be sure to leave by about 3pm, so you will still have a little light when you get there. There's a petrol station just south of town.

TULAMBEN TO YEH SANIH

North of Tulamben, the road continues to skirt the slopes of Gunung Agung, with frequent evidence of lava flows from the 1963 eruption. Further around, the outer crater of Gunung Batur slopes steeply down to the sea. The rainfall is low and you can generally count on sunny weather. The scenery is very stark in the dry season and it's thinly populated. The route has public transport, but it's easier to make stops and detours with your own wheels.

At **Les**, a road goes inland to lovely **Air Terjun Yeh Mampeh** (Yeh Mampeh Waterfall), at 40m one of Bali's highest. Look for a large sign on the main road and then turn inland for about 1km. Walk the last 2km or so on an obvious path by the stream, shaded by rambutan trees. A 2000Rp donation is requested; there's no need for a guide.

The next main town is **Tejakula**, famous for its stream-fed public bathing area, said to have been built for washing horses and often called the 'horse bath'. The renovated bathing areas (separate for men and women) are behind walls topped by rows of elaborately decorated arches, and are regarded as a sacred area. The baths are 100m inland on a narrow road with lots of small shops – it's a quaint village, with some finely carved *kulkul* (hollow tree-trunk warning drum) towers. Take a stroll above the baths, past irrigation channels flowing in all directions.

At **Pacung**, about 10km before Yeh Sanih, you can turn inland 4km to **Sembiran**, which is a Bali Aga village, although it doesn't promote itself as such. The most striking thing about the place is its hillside location and brilliant coastal views.

Sleeping

Bali's remote northeast coast has a growing number of resorts where you can indeed get away from it all. These are places to settle in for a few days and revive your senses. Getting here from the airport or South Bali can take three hours or more via two routes: one up and over the mountains via Kintamani and then down a rustic, scenic road to the sea near Tejakula; the other going right round East Bali on the coast road via Candidasa and Tulamben.

Poinciana Resort (☎ 0812 398 6458; www.poinciana-resort.com; villas US$40-155; 🔀 ⚐) A remote retreat, isolated from the coast road amid palms, Poinciana is absolutely spotless and has seven villas on large, lavishly planted grounds. Beach villas (US$60) are excellent value and have large tubs, fridges and relaxing indoor/outdoor seating. Many cyclists stay here as they circumnavigate the island.

Alam Anda (☎ 0361-750444; www.alamanda.de; r €40-160; 🔀 ⚐) The tropical architecture at this oceanside resort, near Sambirenteng, is striking thanks to the efforts of the German architect owner. A reef just offshore keeps the dive shop busy. The 30 units come in various sizes, from losmen rooms to cottages with views. All are well-equipped and have artful thatch and bamboo motifs. The resort is 1km north of Poinciana.

Tembok Spa Village Resort (☎ 0362-32033; www.spavillage.com; full board r from US$400; 🔀 ⚐ 🖳) When you arrive at this beachside resort, you realise you're in for an experience. Guests are asked to choose a path: balance, creativity or vigour (there's no 'leave me alone'). Extensive spa treatments and daily activities are geared to your path. The 27 rooms have a traditional feel with a coffee-and-cream theme accented by carving. Meals are healthful and focus on simple, local ingredients.

Central Mountains

Bali has a hot soul. The volcanoes stretching along the spine of the island are more than just cones of silence; their active spirits are literally just below the surface, eager for expression.

Gunung Agung's (3142m) deadly eruptions are legend. Gunung Batur (1717m) takes a steadier approach – it's constantly letting off steam. You may want to do the same if you undertake a visit with its attendant hassles, but the otherworldly beauty of the place may just convince you to give it a go. You can now canoe the azure beauty of Danau Batur while taking in the beauty of a rare double caldera.

To the east, narrow jungle roads lead to a series of lakes in the shadow of Gunung Batukau (2276m). Danau Bratan has sacred Hindu temples and its shore is lined with strawberry farms. The village of Candikuning makes a good stop and has good cafés and an engrossing botanic garden.

Throughout the mountains you can organise myriad treks. But the centre for such things is the old colonial village of Munduk, where views down the hills to the coast of North Bali match the beauty of the many nearby waterfalls and plantations. On the south side of the slopes, the Unesco-nominated ancient rice terraces in and around Jatiluwih bedazzle.

Amid it all, little roads lead to untouched villages and the occasional hidden retreat where you can truly get away from it all.

HIGHLIGHTS

- Claiming your own waterfall while trekking around **Munduk** (p250)
- Identifying each ancient variety of rice grown at **Jatiluwih** (p252)
- Hearing the chant of priests at one of Bali's holiest temples, **Pura Luhur Batukau** (p252)
- Luxuriating among the hundreds of rare plants at the **Bali Botanical Gardens** (p247)
- Finding your own serenity in the lakeside village of **Toya Bungkah** (p245)

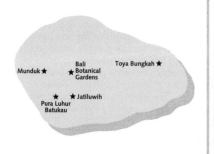

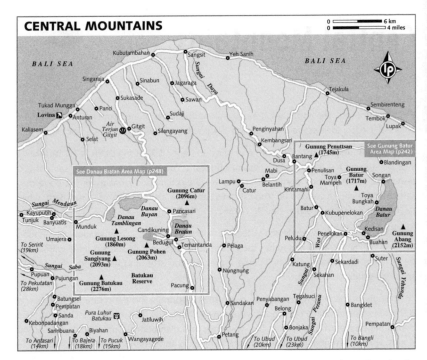

GUNUNG BATUR AREA

☎ 0366

This area is like a giant bowl, with the bottom half covered by water and a set of volcanic cones jutting out of the middle. Sounds a bit spectacular? It is. On clear days – vital to appreciating the spectacle – the turquoise waters wrap around the newer volcanoes, which have obvious old lava flows oozing down their sides.

The road around the southwestern rim of the Gunung Batur crater is one of Bali's most important north–south routes and has one of Bali's most stunning vistas. Most people intending to do some trekking stay in the villages around the shores of Danau Batur, and plan an early start to climb the volcano.

Even day-trippers should bring some sort of wrap in case the mist closes in and it hits 18°C.

Orientation

The villages around the Gunung Batur crater rim have grown together in a continuous, untidy strip. The main village is Kintamani, though the whole area is often referred to by that name. Coming from the south, the first village is Penelokan, where tour groups stop to gasp at the view, eat a buffet lunch and be hassled by souvenir-sellers.

Penelokan is also where you can take a short road down into the crater. From here, a road loosely follows the shore of Danau Batur, linking the villages of Kedisan and Toya Bungkah. You can travel between the Gunung Batur and Danau Bratan areas using a beautiful mountain lane (see the boxed text p249).

Entry Tickets

If you arrive by private vehicle, you will be stopped at ticket offices at Penelokan or Kubupenelokan. Entry is 6000/3000Rp per adult/child. Bicycles are free (and should be, given the climb needed to get here). This ticket is for the whole Gunung Batur area; you shouldn't be charged again – save your stub.

Information

Services are few in the Gunung Batur area. There is an ATM in the car-parking area for the Lakeview Hotel in Penelokan. In Kubupenelokan there is a post office and in Kintamani there is a Bank BPD. There are no services in the villages around Danau Batur. The moral here is bring lots of cash from the lowlands.

Getting There & Around

From Batubulan terminal in Denpasar, bemo (small minibuses) travel regularly to Kintamani (18,000Rp). You can also get a bus on the busy Denapsar (Batabulan)–Singaraja route, which will stop in Penelokan and Kintamani (about 18,000Rp). Alternatively, you can just hire a car or use a driver. From South Bali expect to pay at least 450,000Rp.

Orange bemo regularly shuttle back and forth around the crater rim, between Penelokan and Kintamani (8000Rp for tourists). Public bemo from Penelokan down to the lakeside villages go mostly in the morning (tourist price is about 6000Rp to Toya Bungkah). Later in the day, you may have to charter transport (40,000Rp or more).

TREKKING GUNUNG BATUR

Vulcanologists describe Gunung Batur as a 'double caldera', ie one crater inside another. The outer crater is an oval about 14km long, with its western rim about 1500m above sea level. The inner crater is a classic volcano-shaped peak that reaches 1717m. Activity over the last decade has spawned several smaller cones on its western flank, unimaginatively named Batur I, II, III and IV. More than 20 minor eruptions were recorded between 1824 and 1994, and there were major eruptions in 1917, 1926 and 1963. Geological activity and tremors have continued to occur regularly.

Statistics aside, you really have to see it to believe it. One look at this otherworldly spectacle and you'll understand why people want to go through the many hassles and expenses of taking a trek. Note that the odds of clouds obscuring your reason for coming are greater July to December, but any time of year you should check conditions with a trekking agency before committing to a trip, or even coming up the mountain.

HPPGB

The **HPPGB** (Mt Batur Tour Guides Association; Map p242; ☎ 52362; ◷ 3am-noon) has a monopoly on guided climbs up Gunung Batur. The HPPGB requires that all trekking agencies that operate on the mountain hire at least one of its guides for trips up the mountain. In addition, the cartel has developed a reputation for intimidation in requiring climbers to use its guides and during negotiations for its services.

Reported tactics have ranged from dire warnings given to people who inquired at its offices to physical threats against people attempting to climb without a guide. There have also been reports of guides stationing themselves outside hotels to intercept climbers.

Pinning these guys down on rates can be like trying to keep pace with the pea in a shell game, but expect to pay the following:

Trek	Duration	Cost
Batur Sunrise	4-8am	300,000-400,000Rp
Gunung Batur Main Crater	4-10am	300,000-400,000Rp

Trekking Agencies

Even reputable and highly competent adventure-tour operators from elsewhere in Bali cannot take their customers up Gunung

---

WARNING

The Gunung Batur area has a reputation as an avaricious place and many visitors leave vowing never to return. One travel agent told us that he gets more complaints about this area than the rest of Bali combined, which is a shame, as properly briefed you can enjoy the stunning natural beauty of this region.

Keep an eye on your gear and don't leave any valuables in your car, especially at the start of any trail up the volcano. Break-ins are common.

Be wary of touts on motorcycles, who will attempt to steer you to a hotel of *their* choice as you descend into the Danau Batur area from the village of Penelokan. Vendors in the area can be highly aggressive and irritating. Guide services are controlled by the HPPGB (Mt Batur Tour Guides Association; see above).

Batur without paying the HPPGB to have one of their guys tag along, so these tours are relatively expensive.

Pretty much all the accommodation in the area can help you put together a trek. They can recommend alternatives to the classic Batur climb, such as the outer rim of the crater, or treks to other mountains such as Gunung Agung.

Trekking agencies can also arrange other treks in the area, to Gunung Abang or the outer rim of the crater, or to other mountains such as Gunung Agung. All of the agencies listed here can get you up Gunung Batur for rates starting from about US$30 (not including HPPGB fees); everything is negotiable.

Hotel Miranda (Map p242; ☎ 52022; Jl Raya Kintamani, Kintamani) Will take solo climbers; the owner Made Senter is a gem.

Hotel Segara (Map p242; ☎ 51136; hotelsegara@plasa .com; Kedisan) Popular with larger groups.

Jero Wijaya Tourist Service (Map p246; ☎ 51249; www.lakesidebali.com; Lakeside Cottages, Toya Bungkah) Wijaya is an expert and his website is a great resource.

Volcano Breeze (Map p246; ☎ 51824; Toya Bungkah) Located in the café of the same name; offers many treks.

Equipment

If you're climbing before sunrise, take a torch (flashlight) or be absolutely sure that your guide provides you with one. You'll need good strong footwear, a hat, a jumper (sweater) and drinking water.

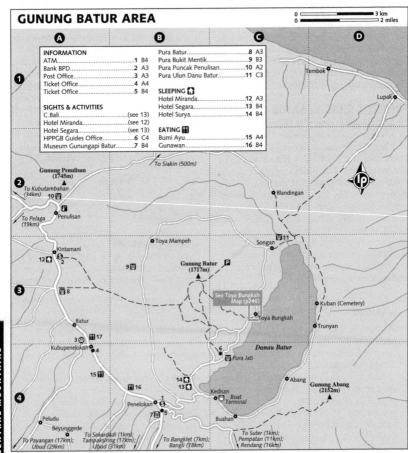

UNPLANNED EXCITEMENT

The volcanically active area west of the main peak can be deadly, with explosions of steam and hot lava, unstable ground and sulphurous gases. To find out about current conditions, ask at the trekking agencies (p241), or alternatively look at the website of the **Directorate of Volcanology & Geographical Hazard Mitigation** (www.vsi .esdm.go.id), although much is in Indonesian. The active areas are sometimes closed to visitors for safety reasons.

Trekking Routes

The climb to see the sunrise from Gunung Batur is still the most popular trek, even with the hassles of the HPPGB; see p241.

Ideally, trekkers should get to the top for sunrise (about 6am), before mist and cloud obscure the view. It is a magnificent sight, although hardly a wilderness experience – as it's not uncommon to have 100 people on top for sunrise in the tourist season. Nor is it necessary to be at the top for sunrise – a halfway point is fine. If you start at 5am, you'll avoid the crowds.

Guides will provide breakfast on the summit for a fee (50,000Rp), and this often includes the novelty of cooking an egg or banana in the steaming holes at the top of the volcano. There are several refreshment stops along the way, but bottled beverages can be pricey. Water sources may be dubious, so bring some.

FROM TOYA BUNGKAH

The basic trek is to start climbing from Toya Bungkah at about 3am, reach the summit for sunrise, and possibly walk right around the main cone, then return to Toya Bungkah. The route is pretty straightforward – walk out of the village towards Kedisan and turn right just after the car park. After about 30 minutes, you'll be on a ridge with a well-defined track; keep going up. It gets pretty steep towards the top and it can be hard walking over the loose volcanic sand. Allow about two hours to reach the top, which is at the northern edge of the inner crater.

Climbers have reported that they've easily made the journey without an HPPGB guide, though it shouldn't be tried while dark. The major obstacle is actually avoiding any hassle from the guides themselves.

You can follow the rim to the western side – where you can view the most recent volcanic activity – continue to the southern edge, and then return to Toya Bungkah by the route you climbed up.

Longer trips go around the recent volcanic cones southwest of the summit. This has the most exciting volcanic activity, with smoking craters, bright-yellow sulphur deposits, and steep slopes of fine black sand. If the activity is *too* exciting, the area may be closed for trekking, although the summit can still be OK.

Climbing up Gunung Batur, spending a reasonable time on the top and then strolling back down takes four or five hours; for the longer treks around the newer cones, allow around eight hours.

FROM PURA JATI

A huge parking lot (and HPPGB office) near Pura Jati makes this the main entrance for groups and day-trippers. The shortest trek is basically across the lava fields, then straight up (allow about two hours to the top). If you want to see the newer cones west of the peak (assuming the area is safe to visit), go to the summit first – do not go walking around the active area before sunrise.

FROM THE NORTHEAST

The easiest route is from the northeast – that's if you can get transport to the trailhead at 4am. From Toya Bungkah take the road northeast towards Songan and take the left fork after about 3.5km. Follow this small road for another 1.7km to a badly signposted track on the left – this climbs another kilometre or so to a parking area. From here, the walking track is easy to follow to the top, and should take less than an hour.

FROM KINTAMANI

From the western edge of the outer crater, trails go from Batur and Kintamani down into the main crater, then up Gunung Batur from the west side. This route passes close to the rather exciting volcanically active area and may be closed for safety reasons. Check the current status with Made Senter at Hotel Miranda (p244).

THE OUTER CRATER

A popular place to see the sunrise is on the outer crater rim northeast of Songan. You'll need transport to Pura Ulun Danu Batur, near the northern end of the lake. From there you can climb to the top of the outer crater rim in under 30 minutes, from which you can see Bali's northeast coast, about 5km away. At sunrise, the silhouette of Lombok looms across the water, and the first rays strike the great volcanoes of Batur and Agung. If you can reconnoitre this route in daylight, you'll be able to do it without a guide.

VILLAGES AROUND GUNUNG BATUR CRATER

There are several small villages on the ridge around Gunung Batur crater. The Penelokan area is filled with bus-tour restaurants. Generally places on the west side of the road enjoy views down to South Bali while those on the east side look into the double caldera.

Penelokan

Penelokan means 'Place to Look' – and you will be stunned by the view across to Gunung Batur and down to the lake at the bottom of the crater. Apart from the vista (check out the large lava flow on Gunung Batur), there's the welcome new addition of the **Museum Gunungapi Batur** (☎ 51152; admission 10,000Rp; ☯ 8am-5pm). This large new facility combines the serious with the hokey. In the former category there are displays about the volcanoes and the legends around them. In the latter category there is a model volcano that erupts on command in a manner that would do Peter Brady proud.

EATING

Bring a shovel for the chow served at a lot of the ugly monolithic restaurants that line the crater rim. These places are geared for tourists and have fine views. Buffet lunches cost 60,000Rp to 80,000Rp or more (your guide often gets half of that as a commission).

But there are some acceptable choices, including many humble places where you can sit on a plastic chair and have a simple meal while enjoying a priceless view. Places with *ikan mujair* signs are probably good bets, as they are selling the small, sweet fish that are caught in the lake below and then barbecued to a crisp with onion, garlic and bamboo sprouts. This beats the corn syrup off the gloopy sweet-and-sour pork and other nightmares at some of the bus-tour joints.

Otherwise, **Bumi Ayu** (☎ 52345; meals 30,000-70,000Rp; ☯ 8am-5pm) has a terrace looking both ways. For views into the crater, consider

Gunawan (☎ 51404; meals 30,000-80,000Rp; ☯ 8am-5pm), which also has the benefit of being high above the road.

Batur & Kintamani

The villages of Batur and Kintamani now virtually run together. Kintamani is famed for its large and colourful **market**, which is held every three days. The town is like a string bean: long, with pods of development. Activity starts early and by 11am the town is all packed up. If you don't want to go on a trek, the sunrise view from the road here is pretty good.

The original village of Batur was in the crater, but was wiped out by a violent eruption in 1917. It killed thousands of people before the lava flow stopped at the entrance to the village's main temple.

Taking this as a good omen, the village was rebuilt, but Gunung Batur erupted again in 1926. This time, the lava flow covered everything except for the loftiest temple shrine. Fortunately, there were evacuations and few lives were lost. The village was relocated up onto the crater rim, and the surviving shrine was also moved up there and placed in the new temple, **Pura Batur** (admission 6000Rp, sarong & sash rental 2000Rp).

Spiritually, Gunung Batur is the second most important mountain in Bali (only Gunung Agung outranks it), so this temple is of considerable importance. It's a great stop, as there are always a few colourful mountain characters hanging around. Within the complex is a Taoist shrine.

Hotel Miranda (☎ 52022; Jl Raya Kintamani, Kintamani; s/d 40,000/70,000Rp) is the only accommodation here. The six rooms are clean and very basic with squat toilets. It has good food and a welcome open fire at night. The informative owner, Made Senter, is an excellent trekking guide (see p241).

Penulisan

The road gradually climbs along the crater rim beyond Kintamani, and is often shrouded in clouds, mist or rain. Penulisan is where the road bends sharply and heads down towards the split for the north coast and the remote scenic drive to Bedugal (p249). A viewpoint about 400m south from here offers an amazing panorama over three mountains: Gunung Batur, Gunung Abang and Gunung Agung. If you're coming from the north, this is where you'll first see what all the tourism fuss is about.

Near the road junction, several steep flights of steps lead to Bali's highest temple, **Pura Puncak Penulisan** (1745m). Inside the highest courtyard are rows of old statues and fragments of sculptures in the open *bale* (pavilions). Some of the sculptures date back to the 11th century. The temple views are superb: facing north you can see over the rice terraces clear to the Singaraja coast (weather permitting).

VILLAGES AROUND DANAU BATUR

The little villages around Danau Batur have a crisp lakeside setting and views up to the surrounding peaks. There's a lot of fish-farming here and the air is redolent with the smell of onions from the many farms. You'll also see chillies, cabbage and garlic growing, a festival for those who like assertively flavoured food.

A hairpin road winds its way down from Penelokan to the shore of Danau Batur. At the lakeside you can go left along the good road that winds its way through lava fields to Toya Bungkah, the usual base for climbing Gunung Batur.

Kedisan & Buahan

The villages around the southern end of the lake have a few inns available for stays in a fairly isolated setting. Buahan is a pleasant 15-minute stroll from Kedisan, and has market gardens going right down to the lakeshore.

Beware of the motorcycle touts who will follow you down the hill from Penelokan, trying out the various guide and hotel scams. Local hotels ask that you call ahead and reserve so that they can have your name on record and thus avoid paying a bounty to the touts.

ACTIVITIES

`our pick` **C.Bali** (☎ 0813 5320 0251; www.c-bali.com; Hotel Segara, Kedisan) is a ground-breaking tour company (operated by an Australian-Dutch couple) that offers bike tours around the craters and canoe tours on the lake. Prices start at US$40 and include pick-up across South Bali (discounts if you're already staying in the area). Packages include multiday trips. The pair also sponsors charity drives for local schools and neighbourhood clean-ups.

SLEEPING & EATING

The restaurants at these two hotels are good places to sample the garlic-infused local fish.

Hotel Surya (☎ 51139; Kedisan; r 60,000-100,000Rp) All but the very cheapest of the 28 rooms here have hot water. The best have lake views and bathtubs and are located on the top floors of the buildings around the small multilevel compound.

Hotel Segara (☎ 51136; hotelsegara@plasa.com; Kedisan; r 80,000-200,000Rp;) The Segara has bungalows set around a courtyard. The cheapest rooms have cold water; the best have hot water and bathtubs – perfect for soaking away the hypothermia.

Trunyan & Kuban

The village of Trunyan is squeezed between the lake and the outer crater rim. It is inhabited by Bali Aga people. But unlike Tenganan (p224), it is not a welcoming place.

Trunyan is known for the **Pura Pancering Jagat**, with its 4m-high statue of the village's guardian spirit, but tourists are not allowed to go inside. Touts and guides, however, hang about soliciting exorbitant tips. Our advice: don't go.

A little beyond Trunyan, and accessible only by boat, is the **cemetery** at Kuban. The people of Trunyan do not cremate or bury their dead – they lie them out in bamboo cages to decompose. This is a tourist trap for those with macabre tastes and you'll be met by characters demanding huge fees. Our advice: don't go.

Boats leave from a jetty near Kedisan, where there is a ticket office and a car park (2000Rp) with pushy vendors. The price for a four-hour return trip (Kedisan–Trunyan–Kuban–Toya Bungkah–Kedisan) depends on the number of passengers, with a maximum of seven (300,000Rp, although extra 'fees' may be added). Our advice: don't go. However, if you'd like to spend time out on the lake, go on one of the canoe trips with C.Bali (left).

Toya Bungkah

The main tourist centre is Toya Bungkah (also known as Tirta), which boasts hot springs (*tirta* and *toya* both mean water). It's a simple village, and travellers stay here so they can climb Gunung Batur early in the morning. But if you take a moment to smell the onions (and take in the azure lake view), you may decide to stay awhile, even if you don't climb the mountain.

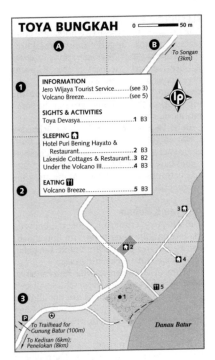

TOYA BUNGKAH

0 ——— 50 m

To Songan (3km)

INFORMATION
Jero Wijaya Tourist Service........(see 3)
Volcano Breeze.........................(see 5)

SIGHTS & ACTIVITIES
Toya Devasya...............................1 B3

SLEEPING
Hotel Puri Bening Hayato &
Restaurant...............................2 B3
Lakeside Cottages & Restaurant..3 B2
Under the Volcano III.................4 B3

EATING
Volcano Breeze...........................5 B3

Danau Batur

To Trailhead for
Gunung Batur (100m)
To Kedisan (6km);
Penelokan (8km)

ACTIVITIES

Hot springs bubble in a couple of spots, and have long been used for bathing pools. Beside the lake, **Toya Devasya** (☎ 51204; adult/child US$10/5; ☻ 8am-8pm) is built around a spring. The huge hot pool is 38°C while the comparatively brisk lake-fed pool is 20°C. Admission includes refreshments and the use of loungers. Investors have big plans for this site; in the meantime, you can camp here – a rarity in Bali – for US$90, which includes two days of soaking and one night shivering in a provided tent.

SLEEPING & EATING

Avoid rooms near the noisy main road through town and opt for placid ones with lake views. Unless noted, hotels only have cold water, which can be a boon for waking up for a sunset climb. For camping, see Toya Devasya (above).

Small, sweet lake fish known as *ikan mujair* are the local delicacy. They are barbecued to a crisp with onion, garlic and bamboo sprouts.

Under the Volcano III (☎ 0813 386 0081; r 70,000Rp) With a lovely, quiet lakeside location opposite vegetable plots, this inn has eight clean and pretty rooms; go for Room 1 right on the water. There are two other nearby inns in the Volcano empire, all run by the same lovely family.

Lakeside Cottages & Restaurant (☎ 51249; www .lakesidebali.com; r US$10-35; ☻) The lakeside pool at this option, at the end of the lane on the water's edge, makes it a top pick. Of the 11 rooms, the best have hot water and satellite TV. The restaurant serves home-style Japanese dishes.

Hotel Puri Bening Hayato & Restaurant (☎ 51234; www.indo.com/hotels/puribeninghayato; r from US$25; ☻) An incongruously modern place for rustic Toya Bungkah. The 21 rooms are motel-like and have been spiffed up a bit of late. The hotel lists services that include free fishing gear and leaves the door open for a lot more with 'etc'. The pool is small, but there's also a hot-spring-fed whirlpool.

Volcano Breeze (☎ 51824; dishes 15,000-25,000Rp) This sociable travellers café with local art on the walls serves fresh lake fish in many forms. It's a good place to just hang out, and to gather and plan volcano treks.

Songan

Two kilometres around the lake from Toya Bungkah, Songan is a large and interesting village with market gardens extending to the lake's edge. At the lakeside road end is the temple **Pura Ulun Danu Batur**, under the edge of the crater rim.

DETOUR

A turn-off in Songan takes you on a rough but passable road around the crater floor. Much of the area is very fertile, with bright patches of market garden and quite strange landforms. On the northwestern side of the volcano, the village of **Toya Mampeh** (Yeh Mampeh) is surrounded by a vast field of chunky black lava – a legacy of the 1974 eruption. Further on, **Pura Bukit Mentik** was completely surrounded by molten lava from this eruption, but the temple itself, and its impressive banyan tree, were quite untouched – it's called the 'Lucky Temple'.

CENTRAL MOUNTAINS

DANAU BRATAN AREA

Approaching from the south, you gradually leave the rice terraces behind and ascend into the cool, often misty mountain country around Danau Bratan. Candikuning is the main village in the area, and has an important and picturesque temple. Bedugul is at the south end of the lake, with the most touristy attractions. Danau Buyan and Danau Tamblingan are pristine lakes northwest of Danau Bratan that offer good trekking possibilities, while marvellous Munduk anchors a region with fine trekking to waterfalls and cloud-cloaked forests.

The choice of accommodation near the lake is limited as much of the area is geared towards domestic, not foreign, tourists. On Sundays and public holidays, the lakeside can be crowded with courting couples and Toyotas bursting with day-tripping families. Many new inns are opening around Munduk.

Wherever you go, you are likely to see the blissfully sweet local strawberries on offer. Note that it is often misty and can get chilly up here.

BEDUGUL
☎ 0368
'Bedugul' is sometimes used to refer to the whole lakeside area, but strictly speaking it's just the first place you reach at the top of the hill when coming from South Bali.

Activities
TAMAN REKREASI BEDUGUL
Lakeside eateries, a souvenir market and a selection of water sports – parasailing, water- and jet-skiing plus speedboats – are the features at this **recreation park** (☎ 21197; admission 7000Rp, parking 2000Rp), which attracts busloads of locals to its classic carnival charms.

TREKKING
From the water-sports area, a trail around the south side of the lake goes to the mundane **Goa Jepang** (Japanese Cave), which was dug during WWII. From there, a difficult path ascends to the top of **Gunung Catur** (2096m), where the old **Pura Puncak Mangu** temple is popular with monkeys. Allow about four hours to go up and back from Taman Rekreasi Bedugul.

Sleeping & Eating
Upmarket hotels on the slope 9km south of Bedugul offer outstanding views to the south. And they are good choices for a snack or a refreshment if you're just passing by. Beware of a string of run-down places up at the ridge around Bedugul.

Pacung Indah (☎ 21020; www.pacungbali.com; r 230,000-600,000Rp; 🏊) Across the street from the slightly more upscale Saranam Eco-Resort, this hotel has rice-terrace views and the cosy rooms have some style – all include a private courtyard. Treks are offered in the green, green, green countryside.

Strawberry Hill (Bukit Stroberi; ☎ 21265; dishes 14,000-25,000Rp) Opposite the Taman Rekreasi turn-off, this café has polished floorboards and on a clear day you can see Kuta. The Indo menu includes soul-healing *soto ayam* (chicken soup) and *gudeg yogya* (jackfruit stew). Hot drinks chase away the mists.

Getting There & Away
Any minibus or bemo between South Bali and Singaraja will stop at Bedugul on request (see p250 for details).

CANDIKUNING
☎ 0368
Dotting the western side of the lake, Candikuning is a haven for plant lovers. Its **market** (parking 1000Rp) is touristy but among the eager vendors of tat, you'll find locals shopping for fruit, veg, herbs, spices and potted plants. You'll find good cafés hidden in the corners and a few worthwhile stalls like Smile for Life, a T-shirt shop run by widows of the 2002 Kuta bombings. Privately run toilets in the southwest corner (5000Rp) are the cleanest for miles.

Bali Botanical Gardens
This **garden** (Kebun Raya Eka Karya Bali; ☎ 21273; admission walking/driving 7000/12,000Rp, car parking 6000Rp; ⏰ 7am-6pm) is a showplace. Established in 1959 as a branch of the national botanical gardens at Bogor, near Jakarta, it covers more than 154 hectares on the lower slopes of Gunung Pohen. The garden boasts an extensive collection of trees and flowers. Some plants are labelled with their botanical names, and a booklet of self-guided walks (20,000Rp) is helpful. The gorgeous orchid area is often locked to foil flower filchers; ask that it be unlocked.

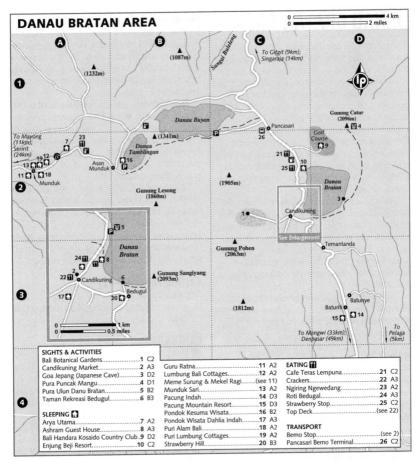

DANAU BRATAN AREA

SIGHTS & ACTIVITIES

Bali Botanical Gardens	1 C2
Candikuning Market	2 A3
Goa Jepang (Japanese Cave)	3 D2
Pura Puncak Mangu	4 D1
Pura Ulun Danu Bratan	5 B2
Taman Rekreasi Bedugul	6 B3

SLEEPING

Arya Utama	7 A2
Ashram Guest House	8 A3
Bali Handara Kosaido Country Club	9 D2
Enjung Beji Resort	10 C2

Guru Ratna	11 A2
Lumbung Bali Cottages	12 A2
Meme Surung & Mekel Ragi	(see 11)
Munduk Sari	13 A2
Pacung Indah	14 D3
Pacung Mountain Resort	15 D3
Pondok Kesuma Wisata	16 B2
Pondok Wisata Dahlia Indah	17 A3
Puri Alam Bali	18 A2
Puri Lumbung Cottages	19 A2
Strawberry Hill	20 B3

EATING

Cafe Teras Lempuna	21 C2
Crackers	22 A3
Ngiring Ngewedang	23 A2
Roti Bedugal	24 A3
Strawberry Stop	25 C2
Top Deck	(see 22)

TRANSPORT

Bemo Stop	(see 2)
Pancasari Bemo Terminal	26 C2

Within the park, you can cavort like a bird or a squirrel at the **Bali Treetop Adventure Park** (www.balitreetop.com; adult/child US$20/13). Winches, ropes, nets and more let you explore the forest well above the ground. And it's not passive – you hoist, jump, balance and otherwise circumnavigate the park. Special programs are geared to different ages.

Coming northwest from Bedugul, at a junction conspicuously marked with a large, phallic corn-cob sculpture, a small side road goes 600m west to the garden. It gets crowded on Sundays with local families.

Pura Ulun Danu Bratan

This very important Hindu-Buddhist **temple** (adult/child 10,000/5000Rp, parking 2000Rp; ⏰ tickets 7am-5pm, site 24hr) was founded in the 17th century. It is dedicated to Dewi Danu, the goddess of the waters, and is actually built on small islands, which means it is completely surrounded by the lake. Pilgrimages and ceremonies are held here to ensure that there is a supply of water for farmers all over Bali.

The tableau includes classical Hindu thatch-roofed *meru* (multiroofed shrines) reflected in the water and silhouetted against the often-cloudy mountain backdrop – a true Bali-photo-cliché. A large banyan tree shades the entrance, and you walk through manicured gardens and past an impressive Buddhist stupa to reach the lakeside.

There's a bit of a sideshow atmosphere, however. Animals in small cages and oppor-

CENTRAL MOUNTAINS

tunities to caress a snake or hold a huge bat amuse the punters.

Water Tours

At the temple gardens, you can hire a four-passenger speedboat with a driver (150,000Rp per 30 minutes), a five-person rowboat with rower (100,000Rp per 30 minutes), or a two-person pedal boat (35,000Rp per 30 minutes).

For an almost surreal experience, take a quiet paddle across the lake and see Pura Ulun Danu Bratan at sunrise – arrange it with a boatman the night before.

Sleeping

Ashram Guest House (☎ 21450; r 60,000-175,000Rp) Overlooking the lake, Ashram has tidy grounds of closely cropped grass. Prices for the 20 rooms start with shared cold-water bathrooms. Much nicer are the rooms up the terraced hill with sweeping views and hot-water bathrooms with tubs for soaking away the chill.

Pondok Wisata Dahlia Indah (☎ 21233; r 80,000-125,000Rp) In the village along a lane near the road to the botanical gardens, this is a decent budget option with 17 comfortable, clean rooms with hot-water showers set in a garden of mountain flowers.

Enjung Beji Resort (☎ 21490; cottages 250,000-500,000Rp) Just north of the temple and overlooking Danau Bratan is this peaceful, pleasant option. The 23 cottages are modern and clean. The nicest have outdoor showers and sunken baths.

Eating

From simple market snacks to meals featuring the region's fresh strawberries, you'll have much to choose from. At the entrance to Pura Ulun Danu Bratan are several Padang warung (food stalls), and there's a café with a view on the grounds.

Roti Bedugal (☎ 21838; snacks 5000Rp; ☽ 8am-6pm) Just north of the market, this tiny bakery produces fine versions of its namesake as well as croissants and other treats all day.

Strawberry Stop (☎ 21060; dishes 7000-20,000Rp; ☽ 8am-7pm) Here, north of the temple, locally grown strawberries star in milkshakes, juices, pancakes and more. Bananas are used when berries are out of season, which might drive you to drink the self-proclaimed 'dry' – ha! – strawberry wine (100,000Rp).

Cafe Teras Lempuna (☎ 0362-29312; dishes 15,000-40,000Rp; ☽) Also north of the temple, this indoor/outdoor café is stylish and modern. The menu ranges from burgers to Japanese and the coffees, teas and juices refresh no matter the temperature. When it's sunny, enjoy the inviting covered patio; when it's cool, put on the heat with the hot chilli soup.

Crackers (☎ 0811 388 697; mains 20,000-35,000Rp; ☽ 9am-5pm) A small sports bar hidden in the back of the market, Crackers has barbecued mains and comfy wicker seating.

Top Deck (☎ 0811 388 697, 0361-877 9633; mains 20,000-50,000Rp; ☽ 9am-5pm) Hovering above Crackers, and with the same Australian owners, this airy café with an open kitchen

---

THE ROAD NEVER TRAVELLED

A series of narrow roads links the Danau Bratan area and the Gunung Batur region. Few locals outside of this area even know the roads exist, and if you have a driver, you might need to do some convincing. Over a 30km route you not only step back to a simpler time but also leave Bali altogether for something resembling less-developed islands like Timor. The scenery is beautiful and may make you forget you had a destination.

South of Bedugul, you turn east at Tementanda and take a small and winding road down the hillside into some lush ravines cut by rivers. After about 6km you'll come to a T-junction;, turn north and after about 5km you'll come to the pretty village of **Pelaga**. This area is known for its organic coffee and cinnamon plantations. You'll both see and smell them.

Consider a tour and homestay in Pelaga organised by **JED** (Village Ecotourism Network; ☎ 0361-735320; www.jed.or.id; tours US$70-100), a non-profit group that organises rural tourism (see p346).

From Pelaga, you again ascend the mountain, following terrain that alternates between jungle and rice fields. Most of the bridges are modest except for a new one over a deep gorge that is the highest in Bali. Continue north to Catur, then veer east to the junction with the road down to North Bali and continue east 1km to Penulisan. Expect arm and smile fatigue, as you'll be doing a lot of waving to the locals.

CENTRAL MOUNTAINS

looks over the market and has a full menu of creative Indo fare. At lunch there's a buffet option.

Getting There & Away

Danau Bratan is beside the main north–south road, so it's easy to reach from South Bali or Singaraja.

Although the main terminal is in Pancasari, most minibuses and bemo will stop along the road in Bedugul and Candikuning. There are frequent connections from Denpasar's Ubung terminal (18,000Rp) and Singaraja's Sukasada terminal (18,000Rp). For Gunung Batur, you have to connect through Singaraja or hire transport.

PANCASARI

The broad, green valley northwest of Danau Bratan is actually the crater of an extinct volcano. In the middle of the valley, on the main road, Pancasari is a nontourist town with a bustling market and the main terminal for public bemo.

Just south of Pancasari, you will see the entrance to **Bali Handara Kosaido Country Club** (☎ 0362-22646; www.balihandarakosaido.com; r from US$120), a well-situated (as opposed to South Bali courses, there's plenty of water here), top-flight 18-hole golf course. It offers comfortable accommodation in the sterile atmosphere of a 1970s resort, reminiscent of the villain's grand lair in an old James Bond movie.

DANAU BUYAN & DANAU TAMBLINGAN

Also northwest of Danau Bratan are two more lakes, Danau Buyan and Danau Tamblingan – neither has been developed for tourism, which is a plus. There are several tiny villages and abandoned temples along the shores of both lakes, and although the frequently swampy ground makes it unpleasant in parts to explore, this is still a good place for a hike.

Sights & Activities

Danau Buyan (admission 5000Rp, parking 2000Rp) has parking right at the lake, a pretty 1.5km drive off the main road – when you park, an attendant will find you for the fees. The entire area is home to market gardens growing strawberries and other high-value crops such as the orange and blue flowers used in offerings.

A 4km **hiking** trail goes around the southern side of Danau Buyan from the car park, then over the saddle to Danau Tamblingan, and on to Asan Munduk. It combines forest and lake views.

Danau Tamblingan (adult/child 6000/3000Rp, parking 2000Rp) also has parking at the end of the road from the village of Asan Munduk. The lake is a 400m walk and this is where you can catch the trail to Danau Buyan. If you have a driver, a convenient option is to walk this path in one direction and be met at the other end. There are usually a couple of guides hanging around the car park (you don't need them for the lake path) who will gladly take you up and around **Gunung Lesong** (per 6hr 350,000Rp).

Sleeping & Eating

Pondok Kesuma Wisata (☎ 0817 472 8826; r 200,000Rp) This nice guesthouse features clean rooms with hot water and a pleasant café (dishes 8000Rp to 20,000Rp) and is just up from the Danau Tamblingan parking lot.

MUNDUK & AROUND
☎ 0362

The simple village of Munduk is one of Bali's most appealing mountain retreats. It has a cool misty ambience set among lush hillsides covered with jungle, rice, fruit trees and pretty much anything else that grows on the island. Waterfalls tumble off precipices by the dozen. There are hikes and treks galore and a number of really nice places to stay, from old Dutch summer homes to retreats where you can plunge full-on into local culture. Many people come for a day and stay for week.

Archaeological evidence suggests there was a developed community in the Munduk region between the 10th and 14th centuries. When the Dutch took control of North Bali in the 1890s, they experimented with commercial crops, establishing plantations for coffee, vanilla, cloves and cocoa. Quite a few Dutch buildings are still intact along the road in Munduk and further west. Look for shrines nestled in the crooks of hills.

Sights & Activities

Heading to Munduk from Pancasari, the main road climbs steeply up the rim of the old volcanic crater. It's worth stopping to enjoy the **views** back over the valley and

CENTRAL MOUNTAINS

lakes – watch out for monkey business from the simians on the road. Turning right (east) at the top will take you on a scenic descent to the coastal town of Singaraja, via the Gitgit waterfalls (p260). Taking a sharp left turn (west), you follow a ridge-top road with Danau Buyan on one side and a slope to the sea on the other. Coffee is a big crop in the area.

At Asan Munduk, there's another T-junction. If you turn left a trail leads to near Danau Tamblingan, among forest and market gardens. Turning right takes you along beautiful winding roads to the main village of Munduk. Watch for superb panoramas of North Bali and the ocean. Consider a stop at **Ngiring Ngewedang** (☎ 0828 365 146; dishes 15,000-40,000Rp; ⏱ 10am-5pm), a coffeehouse 5km east of Munduk that grows its own coffee on the surrounding slopes. Staff are happy to show you the process that puts it in your cup.

About 2km east of Munduk look for signs indicating parking for a 15m **waterfall** near the road. This is the most accessible of many in the immediate area.

Almost everything in the Munduk area is at an elevation of at least 1000m. Numerous trails are suitable for **treks** of two hours or much longer to coffee plantations, rice paddies, waterfalls, villages, or around both Danau Tamblingan and Danau Buyan. You will be able to arrange a guide through your lodgings.

Sleeping & Eating

Like mushrooms after the rain (they grow up here), accommodation is proliferating around Munduk. Enjoy simple old Dutch houses in the village or more naturalistic places in the countryside. Most have cafés, usually serving good local fare. There's a couple of cute warung along the road down to Seririt and North Bali.

Arya Utama (bungalow 100,000Rp) There are two simple cold-water bungalows here in the middle of coffee trees. The big activity: sit on your porch, gaze out and just listen. There's no café, just sleep. It's 2.8km east of Munduk.

Guru Ratna (☎ 92182; r 100,000-200,000Rp) The cheapest place in the village, this has five comfortable cold-water rooms in a colonial Dutch house. The best rooms have some

style and nice porches. Ponder the distant ocean from the café.

Meme Surung & Mekel Ragi (☎ 92811; r US$20-24) These atmospheric old Dutch houses adjoin each other in the village and have two rooms. There are seven more rooms – all with hot showers – next door to the pair. Meme Surung has views.

Puri Alam Bali (☎ 0812 465 9815; www.purialambali.com; r 200,000-250,000Rp) Perched on a precipice at the east end of the village, Puri Alam Bali's eight rooms (all hot-water) have better views the higher you go. The rooftop café surveys the local scene from on high. Think of the long concrete stairs down from the road as trekking practice.

Munduk Sari (☎ 0361-297123; www.munduksari.com; s/d 300,000/400,000Rp) The polished rooms at this modern, slightly soulless inn have classic views of the hills and large tubs with hot water. It's just east of the village.

Lumbung Bali Cottages (☎ 92818; www.lumbung-bali.com; r US$45-125) About 800m east of Munduk, this country inn has nine traditional cottages overlooking the lush local terrain. The open-air bathrooms (with tubs) are as refreshing as the porches are relaxing. A short trail leads to a small waterfall.

our pick Puri Lumbung Cottages (☎ 92810; www.purilumbung.com; cottage US$68-160; 🖵 wi-fi) Founded by Nyoman Bagiarta to develop sustainable tourism, this lovely hotel has 14 bright two-storey cottages set among rice fields. Enjoy intoxicating views (units 3, 8, 10 and 11 have the best) down to the coast from the upstairs balconies. Dozens of trekking options and courses, including dance and cooking, are offered. The hotel's restaurant, Warung Kopi Bali, has an interesting menu that includes the local dish *timbungan bi siap* (chicken soup with sliced cassava and fried shallots). The hotel is on the right-hand side of the road, 700m before Munduk from Bedugul.

Getting There & Away

Bemo leave Ubung terminal in Denpasar for Munduk frequently (22,000Rp). Morning bemo from Candikuning also stop in Munduk (13,000Rp). If you're driving to or from the north coast, a decent road west of Munduk goes through a number of picturesque villages to Mayong (where you can head south to West Bali; see p253). The road then goes down to the sea at Seririt in North Bali.

GUNUNG BATUKAU AREA

Often overlooked (probably a good thing given what the vendor hordes have done to Gunung Agung), Gunung Batukau is Bali's second-highest mountain (2276m), the third of Bali's three major mountains and the holy peak of the island's western end.

You can climb its slippery slopes from one of the island's holiest and most underrated temples, Pura Luhur Batukau, or just revel in the ancient rice-terrace greenery around Jatiluwih, which would be a fantasy if it wasn't real. Extend your stay at two ecolodges far up the slopes of the volcano.

ORIENTATION

There are two main approaches to the Gunung Batukau area. The easiest is to go via Tabanan (see p273) and take the Pura Luhur Batukau road north 9km to a fork in the road. Take the one on the left (towards the temple) and go a further 5km to a junction near a school in Wangayagede village. Here you can continue straight to the temple or turn right (east) for the rice fields of Jatiluwih.

The other way is to approach from the east. On the main Denpasar–Singaraja road, look for a small road to the west, just south of the Pacung Indah hotel (p247). Here you follow a series of small, paved roads west until you reach the Jatiluwih rice fields. You'll get lost, but locals will quickly set you right and the scenery is superb anyway.

SIGHTS & ACTIVITIES
Pura Luhur Batukau

On the slopes of Gunung Batukau, **Pura Luhur Batukau** (donation 10,000Rp) was the state temple when Tabanan was an independent kingdom. It has a seven-roofed *meru* (multi-roofed shrine) dedicated to Maha Dewa, the mountain's guardian spirit, as well as shrines for Bratan, Buyan and Tamblingan lakes. Surrounded by forest, it's often damp and misty. Sarongs can be borrowed; a sign listing those not allowed to visit includes 'Mad Ladies/Gentlemen'. Look happy.

This is certainly the most spiritual temple you can easily visit in Bali. The main pagoda-like structures have little doors shielding small ceremonial items. There's a general lack of touts and other characters – including hordes of tourists. The atmosphere is cool and misty; the chants of priests are backed by birds singing. Facing the temple, take a short walk around to the left to see a small white-water stream. The air resonates with the tumbling water.

For tips for respecting traditions and acting appropriately while visiting temples, see the boxed text, p348. For a directory of important temples, see p51.

Gunung Batukau

At Pura Luhur Batukau you are fairly well up the side of **Gunung Batukau**, and you may wish to go for a climb. But to **trek** to the top of the 2276m peak, you'll need a guide, which can be arranged at the temple ticket booth. Expect to pay 800,000Rp or more for a muddy and arduous journey that will take at least seven hours in one direction. The rewards are amazing views alternating with thick, dripping jungle and the knowledge that you've taken the trail that is much less travelled compared with the peaks in the east.

Jatiluwih Rice Fields

At **Jatiluwih**, which means 'Truly Marvellous', you will be rewarded with vistas of centuries-old rice terraces that exhaust your ability to describe green. The locals will also be rewarded with your 'green', as there's a road toll for visitors (per person 10,000Rp, plus 5000Rp per car).

The terraces have been nominated for Unesco status. You'll understand why just viewing the panorama from the narrow, twisting 18km road, but get out for a **rice-field walk**. Follow the water as it runs through channels and bamboo pipes from one plot to the next. Much of the rice you see is not the hybrid version grown elsewhere in Bali and instead is traditional varieties. Look for heavy, short husks of red rice.

Along the drive you'll pass a couple of warung with simple food (good rice!) served at tables overlooking the terraces.

Sleeping

Two remote lodges are hidden away on the slopes of Gunung Batukau. You reach both via a spectacular small and twisting road that makes a long, inverted V far up the mountain from Bajera and Pucuk on the main Tabanan–Gilimanuk road in West Bali.

SCENIC ROUTES BETWEEN THE COASTS

Although most people cross the mountains via Candikuning or Kintamani, there is a very scenic third alternative that links Bali's south and north coasts. Small but paved roads run via **Pupuan**, west of Gunung Batukau.

From the Denpasar–Gilimanuk road in West Bali, one road goes north from **Antosari** and another road goes north from **Pulukan**; the two roads meet at Pupuan then drop down to Seririt, west of Lovina in North Bali.

The road from Antosari starts through rice paddies, climbs into the fragrant spice-growing country via **Sanda** and then descends through the coffee plantations to Pupuan. From Pupuan, if you continue 12km or so towards the north coast you reach Mayong, where you can turn east to Munduk and on to Danau Bratan.

The Pulukan–Pupuan road climbs steeply up from the coast providing fine views back down to West Bali and the sea. The route also runs through spice-growing country – you'll see (and smell) spices laid out on mats by the road to dry. After about 10km and just before Manggissari, the narrow and winding road actually runs right through **Bunut Bolong** – an enormous tree that forms a complete tunnel (the *bunut* is a type of ficus; *bolong* means 'hole').

Further on, the road spirals down to Pupuan through some of Bali's most beautiful rice terraces. It is worth stopping off for a walk to the magnificent **waterfalls** near Pujungan, a few kilometres south of Pupuan. Follow signs down a narrow, rough road and then walk 1.5km to the first waterfall. It's nice, but before you say 'is that all there is?' follow your ears to a second that's 50m high.

The road meets the Munduk road near Mayong before going on to Seririt.

Deep in the foothills of Gunung Batukau, **Sanda Bukit Villas & Restaurant** (☎ 0828 369 137; www.sandavillas.com; bungalows from US$100; 🏊 🍴) offers a serene escape. Some 8km south of Pupuan at Sanda, this boutique hotel has a large infinity pool that seems to disappear into the rice terraces. The engaging owners will recommend walks among the coffee plantations and rice fields.

Bali Mountain Retreat (☎ 0361-789 7553; www.balimountainretreat.com; Biyahan; r US$90-200; 🏊) Luxurious rooms set in refined cottages are arrayed artistically in a hillside location. A pool and gardens mix with mannered architecture that combines new and old influences. The rooms have video and music systems plus large verandahs perfect for contemplating the views.

Sarinbuana Eco-Lodge (☎ 0361-743 5198; www.baliecolodge.com; Satinbuana; r US$100) A protected rainforest preserve is just a 10-minute walk from these beautiful two-level bungalows built on the side of a hill. Notable amenities include fridges, marble bathrooms and handmade soap. There are extensive cultural workshops and trekking opportunities. A simple cold-water bungalow in the village costs US$10. The lodge has a long list of green practices.

GETTING THERE & AWAY

The only realistic way to explore the Gunung Batukau area is with your own transport.

North Bali

The land on the other side, that's North Bali. Although one-sixth of the island's population lives here, the vast region, centred on Singaraja and the Buleleng regency, is overlooked by many visitors who stay trapped in the South Bali–Ubud axis. And that's ironic because the north was once the gateway to Bali, with Dutch steamers bringing the island's first visitors to the port in Singaraja. Only the really adventurous ones ventured as far as Sanur – or horror, Kuta.

Today, tourism in the north is focused on Lovina, the mellow beach town with cheap hotels and even cheaper sunset beer specials. To the west, Pemuteran charms all who discover the crescent of appealing resorts around a cute little bay. Diving is big here and all along the north coast. Although the sites at Menjangan in West Bali are the destination for many, the Buleleng reefs swarm with sea life day and night.

Getting to North Bali for once lives up to the cliché: it's half the fun. Routes follow the thinly populated coastlines east and west, or, you can go up and over the mountains by any number of routes, marvelling at crater lakes and maybe stopping for a misty trek on the way.

Once north, sacred temples, waterfalls and many other seldom-visited treasures await. Pick a back road for a ride or a drive, wave to the villagers and discover a new, more relaxed side of Bali.

HIGHLIGHTS

- Exploring underwater marvels at **Pemuteran** (p267)
- Losing track of time at **Lovina** (p260)
- Getting dirty in the healthy mud of **Air Panas Banjar** (p267)
- Savouring Buleleng's rich culture at the museums of **Singaraja** (opposite)
- Marvelling at the carving all around the artful temple **Pura Maduwe Karang** (p260)

YEH SANIH

☎ 0362

On the coast road to the beach towns of East Bali, Yeh Sanih (also called Air Sanih) is a hassle-free seaside spot with a few guesthouses on the beachfront. It's named for its freshwater springs, **Air Sanih** (adult/child 3000/1000Rp; ☽ 8am-6pm), which are channelled into large swimming pools before flowing into the sea. The pools are particularly picturesque at sunset, when throngs of locals bathe under blooming frangipani trees – most of the time they're alive with frolicking kids. It's about 15km east of Singaraja.

Pura Ponjok Batu has a commanding location between the sea and the road, some 7km east of Yeh Sanih. It has some very fine limestone carvings in the central temple area. Legend has it that it was built to provide some spiritual balance for Bali, what with all the temples in the south.

Between the springs and the temple, the road is often close to the sea. It's probably Bali's best stretch of coast driving, with water crashing onto the breakwater and great views out to sea.

Completely out of character for the area is a place run by quite a character: **Art Zoo** (☽ 8am-6pm) is 5.7km east of Yeh Sanih on the Singaraja road. Symon, the irrepressible American artist (who also has a gallery in Ubud; p178), owns this gallery and studio, bursting with his own creativity that's at times vibrant, exotic and erotic.

Sleeping & Eating

A few warung (food stalls) hover near the entrance of Yeh Sanih and do a brisk business with the local trade. Otherwise, options are few and scattered.

Pondok Wisata Cleopatra (☎ 0812 362 2232; r 100,000Rp) This modern budget place has nine clean, cold-water rooms with showers and tubs. The big, flowery grounds are about 1.1km west of the springs.

Pondok Sembiran (☎ 24437; r 300,000-450,000Rp; ✖ ☒) This inn is bifurcated: one is 20m from the sea and has a pool and four rooms, the other has seven bungalows and is located right on the seawall. All are large, good for families and have kitchens and hot water. The hotel is off the main road in Alassari, 1km east of the temple and 8.3km east of Yeh Sanih. It's popular with the frugal Dutch travellers.

our pick **Cilik's Beach Garden** (☎ 26561; www.ciliks beachgarden.com; s/d €40/60, villas €60-160; ☐) Coming here is like visiting your rich friends, albeit ones with good taste. These custom-built villas, 3km east of Yeh Sanih, are large and have extensive private gardens. Other accommodation is in stylish *lumbung* (rice barns with round roofs) set in a delightful garden facing the ocean. There's a real emphasis on local culture; the owners have even more remote villas further south on the coast.

Puri Bagus Ponjok Batu (☎ 21430; dishes 15,000-30,000Rp) This lovely spot 6.8km east of Yeh Sanih is next to Pura Ponjok Batu and overlooks the water. It serves grilled seafood in covered pavilions and offers an array of fresh juices. Call to confirm hours before making a special trip.

Getting There & Away

Yeh Sanih is on the main road along the north coast. Frequent bemo (small minibuses) and buses from Singaraja stop outside the springs (8000Rp).

If heading to Amed or Tulamben, make certain you're on your way south from here by 4pm in order to arrive while there's still some light.

SINGARAJA

☎ 0362

With a population of more than 100,000 people, Singaraja (which means 'Lion King' and somehow hasn't caused Disney to demand licensing fees) is Bali's second-largest city. With its tree-lined streets, surviving Dutch colonial buildings and charmingly moribund waterfront area north of Jl Erlangga, it's worth exploring for a few hours. Most people stay in nearby Lovina, however.

Singaraja was the centre of Dutch power in Bali and remained the administrative centre for the Lesser Sunda Islands (Bali through to Timor) until 1953. It is one of the few places in Bali where there are visible traces of the Dutch period, as well as Chinese and Muslim influences. Today, Singaraja is a major educational and cultural centre, and its two university campuses provide the city with a substantial, and sometimes vocal, student population.

The village of Beratan, to the south of Singaraja, is the silverwork centre of northern Bali. You'll find a few traditional pieces such as *cucuk* (gold headpieces) on display, but it mostly has uninspiring tourist jewellery. A

NORTH BALI

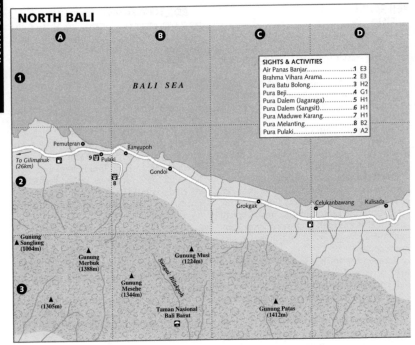

SIGHTS & ACTIVITIES	
Air Panas Banjar.....................1 E3	
Brahma Vihara Arama.............2 E3	
Pura Batu Bolong....................3 H2	
Pura Beji.................................4 G1	
Pura Dalem (Jagaraga)............5 H1	
Pura Dalem (Sangsit)..............6 H1	
Pura Maduwe Karang..............7 H1	
Pura Melanting.......................8 B2	
Pura Pulaki............................9 A2	

few workshops in and around Singaraja produce hand-woven sarongs – especially *songket* (cloth woven with silver or gold threads).

Orientation

The main commercial areas are in the northeastern part of town, south of the old harbour. Traffic does a few complicated one-way loops around town, but it's easy enough to get around on foot or by bemo. Between the museums in the government compound on Jl Veteran and the commercial areas around Jl Jen Achmed Yani are long streets sparse in interest.

Information

EMERGENCY
Police station (☎ 41510; Jl Pramuka)

INTERNET ACCESS & TELEPHONE
There is **internet access** (per min 400Rp) at the rear of the post office.

MEDICAL SERVICES
RSUP Hospital (☎ 22046; Jl Ngurah Rai; 🕑 24hr)
Singaraja's hospital is the largest in northern Bali.

MONEY
There are numerous banks that will change money and have ATMs.

POST OFFICE
Post office (Jl Imam Bonjol)

TOURIST INFORMATION
Diparda (☎ 25141; cnr Jl Veteran & Jl Gajah Mada; 🕑 7.30am-3.30pm Mon-Fri) Near the museum, the regional tourist office loves visitors and has some booklets. Ask about dance and other cultural events.

Sights & Activities

OLD HARBOUR & WATERFRONT
The conspicuous **Yudha Mandala Tama** monument commemorates a freedom fighter killed by gunfire from a Dutch warship early in the struggle for independence. Close by, there's the colourful Chinese temple, **Ling Gwan Kiong**. There are a few old canals here as well and you can still get a little feel of the old colonial port that was the main entrance to Bali before WWII. Some warung have been built on stilts over the water. Walk up

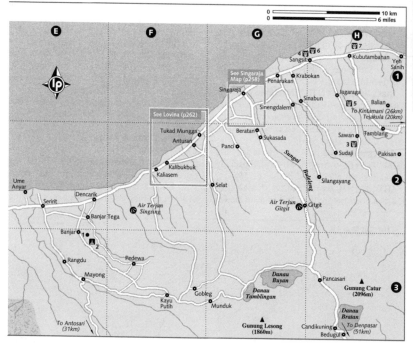

Jl Imam Bonjol and you'll see the art deco lines of late-colonial Dutch buildings.

GEDONG KIRTYA LIBRARY & MUSEUM BULELENG

This small historical **library** (☎ 22645; admission 10,000Rp; ⏰ 8am-4pm Mon-Thu, 8am-1pm Fri) was established in 1928 by Dutch colonialists and named after the Sanskrit word 'to try'. It has a collection of *lontar* (dried palm leaves) books (see p260), as well as some even older written works in the form of inscribed copper plates called *prasasti*. Dutch publications, dating back to 1901, may interest students of the colonial period.

The nearby **Museum Buleleng** (admission 10,000Rp; ⏰ 9am-3.30pm, Mon-Fri) recalls the life of the last Radja (rajah; prince) of Buleleng, Pandji Tisna, who is credited with developing Lovina's tourism. Among the items here is the Royal (brand) typewriter he used during his career as a travel writer (obviously, the rajah was a smart, if poorly remunerated guy) before his death in 1978. It also traces the history of the region back to when there was no history.

Down a small lane in the compound you'll find displays of local weaving.

PURA JAGAT NATHA

Singaraja's main temple, the largest in northern Bali, is not usually open to foreigners. You can appreciate its size and admire the carved stone decorations from the outside.

Festivals & Events

Every May or June, the **Bali Art Festival of Buleleng** is held in Singaraja and surrounding villages. Over one week dancers and musicians from some of the region's most renowned village troupes, such as those of Jagaraga, perform. In August, the **North Bali Festival** is a celebration of the traditional arts of the regency. Consult with the Diparda tourist office (opposite) for details on both.

Sleeping & Eating

There are slim accommodation pickings in Singaraja, and there's no real reason to stay here as it's just a short drive from Lovina. For supplies and sundries, head to **Hardy's Supermarket** (Jl Pramuka; ⏰ 6am-10pm). In the evening, there are food stalls in the **night market** (Jl Durian; ⏰ 5pm-1am).

Hotel Wijaya (☎ 21915; fax 25817; Jl Sudiman 74; r 60,000-160,000Rp; 🌀) This is the most comfortable place in town; economy fan rooms have an outside bathroom. It also has a small café. The bus terminal is a three-minute walk away.

Istana Bakery (☎ 21983; Jl Jen Achmed Yani; snacks 3000Rp; ⏰ 8am-6pm) Fallen in love in Lovina? Get your wedding cake here. For lesser life moments like the munchies, choose from an array of tasty baked goods.

Café Lima Lima (☎ 21769; Jl Jen Achmed Yani; dishes 5000-10,000Rp) Enjoy fresh local food, especially chicken, at simple open-air tables.

SFFC (☎ 24474; Jl Jen Achmed Yani 57; dishes 4000-10,000Rp) Fortunately the food is a lot better than the name, which means quite literally 'Special Fish & Fried Chicken'. There are tables in a small garden and the menu extends to a full range of Indonesian standards.

Warung Kota (☎ 700 9737; Jl Ngurah Rai 22; meals 5000-15,000Rp; ⏰ 24hr) The kool kats hang-out, this café is popular with students from the university. Grab a table amidst the bamboo decor and make some friends. There's live music some nights, movies others.

Getting There & Away
BEMO & BUS
Singaraja is the main transport hub for the northern coast, with three bemo/bus terminals. From the **Sukasada terminal**, 3km south of town, minibuses go to Denpasar (Ubung

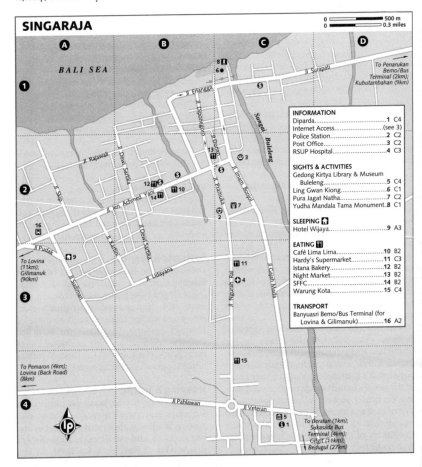

SINGARAJA

0 ——— 500 m
0 ——— 0.3 miles

BALI SEA

To Penarukan
Bemo/Bus
Terminal (2km);
Kubutambahan (9km)

INFORMATION
Diparda..1 C4
Internet Access...................(see 3)
Police Station...........................2 C2
Post Office................................3 C2
RSUP Hospital..........................4 C3

SIGHTS & ACTIVITIES
Gedong Kirtya Library & Museum
 Buleleng................................5 C4
Ling Gwan Kiong.....................6 C1
Pura Jagat Natha......................7 C2
Yudha Mandala Tama Monument..8 C1

SLEEPING
Hotel Wijaya............................9 A3

EATING
Café Lima Lima.......................10 B2
Hardy's Supermarket..............11 C3
Istana Bakery..........................12 B2
Night Market...........................13 B2
SFFC..14 B2
Warung Kota...........................15 C4

TRANSPORT
Banyuasri Bemo/Bus Terminal (for
 Lovina & Gilimanuk)..............16 A2

To Lovina
(11km);
Gilimanuk
(90km)

To Pemaron (4km);
Lovina (Back Road)
(8km)

To Beratan (1km);
Sukasada Bus
Terminal (4km);
Gitgit (11km);
Bedugul (27km)

CARING FOR ORPHANS

Kim Butler was just down the road from the Sari Club when the 2002 bombings occurred. It was the scene of the worst carnage, and she was soon at Bali's main hospital helping care for the victims. On subsequent visits to Bali, she has organised aid, clothes and supplies for victims and their families, many living in impoverished villages where they had little.

More recently, Butler has 'adopted' an orphanage in Singaraja in North Bali, and has done much to improve the lives of the kids there. Besides improving the building and giving the kids the basic items they lack, like clothing and furniture, she's added in a few extras. 'We bought every child an ice cream. Have you ever seen 80 kids all eating ice cream at once? You could have heard a pin drop.'

For her work helping bombing victims, Butler received the Medal of the Order of Australia honour in 2005. Her next goal is to line up sponsors for every child in the orphanage, which costs about A$300 per year. She urges anyone who'd like to help to contact her (kimbalibabe @hotmail.com). And most importantly, she says, everyone visiting Bali can help the people on the island.

'Imagine if everyone going to Bali filled their suitcases with clothes, shoes, hats etc to give to the Balinese – that's a lot of clothing and good karma. Contact me. I can tell you where to donate your goods.'

For more on volunteering, see p346.

terminal, 30,000Rp) via Bedugul/Pancasari (15,000Rp) sporadically through the day.

The **Banyuasri terminal**, on the western side of town, has buses heading to Gilimanuk (22,000Rp, two hours) and Java, and plenty of blue bemo to Lovina (7000Rp).

The **Penarukan terminal**, 2km east of town, has bemo to Yeh Sanih (8000Rp) and Amlapura (18,000Rp, three hours) via the coastal road; and also minibuses to Denpasar (Batubulan terminal, 30,000Rp, three hours) via Kintamani.

To Java

From Singaraja, several companies have overnight services to Surabaya (150,000Rp, 13 hours), which include the ferry trip across the Bali Strait. Other buses go as far as Yogyakarta (210,000Rp, 16 hours) and Jakarta (300,000Rp, 24 hours), usually travelling overnight – book at Banyuasri terminal a day before.

Getting Around

Plenty of bemo link the three main bemo/bus terminals, and zip along all main roads in between. The bemo are all well signed and colour-coded and cost about 5000Rp for a ride anywhere around town. The green Banyuasri–Sukasada bemo goes along Jl Gajah Mada to the tourist office; this bemo, and the brown one between Penarukan and Banyuasri terminals, also goes along Jl Jen Achmed Yani.

AROUND SINGARAJA

The interesting sites around Singaraja include some of Bali's most important temples.

Sangsit

A few kilometres northeast of Singaraja, you can see an excellent example of the colourful architectural style of North Bali. Sangsit's **Pura Beji** is a temple for the *subak* (village association for rice-growers), dedicated to the goddess Dewi Sri, who looks after irrigated rice fields. The over-the-top sculptured panels along the front wall set the tone with their cartoonlike demons and amazing *naga* (mythical snakelike creatures). The inside also has a variety of sculptures covering every available space. It's 500m off the main road towards the coast.

The **Pura Dalem** shows scenes of punishment in the afterlife, and other humorous, sometimes erotic, pictures. You'll find it in the rice fields, about 500m northeast of Pura Beji.

Buses and bemo going east from Singaraja's Penarukan terminal will stop at Sangsit.

Jagaraga

It was the capture of the local rajah's stronghold at Jagaraga that marked the arrival of Dutch power in Bali in 1849. The village, a few kilometres south of the main road, also has a **Pura Dalem**. The small, interesting temple has delightful sculptured panels along its front wall, inside and out. On the outer wall, look for a vintage car driving sedately past,

NORTH BALI

a steamer at sea and even an aerial dogfight between early aircraft. Jagaraga is also famous for its Legong troupe, said to be the best in North Bali, but performances are irregular.

Bemo from the Penarukan terminal in Singaraja stop at Jagaraga on the way to Sawan.

Sawan

Several kilometres inland from Jagaraga, Sawan is a centre for the manufacturing of gamelan gongs and instruments. You can see them being cast and the intricately carved gamelan frames being made. **Pura Batu Bolong** (Temple of the Hollow Stone) and its baths are also worth a look. Around Sawan there are cold-water springs that are believed to cure all sorts of illnesses.

Regular bemo to Sawan leave from Penarukan terminal in Singaraja.

Kubutambahan

About 1km east of the turn-off to Kintamani is **Pura Maduwe Karang** (Temple of the Land Owner). Like Pura Beji at Sangsit, this temple of dark stone is dedicated to agricultural spirits, but this one looks after nonirrigated land.

This is one of the most intriguing temples in North Bali and is particularly noted for its sculptured panels, including the famous bicycle stone-carved relief that depicts a gentleman riding a bicycle with a lotus flower serving as the back wheel. It's on the base of the main plinth in the inner enclosure. The

---

LONTAR BOOKS

Lontar is made from the fan-shaped leaves of the *rontal* palm. The leaf is dried, soaked in water, cleaned, steamed, dried again, then flattened, dyed and eventually cut into strips. The strips are inscribed with words and pictures using a very sharp blade or point, then coated with a black stain which is wiped off – the black colour stays in the inscription. A hole in the middle of each *lontar* strip is threaded onto a string, with a carved bamboo 'cover' at each end to protect the 'pages', and the string is secured with a couple of pierced Chinese coins, or *kepeng*.

The Gedong Kirtya Library in Singaraja has the world's largest collection of works inscribed on *lontar*, see p257.

---

cyclist may be WOJ Nieuwenkamp, a Dutch artist who, in 1904, brought what was probably the first bicycle to Bali.

The temple is easy to find in the village – look for the 34 carved figures from the *Ramanyana* outside the walls. Kubutambahan is on the road between Singaraja and Amlapura, and there are regular bemo and buses passing through.

Gitgit

About 11km south of Singaraja, the well-signposted path goes 800m west from the main road to the touristy waterfall, **Air Terjun Gitgit** (adult/child 6000/3000Rp). The path is lined with souvenir stalls and guides to nowhere. The 40m waterfalls pound away and the mists are more refreshing than any air-con.

About 2km further up the hill, there's a multi-tiered **waterfall** (donation 5000Rp) about 600m off the western side of the main road. The path crosses a narrow bridge and follows the river up past several small sets of waterfalls, through verdant jungle.

Regular bemo and minibuses between Denpasar (Ubung terminal) and Singaraja (Sukasada terminal) stop at Gitgit. Gitgit is also a major stop on organised tours of central and North Bali.

LOVINA
☎ 0362

Relaxed is how people most often describe Lovina and they are correct. This low-key, low-rise beach resort is the polar opposite of Kuta. Days are slow and so are the nights. The waves are calm, the beach is thin and over-amped attractions nil.

This is where you catch up on your journal and get plenty of R&R, finish a book or make new friends at a laid-back beachside café. There's some good diving in the area, and if you want to get you motor revving – literally – there's early-morning dolphin watching. The beaches are made up of washed-out grey and black volcanic sand, and while they're mostly clean near the hotel areas, they're not spectacular. Reefs protect the shore, calming the waves and keeping the water clear.

While not arid, Lovina is also not a tropical jungle. It's sun-drenched, with patches of shade from palm trees. It is spread out –

don't plan on walking from one end to the other in a quick jaunt.

A highlight every afternoon at fishing villages like Anturan is watching *prahu* (traditional outrigger canoes) being prepared for the night's fishing; as sunset reddens the sky, the lights of the fishing boats appear as bright dots across the horizon.

Orientation

The Lovina tourist area stretches over 8km, and consists of a string of coastal villages – Kaliasem, Kalibukbuk, Anturan, Tukad Mungga – collectively known as Lovina. The main focus is Kalibukbuk, 10.5km west of Singaraja and often thought of as the heart of Lovina. The main street is also the main east–west road. It goes by various names, including Jl Raya Lovina and Jl Raya Kaliasem. Traffic in the daytime can be loud and constant.

For trips to Singaraja, back roads offer scenic alternatives.

Information

If you're planning a reading holiday in Lovina, come prepared. Other than some used-book stalls, there's no good source for new books or newspapers (the urchins selling overpriced papers in the south are missing a market opportunity here).

EMERGENCY
Police station (Jl Raya Lovina) Near the tourist office.

INTERNET ACCESS
Fast internet access is common.

Bits and Bytes (☎ 0817 552 511; Jl Raya Lovina; per hr 25,000Rp; ☽ 8am-8pm) Fast connections plus wi-fi and laptop connections.

I-net (Jl Pantai Banyualit; per 5min 500Rp; ☽ 8am-midnight) Open-air internet place with fast connections and services like CD burning.

Spice Cyber (☎ 41305; Jl Bina Ria; per min 300Rp; ☽ 8am-midnight; ⛶) Wi-fi and printing.

MONEY
There is a **Bank BCA ATM** at the corner of Jl Bina Ria and Jl Raya Lovina, plus many more in Singaraja.

POST
The **main post office** is 1km west of central Kalibukbuk.

Sights & Activities

BEACHES
A sweet paved beach path runs along the sand in Kalibukbuk and extends in a circuitous path along the seashore. Enjoy the postcard view to the east of the mountainous North Bali coast.

Otherwise, the best beach areas include the main beach east of the **Dolphin Monument** as well as the curving stretch a bit west. The cluster of cheap hotels in Anturan also enjoy fun on the sand. While moored near shore, the fishing boats can fascinate with their large, bare engines, menacing-looking props and individual paint schemes.

CYCLING
The roads south of Jl Raya Lovina are excellent for biking, with limited traffic and enjoyable rides amidst the rice fields and into the hills for views. Many of the sites beyond Lovina to the west are easily reached by bike.

Most hotels can rent you a bike. **Sovina Shop** (☎ 41402; Jl Ketapang) has a good selection of bicycles for hire from 20,000Rp per day. Motorbikes are 35,000Rp per day.

DOLPHIN WATCHING
Sunrise boat trips to see dolphins are Lovina's much-hyped tourist attraction – so much so that a large concrete-crowned monument has been erected in their honour. Some days no dolphins are sighted, but most of the time at least a few surface.

Expect constant hassle from your hotel and touts selling dolphin trips. The price is fixed at 50,000Rp per person by the boat-owners' cartel. Trips start at a non-holiday-like 6am and last about two hours. Note that the ocean can get pretty crowded with loud, roaring powerboats.

There's great debate about what all this means to the dolphins. Do they like being chased by boats? If not, why do they keep coming back? Maybe it's the fish, of which there are plenty off Lovina. For a dolphin, maybe the buzzing boats are on par with someone yakking on a mobile phone at dinner. Or maybe not.

DIVING
Scuba diving on the local reef is better at lower depths and night diving is popular. Many people stay here and dive Pulau Menjangan (p280), a two-hour drive west.

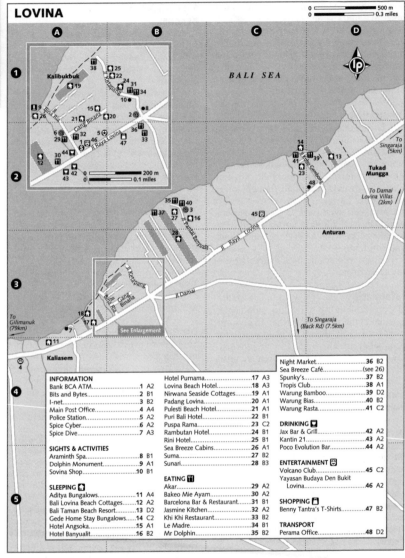

LOVINA

BALI SEA

Kalibukbuk

Tukad
Mungga

To
Singaraja
(5km)

To Damai
Lovina Villas
(2km)

Anturan

See Enlargement

To
Gilimanuk
(79km)

To Singaraja
(Back Rd) (7.5km)

Kaliasem

INFORMATION		Hotel Purnama....................17 A3	Night Market....................36 B2
Bank BCA ATM....................1 A2		Lovina Beach Hotel............18 A3	Sea Breeze Café..............(see 26)
Bits and Bytes....................2 B1		Nirwana Seaside Cottages...19 A1	Spunky's..........................37 B2
I-net...............................3 B2		Padang Lovina...................20 A1	Tropis Club........................38 A1
Main Post Office.................4 A4		Pulesti Beach Hotel............21 A1	Warung Bamboo...............39 D2
Police Station....................5 A2		Puri Bali Hotel...................22 B1	Warung Bias.....................40 B2
Spice Cyber......................6 A2		Puspa Rama.....................23 C2	Warung Rasta...................41 C2
Spice Dive.......................7 A3		Rambutan Hotel.................24 B1	
		Rini Hotel........................25 B1	DRINKING
SIGHTS & ACTIVITIES		Sea Breeze Cabins..............26 A1	Jax Bar & Grill...................42 A2
Araminth Spa....................8 B1		Suma.............................27 B2	Kantin 21.........................43 A2
Dolphin Monument.............9 A1		Sunari............................28 B3	Poco Evolution Bar.............44 A2
Sovina Shop....................10 B1			
		EATING	ENTERTAINMENT
SLEEPING		Akar..............................29 A2	Volcano Club.....................45 C2
Aditya Bungalows...............11 A4		Bakeo Mie Ayam................30 A2	Yayasan Budaya Den Bukit
Bali Lovina Beach Cottages...12 A2		Barcelona Bar & Restaurant...31 B1	Lovina.........................46 A2
Bali Taman Beach Resort......13 D2		Jasmine Kitchen................32 A2	
Gede Home Stay Bungalows...14 C2		Khi Khi Restaurant.............33 B2	SHOPPING
Hotel Angsoka..................15 A1		Le Madre........................34 B1	Benny Tantra's T-Shirts........47 B2
Hotel Banyualit.................16 B2		Mr Dolphin......................35 B2	
			TRANSPORT
			Perama Office...................48 D2

For a two-dive trip, including transport and all equipment, expect to pay about US$40 for a Lovina reef or night dive; and around US$60 to Amed, Tulamben or Pulau Menjangan.

Spice Dive (☎ 41509; www.balispicedive.com) offers PADI open-water certificate courses for about US$350. It's based at the west end of the beach path.

SNORKELLING

Generally, the water is clear and some parts of the reef are quite good for snorkelling, though the coral has been damaged by bleaching and, in places, by dynamite fishing. The best place is to the west, a few hundred metres offshore from Billibo Beach Cottages. A boat trip will cost about

50,000Rp per person for two people for two hours, including equipment. Snorkelling gear costs about 30,000Rp per day.

MASSAGE & SPAS

Araminth Spa (☎ 0812 384 4655; Jl Ketapang; massage from 105,000Rp; ⏱ 10am-7pm) offers Balinese, Ayurveda and foot massage in a simple but soothing setting. It promotes 'vagina steaming', which involves dry, herbal smoke (75,000Rp).

Sleeping

Hotels are spread out along Jl Raya Lovina, and on the side roads going off to the beach. There are decent places to stay in every price range.

Anturan is largely a backpackers' beach with a mellow charm. There are some nice places grouped from Anturan to Kalibukbuk, which is jammed with all manner of accommodation and services. West of Kalibukbuk the hotel density again diminishes right along with the beach.

During slow periods in Lovina, all room prices are negotiable.

BUDGET
Anturan

A few tiny side tracks and one proper sealed road, Jl Kubu Gembong, lead to this lively little fishing village, busy with swimming locals and moored fishing boats. It's a real travellers' hang-out. It's a long way from Lovina's evening delights though – expect to pay around 20,000Rp for transport back to Anturan from Kalibukbuk after 6pm when the bemo stop operating.

Puspa Rama (☎ 42070; Jl Kubu Gembong; s/d incl breakfast 60,000/70,000Rp) One of several budget places on this street, Puspa Rama has grounds a few cuts above the others. The six rooms have hot water. Fruit trees abound – why not pick your own breakfast?

Gede Home Stay Bungalows (☎ 41526; Jl Kubu Gembong; r 70,000-120,000Rp; ⏹) Don't forget to shake the sand off your feet as you enter this beachside nine-room homestay. Cheap rooms have cold water while better ones have hot water and air-con.

Anturan to Kalibukbuk

Jl Pantai Banyualit has many hotels, although the beachfront area is not very inspiring.

Suma (☎ 41566; www.sumahotel.com; Jl Pantai Banyualit; r 150,000-400,000Rp; ⏹ ⏹ ⏹) In a mannered stone building, Suma has views of the sea from its upstairs rooms; the best have air-con and hot water. The pool is large and naturalistic; there's also a pleasant café. A much-renovated temple is nearby.

Kalibukbuk

A little over 10km from Singaraja, the 'centre' of Lovina is the village of Kalibukbuk. Jl Ketapang is marginally quieter and more pleasant than Jl Bina Ria. There are small *gang* (alleys) lined with cheap places to stay off both streets.

Hotel Angsoka (☎ 41841; www.angsoka.com; Gang Binaria; r 40,000-200,000Rp; ⏹ ⏹) The 44 rooms here span a large range, from cold-water, fan singles to large units with air-con and tubs for you and a fridge for your beer. All enjoy a good-sized pool, café and quiet gardens.

Padang Lovina (☎ 41302; Gang Binaria; r 80,000-250,000Rp; ⏹) Down a narrow lane in the very heart of Kalibukbuk. There's no pretension at all around the 12 comfortable bungalow-style rooms set around spacious grounds teeming with flowers. The best rooms have air-con and tubs.

Pulesti Beach Hotel (☎ 41035; Jl Bina Ria; r 100,000-300,000Rp; ⏹ ⏹) Rooms here are arranged in rows on a cramped plot, however all is forgiven once you check out the good-sized pool and patio. If it isn't large enough, the rather larger pool – the ocean – is three minutes north.

Rini Hotel (☎ 41386; rinihotel@telkom.net; Jl Ketapang; r 120,000-250,000Rp; ⏹ ⏹) This tidy 30-room place has a large saltwater pool. Cheaper rooms have fans and cold water but the more expensive ones are huge, with air-con and hot water. In fact, should you come across a keg, you could have a party.

Puri Bali Hotel (☎ 41485; www.puribalilovina.com; Jl Ketapang; r 130,000-250,000Rp; ⏹ ⏹) The pool area is set deep in a lush garden – you may hang out here all day. The better of the 30 rooms, with hot water and air-con, are simple but comfortable. The cheapest, with fans and cold water, are simply simple.

Nirwana Seaside Cottages (☎ 41288; www.nirwanaseaside.com; bungalows 150,000-200,000Rp, r 250,000-500,000Rp; ⏹ ⏹) On large and lovely beachfront grounds, the 58-unit Nirwana offers a wide range of rooms. The bungalows are a bit musty but have hot water; those with

NORTH BALI

beach views are a great deal. A modern wing has hotel-style air-con rooms with satellite TV. Flip coins to choose your pool.

Sea Breeze Cabins (☎ 41138; r US$20, bungalows US$30-40; ❄ ⚊) One of the best choices in the heart of Kalibukbuk and right off Jl Bina Ria, the Sea Breeze has three appealing bungalows right on the pool and beach, some with sensational views from their verandahs. The two economy rooms have fans and hot water.

West of Kalibukbuk

Hotel Purnama (☎ 41043; Jl Raya Lovina; s/d 40,000/50,000Rp) One of the best deals on this stretch, Purnama has seven clean cold-water rooms. The beach is a two-minute walk away. However, the name is a misnomer: this is a family compound, and a friendly one at that.

Lovina Beach Hotel (☎ 41005; www.lovinabeachhotel.com; Jl Raya Lovina; r 75,000-250,000Rp, bungalows 250,000Rp; ❄ ⚊) The classic deal so good it's a steal. This beach place has 24 rooms in a two-storey block and bungalows – the latter are nicer, with lots of carving and Balinese details. The grounds feel like a park.

MIDRANGE
Anturan

Bali Taman Beach Resort (☎ 41126; www.balitamanlovina.com; Jl Raya Lovina; r US$40-75; ❄ ⚊ ▣) Facing the busy road, but extending down to the beach, the Bali Taman has 30 rooms that vary widely – although all have pretty simple interiors. The best ones are bungalows with ocean views. The large pool faces the ocean and is surrounded by leafy gardens.

Anturan to Kalibukbuk

This quiet area has several midrange choices on little parallel lanes running to the beach.

Hotel Banyualit (☎ 41789; www.banyualit.com; Jl Pantai Banyualit; r 250,000-700,000Rp; ❄ ⚊) About 100m back from the beach, the Banyualit has a lush garden, statues and a large pool. The 22 rooms (all with air-con) offer great choice; best are the villas with whirlpools, fridges and large, shady patios. There's also a small spa.

Sunari (☎ 41775; www.sunari.com; r US$40-100, villas US$80-200; ❄ ⚊ ▣) Off Jl Raya Lovina, the imposing entrance to this 129-room place leads to a large resort with many room choices. The garden-view rooms are basic, and the best are the deluxe private villas with whirlpools and views of the (small) waves. There are multiple bars and cafés.

Kalibukbuk

Bali Lovina Beach Cottages (☎ 41285; www.balilovinahotel.com; Jl Raya Lovina; r US$40-60; ❄ ⚊) The 30 rooms here are in mixed two-storey and bungalow-style units. Several surround the large pool (complete with dolphin statue) or face the beach. Room styles are basic but clean.

Rambutan Hotel ☎ 41388; www.rambutan.org; Jl Ketepang; r US$12-65, villas from US$110; ❄ ⚊) The hotel, on one hectare of lush gardens, features two pools, a playground and games for all ages. The 31 rooms and villas are tasteful with lashings of Balinese style. The very cheapest have fans and cold water.

West of Kalibukbuk

Aditya Bungalows (☎ 41059; www.adityalovina.com; r 300,000-600,000Rp; ❄ ⚊) There are 64 rooms at this big place on a sandy beach. The best ones have views of the ocean and all have a good range of amenities and attractive bathrooms. Swim in the large pool or in the ocean? Sit on your patio while you're deciding.

TOP END

Damai Lovina Villas (☎ 41008; www.damai.com; villas from US$200; ❄ ⚊) Set back on a hillside behind Lovina, Damai has the kind of sweeping views you'd expect. It has eight luxury bungalows with antiques accented by beautiful Balinese fabrics. The pool seemingly spills onto a landscape of peanut fields, rice paddies and coconut palms. The restaurant is lauded for its organic fusion cuisine. Call for transport or, at the main junction in Kalibukbuk, go south on Jl Damai and follow the road for about 3km.

Eating

Just about every hotel has a café or restaurant. Close to the centre of Lovina you can find several places that go beyond the usual travellers' fare. Beachside places are good just for drinks if you're planning to do some hopping.

A small **night market** (Jl Raya Lovina; ☽ 5-11pm) is a good choice for fresh and cheap local food.

ANTURAN

Warung Bamboo (dishes 7000-30,000Rp) A small, open-fronted place, Bamboo fronts a lively section of beach; watch fisherfolk prepping boats, travellers grinding on the sand etc. It serves classic fare, cheap beer and fish right off the boats. To find it, walk east along the beach from the end of Jl Kubu Gembong.

Warung Rasta (mains 15,000-30,000Rp) Right on a strip of beach lined with fishing boats. The menu not surprisingly leans towards simply grilled fresh seafood; given the name, the endless loop of music shouldn't surprise either. It's run by dudes who have clearly realised that lounging around here all day beats fishing.

ANTURAN TO KALIBUKBUK
Mr Dolphin (☎ 0813 5327 6985; Jl Pantai Banyualit; dishes 15,000-40,000Rp) Right on the beach, this cheery hang-out for dolphin-tour skippers serves a killer grilled seafood platter (which was probably caught by the guy next to you). There's live acoustic music most nights.

Warung Bias (☎ 411692; Jl Pantai Banyualit; dishes 15,000-40,000Rp; ☒ 5-9pm) Worth a trip for the talented chef, Bias serves homemade baked goods, as well as Indian curries, European dishes like Wiener schnitzel, pastas and pizzas. It's in a simple open-air setting surrounded by a carp pond.

Spunky's (☎ 41134; Jl Pantai Banyualit; dishes 20,000-50,000Rp) A real comer in the sunset drinks department, sprightly Spunky's serves Indonesian classics right on the beach. Take a dip, take a drink, take off your…

KALIBUKBUK
This is ground zero for nightlife. There's a good range of restaurants, beachside cafés, bars where you can get a burger and maybe hear some music, or fun places that defy description.

Bakeo Mie Ayam (Jl Raya Lovina; meals from 3000Rp) A few pavement chairs make up the decor at this pristine stall serving the best chicken in town. It comes in many forms but we always like the soup.

Khi Khi Restaurant (☎ 41548; dishes 8000-100,000Rp) Well off Jl Raya Lovina and behind the night market, this barn of a place specialises in Chinese food and grilled seafood, including lobster. It's always popular in a rub-elbows-with-your-neighbour kind of way.

Akar (☎ 0817 972 4717; Jl Bina Ria; snacks from 18,000Rp) The many shades of green at this cute-as-a-baby-frog café aren't just for show. They reflect the earth-friendly ethics of the owners. Refill your water containers here and then enjoy organic smoothies and other refreshing treats. A tiny back porch overlooks the river.

Barcelona Bar & Restaurant (☎ 41894; Jl Ketapang; dishes 10,000-40,000Rp) This quiet and restful restaurant has a shady garden area out the back

that is the preferred seating option. Despite the name, it has an ambitious and good Balinese menu.

Sea Breeze Café (☎ 41138; dishes 12,000-45,000Rp) Right by the beach off Jl Bina Ria, this café has a range of Indonesian and Western dishes and excellent breakfasts. It's a good spot for sunset drinks and ocean views.

Tropis Club (☎ 42090; Jl Ketepang; dishes 15,000-35,000Rp) The long menu at this beachside place includes wood-fired pizza. Choose a table under the soaring roof or out along the beach walkway. Sunset specials include cheap Bintang.

Jasmine Kitchen (☎ 41565; Gang Binaria; dishes 15,000-35,000Rp) As good as ever, the Thai fare at this elegant two-level restaurant is excellent. The menu is long and authentic and the staff gracious. While soft jazz plays (and trays of peppers dry near the entrance), try the homemade ice cream for dessert.

Le Madre (☎ 0817 554 399; Jl Ketapang; mains 20,000-40,000Rp) Two married chefs who worked at some of South Bali's best Italian restaurants run this cute little bistro that looks like somebody's home (actually it is). Get a table in the garden and enjoy fresh pastas and seafood with crusty Italian bread that's baked daily.

SOUTH OF LOVINA
Damai Lovina Villas (☎ 41008; www.damai.com; lunch US$4-12, 5-course dinner from US$45) Enjoy the renowned organic restaurant at this boutique hotel (opposite).

Drinking
Plenty of places to eat are also good for just a drink, especially those on the beach. Happy hours abound. The following are some of the top picks in Kalibukbuk.

Jax Bar & Grill (Jl Raya Lovina; ☒ 6pm-midnight) The big open bar serves a long list of creative drinks made with fruit. Lounge on pillow-bedecked *bale* (pavilions) while listening to cover rock. This being Lovina, they told us 'sometimes we go late, like to 12.30pm…'.

Kantin 21 (☎ 0812 460 7791; Jl Raya Lovina; ☒ 11am-1am) Funky open-air place where you can watch traffic by day and groove to acoustic guitar or garage-band rock by night. There's a long drinks list (jugs of Long Island iced tea for 75,000Rp), fresh juices and a few local snacks.

Poco Evolution Bar (☎ 41535; Jl Bina Ria; dishes 12,000-25,000Rp; ☒ 11am-1am) Movies are shown at various times, and cover bands perform at this popular bar-café. Classic travellers' fare is served at tables open to street life in front and the river in back.

Entertainment

Some of the joints on Jl Bina Ria have live music.

Volcano Club (Jl Raya Lovina; 🕙 9pm-late Wed-Sat) There's nothing fancy about this big tropical disco in Anturan, where local and visiting partiers mix it up to local DJs until all hours.

Yayasan Budaya Den Bukit Lovina (Lovina Culture Foundation; ☎ 41293; Jl Raya Lovina) This foundation in Kalibukbuk organises Kecak dances on Tuesday nights from good local troupes, and Gong Kebyar dances on Saturday nights. Ask about Legong and bull races (see p277).

Shopping

Shops on the main streets of Kalibukbuk sell a range of souvenirs, sundries and groceries.

Benny Tantra's T-Shirts (Jl Raya Lovina) Better than a Bintang T-shirt, Benny paints amusing shirts and postcards, satirising local tourism and other topics.

Getting There & Away

BUS & BEMO

To reach Lovina from South Bali by public transport, you'll need to change in Singaraja (see p258). Regular blue bemo go from Singaraja's Banyuasri terminal to Kalibukbuk (about 7000Rp) – you can flag them down anywhere on the main road.

If you're coming by long-distance bus from the west you can ask to be dropped off anywhere along the main road.

TOURIST SHUTTLE BUS

Perama buses stop at its office, in front of **Hotel Perama** (☎ 41161) on Jl Raya Lovina in Anturan. Passengers are then ferried to other points on the Lovina strip (10,000Rp).

Destination	Fare	Duration
Candidasa	150,000Rp	5½hr
Kuta	125,000Rp	4hr
Padangbai	150,000Rp	4¾hr
Sanur	125,000Rp	3¾hr
Ubud	125,000Rp	2¾hr

Getting Around

The Lovina strip is *very* spread out, but you can easily travel back and forth on bemo

(3000Rp). Bikes are easily rented around town for about 30,000Rp per day.

WEST OF LOVINA

The main road west of Lovina passes temples, farms and towns while it follows the thinly developed coast. You'll notice a lot of vineyards, where the grapes work overtime producing the sugar that's used in Bali's very sweet local vintages. The road continues to the Taman Nasional Bali Barat (p280) and the port of Gilimanuk (p279).

Air Terjun Singsing

About 5km west of Lovina, a sign points to **Air Terjun Singsing** (Daybreak Waterfall). About 1km from the main road, there is a warung on the left and a car park on the right. Walk past the warung and along the path for about 200m to the lower falls. The waterfall is not huge, but the pool underneath is ideal for swimming. The water isn't crystal clear, but it's cooler than the sea and very refreshing.

Clamber further up the hill to another waterfall, **Singsing Dua**, which is slightly bigger and has a mud bath that is supposedly good for the skin (we'll let you decide about this freelance spa). These falls also cascade into a deep swimming pool.

The area is thick with tropical forest and makes a nice day trip from Lovina. The falls are more spectacular in the wet season (October to March), and may be just a trickle other times.

Brahma Vihara Arama

Bali's single Buddhist monastery is only vaguely Buddhist in appearance, with colourful decorations, a bright orange roof and statues of Buddha – it also has very Balinese decorative carvings and door guardians plus elaborately carved dark stones. It is quite a handsome structure in a commanding location, with views that reach down into the valley and across the rice fields to the sea. You should wear long pants or a sarong, which can be hired for a small donation. The monastery does not advertise any regular courses or programs, but visitors are more than welcome to meditate in special rooms.

The temple is 3.3km off the main road – take the obvious turn-off in Dencarik. If you don't have your own transport, arrange it with an *ojek* (motorcycle) driver at the turn-off (10,000Rp). The road continues past the monastery, winding further up into the hills to Pedewa, a Bali Aga village.

Air Panas Banjar
☎ 0362

Not far from Brahma Vihara Arama, these **hot springs** (adult/child 6000/3000Rp, parking 2000Rp; ☼ 8am-6pm) percolate amid lush tropical plants. You can relax here for a few hours and have lunch at the restaurant, or even stay the night.

Eight fierce-faced carved stone *naga* (mythical serpents) pour water from a natural hot spring into the first bath, which then overflows (via the mouths of five more *naga*), into a second, larger pool. In a third pool, water pours from 3m-high spouts to give you a pummelling massage. The water is slightly sulphurous and pleasantly hot (about 38°C), so you might enjoy it more in the morning or the evening than in the heat of the Balinese day. You must wear a swimsuit and you shouldn't use soap in the pools, but you can do so under an adjacent outdoor shower.

In a verdant setting on a hillside very close to the baths, the rooms at **Pondok Wisata Grya Sari** (☎ 92903; r 100,000-150,000Rp) are rustic at best and have outdoor bathrooms. Treks into the surrounding densely-grown countryside can be organised from here.

Overlooking the baths, a casual **café** (dishes 8000-20,000Rp) has the usual Indonesian menu, which only gets better thanks to the view.

It's only about 3km from the Buddhist monastery to the hot springs if you take the short cut – go down to Banjar Tega, turn left in the centre of the village and follow the small road west, then south to Banjar village. From there, it's a short distance uphill before you see the 'Air Panas 1km' sign on the left (on the corner by the police station). From the bemo stop on the main road to the hot springs you can take an *ojek;* going back is a 2.4km downhill stroll.

Seririt

This town is a junction for roads that run south over the mountains to Munduk and the central mountains (p250) or to Papuan and West Bali (see the boxed text, p253). They are beautiful drives.

The road continuing west along the coast towards Gilimanuk is in good shape. In Seririt, there's a Bank BCA ATM at the Lovina end of town and a large Hardy's supermarket. There are many warung in the market area,

just north of the bemo stop, and you can find petrol stations on the main road. Temple-offering stalls here brim with orange and pale-blue beauty.

The name says it all – albeit very calmly – at **Zen Resort Bali** (☎ 93578; www.zenresortbali.com; s/d €60/80; ☒), a seaside resort devoted to internal and mental well-being. Rooms in traditional bungalows have a minimalist look designed to not tax the synapses, and gardens are dotted with water features. Activities start with yoga and end with a good Ayurvedic cleansing. It's just west of Seririt in the seaside village of Ume Anyar.

Celukanbawang

Celukanbawang is the main cargo port for North Bali, and has a large wharf. Bugis schooners – the magnificent sailing ships that take their name from the seafaring Bugis people of Sulawesi – can sometimes be seen anchoring here.

Pulaki

Pulaki is famous for its grape vines, watermelons and for **Pura Pulaki**, a coastal temple that was completely rebuilt in the early 1980s, and is home to a large troop of monkeys as well as troops at a nearby army base.

About 600m east of the temple, a well-signposted 1.7km paved road leads to **Pura Melanting**. This temple has a dramatic setting with steps leading up into the foothills. It's dedicated to good fortune in business. A donation is expected as entry to the complex, although you're not permitted in the main worship area. Look for the dragon statue with the lotus blossom on its back near the entrance as well as villa owners hoping for rentals. Sarong rentals are 5000Rp.

PEMUTERAN
☎ 0362

This oasis in the far northwest corner of Bali has a number of artful resorts set on a little bay that's alive with local life such as kids playing soccer until dark. The villagers, once impoverished, have realised that healthy reefs and sea life draw visitors, so they've found relative prosperity as good stewards to the local environment.

This is the place to come for a real beach getaway. Most people dive or snorkel the underwater wonders at nearby Menjangan (p280) while here.

NORTH BALI

WANT A NEW REEF? CHARGE IT!

Pemuteran is set among a fairly arid part of Bali where people have always had a hard-scrabble existence. In the early 1990s, tourism began to take advantage of the excellent diving in the area. Locals who'd previously been scrambling to grow or catch something to eat began getting language and other training to welcome people to what would become a collection of resorts.

But there was one big problem: dynamite and cyanide fishing was rampant. After a few fits and starts though, the community managed to control this. Then came the late 1990s and the El Niño warming of the water, which bleached and damaged large parts of the reef.

A group of local hotels, dive-shop owners and community leaders hit upon a novel solution: charge a new reef! Not with plastic, of course, but with electricity. The idea had already been floated by scientists internationally, but Pemuteran was the first place to implement it on a wide – and hugely successful – scale.

Using local materials, the community built dozens of large metal cages that were placed out among the threatened reef. Then, they were literally hooked to *very* low-wattage generators on land (you can see the cables running ashore near the Taman Sari Bali Cottages). What had been a theory became a reality. The low current stimulated limestone formation on the cages which in turn quickly grew new coral. All told, Pemuteran's small bay is getting new coral at five to six times the rate it would take to grow naturally.

The results are win-win all around. Locals and visitors are happy and so are the reefs.

For much more on Pemuteran's reef project follow the links at www.balitamansari.com/reef.htm.

Sights & Activities

The extensive coral reefs are about 3km offshore. Coral that's closer in is being restored as part of a unique project (see the boxed text, above). Diving and snorkelling on the local reefs is universally popular.

Pemuteran is home to the non-profit Reef Seen Turtle Project, run by the Australian-owned **Reef Seen Aquatics** (☎ 93001; www .reefseen.com). Turtle eggs and small turtles purchased from locals are looked after here until they're ready for ocean release. More than 7000 turtles have been released since 1994. You can visit the small hatchery and see Boomer, the turtle who wouldn't leave, and make a donation to sponsor and release a tiny turtle. It's just off the main road east of Pondok Sari.

Reef Seen also offers diving, boat cruises and horse riding. A PADI introductory dive costs US$60 and dives at Pemuteran/Pulau Menjangan are US$60/70 for two dives. Sunset and sunrise cruises and glass-bottomed boat trips (per person 200,000Rp) are offered. Horse-riding treks pass through the local villages and beaches (from 300,000Rp for two hours). Accommodation is also available (right).

Easy Divers (☎ 94736; www.easy-divers.eu) comes well recommended and the founder, Dusan Repic, has befriended many a diver new to Bali. Prices are similar to Reef Seen. It is on the main road near the Taman Sari and Pondok Sari hotels.

Pemuteran's hotels all have their own dive operations.

Sleeping & Eating

Pemuteran has many mellow midrange and top-end choices, all located on the bay, which has nice sand and is good for swimming. There are small warung along the main drag, otherwise all the hotels have good, mostly modestly priced, restaurants. You can wander between them along the beach debating which one to choose.

Some of the hotels are accessed directly off the main road, others are off of a small road the follows the west side of the bay.

Jubawa Home Stay (☎ 94745; r 180,000-270,000Rp; 🔀) Not far from the Matahari on the south (hill) side of the road, this clean hotel is a good budget choice. The best of the 12 rooms have hot water and air-con. The café serves Balinese and Thai food and there is a popular bar.

Reef Seen (☎ 93001; www.reefseen.com; r 450,000Rp; 🔀) Five solid Balinese-style brick bungalows have air-con and open-air bathrooms with showers. This is a well-regarded dive centre (see left) and it's located on the small bay. The turtles are a diverting attraction.

Taman Sari Bali Cottages (☎ 93264; www.balitaman sari.com; bungalows US$50-200; 🔀 🛢 🖳) Thirty-one rooms are set in gorgeous bungalows (some quite grand) that feature intricate carvings and traditional artwork inside and out. The open-air bathrooms inspire extended ablutions. Most rooms are under US$100 – those over are quite grand. It's located on a long stretch of quiet beach on the bay. It's also part of the reef restoration project (see the boxed text, opposite).

Pondok Sari (☎ 92337; www.pondoksari.com; r US$50-160; ❄ ⚤) There are 30 rooms here set in densely-planted gardens that assure privacy. The pool is down by the beach; the café has sweet water views through the trees. Traditional Balinese details abound; the bathrooms are open-air and are a calling card for the stone-carvers. Deluxe units have elaborate stone tubs among other details. The resort is just off the main road.

Taman Selini Beach Bungalows (☎ 94746; www .tamanselini.com; r US$90-200; ❄ ⚤) The 11 bungalows recall an older, refined Bali, from the quaint thatched roofs down to the antique carved doors and detailed stonework. Rooms, which open onto a small garden area, have four-poster beds and large outdoor bathrooms. The outdoor daybeds can be addictive. It's immediately east of Pondok Sari, on the beach and right off the main road.

Matahari Beach Resort & Spa (☎ 92312; www .matahari-beach-resort.com; r US$240-600; ❄ ⚤ ☐) One of Bali's best hotels, the Matahari is an elegant place in an isolated location on the eastern outskirts of Pemuteran (just off the main road). Bungalow-style rooms open onto private gardens; details are a regal version of traditional Balinese. The large pool overlooks a black-sand beach. The spa is like a grand water palace; it's open to non-guests.

Puri Ganesha Villas (☎ 94766; www.puriganesha bali.com; villas US$400-500; ❄ ⚤ ☐) Four two-storey villas on sweeping grounds at the west end of the bay are the basics at Puri Ganesha. Ahh, but the details: each has a unique style that mixes antiques with silks and relaxed casual comfort. Outside the air-con bedrooms, life is in the open air, including your time in your private pool. You can dine in the small restaurant or in your villa; the spa is lavish.

Getting There & Away

Pemuteran is served by any of the buses and bemo on the Gilimanuk–Lovina run. Labuhan Lalang (p282) and Taman Nasional Bali Barat are 12km west. It's a three- to four-hour drive from South Bali, either over the hills or around the west coast.

West Bali

Like Heather Graham – or Brazil – West Bali always seems to be on the verge of hitting it big. But like the sunsets that paint the shore a nightly flamingo pink, the date for this success is ever-receding.

A new airport, vast tourist developments, a new highway and more are often discussed. In the meantime, the waves keep pounding the rocky shore, surfers keep hitting the breaks at funky beaches like Balian and Medewi, and everybody else just gets on with business. The tidy town of Tabanan is at the apex of Bali's *subak*, the system of irrigation that ensures everybody gets a fair share of the water. The verdant, green fields all around attest to its success.

Some of Bali's most sacred sites are here, from the ever-thronged Pura Tanah Lot to the Unesco-nominated Pura Taman Ayun and on to the wonderful isolation of Pura Rambut Siwi. In between you can cruise along beside coursing streams on rural roads with bamboo arching overhead and fruit piling up below.

But the real star of the under-achieving west is Taman Nasional Bali Barat (West Bali National Park), the only protected place of its kind on the island. Few who dive or snorkel the rich and pristine waters around Pulau Menjangan forget the experience. Others go for the challenge and trek through the savannah flats, mangroves and hillside jungles.

Amid it all you'll find isolated resorts and hideaway inns. Soon you'll hope West Bali doesn't change at all.

HIGHLIGHTS

- Plunging into the depths at Bali's renowned dive spot, **Pulau Menjangan** (p280)
- Nailing the long left break at **Medewi Beach** (p276)
- Finding your own corner of serenity at **Pura Taman Ayun** (opposite)
- Discovering, by foot or boat, Bali's national park, **Taman Nasional Bali Barat** (p280)
- Joining the beach bums at **Balian Beach** (p276)

PURA TANAH LOT

☎ 0361

One of the most popular day trips from South Bali, **Pura Tanah Lot** (adult/child 10,000/5000Rp, car park 5000Rp) is the most visited and photographed temple in Bali. It's an obligatory stop, especially at sunset, and it is very commercialised. It has all the authenticity of a stage set – even the tower of rock that the temple sits upon is an artful reconstruction (the entire structure was crumbling). Over one-third of the rock you see is artificial.

For the Balinese, Pura Tanah Lot is one of the most important and venerated sea temples (p51). Like Pura Luhur Ulu Watu, at the tip of the southern Bukit Peninsula, and Pura Rambut Siwi to the west, it is closely associated with the Majapahit priest, Nirartha. It's said that each of the 'sea temples' was intended to be within sight of the next, so they formed a chain along Bali's southwestern coast – from Pura Tanah Lot you can usually see the cliff-top site of Pura Ulu Watu far to the south, and the long sweep of sea shore west to Perancak, near Negara.

But at Tanah Lot itself you may just see from one vendor to the next. To reach the temple, a walkway runs through a sideshow of souvenir shops down to the sea. To ease the task of making purchases, there is an ATM.

Why not skip it? Because it is an important spiritual site, and if you arrive before noon you'll beat the crowds and the vendors will still be asleep. Besides, you can see the sunset from many other places – like a beachfront bar south towards Kuta.

You can walk over to the temple itself at low tide, but non-Balinese people are not allowed to enter. One other thing: local legend has it that if you bring a partner to Tanah Lot before marriage, you will end up as split as the temple. Let that be a warning – or an inducement.

Since you really want to just drop in on Tanah Lot, there's no need to worry about food or drink – although there's no shortage of warung (food stalls). You won't be able to miss the looming Le Meridien Nirwana resort with its water-sucking golf course. It has been controversial since the day it was built as many feel it shows the temple disrespect (it's higher).

For info about respecting traditions and acting appropriately while visiting temples, see p348.

Getting There & Away

Coming from South Bali with your own transport, take the coastal road west from Kerobokan, north of Seminyak, and follow the signs or the traffic. From other parts of Bali, turn off the Denpasar–Gilimanuk road near Kediri and follow the signs. During the pre- and post-sunset rush, traffic is awful.

By bemo (small minibus), go from Denpasar's Ubung terminal to Tanah Lot (7000Rp) via Kediri, noting that bemo stop running by nightfall.

KAPAL

About 10km north of Denpasar, Kapal is the garden-feature and temple doodad centre of Bali. If you need a polychromatic tiger or other decorative critter (we saw a pink beaver) rendered in colours not found in nature, then this your place! (Although shipping might be a bitch.) This is on the main road to the west, so it might be worth getting out of the traffic just to walk with the animals.

The most important temple in the area is **Pura Sadat**. It was possibly built in the 12th century, then damaged in an earthquake early in the 20th century and subsequently restored after WWII.

Throughout this part of Bali you will see peanuts and corn growing in rotation with rice. Bananas and other fruits grow wild alongside the roads.

PURA TAMAN AYUN

The huge state temple of **Pura Taman Ayun** (adult/child 5000/2500Rp; ☯ 8am-6pm), surrounded by a wide, elegant moat, was the main temple of the Mengwi kingdom, which survived until 1891, when it was conquered by the neighbouring kingdoms of Tabanan and Badung. The large, spacious temple was built in 1634 and extensively renovated in 1937. It's a lovely place to wander around and its size means you can get away from speed-obsessed group-tour mobs ('Back on the bus!'). The first courtyard is a large, open, grassy expanse and the inner courtyard has a multitude of *meru* (multiroofed shrines).

Owing to its heritage, the temple has been nominated for Unesco recognition.

Getting There & Away

Any bemo running between Denpasar (Ubung terminal) and Bedugul or Singaraja can drop you off at the roundabout in Mengwi, where

WEST BALI

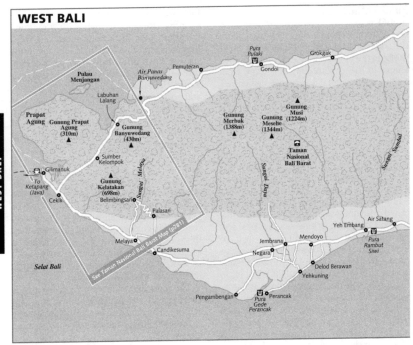

signs indicate the road (250m) to the temple. Pura Taman Ayun is a stop-off on many organised tourist tours.

BELAYU

Traditional *songket* (silver- or gold-threaded cloth) sarongs are intricately woven with gold threads. These are for ceremonial use only and not for everyday wear. You'll find them in the small village of Belayu (or Blayu), 3km north of Mengwi.

MARGA

Between the walls of traditional family compounds in the village of Marga, there are some beautifully shaded roads – but this town wasn't always so peaceful. On 20 November 1946, a much larger and better-armed Dutch force, fighting to regain Bali as a colony after the departure of the Japanese, surrounded a force of 96 independence fighters. The outcome was similar to the *puputan* (warrior's fight to the death) of 40 years earlier – Ngurah Rai, who lead the resistance against the Dutch (and later had an airport named after him), and every one of his men,

was killed. There was, however, one important difference – this time the Dutch suffered heavy casualties as well, and this may have helped weaken their resolve to hang onto the rebellious colony.

The independence struggle is commemorated at the **Margarana** (admission 5000Rp; ☼ 9am-5pm), northwest of Marga village. Tourists seldom visit, but every Balinese schoolchild comes here at least once, and a ceremony is held annually on 20 November. In a large compound stands a 17m-high pillar, and nearby there's a **museum** with a few photos, homemade weapons and other artefacts from the conflict. Behind is a smaller compound with 1372 small stone memorials to those who gave their lives for the cause of independence – they're headstone markers in a military cemetery, though bodies are not actually buried here. Each memorial has a symbol indicating the hero's religion, mostly the Hindu swastika, but also Islamic crescent moons and even a few Christian crosses. Look for the memorials to 11 Japanese who stayed on after WWII and fought with the Balinese against the Dutch.

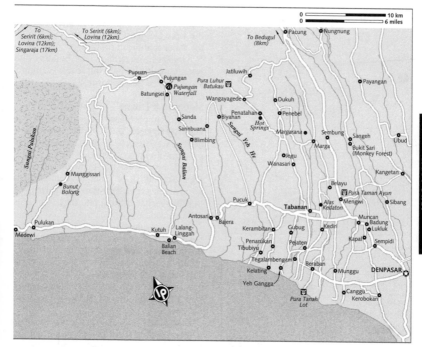

Getting There & Away

Even with your own transport it's easy to get lost finding Marga and the memorial, so, as always, ask directions. You can easily combine this with a tour of the amazing Jatiluwih rice terraces (p252).

SANGEH

If you love monkeys, you'll love the 14-hectare monkey forest of **Bukit Sari**. But if you're put off by the thieving, copulating little buggers, than perhaps you should give it a miss. Actually we're among the former, and the monkeys here are all rather workmanlike: they eat three square meals a day (breakfast is bananas, lunch is cassava and dinner is rice – a very Balinese diet, in fact), and when tourists leave they relax after a day of high jinks ('Those glasses you stole make you look fat.').

Also noteworthy, but not as exciting, are a rare grove of **nutmeg trees** in the monkey forest and a **temple**, Pura Bukit Sari, with an interesting old Garuda (mythical man-bird) statue. This place is touristy, but the forest is cool, green and shady. The souvenir sellers are restricted to certain areas, hence easy to avoid.

Getting There & Away

Most people visit on an organised tour or drive themselves; it's about 20km north of Denpasar.

TABANAN

☎ 0361

A renowned centre for dancing and gamelan playing, Tabanan, like most regional capitals in Bali, is a large, well-organised place. Mario, the renowned dancer of the pre-war period, hailed from Tabanan. His greatest achievement was to perfect the Kebyar dance. He is featured in Miguel Covarrubias' classic book, *Island of Bali*. Nowadays it's hard for visitors to find performances here on a regular basis, but you can enjoy the vibrant rice fields and related museum.

Orientation & Information

The main road thankfully bypasses the centre, where you'll find ATMs, a hospital, a **police station** (☎ 91210), a post office and solid blocks of shops. The road to Pura Luhur Batukau and the amazing rice terraces of Jatiluwih (p252) heads north from the centre.

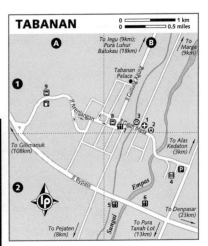

INFORMATION
Hospital...1 B1
Police Station...2 B1
Post Office...3 B1

SIGHTS & ACTIVITIES
Mandala Mathika Subak.................................4 B2

EATING 🍴
Babi Guling Stall..5 B2
Hardy's...6 B2
Market..7 B1
Night Market...(see 6)

TRANSPORT
Bemo Terminal..8 B1
Bus Terminal..9 A1

Sights

Playing a critical role in rural Bali life, the *subak* is a village association that deals with water, water rights and irrigation. The **Mandala Mathika Subak** (☎ 810315; Jl Raya Kediri; admission 5000Rp; ⏱ 7am-4.30pm) is quite a large complex devoted to Tabanan's *subak* organisations. Within this is the **Subak Museum** with displays about the irrigation and cultivation of rice and the intricate social systems that govern it. The staff here are very sweet and will show you around; the exhibits themselves could use a little love.

With water passing through many, many scores of rice fields before it drains away for good, there is always the chance that growers near the source would be water-rich while those at the bottom would be selling carved wooden critters at Tanah Lot. Regulating a system that apportions a fair share to every-

one is a model of mutual cooperation and an insight into the Balinese character. (One of the strategies used is to put the last guy on the water channel in control.)

Exhibits are housed in a large building with water coursing by right out front. For more, see the boxed text, opposite.

Sleeping & Eating

You can sample village life as part of the **Bali Homestay Program** (☎ 0817 067 1788; www.bali-homestay.com; Jegu, Penebel; s/d US$10/20), an innovative program that places travellers in the homes of residents of the rice-growing village of Jegu, 9km north of Tabanan. Guests (who normally stay at least three nights) participate in activities like making offerings. All meals are included.

There are plenty of basic warung in the town centre as well as at the bustling regional market; a tasty **night market** (⏱ 5pm-midnight) sets up on the south side. Out on the main road, **Babi Guling Stall** (dishes 5000-10,000Rp; ⏱ 7am-7pm) has batches of fresh-roasted seasoned young pork throughout the day. It's a savoury treat Balinese love.

Hardy's (☎ 819850), also on the main road, is a huge, modern supermarket with groceries and sundries. Good if you're heading to one of the surf sites in the west.

Getting There & Away

All bemo and buses between Denpasar (Ubung terminal) and Gilimanuk stop at the terminal at the western end of Tabanan (7000Rp). The bemo terminal in the town centre only has transport to nearby villages. If you're driving, note that most main streets are one way, with traffic moving in a clockwise direction around the central blocks.

SOUTH OF TABANAN

Driving in the southern part of Tabanan district takes you though many charming villages and past a lot of vigorously growing rice. The fields are revered by many as the most productive in Bali.

Just south of Tabanan, **Kediri** has Pasar Hewan, one of Bali's busiest cattle markets. About 10km south of Tabanan is **Pejaten**, a centre for the production of traditional pottery, including elaborate ornamental roof tiles. Porcelain clay objects, which are made purely for decorative use, can be seen in a few workshops in the village. Check out the small showroom of **CV Keramik Pejaten** (☎ 0361-831997), one of several local producers. The trademark pale-green pieces are lovely, and when you see the prices, you'll at least buy a toad.

A little west of Tabanan, a road goes 8km south via Gubug to the secluded coast at **Yeh Gangga**, where there are some good accommodation choices and **Island Horse** (☎ 0361-730218; www.baliislandhorse.com; rides from US$50), which offers horse rides along the long flat beach and surrounding countryside.

The next road west from Tabanan turns down to the coast via **Kerambitan**, a village noted for its dance troupe and musicians who perform across the south and Ubud. Banyan trees shade beautiful old buildings, including two 17th-century palaces. **Puri Anyar Kerambitan** accepts guests (see right) and is an attraction in itself with a vast shambolic compound filled with antiques and populated by genial characters. The other palace, **Pura Agung Kerambitan**, is tidy and dull.

South of Kerambitan, you will pass through **Penarukan**, known for its stone carvers and woodcarvers, and also its dancers. Continue to the coast, where you'll find the beach at **Kelating** wide, black and usually deserted.

About 4km from southern Kerambitan is **Tibubiyu**. For a gorgeous drive through huge bamboo, fruit trees, rice paddies and more, take the scenic road northwest from Kerambitan to the main Tabanan–Gilimanuk road.

Sleeping

Bali Wisata Bungalows (☎ 0361-7443561; www.bali wisatabungalows.com; Yeh Gangga; bungalows 200,000-400,000Rp; 🔊) West of Tabanan and on the coast at Yeh Gangga, this attractive accommodation has excellent views in a superb setting on 15km of rock and black-sand beach. The cheapest of the 12 rooms have cold water; the best have dramatic oceanfront vistas. It's family-run, and there's nothing fancy here.

Puri Anyar Kerambitan (☎ 0361-812668; giribali @yahoo.co.id; r from 300,000Rp; 🔊) Join Anak Agung, the leader of the royal family that lives sit-com style in this intriguing compound. Anak will teach you about kite culture while his son the prince will offer to paint you or do a figure study. Children wandering about provide cute punchlines. The four rooms are filled with royal antiques and vary in tidiness. At your command, Balinese feasts and cultural shows fit for a king will be arranged.

NORTH OF TABANAN

The area north of Tabanan is good to travel around with your own transport. There are some strictly B-level attractions; the real appeal here is just driving the fecund back roads where the bamboo arches templelike over the road.

About 9km north of Tabanan the road reaches a fork. The left road goes to Pura Luhur Batukau, via the **hot springs** at Penatahan. Here you'll find the simple **Yeh Panas Resort** (☎ 0361-262356; espa_yehpanes@telkom .net; r from 250,000Rp; 🔊), 4km from the fork, by Sungai Yeh He (Yeh He River). The resort has a small, cool pool, which non-guests can enjoy for 30,000Rp. Another pool has water from the hot springs and costs 150,000Rp. Rooms are basic, you may just want to literally dip in…

INTERVIEW WITH A RICE FARMER

Made Suarnata is a rice farmer in the tiny village of Tegalambengam south of Tabanan. A place he says is 'the best place for growing rice in Bali. You see the green fields everywhere you look. My whole family lives near each other as we've always done for hundreds of years.'

Recent decades have seen more change in a rice-farmer's life than during all the previous centuries, he adds. 'We used to only get two crops of rice per year and all the work was by hand, unless you could rent a cow to help with the ploughing. Now we have hybrid rice that yields more and allows us a third crop each year.'

'When I was little, rice was special, something you added to the daily diet of casaba. Now you can have rice for every meal and we have money for things like meat and better houses.'

As villas creep north and west from Canggu, covering once-productive rice fields, Made says he tries to keep things in balance. 'It is sad to see rice fields disappear but the farmers need money. They never had any at all.'

ANTOSARI & BAJERA

At Antosari, the main road takes a sharp turn south to the welcoming breezes of the ocean. Turn north and you enjoy a scenic drive to North Bali; see the boxed text, p253. Nearby Bajera is renowned for the quality of its market and warung. The *nasi campur* is much vaunted. A narrow road goes north up the river valley and eventually reaches tiny villages on the side of Gunung Batukau with good places to stay. See p252 for details.

BALIAN BEACH & LALANG-LINGGAH
☎ 0361

Some 10km west of Antosari is Lalang-Linggah. Here a road (toll 2000Rp) leads 800m to the surf breaks near the mouth of Sungai Balian (Balian River) and the ever-more-popular scene at Balian Beach.

A rolling area of dunes and knolls overlooks the pounding surf here, which predictably is popular with surfers (see p94 for details). A sort of critical mass of villas and beach accommodation has appeared here, and you can wander about between a few cafés and join other travellers for a beer and sunset.

Sleeping & Eating

All of the places listed below are close together. The way things are going, there will be more choices by the time you arrive. Warung and simple cafés mean a bottle of Bintang is never more than one minute away.

Made's Homestay (☎ 0812 396 3335; r 100,000Rp) Three basic bungalow-style units are surrounded by banana trees back from the beach. The rooms are basic, clean, large enough to hold numerous surfboards and have cold-water showers.

Balian Segara Homestay (☎ 0819 1645 6147; r 150,000-200,000Rp) Right down by the grey-sand beach, the three simple, clean cottages are in a row, although views are a little obscured by dunes. The top unit has hot water. Try to overlook the marketing materials, which show the perils of Photoshop: huge waves break right over the homestay.

Kubu Balian Beach (☎ 0361-485094; r 220,000Rp) You might decide to stay a spell at these four apartments based in two villas at the start of the road to Gajah Mina hotel. The large units are cheap for what you get: full kitchens, satellite TV, huge porches, stylish furniture and more. Stay on the upper level and you can see the sea through the palms.

Pondok Pisces (☎ 0812 360 0680; www.pondokpisces bali.com; r 285,000-650,000Rp) You can certainly hear the sea, even if you can't see it, at this tropical fantasy of thatched cottages and flower-filled gardens. The five rooms have hot-water showers, fans and large patios. A large beach house goes for the top rate. That blockbuster you missed five years ago awaits in the DVD library. The café has grilled seafood.

Gajah Mina (☎ 0812 381 1630; www.gajahminaresort .com; bungalows US$85-145; ☒ ☒) Designed by the French architect-owner, this eight-unit boutique hotel is close to the ocean. The private, walled bungalows march out to a dramatic outcrop of stone surrounded by surf. The grounds are vast and there are little trails for wandering and pavilions for relaxing. The restaurant overlooks its own little bowl of rice terraces.

JEMBRANA COAST

About 34km west of Tabanan you cross into Bali's most sparsely populated district, Jembrana. The main road follows the south coast most of the way to Negara. There's some beautiful scenery, but little tourist development along the way, with the exception of the surfing action at Medewi. At Pulukan you can turn north and enjoy a remote and scenic drive to North Bali; see the boxed text, p253.

Medewi
☎ 0365

The surf scene at Medewi is centred on one short lane from the road down to the waves. There are a couple of places aimed at surfers and not much else. Nearby along the coast are a few more inns scattered amid the rice fields.

On the main road, a large sign points down the paved road (200m) to the surfing mecca of Pantai Medewi and its *long* left-hand wave. The 'beach' is a stretch of huge, smooth grey rocks interspersed among round black pebbles. Think of it as free reflexology. It's a placid place where cattle graze by the shore, paying no heed to the many people watching the action out on the water. A few local guys have ding-repair and board-rental huts.

SLEEPING & EATING

You'll find accommodation along the main lane to the surf break and down other lanes about 2km east. For a casual meal, some of the finest fare is freshly stir-fried and served up at a cart right by the beach/rocks.

Mai Malu Restaurant & Guesthouse (☎ 43897; s/d 70,000/90,000Rp) Near the highway on the Medewi side road, Mai Malu is a popular (and almost the only) hang-out, serving crowd-pleasing pizza, burgers and Indonesian meals in its modern, breezy upstairs eating area. Eight cold-water rooms have the basics plus fans.

ourpick Homestay CSB (☎ 0813 3866 7288; Pulukan; r 70,000-150,000Rp; 🔀) Some 2km east of the Medewi surf break at Pulukan, look for signs along the main road. Venture 300m down a track and you'll find a great family with the beginnings of an empire. The best of the 10 simply furnished rooms have air-con, hot water and balconies with views that put anything in South Bali to shame. The coast and churning surf curve to the east, backed by jade-green rice fields and rows of palm trees. It's rather idyllic.

Gede Homestay II (☎ 0812 397 6668; Pulukan; r 80,000Rp) At midday it is like off-duty time at Looney Tunes: the dogs, cats, birds and cocks are all sharing the same space, blissfully asleep. You'll share the mood at this very quiet collection of simple bungalows amid rice fields. It's 100m past Homestay CSB.

Medewi Beach Cottages (☎ 40029; r US$45-75; 🔀 🏊) A large pool anchors 27 modern, comfortable rooms (with satellite TV) scattered about nice gardens right down by the surf break. The one off-note: security measures obstruct what should be a good view. Across the lane there's a lively two-storey building ostensibly called 'the party wing' with seven second-rate cold-water rooms (US$10) aimed at surfers.

Puri Dajuma Cottages (☎ 43955; www.dajuma.com; Pulukan; cottage from US$100; 🔀 🏊 💻) Coming from the east, you won't be able to miss this seaside resort, thanks to its prolific signage. Happily, the 18 cottages actually live up to the billing. Each has a private garden, ocean view and a walled outdoor bathroom. The Medewi break is 2km west.

Pura Rambut Siwi

Picturesquely situated on a clifftop overlooking a long, wide stretch of black-sand beach, this superb temple shaded by flowering frangipani trees is one of the important sea temples of West Bali. Like Pura Tanah Lot and Pura Ulu Watu, it was established in the 16th century by the priest **Nirartha**, who had a good eye for ocean

scenery. Legend has it that when Nirartha first came here, he donated some of his hair to the local villagers. The hair is now kept in a box buried in this temple, the name of which means 'Worship of the Hair'. Unlike Tanah Lot, it remains a peaceful and little-visited place.

The caretaker rents sarongs for 2000Rp and is happy to show you around the temple and down to the beach. He then opens the guestbook and requests a donation – a suitable sum is about 10,000Rp (regardless of the much higher amounts attributed to previous visitors). A path along the cliff leads to a staircase down to a small and even older temple, **Pura Penataran**.

GETTING THERE & AWAY

The temple is between Air Satang and Yeh Embang, at the end of a 300m side road. You'll find it's well signposted, but look for the turn-off near a cluster of warung on the main road. Any of the regular bemo and buses between Denpasar and Gilimanuk will stop at the turn-off.

NEGARA
☎ 0365

Set amid the broad and fertile flatlands between the mountains and ocean, Negara is a prosperous little town, and a useful pit stop. Although it's a district capital, there's not much to see. The town springs to life when the famous bull races (p278) are held nearby. Services include a **clinic** (Jl Arjuna). Several banks on the main commercial road (south of the Tabanan–Gilimanuk road), Jl Ngurah Rai, change money and have international ATMs.

Eating

Numerous choices for meals line Jl Ngurah Rai. There are assorted warung in the market area at the traffic circle with Jl Pahlawan.

Warung Lesehan (Jl Ngurah Rai; mains from 4000Rp) A simple open-air place across from Hardy's has excellent fried fish and chicken redolent with local spices.

Depot Natalia (☎ 42669; Jl Ngurah Rai 107; dishes 5000-20,000Rp) In front of Hotel Wira Pada, the Depot is the stop for a sit-down Indonesian meal.

Hardy's Supermarket (☎ 40709; Jl Ngurah Rai; 🔀) Hardy's has a popular albeit cacophonous indoor food court serving fresh, cheap chow. Dishes are generally under 4000Rp. This large supermarket has the best selection of goods in western Bali.

WEST BALI (sidebar)

BULL RACES

This part of Bali is famous for the bull races, known as *mekepung,* which culminate in the Bupati Cup in Negara in early August. The racing animals are actually the normally docile water buffalo, which charge down a 2km stretch of road or beach pulling tiny chariots. Gaily-clad riders stand or kneel on top of the chariots forcing the bullocks on, sometimes by twisting their tails to make them follow the curve of the makeshift racetrack. The winner, however, is not necessarily first past the post. Style also plays a part and points are awarded for the most elegant runner. Gambling is not legal in Bali, but…

Important races are held during the dry season, from July to October. Occasional races are set up for tourist groups at a park in Perancak on the coast, and minor races and practices are held at several Perancak and other sites on Sunday mornings, including Delod Berawan and Yeh Embang. Check with your hotel or the **Jembrana Government Tourist Office** (☎ 0365-41210, ext 224) for details.

Getting There & Away

Most bemo and minibuses from Denpasar (Ubung terminal) to Gilimanuk drop you in Negara (20,000Rp).

AROUND NEGARA

At the southern fringe of Negara, **Loloan Timur** is a largely Bugis community (originally from Sulawesi) that retains 300-year-old traditions. Look for a few distinctive houses on stilts, some decorated with wooden fretwork.

To reach **Delod Berawan**, turn off the main Gilimanuk–Denpasar road at Mendoyo and go south to the coast, which has a black-sand beach and irregular surf. You can see bull-race practices Sunday mornings at the nearby football field.

Perancak is the site of Nirartha's arrival in Bali in 1546, commemorated by a limestone temple, **Pura Gede Perancak**. Bull races are run at **Taman Wisata Perancak** (☎ 0365-42173), and Balinese buffets are sometimes staged for organised tours from South Bali. If you're travelling independently, give the park a ring before you go there. In Perancak, ignore the sad little zoo and go for a walk along the fishing harbour.

Once capital of the region, **Jembrana** is the centre of the *gamelan jegog,* a gamelan using huge bamboo instruments that produce a low-pitched, resonant sound. Performances often feature gamelan groups engaging in musical contest. To hear them in action, time your arrival with a local festival, or ask in Negara where you might find a group practising.

BELIMBINGSARI & PALASARI

Two fascinating religious towns north of the main road are reason enough for a detour.

Christian evangelism in Bali was discouraged by the secular Dutch, but sporadic missionary activity resulted in a number of converts, many of whom were rejected by their own communities. In 1939 they were encouraged to resettle in Christian communities in the wilds of West Bali.

Palasari is home to a Catholic community, which boasts a huge church largely made from white stone and set on a large town square. It is really rather peaceful, and with the gently waving palms it feels like old missionary Hawaii rather than Hindu Bali. The church does show Balinese touches in the spires, which resemble the *meru* (multiroofed shrine) in a Hindu temple, and features a facade with the same shape as a temple gate.

Nearby **Belimbingsari** was established as a Protestant community, and now has the largest Protestant church in Bali, although it doesn't reach for the heavens the way the church does in Palasari. Still, it's an amazing structure, with features rendered in a distinctly Balinese style – in place of a church bell there's a *kulkul* (hollow tree-trunk warning drum) like those in a Hindu temple. The entrance is through an *aling aling*–style (guard wall) gate, and the attractive carved angels look very Balinese. Go on Sunday to see inside.

For a near-religious experience you might consider staying at **Taman Wana Villas & Spa** (☎ 0365-40970; www.bali-tamanwana-villas.com; Palasari; r US$135-300; 🖭 🖭), a striking 2km drive through a jungle past the Palasari church. This architecturally stunning boutique resort has 27 rooms in unusual round structures. Posh only starts to describe the luxuries at this cloistered refuge. Views are panoramic; get one of the rice fields.

The two villages are north of the main road, and the best way to see them is on a loop with your own transport. About 17km west from Negara, look for signs for the Taman Wana Villas. Follow these for 6.1km to Palasari. From the west, look for a turn for Belimbingsari, some 20km southeast of Cekik. A good road leads to the village. Between the two towns, only divine intervention will allow you to tackle the thicket of narrow but passable lanes unaided. Fortunately directional help is readily at hand.

CEKIK

At this junction one road continues west to Gilimanuk and another heads northeast towards North Bali. All buses and bemo to and from Gilimanuk pass through Cekik.

Archaeological excavations here during the 1960s yielded the oldest evidence of human life in Bali. Finds include burial mounds with funerary offerings, bronze jewellery, axes, adzes and earthenware vessels from around 1000 BC, give or take a few centuries. Look for some of this in the Museum Situs Purbakala Gilimanuk (below).

On the southern side of the junction, the pagoda-like structure with a spiral stairway around the outside is a **war memorial**. The memorial commemorates the landing of independence forces in Bali to oppose the Dutch, who were trying to reassert control of Indonesia after WWII.

Cekik is home to the **park headquarters** (☎ 0365-61060; ⏰ 7am-5pm) of the Taman Nasional Bali Barat (p280).

GILIMANUK
☎ 0365

Gilimanuk is the terminus for ferries that shuttle back and forth across the narrow strait to Java. Most travellers to or from Java can get an onward ferry or bus straight away, and won't hang around. The museum is the only attraction – the town is really a place one passes through quickly. It has the closest accommodation to the national park if you want to start a trek early.

Information

There is a Bank BDP Bali (without ATM) on Jl Raya, a post office, a police station and wartel (public telephone office), but not many shops or other services.

Sights

This part of Bali has been occupied for thousands of years. The **Museum Situs Purbakala**

Gilimanuk (☎ 61328; donation 5000Rp; ⏰ 8am-4pm Mon-Fri) is centred on a family of skeletons, thought to be 4000 years old, which were found locally in 2004. The museum is 500m east of the ferry port.

Stop anywhere along the north shore of town to see the huge clash of waves and currents in the strait. It's dramatic and a good reason *not* to have that dodgy curry dish if you're about to board a ferry.

Sleeping

Good sleeping choices are thin on the ground. There's nothing worthwhile close to the ferry terminal, but things improve as you go southeast. The best food is at the bus station warung.

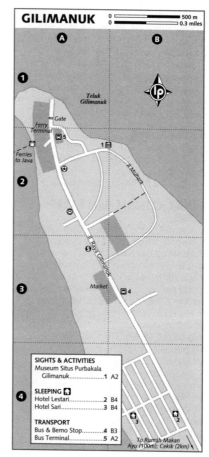

SIGHTS & ACTIVITIES	
Museum Situs Purbakala Gilimanuk	1 A2
SLEEPING 🏠	
Hotel Lestari	2 B4
Hotel Sari	3 B4
TRANSPORT	
Bus & Bemo Stop	4 B3
Bus Terminal	5 A2

WEST BALI

Hotel Lestari (☎ 61504; r 65,000-325,000Rp; ❄) From fan-cooled singles to air-con suites you have your choice of basic accommodation at this 21-room place, which feels strangely suburban. It has a café.

Hotel Sari (☎ 61264; r 100,000Rp, with air-con 175,000Rp; ❄) Among the best of the dubious lot of hotels. On the ocean side of Jl Raya, it has 22 basic rooms, including some where you sleep with your car; the karaoke bar next door can be invasive.

Getting There & Away

Frequent buses hurtle along the main road between Gilimanuk's huge bus depot and Denpasar's Ubung terminal (25,000Rp, two to three hours), or along the north-coast road to Singaraja (22,000Rp).

To get to and from Ketapang on Java (30 minutes), car ferries (adult/child 6000/4500Rp, car and driver 95,000Rp, motorbike 31,000Rp) run around the clock.

If you have wheels, watch out for the numerous police checkpoints around the terminal where commas are counted and the number of dots on i's checked on vehicle documents. Freelance 'fines' are common.

Getting Around

At the ferry, bemo and bus terminals, you can get an *ojek* (motorcycle that takes passengers), car with driver or even a *dokar* (pony cart) for a negotiable 10,000Rp around town.

TAMAN NASIONAL BALI BARAT

☎ 0365

Call it nature's symphony. Most visitors to Bali's only national park, Taman Nasional Bali Barat (West Bali National Park), are struck by the mellifluous sounds from myriad birds with a nice riff from the various rustling trees.

The park covers 19,000 hectares of the western tip of Bali. An additional 55,000 hectares is protected in the national park extension, as well as almost 7000 hectares of coral reef and coastal waters. Together this represents a significant commitment to conservation on an island as densely populated as Bali.

It's a place where you can hike through forests, enjoy the island's best diving at Pulau Menjangan and explore coastal mangroves.

Although you may imagine dense jungle, most of the natural vegetation in the park is not tropical rainforest, which requires rain year-round, but rather coastal savannah, with deciduous trees that become bare in the dry season. The southern slopes receive more regular rainfall, and so have more tropical vegetation, while the coastal lowlands have extensive mangroves.

There are more than 200 species of plants growing in the park. Local fauna includes black monkeys, leaf monkeys and macaques (seen in the afternoon along the main road near Sumber Kelompok); rusa, barking, sambar, Java and mouse deer *(muncak)*; and some wild pigs, squirrels, buffalo, iguanas, pythons and green snakes. There were once tigers, but the last confirmed sighting was in 1937 – and that one was shot. The bird life is prolific, with many of Bali's 300 species found here, including the possibly extinct Bali starling (p282). For more on the park's wildlife, see p80.

Just getting off the road a bit on one of the many trails transports you into the heart of nature. One discordant note: hikes in fuel prices have seen lots of vendors along the road selling firewood snatched from the forest.

Information

The **park headquarters** (☎ 61060; ☽ 7am-5pm) at Cekik displays a topographic model of the park area, and has a little information about plants and wildlife. The **Labuhan Lalang visitors centre** (☽ 7.30am-5pm) is in a hut located on the northern coast, where boats leave for Pulau Menjangan.

You can arrange trekking guides and permits at either place; however, there are always a few characters hanging around, and determining who is an actual park official can be like spotting a Bali starling: difficult.

The main roads to Gilimanuk go through the national park, but you don't have to pay an entrance fee just to drive through. If you want to stop and visit any of the sites within the park, you must buy a ticket (20,000Rp).

Sights & Activities

By land, by boat or by water, the park awaits exploration.

DIVING PULAU MENJANGAN

Bali's best-known dive area, Pulau Menjangan has a dozen superb dive sites. The diving is excellent – iconic tropical fish, soft corals, great visibility (usually), caves and a spectacular drop-off. One of the few complaints we've ever heard came from a reader who said that while snorkelling she kept getting water in her mouth because she was 'smiling so much'.

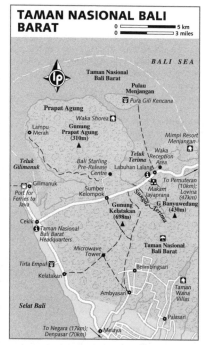

TAMAN NASIONAL BALI BARAT

trip, 400,000Rp) from the tiny dock at Labuhan Lalang (p282) just across the turquoise water from Menjangan. Warung here rent snorkelling gear (50,000Rp for four hours).

BOAT TRIPS

The best way to explore the mangroves of Teluk Gilimanuk (Gilimanuk Bay) or the west side of Prapat Agung is by chartering a boat (maximum of five people) for about 250,000Rp per boat per hour, including guide and entrance fees. You can arrange this at either of the park offices. This is the ideal way to see bird life, including kingfishers, Javanese herons and more.

TREKKING

All trekkers must be accompanied by an authorised guide. It's best to arrive the day before you want to trek, and make inquiries at the park offices in Cekik or Labuhan Lalang.

The set rates for guides in the park depend on the size of the group and the length of the trek – with one or two people it's 250,000Rp for one or two hours, 350,000Rp for three or four hours, and 600,000Rp for five to seven hours; with three to five people it's 350,000Rp, 450,000Rp or 800,000Rp. Food (a small lunchbox) is included but transport is extra and all the prices are negotiable. Early morning, say 6am, is the best time to start – it's cooler and you're more likely to see some wildlife.

Although you can try to customise your hike, the guides are most familiar with the four options listed here. If, once you're out, you have a good rapport with your guide, you might consider getting creative.

Gunung Kelatakan (Mt Kelatakan) From Sumber Kelompok, go up the mountain (698m), then down to the main road near Kelatakan village (six to seven hours). You may be able to get permission from park headquarters to stay overnight in the forest – if you don't have a tent, your guide can make a shelter from branches and leaves which will be an adventure in itself. Clear streams abound in the dense woods.

Kelatakan Starting at the village, climb to the microwave tower, go down to Ambyasari and get transport back to Cekik (four hours). This takes you through the forested southern sector of the park. From the tower you get a feel for what much of Bali looked like centuries ago.

Prapat Agung From Sumber Kelompok, you can trek around here, via the Bali Starling Pre-Release Centre and Batu Lucin – but only from about June to September, when the sensitive Bali starlings move further inland (allow at least five hours). It's easier and quicker to access

Lacy sea fans and various sponges provide both texture and myriad hiding spots for small fish that together form a colour chart for the sea. Few can resist the silly charms of parrotfish and clownfish. Among larger creatures, you may well see whales, whale sharks and manta rays gracefully swimming past.

Of the dozen of so named sites here, most are close to shore and suitable for snorkellers or diving novices. Some decent snorkelling spots are not far from the jetty – ask the boatman where to go. Venture a bit out, however, and the depths turn inky black as the shallows drop off in dramatic cliffs, a magnet for experienced divers looking for wall dives. The Anker Wreck, a mysterious sunken ship, challenges even experts.

This uninhabited island boasts what is thought to be Bali's oldest temple, **Pura Gili Kencana**, dating from the 14th century. You can walk around the island in about an hour and most people who take to the waters here take a break on the unblemished beaches.

The closest and most convenient dive operators are found at Pemuteran (p268). Snorkellers can arrange for a boat (four-hour

---

ON A WING & A PRAYER

Also known as the Bali myna, Rothschild's mynah, or locally as *jalak putih,* the Bali starling is perhaps Bali's only endemic bird (opinions differ – as other places are so close, who can tell?). It is striking white in colour, with black tips to the wings and tail, and a distinctive bright-blue mask. These natural good looks have caused the bird to be poached into virtual extinction. On the black market, Bali starlings command US$7000 or more.

The wild population (maybe in the park) has been estimated at a dozen or none. In captivity, however, there are hundreds if not thousands.

It's possible to visit the **Bali Starling Pre-Release Centre** (8am-3pm), which is a holdover from failed efforts to reintroduce the bird into the wild. Some 6km off the main road through the park, you can see starlings in cages for a negotiable 50,000Rp.

Near Ubud, the Bali Bird Park (p203) has large aviaries where you can see Bali starlings. The park was one of the major supporters of efforts to reintroduce the birds into the wild.

---

the peninsula by chartered boat from Gilimanuk where you will see the mangroves and drier savannah landscape.

Teluk Terima (Terima Bay) From a trail west of Labuhan Lalang, hike around the mangroves here. Then partially follow Sungai Terima (Terima River) into the hills and walk back down to the road along the steps at Makam Jayaprana. You might see grey macaques, deer and black monkeys. The most popular hike, it takes three to four hours.

MAKAM JAYAPRANA

A 20-minute walk up some stone stairs from the southern side of the road, a little west of Labuhan Lalang, will bring you to Jayaprana's grave. There are fine views to the north at the top. Jayaprana, the foster son of a 17th-century king, planned to marry Leyonsari, a beautiful girl of humble origins. The king, however, also fell in love with Leyonsari and had Jayaprana killed. Leyonsari learned the truth of Jayaprana's death in a dream, and killed herself rather than marry the king. This Romeo and Juliet story is a common theme in Balinese folklore, and the grave is regarded as sacred, even though the ill-fated couple were not gods.

Sleeping

Park visitors will want to spend the night as close to the park as possible in order to get an early start. Gilimanuk (p279) is closest and has basic choices. Much nicer are the luxury hotels in Labuhan Lalang (right). The best all-round choice is in Pemuteran (p268), 12km further east.

There is free camping at the park headquarters in Cekik (p279). The grounds are not pristine, but the bathroom is clean enough and the toilets decent. A gratuity to the staff is greatly appreciated. You'll need some sort of gear, however.

Getting There & Away

The national park is too far for a comfortable day trip from Ubud or South Bali, though many dive operators do it. Better to stay at one of the places suggested under Sleeping left.

If you don't have transport, any Gilimanuk-bound bus or bemo from North or West Bali can drop you at park headquarters at Cekik (those from North Bali can also drop you at the Labuhan Lalang visitors centre).

LABUHAN LALANG

To catch a boat to Pulau Menjangan (p280), head to the jetty at this small harbour in the national park. There's also a small park **visitors centre** (7.30am-5pm) in a hut on the northern coast, and there are warung and a pleasant beach 200m to the east. The resorts and dive shops of Pemuteran (p267) are 11km northeast.

Sleeping

The closest choices are quite luxurious and have diver operations for your days at Pulau Menjangan.

Mimpi Resort Menjangan (0362-94497, 0361-701070; www.mimpi.com; r US$80-120, villas US$180-350;) At isolated Banyuwedang, this 54-unit resort extends down to a small, mangrove-fringed, white-sand beach. The rooms have an unadorned monochromatic motif with open-air bathrooms. Hot springs feed communal pools and private tubs in the villas.

Waka Shorea (0362-94666; www.wakaexperience .com; r US$165, villas US$230;) Located in splendid isolation in the park, Waka Shorea is a 10-minute boat ride from the hotel's reception area 100m east of Labuhan Lalang. The 16 naturalistic units are hidden in the forest, with decks above the trees and a dreamy pool.

Lombok

If you're weary of Bali's crowds, traffic and beach braids, feel free to exhale and stretch out a little. You're on Lombok now, Bali's much less renowned neighbour to the east, an island rich in white-sand beaches, epic surf and spectacular diving. Oh, and you'll probably notice mighty Gunung Rinjani, Indonesia's second-highest volcano. Rivers and waterfalls gush down its fissured slopes and feed the island's crops (chiefly rice, cashews, coffee and tobacco), while its summit – complete with hot springs and a dazzling crater lake – lures international trekkers, local Balinese Hindu (who once colonised Lombok), and indigenous Sasak Muslim pilgrims hungry for divine blessings.

You won't want to miss the fabled Gili Islands – three exquisite droplets of white sand, sprinkled with coconut palms, surrounded by coral reefs teeming with marine life. On the islands, you'll nest in mod beach huts and feast on everything from humble *nasi campur* to the fresh daily selection of grilled seafood to melt-in-your-mouth sashimi. You can happily burn the daylight hours diving, snorkelling or chilling by the sea, and if you're nocturnal, you'll love Gili Trawangan's bar scene.

Lombok's dramatic south coast is a labyrinth of turquoise bays, white sand, world-class surf breaks, undulating tobacco fields and massive headlands. Given its drop-dead good looks, it's no surprise that it also happens to be the vortex of Lombok's on-rushing US$800 million metamorphosis.

Thankfully, that transformation will take some time. So get Zen, forget about the future and enjoy Lombok's sweet, spacious and wild present.

LOMBOK

HIGHLIGHTS

- Trekking the lush and majestic slopes of **Gunung Rinjani** (p314) to its sacred summit
- Plunging into the deep waters of the **Gili Islands** (p295), where mantas, sharks and sea turtles converge to offer terrific snorkelling and scuba diving
- Grooving under the coconut palms at midnight in sweet **Gili Trawangan** (p304)
- Exploring the beautiful sandy coves and spectacular coastline east and west of **Kuta** (p321), a region that has some of Lombok's best surf and is due for some major development in the near future
- Searching for the perfect beach in the thinly populated **Southeastern Peninsula** (p290), a rugged region with an enormous and pristine bay that resembles Bali's Bukit 30 years ago

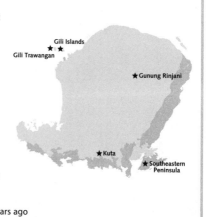

LOMBOK

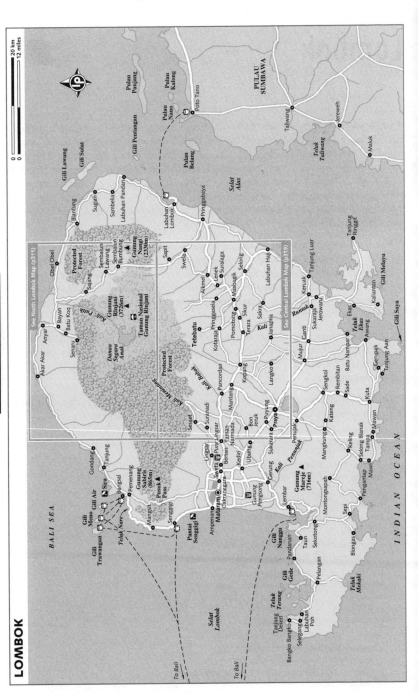

WESTERN LOMBOK

☎ 0370
You'll likely spend some time in western Lombok, if only to catch a plane in Mataram or hop a ferry to Bali from Lembar. Mataram is Lombok's biggest city. It has an off-the-beaten-path charm, and its wild local markets are worth a peek. So is the spectacular coastline around Senggigi, the main island's largest beach resort.

MATARAM

Lombok's capital is actually a conglomeration of several separate towns – Ampenan (the port); Mataram (the administrative centre); Cakranegara (the business centre), which is often shortened to Cakra; and Bertais and Sweta to the east, where you'll find the bus terminal. It's a quintessential Indonesian city, home to over a million people stretching more than 10km from east to west. It's chaotic and can be choked with traffic, but it's also attractive, with broad tree-lined avenues, and exuberant, friendly locals. Since sights are slim, and the Senggigi beaches are so close, very few visitors choose to stay here – which is exactly why you should.

Orientation
The five towns are spread along one main road – it starts as Jl Pabean in Ampenan, becomes Jl Yos Sudarso, then changes to Jl Langko, Jl Pejanggik and travels from Sweta to Bertais as Jl Selaparang. It's one-way throughout, running west to east. A parallel one-way road, Jl Tumpang Sari–Jl Panca Usaha–Jl Pancawarga–Jl Pendidikan, brings traffic back to the coast.

Information

EMERGENCY
Police station (Map p286; ☎ 631225; Jl Langko) In an emergency, dial ☎ 110.
Rumah Sakit Umum Mataram (Map p286; ☎ 622254; Jl Pejanggik 6) The best hospital on Lombok; has English-speaking doctors and a special tourist service from 8am to noon.

INTERNET ACCESS
Elian Internet (Map p286; www.elianmedia.net; 1 Panca Usaha Komplek, Mataram Mall; per hr 5000Rp; ☉ 24hr)

MONEY
You'll find plenty of banks with ATMs scattered along Cakra's main drag; most of them will also change cash as well as travellers cheques.

POST
Main post office (Map p286; Jl Sriwijaya 37; ☉ 8am-5pm Mon-Thu, 8-11am Fri, 8am-1pm Sat) Inconveniently located, but has internet and poste restante services.
Sub-post office (Map p286; Jl Langko; ☉ 8am-4.30pm Mon-Thu, 8-11am Fri, 8am-1pm Sat) Near the police station.

TELEPHONE
There are wartel (public telephone offices) on Jl Pejanggik and at the airport.
Telkom Map p286; (☎ 633333; Jl Pendidikan 23; ☉ 24hr) Offers phone and fax services.

TOURIST INFORMATION
West Lombok tourist office (Map p286; ☎ 621658; Jl Suprato 20; ☉ 7.30am-2pm Mon-Thu, 7.30-11am Fri, 8am-1pm Sat) A slim selection of maps and leaflets. Ultimately not particularly informative.
West Nusa Tenggara tourist office (Map p286; ☎ 634800; Jl Singosari 2; ☉ 8am-2pm Mon-Thu, 8-11am Fri, 8am-12.30pm Sat) The friendly staff here offer limited information about Lombok.

Sights
MUSEUM NEGERI NUSA TENGGARA BARAT
This dusty, yet terrific **museum** (Map p286; ☎ 632519; Jl Panji Tilar Negara 6; admission 20,000Rp; ☉ 8am-2pm Tue-Thu & Sat-Sun, 8-11am Fri) has exhibits on the geology, history and culture of Lombok and Sumbawa, an island east of Lombok. There's an interesting collection of prehistoric pottery, ancient bronze kettledrums, and a captivating assortment of kris (traditional daggers), *songket* (silver- or gold-threaded cloth), baskets and masks. For an extra 40,000Rp you can explore a locked wing full of gold swords and jewellery that once belonged to Sumbawan sultans and Javanese kings.

MAYURA WATER PALACE
Built in 1744, this **palace** (Map p286; Jl Selaparang; admission by donation; ☉ 7am-7.30pm) includes the former king's family temple, which is a pilgrimage site for Lombok's Hindus on December 24. In 1894 it was the site of bloody battles between the Dutch and Balinese. Unfortunately its regal past is long gone and

LOMBOK

MATARAM

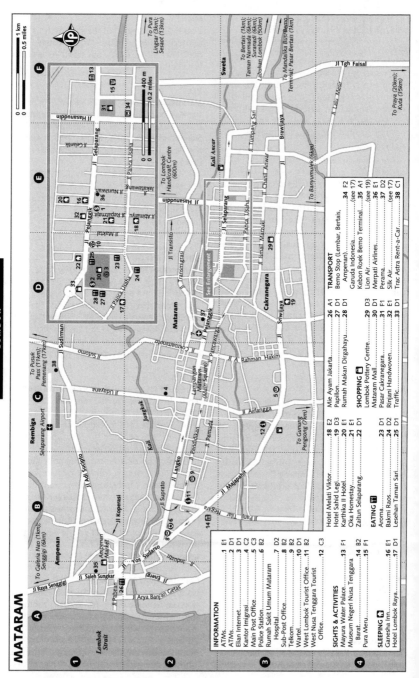

INFORMATION

ATMs..1	E1
ATMs..2	D1
Elian Internet...............................3	D1
Kantor Imigrasi............................4	C2
Main Post Office..........................5	C3
Police Station..............................6	B2
Rumah Sakit Umum Mataram	
Hospital..................................7	D2
Sub-Post Office...........................8	B2
Telkom..9	B2
Wartel.......................................10	D1
West Lombok Tourist Office.....11	B2
West Nusa Tenggara Tourist	
Office....................................12	C3

SIGHTS & ACTIVITIES

Mayura Water Palace..............13	F1
Museum Negeri Nusa Tenggara	
Barat.....................................14	B2
Pura Meru................................15	F1

SLEEPING

Ganesha Inn............................16	E1
Hotel Lombok Raya..................17	D1

Hotel Melati Viktor..................18	E2
Hotel Sahid Legi.......................19	D3
Karthika II Hotel.......................20	E1
Oka Homestay..........................21	E1
Zaitun Selaparang....................22	D1

EATING

Aroma.......................................23	D1
Bakmi Raos...............................24	D2
Lesehan Taman Sari..................25	D1
Mie Ayam Jakarta.....................26	A1
Papillon....................................27	D1
Rumah Makan Dirgahayu.........28	D1

SHOPPING

Lombok Pottery Centre.............29	D3
Mataram Mall............................30	D1
Pasar Cakranegara....................31	F1
Rinjani Handwoven..................32	E1
Traffic.......................................33	D1

TRANSPORT

Bemo Stop (Lembar, Bertais,	
Ampenan)..............................34	F2
Garuda Indonesia.....................35	A1
Kebon Roek Bemo Terminal.....(see 17)	
Lion Air.....................................36	E1
Merpati Airlines........................37	D2
Perama.....................................(see 19)	
Silk Air......................................38	C1
Trac Astra Rent-a-Car...............38	C1

it's become a neglected public park with a polluted artificial lake.

You'll find the entrance on the western side, off Jl Selaparang.

PURA MERU

Opposite the water palace, **Pura Meru** (Map p286; admission by donation; 8am-5pm) is the largest and most important Hindu temple on Lombok. Built in 1720 by Balinese prince Anak Agung Made Karang, it's dedicated to the Hindu trinity of Brahma, Vishnu and Shiva.

Wooden drums are beaten to call believers to ceremonies (the June full moon is the most important of these, but the grounds are also packed on Christmas Eve) in the outer courtyard. The inner court has one large and 33 small shrines, and three thatched, teak wood *meru* (multi-tiered shrines). The central *meru,* with 11 tiers, is Shiva's house; the *meru* to the north, with nine tiers, is Vishnu's; and the seven-tiered *meru* to the south is Brahma's. The *meru* are also said to represent the three great mountains, Rinjani, Agung and Bromo, and the mythical Mount Meru.

The caretaker will lend you a sash and sarong if you need one. Don't miss it.

Sleeping

Most folks nest among Cakranegara's quiet streets off Jl Pejanggik/Selaparang, east of Mataram Mall.

BUDGET

Ganesha Inn (Map p286; 624878; Jl Subak 1; s/d 30,000/40,000Rp) Stylish exterior, nice location, but some of the rooms are yellow at the edges. It's the kind of place that begs the question, why are these walls so dirty?

Oka Homestay (Map p286; 622406; Jl Repatmaja 5; d from 40,000Rp) Balinese-owned, this garden compound, patrolled by three friendly poodles, is a great deal. Rooms are fan-cooled and quite clean.

Karthika II Hotel (Map p286; 641776; Jl Subak I 16; s/d/tr 65,000/70,000/80,000Rp;) A nice courtyard and a Balinese theme. Choose rooms wisely though – some of the standard rooms are in better shape than the VIPs. Air-con rooms cost 20,000Rp more.

Hotel Melati Viktor (Map p286; 633830; Jl Abimanyu 1; d from 80,000Rp;) The high ceilings, clean rooms and Balinese-style courtyard, complete with Hindu statues, make this the best value in town.

Zaitun Selaparang (Map p286; 632235; www.zaitun.hotels.com; Jl Pejanggik 41; standard/superior/deluxe r 225,000/235,000/400,000Rp) In the thick of Cakra's commercial district, this mini-mall atrium hotel isn't fabulous, but it has new, recently remodelled rooms.

MIDRANGE

Hotel Sahid Legi (Map p286; 636282; sahid@mataram.wasantara.net.id; Jl Sriwijaya 81; r/deluxe 365,000/580,000Rp;) Once Mataram's grand dame of business hotels, thanks to the blend of modern and Indonesian design influences, three restaurants, international TV and a circular pool. The halls are dark though and even the deluxe rooms can be a bit musty.

Hotel Lombok Raya (Map p286; 632305; lora@mataram.wasantara.net.id; Jl Panca Usaha 11; s/d from 390,000/525,000Rp, plus 21% tax;) This well-located hotel has spacious, comfortable rooms with balconies and all the mod cons including a terrific spa.

Eating

You'll find plenty of Western fast-food outlets and Indonesian staples in the Mataram Mall.

Rumah Makan Dirgahayu (Map p286; 637559; Jl Cilinaya 19; rice dishes from 7000Rp, seafood from 25,000Rp) A popular Makassar-style place opposite the mall, with gurgling fountains and twirling fans. An ideal lunch oasis on sweaty afternoons.

our pick **Bakmi Raos** (Map p286; 6610499; Jl Panca Usaha; dishes 9000-20,000Rp; 10am-10pm) An authentic and modern Indonesian noodle and soup joint behind the mall that attracts a steady stream of Mataram's hip, young and beautiful. And the food rocks!

Aroma (Map p286; off Jl Pejanggik; meals from 15,000Rp; 11am-10pm) This modern, spotless Chinese seafood restaurant serves an outstanding fried gourami (fish; 35,000Rp) accompanied by a fiery sweet chilli sauce. It's popular among Mataram's Chinese Indonesian families.

Lesehan Taman Sari (Map p286; 629909; Mataram Mall; meals 25,000Rp; 11am-10pm) Attached to the mall, this place wins with ambience and multi-course, traditional Sasak meals served on banana leaves and enjoyed in stilted, thatched *beruga* (open-sided pavilions).

Other recommendations:
Mie Ayam Jakarta (Map p286; Jl Pabean; dishes 5000-12,000Rp) Scores for tasty, inexpensive Javanese food.
Papillon (Map p286; 632308; Jl Cilinaya 1; dishes 19,000-45,000Rp) An upstart restaurant off the mall, with lamp-lit tables, red vinyl booths and an international menu.

Shopping

For handicrafts try the many stores on Jl Raya Senggigi, the road heading north from Ampenan.

Lombok Handicraft Centre (Jl Hasanuddin) At Sayang Sayang (2km north of Cakra), there's a wide range of crafts including masks, textiles, and ceramics from across Nusa Tenggara.

Mataram Mall (Map p286; Jl Pejanggik; 7am-7pm) A multi-storey shopping mall with a super-market, electrical goods and clothes stores as well as food stalls.

Traffic (Map p286; ☎ 0819 179 28974; Jl Selaparang; 9am-9.30pm) Get your hipster, skate-punk fashion here.

Galeria Nao (☎ 626835; Jl Raya Senggigi 234) Beautifully finished contemporary wooden furniture and artefacts that wouldn't look out of place in *Wallpaper** magazine.

Lombok Pottery Centre (Map p286; ☎ 640351; Jl Sriwijaya 111) Offers a vast range of Lombok pot-tery for reasonably competitive prices.

Rinjani Handwoven (Map p286; ☎ 633169; Jl Pejanggik 44) You can see weavers in action and buy their handiwork at this workshop.

Pasar Cakranegara (Map p286; cnr Jl Hasanuddin & Jl Selaparang; 6am-5.30pm) A charming tumble of warehouse stalls, some of which sell good-quality ikat. Penetrate the dank halls and you'll find an interesting food market upstairs.

Pasar Bertais (Map p286; 7am-5pm) This place, near the bus terminal, is a great spot to get localised after you've overdosed on the *bule* (Westerner) circuit. There are no tourists here, but it's got everything else: fruit and veggies;w fish (fresh and dried); baskets full of colourful, aromatic spices and grains; freshly butchered beef; palm sugar; enormous, pungent bricks of shrimp paste; and cheaper handicrafts than anywhere else on Lombok.

Getting There & Away

AIR

The following airlines serve Lombok's Selaparang Airport (AMI), which has a de-cent terminal with a few cafés and shops to keep you busy when your flight is inevitably delayed (unless you're on the first flight out). Domestic departure tax is now 30,000Rp; and international departure tax is 150,000Rp. There has been wind blowing about a new international airport to be built near Praya for a number of years now, and with the im-pending south Lombok development, those rumours may finally be coming true – no

significant construction had begun at the time of research.

Garuda Indonesia (Map p286; ☎ 0804 1807 807; www.garuda-indonesia.com; Jl Panca Usaka 11, Hotel Lombok Raya) Daily flights to Jakarta, Surabaya and Bali.

Lion Air (Map p286; ☎ 629333, www.lionair.co.id; Hotel Sahid Legi, Mataram) Flights to Surabaya.

Merpati Airlines (Map p286; ☎ 621111; www.merpati .co.id; Jl Pejanggik 69, Mataram) Flies to Bali at least twice daily.

Silk Air (Map p286; ☎ 628254; www.silkair.com; Jl Panca Usaka 11, Hotel Lombok Raya) Serves Singapore direct.

Trigana Airlines (☎ 6162433; www.trigana-air.com) Three flights a day to Bali.

Wings Air (see Lion Air, above) This is a branch of Lion Air.

BUS

The sprawling, dusty Mandalika bus station in Bertais is the main bus and bemo (small minibus) terminal for the entire island, and also for long-distance buses to Sumbawa, Bali and Java (p352).

The terminal is fairly chaotic, so be sure to keep a level head to avoid the 'help' of the commission-happy touts. Long-distance buses leave from behind the main terminal building, while bemo and smaller buses leave from one of two car parks on either side.

Some distances and fares for buses and bemo from Mandalika terminal:

Destination	Distance	Fare	Duration
Kuta (via Praya & Sengkol)	54km	10,000Rp	90min
Labuhan Lombok	69km	8000Rp	2hr
Lembar	22km	3500Rp	30min
Pemenang (for Bangsal)	30km	6000Rp	40min
Praya	27km	5000Rp	30min

Kebon Roek bemo terminal in Ampenan has bemo to Bertais (1500Rp) and services to Senggigi (3000Rp).

TOURIST SHUTTLE BUS

Perama (Map p286; ☎ 635928; www.peramatour.com; Jl Pejanggik 66) operates shuttle buses to popular destinations on Lombok (including Bangsal, Senggigi and Kuta), and to Bali.

Getting Around

TO/FROM THE AIRPORT

Lombok's Selaparang Airport is on the north side of the city, 5km from Cakra. A taxi desk sells prepaid tickets to locations around the island: 30,000Rp to anywhere in Mataram; 85,000Rp to Senggigi; 125,000Rp to Bangsal and Lembar; 250,000Rp to Kuta; 400,000Rp to Senaru. Alternatively, walk out of the airport to Jl Adi Sucipto and take one of the number 7 bemo that run frequently to Ampenan.

BEMO

Mataram is *very* spread out. Yellow bemo shuttle between Kebon Roek terminal in Ampenan and Mandalika terminal in Bertais (6km away), along the two main thoroughfares. Bemo terminals are good places to organise a charter trip. Outside the Pasar Cakranegara there is a handy bemo stop for services to Bertais, Ampenan, Sweta and Lembar. The standard fare is 1500Rp, regardless of distance.

CAR & MOTORCYCLE

Most hotels can arrange car hire, but you'll almost certainly find a much better deal in Senggigi. If you'd rather someone else did the driving, there are legions of drivers in Mataram who would be happy to help. Most charge between 350,000Rp and 525,000Rp per day. You'll have to negotiate. For care hire, try **Trac Astra Rent-a-Car** (Map p286; ☎ 626363; www.trac .astra.co.id; Jl Adi Sucipto 5, Rembiga Mataram; self-drive per day 360,000Rp, Avanza with driver 525,000Rp).

TAXI

For a metered taxi, call **Lombok Taksi** (☎ 627000).

AROUND MATARAM

There are some gorgeous villages, rice fields and temples, reminiscent of some of the best landscapes and scenery that Bali has to offer, east of Mataram. You can easily visit all of the following places in half a day with your own transport.

Pura Lingsar

This large **temple compound** (admission by donation; ☻ 7am-6pm) is the holiest on Lombok. Built in 1714 by King Anak Agung Ngurah, and nestled beautifully in the lush rice paddies, it's multi-denominational, with a temple for Balinese Hindus and one for followers of Lombok's mystical take on Islam, Wektu Telu (p312). It's not uncommon to happen upon pilgrims of both religions making offerings and sipping holy water.

The Hindu temple (Pura Gaduh) in the northern half is higher than the Wektu Telu temple in the southern section. Pura Gaduh has four shrines: one oriented to Gunung Rinjani (seat of the gods on Lombok), one to Gunung Agung (seat of the gods in Bali) and a double shrine representing the union between the two islands.

The Wektu Telu temple is noted for its enclosed pond devoted to Lord Vishnu, and the holy eels, which can be enticed from their hiding places with hard-boiled eggs (available at stalls outside) – it's considered good luck to feed them. You will be expected to rent a sash and/or sarong (or bring your own) to enter the temple.

A huge ritual battle, Perang Topat, is held here every year in November or December (the exact date depends on the lunar month). After a costumed parade, Hindus and Wektu pelt each other with *ketupat* (sticky rice in coconut leaves).

Pura Lingsar is 9km northeast of Mandalika. First take a bemo from the terminal to Taman Narmada, and another to Lingsar. Ask to be dropped off near the entrance to the temple complex, which is 300m down a well-marked path from the main road.

Suranadi

Suranadi is a pleasant little village surrounded by picturesque countryside. It has a temple, a small pocket of forest and a swimming pool, making it a popular spot for locals on weekends.

SIGHTS

Set amid gorgeous countryside, **Pura Suranadi** (admission by donation; ☻ 7.30am-6pm) is one of the holiest Hindu temples on Lombok. It's worth a visit for its lovely gardens, with a bubbling, icy natural spring and restored baths with ornate Balinese carvings (plus the obligatory holy eels).

Just opposite the village market, an entrance leads to **Hutan Wisata Suranadi** (admission 1000Rp; ☻ 8am-5pm), a quiet forest sanctuary good for short hikes and birdwatching.

Several restaurants dot the main road close to the temple and there are plenty of cheap warung (food stalls) in the neighbouring village of Surandi.

The temple is 6km northwest of Taman Narmada and served by frequent public bemo. Failing that, charter one.

LOMBOK

Sesaot & Around

Some 4km northeast of Suranadi is Sesaot, a charming market town with an ice-cold holy river that snakes from Gunung Rinjani into the forest. There are some gorgeous picnic spots and enticing swimming holes here. Regular transport connects Taman Narmada with Sesaot, and bites are available at the warung along the main street.

Further east, **Air Nyet** is another pretty village with more options for swimming and picnics. Ask for directions to the unsigned turn-off in the middle of Sesaot. The bridge and road to Air Nyet are rough, but it's a lovely stroll (about 3km) from Sesaot; otherwise, charter a vehicle.

Gunung Pengsong

This Balinese hilltop **temple** (admission by donation; 7am-6pm), 9km south of Mataram, has spectacular views across undulating rice fields towards distant volcanoes and the sea. Japanese soldiers hid here towards the end of WWII, and remnants of cannons can be found, as well as plenty of playful monkeys.

Once a year, generally in March or April, a buffalo is taken up the steep slope and sacrificed to give thanks for a good harvest. The **Desa Bersih festival** also occurs here at harvest time – houses and gardens are cleaned, fences whitewashed, and roads and paths repaired. Once part of a ritual to rid the village of evil spirits, it's now held in honour of the rice goddess, Dewi Sri.

It's a 15-minute walk up to the temple top from the entrance. You'll need your own wheels to get here.

Banyumulek

One of the two main pottery centres on Lombok, here they specialise in decorated pots, pots with a woven fibre covering, as well as more traditional urns and water flasks. It's close to the city – head south of Sweta on the main road to Lembar. After 6km, veer right to Banyumulek, a couple of kilometres to the west.

LEMBAR

Lembar is Lombok's main port for ferries, tankers and Pelni liners coming in from Bali and beyond. Though the ferry port itself is watch-your-back scruffy, the setting – think azure inlets ringed by soaring green hills – places Lembar among Indonesia's most beautiful harbours. That doesn't mean you'll want to crash here, and since bus connections to Mataram and Senggigi are abundant, and bemo run regularly to the Mandalika bus terminal (3500Rp), you won't have to. If you do manage to get stuck, or need a bite to eat, the clean and hospitable **Hotel Tigadara** (681444; Jl Raya Pelabuhan; s/d with bathroom 50,000Rp; cottages 135,000Rp, all incl breakfast), 1km north of the ferry port, is an excellent deal.

To get to Lembar, hop on one of the many bemo that shuttle there from the Mandalika terminal in Bertais (3500Rp), or you can catch one at the market stop in Cakra. See p349 for details on the ferries and boats between Bali and Lembar, including the public ferries from Padangbai (p219).

SOUTHWESTERN PENINSULA

The jagged coastline west of Sekotong is blessed with deserted beaches and tranquil offshore islands, which is why it has long been hyped as Lombok's next big tourist destination. And while vacation villas are beginning to sprout, it remains laid-back and pristine. The road hugs the coast, passing white-sand beach after turquoise cove. It's narrow but paved until Selegang. A track continues to the west past Bangko Bangko to Tanjung Desert; for details on Desert Point, one of Asia's legendary surf breaks, see p97.

A few of the palm-dappled offshore islands with silky beaches and fine snorkelling are inhabited. Gili Nanggu and Gili Gede both have accommodation. Gede is also home to Bugis craftsman who build gorgeous wooden schooners.

Sleeping & Eating

Places to stay and restaurants are slim on the ground in this region, and be aware that some close in the rainy season.

MAINLAND

Bola Bola Paradis (bolabolaparadis.com; Jl Raya Palangan Sekotong; r 210,000-450,000Rp;) Just west of Pelangan, this funky spot has sweet octagonal bungalows, comfortable air-con rooms, and a chic restaurant-lounge (mains 20,000Rp to 55,000Rp) set on a fine stretch of sand.

Nirvana Roemah Air (6608060; www.floatingvilla .com; Jl Raya Medang, Sekotong Barat; villas incl airport transfers US$100-125;) Enjoy secluded, floating luxury in the mangroves, 2km west of Sekotong. Book online for substantial low-season discounts.

AVOIDING OFFENCE

Most of Lombok is culturally conservative, and immodest dress and public displays of affection between couples can cause offence. Both men and women should dress appropriately away from Senggigi and the Gilis. Nude or topless bathing anywhere is very offensive.

Islamic law forbids drinking alcohol and, although booze is widely available on Lombok, public drunkenness is frowned upon. It's particularly offensive to drink alcohol near a mosque. Ramadan is a time to be particularly sensitive toward local sensibilities – most locals fast during daylight hours during this month, and there are no parties on Gili Trawangan.

ISLANDS
Secret Island Resort (☎ 0818 037 62001; www.secret islandresort.com; r 200,000Rp, bungalow 250,000Rp, 2-bed villas 1 million Rp; 🟦) Gili Gede's best accommodation comes with fine sea or mountain views. The restaurant grills up dynamite seafood. Kayak, hiking, snorkelling and diving trips can be arranged here. Call ahead for airport pick-up and/or free boat transfer from Tembowong beach.

Gili Nanggu Cottages (☎ 623783; www.gilinanggu .com; cottages s/d 240,000/250,000Rp, bungalows 350,000Rp; 🟦) Nobody ever regrets boating across the Lembar channel to these rustic two-storey *lumbung* (rice barn) cottages just off the beach. Meals are 16,000Rp to 38,000Rp.

Getting There & Away
Bemo buzz between Lembar and Pelangan (one hour to Lembar and 45 minutes to Pelangan, every 30 minutes) via Sekotong (25 minutes). West of Pelangan, transport is less regular, but the route is still served by infrequent bemo services until Selegang.

To reach Gili Nanggu, a return charter on a *prahu* (outrigger fishing boat) from Taun costs 250,000Rp. Chartered boats connect Tembowong with the islands of Gili Gede and Gili Ringit (150,000Rp to 200,000Rp).

SENGGIGI
You can spend a lifetime of travel in search of the perfect beach, and it would be hard to top those around Senggigi, Lombok's original tourist town. Think: a series of sweeping bays with white-sand beaches, coconut palms, cliff and mountain backdrops, and blood-red views of Bali's Gunung Agung at sunset when locals congregate on the cliffs and watch another day turn into night. As darkness descends, the bright lanterns of the local fishing fleet glint like fallen stars against the black sea.

There are sweet, inexpensive guesthouses, a few luxury hotels and dozens of restaurants and bars. Senggigi has everything, save a steady flow of tourists. However, with Lombok's growing popularity, that appears to be changing little by little. And even if it is a relative ghost town when you roll through, and the beach hawkers feel overbearing, the sheer beauty of the place is still worth a night or two.

Orientation
The Senggigi area spans 10km of coastal road. Most shops, facilities, and hotels, are on the main road, Jl Raya Senggigi, which starts about 6km north of Ampenan. Street numbers are not used in Senggigi.

Information
EMERGENCY
The nearest hospitals are in Mataram.
Police station (Map p292; ☎ 110) Next to the Pasar Seni.
Senggigi Medical Clinic (Map p292; ☎ 693856; 🕑 8am-7pm) Based at the Senggigi Beach Hotel.
Tourist Police (☎ 632733)

INTERNET ACCESS & TELEPHONES
Internet cafés on the main strip also double as wartel.
Millennium Internet (Map p292; ☎ 693860; Jl Raya Senggigi; per min 500Rp; 🕑 24hr)

MONEY
Bank Central Asia (BCA) and Bank Negara Indonesia (BNI) on Jl Raya Senggigi both have ATMs and will exchange cash and travellers cheques.

POST
Post office (Map p292; Jl Raya Senggigi; 🕑 8am-6pm)

Sights
PURA BATU BOLONG
It may not be the grandest, but it is Lombok's sweetest Hindu **temple** (admission by donation; 🕑 7am-7pm). Join an ever-welcoming Balinese

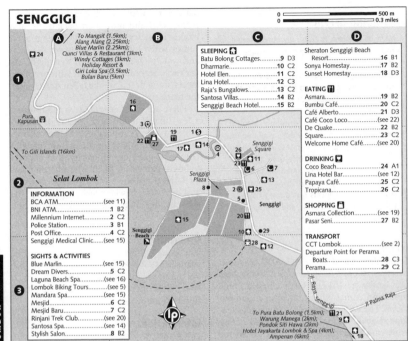

SENGGIGI

SLEEPING 🛏
Batu Bolong Cottages...........**9** D3
Dharmarie...........................**10** C2
Hotel Elen..........................**11** C2
Lina Hotel..........................**12** C3
Raja's Bungalows................**13** C2
Santosa Villas.....................**14** B2
Senggigi Beach Hotel..........**15** B2
Sheraton Senggigi Beach
  Resort..............................**16** B1
Sonya Homestay..................**17** B2
Sunset Homestay.................**18** D3

EATING 🍴
Asmara...............................**19** B2
Bumbu Café.........................**20** C2
Café Alberto........................**21** D3
Café Coco Loco................(see 22)
De Quake............................**22** B2
Square................................**23** C2
Welcome Home Café........(see 20)

DRINKING 🍷
Coco Beach..........................**24** A1
Lina Hotel Bar.................(see 12)
Papaya Café.........................**25** C2
Tropicana............................**26** C2

SHOPPING 🛍
Asmara Collection.............(see 19)
Pasar Seni...........................**27** B2

TRANSPORT
CCT Lombok....................(see 2)
Departure Point for Perama
  Boats................................**28** C3
Perama...............................**29** C2

INFORMATION
BCA ATM.........................(see 11)
BNI ATM............................**1** B2
Millennium Internet.............**2** C2
Police Station.....................**3** B1
Post Office.........................**4** C2
Senggigi Medical Clinic......(see 15)

SIGHTS & ACTIVITIES
Blue Marlin.......................(see 15)
Dream Divers......................**5** C2
Laguna Beach Spa.............(see 16)
Lombok Biking Tours..........(see 5)
Mandara Spa....................(see 15)
Mesjid.................................**6** C2
Mesjid Baru........................**7** C2
Rinjani Trek Club..............(see 20)
Santosa Spa......................(see 14)
Stylish Salon.......................**8** B2

To Mangsit (1.5km);
Alang Alang (2.25km);
Blue Marlin (2.25km);
Qunci Villas & Restaurant (3km);
Windy Cottages (3km);
Holiday Resort &
Giri Loka Spa (3.5km);
Bulan Baru (5km)

Pura
Kapusan

To Gili Islands (16km)

Selat Lombok

Senggigi
Square

Senggigi
Plaza

Senggigi
Beach

Senggigi

To Pura Batu Bolong (1.5km);
Warung Manega (2km);
Pondok Siti Hawa (2km);
Hotel Jayakarta Lombok & Spa (4km);
Ampenan (6km)

community as it leaves offerings at the 14 altars and pagodas that tumble down a rocky volcanic outcropping that spills into the foaming sea about 2km south of central Senggigi. The temple is oriented towards Gunung Agung, Bali's holiest mountain, and is a perfect sunset spot. The rock underneath the temple has a natural hole that gives it its name – *batu bolong* (literally, 'rock with hole').

Activities
SNORKELLING & DIVING
There's reasonable snorkelling off the point in Senggigi, in the sheltered bay around the headland, and in front of Windy Cottages, a few kilometres north of the town. You can rent snorkelling gear (25,000Rp per day) from several spots along the beach near Senggigi Beach Hotel.

Diving trips from Senggigi normally visit the Gili Islands, so you may want to consider basing yourself there. Professional dive centres include:

Blue Marlin (☎ 0812 376 6496; www.bluemarlindive.com; Jl Raya Senggigi; Holiday Resort Lombok; Alang Alang, Senggigi Beach Hotel)

Dream Divers (Map p292; ☎ 692047; www.dreamdivers.com; Jl Raya Senggigi)

BIKING & HIKING
Lombok Biking Tours (Map p292; ☎ 6605792; Jl Raya Senggigi; day excursions per person from 200,000Rp) offers fun, interesting guided rides through the rural Sekotong region and the countryside around Lingsar and Surandi.

Drop by the **Rinjani Trek Club** (Map p292; ☎ 693202; rtc.senggigi@gmail.com; Jl Raya Senggigi) if you're interested in climbing the sacred volcano. It's well informed about routes and trail conditions.

MASSAGES, SPAS & SALONS
Local masseurs armed with mats, oils and attitude hunt for business on Senggigi Beach. Expect to pay about 50,000Rp for one hour after bargaining. Almost all hotels can also arrange for a masseur to come to your room; rates start at about 60,000Rp.

If you care to indulge, visit one of the many hotel-based spas in the area. **Giri Loka Spa** (☎ 693444; Holiday Resort; ☀ 8am-9pm) offers delicious warm stone massages (one hour;

US$45). First, rosemary and orange oils are applied to your body, then a masseur rubs the heated stones over your 'chakra' points, stimulating the lymph nodes, blood and muscles. Divine.

Laguna Beach Spa (Map p292; ☎ 693333; Sheraton Senggigi Beach Resort; ☻ 9am-9pm) has Balinese milk-and-honey body scrub treatments (1½ hours; US$50) and massages (one hour; US$25). The **Mandara Spa** (Map p292; ☎ 693210; Senggigi Beach Hotel; ☻ 10am-9pm) offers a comprehensive range of treatments and massages (from US$36), including Balinese aromatherapy and reflexology. Rates at the **Jayakarta Spa** (☎ 693048; Hotel Jayakarta Lombok; ☻ 8am-11pm) are the most reasonable at 121,000Rp for a traditional massage and 272,000Rp for a Lulur bath, exfoliation and 'body polishing' treatment. The newest addition to Senggigi's luxury armada, the **Santosa Spa** (Map p292; ☎ 693090; Santosa Villas; ☻ 8am-11pm), offers a variety of massage styles including a hot stone treatment from US$26. Two-hour packages start at US$39.

For a manicure, pedicure or other beauty treatments in humbler, storefront environs, hit **Stylish Salon** (Map p292; ☎ 6194240; Senggigi Plaza Blok 1 No 4; ☻ 10am-8pm) for treatments and massages from 55,000Rp.

Sleeping

Senggigi has no shortage of excellent accommodation spread up and down the coastal road. If you want to walk everywhere, choose a place on the main strip. Many of the more upscale places north of here in Mangsit are also definitely worth considering, and some offer free transport into central Senggigi.

Outside peak times, room rates are in constant flux, and discounts of up to 50% are common.

DETOUR

North of Senggigi is a succession of wonderful, near-deserted fishermen's coves where you can pretty much guarantee to have a beach all to yourself. Cruise just west of the Bulan Baru hotel, about 7km from central Senggigi, for some beautiful beaches; Pantai Setangi is one fine example. From there, the coastal road from Mangsit to Pemenang is a spectacular drive. The road slaloms the coastal contours, and serves up sweeping ocean views.

BUDGET
Senggigi

Sonya Homestay (Map p292; ☎ 0813 398 99878; Jl Raya Senggigi; d from 40,000Rp) A family-run enclave of six rooms with nice patios and bright pink beds. Nathan, the owner, offers free driving tours of Mataram and the surrounding area. He'll even shuttle you to Bangsal harbour for a song.

Pondok Siti Hawa (☎ 693414; Jl Raya Senggigi; d 40,000Rp) This isn't a homestay, it's a novelty act, starring an eccentric European expat and his family, a captive monkey, and ramshackle bamboo cottages set on one of the most beautiful beaches in Senggigi.

Hotel Elen (Map p292; ☎ 693077; Jl Raya Senggigi; d from 55,000Rp; ☒) Elen is the long-time backpackers' choice. Rooms are basic, but those facing the waterfall fountain and koi pond come with spacious tiled patios that catch ocean breezes.

Lina Hotel (Map p292; ☎ 693237; Jl Raya Senggigi; s/d from 60,000/75,000Rp; ☒) Rooms are bland and simple, but they all come with views of the point break.

Raja's Bungalows (Map p292; ☎ 0812 377 0138; d 85,000Rp) Rooms are big, clean, and tastefully decorated with high ceilings, gecko sculptures on the walls, and outdoor bathrooms. But it's well within range of the mosque's loudspeaker and 300m from the sand.

Batu Bolong Cottages (Map p292; ☎ 693065; Jl Raya Senggigi; s/d 150,000/300,000Rp; ☒) Bamboo is the decor du jour at this charming bungalow-style hotel set on both sides of the road south of the centre. Beachfront rooms open onto a manicured lawn that fades into white sand.

Mangsit

Windy Cottages (☎ 693191; cottages with cold/hot water 110,000/150,000Rp, r 140,000Rp; ☒) These attractive thatched cottages with sea views have been popular for years. There's decent snorkelling offshore.

Bulan Baru (☎ 693786; r 180,000Rp; ☒ ☒) Set in a lovely garden a short walk from a fine sandy beach, this welcoming hotel has spacious, well-furnished rooms, all with minibars, air-con and hot-water bathrooms. No children allowed.

MIDRANGE

Senggigi's midrange runs plush thanks to the excess of luxury hotels. Ask for discounts in the low season.

LOMBOK

Senggigi

our pick **Sunset Homestay** (Map p292; ☎ 692020; www.sunsethouse-lombok.com; r 275,000/400,000Rp; 🗙) These six, tastefully simple bungalows on a quiet stretch of shore come with all the mod cons and homey touches.

Dharmarie (Map p292; ☎ 693050; www.dharmarie.com; r 300,000Rp; 🗙) These comfy sea-view cottages with French doors and indoor/outdoor bathrooms are great value. Breakfast is included but you could skip it.

Senggigi Beach Hotel (Map p292; ☎ 693210; www.senggigibeach.aerowisata.com; r US$70, beach bungalows US$80 plus 21% tax; 🗙 🖳) Detached bungalows surrounded by a lush garden are set back from the beach. The complex includes a large pool situated close to the shore, a spa and tennis courts.

Hotel Jayakarta Lombok (☎ 693048; www.indo.com/hotels/jayakartalombok; standard/superior r 400,000/450,000Rp. ste 1 million Rp; 🗙 🖳) This large Indonesian chain hotel, 5km south of the centre, is popular among Javanese families. The theme-park kitsch is offset by the gorgeous stretch of sand.

Sheraton Senggigi Beach Resort (Map p292; ☎ 693333; www.sheraton.com; r from 775,000Rp; 🗙 🖳) Just north of the centre, the Sheraton has, until relatively recently, been Senggigi's top resort. And although the newer, hipper spots have stolen some of its thunder, rooms still come with terraces or balconies. There's a palm-fringed swimming pool and a kids' pool, two restaurants and a well-regarded spa (Laguna Beach Spa, p293) and health club. Families love it.

Mangsit

Qunci Villas (☎ 693800; www.quncivillas.com; r garden/ocean view US$70/95 plus 21% tax; 🗙 🖳) Senggigi's most stylish hotel is also a great deal. Rooms have indoor and outdoor living rooms and bathrooms; the pool bar and tasty restaurant (opposite) are outfitted with cool block-wood furnishings; and the staff are warm and friendly. Book ahead during high season.

Alang Alang (☎ 693518; www.alang-alang-villas.com; s/d bungalows US$95/100; 🗙 🖳) If you're looking for more of a classic Indonesian themed hotel, you'll like it here. Its 20 rooms come with teak furnishings and are set in a lush, flowering garden. The small pool overlooks a thin sliver of beach where fishermen cast into the waves.

Senggigi

Santosa Villas (Map p292; ☎ 693090; www.santosavillas.com; standard/superior/deluxe r 560,000/650,000/1.5 million, villas 3 million Rp; 🗙 🖳) The recently renovated and rebranded Santosa resort has a range of accommodation from midrange to luxury villas. On a nice beach, it's smack in the centre of the Senggigi strip.

Eating

Central Senggigi has far more restaurants than necessary, varying from local warung to contemporary fine dining. Most offer free transport for evening diners – phone for a ride.

For authentic Indonesian street food, head to the hillside warung on the route north to Mangsit – *sate* (satay) sizzles, pots of noodles bubble, and corn on the cob roasts at dusk.

SENGGIGI

Asmara (Map p292; ☎ 693619; Jl Raya Senggigi; mains 18,000-75,000Rp; 🗙) Asmara spans the culinary globe, from tuna carpaccio to Wiener schnitzel to Lombok's own *sate pusut* (minced fish, chicken or beef mixed with fresh coconut, chilli and spices, moulded and grilled on lemongrass stalks). It's an ideal family choice, with a playground and kids' menu.

De Quake (Map p292; ☎ 693694; mains from 23,000Rp; ⏰ 10am-10pm) Like Square (below), this new spot blends pan-Asian cuisine with ambitious high design. It's right on the beach behind the art market.

Café Coco Loco (Map p292; ☎ 693396; mains from 23,000Rp) Munch on tempura, curries and fresh fish done up Lombok-style at this popular new café in the art market.

Café Alberto (Map p292; ☎ 693039; mains from 30,000Rp; ⏰ 11am-11pm) Eat beachfront at this popular pizzeria on the sand.

Welcome Home Café (Map p292; ☎ 693833; Jl Raya Senggigi; mains 30,000Rp) Gives you that Jimmy Buffet feeling, with a fantastic knotted-wood bar, bamboo furniture, coral floors, and fresh fish on the grill at reasonable prices.

Bumbu Café (Map p292; Jl Raya Senggigi; mains 35,000Rp) Popular choice for tasty pan-Asian fare. The owner says, 'We always full!' It's no coincidence.

Square (Map p292; ☎ 693688; Senggigi Square; mains 35,000Rp; ⏰ 11am-11pm) Uberhip design with lounge seating, a blue-lit, open dining room and sea views. Lombok expats rave about the food. Try the wok-tossed calamari with bok choy.

our pick **Warung Manega** (Jl Raya Senggigi 6; meals 75,000-250,000Rp; ☺ 11am-11pm) If you fled Bali before experiencing the Jimbaran fish grills, you can make up for it at this sister restaurant to one of Jimbaran's finest. Choose from a fresh daily catch of barracuda, squid, snapper, grouper, lobster, tuna and prawns – all are grilled over coconut husks and served to you on candlelit tables in the sand. Superb.

MANGSIT
Qunci restaurant (☎ 693800; www.quncivillas.com; mains 46,000-64,000Rp) Abutting the beach in Mangsit, this terrific, hip hotel-restaurant (opposite) has a modern menu with both Asian and European dishes.

Drinking & Entertainment
Senggigi's nocturnal activity is mellow midweek with a mild spike on weekends. It revolves around a handful of bars with live music and a disco or two.

our pick **Coco Beach** (Map p292; ☎ 0817 578 0055; Pantai 2 Kerandangan Jl Raya Senggigi; ☺ noon-10pm) Rent comfortable beachside bamboo *beruga* (open-sided pavilions) for sunset drinks where the coconut groves meet the sand north of Senggigi. Sip from a bar that serves traditional Jamu tonics, fresh organic juices and terrific tropical cocktails. It's very popular with the moneyed Mataram set.

Lina Hotel Bar (Map p292; Lina Hotel; beer small/large 10,000/13,000Rp) Another great spot for a sundowner is Lina's seafront bolat. Happy hour starts at 4pm and ends an hour after dusk.

Papaya Café (Map p292; ☎ 693136; Jl Raya Senggigi) The decor is slick, with exposed stone walls, rattan furniture and evocative Asmat art from Papua; there's a nice selection of liquor; and it has a tight house band that rocks.

Tropicana (Map p292; ☎ 693432; www.tropicanalombok.com; Jl Raya Senggigi; admission 25,000Rp) Your cliché, cheeseball disco with DJs spinning Western pop, rock and a few Indonesian hits plus live acts and bands. Be warned, you may be asked to participate in the 'Mr & Miss Tropicana' contests. Yikes.

Shopping
Senggigi's shops are not well patronised. The **Pasar Seni** (Art Market; Map p292; Jl Raya Senggigi) has some cheap handicraft stalls, but most of the wares aren't worth your time. The **Asmara Collection** (Map p292; ☎ 693619; Jl Raya Senggigi; ☺ 8am-11pm), on the other hand, is sensational. You'll find authentic, hand-woven Lombok textiles, intense tribal masks, carved hair combs and a lovely collection of jewellery.

The warehouses and craft shops along the main road to Ampenan are also worth stopping for.

Getting There & Away
BOAT
Perama (Map p292; ☎ 693007; Jl Raya Senggigi) operates a daily boat service from Padangbai in Bali to Senggigi (p222; 300,000Rp, six hours). There's also a daily Perama boat from Senggigi to the Gili Islands (70,000Rp to 100,000Rp, 60 to 90 minutes) at 9am, which means you avoid having to deal with Bangsal. The dive schools (p292) also operate speedboat shuttles (from 120,000Rp per person) to the Gilis most days – contact them in advance.

BUS
Regular bemo travel between Senggigi and Ampenan's Kebon Roek terminal (3000Rp, 10km). You can easily wave them down on the main drag. Headed to the Gilis? Organise a group and charter a bemo to Bangsal harbour (60,000Rp).

Perama (above) has a few tourist shuttle-bus/boat services daily between Senggigi and Bali – Kuta (Bali) and Bali airport (150,000Rp), Ubud (150,000Rp) – and other places on Lombok including Kuta (185,000Rp).

Getting Around
If you stay within walking distance of the main drag, you won't need wheels. Besides, many restaurants offer free lifts if you call ahead.

Motorbikes are readily available for hire in Senggigi and are the easiest way to get around. Mopeds rent for 35,000Rp per day plus petrol. Motorcycles go for 60,000Rp. Ask about rental at your hotel or call Dino at **CCT Lombok** (Map p292; ☎ 6681864, 0819 171 59365); he can also help you hire a car and driver for chartered trips around Lombok.

GILI ISLANDS
☎ 0370
For decades travellers have made the hop from Bali for a quick dip in the turquoise-tinted, bathtub-warm waters of the tiny, irresistible Gili Islands, and stayed longer than they anticipated. Perhaps it's the deep-water coral reefs teeming with sharks, rays

and reasonably friendly turtles? Maybe it's the serenity that comes with no motorised traffic? Or it could be the beachfront bungalows, long stretches of white sand, and the friendly locals. Each of these pearls, located just off the northwestern tip of Lombok, have their own unique character, but they have one thing in common: they are all hard to leave.

Gili Air is the closest to the mainland, with plenty of stylish bungalows dotted among the palms. Mellow Gili Meno, the middle island, is the smallest and quietest, and makes for a wonderful chilled-out retreat.

Gili Trawangan (population 800), the furthest out, has been tagged as the 'party island'. And with three weekly parties and a groovy collection of beach bars, you can get loose here. But Trawangan is growing up, with stylish accommodation, including a number of inland vacation villas, a fun expat community and outstanding dining.

Information

INTERNET & TELEPHONE

There is mobile-phone coverage, and all islands have a wartel and internet cafés, but surfing (500Rp to 600Rp per minute) is woefully slow in most places.

MONEY

There are no banks or ATMs on the Gilis, and though each island has shops and hotels that will change money and arrange cash advance from credit and debit cards, rates are low and commissions are high. Bring ample rupiah with you – enough for a few extra days, at least.

Try to bring as many small-denomination notes as possible, as there's often a problem changing the bigger notes.

Dangers & Annoyances

There are no police on any of the Gilis, so report theft to the island *kepala desa* (village head) immediately. They will stop all boats out and search passengers before they can leave the island. If you need help locating them, or need help translating, dive schools are a good point of contact. If you are on Gili Trawangan, notify Satgas, the community group that runs island affairs, via your hotel or dive centre. Satgas uses its community contacts to fix problems or locate stolen property with a minimum of fuss.

Incidents are very rare, but some foreign women have experienced sexual harassment and even assault while on the Gilis – it's best to walk home in pairs to the quieter parts of the islands.

Jellyfish are common when strong winds blow from the mainland, and the larger ones leave a painful rash. See p370.

And beware of non-commercial arak, the potent rice or palm hootch. There have been incidents of poisoning.

Getting There & Away

Much of the Gili's recent tourist boom is due in large part to the three speedboats that carry passengers directly from Bali. **Gili Cat** (0361-271680; www.gilicat.com) leaves from Padangbai at 9am daily (660,000Rp, 2½ hours). **Blue Water Express** (0361-3104558; www.bwsbali.com) leaves from Benoa harbour (690,000Rp, 2½ hours).

You can also book passage directly from Serangan (near Sanur) to Gili Trawangan on the Mahi Mahi (580,000Rp, 2½ hours). The **Gili Paradise Shop** (Map p100; 0361-753241; www.gili-paradise.com; Poppies Gang I, Kuta) in Bali has info. Its shop and website have objective, timely information about all the Gilis. Given the time you save, the new fast boats make a lot more sense than flying, which is why seats

---

BANGSAL GAUNTLET

If you arrive to the principal Gili Islands port by bus, bemo or taxi, you will be dropped off at the Bangsal terminal – nearly a kilometre from the harbour. From which point irrepressible touts hustling a dishonest buck will harass you non-stop. It's not fun. Just ignore them and do not buy a ticket from them or from anyone else on the road. There is but one official Bangsal harbour ticket office, the Koperasi harbour office: it is on the beach left of the dirt road, and arranges all local boat transport – shuttle, public and chartered – to the Gilis. Buy a ticket anywhere else and you're taking a hit. You could also avoid Bangsal altogether by booking a speedboat transfer from Senggigi via one of the dive schools, taking one of the new fast-boat services direct from Bali (the best choice), or by travelling with Perama from Bali or Mataram, Kuta (Lombok) or Senggigi.

sell out during July and August. Be sure to book ahead.

There's also a cheaper direct service from Bali. Perama buses and their slow boat head to the Gilis via Padangbai (see p222) and Senggigi. Or you can fly to Mataram and make arrangements from there.

Coming from other parts of Lombok, you can travel via Senggigi; via the public boats that leave from Bangsal (the cheapest route); you can charter your own boat from Bangsal (195,000Rp), or you can book passage on a private speedboat. Blue Marlin and Manta Dive (p304) on Gili Trawangan can arrange transfers (500,000Rp for up to three people). Speedboats use the lovely Teluk Nare harbour south of Bangsal.

Coming by public transport, catch a bus or bemo to Pemenlombok. It's about 1 km by *ci-domo* (pony cart; 3000Rp) to Bangsal harbour. Bangsal is beyond annoying; see opposite for tips on dealing with the inevitable hassle there. Suffice it to say, these touts are adept at rais-ing blood pressures, and you should sooner ignore than trust them. Boat tickets are sold at the Koperasi harbour office on the beach. Public boats run from roughly 8am to 5pm, but don't leave until full (about 18 people). The one-way fares at the time of research were 8000Rp to Gili Air, 9000Rp to Gili Meno and 10,000Rp to Gili Trawangan. Special charters can also be organised in Bangsal.

All boats pull up on the beach when they get to the Gilis, so you'll have to wade ashore with your luggage.

Getting Around
CIDOMO
Hiring a *cidomo* for a clip-clop around an island is a great way to explore the terrain; a short trip costs between 20,000Rp and 35,000Rp. You'll pay 50,000Rp or more for a two-hour jaunt.

ISLAND-HOPPING
There's a twice-daily island-hopping boat service that loops between all three islands (20,000Rp to 23,000Rp), meaning you can spend the day snorkelling and exploring Meno and get back to Air or Trawangan in time for a sundowner. The morning boat leaves Air at 8.30am, stopping on Meno at 8.45am, Trawangan at 9.30am, Meno again at 9.45am and returning to Air at 9.45am. In the af-ternoons, the boat leaves Air at 3pm, Meno

---

> ### GILI ISLANDS CURRENTS: WARNING
> Currents between the Gili Islands are very strong. Take care when snorkelling offshore and do not attempt to swim between the islands – this goes double after a night on the ale.

at 3.15pm, Trawangan at 3.30pm, Meno at 4.15pm and gets back to Air at 4.30pm. Check the latest timetable at the islands' docks. You can also charter your own island-hopping boat (170,000Rp to 195,000Rp).

WALKING
The Gilis are flat and easy enough to get around by foot (or bicycle, p298). A torch (flashlight) is useful at night. You can buy one at local shops for around 25,000Rp.

GILI AIR
Closest to Lombok, Gili Air falls between Gili T's sophistication and less-is-more Meno. It's a rural island and, like the others, was settled by Sasak and Bugis farmers who planted the lovely coconut groves that domi-nate the flat interior and cloak some of the better bungalows. On clear mornings you'll have stunning views of both Gunung Rinjani and Gunung Agung in Bali. The white-sand beaches are beautiful here, and although they're relatively thin, the turquoise water and laid-back beach bars and cafés make up for it. Traditionally, families have made Gili Air their offshore Lombok base, but Gili T has been gobbling up that market, so it's mostly couples lazing in the sun these days. Although it feels delightfully empty at times, Air is still the most populous of the Gili islands with 1800 inhabitants.

Orientation
The main harbour is located at the southern end of the island, near the jetty; the **Koperasi** (Map p298; ☾ 8am-5.30pm), the public boat office, has a hut here with prices marked clearly out-side. Almost all accommodation and restau-rants are on the east and south coasts, which have the best swimming beaches. A network of sand and dirt tracks criss-cross the island, but can get quite confusing. Keep it simple and stick to the coastal path around the island – it's a gorgeous 90-minute walk, especially around sunset.

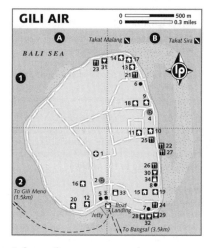

INFORMATION
Clinic...1 A2
Gecko Café..2 A2
Koperasi...3 A2
Ozzy's Shop..4 B1
Perama..5 A2

SIGHTS & ACTIVITIES
Blue Marlin Dive Centre............................6 B1
Dream Divers..7 B2
Manta Dive...8 B1

SLEEPING
Abdi Fantastik..9 B1
Corner Bungalows....................................10 B2
Gili Air Santay..11 B2
Gili Indah Hotel..12 A2
Gusung Indah...13 B1
Hotel Gili Air..14 B1
Manta Dive...(see 8)
Mawar Bungalows....................................15 B2
Resota Bungalows....................................16 A2
Sandy Cottages..17 B1
Sejuk Cottages...18 B1
Sunrise Hotel..19 B2
Villa Karang..20 A2

EATING
Ali Baba..21 B1
Green Café..22 B2
Gusung Indah.....................................(see 13)
Harmony Café...23 A1
Hikmah's..24 B2
Munchies...25 B2
Santay..(see 11)
Tami's...26 B2
Wiwin Café...27 B2

DRINKING
Blue Bar...28 B2
Chill Out Bar..29 B2
Gita Gili..30 B2
Legend Pub..31 A1
Zipp Bar...32 B2

SHOPPING
Art Shop...33 B2
Coconut Handicraft..................................34 B2

Information

There's a small **Perama** (Map p298; ☎ 637816) office next to the Gili Indah Hotel. **Gecko Café** (Map p298; per min 500Rp; ✆ 8am-9pm) has by far the best web connection on the island. **Ozzy's Shop** (Map p298; ☎ 622179; ✆ 8am-8pm), about halfway up the east coast, has a wartel and will change money, as will Hotel Gili Air, but exchange rates are poor. The Blue Marlin Dive Centre charges 7% for cash advances on credit cards. There's a **clinic** (Map p298; ✆ 8am-6pm) in the village for medical services.

Activities

SNORKELLING & DIVING

There's great snorkelling all along the east coast reef, with plenty of colourful fish. Gear can be hired from Ozzy's Shop and a number of beach bars for 20,000Rp a day. Check with dive centres about currents, as sometimes they can be extremely strong (p297). Ozzy's Shop also operates **glass-bottomed boat tours** (per person 40,000Rp, minimum 4 people) around all three islands.

Scuba diving is excellent throughout the Gilis, and no matter where you stay, you'll dive the same sites. See p302 for more information. Gili Air now has three dive schools, **Blue Marlin Dive Centre** (Map p298; ☎ 634387, 0812 377 0288; www.bluemarlindive.com), **Dream Divers** (Map p298; ☎ 634547; www.dreamdivers.com), and **Manta Dive** (Map p298; ☎ 0813 530 50462, 0813 377 89047; www.manta-dive.com) who just opened their Gili Air branch (complete with sweet bungalows) on the east coast.

SURFING

Directly off the southern tip of the island there's a long, peeling right-hand break that can get big at times. The dive schools will help you get your hands on a board.

CYCLING

Ozzy's Shop has bikes for hire for 25,000Rp a day. Pedalling on Air can be fun. You'll have to walk it when you inevitably land in deep sand, and you're sure to roll into villagers' back yards if you explore the inland trails, but isn't that kind of accidental mingling why you're here?

Sleeping

Most places are spread up and down the east coast, where the best swimming is. Prices quoted are high-season rates – you can negotiate big discounts in low season. Breakfast is almost always included.

BUDGET

Gili Air Santay (Map p298; ☎ 0818 0375 8695, 0819 1599 3782; www.giliair-santay.com; d 80,000-180,000Rp) Set back from the beach in a quiet coconut grove, these spacious bamboo-and-timber huts are a good budget choice, especially if you dig rocking in a hammock on the beach. The shoreside restaurant is the only one on the island serving authentic Thai food (see right).

Mawar Bungalows (Map p298; ☎ 0813 6225 3995; bungalows 130,000-220,000Rp) Basic, thatched bungalows set 30m from the sea in the coconut grove. The new ones have Western toilets, and all have hammocks and come with breakfast in a stylish dining area. It also serves family dinners for guests and staff every night (50,000Rp).

Gili Indah Hotel (Map p298; ☎ 637328; gili_indah @mataram.wasantara.net.id; bungalows 150,000-300,000Rp; ✄) These Indonesian-owned bungalows near the jetty could be cleaner. The nicer wooden ones on the beach have air-con and hot water and are a good deal.

Resota Bungalows (Map p298; ☎ 0818 0571 5769; bungalows 250,000Rp) Nestled in the coconut palms near the harbour is this charming bungalow property. They feel new and come with a stocked minibar and inviting hammocks on the porch.

Sunrise Hotel (Map p298; ☎ 642370; bungalows 250,000-350,000Rp) Charming, if a bit aged, these two-storey thatched bungalows have outdoor living rooms and are set back from the beach.

Also worth considering:

Gusung Indah (Map p298; ☎ 0812 378 9054; bungalows 100,000-150,000Rp) Nice bungalows, most with a sea view, served with a touch of attitude by the man in charge.

Abdi Fantastik (Map p298; ☎ 636421; r 150,000Rp) Family-owned bungalows strung with hammocks, steps from the sea.

MIDRANGE

Sandy Cottages (Map p298; ☎ 0812 378 9832; bungalows 250,000-400,000Rp; ✄) New stone and low-slung thatched bungalows. They offer great low-season deals.

Hotel Gili Air (Map p298; ☎ 634435; www.hotelgiliair .com; r US$34-90; ✄ ▣) Setting itself up as the island's 'proper' hotel, but it's obvious that standards have slipped. But it does have gorgeous sunset and sunrise views.

Corner Bungalows (Map p298; ☎ 0819 172 29543; bungalows 350,000Rp) Owned by a welcoming local family, these new (at the time of research) bamboo bungalows each have hammocks swinging on a varnished deck.

Manta Dive (Map p298; ☎ 0813 5305 0462, 0813 3778 9047; www.manta-dive.com; bungalows US$50-65; ✄ ▣) Manta is the innovator of the Zen mod-hut motif that has been replicated throughout the Gilis. These were brand-new at research time with arched roofs, minimalist interiors, decks and outdoor baths.

our pick Sejuk Cottages (Map p298; ☎ 636461, 0813 3953 5387; bungalows 450,000-650,000Rp; ✄ ▣) A stunning French-owned property, this option may offer the best bungalows on any Gili. Your experience will begin with an ice-blended latte – the welcome drink, which you'll slurp on the deck of your low-slung *lumbung* cottage or in the rooftop living room of your split-level bungalow, which has ocean views. They all have outdoor baths, superb lighting and homey touches like hand-painted wardrobes and a bouquet of glittering silver dragonflies in a ceramic floor vase. And they open onto a flower garden that fades into a coconut grove that sways to the sand. *Magnifique!*

Villa Karang (Map p298; ☎ 0813 3990 4440; bungalows from 500,000Rp; ✄) This ambitious harbour resort is a mishmash of newer concrete and tile rooms, and older thatched wood bungalows. For the money, it's not the best value. But it does have a lovely pool area, and it does book up fast.

Eating

Gili Air eats pretty well. It isn't fancy, and service tends to be slow (painfully, at times) but you'll be seated cross-legged on cushions atop beachfront *beruga* (open-sided pavilions), so no bitching! Most cafés serve simple Indonesian and Western dishes, and they almost all have wood-fired pizza ovens…for some unexplained reason.

Ali Baba (Map p298; dishes 10,000-50,000Rp) A creative beachside warung infused with wacky sea- and coconut-shell sculpture on a lovely rocky beach. It has the usual Indonesian, seafood and Western fare, and pizza, of course.

LOMBOK

Tami's (Map p298; dishes 10,000-40,000Rp) A funky Sasak-themed café decorated with masks, bamboo furniture, dining platforms and shaggy new *beruga*. Try the *ayam taliwang* (whole split chicken roasted over coconut husks served with a tomato-chilli-lime dip). It also has a nightly fish grill.

Santay (Map p298; ☎ dishes 12,000-30,000Rp) The only Thai kitchen on Gili Air, and it has the typical Indo-Western offerings too. Meals are served with gorgeous Rinjani views if the gods allow.

Harmony Café (Map p298; dishes 15,000-100,000Rp; ☻ 4-9pm) This is the island's classiest dinner spot. It's set on a bamboo pier, with pink tablecloths, candlelight, platforms with ample pillows to lean into, and exquisite sunset views. Come for a sundowner at happy hour (cocktails 25,000Rp) or for a full grilled fish dinner (50,000Rp to 100,000Rp).

Green Café (Map p298; dishes 15,000-25,000Rp; ☻ 11am-9pm) The pink-washed, waterfront *beruga* dangle with hand-painted coconuts, and the kitchen serves up decent Sasak cuisine, pasta, pizza and kebabs.

Wiwin Café (Map p298; dishes 25,000-45,000Rp) Its wood-fired pizzas smell divine, and it has the most extensive veggie menu on the island.

Hikmah's (Map p298; ☎ 0818 0578 4565; baguettes 35,000-40,000Rp) Set on the island's southeast corner, Hikmah's specialises in homemade baguettes. Choices include chicken and asparagus; smoked salmon and cream cheese; and brie with green pepper. It also rents snorkel gear for 20,000Rp a day.

Or try one of the following:

Munchies (Map p298; dishes 7500-26,000Rp; ☻ noon-11pm) Serves good curries, fish and overflowing sandwiches.

Gusung Indah (Map p298; ☎ 0812 3789 054; dishes 15,000-40,000Rp) Sit under a beachfront *beruga* and feast on local food such as *opor ayam* (braised chicken in coconut milk), sandwiches or pasta.

Drinking

On full and dark moons, the island can rock, but usually Gili Air is as mellow as Meno.

ourpick **Zipp Bar** (Map p298; ☎ 0819 1593 5205; ☻ 7am-late) This beautiful teak island bar, set on a sandy beach perfect for swimming, is the island's main hub of activity. It has an excellent booze selection, outstanding fresh-fruit cocktails and decent pub grub. It throws a beach party every full moon.

Chill Out Bar (Map p298; ☻ 11-2am) Popular with visitors and locals, it has a good selection of spirits and cocktails.

Gita Gili (Map p298; ☻ 11-1am) A friendly bar where you can request a DVD to watch while you sink a cold one.

Blue Bar (Map p298; ☻ 8.30am-late) You'll find comfy beach *beruga* and a great vibe here.

Legend Pub (Map p298; ☻ 10am-11.30pm Thu-Tue, happy hour 5-7pm, dark moon party 10pm-2am) Your standard-issue island reggae bar. It throws monthly dark moon parties.

Shopping

The **Art Shop** behind the harbour is worth a look if you're interested in Sasak masks. It has a wide array of styles and sizes. **Coconut Handicraft** (Map p298; ☎ 0813 622 53995; ☻ 10am-8pm) deals in high-quality coconut-shell necklaces, rings, bowls and cups. The proprietor teaches his craft and sells lovely mosaic mirrors as well.

GILI MENO

Gili Meno is the smallest of the three islands and the perfect setting for your Robinson Crusoe fantasy. Its beaches are the best in the archipelago and, with a population of just 300, it's gloriously quiet day and night. Most of the accommodation is strung out along the eastern coast, near the widest and most picturesque beach. Inland you'll find scattered homesteads, coconut plantations and salt flats.

Information

There are a couple of minimarkets by the boat landing, so you'll be able to pick up the most basic supplies. **Internet** (Map p301; per min 600Rp) and a wartel are available near the boat landing. Money can be exchanged at the Kontiki Meno hotel, among others, at poor rates. For tours and shuttle-bus/boat tickets, the travel agent **Perama** (☎ 632824) is based at Kontiki Meno. A resident nurse attends the medical clinic near the bird park. Doctors are on call in Mataram.

Sights & Activities
TAMAN BURUNG

Gili Meno's 2500-sq-metre **bird park** (Map p301; ☎ 642321; admission 50,000Rp; ☻ 9am-5pm) is home to 300 exotic birds from Asia and Australia, three demure kangaroos and a komodo dragon. Birds are liberated from their cages for three hours a day to fly around an expansive atrium covered in netting.

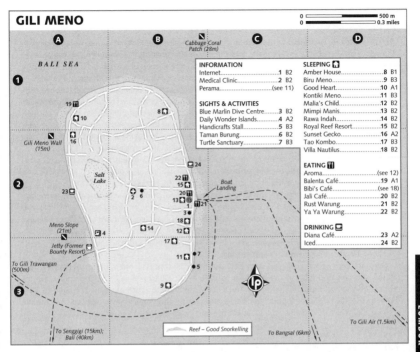

GILI MENO

0 — 500 m
0 — 0.3 miles

INFORMATION
Internet.........................1 B2
Medical Clinic...............2 B2
Perama......................(see 11)

SIGHTS & ACTIVITIES
Blue Marlin Dive Centre.......3 B2
Daily Wonder Islands...........4 A2
Handicrafts Stall...............5 B3
Taman Burung.................6 B2
Turtle Sanctuary.................7 B3

SLEEPING
Amber House....................8 B1
Biru Meno.......................9 B3
Good Heart......................10 A1
Kontiki Meno....................11 B3
Malia's Child....................12 B2
Mimpi Manis....................13 B2
Rawa Indah....................14 B2
Royal Reef Resort...............15 B2
Sunset Gecko....................16 A2
Tao Kombo.....................17 B3
Villa Nautilus....................18 B2

EATING
Aroma.........................(see 12)
Balenta Café....................19 A1
Bibi's Café.....................(see 18)
Jali Café.......................20 B2
Rust Warung....................21 B2
Ya Ya Warung...................22 B2

DRINKING
Diana Café.....................23 A2
Iced...........................24 B2

BALI SEA

Cabbage Coral Patch (28m)

Gili Meno Wall (15m)

Salt Lake

Boat Landing

Meno Slope (21m)

Jetty (Former Bounty Resort)

To Gili Trawangan (500m)

To Senggigi (15km); Bali (40km)

Reef – Good Snorkelling

To Bangsal (6km)

To Gili Air (1.5km)

LOMBOK

TURTLE SANCTUARY

Meno's **turtle sanctuary** (Map p301; www.gilimenoturtles
.com) is a complex of kiddie pools and bathtubs
on the beach, bubbling with filters and teeming
with baby turtles. The cute critters are nurtured
until they're strong enough to be released into
the wild with a minimum of predatory risk. It
releases about 250 turtles a year.

SNORKELLING & DIVING

There's good snorkelling off the northeast
coast near Amber House, on the west coast
near Good Heart and also around the former
jetty of the (abandoned) Bounty resort. Gear
is available for 20,000Rp per day from several
places on the eastern strip. Always ask about
the currents first. For more on snorkelling
and diving, see p302. **Daily Wonder Islands** (Map
p301; ☎ 0818 036 12402; ⏰ tours depart 9am & 2pm) offers half-day snorkelling tours (235,000Rp
per person for four hours). Price includes
hotel pick-up.

Blue Marlin Dive Centre (Map p301; ☎ 639979, 0819
171 93285; www.bluemarlindive.com) offers fun dives
and courses, from the introductory 'Discover
Scuba' to dive master.

WALKING & SHOPPING

A late-afternoon stroll around tiny Meno is
a must. It can be completed in an hour and
is best done with a few stops for sundowners
along the way. Look for the ramshackle **handicrafts stall** just south of Kontiki. You'll find
very cool, traditional Sasak water baskets and
gourds. Blink and you'll miss it though.

Sleeping

In terms of value, lodging on Meno doesn't
compete with what you'll find on Air and Gili
T, but if you reserve ahead (an absolute must in
the high season), you can land in a sweet spot.
Prices quoted are high-season rates – reductions
of up to 50% are possible the rest of the year.

BUDGET

Tao Kombo (Map p301; ☎ 0812 372 2174; tao_kombo
@yahoo.com; bungalows 100,000-300,000Rp) About
200m inland, you'll find the most original
of Meno's bungalow properties. There are
open huts with bamboo screens instead
of walls, and nicer, enclosed cottages with
vaulted ceilings, thatched roofs and stone
floors. An intriguing option.

LOMBOK

UNDERWATER GILIS

The Gili Islands are a superb dive destination as the marine life is plentiful and varied. Turtles and black- and white-tip reef sharks are common, and the macro life (small stuff) is excellent, with seahorses, pipefish and lots of crustaceans. Around the full moon, large schools of bumphead parrotfish appear to feast on coral spawn; at other times of the year scores of manta rays soar through dive sites.

Though years of bomb fishing and an El Niño–inspired bleaching damaged soft corals above 18m, the reefs are now in recovery. In front of every dive shop, an electric current runs to a Biorock reef, which over time will evolve into a natural coral reef. This is a project of the Gili Eco Trust, a partnership between dive operators and the local community, aiming to improve the condition of the reefs and protect them in perpetuity. All divers help fund the trust by paying a one-off fee of 30,000Rp with their first dive – part of those funds goes to locals who are actually paid not to fish.

The Gilis also have their share of virgin coral. Hidden Reef, a recently discovered site, pops with colourful coral life above 20m, and there's also an abundance of deep coral shelves and walls at around 30m, where the coral is, and always has been, pristine.

Safety standards are high on the Gilis despite the modest dive costs – there are no dodgy dive schools, and instructors and training are professional. Rates are fixed (no matter who you dive with) at US$35 a dive, with discounts for packages of five dives or more. A PADI open-water course costs US$350 and the advanced course is US$275. A dive master course starts at US$650. Blue Marlin and Trawangan Dive also offer nitrox and trimix dives and courses. For contact details of dive schools, see individual island entries.

Surrounded by coral reefs and with easy beach access, the Gilis offer superb snorkelling too. Masks, snorkels and fins can be hired for as little as 20,000Rp per day. On Trawangan, turtles appear on the reef right off the beach. You'll likely drift with the current, so be prepared to walk back to the starting line. Around Gili Meno, the pier by the Bounty resort (closed) has prolific marine life, while over on Air, the walls off the east coast are good.

Kontiki Meno (Map p301; ☎ 632824; cottages with fan/air-con 200,000/300,000Rp; 🛰) The beach is gorgeous, the seaside wooden platforms demand sunbathing, but the cold water, cinderblock cottages are just okay.

Good Heart (Map p301; ☎ 0813 395 56976; bungalows 200,000Rp) Excellent, friendly Balinese-owned place with a row of twin-deck *lumbung*-like bungalows with open-air fresh-water bathrooms. It's opposite a slim stretch of beach that faces Gili Trawangan.

Royal Reef Resort (Map p301; ☎ 642340; bungalows 300,000Rp) The name makes it sounds like some old school yacht club. It's really just a faded yellow sign and six large but basic, thatched bamboo bungalows opposite the marina. Um, that's a good thing.

Other recommendations:

Rawa Indah (Map p301; ☎ 0819 179 38813; bungalows 150,000Rp) Basic, bamboo, thatched, palm-shaded and dangling with seashell wind chimes.

Mimpi Manis (Map p301; ☎ 642324; s/d 200,000Rp) Basic bamboo bungalows set back from the beach.

Amber House (Map p301; ☎ 0813 375 69728; bungalows 250,000Rp) Attractive, circular bungalows with outdoor showers on the island's quiet north end.

MIDRANGE

our pick **Sunset Gecko** (Map p301; ☎ 0813 535 66774 www.thesunsetgecko.com; bungalows 350,000Rp; 🛰) These attractive, thatched two-storey A-frame bungalows have outdoor and indoor bedrooms, wood shutters, and the best views on Meno.

Malia's Child (Map p301; ☎ 622007; www.gilimeno -mallias.com; bungalows US$35) Some of the best bungalows on this end of Meno – they're thatched, bamboo and lined up along the deep white sand. If you want one, you'd better book ahead. They'll negotiate a lower daily rate for long stays.

Biru Meno (Map p301; ☎ 0813 365 7322; bungalows 450,000Rp) The staff are friendly, the bungalows are tastefully crafted from mostly native materials like bamboo and coral, and their beach is stunning. But considering there's no hot water, it's a touch over-priced.

Villa Nautilus (Map p301; ☎ 642143; www.villanau tilus.com; r €66; 🛰) Five deluxe detached villas, finished in contemporary style with natural wood, marble and limestone. The design allows plenty of natural light to flood the lounge level, which has doors opening to a decked terrace.

Some of the best dive sites include the following:

- **Bounty Pier** At 12m to 18m, this sunken pontoon site is ideal for beginners, and you can glimpse rare frogfish here regularly.

- **Deep Halik** This canyon-like site is ideally suited to drift diving. Black- and white-tip sharks are often seen at 28m to 30m.

- **Deep Turbo** At around 30m, this site is ideally suited to nitrox diving. It has impressive sea fans and leopard sharks hidden in the crevasses.

- **Hans Reef** Off the northeast coast of Gili Air, this reef is great for macro life including frogfish, ghostfish, sea horses and pipefish.

- **Hidden Reef** Nestled between Meno and Air, and not yet flagged on most dive maps, this 12m to 25m site has vibrant, pristine soft corals.

- **Japanese Wreck** For experienced divers only (it lies at 45m), this shipwreck of a Japanese patrol boat (c WWII) is another site ideal for nitrox divers. You'll see prolific soft coral, and lots of nudibranches. Look out for lionfish and frogfish.

- **Shark Point** From 15m to 30m, this is perhaps the most exhilarating dive on the Gilis: reef sharks and turtles are very regularly encountered, as well as schools of bumphead parrotfish and mantas. Look out too for cuttlefish and octopuses. At shallow depths there can be a strong surge.

- **Simon's Reef** The reef here is in excellent condition; from 16m to 30m you can see schools of trevally, and occasionally barracuda and leopard sharks.

- **Sunset (Manta Point)** The sloping reef has good coral growth below 18m, including impressive table coral. Large pelagics are frequently encountered and strong currents are rarely an issue.

Eating & Drinking

The beachfront restaurants near the boat landing all offer fine views for your meal, which is just as well as service can be slow. Most places are locally owned, which is always nice.

our pick **Rust Warung** (Map p301; ☎ 642324; mains 8000-75,000Rp; 7am-10am, 11am-3.30pm, 6pm-late) This restaurant, attached to the islands' best allpurpose shop, has beachfront *beruga* and a terrific assortment of fresh daily catch. Fish is perfectly grilled, glazed with garlic or sweetand-sour sauce and served with grilled corn, cabbage salad and baked potato. The only problem is the nearby bar's soundtrack, bouncing from Bollywood classics to techno club anthems to death metal. At least the fish is good.

Iced (Map p301; scoops 6000Rp, coffees 10,000-12,000Rp, sundaes 15,000-28,000Rp; 8am-sunset) A half-dozen tables tastefully scattered on the white sand and shaded by parasols make this the perfect setting for iced coffee and… *ice cream*!

Jali Café (Map p301; ☎ 639800; dishes 10,000-20,000Rp) The friendly owners serve up tasty Indonesian, Sasak and curry dishes. At night they grill fresh fish and strum guitars by the fire. Everyone is welcome.

Ya Ya Warung (Map p301; dishes 10,000-20,000Rp) It looks like a stiff breeze might blow this lean-to beach warung over, but it's part of the charm. It serves all your Indonesian faves and a huge selection of pasta dishes.

Aroma (Map p301; ☎ 622007; dishes 15,000-40,000Rp) Um, yeah, that's right, more wood-fired pizza. Settle into a *beruga* and devour the pizza Lombok – it's got mushies, onions and fiery Lombok chilli.

Bibi's Café (Map p301; ☎ 642143; mains 15,000-27,000Rp) Attached to the Villa Nautilus, Bibi's is touted as having the best wood-fired pizza on an island of wood-fired pizzas.

Balenta Café (Map p301; mains from 20,000Rp, fish at market price) Next to the Good Heart, this fantastic café has a full menu of Sasak and international food and a great seafood barbecue nightly.

Diana Café (Map p301; ☎ 0818 057 7622, drinks 12,000-25,000Rp) A hippie bar deluxe and your perfect pit stop for an ice-cold Bintang at sunset. The stilted *beruga* have cushions, coffee tables and ideal sunset views. It also has great snorkelling nearby and rents gear on the cheap (12,500Rp). Bring a book and hang awhile.

LOMBOK

GILI TRAWANGAN

Social but not trashy, relaxed but not boring, all natural, yet updated with technology – internet, DVD pavilions, and top-range sound-systems – and sprinkled with a collection of restaurants and bars that would satisfy any devout cosmopolitan, Gili T is the road-weary rambler's lucid fantasy.

Gili Trawangan, the largest and most popular of the car-less Gilis Islands, first blipped onto the tourism radar during the '90s, when Bali rose to global prominence and backpackers descended in search of white sand, warm water, rich reefs and a good party. Expectations were exceeded across the board. But thanks to an overt, entrenched weed and 'shrooms trade, and three all-night rave-like events a week, it was that party label which stuck. Gili T is a lot more than that now.

Part of this latent maturity is due to a recent drug bust sparked by undercover cops who posed as humble DVD hawkers. But it also has something to do with the fast boats from Bali, shepherding over a diversified clientele of young families and moneyed weekenders from Singapore and Jakarta. Then there's the, ahem, 'maturing' expat community.

Yes, the once carefree dive entrepreneurs have families now. And they're building swank villas, upscale dive schools and shabby-chic cafés. Trawangan's Indonesian community has benefited from the surge in tourism here, as well. Some of the best new bars and bungalows are locally owned.

But agoraphobics needn't worry. Even with the new construction boom, the lightly developed northwest coast – where the crowds are (much!) thinner, the water is the turquoise shade you dream about, and the snorkelling is superb – remains pristine. Nest here and you're still just a 20-minute beach stroll from that scrum of dive shops, sushi bars, lounges, reggae joints, and beachfront dining rooms that are simply impossible to resist.

Orientation & Information

Boats dock on the eastern side of the island, which is also home to most of Trawangan's accommodation, restaurants and facilities. The best stretch of beach is on the stunning northwest corner of the island, but be aware that if you stay here you'll have a longer trek to the action.

Several stores will change cash or travellers cheques, but rates are notoriously poor. Dive shops give cash advances on credit cards for a hefty commission of 7% to 10%.

There is no post office, but stamps and postcards are sold in the wartel and Pasar Seni, a local mini-mall filled with souvenirs, cheap handicrafts, mobile-phone kiosks, tasty local food and one surf shop.

EMERGENCIES

Clinic (Map p305; ☽ 9am-5pm) Just south of Hotel Vila Ombak.

Satgas Contact Satgas, a community organisation that controls security on the island, via your hotel or dive school.

INTERNET ACCESS & TELEPHONE

Also offering a wartel, **Lightening** (Map p305; internet access per min 500Rp) has a satellite-fed broadband connection, but it ain't swift. If you have a laptop, find Scallywag's (p309), one of Trawangan's most popular new restaurants. It has the only wireless connection on the Gilis.

TRAVEL AGENCIES

Located just north of the jetty, **Perama** (Map p305; ☎ 638514; www.peramatour.com) offers boat tickets to Pandangbai in Bali, Senggigi, and additional Lombok destinations by shuttle bus. Trips to Komodo can also be arranged here (see the boxed text, p362).

Activities

DIVING

Trawangan is made for divers, with seven established scuba schools – including one of the best tech diving schools in the world – and reasonable prices (see p302).

Big Bubble (Map p305; ☎ 625020; www.bigbubble diving.com)

Blue Marlin Dive Centre (Map p305; ☎ 632424, 0813 3993 0190; www.bluemarlindive.com)

Buddha Dive (Map p305; ☎ 642289; www.buddha dive.com)

Dream Divers (Map p305; ☎ 634496; www.dream divers.com)

Manta Dive (Map p305; ☎ 643649; www.manta-dive.com)

Trawangan Diving (Map p305; ☎ 649220, 0813 3770 2332; www.trawangadive.com)

Villa Ombak Diving Academy (Map p305; ☎ 638531)

BOAT TRIPS & SNORKELLING

Glass-bottomed boat trips (60,000Rp per person, including snorkelling equipment) to coral reefs can be booked at many stores on the main strip.

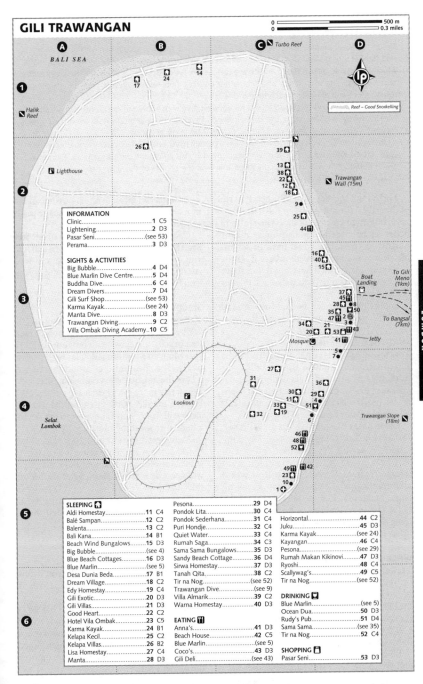

GILI TRAWANGAN

0 _____ 500 m
0 _____ 0.3 miles

BALI SEA

Halik
Reef

Lighthouse

Turbo Reef

Reef – Good Snorkelling

Trawangan
Wall (15m)

To Gili
Meno
(1km)

Boat
Landing

To Bangsal
(7km)

Jetty

Mosque

Selat
Lombok

Lookout

Trawangan
Slope
(18m)

LOMBOK

INFORMATION
Clinic..**1** C5
Lightening..................................**2** D3
Pasar Seni..........................(see **53**)
Perama..**3** D3

SIGHTS & ACTIVITIES
Big Bubble...................................**4** D4
Blue Marlin Dive Centre..............**5** D4
Buddha Dive................................**6** C4
Dream Divers...............................**7** D4
Gili Surf Shop......................(see **53**)
Karma Kayak........................(see **24**)
Manta Dive..................................**8** D3
Trawangan Diving........................**9** C2
Villa Ombak Diving Academy.....**10** C5

SLEEPING
Aldi Homestay...........................**11** C4
Balé Sampan..............................**12** C2
Balenta......................................**13** C2
Bali Kana...................................**14** B1
Beach Wind Bungalows.............**15** D3
Big Bubble...........................(see **4**)
Blue Beach Cottages.................**16** D3
Blue Marlin..........................(see **5**)
Desa Dunia Beda.......................**17** B1
Dream Village............................**18** C2
Edy Homestay............................**19** C4
Gili Exotic..................................**20** D3
Gili Villas...................................**21** D3
Good Heart.................................**22** C2
Hotel Vila Ombak......................**23** C5
Karma Kayak..............................**24** B1
Kelapa Kecil...............................**25** C2
Kelapa Villas..............................**26** B2
Lisa Homestay............................**27** C4
Manta...**28** D3

Pesona.......................................**29** D4
Pondok Lita...............................**30** C4
Pondok Sederhana.....................**31** C4
Puri Hondje...............................**32** C4
Quiet Water...............................**33** C4
Rumah Saga...............................**34** C3
Sama Sama Bungalows...............**35** D3
Sandy Beach Cottage.................**36** D4
Sirwa Homestay.........................**37** D3
Tanah Qita.................................**38** C2
Tir na Nog............................(see **52**)
Trawangan Dive....................(see **9**)
Villa Almarik..............................**39** C2
Warna Homestay........................**40** D3

EATING
Anna's.......................................**41** D3
Beach House...............................**42** C5
Blue Marlin...........................(see **5**)
Coco's..**43** D3
Gili Deli................................(see **43**)

Horizontal..................................**44** C2
Juku...**45** D3
Karma Kayak........................(see **24**)
Kayangan...................................**46** C4
Pesona.................................(see **29**)
Rumah Makan Kikinovi................**47** D3
Ryoshi..**48** C4
Scallywag's................................**49** C5
Tir na Nog............................(see **52**)

DRINKING
Blue Marlin..........................(see **5**)
Ocean Dua.................................**50** D3
Rudy's Pub.................................**51** D4
Sama Sama...........................(see **35**)
Tir na Nog.................................**52** C4

SHOPPING
Pasar Seni..................................**53** D3

GILI T'S TECHNICALITIES

Simon Liddiard, founder and owner of Blue Marlin and the first Westerner with a Gili address, also happens to be one of the world's best tech dive instructors. The Gilis' vibrant coral walls, which descend to over 1000m beneath the surface, are his classrooms, and his curriculum includes nitrox, trimix, extended range and rebreather courses. Rebreathers recycle your air, are almost totally silent and allow for much longer dives.

Liddiard once held the world record for deepest dive with a rebreather (170m), and his affable lead instructor Will Goodman, the perfect blend of London punk and dive god, owns the current record for the longest dive ever (30 hours). You'll be in good hands.

Just remember going deep (over 45m) has a certain psychedelic affect on the brain. Technicolor coral throbs and sways, and you will be forgiven if you commune with a glowing, fluorescent green nudibranch and become convinced it knows the secrets of the universe.

There's fun snorkelling off the beach north of the jetty – the coral isn't in the best shape here, but there are tons of fish. The reef is in better shape close to the lighthouse off the northwest coast, but you'll have to scramble over some low coral to access it. If the current is quick, you'll have fun flying above the reef...until you have to walk back to your starting point.

Snorkelling gear can be hired for around 25,000Rp per day from shacks near the jetty.

SURFING & KAYAKING

Trawangan has a fast right break that can be surfed year-round and at times swells overhead. It's just south of Villa Ombok; for details, see p97. For more information and board rental, head to **Gili Surf Shop** (Map p305; ☎ 0812 372 7615) in the Pasar Seni.

Karma Kayak (Map p305; ☎ 0818 055 93710; tours 300,000Rp), a hotel, tapas bar and kayaking school, is set on the northern end of Gili T, where Astrid, a former champion stunt kayaker (she took silver at the 1991 world championships), leads half-day kayaking trips (maximum four paddlers) around the Gilis. If you're looking to build your paddling skills, she also teaches three-day courses upon request.

WALKING, CYCLING, RIDING

Trawangan is perfect for exploring on foot or by bike. You can walk around the whole island in a couple of hours – if you finish at the hill on the southwestern corner (which has the remains of an old Japanese gun placement c WWII), you'll have terrific sunset views of Bali's Gunung Agung.

Bikes are the preferred mode of transport, and are easily hired from 25,000Rp per day.

Your hotel can arrange rental or you can approach the bike shops directly. They're easily spotted along the main drag.

Or maybe you'd rather mount a steed? **Stud Horse Riding Adventures** (☎ 0817 574 6079) will lead you on long rides down the north and west coasts and through the inland coconut groves. You'll probably see them clop by.

Sleeping

There are now over 100 places to stay on Gili T. They range from simple village huts to mod Zen beach bungalows with outdoor baths, to sprawling air-conditioned villas with private pools. The cheapest digs are in the village, where the mosque is everyone's alarm clock. You'll pay more for a beachside address. We like the island's north coast, where you can sleepwalk from your bungalow to the sea for a hangover-soothing morning dip.

All budget and most midrange places have brackish tap water. Pure water is available in some bungalows and rumour has it that there will soon be a public fresh-water service on the Gilis.

These high-season rates can drop up to 50% off-peak. Breakfast is included unless stated otherwise.

BUDGET
Village

If the following places are full, you'll find a dozen or so comparable alternatives in the village.

Aldi Homestay (Map p305; ☎ 0813 395 41102; s/d 60,000/100,000Rp) A village bargain. Some rooms are nicer than others, so look around. Look for the ripped-off logo of the German supermarket chain Aldi, which is also the name of the owner's son.

Lisa Homestay (Map p305; ☎ 0813 395 23364; r 75,000Rp) Very friendly little place with light and airy tiled rooms that overlook a garden.

Pondok Lita (Map p305; ☎ 648607; s/d 80,000/120,000Rp) Popular family-run place in the village with spacious courtyard rooms, a library and in-house laundry service.

Sandy Beach Cottage (Map p305; ☎ 625020; d from 100,000Rp) A shady hideaway, close to the action.

Edy Homestay (Map p305; d from 120,000Rp) The best of the village cheapies. Rooms are very clean and come with ceiling fans and a big breakfast.

Pondok Sederhana (Map p305; ☎ 0813 3860 9964; r 120,000Rp) Run by a house-proud, friendly Balinese lady, the spotless rooms here face a neat little garden.

Puri Hondje (Map p305; r 150,000Rp; 🖵) Tucked away down a quiet village lane, these very stylish rooms overlook a small koi pond surrounded by bougainvillea and palms.

Quiet Water (Map p305; ☎ 0812 375 0687; d from 150,000) A plush yet affordable village choice with queen-size beds, soft linens, air-con, hot water, and in-room DVD players.

Beachside

Sirwa Homestay (Map p305; s/d 40,000/45,000Rp) This homestay offers spacious rooms (some have two double beds) with prices to suit those on a strict budget. There's a simple restaurant up front.

Warna Homestay (Map p305; ☎ 623859; d from 150,000Rp) Arguably the best value on the island, Warna has five sweet, tropical-flower-garden bungalows mere steps from the sea.

Balenta (Map p305; ☎ 0818 0520 3464; d from 180,000Rp) On the northwest coast, north of the upmarket Good Heart, Balenta is one of Gili T's better-value options. It's opposite a great stretch of beach and the rooms are large and immaculate.

MIDRANGE
Main Strip

Blue Marlin (Map p305; ☎ 632424, 0813 3993 0190; www.bluemarlindive.com; d from US$35) The air-con rooms are nice and convenient if you're enrolled in a dive course here. The cheaper digs could use an update.

Tir na Nog (Map p305; ☎ 639463; tirnanog@mataram.wasantara.net.id; r from 300,000Rp; 🖵) At the rear of the bar, these huge rooms with air-con have been thoughtfully designed and decorated;

most have spacious private terraces and swanky modern bathrooms.

Pesona (Map p305; ☎ 6607233; www.pesonaresort.com; r 400,000-600,000Rp, 🖵) You'll enjoy these sweet, brand-new (at research time) concrete-and-tile bungalows with inviting hammocks laced porch-side. The rooms, which are named for flowers, all have TVs, DVD and safety boxes, and the bathrooms are four-star quality with shell-embedded marble sinks.

Big Bubble (Map p305; ☎ 625020; www.bigbubblediving.com; d from 500,000Rp; 🖵 🗔) Native wood and thatched modernism can be found in this row of beautiful rooms behind the dive school. These have hammocks on the front terrace.

Village

Rumah Saga (Map p305; ☎ 648604, 0818 057 14315; www.rumahsaga.com; cottages 350,000/500,000Rp; 🖵) Clean, modern cottages with TV, air-con and hot water are set around a lovely garden area with a nice pool. The large bungalows sleep up to three people.

Beachside

Good Heart (Map p305; ☎ 0812 239 5170; r 100,000; bungalows 350,000-500,000Rp; 🖵) A great choice, with superb-value budget rooms (each with large beds) and some very stylish thatched A-frame bungalows with pebble-floored open-air bathrooms and all the mod cons.

Beach Wind Bungalows (Map p305; ☎ 0812 376 4347; standard/deluxe bungalows 350,000/600,000Rp; 🖵) Two levels of bungalows can be found here. The best are the wood, thatched variety with wide verandahs. The others are concrete and tile and overpriced. Table tennis, a book exchange, laundry service and snorkelling gear are available for guests.

Sama Sama Bungalows (Map p305; ☎ 0812 376 3650; r with air-con 400,000, deluxe lumbung 650,000Rp; 🖵) Combining natural materials with mod cons, these stylish rooms, though set back from the beach, make a comfortable base.

Tanah Qita (Map p305; ☎ 639159; bungalows 500,000Rp) Perhaps Trawangan's best new addition, these thatched, teak *lumbung* have high ceilings, outdoor bathrooms and style and grace to spare. The staff are marvellous. If they invite you to share a home-cooked Sasak meal, say 'yes please'.

Balé Sampan (Map p305; ☎ 0813 398 82153, 0813 377 48469; www.balesampanbungalows.com; garden/seaview bungalows 500,000/800,000Rp; 🖵 🗔) The name means boathouse, but there are no broken outboards, fishing nets and oily concrete floors here – just fine modern-edge beach bungalows. Only days old at the time of research, they were already sold out. The Jogja stone baths, fresh-water pool, plush duvet covers and proper English breakfast might have something to do with it. It's co-owned by some of Manta's best dive masters and the co-owner of Tir Na Nog and Coco's.

our pick Karma Kayak (Map p305; ☎ 0818 0559 3710; bungalows 550,000Rp) A new, beautiful bungalow property on the tranquil north end, run by a former champion kayaker who leads kayak tours of the island (p306). The staff are lovely, the well-lit bungalows spotless and the beach is absolutely gorgeous, especially at sunset.

Blue Beach Cottages (Map p305; ☎ 623538; bungalows from 550,000Rp, 🖳) Native thatch meets mod-minimalist at this locally owned collection of sea-view cottages on the north end of the strip. There are outdoor bathrooms, queen-size beds, wide decks and glass doors. Can bungalows look any smoother? Large long-term and low-season discounts are available if you negotiate.

Kelapa Kecil (Map p305; ☎ 0812 376 6496; bungalows US$70–90; 🖳🖳) These sleek, minimalist mod bungalows have little luxuries like security boxes, limestone baths and a plunge pool, and they're just steps from the sea.

Manta (Map p305; ☎ 643649 or 0812 376 4780; www .manta-dive.com; bungalows 550,000Rp; 🖳🖳) This laid-back English-run dive centre introduced the mod-bungalow motif to the Gilis, and theirs remain some of the most stylish. It's a fun place to be after the afternoon dive when the beers flow.

Bali Kana (Map p305; ☎ 622386; s/d/t 600,000/700,000/ 800,000Rp; 🖳🖳) Well-situated on the quiet north end are some of the most unique bungalows on the island. They're fashioned after traditional Sasak *lumbung*, and the two-storey variety have an upper deck terrace.

Trawangan Diving (Map p305; ☎ 649220, 0813 377 02332; www.trawangadive.com; bungalows US$60–80; 🖳🖳) The swankiest dive school on the island – think: luxe locker rooms with stone floors and a climate-controlled rebreather room – has just opened 12 stylish new rooms decked out in Indian limestone. They have fresh-water showers, a Western chef, and a sunken pool bar.

Dream Village (Map p305; ☎ 0818 546 591; www. dreamvillagetrawangan.com; bungalows 800,000Rp; 🖳🖳) Popular among Italian and French families

who love *lumbung*-chic living. Bungalows come with TVs, security box and gorgeous fresh-water outdoor bathrooms.

TOP END

Desa Dunia Beda (Map p305; ☎ 641575; www.desa duniabeda.com; bungalows US$110–140 plus 21% tax; 🖳) These astonishing rebuilt Javanese Joglo bungalows are beautifully isolated on the north end. Each is decked out with colonial-era antiques, including a four-poster bed, writing desk and sofa, and you'll dig the back-to-nature open-air bathrooms. The infinity pool is small, but you have your own beach, so why quibble. This is an eco-retreat, so there's no air-con and no fresh water. But you won't mind at all.

Hotel Vila Ombak (Map p305; ☎ 642336; www.hotel ombak.com; r US$110–170 plus 21% tax; 🖳🖳) Just south of the main drag, this highly attractive resort occupies a leafy garden plot partly shaded by yuccas and palms. The faux-traditional two-storey A-frame bungalows are not that large for the price, but they do have real character. The stunning superior rooms are more minimalist in design. The hotel has a great pool, spa, diving academy, restaurant and beach bar, too.

Villa Almarik (Map p305; ☎ 638520; www.almarik -lombok.com; r US$135–160; 🖳🖳) Now owned by the ever-growing Lotus brand, this four-star hotel has huge, light and airy, high-ceilinged bungalows with a dining/living-room area and modern bathroom, TV and minibar.

Kelapa Villas (Map p305; ☎ 632424, 0812 375 6003; www.kelapavillas.com; villas US$150–550 plus 21% tax; 🖳🖳) The villa complex that started the Trawangan luxe development boom. During research there were 14 villas, all privately-owned, varying in size from one-bedroom to five, less than half a click from the deserted western shore. The largest (which sleep up to eight people) are tropical palaces with granite kitchens, terrazzo baths and massive open-air great rooms that spill onto a private pool deck, tropical flower garden and manicured lawns that roll toward the swaying palms. Future plans include tennis courts and a fitness centre. Bring a big group and that gaudy price tag won't hurt too much.

Gili Villas (Map p305; ☎ 0812 376 4780; www.gili villasindonesia.com; villas US$250; 🖳🖳) Hidden in the village, just inland from the art market, is the latest villa development on Trawangan. These are ultra-modern two-bedroom villas with Jogja stone floors, indoor-outdoor kitchen, living room and dining room, attentive staff and a sweet pool deck. They're well-located in the middle of the action.

Gili Exotic (Map p305; ☎ 692113; 0818 360 019; www.giliexotic.com; villas 1.5 million Rp; ❷ ❷) Sasak-owned and adjacent to the Gili Villas are these luxe wood, one-bedroom villas with classic Indonesian style and modern accents like satellite TV and wireless web access.

Eating

It's easy to munch your way around the world – from Indonesia to Ireland, India and Japan – in tiny Trawangan. In the evenings, several places display and grill fresh seafood on the main strip.

Anna's (Map p305; dishes from 8000Rp; ❷ 24hr) Backpackers rejoice – opposite the harbour is a tasty, high-turnover local warung serving *nasi campur* for 10,000Rp. It's the cheapest meal in town, and it's damn good.

Blue Marlin (Map p305; mains 9000-35,000Rp) It has one of the two best fish grills on the island. Choose your catch and enjoy it with a limitless buffet of salads and sides. It's always cooked to perfection.

Rumah Makan Kikinovi (Map p305; nasi campur 12,000Rp) Another local warung with cheap, satisfying meals, north of the art market.

Beach House (Map p305; ☎ 642352; dishes 17,000-60,000Rp) This once great restaurant isn't cheap, but with a plush sand floor, seaside digs, a terrific fresh fish and salad-bar selection, and a solid jazz and rock soundtrack, people keep coming back. The food has

MANDI SAFAR

Many of Trawangan's locals don't visit the island's beach frequently, but during an annual ceremony held at the end of the second month of the Islamic calendar, they flock there. This ceremony, a ritual purification called Safar, takes place as hundreds of villagers take a dip in the ocean to symbolise the Prophet Muhammad's final bath. It includes the construction of a *pondok pisang* (banana house), drumming, seated dancing and reading from the Koran. Prayers are then written on mango leaves before participants take to the sea, taking their prayers with them.

slipped a touch but the barmen are exceptional and it's still a fun scene.

Ryoshi (Map p305; ☎ 639463; dishes 17,000-48,000Rp) Another delectable Bali import. The melt-in-your-mouth tuna carpaccio should not be missed.

Pesona (Map p305; ☎ 6607233; dishes 25,000-55,000Rp) The only Indian restaurant on the Gilis. It makes its own naan in the authentic tandoor, and serves curries like *tikka masala*, and kebabs on sizzling plates. Dishes are spiced to order. Did we mention the homemade yoghurt and ice cream?

Horizontal (Map p305; ☎ 639248; dishes 25,000-65,000Rp) With more than a nod to Seminyak style, this lounge-bar-restaurant boasts luxe scarlet lounges, sculptured white pods, and a post-modern take on the beach bonfire at sunset. The chef was new at the time of research and his food has won rave reviews from local expats.

Coco's (Map p305; espresso drinks from 15,000Rp; sandwiches 25,000Rp; ❷ 8am-6pm) If only there was a café like this in every town. Mouth-watering bacon and egg baguettes for breakfast and roast turkey or meatball sandwiches at lunch; the brownies, cakes, smoothies and shakes are incredible too.

Karma Kayak (Map p305; ☎ 0818 055 93710; tapas from 35,000Rp) Tasty Spanish tapas (including house-cured olives, exquisite garlic prawns and delicious meatballs) are served on the beach, in *beruga* (open-sided pavilions) or on tables and lounges made from driftwood. It's a popular spot at sunset.

Gili Deli (Map p305; ☎ 0812 376 4443; meals from 35,000Rp; ❷ 8am-6pm) Owned by Caswell's of Bali and Jakarta fame, it serves wraps, salads, baguettes and homemade bagels. The Gili Deli bagel sandwich comes with shrimp, crab, tuna and rocket dressed with lime mayo.

ourpick Juku (Map p305; grilled fish from 35,000Rp) Among local expats, Juku has long been known as the most affordable and possibly the best fish grill on the island. Exceptional dishes like grilled barracuda with ginger glaze made its reputation. Business has been booming, it took on new Western partners, doubled in size, and replaced its humble *beruga* with white tablecloths and candlelit tables. So far it hasn't lost its culinary edge. Here's hoping it stays that way.

Scallywag's (Map p305; ☎ 631945; meals from 45,000Rp; ❷ wi-fi) Its open, shabby-chic decor and plush patio seating make this new hot spot a major draw. It has a daily selection of Aussie pies, an organic ethos, a full bar and exceptional desserts. It doesn't have timely service but you won't mind waiting here.

Other recommendations:

Kayangan (Map p305; dishes from 20,000Rp) Across from Ryoshi is a cheap and cheerful expat fave. Known for its tasty curries, satays and *gado-gado*.

Tir na Nog (Map p305; ☎ 639463; dishes 21,000-37,000Rp) Ideal for enormous portions of comfort food such as Irish stew and fish 'n' chips, and desserts like banoffi (banana and condensed milk) pie.

Drinking & Entertainment

Trawangan's rotating parties are no secret. They fire up around 11pm and go on until 4am or so, as imported DJs from Bali and beyond mix techno, trance and house music (except during Ramadan when the action is completely curtailed out of respect for local culture). At the time of research, the party schedule shifted between Blue Marlin (Monday), Tir na Nog (Wednesday), and Rudy's (Friday). But with this many cool beach bars, every night can be a party, should you so desire.

Blue Marlin (Map p305; ☼ 8am-midnight Tue-Sun, 8am-3am Mon) Of all the party bars, this upper-level venue has the largest dance floor and the meanest sound system – it pumps out trance and tribal sounds on Monday.

Tir na Nog (Map p305; ☼ 7am-2am Wed-Mon, 7am-4am Tue) Known simply as 'The Irish Pub', it has a barn-like, sports-bar interior with big screens, private, thatched DVD lounges that guests can use free (the film selection is huge), and a brilliant outdoor bar with a live DJ that draws the biggest crowds in town. Jameson comes cheap and Wednesday is the blowout night.

Rudy's Pub (Map p305; ☼ 8am-4am Fri, 8am-11pm Sat-Tue) Rudy's has as much to do with Gili T's party-hard reputation as all the other bars combined. It's mostly due to its weekly debaucherous Friday-night throwdowns and a preponderance of drinks and dishes involving a certain fungus. Drug bust? What drug bust?

Sama Sama (Map p305; ☼ 8am-late) Locally owned and easily the best reggae bar in Indonesia (and probably Southeast Asia), this was Gili T's reigning hot spot at the time of research. It has a top-end sound system, a killer live band at least six nights a week, and great barmen who mix tasty mojitos.

Ocean Dua (Map p305; drinks from 13,000Rp; ☼ open til the last guy leaves) With football on the TV, fun-loving bartenders, a good crowd and no discernable closing time, this is the kind of place Charles Bukowski would have loved.

NORTH & CENTRAL LOMBOK

☎ 0370

Lush and fertile, Lombok's scenic interior is stitched together with rice terraces, undulating tobacco fields (destined for those Marlboro Reds), too many varieties of fruit and nut orchards to count, swatches of monkey forest, and capped by sacred Gunung Rinjani, which haemorrhages springs, rivers and waterfalls. Entwined in all this big nature are traditional Sasak settlements, some of which are known for their handicrafts. Public transport is not frequent or consistent enough to rely on, but the main road is in good condition. With your own wheels you can explore the black-sand fishing beaches, inland villages and waterfalls, and if you're here in August, you can attend the annual Sasak stick-fighting tournament. Bottom line: if you get bored here you may need to seek psychological help.

BANGSAL TO BAYAN

The port of Bangsal is a hassle (see p296), and public transport north from here is infrequent. Several minibuses a day go from Mandalika terminal in Bertais (Mataram) to Bayan, but you'll have to get connections in Pemenang and/or Anyar, which can be difficult to navigate. Simplify things and get your own wheels.

Sira

This peninsula has an insanely gorgeous, sweeping white-sand beach, some snorkelling offshore where the reef is under recovery, and Lombok's finest hotel, the **Oberoi Lombok** (☎ 638444; www.oberoihotels.com; r from US$240, villas from US$350, plus 21% tax; ☒ ☒). The rooms, villas and pavilions here ooze classic Indonesian luxury, with sunken marble bathtubs, worn teak floors, antique entertainment armoires, oriental rugs and time-stopping verandahs with gorgeous sea and sunset views. The bathrooms alone are worth the splurge. There's a fine spa, good sports

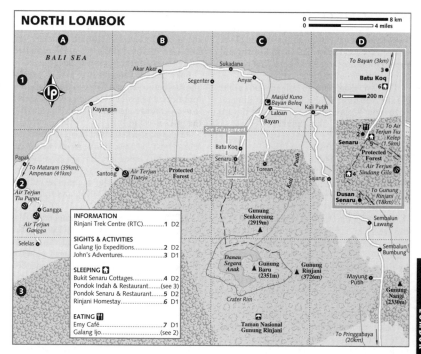

NORTH LOMBOK

INFORMATION
Rinjani Trek Centre (RTC)............**1** D2

SIGHTS & ACTIVITIES
Galang Ijo Expeditions..................**2** D2
John's Adventures........................**3** D1

SLEEPING
Bukit Senaru Cottages..................**4** D2
Pondok Indah & Restaurant........(see 3)
Pondok Senaru & Restaurant.......**5** D2
Rinjani Homestay.........................**6** D1

EATING
Emy Café......................................**7** D1
Galang Ijo.................................(see 2)

facilities including tennis courts, and a terrific poolside restaurant if you just want to pop in for lunch.

Close by, signposted from the road south to Bangsal, the **Lombok Golf Kosaido Country Club** (☎ 640137; per round incl caddy & cart US$80) is an attractive seaside 18-hole, 72-par course. Hole 9 faces glorious Sira Bay, while holes 10 to 18 have exceptional Rinjani views. Guests who stay at Manta Dive (on Gili T and Gili Air) or Gili Villas (on Gili T) are considered club members and pay discounted rates.

Gondang & Around

Just northeast of Gondang village, a 6km trail heads inland to **Air Terjun Tiu Pupas**, a 30m waterfall that's only worth seeing in the wet season. Trails continue from here to other wet-season waterfalls including **Air Terjun Gangga**, the most beautiful of all. A guide is useful to navigate the confusing trails in these parts. Don't worry, they'll find you.

Bayan

Wektu Telu (p312), Lombok's animist-tinted form of Islam, was born in humble thatched mosques nestled in these Rinjani foothills. The best example is **Masjid Kuno Bayan Beleq**, next to the village of Baleq. Its low-slung roof, dirt floors and bamboo walls reportedly date from 1634, making this mosque the oldest on Lombok. It's built on a square platform of river stones with a pagoda-like upper section. Inside is a huge old drum which served as the call to prayer before PA systems. Ah, the good old days. Access to the interior of the mosque is not permitted, and with the exception of an annual pilgrimage, the mosque is usually dormant. Some of the outlying buildings are tombs, including one for the mosque's founding haj. You will be asked to sign a visitors book and make a donation for mosque maintenance.

Senaru & Batu Koq

These picturesque villages merge into one along a ridge with sweeping Rinjani and sea views. They are also way stations for would-be climbers who have Rinjani in their sights. But even without a peak-bagging itch, the beautiful walking trails and spectacular waterfalls are worth a day or so.

LOMBOK

INFORMATION & ORIENTATION
Rinjani Trek Centre (RTC; Map p311; ☎ 0868 1210 4132; www.info2lombok.com), at the southern end of the village, has good information on Rinjani and the surrounding area. It's not all that hard to figure out solo though.

The two villages are spread out along a single steep road which heads south to Rinjani. Batu Koq is about 3km south from Bayan, Senaru is a further 3km uphill.

SIGHTS & ACTIVITIES
Do not miss **Air Terjun Sindang Gila** (2000Rp), a spectacular set of falls 20 minutes' walk from Senaru. You'll stroll through forest and alongside an irrigation canal that follows the contour of the hill, occasionally disappearing into tunnels where the cliffs are too steep. Locals love to picnic by Sindang Gila. The hearty and the foolish make for the creek, edge close and then get pounded by the hard foaming cascade that explodes over black volcanic stone 40m above. If you crave a shot of life, do yourself a favour and join them.

A further 50 minutes or so uphill is **Air Terjun Tiu Kelep**, another waterfall with a swimming hole. The track is steep and tough at times. Guides are compulsory (25,000Rp).

Six kilometres south of Bayan is the traditional village of Dusun Senaru where locals will invite you to chew betel nut (or tobacco) and show you around.

Community tourism activities can be arranged in most guesthouses – they include a **rice-terrace and waterfalls walk** (50,000Rp), which takes in Sindang Gila, and the **Senaru Panorama Walk** (75,000Rp), which is led by female guides and incorporates stunning views and insights into local traditions.

SLEEPING & EATING
Mountain lodging is improving slowly but surely, and since the climate's cooler, you won't need fans. All these places are dotted along the road from Bayan to Senaru.

Bukit Senaru Cottages (Map p311; r 75,000Rp) Shortly before Dusan Senaru, this place has four decent semidetached bungalows nestled in a sweet flower garden. There's no view, but the price is right.

Pondok Indah & Restaurant (Map p311; ☎ 0817 578 8018; s/d 75,000/100,000Rp) Simple rooms with great views of the valley and the sea beyond. It's owned and operated by the 'Rinjani Master'. There's ample parking, a good restaurant (dishes 7000Rp to 18,000Rp), and free internet (when it works).

ourpick Pondok Senaru & Restaurant (Map p311; ☎ 622868, 0868 121 04141; r 200,000-350,000Rp) Perfectly perched on a cliff near the trail to the waterfalls, it offers great easterly views of the rice-terraced valley from its recommended restaurant (dishes 13,000Rp to 21,000Rp) and spacious, spotless rooms that may be a little overpriced but are still by far the most comfortable digs in town.

Also worth considering:
Rinjani Homestay (Map p311; ☎ 0817 575 0889; r 60,000Rp) A little further uphill, it has basic bamboo-and-tile bungalows with twin beds, and amazing views.

Head to **Emy Café** (Map p311; dishes 5000-12,500Rp) or warung **Galang Ijo** (Map p311; dishes 13,000-18,500Rp), both midway between Batu Koq and Senaru for simple food, some Sasak specials and cold drinks.

GETTING THERE & AWAY
From Mandalika terminal in Mataram, catch a bus to Anyar (20,000Rp, 2½ hours). Bemo

---

WEKTU TELU
Believed to have originated in the northern village of Bayan, Wektu Telu is a complex mixture of Hindu, Islamic and animist beliefs, though it's classified as a sect of Islam. At its forefront is a rather physical concept of the Holy Trinity. The sun, moon and the stars represent heaven, earth and water; while the head, body and limbs represent creativity, sensitivity and control.

As recently as 1965, the vast majority of Sasaks in northern Lombok were Wektu Telu, but under Soeharto's New Order government, indigenous religious beliefs were discouraged and considered backward, and it was mortally dangerous to practise it overtly – hence the Islam classification.

Most of the Wektu Telu religious festivals take place at the beginning of the rainy season (from October to December), or at harvest time (April to May), with celebrations in villages all over the island. Though these ceremonies and rituals are annual events, they are based on a lunar calendar and do not fall on specific days. Getting to see one is a matter of divine coincidence.

leave Anyar for Senaru (7000Rp) about every 20 minutes until 4.30pm. If you're coming from, or going to, eastern Lombok, get off at the junction near Bayan (your driver will know it), from where bemo go to Senaru.

SEMBALUN VALLEY
☎ 0376

High on the more arid but still agrarian eastern side of Gunung Rinjani is the beautiful Sembalun Valley, surrounded by farmland and golden foothills that turn green in the wet season. When the high clouds part, Rinjani goes full frontal from all angles. The valley has two main settlements, Sembalun Lawang and Sembalun Bumbung. Bumbung is wealthier but has no tourist facilities. Lawang is the best launch pad for Rinjani summit attempts, but that doesn't mean it's a tourist magnet. Most trekkers sleep in and hike from Senaru. That's reason enough to consider nesting here, among the relatively shy sun-baked local Sasaks and Hindu Javanese who work in the garlic fields for a Chinese-Indonesian agribusiness firm. It's always interesting being the only foreigner(s) in town.

Information & Activities

The national park rangers who staff the **Rinjani Information Centre** (RIC; ✆ 6am-6pm) speak decent English and are very well informed about the area. They can hook you up with guides for day treks such as a not-too-demanding four-hour **Village Walk** (150,000Rp, minimum 2 people), and the strenuous slog to the **Crater Rim** (250,000Rp for guide & park entrance fee). You should also consider the challenging **Wildflower Walk** (per person 550,000Rp incl a guide, porters, meals & all camping gear), a delightful two-day trek inside the national park past flowery grasslands. If you abhor package climbs, have your own gear and just wish to hire guides and porters at day rates, the rangers can help get you sorted for a summit attempt. Guides cost 100,000Rp per day and porters are 80,000Rp per day.

The RIC has also helped local women revive traditional weaving in Sembalun Lawang. Follow the signs from the village centre to their workshops.

Sleeping & Eating

The local hotel market is a bit bleak, but the RIC and its network of guides can help you find a homestay (75,000Rp). Wherever you stay you will wash in frigid Rinjani water.

Pondok Sembalun (☎ 0852 3956 1340; r 75,000Rp) Stay in thatched, brick-and-bamboo bungalows set in a lovely garden. The restaurant serves basic Indo and Western fare. Of course, that massive mobile-phone tower is a bit of an eyesore.

Lembah Rinjani (☎ 0818 0365 2511; r 150,000Rp) The better of the two hotels in town. Queensize beds, spotless bathrooms and breathtaking mountain and sunrise views.

Warung Madiya (Jl Pariswata-Sembalun; meals from 10,000Rp) The rangers' choice for local food, it's across the street from the police station.

Getting There & Away

From Mandalika bus terminal take a bus to Aikmel (12,000Rp) and change there for Sembalun Lawang (12,000Rp). Hourly pickups connect Lawang and Bumbung.

There's no public transport between Sembalun Lawang and Senaru, so you'll have to charter an *ojek,* or a bemo for around 100,000Rp. Roads to Sembalun are sometimes closed in the wet season due to landslides.

SAPIT
☎ 0376

On the southeastern slopes of Gunung Rinjani, Sapit is a tiny, very relaxed village with views across to Sumbawa. Tobacco-drying *open* (tall red-brick buildings) loom above the beautifully lush landscape, and thick blocks of the local cash crop can be found in the market.

Sights

Between Swela and Sapit, a side road leads to **Taman Lemor** (admission 3000Rp; ✆ 8am-4pm), a park with a refreshing spring-fed swimming pool and some pesky monkeys. Further towards Pringgabaya, **Makam Selaparang** is the burial place of ancient Selaparang kings.

You can also visit hot-water springs and small waterfalls near Sapit. Ask at the homestay for directions.

Sleeping & Eating

Hati Suci Homestay (☎ 0818 545 655; www.hatisuci.tk; s 40,000-45,000Rp, d 75,000-85,000Rp) The budget bungalows come with en-suite bathrooms set in a blossoming garden. The accommodation and restaurant (dishes 8000Rp to 18,000Rp) both offer stunning views over the sea to Sumbawa. Breakfast is included and hikes to Rinjani can be organised here.

Getting There & Away

To reach Sapit from Mataram or central Lombok first head to Pringgabaya, which has frequent bemo connections to Sapit. Occasional bemo also go to Sapit from the Sembalun Valley in the north.

GUNUNG RINJANI

Rising over the northern half of Lombok is the mighty 3726m Gunung Rinjani, Indonesia's second-tallest volcano (the tallest, Gunung Kerinci, is in Sumatra). The mountain has spiritual gravitas. Balinese Hindus and Sasak Muslims consider it sacred and make pilgrimages to its peak and lake (in flip-flops amazingly enough) to leave offerings for the gods. To the Balinese, Rinjani is one of three sacred mountains, along with Bali's Agung and Java's Bromo. They come once a year. Sasaks ascend throughout the year around the full moon. Tourists from all over the world also make the gruelling three-day trek. But we're generally after a more earthly satisfaction, wear high-tech hiking boots, and take pictures.

The mountain also has climatic significance. Its peak attracts a steady stream of swirling rain clouds that shower the valley and feed a tapestry of rice paddies, tobacco fields, cashew and mango trees, and banana and coconut palms.

Inside the immense caldera, sitting 600m below the rim, is a stunning, 6km-wide, cobalt-blue crescent lake, Danau Segara Anak (Child of the Sea). The Balinese toss their jewellery into the lake in a ceremony called *pekelan*, before they slog their way towards the sacred summit. The mountain's newest cone, Gunung Baru (or Gunung Barujari), which only emerged a couple of hundred years ago, seems to rise from the water in all its scarred, ominous glory. It remains highly active and erupted as recently as October 2004. Also in the crater is a series of natural hot springs known as Aiq Kalak. Locals suffering from skin diseases trek here with a satchel of medicinal herbs to bathe and scrub in the bubbling mineral water.

Treks to the rim, lake and peak should not be taken lightly, and guides are mandatory. Climbing Rinjani during the wet season (November to March), when the tracks are often treacherously slippery and there's a real risk of landslides, is not at all advisable – the national park office often completely forbids access to Rinjani for the first three months

of each year. June to August is the only time you are (almost) guaranteed minimal rain or clouds, but be prepared with layers and a fleece because it can still get extremely cold at the summit.

Senaru (p311) has the best services for trekkers and many treks begin there. Of course, this does add about 1000 vertical metres to the itinerary, so the smart ones drive to Sembalun Lawang on the eastern slope and begin hiking from there.

Organised Treks

The best and most inexpensive way to organise a trip is to head to either the Rinjani Trek Centre (RTC; p312) in Senaru or the Rinjani Information Centre (RIC; p313) in Sembalun Lawang. Anyone passing through Senggigi can first contact the Rinjani Trek Club's office there (p292). Funded by the New Zealand government, the centres use a rotation system so that all local guides get a slice of the trekking purse. And though guides are always eager for a gig, they're laid-back and easy to work with. The vibe on Rinjani is a far cry from the aggressive guiding environment that dominates Bali's Agung.

Whether you book through your losmen (basic accommodation) or directly at the RTC or RIC, the same trek packages are offered, but in Senaru the prices often vary depending upon demand and level of luxury. The most popular is the three-day, two-night trek from Senaru to Sembalun Lawang via the summit. It includes food, equipment, guide, porters, park fee and transport back to Senaru. This costs about 1.75 million rupiah per person. An overnight trek to the crater rim from Senaru costs 1 million rupiah for one, 900,000Rp per person for two, and 750,000Rp per person for three. Deals on all itineraries get cheaper the larger the party.

Two local Senaru outfitters stand out. **John's Adventures** (Map p311; ☎ 0817 578 8018; www.lombok -rinjanitrek.com; per person 1.75 million Rp) has been leading Rinjani climbs since 1982. He has toilet tents, offers four meals a day, provides thick sleeping mats, and starts hiking from Sembalun (which you will definitely appreciate). **Galang Ijo Expedition** (Map p311; ☎ 0819 1740 4198; 2.3 million Rp for two people) is an upstart outfitter with competitive prices and a network of experienced guides.

In Sembalun Lawang, the prices are uniform. Summit attempts cost 2.3 million ru-

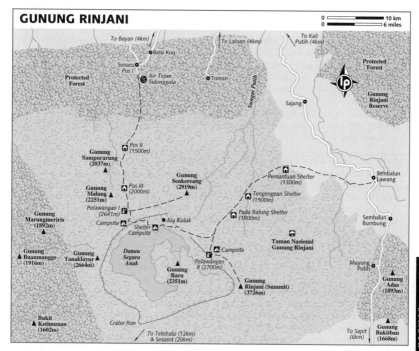

GUNUNG RINJANI

piah for one or two people, the per-person price falls for larger groups. All day hikes to the crater rim (6am to 6pm) cost 1.5 million rupiah.

A number of agencies in Mataram, Senggigi and the Gili Islands can organise all-inclusive treks. Prices usually include everything outlined above, plus return transport from the point of origin. For example, **Perama** (www.peramatour.com), with offices in all of these locations, has a trekking package that leaves from any of the places above, via Senaru using official RTC guides, for 2.5 million rupiah per person (minimum two people).

Guides & Porters

Hiking independently is simply not allowed, but if you don't want to do an all-inclusive trekking package with RTC or RIC, you can hire guides (100,000Rp per day) and porters (80,000Rp per day) at day rates. You'll have to bring your own camping gear and supplies for you and your support team. Make sure you take a radio (10,000Rp per day) as well. Contract your guides and porters directly from the centres in Senaru or

Sembalun Lawang, as they are licensed for your security. Guides are knowledgable and informative, but won't carry anything for you, so you'll need to take at least one porter. You'll also need to arrange transport, bring ample food and water, and you'll get a smile out of your guides if you bring them a case of cigarettes.

Entrance Fee & Equipment

The entrance fee for the Rinjani National Park has ballooned to 150,000Rp – register and pay at the RTC in Senaru or the RIC in Sembalun Lawang before you start your trek.

Sleeping bags and tents are essential and can be hired at either RTC or RIC. You'll also need solid footwear, layers of warm clothing, wet-weather gear, cooking equipment and a torch (flashlight), but these can also be hired from the RTC. Expect to pay about 75,000Rp a head per day for all your equipment.

Poaching firewood at high altitude is an environmental no-no, so take a stove. And pack out your rubbish, including toilet tissue. As the saying goes, 'take only pictures, leave only footprints'.

CLIMBING GUNUNG RINJANI

The two most popular ways to climb Gunung Rinjani are a five-day trek (described below) that starts at Senaru and finishes at Sembalun Lawang, or a strenuous three-day dash from Senaru to the crater rim and back. A guide is essential from the hot springs to Sembalun Lawang, as the path is indistinct. This trek is outlined on the Gunung Rinjani map (p315). Another good map is the one from the Rinjani Trek Centre (RTC) – it's large, in colour, glossy and easy to understand.

It's often not possible to climb Rinjani during the wet season (November to March), particularly after heavy rainfall when the trail around the lake is very dangerous due to potential landslides and rockslides.

Day One: Senaru Pos I to Pos III (five to six hours)

At the southern end of Senaru is the Rinjani Trek Centre (Pos I, 601m), where you register and pay the park fee. Just beyond the post, the trail forks – continue straight ahead on the right fork. The trail climbs steadily through scrubby farmland for about half an hour to the sign at the entrance to Gunung Rinjani National Park. The wide trail climbs for another 2½ hours until you reach Pos II (1500m), where there's a shelter. Water can be found 100m down the slopes from the trail, but it should be treated or boiled.

Another 1½ hours' steady walk uphill brings you to Pos III (2000m), where there are two shelters in disrepair. Water is 100m off the trail to the right, but it sometimes evaporates in the dry season. Pos III is usually the place to camp at the end of the first day.

Day Two: Pos III to Danau Segara Anak & Aiq Kalak (four hours)

From Pos III, it takes about 1½ hours to reach the rim, Pelawangan I, at an altitude of 2641m. Set off very early for the stunning sunrise. It's possible to camp at Pelawangan I, but there are drawbacks: level sites are limited, there's no water and it can be very blustery.

It takes about two hours to descend to Danau Segara Anak and around to the hot springs, Aiq Kalak. The first hour is a very steep descent and involves low-grade rock-climbing in parts. From the bottom of the crater wall it's an easy 30-minute walk across undulating terrain around the lake's edge. There are several places to camp, but most locals prefer to be near the hot springs to soak their weary bodies and recuperate. There are also some caves nearby which are interesting, but are not adequate shelter. The nicest campsites are at the lake's edge, and fresh water can be gathered from a spring near the hot springs. Some hikers spend two nights or even more at the lake, but most who are returning to Senaru from here head back the next day. The climb back up the rim is certainly taxing – allow at least three hours and you'll have to start early to make it back to Senaru in one day. Allow five hours from the rim down to Senaru. Instead of retracing your steps, the best option is to complete the Rinjani trek by continuing to Sembalun Lawang and arranging transport back to Senaru.

Day Three: Aiq Kalak to Pelawangan II (three to four hours)

The trail starts beside the last shelter at the hot springs and heads away from the lake for about 100m before veering right. It then traverses the northern slope of the crater, and it's an easy one-hour walk along the grassy slopes before you hit a steep, unforgiving rise; from the lake it takes about three hours to reach the crater rim (2639m). At the rim, a sign points the way back to Danau Segara Anak. Water can be found down the slope near the sign. The trail forks here – go straight on to Lawang or continue along the rim to the campsite of Pelawangan II (2700m). It's only about 10 minutes more to the campsite, which is located on a bare ridge.

Day Four: Pelawangan II to Rinjani Summit (five to six hours return)

Gunung Rinjani stretches in an arc above the campsite at Pelawangan II and looks deceptively close. Start the climb at 3am in order to reach the summit in time for the sunrise and before the clouds roll in.

It takes about 45 minutes to clamber up a steep, slippery and indistinct trail to the ridge that leads to Rinjani. Once on the ridge it's a relatively easy walk uphill. After about an hour heading towards what looks like the peak, the real summit of Rinjani (3726m) looms behind, and as you gain altitude you'll see it towering above you.

The trail then gets steeper and steeper. About 350m before the summit, the scree is composed of loose, fist-sized rocks – it's easier to get along by scrambling on all fours. This section can take about an hour. The views from the top are truly magnificent on a clear day. The descent is much easier, but again, take it easy on the scree. In total it takes three hours or more to reach the summit, and two to get back down.

Day Four/Five: Pelawangan II to Sembalun Lawang (five to six hours)

After negotiating the peak, it's still possible to reach Lawang the same day. After a two-hour descent, it's a long and hot three-hour walk to the village. Head off early to avoid as much of the heat of the day as possible and make sure you've brought along plenty of water. From the campsite, head back along the ridge-crest trail. A couple of hundred metres past the turn-off to Danau Segara Anak, there is a signposted right turn leading down a subsidiary ridge to Pada Balong and Sembalun Lawang. Once on the trail, it's easy to follow and takes around two hours to reach the bottom.

At the bottom of the ridge (where you'll find Pada Balong shelter; 1800m) the trail levels out and crosses undulating to flat grassland all the way to Sembalun Lawang. After about an hour you'll hit the Tengengean shelter (1500m); it's then another 30 minutes to Pemantuan shelter (1300m). Early in the season, long grass obscures the trail until about 30 minutes beyond Pemantuan. The trail crosses many bridges; at the final bridge, just before it climbs uphill to a lone tree, the trail seems to fork; take the right fork and climb the rise. From here, the trail follows the flank of Rinjani before swinging around to Sembalun Lawang at the end. A guide is essential for this part of the trip.

Variations

There are a few possible variations to the route to the top of Gunung Rinjani described above. They're outlined here:

- Compress the last two days into one (racking up a hefty 10 to 11 hours on the trail). On the plus side, it's downhill all the way after the hard climb to the summit.

- Retrace your steps to Senaru after climbing to the summit, making a five-day circuit that includes another night at the hot springs.

- Another popular route, because the trail is well defined and (if you're experienced) can be trekked with only a porter, is a three-day trek from Senaru to the hot springs and back. The first night is spent at Pos III and the second at the hot springs. The return to Senaru on the final day takes eight to nine hours.

- For (almost) instant gratification (if you travel light and climb fast) you can reach the crater rim from Senaru in about six hours. You'll gain an altitude of approximately 2040m in 10km. Armed with a torch (flashlight), some moonlight and a guide, set off at midnight to arrive for sunrise. The return takes about five hours.

- If you reach Pelawangan I early in the day, consider taking a side trip along the crater rim, following it around to the east for about 3km to Gunung Senkereang (2919m). This point overlooks the gap in the rim where the stream that comes from the hot springs flows out of the crater and northeast towards the sea. It's not an easy walk, however, and the track is narrow and very exposed in places – if you do decide to give it a go, allow around two hours to get there and back.

- Start trekking from Sembalun Lawang (a guide is essential), from where it takes six or seven hours to get to Pelawangan II. This is a shorter walk to the rim than from Senaru, with only a three-hour trek up the ridge.

LOMBOK

Your suitcases and excess gear can be left at most losmen in Senaru or the RTC for around 5000Rp per day.

Food & Supplies

Trek organisers at RTC and RIC arrange trekking food, or you can take your own. Obviously it's much better to buy most of your supplies in the Mataram markets, where it's cheaper and there's more choice, but some provisions are available in Senaru. Take more water than seems reasonable (dehydration can spur altitude sickness) and a lighter.

Getting There & Away

For transport options from Sembalun Lawang to Senaru, see p313. If you've purchased a trekking package, transport back to the point of origin is usually included.

TETEBATU
☎ 0376

Laced with Rinjani mountain-spring-fed streams and canals, sprinkled with traditional villages and blessed with rich soil, Tetebatu is a Sasak breadbasket. The surrounding countryside is quilted with tobacco and rice fields, fruit orchards and cow pastures that fade into remnant monkey forest where you'll find some fabulous waterfalls; this all makes Tetebatu ideal for long country walks. At 400m it's also high enough on Rinjani's lower slopes to mute that hot sticky coastal mercury. Dark nights come saturated with sound courtesy of a frog orchestra accompanied by countless gurgling brooks. Even insomniacs snore here.

Though small, the town is actually quite spread out, with facilities on roads north and east (nicknamed 'waterfall road') of the *ojek* stop in the centre of the village. There's a **wartel** (🕑 9am-9pm) next to Salabuse Café, and there's halfway-decent mobile-phone coverage, but the internet has yet to colonise tiny Tetebatu.

Sights & Activities
TAMAN WISATA TETEBATU

A shady 4km track leading from the main road, just north of the mosque, heads into the **Taman Wisata Tetebatu** (Monkey Forest; Map p319) with black monkeys and waterfalls – you'll need a guide to find both.

WATERFALLS

On the southern slopes of Taman Nasional Gunung Rinjani, there are two waterfalls. Both are accessible by private transport or a spectacular two-hour walk (one way) through rice fields from Tetebatu. If walking, hire a guide (80,000Rp to 100,000Rp) through your hotel. The best ones describe the vegetation and village life, and make the experience even richer.

A 2km walk from the car park at the end of the road, **Air Terjun Jukut** (Jeruk Manis, Air Temer; admission 20,000Rp) is still popular with locals as they believe its water will increase hair growth. So if baldness frightens you, wade over and let the frigid cascade rain down on your man-scalp.

Northwest of Tetebatu, **Air Terjun Joben** (Otak Kokok Gading; admission 20,000Rp) is more of a public swimming pool, so less alluring.

Sleeping & Eating

Pondok Tetebatu (Map p319; ☎ 632572; s/d 60,000/80,000Rp) North of the intersection, these detached and ranch-style rooms set around a flower garden are basic and could frankly be cleaner. But, the staff are fantastic, the Sasak-specialising restaurant is a good bet, and it offers guided walks through the villages (50,000Rp) and to the falls (80,000Rp). It can also help you find transport (right).

our pick Cendrawasih Cottages (Map p319; ☎ 0818 0372 6709; r 90,000Rp) Sweet little *lumbung*-style cottages nestled in the rice fields. You'll sit on floor cushions in the stunning stilted restaurant, which has Sasak, Indonesian or Western grub (7000Rp to 22,000Rp) and 360-degree paddy views. It's about 500m east of the intersection.

Wisma Soedjono (Map p319; ☎ 21309; r 150,000Rp, cottages 200,000Rp; 🏊) About 2km north of the intersection, these basic, functional rooms (with thin walls) and lovely two-storey chalet-style cottages (with both balconies and verandahs) are scattered around the grounds of a rambling family farm.

Green Orry (Map p319; ☎ 632233; cottages incl breakfast 175,000Rp) Twenty of the newest and cleanest rooms in town. It's a large, family-run place that is short on views but has some character. Even when the town is blacked out (a frequent occurrence), they have juice, which is why large tour groups favour it.

Bale Bale (Map p319; ☎ 0828 375 8688; dishes 10,000-22,000Rp) Tastefully candlelit, this sweet street-side café has outstanding local food, such as fiery *pelecing kangkung* (spinach in tomato sauce) and Lombok-style *gado-gado*. The friendly owner also pours free shots of rice wine when the electricity falters.

LOMBOK

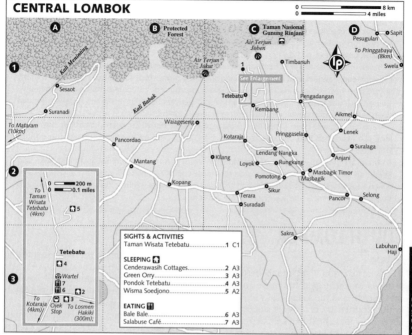

SIGHTS & ACTIVITIES
Taman Wisata Tetebatu.................1 C1

SLEEPING
Cenderawasih Cottages.................2 A3
Green Orry.................3 A3
Pondok Tetebatu.................4 A3
Wisma Soedjono.................5 A2

EATING
Bale Bale.................6 A3
Salabuse Café.................7 A3

LOMBOK

Salabuse Café (Map p319; ☎ 0817 573 1143; dishes 6000-17,500Rp) Cheery, cheap place serving Western, Indonesian and Sasak meals.

Getting There & Around

Public transport to this end of Lombok is infrequent and unpredictable. Buses do go from Mandalika to Pomotong (10,000Rp), which is on the main east–west highway. And on market days (Monday and Wednesday), there are bemo from here to Kot-araja (2000Rp), where you can get an *ojek* (3000Rp) or *cidomo* (4000Rp) to Tetebatu. You'll feel much better though if you book your own transport.

Private cars (with drivers) can be arranged at Pondok Tetebatu (left) to all of Lombok's main destinations (250,000Rp to 500,000Rp for up to four passengers).

Pondok Tetebatu also rents bicycles and motorbikes for 15,000Rp and 50,000Rp per day, respectively.

SOUTH OF TETEBATU

The nearest market town to Tetebatu is **Kotaraja**, which is also the transport hub of

the area. It's known for its skilled blacksmiths, and in August, you can take in the annual **Sasak stick-fighting** festivities. The fights are both fierce and real, and end gracefully at the first sight of blood. There's a market in town on Monday and Wednesday mornings.

Loyok, heading south, is noted for its fine basketry and **Rungkang** is known for its pottery made from local black clay. You'll find home workshops in both villages.

Masbagik is a large town on Lombok's east–west highway with a daily morning market, a huge cattle market on Monday afternoon, an imposing new mosque with elegant minarets, and the region's only reliable ATM. Look for the BCA sign opposite the mosque. **Masbagik Timor**, 1km east, is a centre for black-clay pottery and ceramic production.

Lendang Nangka is a Sasak village surrounded by picturesque countryside, 3km north of the highway. In and around the village you can see blacksmiths who make knives, hoes and other tools using traditional techniques. A few silversmiths are also based here.

It's best to charter private transport from Tetebatu to visit the artisans.

SASAK LIFE

Lombok's indigenous Sasak people comprise about 90% of the island's population. Virtually all are now orthodox Muslims, though before 1965, many Sasaks in remote areas were Wektu Telu (see the boxed text, p312).

Sasak houses are made of bamboo, and sit on a base of compacted mud and cow dung; they have a steeply angled and rather low-slung thatched roof, which forces guests to bow humbly before their hosts. Husbands and wives share a home, but not a bed (ie bamboo mat). They only spend the night together when they are trying to get pregnant. Once the job is done, the men sleep outside, and the women and children huddle indoors.

Each village will have *lumbung,* stilted rice-storage barns, to keep rodents at bay. They look like little thatched cottages, and have been mimicked by bungalow resorts throughout Lombok.

There are several examples of traditional villages in northern Lombok, including Sade and Rembitan (below) near Kuta. Villages on the north end of Lombok still maintain a caste system, which heavily influences courtship, and marriage between the highest castes – *Datu* (men) and *Denek Bini* (women) – and lower castes are quite rare.

SOUTH LOMBOK

☎ 0370

Beaches just don't get much better: the water is warm, striped turquoise and curls into barrels, and the sand is silky and snow-white, framed by massive headlands and sheer cliffs that recall Bali's Bukit Peninsula 30 years ago. Village life is still vibrant in south Lombok as well. You'll see seaweed and tobacco harvests, duck into tribal homes, and listen to Sasak drum corps. The south is noticeably drier than the rest of Lombok and more sparsely populated, with limited roads and public transport, for now. But, with long-anticipated hotel development on the immediate horizon, authentic tropical tranquillity may be on its way out. Especially in Kuta, which is the antithesis of Bali's version and the south coast's best base. Get here soon!

PRAYA

pop 35,000

Praya is the south's main town. It sprawls, with tree-lined streets and a few Dutch colonial relics. There's nothing of much interest to visitors right now however, except for a couple of ATMs on Jl Jend Sudirman, but soon, Lombok's new international airport will be close by, boosting the local economy – especially in the surrounding crafts villages. Till then, the bemo terminal, on the north-west side of town, is the transport hub for the region.

AROUND PRAYA

Sukarara

The main street here is the domain of textile shops, where you can watch weavers work their old looms. **Dharma Setya** (☎ 6605204; 8am-5pm) has an incredible array of hand-woven Sasak textiles, including ikat and *songkat.*

To reach Sukarara, take a bemo to Puyung along the main road. From there, hire a *cidomo* or walk the 2km to Sukarara.

Penujak

Penujak is well known for its traditional *gerabah* pottery. Made from chocolatey terracotta-tinted local clay, it's hand-burnished and topped with braided bamboo. The pots are gorgeous and dirt-cheap. Even the 1m-tall floor vases are under US$5 each. There are also plates and cups on offer from the potters' humble home studios. The best of the bunch belongs to **Wadiah** (☎ 0819 331 60391), a sweet local potter who is all smiles and has a terrific inventory. Her home is across from the cemetery.

Penujak is on the main road from Praya to the south coast; any bemo to Sengkol or Kuta will drop you off.

Rembitan & Sade

The area from Sengkol down to Kuta is a centre for traditional Sasak culture – you can tour working Sasak villages, meet the villagers, check out their decorative *lumbung* (rice barns) and even sip coffee in their homes, called *bale tani,* which are made from bamboo, cow and buffalo dung, and mud. Regular bemo cover this route.

Rembitan, aka Sasak Village, is on a hill just west of the main road. Don't fear the theme-park moniker – it boasts an authentic cluster of thatched houses and *lumbung*. Teens from the village offer short but interesting walking tours where they'll fill you in on village life. **Masjid Kuno**, an ancient thatched-roof mosque, crowns the nearby hill. It's a pilgrimage destination for Lombok's Muslims as one of the founding fathers of Indonesian Islam is buried here.

A little further south is Sade, another traditional, picturesque village that has been extensively renovated. Many Sade villagers actually work and live part-time in Kuta. Donations are 'requested' by guides at both villages – 30,000Rp is enough, but you may have to pay extra for photos.

KUTA

Imagine a crescent bay – turquoise in the shallows and deep blue further out. It licks a huge, white-sand beach, wide as a football pitch, backed by swaying trees and framed by dome-like headlands. It's deserted, save for a few fishermen, seaweed farmers and their children. Now imagine a coastline of nearly a dozen just like it, all backed by a dry, rugged range of coastal hills spotted with lush patches of banana trees and tobacco fields, and you'll have a vague idea of Kuta's majesty.

For years it's been an under-the-radar surf paradise, thanks to the limitless world-class beach and reef breaks within 30 minutes of town, and the international packs of surfers who tend to congregate here in August. It's not all about the waves though. The locals, engaging and fun-loving Sasaks, saturate Kuta with their charm. And the motley assortment of barefoot bars and cafés serves some terrific meals and good conversation. Unfortunately, this incarnation of Kuta is on the clock.

There have been whispers linking five-star resort developers to Kuta's pristine coastline for nearly a decade, but there's a different feel to this round of rumour. Now a Dubai development firm is publicly involved, US$600 million has been put on the table, and construction of a Ritz Carlton is slated to begin in January 2009 (see p324). Will it be a few well-placed, exclusive resorts or another Nusa Dua? Nobody but the suits knows for sure. What is clear though is that if you want to catch the last throes of Kuta natural, you better book now.

LOMBOK

SASAK FESTIVALS & CEREMONIES

As more and more Sasaks have adopted orthodox Islam, many ancient cultural rituals and celebrations based on animist and Hindu traditions have dwindled in popularity. Nevertheless, some festivals and events have endured, and are being promoted by local authorities. In addition to these festivals, there are also events celebrating the harvesting of a sea worm called *nyale* (p323) in Kuta, and the riotous Hindu-Wektu Telu 'rice war' known as **Perang Topat** held at Pura Lingsar (p289).

Lebaran Topat, held in the seven days after the end of the fasting month (Idul Fitri; Ramadan) in the Islamic calendar, is a Sasak ceremony thought to be unique to west Lombok. Relatives gather in cemeteries to pour water over family graves, and add offerings of flowers, betel leaves and lime powder. Visitors can observe ceremonies at the Bintaro cemetery on the outskirts of Ampenan.

Malean Sampi (meaning 'cow chase' in Sasak) are highly competitive buffalo races held over a 100m waterlogged field in Narmada, just east of Mataram. Two buffalo are yoked together and then driven along the course by a driver brandishing a whip. The event takes place in early April, and commemorates the beginning of the planting season.

Gendang Beleq (big drum) performances were originally performed before battles. Today many villages in central Lombok have a *gendang* battery, some with up to 40 drummers, who perform at festivals and ceremonies. The drums themselves are colossal, up to a metre in length and not unlike an oil drum in shape or size. The drummers support the drums using a sash around their necks.

Peresean (stick fighting) are martial-art performances by two young men stripped to the waist, armed with rattan sticks and square shields made of cowhide. The Sasak believe that the more blood shed on the earth, the better the rainfall will be in the forthcoming wet season. In late July, demonstrations can be seen in Senggigi, and in late December there's a championship in Mataram.

Information & Orientation

Several places change money, including the Kuta Indah Hotel and **Segare Anak Cottages** (☎ 654846), which is also a postal agency.

There's a wartel in town and **Ketapang Café** (☺ 8am-11pm) has slow but functional internet access. The market fires up on Sunday and Wednesday. **Perama** (☎ 654846), based at Segare Anak Cottages, runs tourist buses to Mataram (75,000Rp), with connections to Senggigi and elsewhere.

Virtually everything in Kuta is on a single road that parallels the beach, either east or west of the junction where the road from Praya hits town.

Danger & Annoyances

If you decide to rent a bicycle or motorbike, take care whom you deal with – arrangements are informal and no rental contracts are exchanged. We have received reports of some visitors having motorbikes stolen, and then having to pay substantial sums of money as compensation to the owner (who may or may not have arranged the 'theft' himself). If you rent your motorbike from your guesthouse though, you'll have no worries.

As you drive up the coastal road west of Kuta, watch your back –there have been reports of muggings in the area (see p325). Not that it's rampant, but when we (the royal version) visited, two aggressive locals roared up on motorcycles right alongside and tried to intimidate. We stayed relaxed, laughed it off, and soon they were on their way. But yes, it was odd.

Activities

SURFING

Plenty of good waves break on the reefs, including lefts and rights, in Teluk Kuta, Kuta bay, and more on the reefs east of Tanjung Aan. If you're after a reef break, use local boatmen to tow you out for around 70,000Rp. About 7km east of Kuta is the fishing village of **Gerupak**, where there are five reef breaks, including those way out by the mouth of the bay that demand a boat. The current charter rate is a negotiable 200,000Rp per day. West of Kuta, **Mawi** is absolutely gorgeous and offers consistent world-class surf. It's no secret, so expect company in the high season. Local

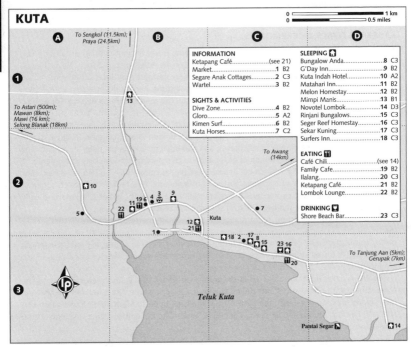

KUTA

0 ——— 1 km
0 ——— 0.5 miles

INFORMATION	
Ketapang Café	(see 21)
Market	1 B2
Segare Anak Cottages	2 C3
Wartel	3 B2

SIGHTS & ACTIVITIES	
Dive Zone	4 B2
Gloro	5 A2
Kimen Surf	6 B2
Kuta Horses	7 C2

SLEEPING	
Bungalow Anda	8 C3
G'Day Inn	9 B2
Kuta Indah Hotel	10 A2
Matahari Inn	11 B2
Melon Homestay	12 B2
Mimpi Manis	13 B1
Novotel Lombok	14 D3
Rinjani Bungalows	15 C3
Seger Reef Homestay	16 C3
Sekar Kuning	17 C3
Surfers Inn	18 C3

EATING	
Café Chili	(see 14)
Family Cafe	19 B2
Ilalang	20 C3
Ketapang Café	21 B2
Lombok Lounge	22 B2

DRINKING	
Shore Beach Bar	23 C3

To Sengkol (11.5km);
Praya (24.5km)

To Astari (500m);
Mawan (8km);
Mawi (16 km);
Selong Blanak (18km)

To Awang
(14km)

To Tanjung Aan (5km);
Gerupak (7km)

Teluk Kuta

Kuta

Pantai Segar

surfers are privy to another handful of hidden breaks, so if you happen to befriend one, you'll likely dodge the crowds and surf in relative peace. For details, see p97.

Drop by the friendly, professional **Kimen Surf** (Map p322; ☎ 655064; www.kuta-lombok.net) just west of the junction for swell forecasts, tips and information. Boards can be rented here (50,000Rp per day) and repairs undertaken. Lessons are offered (360,000Rp, four hours) and so are guided day trips. **Gloro** (Map p322; ☎ 0818 057 65690), Indonesian for swell, is the upstart surf shop in town. It rents boards (35,000Rp per day) and offers lessons (200,000Rp, four hours)

DIVING

Dive Zone (Map p322; ☎ 6603205; www.divezone-lombok .com) has two locations, one in town and the other at the Novotel. It dives in the bay (US$80 for two tanks), and at a site known as Magnet (US$120 for two tanks), which is famous for schooling hammerheads. Diving is best in the dry season but visibility is decent all year round.

HORSE RIDING

If you're partial to horseback riding, through Sasak villages or on the beach, call **Kuta Horses** (Map p322; ☎ 0819 159 99436; 1hr ride 300,000Rp; ⏰ rides 8am & 4pm).

Sleeping

Breakfast is included at those listed here. All accommodation is on or within walking distance of the beach, except Mimpi Manis.

BUDGET

our pick **Seger Reef Homestay** (Map p322; ☎ 655528; s/d 80,000/100,000Rp) Ignore the ramshackle courtyard because these bright, spotless, family-owned bungalows are the sweetest deal in town, and are nestled across the street from the beach.

Mimpi Manis (Map p322; ☎ 0818 369 950; www .mimpimanis.com; r 80,000-130,000Rp; ⚂) An extremely welcoming English-Balinese-owned guesthouse with two spotless, bright rooms in a two-storey house, both with en-suite showers and TV/DVD player. There's home-cooked food, a dartboard and plenty of good books to browse through and DVDs to borrow. It's 2km inland from the beach, but the owners offer a free drop-off service and arrange bike and motorbike rental.

Rinjani Bungalows (Map p322; ☎ 654849; s/d with fan 80,000/95,000Rp, with air-con 200,000/250,000Rp; ⚂) This well-run place, 1km east of the junction, offers very clean bamboo bungalows with ikat bedspreads. The spacious, newer concrete bungalows have two double beds, hot water, hardwood furniture and cable TV.

G'Day Inn (Map p322; ☎ 655342; s/d 90,000/100,000Rp) This friendly, family-run place offers clean, recently renovated rooms, some with hot water, as well as a café. Located about 300m east of the junction.

Melon Homestay (Map p322; ☎ 0817 367 892; r/apt 100,000/150,000Rp) This place has two lovely apartments with a lounge and self-catering facilities, one with sea views from its balcony. There are a couple of smaller modern rooms with verandah and bathroom. It's about 400m east of the junction.

Surfers Inn (Map p322; ☎ 655582; www.lombok -surfersinn.com; r with fan 100,000Rp, with air-con 180,000- 400,000Rp; ⚂ ⚃) A very smart, stylish and orderly place with five classes of modern rooms, each with huge windows and large beds, and some with sofas. Book ahead as it's very popular.

Bungalow Anda (Map p322; ☎ 655049; r with fan 120,000Rp, with air-con 150,000Rp; ⚂) The tiled bungalows are relatively charmless, but management is friendly. They're on the beach road and they tend to have vacancies during the August rush.

Sekar Kuning (Map p322; ☎ 654856; r with 150,000Rp; ⚂) A charming beach-road inn. Top-floor rooms have ocean views.

LOMBOK

THE KUTA SITUATION

Emaar Property, a Dubai development concern, is poised to transform Kuta's pristine coast. The team planned its US$800 million takeover from Astari. Gaz, one of Astari's owners, watched unnoticed as they unfurled blueprints and eyed a plot of land that stretches from the west end of Kuta Bay to the east end of Tanjung Aan. Construction is slated to begin on a luxury five-star hotel at Tanjung Aan in January 2009, and all the small businesses on the main road are in danger of being bulldozed when the road doubles in size.

Of course, Kuta's sea change was just a matter of time. Tommy Soeharto, the former president's son, stockpiled Kuta coastal property for years under an Indonesian law that allows government ministers to force owners to sell their land at will. But every time he began to build, a local torched the construction site. Rather than persist, he sold out to Dubai. Whether the Dubai developers will bring economic opportunity, ecological indifference or a cocktail of the two remains to be seen.

Nobody in Kuta really knows what's going to happen. In Indonesia, developers aren't required to divulge information to the public – there is no public voice, and there are no development standards. But the Emaar Property spokesman in Jakarta did tell us that 'this project involves multiple luxury hotels and golf courses and will be rolled out over the next 10 to 15 years'.

MIDRANGE

Matahari Inn (Map p322; ☎ 655000; www.matahariinn .com; r 175,000-550,000Rp; ✼ ▓) Sure, they've OD'd on knick-knacks, but the lush tropical gardens and Balinese polish make it one of Kuta's better options.

Kutah Indah Hotel (Map p322; ☎ 653781; kutaindah @indonet.id; r 100,000-500,000Rp; ✼ ▓) An aging bungalow resort that on empty days has a certain *Shining* aesthetic – the bungalows have been recently re-tiled though, it's on a quiet stretch of beach, and the staff are warm and welcoming.

Novotel Lombok (Map p322; ☎ 653333; www.novotel -lombok.com; r without/with terrace US$105/120, villas US$195, plus 21% tax; ✼ ▓) This appealing, Sasak-themed four-star resort spills onto a superb beach 3km east of the junction. Rooms have high, sloping roofs and modern interiors. There are two pools, a wonderful spa, good restaurants, a swank bar and a plethora of activities on offer including catamaran sailing, fishing and scuba diving. European families love it. It really is in a league of its own.

Eating & Drinking

From the looks of the backpacker/surf-ghetto environs, you may be surprised to hear that there are some exceptional dishes hidden within Kuta's largely bland dining scene.

Ilalang (Map p322; dishes 11,000-35,000Rp) Looks exactly like a tropical beach shack should. Cold beer and sea views await.

Family Cafe (Map p322; ☎ 653748; mains 12,000-30,000Rp) You won't need that thick notebook of a menu – just order the *sate pusut*

(minced fish, chicken or beef mixed with fresh coconut, chilli and spices, moulded and grilled on lemongrass stalks) and *kangkung pelecing* (sautéed water spinach and bean sprouts, topped with tomato sauce and shredded coconut).

Ketapang Café (Map p322; ☎ 0878 654 15209; meals 12,000-50,000Rp) There are three charming dining pagodas shaded by grass umbrellas at this café, but you should belly up to the fine bamboo bar. The Indonesian fare is tasty and pizzas get rave reviews by the expat locals who buzz over to munch and sip almost every night. It rents out a couple of rooms as well.

Astari (dishes 18,000-25,000Rp; ⊙ 8.30am-6pm Tue-Sun) Perched on a mountaintop 2km west of town on the road to Mawan, this breezy, Moroccan-themed vegetarian lounge-restaurant has spectacular vistas of pristine bays and rocky peninsulas that take turns spilling further out to sea. The delicious, health-conscious menu lives up to the setting. The blackboard always has a daily dish and drink of the day, but the mainstays are the focaccia sandwiches, salads and superb shakes (the coconut shake will make your beverage hall of fame immediately). Trust us, you will not eat and run.

⬛ourpick⬛ Lombok Lounge (Map p322; ☎ 655542; chilli crab 50,000Rp) Yes, it has inexpensive Indonesian food and scrolls of pedestrian Western dishes. But you won't need to search the menu because you're here for the scintillating, finger-licking, meaty chilli crab, a Chinese-Indonesian classic. It's more than just the best meal in town. It's a full body experience. Wash it down with icy Bintang. *Enak!*

Café Chili (Map p322; breakfast buffet US$10; 8am-10.30am) Breakfast lovers rejoice! The Novotel opens its bottomless array of Western breakfast delights to all comers. Grab a table seaside and munch deeply.

Shore Beach Bar (Map p322; 10am-late, live band on Sat night) Kimen, Kuta's original surf-shop entrepreneur, had just opened this bar at research time, and it was rocking. The open dance-hall interior has been recently renovated, the sound system is fantastic, there's breezy patio seating, cushy red booths and an expansive bar. If you're in town on a Saturday night, you'll probably wind up here.

Getting There & Away

Kuta is a hassle to reach by public transport – from Mandalika terminal in Mataram you'll have to go via Praya (5000Rp), then to Sengkol (3000Rp) and finally to Kuta (2000Rp), usually changing buses at all these places. Most opt for the Perama shuttle-bus option – from Mataram (125,000Rp, two hours), Senggigi (150,000Rp, 2½ hours), and the Gilis (225,000Rp, 3½ hours), or hire private transport.

Getting Around

Ojek congregate around the main junction as you enter Kuta. Bemo go east of Kuta to Awang and Tanjung Aan (5000Rp), and west to Selong Blanak (10,000Rp), or can be chartered to nearby beaches. Most guesthouses rent motorbikes for 40,000Rp to 50,000Rp per day. See p322 for information about bike-hire scams.

EAST OF KUTA

Decent roads traverse the coast to the east, passing a seemingly endless series of beautiful bays punctuated by headlands. It's a terrific motorbike ride.

Pantai Segar, a lovely beach about 2km east around the first headland, is within walking distance of town. The enormous rock of **Batu Kotak**, 2km further on, divides two glorious white-sand beaches. Continuing east, **Tanjung Aan** is an idyllic turquoise, horseshoe bay with five powder-sand beaches. It's also the best swimming beach on this end of Kuta. Regrettably, it's not gonna look like this too much longer (see opposite). The road continues another 2km to the fishing village of **Gerupak** where there's a market on Tuesday, a restaurant on the beach and five exceptional surf breaks. Alternatively, turn northeast just before Tanjung Aan and go to **Awang**, a busy fishing village with a sideline in seaweed harvesting. You could take a boat from Awang across to Ekas (a charter costs around 120,000Rp) or to some of the other not-so-secret surf spots in this bay.

WEST OF KUTA

West of Kuta is yet another series of awesome beaches that all have sick surf when conditions are right. It's possible that the region may eventually be developed when Kuta's metamorphosis strikes, but for now, it remains almost pristine and often deserted. The road, which is potholed and very steep in places, detours inland and skirts tobacco, sweet potato and rice fields in between turn-offs to the sand.

The first left after Astari leads to **Mawan** (parking motorbike/car 3000/5000Rp), a sweet cove with a majestic old shade tree, a wide stretch of white sand that extends into the deep sea, and views of offshore islands. It's a terrific swimming beach when the undertow isn't too treacherous.

The very next left – although it's quite a bit further down the road – leads through a gate (admission 5000Rp) down a horribly rutted track to **Mawi** (parking 5000Rp), 16km from Kuta. This is a surf paradise. Although the white-sand beach is relatively thin, it's still a stunning scene, with several beaches scattered around the bay. Surfers descend for the legendary barrels that roll in liberally. There can be a very strong riptide, so be extra careful sans board. Sadly, thefts have been reported here.

After Mawi, head back to the main road and when it forks, make a left into **Selong Blanak** village. Park and cross the rickety pedestrian bridge to a wide, sugar-white beach with water streaked a thousand shades of blue, ideal for swimming. Fishing boats gather near the beachfront warung, others bob on the tides.

From **Pengantap**, the road climbs across a headland then descends to a superb bay; follow this around for 1km then look out for the turn-off west to **Blongas**, which is a steep, rough and winding road with breathtaking scenery.

> ### SOUTH LOMBOK SECURITY WARNING
>
> Tourists have been threatened and robbed at knifepoint on the back roads of south Lombok, in particular around Mawi. Ask around about the latest situation and try not to leave your vehicle unattended – find a local to watch it for a tip.

LOMBOK

EAST LOMBOK

☎ 0376

All most travellers see of the east coast of Lombok is Labuhan Lombok, the port for ferries to Sumbawa. But the road around the northeast coast is pretty good, and can be traversed if you're hoping to complete a circumnavigation. The real highlight here is the remote southeastern peninsula. If you've ever wondered what Bali's Bukit looked like before all the villas and surf rats, here's your chance.

LABUHAN LOMBOK

Labuhan Lombok (Labuhan Kayangan) is the port for ferries and boats to Sumbawa. The town centre of Labuhan Lombok, 3km west of the ferry terminal, is a scruffy place but it does have great views of Gunung Rinjani.

Sleeping & Eating

Try to avoid staying overnight as there's only one decent place. There are warung in town and around the ferry terminal.

Losmen Lima Tiga (☎ Jl Raya Kayangan; r 55,000Rp) About 2.5km inland from the port on the main road, this is a family-run place with small rooms and shared bathrooms.

Getting There & Away

BUS & BEMO

Frequent buses and bemo travel between Labuhan Lombok and Mandalika terminal in Mataram (11,000Rp, two hours). Public transport to and from Labuhan Lombok is often marked 'Labuhan Kayangan' or 'Tanjung Kayangan'. Buses and bemo that don't go directly to Labuhan Lombok will only drop you off at the port entrance. You'll have to catch another bemo to the ferry terminal. Don't walk – it's too far.

FERRY

See p352 for details of ferry connections between Lombok and Sumbawa and p288 for bus connections between Mataram and Sumbawa.

NORTH OF LABUHAN LOMBOK

This road has limited public transport and becomes very steep and windy as you near Anyar. There are isolated black-sand beaches along the way, particularly at Obel Obel.

Leaving Labuhan Lombok, look out for the giant mahogany trees about 4km north of the harbour. From Labuhan Pandan, or from further north at Sugian, you can charter a boat to the uninhabited **Gili Sulat** and **Gili Pentangan**. Both islands have lovely white beaches and good coral for snorkelling, but no facilities.

SOUTH OF LABUHAN LOMBOK

Selong, the capital of the East Lombok administrative district, has some dusty Dutch colonial buildings. The transport junction for the region is just to the west of Selong at **Pancor**, where you can catch bemo to most points south.

Tanjung Luar is one of Lombok's main fishing ports and has lots of quaint Bugis-style houses on stilts. From there, the road swings west to **Keruak**, where wooden boats are built, and continues past the turn to **Sukaraja**, a traditional Sasak village where you can buy woodcarvings. Just west of Keruak a road leads south to **Jerowaru** and the spectacular southeastern peninsula. You'll need your own transport; be warned that it's easy to lose your way around here and that the roads go from bad to worse.

A sealed road branches west past Jerowaru to **Ekas**, where you'll find a huge bay framed by stunning sheer cliffs on both sides. There are two sensational surf breaks (Inside and Outside) at Ekas and boat charters to Awang across the bay. Or, you could just find **Heaven on the Planet** (☎ 0812 3705 393; www.heaventhe planet.co.nz; all-inclusive per person, per night AU$120-150; 🖭). Chalets are scattered among the cliffs (there is one beach chalet) from where you'll have mind-blowing bird's-eye views of the sea and swell lines. It's especially magical at sunset, when the rippled bay flashes hot pink then melts into a deep purple before the light fades and stars carpet a black dome sky. Although Heaven does offer fun-dives (AU$45) on a wall lit by colourful soft corals, it's primarily a surf resort. From here you can paddle out to the Inside break at Ekas or take the house boat to Outside. Heaven's groovy Kiwi owners recently opened a second resort, **Ocean Heaven**, right on Ekas Beach. Both have tasty food, a full bar, friendly staff, and guests receive massages every second day. Room rates and contact details are the same at both resorts.

The road to Heaven is pretty terrible, but if you reserve ahead, their angels provide free airport transfer. If you'd rather wing it and you're already in Kuta, just charter a boat from Awang (see p325).

Directory

CONTENTS

Accommodation	327
Activities	330
Business Hours	330
Children	330
Climate Charts	331
Courses	332
Customs	332
Dangers & Annoyances	333
Embassies & Consulates	335
Festivals & Events	335
Food	337
Gay & Lesbian Travellers	337
Holidays	337
Insurance	338
Internet Access	338
Legal Matters	338
Maps	338
Money	339
Photography & Video	340
Post	340
Shopping	340
Solo Travellers	342
Telephone	343
Time	344
Toilets	344
Tourist Information	344
Travellers with Disabilities	344
Visas	344
Volunteering	346
Women Travellers	347
Work	347

ACCOMMODATION

Bali has a huge range of accommodation, primarily in hotels of every shape, size and price. It has great-value lodging no matter what your budget.

All accommodation attracts a combined tax and service (called 'plus plus') charge of 21%. In budget places, this is generally included in the price, but check first. Many midrange (but not all) and top-end places will add it on, which can add substantially to your bill.

In this guide, the rates quoted are those that travellers are likely to pay during the high season and include tax. Nailing down rates is difficult as some establishments publish the rates they actually plan to charge, while others publish rates that are pure fantasy, fully expecting to discount 50%.

The range of prices used in this book are as follows:

Budget Most rooms cost less than 280,000Rp (less than US$30) per night.

Midrange Most rooms cost between 280,000Rp (around US$30) and 1,100,000Rp (around US$120).

Top End Most rooms cost more than 1,100,000Rp (more than US$120).

Rates are almost always negotiable, especially outside the main peak season, and if you are staying for a few days or longer, you should always seek a discount. In the low season, discounts between 30% and 50% aren't uncommon in many midrange and top-end hotels. Note that a high-season surcharge applies in many top-end hotels during holiday periods such as Christmas. With Bali enjoying record visitor numbers, rates have been climbing sharply after years of staying flat.

Rates are often given in US dollars (US$) – and sometimes euros (€) – as opposed to rupiah (Rp), especially at higher-end places. Sometimes rates are in both currencies, meaning you should offer to pay in the one offering the best deal based on current conversion rates.

Camping

The only camping ground on the island is at the headquarters of the Taman Nasional Bali Barat (West Bali National Park) at Cekik in western Bali. It's only useful if you want to trek in the park, and you'll have to bring your own camping and cooking equipment.

BOOK YOUR STAY ONLINE

For more accommodation reviews and recommendations by Lonely Planet authors, check out the online booking service at www.lonelyplanet.com/hotels. You'll find the true, insider low-down on the best places to stay. Reviews are thorough and independent. Best of all, you can book online.

Even if you're trekking in the central mountains, or in the national park, you will rarely find use for a tent – there are usually shelters of some sort, and most hikes can be completed in one day anyway.

Hotels

Pretty much every place to stay in Bali and Lombok can arrange tours, car rental and other services. Laundry service is universally available, often cheap and sometimes free. Note that service and cleanliness at hotels on Lombok is a touch below Bali standards.

BUDGET HOTELS

The cheapest accommodation in Bali is in small places that are simple, but clean and comfortable. A losmen is a small hotel, often family-run, which rarely has more than about a dozen rooms; names usually include the word 'losmen', 'homestay,' 'inn' or 'pondok'. Losmen – or homestays – are often built in the style of a Balinese home, ie a compound with an outer wall and separate buildings around an inner garden.

There are losmen all over Bali, and they vary widely in standards and price. In a few places you'll find a room for as little as 40,000Rp, but they're generally in the 50,000Rp to 180,000Rp range. Some of the cheap rooms are definitely on the dull side, but others are attractive, well kept and excellent value for money. A lush garden can be one of the most attractive features, even in very cheap places. The price usually includes a light breakfast, and rooms have an attached bathroom with a shower (sometimes cold water only), basin and generally a Western-style toilet and a fan.

Many budget places also resemble hotels and as competition in Bali has heated up, it's quite common to find amenities such as pools, hot water and air-con in budget places with rooms under 280,000Rp. Don't expect great levels of service in any of these places – although smiles abound.

MIDRANGE HOTELS

Midrange hotels are often constructed in Balinese bungalow style or in two-storey blocks and are set on spacious grounds with a pool. In the less-expensive midrange hotels, rooms are priced from about 280,000Rp to 500,000Rp, which includes breakfast and a private bathroom. Midrange hotels may have a variety of rooms and prices, with the main difference being air-con and hot water versus a fan and cold water. Pools are near-universal and small fridges are common.

Upper-midrange hotels normally give their price in US dollars. Prices range from US$50 to US$120, and should include hot water, air-con, satellite TV and the like. Rooms at the top end of the this price range are likely to have a sunken bar in the swimming pool (usually unattended, but it looks good on the brochure). Many have a sense of style that is beguiling and which may help postpone your departure.

PRACTICALITIES

- Current issues of English-language dailies (*Jakarta Post* and the *International Herald Tribune*) and major news magazines can be found at bookshops and minimarts in South Bali and Ubud. Don't buy either newspaper at more than the cover price from street vendors, who are also the only source for Australian newspapers, which they sell for outrageous prices.

- Pop radio in Bali often has DJs jamming away in English. Stations include 87.8FM Hard Rock Radio, Oz101.2FM and Paradise 100.9FM (which has ABC news from Australia). Short-wave broadcasts such as Voice of America and the BBC World Service can be picked up in Bali. Many hotels and some bars have satellite TV with international channels.

- Indonesia uses the PAL broadcasting standard, the same as Australia, New Zealand, the UK and most of Europe; for DVDs you buy here though, be aware that you may need a multi-region DVD player.

- Electricity is usually 220V to 240V AC in Bali. Wall plugs are the standard Western European variety – round with two pins. Service is usually reliable.

- Indonesia follows the metric system. There is a conversion table for the imperial system on the inside front cover.

TOP-END HOTELS

Top-end hotels in Bali are world-class. You can find excellent places in Seminyak, Jimbaran, the resort strip of Nusa Dua and Tanjung Benoa, and Ubud. Posh resorts can be found around the coast of East Bali and around Pemuteran in North Bali. Service is refined and you can expect decor plucked from the pages of a glossy magazine. Views are superb – whether they're of the ocean or of lush valleys and rice paddies. At the best places, you can expect daily deliveries of fresh fruit and flowers to your room. Several places in Bali are regularly featured in surveys of top hotels such as those done by *Conde Nast Traveller*.

Although top end in this book usually means a place where the average room costs at least US$120, you can multiply that by a factor of five at some of the world-class resorts. Great deals for these places can be found from many sources: hotel websites, internet booking services or as part of holiday packages. It pays to shop around.

Villas & Long-Term Accommodation

Like frangipani blossoms after a stiff breeze, villas litter the ground of South Bali. Often they land in the midst of rice paddies seemingly overnight. The villa boom has been quite controversial for environmental, aesthetic and economic reasons. Many skip collecting government taxes from guests, which has raised the ire of their luxury hotel competitors and brought threats of crack-downs.

Most villas are available for longer stays. At the minimum they have a kitchen, living room and private garden, and often two or more bedrooms, so they are suitable for a family or a group of friends.

But many villas go far beyond the norm. Some are literally straight out of the pages of *Architectural Digest* and other design magazines, and come with pools, views, beaches and more. Often the houses are staffed and you have the services of a cook, driver etc. Some villas are part of developments – common in Seminyak – and may be linked to a hotel, which gives you access to additional services. Others are free-standing homes in rural areas such as the coast around Canggu.

Rates typically range anywhere from US$500 to US$4000 per week for a modest villa and beyond for your own tropical estate. There are often deals, especially in the low

---

FINDING A ROOM DEAL

For hotels, especially midrange and top-end places, you can often find the best deal by shopping around online. Some hotels offer internet deals on their websites; many more work with agents and brokers to sell their rooms at discounts off the published rates.

Bali Discovery (www.balidiscovery.com) has discount rates for hundreds of places. Besides the main internet travel bookers such as Expedia and Travelocity, the following sites often have good rates on Bali rooms.

- www.asiarooms.com
- www.directrooms.com
- www.hotelclub.net
- www.otel.com
- www.zuji.com

season. For longer stays, you can find deals easily for US$800 a month. Look in the *Bali Advertiser* (www.baliadvertiser.biz) and on bulletin boards popular with expats such as ones in Ubud (p173). If your tastes run simple, you can find basic bungalows among the rice fields in Ubud for US$200 a month.

You can sometimes save quite a bit by waiting until the last minute, but during the high season the best villas can book up months in advance. The following agencies are among the many in Bali.

Bali Tropical Villas (☎ 0361-732 083; www.bali -tropical-villas.com)

Bali Ultimate Villas (☎ 0361-857 1658; www .baliultimatevillas.com)

Bali Villas (☎ 0361-703060; www.balivillas.com)

Duncan & Edwards (☎ 0812 385 3337; www .duncanedwardsproperty.com)

Exotiq Real Estate (Map p120; ☎ 0361-737358; www .exotiqrealestate.com; Jl Laksmana, Seminyak)

House of Bali (☎ 0361-739541; www.houseofbali.com)

Village Accommodation

In remote villages, you can often find a place to stay by asking the *kepala desa* (village chief or headman) – it will usually be a case of sleeping in a pavilion in a family compound. The price is negotiable, maybe about 50,000Rp per person per night. Your hosts may not even ask for payment, and in these cases you should definitely offer some gifts, like bottled water, sweets or fruit.

AHHH, A SPA

Whether it's a total fix for the mind, body and spirit, or simply the desire for some quick-fix serenity, lots of travellers in Bali are spending hours (and sometimes days) being massaged, scrubbed, perfumed, pampered, bathed and blissed-out. Sometimes this happens on the beach or in a garden, other times you'll find yourself in stylish, even lavish surroundings.

Every upmarket hotel worth its stars has spa facilities (almost always open to non-guests) offering health, beauty and relaxation treatments. Day spas are also common, many of the best booked up days in advance during high season. The cost can be anything from a 20,000Rp beach rub to a multihour sybaritic soak for US$100 or more. In general however, the costs are quite low compared with other parts of the world and the Balinese have just the right cultural background and disposition to enhance the serenity.

The Balinese massage techniques of stretching, long strokes, skin rolling and palm and thumb pressure result in a lowering of tension, improved blood flow and circulation, and an all-over feeling of calm. Based on traditional herbal treatments, popular spa options include the *mandi rempah* (spice bath) and the *mandi susu* (milk bath). The *mandi rempah* begins with a massage, followed by a body scrub with a paste made from assorted spices, and ending with a herbal-and-spice hot bath.

Good spas can be found wherever there are tourists. Day spas are particularly common in Ubud (p180), Kuta and Legian (p108) and Seminyak (p120).

A good way to arrange a village stay is through the JED Village Ecotourism Network, see p362 for details. Another good option is Bali Homestay Program, north of Tabanan (p274).

ACTIVITIES

There are loads of things to do on land and at sea. See p86 for details.

Enriching yourself through courses is another popular way of enjoying your stay in Bali. See p332.

BUSINESS HOURS

Government office hours in Bali and Lombok are roughly from 8am to 3pm Monday to Thursday and from 8am to noon on Friday, but they are not completely standardised. Postal offices are open from about 8am to 2pm Monday to Friday; in tourist centres, the main post offices are often open longer and/or on weekends. Banking hours are generally from 8am to 2pm Monday to Thursday, from 8am to noon Friday and from 8am to about 11am Saturday. The banks enjoy many public holidays.

In this book it's assumed that restaurants and cafés are usually open from about 8am to 10pm daily. Shops and services catering to tourists are open from 9am to about 8pm. Where the hours vary from these, they are noted in the text.

CHILDREN

Travelling anywhere with *anak-anak* (children) requires energy and organisation (see Lonely Planet's *Travel with Children* by Cathy Lanigan), but in Bali these problems are lessened by the Balinese affection for children. They believe that children come straight from God, and the younger they are, the closer they are to God. To the Balinese, children are considered part of the community and everyone, not just the parents, has a responsibility towards them. If a child cries, the Balinese get most upset and insist on finding a parent and handing the child over with a reproachful look. Sometimes they despair of uncaring Western parents, and the child will be whisked off to a place where it can be cuddled, cosseted and fed. In tourist areas this is less likely, but it's still common in traditional environments. A toddler may even get too much attention!

Children are a social asset when you travel in Bali, and people will display great interest in any Western child they meet. You will have to learn your child's age and sex in Bahasa Indonesia – *bulau* (month), *tahun* (year), *laki-laki* (boy) and *perempuan* (girl). You should also make polite inquiries about the other person's children, present or absent.

Lombok is generally quieter than Bali and the traffic is less dangerous. People are fond of kids, but less demonstrative about it than the Balinese. The main difference is that services for children are much less developed.

Practicalities
ACCOMMODATION
A hotel with a swimming pool, air-con and a beachfront location is fun for kids and very convenient, and still provides a good break for the parents. Sanur, Nusa Dua and Lovina are all good places for young kids as the surf is placid and the streets quieter than the Kuta and Seminyak area. The Gilis and Senggigi are the best spots for kids on Lombok owing to the calm beaches and many tourism services.

Most places, at whatever price level, have a 'family plan', which means that children up to about 12 years old can share a room with their parents free of charge. The catch is that hotels may charge for extra beds, although some offer family rooms. If you need more space, just rent a separate room for the kids.

As noted in the text, many top-end hotels offer special programs or supervised activities for kids, and where this isn't the case, most hotels can arrange a babysitter.

Hotel and restaurant staff are usually very willing to help and improvise, so always ask if you need something for your children.

FOOD
The same rules apply as for adults – kids should drink only clean water and eat only well-cooked food or fruit that you have peeled yourself. If you're travelling with a young baby, breastfeeding is much easier than bottles. For older babies, mashed bananas, eggs, peelable fruit and *bubur* (rice cooked to a mush in chicken stock) are all generally available. In tourist areas, supermarkets do sell jars of Western baby food and packaged UHT milk and fruit juice. Bottled drinking water is available everywhere. Bring plastic bowls, plates, cups and spoons for do-it-yourself meals.

SAFETY PRECAUTIONS
The main danger is traffic, so try to stay in less busy areas. If your children can't look after themselves in the water, they must be supervised – don't expect local people to act as life-savers.

The sorts of facilities, safeguards and services that Western parents regard as basic may not be present. Not many restaurants provide a highchair, many places with great views have nothing to stop your kids falling over the edge, and shops often have breakable things at kiddie height.

WHAT TO BRING
Apart from those items mentioned in the Health chapter (p363), bring some infant analgesic, anti-lice shampoo, a medicine measure and a thermometer.

You can take disposable nappies (diapers) with you, but they're widely available in Bali and to a lesser degree on Lombok.

For small children, bring a folding stroller, or you will be condemned to having them on your knee constantly, at meals and everywhere else. However, it won't be much use for strolling, as there are few paved footpaths that are wide and smooth enough. A papoose or a backpack carrier is a much easier way to move around with young children.

Sights & Activities
Many of the things that adults want to do in Bali will not interest their children. Have days when you do what they want, to offset the times you drag them to shops or temples. Encourage them to learn about the islands so they can understand and enjoy more of what they see. For coverage of activities kids are likely to enjoy in Bali, see the boxed text, p98.

CLIMATE CHARTS
Just 8 degrees south of the equator, Bali and Lombok have tropical climates – the average temperature hovers around 30°C (86°F) all year round. Direct sun feels incredibly hot, especially in the middle of the day. In the wet season, from October to March, the humidity can be very high and quite oppressive. The almost-daily tropical downpours come as a relief, but pass quickly, leaving flooded streets and renewed humidity. The dry season (April to September) is generally sunnier, less humid and, from a weather point of view, the best time to visit, though downpours can occur at any time.

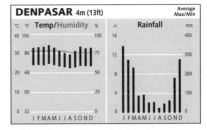

There are marked variations across the islands. The coast is hotter, but sea breezes can temper the heat. As you move inland, you also move up, so the altitude works to keep things cool – at times it can get chilly up in the highlands, and a warm jumper (sweater) or light jacket can be a good idea in mountain villages such as Kintamani and Candikuning. The northern slopes of Gunung Batur always seem to be wet and misty, while a few kilometres away, the east coast is nearly always dry and sunny.

Lombok is broadly similar but generally drier.

COURSES

More and more people are finding it rewarding to take one of the many courses available in Bali. The rich local culture and activities make for plenty of opportunities to learn something new. Whether it's exploring a food market, learning basic language skills, delving into the profusion of arts or honing your aquatic skills, you'll find plenty of options to expand your horizons and take home a new talent.

Arts & Crafts

The Ubud area is the best place for art courses, see p183. A wide range of courses is available, including batik, jewellery making and painting.

Cooking

See p77 for information on learning how to exploit the fresh flavours of Balinese food.

Language

The best place for courses in Bahasa Indonesia is the **Indonesia Australia Language Foundation** (IALF; Map p132; ☎ 225243; www.ialf.edu; Jl Raya Sesetan 190, Denpasar), which has a language lab, library, and four-week 40-hour course (two hours per day Monday to Friday, costing from 600,000Rp). There are six levels of courses available.

Ubud (p183) is also a good place to learn the local lingo.

Meditation & Spiritual Interests

For the Balinese, everything on the island is imbued with spiritual significance, and this ambience is an attraction for travellers looking for an alternative holiday experience. Ubud (p183) is a good place to go for spiritual enlightenment.

Music & Dance

Sanur (see p150) and Ubud (p183) have schools where you can explore the rich traditions of Balinese music and dance.

Surfing & Diving

See the Bali & Lombok Outdoors chapter for more information on surf (p93) and dive schools (p88).

CUSTOMS

Indonesia has the usual list of prohibited imports, including drugs, weapons, fresh fruit and anything remotely pornographic.

Each adult can bring in 200 cigarettes (or 50 cigars or 100g of tobacco), a 'reasonable amount' of perfume and 1L of alcohol.

Surfers with more than two or three boards may be charged a 'fee', and this could apply

---

TRAVEL ADVISORIES

Government departments charged with foreign affairs maintain websites with travel information and warnings for specific countries and regions. It's a good idea for travellers to check the following websites before a trip in order to confirm local conditions. But note that the advisories often are general to the point of meaninglessness and are guaranteed to allow for bureaucratic cover should trouble occur. Once in Bali, travellers may be able to get updated information through the local consulate or from embassies in Jakarta (p335).

- Australia Department of Foreign Affairs & Trade (www.smartraveller.gov.au)
- Canada Foreign Affairs (www.voyage.gc.ca)
- New Zealand Ministry of Foreign Affairs & Trade (www.safetravel.govt.nz)
- UK Foreign & Commonwealth Office (www.fco.gov.uk)
- US Department of State (www.travel.state.gov)

to other items if the officials suspect that you aim to sell them in Indonesia. If you have nothing to declare, customs clearance is usually quick.

There is no restriction on foreign currency, but the import or export of rupiah is limited to five million rupiah. Amounts greater than that must be declared.

Indonesia is a signatory to the Convention on International Trade in Endangered Species (CITES), and as such bans the import and export of products made from endangered species. In particular, it is forbidden to export any product made from green sea turtles or turtle shells.

DANGERS & ANNOYANCES

It's important to note that compared with many places in the world, Bali is fairly safe. There are some hassles from the avaricious, but most visitors face many more dangers at home. Petty theft occurs but it is not prevalent.

Security increased after the 2002 and 2005 bombings but has tended to fade after a while. The odds you will be caught up in such a tragedy are low. Note that large luxury hotels that are part of international chains tend to have the best security.

As for all destinations, you might want to check your government's travel advisories before you depart, and listen to local advice when you arrive. For more, see left.

In addition to the warnings in this section, see p105 for warnings specific to the Kuta region.

For information on Bali's notorious dogs, see p184. See p363 for details on international clinics and medical care in Bali.

A few other things to note: outside the Mataram/Senggigi area on Lombok, emergency services may be nonexistent, or a long time coming. Don't expect an ambulance to collect injured surfers from the southwest coast. The Gili Islands don't have a formal police force. Bangsal (p296), Mawi (p325) and Kuta (p322) have problems worth noting.

Beware of non-commercial arak, the potent rice or palm hootch. There have been incidents of poisoning and death.

Activities

Don't assume that activities operators are looking out for your well-being. Travellers have died with the sports-activities operators in Tanjung Benoa and dive mishaps occur every

where. The iconic volcanoes claim trekkers, especially Gunung Rinjani on Lombok. The moral: keep a healthy scepticism about you if others bear responsibility for your safety.

Begging

You may be approached by beggars in Kuta, Legian or Ubud – typically a woman with one or more young children. Pause and they might literally latch on.

Drugs

Numerous high-profile drug cases in Bali and on Lombok should be enough to dissuade anyone from having anything to do with illicit drugs. As little as two ecstasy tabs or a bit of pot has resulted in huge fines and multiyear jail sentences in Bali's notorious jail in Kerobokan. Try dealing and you may pay with your life.

You can expect to be offered pot, ecstasy, *shabu-shabu* (methamphetamine), crystal meth *(yabba)*, magic mushrooms and other drugs in nightclubs, beaches and while walking along tourist-area streets. Assume that such offers come from people who may be in cahoots with the police. That some foreigners have been able to buy their way out of jail by paying enormous fines (US$50,000 and up) should indicate that nabbing tourists for drugs is a cottage industry.

It's also worth noting that clubbers have been hit with random urine tests.

Hawkers, Pedlars & Touts

Many visitors regard the persistent attentions of people trying to sell as *the* number one annoyance in Bali (and in tourist areas of Lombok). These activities are officially restricted in many areas but hawkers will still work just outside the fence. Elsewhere, especially around many tourist attractions, visitors are frequently, and often constantly, hassled to buy things. The worst places for this are Jl Legian in Kuta, Kuta Beach, the Gunung Batur area and the over-subscribed temples at Besakih and Tanah Lot. And the cry of 'Transport?!?', that's everywhere. Many touts employ fake, irritating Australian accents, eg 'Oi! Mate!'. Pirate DVDs and CDs often don't work.

The best way to deal with hawkers is to completely ignore them from the first instance. Eye contact is crucial – don't make any! Even a polite *'tidak'* (no) encourages them. Never ask the price or comment on the quality unless you're interested in buying, or you want to spend half an hour haggling. It may seem very rude to ignore people who smile and greet you so cheerfully, but you might have to be a lot ruder to get rid of a hawker after you've spent a few minutes politely discussing his/her watches, rings and prices. Keep in mind though, that ultimately, they're just people trying to make a living and if you don't want to buy anything then you are wasting their time trying to be polite.

Scams

Bali has such a relaxed atmosphere, and the people are so friendly, that you may not be on the lookout for scams. It's hard to say when an 'accepted' practice such as over-charging becomes an unacceptable rip-off, but be warned that there are some people in Bali (not always Balinese) who will engage in a practised deceit to rip you off.

Most Balinese would never perpetrate a scam, but it seems that very few would warn a foreigner when one is happening. Be suspicious if you notice that bystanders are uncommunicative and perhaps uneasy, and one guy is doing all the talking.

Here is a rundown of common scams.

CAR CON

Friendly locals (often working in pairs) discover a 'serious problem' with your car or motorcycle – it's blowing smoke, leaking oil or petrol, or a wheel is wobbling badly (problems that one of the pair creates while the other distracts you). Coincidentally, he has a brother/cousin/friend nearby who can help, and before you know it, they're demanding an outrageous sum for their trouble.

EASY MONEY

Friendly locals will convince a visitor that easy money can be made in a card game. Anyone falling for this one is a prime candidate for what happens to fools and their money.

HIGH RATES – NO COMMISSION

Many travellers are ripped off by money-changers who use sleight of hand and rigged calculators. The moneychangers who offer the highest rates are usually the ones to look out for. Always count your money at least twice in front of the moneychanger, and don't let him touch the money again after you've finally counted it. The best defence is to use

a bank-affiliated currency exchange or stick to ATMs.

Swimming

Kuta Beach and those to the north and south are subject to heavy surf and strong currents – always swim between the flags. Trained lifeguards do operate, but only at Kuta, Legian, Seminyak, Nusa Dua, Sanur and (sometimes) Senggigi. Most other beaches are protected by coral reefs, so they don't have big waves, but the currents can still be treacherous, especially along the coast running north and west from Seminyak. Currents can also cause problems off the Gilis.

Water pollution can also be a problem, especially after rains. Try to swim well away from any open streams you see flowing into the surf.

Be careful when swimming over coral, and never walk on it at all. It can be very sharp and coral cuts are easily infected. In addition, you are damaging a fragile environment.

Theft

Violent crime is relatively uncommon, but there is bag-snatching, pickpocketing and theft from rooms and parked cars in the tourist centres. Don't leave anything exposed in a rental vehicle. Always carry money belts inside your clothes and bags over your neck (not shoulder). Be sure to secure all your money *before* you leave the ATM, bank or moneychanger. Also, beware of pickpockets in crowded places and bemo (small minibuses).

Hotel and guesthouse rooms are often not secure. Don't leave valuables in your room. Thieves will often enter through open-air bathrooms, so be sure to fasten the bathroom door. Most hotels offer some form of secure storage, such as in-room safes or central safety deposit boxes for guests – use it.

Many people lose things by leaving them on the beach while they go swimming.

On Lombok, theft and robbery are more common. Certainly there are hassles in Kuta, east of Kuta and west of Kuta around Mawi (see p325).

Traffic

Apart from the dangers of driving in Bali (see p355), the traffic in most tourist areas is often annoying, and frequently dangerous to pedestrians. Footpaths can be rough, even unusable, so you often have to walk on the road. Never expect traffic to stop because you think you're on a pedestrian crossing.

The traffic is much lighter on Lombok than in Bali, but there is still a danger of traffic accidents.

EMBASSIES & CONSULATES

Indonesian embassies and consulates abroad are listed at Indonesia's department of foreign affairs website (www.deplu.go.id).

Embassies & Consulates in Indonesia

Foreign embassies are in Jakarta, the national capital. Most of the foreign representatives in Bali are consular agents (or honorary consuls) who can't offer the same services as a full consulate or embassy but can at least assist you in figuring out where to go. For some, this means a trek to Jakarta in the event of a lost passport.

BALI

The US, Australia and Japan (visitors from these countries together make up half of all visitors) have formal consulates in Bali. Unless noted, the following offices are open from about 8.30am to noon, Monday to Friday. All telephone area codes are ☎ 0361.

Australia (Map pp164-5; ☎ 241118; www.dfat.gov.au/bali; Jl Tantular 32, Denpasar; ☽ 8am-noon, 12.30-4pm Mon-Fri) The Australian consulate has a consular sharing agreement with Canada, and may also be able to help citizens of New Zealand, Ireland and Papua New Guinea.

France (Map p146; ☎ 285485; consul@dps.centrin.net.id; Jl Mertasari, Gang II 8, Sanur)

Germany (Map p146; ☎ 288535; germanconsul@bali-ntb.com; Jl Pantai Karang 17, Batujimbar, Sanur)

Japan (Map pp164-5; ☎ 227628; konjpdps@indo.net.id; Jl Raya Puputan 170, Renon, Denpasar)

Netherlands (Map pp102-3; ☎ 752777; Jl Raya Kuta 127, Kuta)

Switzerland (Map pp102-3; ☎ 751735; swisscon@telkom.net; Kuta Galleria, Blok Valet 2, 12, Kuta)

UK (Map p146; ☎ 270601; bcbali@dps.centrin.net.id; Jl Tirtanadi 20, Sanur)

USA (Map pp164-5; ☎ 233605; amcobali@indosat.net.id; Jl Hayam Wuruk 188, Renon, Denpasar; ☽ 8am-4.30pm) A consular agent.

JAKARTA

Most nations have an embassy in Jakarta (telephone area code ☎ 021), including the following:

Australia (☎ 2550 5555; www.indonesia.embassy.gov.au; Jl Rasuna Said Kav 15-16)

Canada (☎ 2550 7800; www.international.gc.ca/asia/jakarta; World Trade Centre, 6th fl, Jl Jend Sudirman Kav 29-31)

France (☎ 2355 7600; Jl MH Thamrin 20)

Germany (☎ 3985 5000; Jl MH Thamrin 1)

Japan (☎ 3192 4308; Jl MH Thamrin 24)

Netherlands (☎ 524 8200; Jl HR Rasuna Said Kav S-3)

New Zealand (☎ 570 9460; BRI II Bldg, 23rd fl, Jl Jend Sudirman Kav 44-46)

UK (☎ 315 6264; www.britain-in-indonesia.or.id; Jl M.H. Thamrin 75)

USA (☎ 3435 9000; www.usembassyjakarta.org; Jl Medan Merdeka Selatan 4-5)

FESTIVALS & EVENTS

Try to obtain a *Calendar of Events* booklet – there are several versions published by the government – listing every important temple ceremony and village festival in Bali for the current (Western) year. You can also inquire at tourist offices or at your hotel.

Balinese Calendars, Holidays & Festivals

Apart from the usual Western calendar, the Balinese also use two local calendars, the *saka* calendar and the *wuku* calendar. For more on this, see the boxed text, p66. See the boxed text, p62, for the surprising details about the important holy day of silence, Nyepi.

SAKA CALENDAR

The Hindu *saka* (or *caka*) calendar is a lunar cycle that is similar to the Western calendar in terms of the length of the year. Nyepi (see the boxed text, p62) is the major festival of the *saka* year – it's the last day of the year, ie the day after the new moon of the ninth month. Certain major temples celebrate their festivals by the *saka* calendar.

WUKU CALENDAR

The *wuku* calendar is used to determine festival dates. The calendar uses 10 different types of weeks between one and 10 days long, which all run simultaneously. The intersection of the various weeks determines auspicious days. The seven- and five-day weeks are of particular importance. A full year is made up of 30 individually named seven-day weeks (210 days).

Galungan, which celebrates the death of a legendary tyrant called Mayadenawa, is one of Bali's major festivals. During this 10-day period, held every 210 days, all the gods come down to earth for the festivities. Barong

A GOOD DAY FOR...

Almost every Balinese home and business has a copy of the *Kalendar Cetakan* hanging on the wall. This annual publication tracks the various local religious calendars and overlays them upon your usual 365-day Western calendar. Details are extensive and most importantly, the calendar provides vital details on which days are most fortuitous for myriad activities such as bull castration, building a boat, laying a foundation, drilling a well, starting a long trip and having sex. Many Balinese would not think of scheduling any activity without checking the calendar first and this can lead to many inconveniences since many activities are only condoned for a few days a year (except sex, which is called for at least 10 days a month – a real marketing tool!). For a full discussion of the numerous inputs that produce this calendar, see p66.

(mythical lion-dog creatures) prance from temple to temple and village to village, and locals rejoice with feasts and visits to families. The celebrations culminate with the Kuningan festival, when the Balinese say thanks and goodbye to the gods.

Every village in Bali will celebrate Galungan and Kuningan in grand style. Forthcoming dates (the two days are always separated by 10 days and they occur twice in 2010) are the following:

Year	Galungan	Kuningan
2009	14 Oct	24 Oct
2010	12 May & 8 Dec	22 May & 18 Dec
2011	6 Jul	16 Jul

Bali Events

Although most of the island's energies go to the myriad religious festivals, Bali has a few organised events which have proven popular with locals and visitors alike. Be sure to confirm that the event will happen.

Bali Art Festival of Buleleng May or June, Singaraja (p257)

Bali Arts Festival Mid-June to mid-July, Denpasar (p167)

Bali Kite Festival July, Sanur (p148)

Kuta Karnival Late September and early October, Kuta (p109)

Ubud Writers & Readers Festival October, Ubud (p184)

Lombok Events

Many festivals take place at the start of the rainy season (around October to December) or at harvest time (around April to May). Most of them do not fall on specific days in the Western calendar, including Ramadan, so planning for them isn't really possible.

Ramadan, the month of fasting, is the ninth month of the Muslim calendar. During this period many restaurants are closed, and for-

eigners eating, drinking (especially alcohol) and smoking in public may attract a very negative reaction.

Other occasions observed on Lombok include the following:

Desa Bersih (First Thursday in April) A harvest festival held in honour of Dewi Sri, the rice goddess in the region of Gunung Pengsong.

Nyale Festival (Nineteenth day of the 10th month of the Sasak calendar; generally February/March) Commemorates the legend of a beautiful princess who went out to sea and drowned herself rather than choose between her many admirers – her long hair was transformed into the worm-like fish the Sasak call *nyale*.

Perang Topat (November or December) A harvest festival featuring a mock battle with sticky rice held near Mataram (see p289).

Temple Festivals

Temple festivals in Bali are quite amazing, and you'll often come across them quite unexpectedly, even in the most remote corners of the island. The annual 'temple birthday' is known as an *odalan* and is celebrated once every Balinese year of 210 days. Since most villages have at least three temples, you're assured of at least five or six annual festivals in every village. In addition, there can be special festival days common throughout Bali; festivals for certain important temples and festivals for certain gods. The full moons which fall around the end of September to the beginning of October, or from early to mid-April, are often times for important temple festivals in Bali.

The most obvious sign of a temple festival is a long line of women in traditional costume, walking gracefully to the temple with beautifully arranged offerings of food, fruit and flowers piled in huge pyramids which they carry on their heads.

Meanwhile, the various *pemangku* (temple guardians and priests for temple rituals) suggest to the gods that they should come down for a visit. That's what those little thrones are for in the temple shrines – they are symbolic seats for the gods to occupy during festivals. Women dance the stately Pendet, an offering dance for the gods.

All night long on the island there's activity, music and dancing – it's like a great country fair, with food, amusements, games, stalls, gambling, noise, colour and confusion. Finally, as dawn approaches, the entertainment fades away, the *pemangku* suggest to the gods that it's time they made their way back to heaven and the people wind their weary way back home.

When you first arrive, it's well worth asking at a tourist office or your hotel what festivals will be held during your stay. Seeing one will be a highlight of your trip. Foreigners are welcome to watch the festivities and take photographs, but be unobtrusive and dress modestly. For tips for respecting traditions and acting appropriately while visiting temples, see the boxed text, p348.

FOOD

You can eat well with locals for under US$1, or in touristy places for under US$5. A fabulous meal prepared by a renowned chef will cost somewhat more, but the constant is that at any price range the food is generally very fresh, often quite good and usually much cheaper than you would pay at home. See p70 for details.

In this book, restaurants are listed in order of cheapest to most expensive price for a meal.

GAY & LESBIAN TRAVELLERS

Gay travellers in Bali will experience few problems, and many of the island's most influential expat artists have been more-or-less openly gay. Physical contact between same-sex couples is acceptable and friends of the same sex often hold hands, though this does not indicate homosexuality.

There are many venues where gay men congregate, mostly in Kuta and Seminyak. There's nowhere that's exclusively gay, and nowhere that's even inconspicuously a lesbian scene. Hotels are happy to rent a room with a double bed to any couple. Homosexual behaviour is not illegal, and the age of consent for sexual activity is 16 years. Gay men in Indonesia are referred to as *homo*, or *gay*, and

are quite distinct from the female impersonators called *waria*.

Many gays from other parts of the country come to live in Bali, as it is more tolerant, and also because it offers opportunities to meet foreign partners.

Gay prostitutes are mostly from Java, and some have been known to rip off their foreign clients. Gay Balinese men are usually just looking for nothing more than an adventure, though there is an expectation that the (relatively) wealthy foreign guy will pay for meals, drinks, hotels etc.

On Lombok, gay and lesbian travellers should refrain from public displays of affection (advice that also applies to straight couples). There are gay-friendly places in Senggigi (p291).

Organisations

Bali Pink Pages (www.balipinkpages.com) Website by the Bali Gay & Lesbian Association.
Gaya Dewata (☎ 0361-234079; Denpasar) Bali's gay organisation.
Hanafi (see p105) Kuta-based gay-friendly tour operator and guide; good for the low-down on the local scene.
Utopia Asia (www.utopia-asia.com) Not specific to Bali, but has excellent information about the Bali gay scene.

HOLIDAYS

The following holidays are celebrated throughout Indonesia. Many of the dates change according to the phase of the moon (not by month), and these are estimates.
Tahun Baru Masehi (New Year's Day) 1 January
Idul Adha (Muslim festival of sacrifice) February
Muharram (Islamic New Year) February/March
Nyepi (Hindu New Year) March/April
Hari Paskah (Good Friday) April
Ascension of Christ April/May
Hari Waisak (Buddha's birth, enlightenment and death) April/May
Maulud Nabi Mohammed/Hari Natal (Prophet Mohammed's birthday) May
Hari Proklamasi Kemerdekaan (Indonesian Independence Day) 17 August
Isra Miraj Nabi Mohammed (Ascension of the Prophet Mohammed) September
Idul Fitri (End of Ramadan) November/December
Hari Natal (Christmas Day) 25 December

See Festivals & Events (p335) for additional holidays. The Muslim population in Bali observes Islamic festivals and holidays, including Ramadan. Religious and other holidays on Lombok are as follows.

Anniversary of West Lombok (Government holiday)
April 17
Ramadan Usually October
Founding of West Nusa Tenggara (Public holiday)
December 17

INSURANCE

Unless you are definitely sure that your health coverage at home will cover you in Bali and Lombok, you should take out travel insurance – bring a copy of the policy as evidence that you're covered. Get a policy that pays for medical evacuation if necessary.

Some policies specifically exclude 'dangerous activities', which can include scuba diving, renting a local motorcycle and even trekking. Be aware that a locally acquired motorcycle licence isn't valid under some policies.

INTERNET ACCESS

Internet centres are common anywhere there are tourists in Bali. Expect to pay 300Rp to 500Rp per minute for access. Excellent places can be found in South Bali and Ubud. At these centres you can download your digital camera, burn CDs or chat on Skype. You can also network your laptop. Elsewhere, speed varies but is often slow.

Many hotels have internet centres for their guests. In-room wi-fi access is moving down the price chart in availability but watch out for places with high charges pegged to time or data use (we tried one where two emails exhausted the 80,000Rp connection allowance). Most are free or cheap. In South Bali and Ubud wi-fi access in cafés is increasingly common and is often free.

Indosat (www.indosatm2.com) has deployed a 3G data network across South Bali.

Internet access on Lombok tends to cost 400Rp to 500Rp per minute. However, outside of Mataram and Senggigi, internet access is painfully slow wherever you go on Lombok.

LEGAL MATTERS

Gambling is illegal (although it's common, especially at cockfights), as is pornography. The government takes the smuggling, using and selling of drugs very, *very* seriously. Once you've been caught and put in jail, there is very little that your consulate in Bali (if there's one) can do for you. You may have to wait for up to six months in jail before you even go to trial. See p333 for additional dire details.

Generally, you are unlikely to have any encounters with the police unless you are driving a rented car or motorcycle (see p355).

Some governments (including the Australian government) have laws making it illegal for their citizens to use child prostitutes or engage in other paedophiliac activities anywhere in the world. Foreigners have been prosecuted and penalties are severe. See the boxed text, p56.

There are police stations in all district capitals. If you have to report a crime or have other business at a police station, expect a lengthy and bureaucratic encounter. You should dress as respectably as possible, bring a fluent Indonesian-speaking friend for interpretation and moral support, arrive early and be very polite. You can also call the **Bali Tourist Police** (☎ 0361-224111) for advice. Call ☎ 112 in an emergency in Bali.

Police officers frequently expect to receive bribes, either to overlook some crime, misdemeanour or traffic infringement, or to provide a service that they should provide anyway. Generally, it's easiest to pay up – and the sooner you do it, the less it will cost. You may be told there's a 'fine' to pay on the spot or you can offer to a pay a 'fine' to clear things up. How much? Generally, 50,000Rp can work wonders and the officers are not proud. If things seem unreasonable, however, ask for the officer's name and write it down.

If you're in trouble, contact your consulate as soon as you can – they can't get you out of it, but they can recommend English-speaking lawyers and may have useful contacts.

MAPS

For tourist resorts and towns, the maps in this guidebook are as good as you'll get. If you need a more detailed road map of the island, there are some OK sheet maps available in bookshops. The following are examples of good maps that are available; there are many more which are old and/or useless.

▪ Periplus Travel Maps has a decent *Bali* contour map (1:250,000), with a detailed section on southern Bali, plus maps of the main town areas. However, the labelling and names used for towns are often incomprehensible. The *Lombok & Sumbawa* map is useful.

▪ The Periplus *Street Atlas Bali* may be more than you need, but it is more accurate than the sheet map. Again, there are inexplicable omissions.

MONEY

Indonesia's unit of currency is the rupiah (Rp). There are coins worth 50, 100, 500 and 1000Rp. Notes come in denominations of 1000Rp, 5000Rp, 10,000Rp, 20,000Rp, 50,000Rp and 100,000Rp.

Check out the inside front cover of this book for an idea about current exchange rates of the rupiah. In recent times the currency has been fairly stable. Many midrange hotels and all top-end hotels, along with some tourist attractions and tour companies, list their prices in US dollars or euros, although you can usually pay in rupiah at a poorer exchange rate.

US dollars are usually the most negotiable currency.

Many travellers now rely on ATMs for cash while in Bali. It is a good idea, however, to carry some backup funds in case your card is lost or the network goes down (usually just for a few hours).

Always carry a good supply of rupiah in small denominations with you. Throughout the island, many people will struggle to make change for a 50,000Rp note or larger.

ATMs

There are ATMs all over Bali (with the notable exception of Nusa Lembongan). Most accept international ATM cards and major credit cards for cash advances. The exchange rates for ATM withdrawals are usually quite good, but check to see if your home bank will hit you with outrageous fees. Most ATMs in Bali allow a maximum withdrawal of 600,000Rp to 1.2 million rupiah. Try to avoid ones with a sticker saying '100,000Rp', as that's the denomination you'll get and you'll struggle to break those bills with local traders.

Mataram, Praya and Senggigi on Lombok have ATMs but there are none on the Gilis.

Banks

Major banks have branches in the main tourist centres and provincial capitals. Smaller towns may not have banks at all or have banks that don't exchange currency. Changing money in banks can be time-consuming.

Cash

Changing money in Bali isn't too difficult in tourist areas. It's easiest to exchange US banknotes, especially US$100 bills. However, make certain that your money is new and recent. Older designs and damaged notes will often be refused.

Rupiah bills of 50,000Rp and larger can be hard to break. Always keep lots of small bills for taxis, tips and other services.

Credit Cards

Visa, MasterCard and American Express (Amex) are accepted by most of the larger businesses that cater to tourists. You sign for the amount in rupiah – or dollars – and the bill is converted into your domestic currency. The conversion is at the interbank rate and is usually quite good, though some banks add various usage and exchange fees which are strictly for their own profit. However, be sure to confirm that a business accepts credit cards before you show up cashless.

You can also get cash advances on major credit cards at many ATMs.

Moneychangers

Exchange rates offered by moneychangers are normally better than the banks, plus they offer quicker service and keep much longer hours. The exchange rates are advertised on boards along footpaths or on windows outside shops. It's worth looking around because rates vary a little, but beware of places advertising exceptionally high rates – they may make their profit by short-changing their customers (see p334). In the Kuta area, you can now find international banks with reliable exchange services (see p105). In hotels, the rates can be up to 20% less than a street moneychanger.

Tipping

Tipping a set percentage is not expected in Bali, but restaurant workers are poorly paid; if the service is good, it's appropriate to leave 4000Rp or more. Most midrange hotels and restaurants and all top-end hotels and restaurants add 21% to the bill for tax and service (known as 'plus plus'). This service component is distributed among hotel staff (one hopes), so you needn't tip under these circumstances.

It's also a nice thing to tip taxi drivers, guides, people giving you a massage, fetching you a beer on the beach etc.

Travellers Cheques

Travellers cheques are getting harder and harder to exchange, especially if they are not in US dollars. The exchange rates offered for travellers cheques are often worse than for cash.

PHOTOGRAPHY & VIDEO

Bali is one of the most photogenic places on earth, so be prepared.

Cameras

You can buy additional memory cards for digital cameras at photo shops in the major tourist centres, but you're really better off bringing what you need from home.

The best internet places (p338) will allow you to download your photos onto their computers for distribution to lucky friends and relatives worldwide or for burning onto a CD for storage or printing at a photo shop. It's also a good idea to bring along whatever cable your camera requires. The process is easiest for people who carry their own laptops.

Basic 35mm film is available at reasonable prices – but always check the expiry date first. Developing and printing is going the way of the dodo, however.

Photographing People

Photograph with discretion and manners. It's always polite to ask first, and if they say no, then don't. A gesture, smile and nod are all that is usually necessary.

Restrictions

You are usually welcome to take photos of ceremonies in the villages and temples, but try not to be intrusive. Ask before taking photos inside a temple.

There's one place where you must not take photographs at all – public bathing places. Balinese think of these places as private and do not 'see' one another when they're bathing. To intrude with a camera is very rude voyeurism.

Video

Bring any media you need from home in sealed packages to avoid a customs search for prohibited material.

POST

Sending postcards and normal-sized letters (ie under 20g) by airmail is cheap, but not really fast. A postcard/letter to the USA costs 5000/10,000Rp (allow 13 days); to Australia costs 7500/15,000Rp (15 days); and to the UK costs 8000/18,000Rp (21 days).

For anything over 20g, the charge is based on weight. You can send parcels up to 20kg and you can get them properly wrapped and sealed at any post office.

Every substantial town has a *kantor pos* (post office). In tourist centres, there are also postal agencies. They are often open long hours and provide postal services. Many will also wrap and pack parcels.

Have poste restante mail sent to you via the post offices at Kuta (p105) and Ubud (p176). Mail should be addressed to you with your surname underlined and in capital letters, then 'Kantor Pos', the name of the town, and then 'Bali, Indonesia'. You can also have mail sent to your hotel.

Express companies offer reliable, fast and expensive service.

FedEx (Map p132; ☎ 0361-701 727; Jl Bypass Nusa Dua 100X, Jimbaran) Located south of the airport.

UPS (Map p100; ☎ 0361-766 676; Jl Bypass Ngurah Rai 2005) Has a location near the Bali Galleria.

See p342 for tips on shipping large items.

SHOPPING

For some people Bali is a destination for shopping, for others it becomes their destiny. You'll find a plethora of shops and stalls across the island – everything from a cheap T-shirt and silly wooden carvings of penises to exquisite boutiques with alluring ranges of housewares and fashions by local designers.

Look in Kuta, Legian and Seminyak in the south, and Ubud, for the widest range of goods, including what seems like millions of bead and necklace shops. Generally, Kuta is the place for huge, chain surf shops and Bintang T-shirts. Towards Legian things get more creative and as you go north through Seminyak, shops become more exclusive, with many owned by noteworthy designers.

The best buys on Lombok are handicrafts, such as boxes, basketware, pottery and handwoven textiles.

For more details on the crafts available, see p65.

Ceramics

Nearly all local pottery is made from low-fired terracotta. Most styles are very ornate, even for functional items such as vases, flasks,

---

THE ART OF BARGAINING

Many everyday purchases in Bali require bargaining. This particularly applies to clothing, arts and crafts. Accommodation has a set price, but this is usually negotiable in the low season, or if you are staying at the hotel for several days.

In an everyday bargaining situation, the first step is to establish a starting price – it's usually better to ask the seller for their price rather than make an initial offer. It also helps if you have some idea what the item is worth.

Generally, your first price could be anything from one-third to two-thirds of the asking price – assuming that the asking price is not completely over the top. Then, with offer and counter-offer, you'll move closer to an acceptable price. For example, the seller asks 60,000Rp for the handicraft, you offer 30,000Rp and so on, until eventually you both agree at somewhere around 45,000Rp. If you don't get to an acceptable price, you're quite entitled to walk away – the vendor may even call you back with a lower price.

Note that when you name a price, you're committed – you have to buy if your offer is accepted. Remember, bargaining should be an enjoyable part of shopping in Bali, so maintain your sense of humour and keep things in perspective.

---

ashtrays and lamp bases. Pejaten (p274) near Tabanan also has a number of pottery workshops producing small ceramic figures and glazed ornamental roof tiles. For details of where to buy ceramics, see p68.

Clothing & Fashion

Famous and soon-to-be famous designers have clothing shops in Seminyak (p126). Locally made clothing is sold in hundreds of small shops in all tourist centres, especially Kuta, Legian and Seminyak. It's pretty casual, but it's not just beachwear – you can get just about anything you want, including tailor-made clothing.

Fabrics & Weaving

Gianyar (p208), in eastern Bali, has a few factories where you can watch ikat (cloth in which a pattern is produced by dyeing the individual threads before weaving) sarongs being woven on a hand-and-foot-powered loom.

Any market, especially in Denpasar (p169), will have a good range of textiles as does Jl Arjuna in Legian (p116).

The village of Sukarara (p320) on Lombok is a good place for fabrics.

Furniture

Wood furniture is a big industry, though much of it is actually made in Java and sent to Bali for finishing and sale. Tourists are tempted by contemporary designs and reproduction antiques at much lower prices than they'd find at home. Outdoor furniture made from teak, mahogany and other rainforest timbers is often spectacular and better than you'd get at home for many times the price.

Harvesting timber for the local furniture industry and furniture manufacturing involves a high local value-added content. It probably also has a lesser impact on rainforests than large-scale clearing for export of logs and wood chips, which are much more significant causes of deforestation, and generate a lot less local employment.

The best places to look for furniture are the stores/warehouses along Jl Bypass Ngurah Rai in South Bali and in Kuta (p116). Mas (p205), south of Ubud, is also good.

Jewellery

Celuk (p204) has always been the village associated with silversmithing. The large shops that line the road into Celuk have imposing, bus-sized driveways and slick facilities. If you want to see the 'real' Celuk, go about 1km east of the road to visit family workshops.

Music & Video

Piracy is a major industry in Bali. CDs and DVDs featuring popular artists and entertainment cost as little as 10,000Rp and are widely sold in tourist areas. Quality is often bad (current-release features are made with hand-held cameras in theatres!), the format may not work with your system and many of the discs are no good to begin with. You really will get what you pay for.

Legitimate DVDs are uncommon but authentic CDs are often sold in the same places offering fakes. They are good value at around

SHIPPING LARGE ITEMS

It might just be feasible to carry home a few folding chairs or some artwork, but generally, if you buy large or heavy items, you'll need to have them shipped home. For items that are shipped, you'll pay a 40% or 50% deposit and the balance (plus any taxes or import duties) when you collect the items at home. If possible, arrange for delivery to your door – if you have to pick the items up from the nearest port or freight depot you may be up for extra port charges.

Most stores selling furniture or heavy artwork can arrange packing, shipping and insurance. Shipping costs for volumes less than a full container load vary greatly according to the company, destination and quantity – think in terms of around US$150 plus per cubic metre. Be aware that packing costs, insurance, fumigation (!) and so on are included in some companies' prices but are charged as extras by others.

To get things home quickly and at great expense, see the express freight companies listed under Post, p340.

Rim Cargo (Map p120; ☎ 0361-737670; www.rimcargo.com; Jl Laksmana 32, Seminyak) is a large company adept at dealing with the needs of shopping-mad visitors.

80,000Rp to 90,000Rp. The cost of CDs featuring Balinese and Indonesian artists is generally lower.

Paintings

There are a relatively small number of creative original painters in Bali today, and an enormous number of imitators who produce copies, or near copies, in well-established styles. Many of these imitative works are nevertheless very well-executed and attractive pieces. Originality is not considered as important in Balinese art as it is in the West.

Unfortunately, much of the painting today is churned out for the undiscriminating tourist market. Thus, the shops are packed full of paintings in the various popular styles – some of them quite good and many of them uniformly alike and uniformly poor in quality (think doe-eyed puppies in garish colours).

Before making a purchase, visit the museums and galleries of Ubud (p176) to see the best of Balinese art and some of the European influences that have shaped it. At the galleries you will get an idea of how to value truly deserving Balinese paintings.

Sculpture

Balinese stone is surprisingly light and it's not at all out of the realms of possibility to bring a friendly stone demon back with you in your airline baggage. A typical temple door guardian weighs around 10kg. The stone, however, is very fragile, so packing must be done carefully if you're going to get it home without damage. Some of the Batubulan workshops will pack figures quickly and expertly. There are also many capable packing and forwarding agents, though the shipping costs will almost certainly be more than the cost of the article.

Batubulan, on the main highway from South Bali to Ubud (p203), is a major stone-carving centre. Workshops are found further north along the road in Tegaltamu and Silakarang. Stone figures from 25cm to 2m tall line both sides of the road, and stone carvers can be seen in action in the many workshops here.

Woodcarvings

As with paintings, try to see some of the best-quality woodcarvings in museums and galleries before you consider buying. Again, many standard pieces are produced in the same basic designs, and craft shops are full of them. Even with a basic frog, hand or fisherman design, some are much better than others.

Ubud (p172) and Mas (p205) are good places to look for woodcarvings.

SOLO TRAVELLERS

Bali (and to a lesser degree Lombok) is a good place for solo travellers. Both locals and other travellers tend to be open and friendly, making it easy to hook up with others while exploring the island.

Most places to stay have accommodation for single travellers for a price at least a little cheaper than pairs. Women travelling alone should refer to the Women Travellers section (p347).

TELEPHONE

To call any country direct from Indonesia dial 001 plus the country code followed by the number, or make a call via the international operator (☎ 101). The country code for Indonesia is ☎ 62, the area code for Jakarta is ☎ 021. Bali has six telephone area codes and Lombok two; these are listed in the relevant chapters of this book. Phone numbers beginning with ☎ 08 are mobile (cell) phones.

The telecommunications service within Indonesia is provided by Telkom, a government monopoly. Local directory assistance operators (☎ 108) are very helpful and some of them speak English. If you call directory assistance and have to spell out a name, try to use the 'Alpha, Bravo, Charlie' system of saying the letters.

Calling internationally can easily cost from US$0.25 to US$1 or more a minute no matter which of the methods you choose to opt for as outlined below.

Some foreign telephone companies issue cards that enable you to make calls from Indonesian phones and have the cost billed to your home phone account. However, the catch is that most public telephones, wartel (public telephone offices) and hotels won't allow you to call the toll-free ☎ 008 or ☎ 001 access numbers needed to use these phonecards or other home-billing schemes, and the few hotels and wartel that do permit it charge a fee for doing so.

Internet Calling

Internet connections fast enough to support Voice Over Internet (VOI) services like Skype are now common in South Bali and Ubud. Internet centres are hip to this and some allow it while others add a surcharge for the call to your connection time (perhaps 3000Rp per minute). If you're staying at a place with fast wi-fi in the room, you're really set.

Mobile Phones

The cellular service in Indonesia is GSM. There are several local providers, including Telkomsel and Pro XL. If your phone company offers international roaming in Indonesia, you can use your own mobile telephone in Bali – but check with the company to find out what the rates are (often outrageous).

Alternatively, a mobile phone (called a handphone in Indonesia) using the GSM system can be used more cheaply if you purchase a prepaid SIM card that you insert into your phone in Bali. This will cost about 50,000Rp from shops in South Bali and will give you your own local telephone number. However, make certain the phone you bring is both unlocked and able to take SIM cards. Basic phones bought locally start at US$30.

Usually the person selling you your SIM card will install it and make certain things are working. There is also a requirement that you show some ID so your number can be registered with the government but often busy clerks will suggest you return 'some other time' thus saving you this formality.

Long-distance and international calls from a mobile can be less expensive than through the regular phone system. When you buy your SIM card and usage credit, ask about special access codes that can result in international calls for as low as US$0.25 per minute.

Many shops are adept at getting your mobile access sorted. A convenient one is **Diamond Selular Center** (Map p120; ☎ 0361-736779; Bintang Supermarket, Jl Raya Seminyak 17, Seminyak).

Phonecards

The vast majority of public phones use phonecards. Some use the regular *kartu telepo* (phonecards) with a magnetic strip. Others use a *kartu chip,* which has an electronic chip embedded in it. You can buy phonecards in denominations of 5000Rp, 10,000Rp, 25,000Rp, 50,000Rp and 100,000Rp at wartel, moneychangers, post offices and many shops. An international call from a card phone costs about the same per minute as a call from a wartel.

Telephone Offices

A *kantor telekomunikasi* (telecommunications office) is a main telephone office operated by Telkom, usually only found in bigger towns. Wartel are sometimes run by Telkom, but the vast majority are private, and there are a lot of them. You can make local, *inter-lokal* (long-distance) and international calls from any wartel.

The official Telkom price of a one-minute call is about the equivalent of US$1 to most parts of the world. Many wartel, however, will charge higher per-minute rates.

You can sometimes make reverse-charge (collect) calls from a Telkom wartel, though most private ones don't allow it and those that do will charge a set fee.

TIME

Bali, Lombok and the islands of Nusa Tenggara to the east are all on Waktu Indonesian Tengah or WIT (Central Indonesian Standard Time), which is eight hours ahead of Greenwich Mean Time/Universal Time or two hours behind Australian Eastern Standard Time. Java is another hour behind Bali and Lombok.

Not allowing for variations due to daylight-saving time in foreign countries, when it's noon in Bali and Lombok, it's 11pm the previous day in New York and 8pm in Los Angeles, 4am in London, 5am in Paris and Amsterdam, noon in Perth, 1pm in Tokyo, and 2pm in Sydney and Melbourne.

'Bali time' is an expression that refers to the Balinese reluctance to be obsessed by punctuality.

TOILETS

You'll encounter Asian-style toilets only in the very cheapest accommodation around Bali and Lombok. These toilets have two footrests and a hole in the floor – you squat down and aim. In almost every place catering for tourists, Western-style sit-down toilets are the norm. At some tourist attractions in Bali, there are public toilets that cost about 1000Rp per visit, but they can also be filthy or non-existent.

Apart from tourist cafés and restaurants and most accommodation, you won't find toilet paper, so bring your own. If there is a bin next to the toilet, it's for toilet paper.

TOURIST INFORMATION

The tourist office in Ubud is an excellent source of information on cultural events. Otherwise, the tourist offices in this book are largely hit or miss (mostly the latter). It helps to have a specific question and don't bother asking tourist services like tours. Hotels are often good sources of info.

Some of the best information is found in the many free publications aimed at tourists and expats which are distributed in South Bali and Ubud. These include the following:

Bali Advertiser (www.baliadvertiser.biz) This newspaper and website has voluminous ads, comprehensive information and idiosyncratic columnists.

Hello Bali Big and glossy with good features, restaurant and entertainment reviews.

Lombok Times (www.lomboktimes.com) A newspaper and website with tourist news and features.

The Beat Excellent bi-weekly with extensive entertainment and cultural listings.

What's Up Bali Useful weekly brochure with entertainment listings.

Yak Glossy mag celebrating the expat swells of Seminyak and Ubud.

The website for **Bali Discovery** (www.balidiscovery .com) has a first-rate Bali news section and a wealth of other island information. Use the handy search feature. For more useful websites, see p19.

TRAVELLERS WITH DISABILITIES

Bali is a difficult destination for those with limited mobility. While some of the airlines flying to Bali have a good reputation for accommodating people with disabilities, the airport is not well set-up. Contact the airlines and ask them what arrangements can be made for disembarking and boarding at the airport.

Bemo, minibuses and buses that provide public transport are not accessible. The minibuses used by tourist shuttle bus and tour companies are similar. Ramps and other disabled facilities at hotels and inns are rare. Your best bet are the international chains – and then you should still confirm your needs with the property. Out on the street, the footpaths, where they exist at all, tend to be narrow, uneven, potholed and frequently obstructed.

Bali can be a rewarding destination for people who are blind or vision impaired. Balinese music is heard everywhere, and the languages are fascinating to listen to. The smells of incense, spices, tropical fruit and flowers pervade the island, and are as exotic as you could wish for. With a sighted companion, most places should be reasonably accessible.

VISAS

The visa situation in Indonesia seems to be constantly in flux. It is essential that you confirm current formalities before you arrive in Bali or Lombok. Failure to meet all the entrance requirements can see you on the first flight out.

No matter what type of visa you are going to use, your passport *must* be valid for at least six months from the date of your arrival.

The main visa options for visitors to Bali and Lombok follow:

■ Visa in Advance – citizens of countries not eligible for Visa Free or Visa on Arrival must apply for a visa before they arrive in Indonesia. Typically this is a visitors visa, which comes in two flavours: 30 or 60 days. Details vary by country, so you should contact the nearest Indonesian embassy or consulate in order to determine processing fees and time. Note: this is the only way people from any country can obtain a 60-day visitor visa.

■ Visa on Arrival – citizens of over 50 countries may apply for a visa when they arrive at the airport in Bali. There are special lanes for this at immigration in the arrivals area. The cost is US$25, collectable on the spot. It's easiest to hand them the exact amount in US currency. This visa is only good for 30 days and cannot be extended. Note that only EU citizens who carry passports issued by the countries listed below can use visa on arrival. You can also obtain a seven-day visa this way for US$10, but go with the 30-day one unless you know for sure you'll be out of Indonesia in less than seven days. Eligible countries include Australia, Austria, Belgium, Canada, Denmark, France, Germany, Ireland, Italy, Japan, the Netherlands, New Zealand, Russia, South Africa, South Korea, Spain, Switzerland, Sweden, Taiwan, UK and the USA.

■ Visa Free – citizens of Singapore and a smattering of other countries can receive a nonextendable 30-day visa for free upon arrival.

Whichever type of visa you use to enter Bali or Lombok, you'll be issued with a tourist card that is valid for a 30- or 60-day stay according to your visa (if you have obtained one of the coveted 60-day visas in advance, be sure the immigration official at the airport gives you a 60-day card). Keep the tourist card with your passport, as you'll have to hand it back when you leave the country. Note that some travellers have been fined for overstaying by only a day or so (officially it is US$20 per day for up to 60 days past your visa, after which it can mean jail) or for losing their tourist card.

The vast majority of visitors to Lombok first pass through Bali or another Indonesian city such as Jakarta so they already have tourist cards. There are, however, a few direct flights to Lombok from other countries so in these instances the same visa rules outlined above apply.

Other Requirements

Officially, an onward/return ticket is a requirement for a tourist card (and visitors visa), and visitors are frequently asked to show their ticket on arrival. If you look scruffy or broke, you may also be asked to present evidence of sufficient funds to support yourself during your stay – US$1000 in cash or travellers cheques (or the equivalent in other currencies) should be sufficient.

It's not possible to extend a tourist card unless there's a medical emergency or you have to answer legal charges. If you want to spend more time in Indonesia, you have to leave the country and then re-enter – some long-term foreign residents have been doing this for years. Singapore is the destination of choice for obtaining a new visa on the 'visa run'.

There are two main *kantor imigrasi* (immigration offices) in Bali. The **Denpasar office** (Map pp164-5; ☎ 0361-227828; 🕑 8am-2pm Mon-Thu, 8am-11am Fri, 8am-noon Sat) is just up the street from the main post office in Renon. The airport **immigration office** (☎ 0361-751038) has similar hours.

On Lombok, the **immigration office** (Map p286; ☎ 632520; Jl Udayana 2; 🕑 7am-2pm Mon-Thu, 7am-11am Fri, 7am-12.30am Sat) is in Mataram. If you have to apply for changes to your visa, make sure you're neatly dressed, but don't be overly optimistic.

For visa advice and service, many expats in South Bali use the services of **Bali Mode** (☎ 0361-765162; www.balimode-biz.com). Visa extensions (on legally extendable visas) average 400,000Rp to 500,000Rp.

Social Visas

If you have a good reason for staying longer (eg study or family reasons), you can apply for a *sosial/budaya* (social/cultural) visa. You will need an application form from an Indonesian embassy or consulate, and a letter of introduction or promise of sponsorship from a reputable person or school in Indonesia. It's initially valid for three months, but it can be extended for one month at a time at an immigration office within Indonesia

DIRECTORY

BREAKING THE POVERTY CYCLE

'We have provided scholarships for 520 students because we believe that a good education is the best foundation to break the poverty cycle,' says Helen Flavel, the head of an eponymous foundation that has helped hundreds of people in Bali's impoverished north.

She first visited Bali in 1994 and was struck both by the needs of so many people and the fact that there is no government safety net for the poor. One trip followed another and she now fronts a major charitable group.

'We have a two-storey Learning Centre which is fully paid for, and six qualified teachers who teach English, computing, animal care, cross-cultural studies, music, dance, drama and dressmaking. There are also 33 students from the mountain regions who board at the centre and attend school with scholarships provided by our sponsors.'

'We have also built 143 very basic houses since 2004, given funding for over 20 small businesses and covered the expenses of surgical operations.'

Flavel notes that having the Balinese feel ownership of the projects is critical. 'Without our dedicated team of 16 full-time staff and 20 front-line men in the villages throughout the north, we could not achieve all that is being achieved. The foundation is 'owned' by the Balinese – we (with our sponsors and sister foundations) provide the finance and support to enable them to do the work.'

The Helen Flavel Foundation (www.helenflavelfoundation.org) is always looking for people to help sponsor its students and its many projects.

For more on volunteering, see above.

---

for a maximum of six months. There are fees for the application and for extending the visa too.

VOLUNTEERING

There's a plethora of opportunities to help others in Bali and Lombok. Many people have found that they can show their love for Bali by helping others. We have three stories, including one from a woman who is helping Balinese kids get an education (below), another from a woman who is making life better for orphans (p260) and a third from an American who found a way to do more on her three-week holiday than just get scorched on the beach (p184).

LOCAL ORGANISATIONS

Ubud is a hub for non-profit and volunteer organisations. **Bali Spirit** (☎ 0361-970 992; www.balispirit.com; 44 Jl Hanoman, Ubud) is part of a café (Kafe, see p193). It has information on a number of non-profit and volunteer groups located in Ubud, including the Indonesian Development of Education & Permaculture (IDEP) and the Sumatran Orangutan Society (SOS). The **Pondok Pecak Library & Learning Centre** (Map p186; ☎ 0361-976 194; pondok@indo.net.id; Monkey Forest Rd, Ubud) also has info on local charities.

BIWA (see opposite) is a useful clearing house for information on local charities. If you'd like to help Bali's dogs, see the boxed text, p184.

The following organisations have need for donations, supplies and often volunteers. Check their websites to see their current status.

East Bali Poverty Project (☎ 0361-410071; www.eastbalipovertyproject.org; Denpasar) Works to help children in the impoverished mountain villages of East Bali.

IDEP (Indonesian Development of Education & Permaculture; ☎ 0361-981504; www.idepfoundation.org; Ubud) A large Ubud-based organisation that works on environmental projects, disaster planning and community improvement. Runs the Bali Cares shop (p196).

JED (Village Ecotourism Network; ☎ 0361-737447; www.jed.or.id) Organises highly regarded tours (p361) of small villages. Often needs volunteers to improve its services and work with the villagers.

PPLH Bali (Pusat Pendidikan Lingkungan Hidup; ☎ 0361-288221; www.pplhbali.or.id; Jl Hang Tuah 24, Sanur) Organises a broad range of environmental and education programs, see p145.

ProFauna (☎ 0361-424731; www.profauna.or.id) A large non-profit animal-protection organisation operating across Indonesia; the Bali office has been aggressive in protecting sea turtles. Volunteers needed to help with hatchery releases and editing publications.

SOS (Sumatran Orangutan Society; www.orangutans-sos.org) An Ubud-based group that works to save endangered species throughout Indonesia.

WISNU (☎ 0361-735321; www.wisnu.or.id; Jl Pengubengan Kauh, Kerobokan) An environmental group that teaches tourism-related industries how to be more green. It's set up community-based recycling programs with 25 hotels on the Bukit Peninsula, and always needs volunteers; it runs Depot Organic, a small warung (p128).

Yakkum Bali (Yayasan Rama Sesana; ☎ 0361-247363; www.yrsbali.org; Denpasar) Dedicated to improving reproductive health for women across Bali.

Yayasan Bumi Sehat (☎ 0361-970002; www.bumisehatbali.org; Ubud) Operates a clinic and gives reproductive services to poor women.

YKIP (Humanitarian Foundation of Mother Earth; ☎ 0361-759544; www.ykip.org) Established after the 2002 bombings, it organises health and education projects for Bali's children.

INTERNATIONAL ORGANISATIONS

Another possible source for long-term paid or volunteer work in Bali or Lombok are the following agencies.

Australian Volunteers International (www.australianvolunteers.com) Organises professional contracts for Australians.

Global Volunteers (www.globalvolunteers.org) Arranges professional and paid volunteer work for US citizens.

Voluntary Service Overseas (www.vso.org.uk) British overseas volunteer program accepts qualified volunteers from other countries. Branches in Canada (www.vso canada.org) and the Netherlands (www.vso.nl).

Volunteer Service Abroad (www.vsa.org.nz) Organises professional contracts for New Zealanders.

WOMEN TRAVELLERS

Women travelling solo in Bali will get a lot of attention from Balinese guys, but Balinese men are, on the whole, fairly benign. Generally, Bali is safer for women than most areas of the world and, with the usual care and common sense, women should feel secure travelling alone.

Some precautions are simply the same for any traveller, but women should take extra care not to find themselves alone on empty beaches, down dark streets or in other situations where help might not be available. Late at night in the tourist centres, solo women should take a taxi, and sit in the back. Note that problems do occur and it is a good idea to practise the same precautions you use at home.

If you are going to stay in Bali for longer than a short holiday, the **Bali International Women's Association** (BIWA; ☎ 0361-285 552; www.biwa-bali.org) can prove essential. It was es-tablished by expats to 'foster friendship and mutual understanding' and meets monthly to organise support for local charities. It also works to help members integrate into local life.

Kuta Cowboys

In tourist areas of Bali (and Lombok), you'll encounter young men who are keen to spend time with visiting women. Commonly called Kuta Cowboys, beach boys, bad boys, guides or gigolos, these guys think they're supercool, with long hair, lean bodies, tight jeans and lots of tattoos. While they don't usually work a straight sex-for-money deal, the visiting woman pays for the meals, drinks and accommodation, and commonly buys the guy presents.

It's not uncommon for them to form long-term relationships, with the guy hopeful of finding a new and better life with his partner in Europe, Japan, Australia or the US. While most of these guys around Bali are genuinely friendly and quite charming, some are predatory con artists who practise elaborate deceits. Many of them now come from outside Bali, and have a long succession of foreign lovers. Be healthily sceptical about what they tell you, particularly if it comes down to them needing money.

There's a variation on this theme in Ubud, thanks to the best-selling *Eat, Pray, Love*. See p178 for more.

Lombok

Traditionally, women on Lombok are treated with respect, but in the touristy areas, harassment of single foreign women may occur. Would-be guides/boyfriends/gigolos are often persistent in their approaches, and can be aggressive when ignored or rejected. Clothes that aren't too revealing are a good idea – beachwear should be reserved for the beach, and the less skin you expose the better. Two or more women together are less likely to experience problems, and women accompanied by a man are unlikely to be harassed. It is better not to walk alone at night.

WORK

Quite a lot of foreigners own businesses in Bali – mostly hotels, restaurants and tour agencies. To do so legally, foreigners need

SHOWING RESPECT

Bali has a well-deserved reputation for being mellow; all the more reason to respect your hosts, who are enormously forgiving of faux pas if you're making a sincere effort. Be aware and respectful of local sensibilities, and dress and act appropriately, especially in rural villages and religious sites. When in doubt, let the words 'modest' and 'humble' guide you.

- An increasing number of younger Balinese now adopt the dress of visitors, which means you'll see shorts and skirts everywhere. Overly revealing clothing is still frowned upon though – few want to see your butt crack. And don't look like an ass wandering down the street shirtless quaffing a beer.

- Many women go topless on Bali's main beaches, but bring a top for less touristy beaches as the Balinese are embarrassed by gratuitous nudity by foreigners.

- On Lombok, nude or topless bathing is considered very offensive anywhere, as is public drunkenness.

- If visiting a temple or mosque, cover shoulders and knees. In Bali, a *selandong* (traditional scarf) or sash is usually provided for a small donation.

- Women are asked not to enter temples if menstruating, pregnant or have recently given birth. At these times women are thought to be *sebel* (ritually unclean), as are the recently bereaved and ill.

- Thongs (flip-flops) are acceptable in temples if you're otherwise well dressed, but if going to a government office, say to get a local driving licence or extend your visa, you need to look smarter.

- Don't put yourself higher than a priest, particularly at festivals (eg by scaling a wall to take photos).

- Take off your shoes before entering a mosque or someone's house.

- Don't touch anyone on the head, it's regarded as the abode of the soul and therefore sacred.

- Pass things with your right hand. Even better, use both hands.

- Beware of talking with hands on hips – a sign of contempt, anger or aggression (as displayed in traditional dance and opera).

- Beckon to someone with the hand extended and a downward waving motion. The Western method of beckoning is considered very rude.

- Don't make promises of mailed gifts, books and photographs that are soon forgotten. Pity the poor Balinese checking his or her mailbox everyday.

the appropriate work or business visa, which requires sponsorship from an employer, or evidence of a business that brings investment to Indonesia. Many foreigners are engaged in buying and exporting clothing, handicrafts or furniture, and stay for short periods – within the limits of a 30- or 60-day tourist card. It's illegal to work if you've entered Indonesia on a tourist card, and you'll have to leave the country to change your visa status. Even if you do get work, typically teaching English, payment is often in rupiah, which doesn't convert into a lot of foreign currency. Under-the-table work, such as dive shop and bar jobs, is typically poorly paid.

Transgport

CONTENTS

Getting There & Away	**349**
Entering the Country	349
Air	349
Sea	352
Getting Around	**353**
To/From the Airport	353
Air	353
Bemo	353
Bicycle	354
Boat	354
Bus	355
Car & Motorcycle	356
Hitching	359
Local Transport	360
Tours	361

GETTING THERE & AWAY

Most international visitors to Bali will arrive by air, either directly or via Jakarta. For island-hoppers, there are frequent ferries between eastern Java and Bali, and between Bali and Lombok, as well as domestic flights between the islands. Most people visit Lombok via Bali.

ENTERING THE COUNTRY

Arrival procedures at Bali's airport are straightforward, although it can take some time for planeloads of visitors to clear immigration; afternoons are worst, with waits of up to an hour to get through immigration. At the baggage claim area, porters are keen to help

---

THINGS CHANGE...

The information in this chapter is particularly vulnerable to change. Check directly with the airline or a travel agent to make sure you understand how a fare (and ticket you may buy) works and be aware of the security requirements for international travel. Shop carefully. The details given in this chapter should be regarded as pointers and are not a substitute for your own careful, up-to-date research.

---

get your luggage to the customs tables and beyond, and they've been known to ask up to US$20 for their services – if you want help with your bags, agree on a price beforehand. The formal price is 5000Rp per piece.

Once through customs, you're out with the tour operators, touts and taxi drivers. The touts will be working hard to convince you to come and stay at some place in the Kuta area. If you go with these guys, you'll pay more than you would if you just show up on your own as they get large commissions.

If you are feeling flush and can't bear the thought of a long queue, **Bali Concierge** (☎ 0361-760287; www.thebaliconcierge.com) will meet you as you get off the plane and take you to an air-con lounge where you will enjoy refreshments. Meanwhile, a rep takes your passports and gets your immigration stamps and luggage sorted. You then breeze past the lines and out to your ride. The fee: a very indulgent US$50.

Passport

Your passport *must* be valid for six months after your date of arrival in Indonesia.

AIR

Although Jakarta, the national capital, is the gateway airport to Indonesia, there are also many direct international flights to Bali and a few to Lombok.

Airports & Airlines
BALI AIRPORT

The only airport in Bali, Ngurah Rai Airport (DPS) is just south of Kuta, however it is sometimes referred to internationally as Denpasar or on some internet flight booking sites as Bali.

The **international terminal** (☎ 0361-751011) and **domestic terminal** (☎ 0361-751011) are a few hundred metres apart. In the first, you'll find internet centres and shops with high prices. There is also a slew of private lounges where you can relax in far more comfort than in the crowded terminal. Although supposedly reserved for premium customers, 50,000Rp to an attendant often works for the lowly economy flyer.

CLIMATE CHANGE & TRAVEL

Climate change is a serious threat to the ecosystems that humans rely upon, and air travel is the fastest-growing contributor to the problem. Lonely Planet regards travel, overall, as a global benefit, but believes we all have a responsibility to limit our personal impact on global warming.

Flying & Climate Change

Pretty much every form of motor travel generates CO_2 (the main cause of human-induced climate change) but planes are far and away the worst offenders, not just because of the sheer distances they allow us to travel, but because they release greenhouse gases high into the atmosphere. The statistics are frightening: two people taking a return flight between Europe and the US will contribute as much to climate change as an average household's gas and electricity consumption over a whole year.

Carbon Offset Schemes

Climatecare.org and other websites use 'carbon calculators' that allow jet-setters to offset the greenhouse gases they are responsible for with contributions to energy-saving projects and other climate-friendly initiatives in the developing world – including projects in India, Honduras, Kazakhstan and Uganda.

Lonely Planet, together with Rough Guides and other concerned partners in the travel industry, supports the carbon offset scheme run by climatecare.org. Lonely Planet offsets all of its staff and author travel.

For more information check out our website: lonelyplanet.com.

Plans are afoot to expand both terminals for 2010 or later. The oft-discussed scheme to lengthen the runway keeps running into hurdles such as environmental concerns about destroying more of the mangroves. The present runway is too short for planes flying direct to/from Europe.

International airlines flying to and from Bali regularly change, although service is on the upswing.

Air Asia (airline code AK; ☎ 0361-760116; www.airasia.com; ticket office outside international terminal) Serves Kota Kinabalu, Kuala Lumpur and Kuching in Malaysia.

Cathay Pacific Airways (airline code CX; ☎ 0361-766 931; www.cathaypacific.com) Serves Hong Kong.

China Airlines (airline code CI; ☎ 0361-754856; www.china-airlines.com) Serves Taipei.

Eva Air (airline code BR; ☎ 0361-751011; www.evaair.com) Serves Taipei.

Garuda Indonesia (airline code GA; ☎ 0361-227824; www.garuda-indonesia.com; Denpasar; Map pp164-5; Jl Sugianyar 5, Denpasar; Tuban Map p108; Hotel Kuta Paradisso, Jl Kartika Plaza;) Serves Australia (Darwin, Melbourne, Perth and Sydney), Japan, Korea and Singapore direct.

Japan Airlines (airline code JL; ☎ 0361-757077; www.jal.co.jp) Serves Tokyo.

Jetstar/Qantas Airways (airline code QF; Map p146; ☎ 0361-288331; www.qantas.com.au; Grand Bali Beach Hotel, Sanur) Serves Brisbane, Darwin, Melbourne, Perth and Sydney.

Korean Air (airline code KE; ☎ 0361-768377; www.koreanair.com) Serves Seoul.

Lion Air (airline code JT; ☎ 0804 177 8899; www.lionair.co.id) Serves Singapore.

Malaysia Airlines (airline code MH; ☎ 0361-764995; www.mas.com.my) Serves Kuala Lumpur.

Merpati Airlines (airline code MZ; ☎ 0361-235358; www.merpati.co.id) Serves Dili in East Timor.

Pacific Blue (airline code DJ; ☎ +61 7 3295 2296; www.flypacificblue.com) Offshoot of Australia's Virgin Blue, serving Adelaide, Brisbane and Perth, with plans for more.

Qatar Airways (airline code QR; Map p108; ☎ 0361-752222; Discovery Kartika Hotel; Jl Kartika Plaza, Tuban) Serves Doha.

Royal Brunei (airline code BI; Map p100; ☎ 0361-759736; Jl Bypass Ngurah Rai, Tuban) Serves Bandar Seri Begawan.

Singapore Airlines (airline code SQ; Map p100; ☎ 0361-768388; www.singaporeair.com; GOI Bldg, Airport Parking Lot) Several Singapore flights daily.

Thai Airways International (airline code TG; Map p146; ☎ 0361-288141; www.thaiair.com; Grand Bali Beach Hotel, Sanur) Serves Bangkok.

Domestic airlines serving Bali from other parts of Indonesia change frequently. All have ticket offices at the domestic terminal.

Air Asia (airline code AK; ☎ 0361-760116; www.airasia.com) Serves Jakarta and Kuching.

Batavia Air (☎ 0361-767633; www.batavia-air.co.id) Serves Jakarta.

TRANSPORT

Garuda Indonesia (airline code GA; ☎ 0361-227824; www.garuda-indonesia.com) Serves numerous cities, including Jakarta, Kupang, Makasar and Surabaya.
Lion Air (airline code JT; ☎ 0804 177 8899; www.lionair.co.id) Serves Jakarta, Kupang, Makasar, Surabaya & Yogyakarta.
Mandala Airlines (airline code RI; ☎ 0804 123 4567; www.mandalaair.com) Serves Jakarta and Surabaya.
Merpati Airlines (airline code MZ; ☎ 0361-235358; www.merpati.co.id) Serves many smaller Indonesian cities, in addition to the main ones.
Trigana Airlines (☎ 021-860 4867; www.trigana-air.com) Connects Bali and Lombok.

Money
The rates offered at the exchange counters at the international and domestic terminals are competitive, and as good as the money-changers in the tourist centres. There are ATMs in both terminals as well as before and after immigration.

Luggage
The **left-luggage room** (per piece per day 10,000Rp; ☾ 24hr) is in the international terminal, behind the McDonald's near the departures area.

LOMBOK AIRPORT
Lombok's Selaparang Airport (AMI) is just north of Mataram. See p288 for airlines and details of flying to and from Lombok.

Tickets
Deregulation in the Asian and Indonesian aviation markets means that there are frequent deals to Bali. Check major web-based travel agents, the airlines and watch for special promotions.

ROUND-THE-WORLD TICKETS
Round-the-world (RTW) tickets that include Bali are usually offered by an alliance of several airlines such as **Star Alliance** (www.staralliance.com) and **One World** (www.oneworld.com). These tickets come in many flavours, but most let you visit several continents over a period of time that can be as long as a year. It's also

worth investigating Circle Pacific–type tickets, which are similar to RTW tickets but limit you to the Pacific region.
These tickets can be great deals. Prices for RTW tickets are often under US$2000 – not much different from what you'll pay for the flight to Bali alone from North America or Europe.

Asia
Bali is well connected to major Asian cities such as Hong Kong, Seoul, Singapore, Taipei and Tokyo. Lombok is now linked to Singapore.

Australia
Australia is well served with numerous direct flights from Bali to all major cities on multiple carriers, including Garuda Indonesia, Jetstar/Qantas and Pacific Blue.

Canada
From Canada, you'll change planes at an Asian hub.

Continental Europe
None of the major European carriers fly to Bali at present due to the length of the runway preventing nonstop flights. Singapore is the most likely place to change planes coming from Europe, with Bangkok, Hong Kong and Kuala Lumpur also popular.

New Zealand
You will have to change planes in Australia or Singapore.

Other Indonesian Islands
From Bali, you can get flights to major Indonesian cities, often for under US$50 but definitely not much more than US$100. The ticket area at the domestic terminal is a bit of a bazaar. Specials posted in windows often offer great deals. Deals to Jakarta put the price of a plane ticket in the same class as the bus – with a savings of about 22 hours in transit time.
From Lombok, you can get some decent deals but direct service is mostly limited to Bali, Surabaya and Jakarta.

UK & Ireland
From London, the most direct service to Bali is on Singapore Airlines through Singapore. Other transit points include Bangkok, Hong Kong and Kuala Lumpur.

DEPARTURE TAX
The departure tax from Bali and Lombok is 30,000Rp domestic and 150,000Rp international. Have the exact amount for the officer.

TRANSPORT

USA

The best connections are through any of the major Asian hubs with nonstop service to Bali. No US airline serves Bali.

SEA

You can reach Java, just west of Bali, and Sumbawa, just east of Lombok, via ferries. Through buses can take you all the way to Jakarta. Longer-distance boats serve Indonesia's eastern islands.

Java

When visiting Java from Bali and Lombok, some land travel is necessary.

FERRY

Running constantly, **ferries** (adult/child 6000/4500Rp, car & driver 95,000Rp, motorbike 31,000Rp; ⊗ 24hr) cross the Bali Strait between Gilimanuk in western Bali and Ketapang (Java). The actual crossing takes under 30 minutes, but you'll spend longer than this loading, unloading and waiting around. Car-rental contracts usually prohibit rental vehicles being taken out of Bali.

From Ketapang, bemo (small minibuses) travel 4km north to the terminal, where buses leave for Baluran, Probolingo (for Gunung Bromo), Surabaya, Yogyakarta and Jakarta. There's a train station near the ferry port, with trains to Probolingo, Surabaya, Yogyakarta and Jakarta. Contact the **Train Information Service** (☎ 0361-227131; www.kereta-api.com) for more information (on the website, *Jadwal* means schedule).

BUS

To/From Bali

The ferry crossing is included in the services to/from Ubung terminal in Denpasar offered by numerous bus companies, many of which travel overnight. It's advisable to buy your ticket at least one day in advance from travel agents in the tourist centres or at the Ubung terminal. Note too that fierce air competition has put tickets to Jakarta and Surabaya in the range of bus prices.

Fares vary between operators; it's worth paying extra for a decent seat and air-con. For a comfortable bus ride, typical fares and travel times are Yogyakarta (210,000Rp, 16 hours) and Jakarta (305,000Rp, 24 hours), usually travelling overnight. Some companies travel directly between Java and Singaraja, via Lovina, on the north coast of Bali.

To/From Lombok

Public buses go daily from Mandalika terminal to major cities on Java. Most buses are comfortable, with air-con and reclining seats. Destinations include Surabaya (260,000Rp, 20 hours), Yogyakarta (310,000Rp, 30 hours) and Jakarta (420,000Rp, 38 hours).

Sumbawa

Ferries travel between Labuhan Lombok and Poto Tano on Sumbawa every 45 minutes (passenger 25,000Rp; motorcycle 50,000Rp; car 300,000Rp). They run 24 hours a day and the trip takes 1½ hours. There are direct buses from Mandalika terminal to Bima (175,000Rp, 13 hours) and Sumbawa Besar (100,000Rp, six hours).

Other Indonesian Islands

Services to other islands in Indonesia are often in flux, although Pelni is reasonably reliable. Check for services at the harbour in Benoa.

PELNI

The national shipping line is **Pelni** (www.pelni .co.id), which schedules large boats on long-distance runs throughout Indonesia.

To/From Bali

Three ships from Pelni stop at the harbour in Benoa as part of their regular loops throughout Indonesia. *Dobonsolo* with Java, Nusa Tenggara, Maluku and northern Papua; and *Awu* and *Tilongkabila* with Nusa Tenggara and southern Sulawesi. Prices are dependent on the route and the class of travel, and this can range widely in price. Check for details locally but in general, fares are very low, eg Benoa to Surabaya on Java is US$35.

You can inquire and book at the **Pelni offices** in Tuban (Map p100; ☎ 0361-763963, 021-7918 0606; www.pelni.co.id; Jl Raya Kuta 299; ⊗ 8am-noon & 1-4pm Mon-Fri, 8am-1pm Sat) and at the harbour in Benoa (Map p132; ☎ 0361-721377; ⊗ 8am-4pm Mon-Fri, 8am-12.30pm Sat).

To/From Lombok

Pelni ships link Lembar with other parts of Indonesia. The *Awu* heads to Waingapu, Ende, Kupang and Kalabahi; the *Kelimutu* goes to Bima, Makassar and Papua; and the *Tilongkabila* to Bima, Labuanbajo and Sulawesi. Tickets can be bought at the **Pelni office** (Map p286; ☎ 0370-637212; Jl Industri 1; ⊗ 8am-noon & 1-3.30pm Mon-Thu & Sat, 8-11am Fri) in Mataram.

GETTING AROUND

Especially in Bali, the best way to get around is with your own transport, whether you drive, hire a driver or ride a bike. This gives you the flexibility to explore at will and allows you to reach many places that are otherwise inaccessible.

Public transport is cheap but can be cause for very long journeys if you're not sticking to a major route. In addition, some places are just impossible to reach.

There are also tourist shuttle buses and these combine economy with convenience.

TO/FROM THE AIRPORT

Bali's Ngurah Rai Airport is immediately south of Tuban and Kuta. From the official counters, just outside the terminals, there are supposedly fixed-price taxis. However, efforts may be made to charge you at the high end of each range (eg you're going to the part of Seminyak that is supposed to cost 70,000Rp, and they charge you 80,000Rp), and if you say you don't have a room booking, there will be heavy pressure to go to a commission-paying hotel. The costs are (depending on drop-off point):

Destination	Cost
Denpasar	70,000-90,000Rp
Jimbaran	75,000-95,000Rp
Kuta Beach	45,000-50,000Rp
Legian	55,000-65,000Rp
Nusa Dua	95,000-105,000Rp
Sanur	95,000Rp
Seminyak	70,000-80,000Rp
Ubud	195,000-225,000Rp

If you have a surfboard, you'll be charged at least 35,000Rp extra, depending on its size. Ignore any touts that aren't part of the official scheme. Many hotels will offer to pick you up at the airport, however there's no need to use this service if it costs more than the above rates.

The thrifty can walk from the international and domestic terminals across the airport car park to the right (northeast) and continue a couple of hundred metres through the vehicle exit to the airport road (ignoring any touts along the way), where you can hail a regular cab for about half the above amounts.

If you're really travelling light, Kuta Beach is less than a 30-minute walk north.

Any taxi will take you to the airport at a metered rate that should be much less than what we have listed.

AIR

Garuda Indonesia, Lion Air, Merpati and Trigana have several flights daily between Bali and Lombok. The route is competitive and fares hover around about 400,000Rp – new entrants in the market keep fares low. See p288 for airlines and details of flying between Bali and Lombok.

BEMO

The main form of public transport in Bali and on Lombok is the bemo. A generic term for any vehicle used as public transport, it's normally a minibus or van with a row of low seats down each side. Bemo usually hold about 12 people in very cramped conditions.

Riding bemo can be part of your Bali adventure or a major nightmare depending on your outlook at that moment in time. You can certainly expect journeys to be rather lengthy and you'll find that getting to many places is both time-consuming and inconvenient. It's uncommon to see visitors on bemo in Bali.

On Lombok, bemo are minibuses or pick-up trucks and are a major means of transport for visitors.

See p334 for information on pickpocketing on public bemo.

Fares

Bemo operate on a standard route for a set (but unwritten) fare. Unless you get on at a regular starting point, and get off at a regular finishing point, the fares are likely to be fuzzy. The cost per kilometre is pretty variable, but is cheaper on longer trips. The minimum fare is about 4000Rp. The fares listed in this book reflect what a tourist should reasonably expect to pay.

Make sure you know where you're going, and accept that the bemo normally won't leave until it's full and will usually take a roundabout route to collect and deliver as many passengers as possible. If you get into an empty bemo, always make it clear that you do not want to charter it. (The word 'charter' is understood by all drivers.)

Terminals & Routes

Every town has at least one terminal (*terminal bis*) for all forms of public transport. There

TRANSPORT

TRANSPORT

PUBLIC TRANSPORT IN BALI

Long the sole means of public transport, bemo just haven't kept up with the times. As more and more Balinese get jobs, they find that bemo – which often stop running in the afternoon – can't get them to and from their employment. Routes remain geared to going to markets early in the morning. Places with high employment like Legian and Seminyak are poorly served if at all. Meanwhile, one-third of Balinese own motorbikes, a number that won't surprise anyone caught within their fish-like schools at traffic lights. For under US$30, you can get freedom of the roads and a motorbike is now the second major consumer purchase on the island after a mobile phone. For huge numbers, a motorbike is the only way they can reach their jobs.

In the meantime, the bemo system clings to the past and absurd practices continue, such as the need to transfer up to three times just to get across Denpasar. Not surprisingly, there are now calls to set up a modern public transit system on the ever-more-traffic-choked island.

---

are often several terminals in larger towns, according to the direction the bus or bemo is heading. For example, Denpasar, the hub of Bali's transport system, has four main bus/bemo terminals and three minor ones. Terminals can be confusing, but most bemo and buses have signs and, if in doubt, you will be told where to go by a bemo jockey or driver anyway.

To go from one part of Bali to another, it is often necessary to go via one or more of the terminals in Denpasar, or via a terminal in one of the other larger regional towns. For example, to get from Sanur to Ubud by public bemo, you go to the Kereneng terminal in Denpasar, transfer to the Batubulan terminal, and then take a third bemo to Ubud. This is circuitous and time-consuming, so many visitors prefer the tourist shuttle buses, a driver or a taxi.

BICYCLE

A famous temple carving (p260) shows the Dutch artist WOJ Nieuwenkamp pedalling through Bali in 1904. Bali's roads have improved greatly since then and more and more people are touring the island by *sepeda* (bicycle). Many visitors are using bikes around the towns and for day trips in Bali and on Lombok; good-quality rental bikes are available, and several companies organise full-day cycle trips in the back country. See p86 for more on how cycling can be a great part of your visit to Bali and Lombok.

Hire

There are plenty of bicycles for rent in the tourist areas, but many of them are in poor condition. The best place to rent good-quality mountain bikes in Bali is in the south and

Ubud. On Lombok, you can find good bikes in Senggigi.

Ask at your accommodation about where you can rent a good bike; hotels often have their own. Generally, prices range from 20,000Rp to 30,000Rp per day.

Touring

See Road Conditions (p359) for more information, and make sure your bike is equipped for these conditions. Even the smallest village has some semblance of a bike shop – a flat tyre should cost about 5000Rp to fix.

The Periplus Bali and Lombok maps (p338) are a good place to start your planning. Pick the smallest roads for real peace and remember that no matter how lost you get, locals are always happy to help with directions.

BOAT

Taking the boat is more contemplative than the hassle of flying between Bali and Lombok (p353) and fast boats make it competitive time-wise.

Public ferries (adult/child 28,000/18,000Rp) travel non-stop between Padangbai and Lembar on Lombok. Motorbikes cost 85,000Rp and cars cost 550,000Rp – go through the weighbridge at the west corner of the Padangbai car park. Depending on conditions, the trip can take three to five hours. Boats supposedly run 24 hours and leave about every 90 minutes, but the service is often unreliable – boats have caught on fire and run aground – and oversubscribed (trucks can wait around Padangbai for up to three days).

Anyone who carries your luggage on or off the ferries at both ports will expect to be paid, so agree on the price first or carry your own stuff. Also, watch out for scams where the porter may try to sell you a ticket you've already bought. Lembar is worse for this.

Perama (www.peramatour.com) operates a daily boat service from Padangbai in Bali to Senggigi (300,000Rp, six hours). There's also a daily Perama boat from Senggigi to the Gili Islands (70,000Rp to 100,000Rp, 60 to 90 minutes) at 9am, which means you avoid having to deal with Bangsal.

See p222 for more details on Perama and the ferries in Padangbai.

There are several fast boats operating between Bali and Lombok's Gilis.

Blue Water Express (☺ 0361-3104558; www.bwsbali .com) Leaves from the harbour in Benoa in Bali (690,000Rp, 2½ hours).

Gilicat (www.gilicat.com) Leaves from Padangbai (p222) at 9am daily (660,000Rp, 90 minutes). It has an office in Sanur (Map p146; ☎ 0361-271680; Jl Tamblingan 51; ☺ 8am-6pm) and does pick-ups across South Bali.

Mahi Mahi Runs from Serangan (near Sanur) to Gili Trawangan (580,000Rp, 2½ hours).

Gili Paradise Shop (Map pp102-3; ☎ 0361-753241; www.gili-paradise.com; Poppies Gang I, Kuta) This office in Bali also has info.

The dive schools on the Gilis (p295) operate speedboat shuttles (from 120,000Rp per person) from Bali and Senggigi most days – contact them in advance.

BUS

Distances in Bali and on Lombok are relatively short, so you won't have cause to ride many large buses unless you are transferring between islands or going from one side to another.

Public Bus

BALI

Larger minibuses and full-size buses ply the longer routes, particularly on routes linking Denpasar, Singaraja and Gilimanuk. They operate out of the same terminals as the bemo. Buses are faster than bemo because they don't make as many stops along the way, however with more and more locals riding their own motorbikes, there have been reports of looong delays waiting for buses to fill up at terminals before departing.

LOMBOK

Buses and bemo of various sizes are the cheapest and most common way of getting around Lombok. On rough roads in remote areas, trucks may be used as public transport. Mandalika in Bertais is the main bus terminal for all of Lombok. There are also regional terminals at Praya and Pancor (near Selong). You may have to go via one or more of these transport hubs to get from one part of Lombok to another.

Public transport fares are fixed by the provincial government, and displayed on a noticeboard outside the terminal office of the Mandalika terminal. You may have to pay more if you have a large bag or surfboard.

Tourist Bus

Shuttle buses are quicker, more comfortable and more convenient than public transport. They are popular with budget and midrange travellers. If you're with a group of three or more people (or sometimes even two), it will probably be cheaper to charter a vehicle.

Perama (www.peramatour.com) has a near monopoly on this service in Bali. It has offices or agents in Kuta, Sanur, Ubud, Lovina, Padangbai and Candidasa. At least one bus a day links these Bali tourist centres with more frequent services to the airport. There are also services to Kintamani and along the east coast from Lovina to/from Candidasa via Amed by demand.

Fares are reasonable (for example, Kuta to Lovina is 100,000Rp). Be sure to book your trip at least a day ahead in order to confirm schedules. It is also important to understand where Perama buses will pick you up and drop you off as you may need to pay an extra 5000Rp to get to/from your hotel.

Note that shuttle buses often do not provide a direct service – those from Kuta to Candidasa may stop en route at Sanur, Ubud and Padangbai, and maybe other towns on request. And like the bemo, the service is ossified, resolutely sticking to the routes it ran years ago and not recognising the emergence of new destinations such as the Ulu Watu area or even Seminyak (eg a run from Seminyak to Ubud would be packed out daily).

Perama also operates boats on Lombok (left).

CAR & MOTORCYCLE

Renting a car or motorcycle (almost always a lightweight motorbike) can open up Bali and Lombok for exploration and can also leave you counting the minutes until you return it. It gives you the freedom to explore myriad back roads and lets you set your own schedule.

TRANSPORT

TRANSPORT

CHARTERING A VEHICLE & DRIVER

An excellent way to travel anywhere around Bali is by chartered vehicle. It literally allows you to leave the driving and inherent frustrations to others. If you're part of a group it can make sound economic sense as well. This is also possible on Lombok but less common.

It's easy to arrange a charter: just listen for one of the frequent offers of 'transport?' in the streets around the tourist centres; approach a driver yourself; or ask at your hotel, which is often a good method as it increases accountability.

Chartering a vehicle costs about 350,000Rp to 600,000Rp per day – although this depends greatly on the distance and, more importantly, your negotiating skills. Shorter times – say from Kuta to Ubud –will cost less (one to two hours for about 150,000Rp). If you are planning to start early, finish late and cover an awful lot of territory, then you'll have to pay more. Although a driver may reasonably ask for an advance for petrol, never pay the full fare until you have returned. For day trips, you will be expected to buy meals for the driver, particularly if you stop to eat yourself. Tipping for a job well done is expected.

Drivers that hang around tourist spots and upmarket hotels will tend to charge more and are rarely interested in negotiating or bargaining. Beware of tactics like claiming you must hire the vehicle for a minimum of five hours, or assertions that your destination is 'very far' or that 'the roads are very rough'. Agree clearly on a route beforehand. It should be said that safe and enjoyable drivers are the norm. Often other travellers have great recommendations.

You can sometimes arrange to charter an entire bemo for your trip at a bemo terminal. The cost is about the same as for chartering a vehicle and you will enjoy the adventure of a bemo without the crowds – or chickens.

Most people don't rent a car for their entire visit but rather get one for a few days of meandering. In Bali, it's common to get a car in the south or Ubud and circumnavigate at least part of the island.

See Road Conditions (p359) for details of the at-times harrowing driving conditions on the islands.

Driving Licence

If you plan to drive a car, you're supposed to have an International Driving Permit (IDP). You can obtain one from your national motoring organisation if you have a normal driving licence. Bring your home licence as well – it's supposed to be carried in conjunction with the IDP. If you don't have an IDP, add 50,000Rp to any fine you'll have to pay if stopped by the police (although you'll have to pay this a lot to exceed the cost and hassle of getting an IDP).

MOTORCYCLE LICENCE

If you have a motorcycle licence at home, get your IDP endorsed for motorcycles too.

If you have an IDP endorsed for motorcycles you will have no problems, which is when an IDP is really useful as otherwise you have to obtain a local licence – something of an adventure.

The person renting the bike may not check your licence or IDP, and the cop who stops you may be happy with a nonendorsed IDP or bribe. You might get away without a motorcycle endorsement, but you should have an IDP or local licence. Officially, there's a 2 million rupiah fine for riding without a proper licence, and the motorcycle can be impounded – unofficially, the cop may expect a substantial 'on-the-spot' payment (50,000Rp seems average). And, if you have an accident without a licence, your insurance company might refuse coverage.

To get a local motorcycle licence in Bali, go independently (or have the rental agency/owner take you) to the **Poltabes Denpasar** (Police Station; Map p132; ☎ 0361-1427352; Jl Gunung Sanhyang; ☻ 8am-1pm Mon-Sat) for a permit, which is valid for one year. When you arrive you'll see a mobbed main hall filled with jostling permit-seekers. However, step around to the back of the parking lot and look for a building with a sign reading '*Pemohon Sim Asing*/Foreigner License Applicant' outside a 2nd-floor office. Here you will find cheery English-speaking officials who, for a sum of 250,000Rp, will give you the required written test (in English with the answers provided on a sample test) and issue the permit. Sure it costs more than in the hall of chaos, but who can argue with the service? Just be sure to bring your passport, a photocopy of same and a passport photo (although at times the office will help you with that too!).

Fuel & Spare Parts

Bensin (petrol) is sold by the government-owned Pertamina company, and costs about 6000Rp per litre. Bali has scads of petrol stations. In remote areas, look for little roadside fuel shops that fill your tank from a plastic container (the same as the ones they use for *arak* – fermented rice wine – which seems fitting). On Lombok there are stations in major towns.

Petrol pumps usually have a meter, which records the litres, and a table that shows how much to pay for various amounts. Make sure to check that the pump is reset to zero before the attendant starts to put petrol in your vehicle, and check the total amount that goes in before the pump is reset for the next customer. Regular unleaded fuel is labelled *Premium;* diesel is labelled *Solar.*

Tyre repair services can be found in almost every town.

Hire

Very few agencies in Bali will allow you to take their rental cars or motorcycles to Lombok – the regular vehicle insurance is not valid outside Bali.

See Insurance (p358) for details or rental insurance.

CAR

By far the most popular rental vehicle is a small jeep – they're compact, have good ground clearance and the low gear ratio is well suited to exploring back roads, although the bench seats at the back are uncomfortable on a long trip. The main alternative is the larger Toyota Kijang, which seats six. Automatic transmissions are unheard of.

Rental and travel agencies at all tourist centres rent vehicles quite cheaply. A Suzuki jeep costs about 150,000Rp per day, with unlimited kilometres and very limited insurance. A Toyota Kijang costs from around 180,000Rp per day. These costs will vary considerably according to demand, the condition of the vehicle, length of hire and your bargaining

BALI ROAD DISTANCES (KM)

	Amed	Bangli	Bedugul	Candidasa	Denpasar	Gilimanuk	Kintamani	Kuta	Lovina	Negara	Nusa Dua	Padangbai	Sanur	Semarapura	Singaraja	Tirtagangga
Bangli	59															
Bedugul	144	97														
Candidasa	32	52	88													
Denpasar	57	47	78	31												
Gilimanuk	197	181	148	165	134											
Kintamani	108	20	89	71	67	135										
Kuta	73	57	57	41	10	144	77									
Lovina	89	86	41	139	89	79	70	99								
Negara	161	135	115	126	95	33	163	104	107							
Nusa Dua	81	81	102	55	24	158	91	14	113	109						
Padangbai	45	39	75	13	18	178	58	28	126	154	42					
Sanur	64	40	85	38	7	141	78	15	96	102	22	37				
Semarapura	37	26	61	27	47	181	46	57	112	124	71	14	52			
Singaraja	78	75	30	128	78	90	59	88	11	118	92	115	85	105		
Tirtagangga	14	65	101	13	84	212	85	95	112	179	108	26	91	44	142	
Ubud	68	29	35	54	23	157	29	33	40	120	47	41	30	29	95	67

TRANSPORT

talents. It's common for extra days to cost much less than the first day.

There's no reason to book rental cars in advance over the internet or with a tour package, and it will almost certainly cost more than arranging it locally. Any place you stay can set you up with a car as will the ever-present touts in the street.

Shop around for a good deal, and check the car carefully before you sign up. Rental cars usually have to be returned to the place from where they are rented – you can't do a one-way rental, but some operators will let you leave a car at the airport.

Big international rental operators in Bali have a presence, but are seldom used.

MOTORBIKES

Motorbikes are a popular way of getting around Bali and Lombok – locals ride pillion on a *sepeda motor* (motorcycle) almost from birth. Motorcycling is just as convenient and as flexible as driving and the environmental impact and the cost are much less.

Motorcycles are ideal for Lombok's tiny, rough roads, which may be difficult or impassable by car. And, once you get out of the main centres there's not much traffic, apart from people, dogs and water buffalo.

But think carefully before renting a motorcycle. It is dangerous and every year a number of visitors go home with lasting damage – this is no place to learn to ride a motorbike.

Motorcycles for rent in Bali and Lombok are almost all between 90cc and 200cc, with 100cc the usual size. You really don't need anything bigger, as the distances are short and the roads are rarely suitable for travelling fast. In beach areas, many come equipped with a rack on the side for a surfboard.

Rental charges vary with the motorcycle and the period of rental – bigger, newer motorcycles cost more, while longer rental periods attract lower rates. A newish 125cc Honda in good condition might cost 30,000Rp to 40,000Rp a day, but for a week or more you might get the same motorcycle for as little as 25,000Rp per day. This should include minimal insurance for the motorcycle (probably with a US$100 excess), but not for any other person or property.

Individual owners rent out the majority of motorcycles. Like cars, it is easy to find a motorbike or one will find you.

See Insurance, right, for details on rental insurance.

Riding Considerations

Check the motorbike over before riding off – some are in very bad condition. You must carry the motorbike's registration papers with you while riding. Make sure the agency/owner gives them to you before you head off.

Helmets are compulsory and this requirement is enforced in tourist areas, but less so in the countryside. You can even be stopped for not having the chin-strap fastened – a favourite of policemen on the lookout for some extra cash. The standard helmets you get with rental bikes are pretty lightweight. You may want to bring something more substantial from home or buy one locally. Shops in South Bali sell helmets with Viking horns and other fun decor. They just might not be that crash-worthy though.

Despite the tropical climate, it's still wise to dress properly for motorcycling. Thongs (flip-flops), shorts and a T-shirt are poor protection. And when it rains in Bali, it really rains. A poncho is handy, but it's best to get off the road and sit out the storm.

Insurance

Rental agencies and owners usually insist that the vehicle itself is insured, and minimal insurance should be included in the basic rental deal – often with an excess of as much as US$100 for a motorcycle and US$500 for a car (ie the customer pays the first US$100/500 of any claim). The more formal motorcycle and car-hire agencies may offer additional insurance to reduce the level of the excess, and cover damage to other people or their property, ie 'third-party' or 'liability' cover.

Especially with cars, the owner's main concern is insuring the vehicle. In some cases, a policy might cover the car for 30 million rupiah, but provide for only 10 million rupiah third-party cover. Your travel insurance may provide some additional protection, although liability for motor accidents is specifically excluded from many policies. The third-party cover might seem inadequate, but if you do cause damage or injury, it's usually enough for your consulate to get you out of jail.

A private owner renting a motorbike may not offer any insurance at all. Ensure that your personal travel insurance covers injuries incurred while motorcycling. Some policies specifically exclude coverage for motorcycle riding, or have special conditions.

Road Conditions

Bali traffic can be horrendous in the south, around Denpasar and up to Ubud, and is usually quite heavy as far as Padangbai to the east and Tabanan to the west. Finding your way around the main tourist sites can be a challenge, as roads are only sometimes signposted and maps are often fanciful at best. Off the main routes, roads can be rough, but they are usually surfaced – there are few dirt roads in Bali. Driving is most difficult in the large towns, where streets are congested, traffic can be awful and one-way streets are infuriating.

Roads on Lombok are often very rough but traffic is lighter than Bali.

Avoid driving at night or at dusk. Many bicycles, carts and horse-drawn vehicles do not have proper lights, and street lighting is limited.

POLICE

Police will stop drivers on very slender pretexts, and it's fair to say that they're not motivated by a desire to enhance road safety. If a cop sees your front wheel half an inch over the faded line at a stop sign, if the chin-strap of your helmet isn't fastened, or if you don't observe one of the ever changing and poorly signposted one-way traffic restrictions, you may be waved down. It's not uncommon to see cops stopping a line of visitors on motorcycles while locals fly past sans helmets.

The cop will ask to see your licence and the vehicle's registration papers, and he will also tell you what a serious offence you've committed. He may start talking about court appearances, heavy fines and long delays. Stay cool and don't argue. Don't offer him a bribe. Eventually he'll suggest that you can pay him some amount of money to deal with the matter. If it's a very large amount, tell him politely that you don't have that much. These matters can be settled for something between 10,000Rp and 60,000Rp; although it will be more like 100,000Rp if you don't have an IDP or if you argue. Always make sure you have the correct papers, and don't have too much visible cash in your wallet. If things deteriorate, ask for the cop's name and talk about contacting your consulate.

Road Rules

Visiting drivers commonly complain about crazy Balinese drivers, but often it's because the visitors don't understand the local conventions of road use. For instance the constant use of horns here doesn't mean 'get the @£*&% out of my way!', rather it is a very Balinese way of saying 'hi, I'm coming through'. The following rules are useful.

- Watch your front – it's your responsibility to avoid anything that gets in front of your vehicle. A car, motorcycle or anything else pulling out in front of you, in effect, has the right of way. Often drivers won't even look to see what's coming when they turn left at a junction – they listen for the horn.
- Use your horn to warn anything in front that you're there, especially if you're about to overtake.
- Drive on the left side of the road, although it's often a case of driving on whatever side of the road is available.
- Use seatbelts in the front seat.

HITCHING

You can hitchhike in Bali and on Lombok, but it's not a very useful option for getting around, as public transport is so cheap and frequent and private vehicles are often full.

Bear in mind, also, that hitching is never entirely safe in any country. Travellers who decide to hitch should understand that they are taking a small but potentially serious risk.

LOCAL TRANSPORT
Dokar & Cidomo

Small *dokar* (pony carts) still provide local transport in some remote areas, and even in areas of Denpasar and Kuta, but they're uncommon, extremely slow and are not particularly cheap. Prices start at 5000Rp per person for a short trip, but are negotiable, depending on demand, number of passengers, nearby competition, and your bargaining skills. The tourist price can be high if the driver suspects the tourist will pay big-time for the novelty value.

The pony cart used on Lombok is known as a *cidomo* – a contraction of *cika* (a traditional handcart), *dokar* and *mobil* (because car wheels and tyres are used). They are often brightly coloured and the horses decorated with coloured tassels and jingling bells. A typical *cidomo* has a narrow bench seat on either side. The ponies appear to some visitors to be heavily laden and harshly treated, but they are usually looked after reasonably well, if only because the owners depend on them for their livelihood. *Cidomo* are a very popular form of transport in many parts of Lombok, and often go to places that bemo don't, won't or can't.

Lombok fares are not set by the government. The price will always depend on demand, the number of passengers, the destination and your negotiating skills – maybe 3000Rp to 5000Rp per passenger for a short trip.

Ojek

Around some major towns, and along roads where bemo rarely or never venture, transport may be provided by an *ojek* (a motorcycle that takes a paying passenger). However, with increased vehicle ownership in Bali, *ojek* are becoming less common. They're OK on quiet country roads, but a high-risk option in the big towns. You will find them in remote places like Nusa Lembongan and Nusa Penida. *Ojek* are more common on Lombok.

Fares are negotiable, but about 10,000Rp for 5km is fairly standard.

Taxi

BALI

Metered taxis are common in South Bali and Denpasar (but not Ubud). They are essential for getting around Kuta and Seminyak, where you can easily flag one down. Elsewhere, they're often a lot less hassle than haggling with bemo jockeys and charter drivers.

The usual rate for a taxi is 5000Rp flag fall and 4000Rp per kilometre, but the rate is higher in the evening. If you phone for a taxi, the minimum charge is 10,000Rp. Any driver who claims meter problems or who won't use it should be avoided.

By far the most reputable taxi agency is **Bali Taxi** (☎ 0361-701111; www.bluebirdgroup.com), which uses distinctive blue vehicles with the words 'Bluebird Group' over the windshield (watch out for fakes). Drivers speak reasonable English, won't offer you illicit opportunities and use the meter at all times. There's even a number to call with complaints (☎ 0361-701621). Many expats will use no other firm and the drivers are often fascinating conversationalists.

LOMBOK ROAD DISTANCES (KM)

	Bangsal	Bayan	Kuta	Labuhan Lombok	Labuhanhaji	Lembar	Mataram	Pemenang	Praya	Pringgabaya	Sapit	Senaru	Senggigi
Bayan	57												
Kuta	86	143											
Labuhan Lombok	101	66	75										
Labuhanhaji	157	100	57	39									
Lembar	54	121	64	109	77								
Mataram	32	96	54	69	64	27							
Pemenang	1	56	79	109	105	53	26						
Praya	54	121	26	66	39	39	27	53					
Pringgabaya	102	74	83	8	26	102	75	101	62				
Sapit	106	47	101	25	43	120	92	119	80	18			
Senaru	54	102	140	68	106	116	86	63	117	81	54		
Senggigi	18	81	64	79	74	40	10	25	40	88	106	72	
Tetebatu	76	120	50	45	32	98	44	75	29	46	63	130	54

After Bali Taxi, standards decline rapidly. Some are acceptable, although you may have a hassle getting the driver to use the meter after dark. Others may claim that their meters are often 'broken' or nonexistent, and negotiated fees can be over the odds (all the more reason to tip Bali Taxi drivers about 10%). Recently we saw one taxi driver insist on a fee of 70,000Rp for a trip that would have cost 7000Rp in a Bali Taxi.

Taxis can be annoying with their constant honking to attract patrons. And men, especially single men, will find that some taxi drivers may promote a 'complete massage' at a 'spa'. Drivers will enthusiastically pantomime some of the activities that this entails. At the very least, insist that they keep their hands on the wheel.

LOMBOK
There are plenty of bemo and taxis around Mataram and Senggigi. On Lombok, **Lombok Taksi** (☎ 0370-627000), also owned by the Bluebird Group, always use the meter without you having to ask; they are the best choice. The only place where you would need to negotiate a taxi fare is if you get in a taxi at the harbour at Bangsal (but not on the main road in Pemenang). See 'Bangsal Gauntlet', p296 for details.

TOURS
Many travellers end up taking one or two organised tours because it can be such a quick and convenient way to visit a few places in Bali, especially where public transport is limited (eg Pura Besakih) or nonexistent (eg Ulu Watu after sunset). All sorts of tours are available from the tourist centres – hotels can arrange day tours for guests, while tour companies along the main streets advertise trips for those on a budget.

Most interesting are specialist tour companies that take you to places far from the well-trodden path of tour busses.

There is an extraordinarily wide range of prices for the same sorts of tours. The cheaper ones may have less comfortable vehicles, less-qualified guides and be less organised. Higher priced tours may include buffet lunch, English-speaking guides and air-con, but generally, a higher price is no guarantee of higher quality. Some tours make long stops at craft shops, so you can buy things and the tour company can earn commissions. Tours are typically in white eight- to 12-seat minibuses, which pick you up and drop you off.

Tours can be booked at the desk of any large hotel, but these will often be more expensive than a similar tour booked at a tour agency with the price in rupiah. If you can get together a group of four or more, most tour agencies will arrange a tour to suit you.

Rather than go on an organised tour, it can be much more enjoyable to plan your own itinerary and then hire a car and driver to execute it.

Day Tours
The following are the usual tours sold around Bali. They are available from most hotels and shops selling services to tourists. Typically, you will be picked up in the morning along with other travellers at nearby hotels. You may then go to a central area where you are redistributed to the minibus doing *your* tour.

Prices can range from 40,000Rp to 150,000Rp even if standards seem similar, so it pays to shop around.

Bedugul Tour Includes Sangeh or Alas Kedaton, Mengwi, Jatiluwih, Candikuning and sunset at Tanah Lot.

Besakih Tour Includes craft shops at Celuk, Mas and Batuan, Gianyar, Semarapura (Klungkung), Pura Besakih, and return via Bukit Jambal.

Denpasar Tour Takes in the arts centre, markets, museum and perhaps a temple or two.

East Bali Tour Includes the usual craft shops, Semarapura (Klungkung), Kusamba, Goa Lawah, Candidasa and Tenganan.

Kintamani-Gunung Batur Tour Takes in the craft shops at Celuk, Mas and Batuan, a dance at Batubulan, Tampaksiring and views of Gunung Batur. Alternatively, the tour may go to Goa Gajah, Pejeng, Tampaksiring and Kintamani.

Singaraja-Lovina Tour Goes to Mengwi, Bedugul, Gitgit, Singaraja, Lovina, Banjar and Pupuan.

Sunset Tour Includes Mengwi, Marga, Alas Kedaton and sunset at Tanah Lot.

Specialist Tours
There a number of Bali tour operators that offer tours that vary from the norm. Often these can be excellent ways to see things that are otherwise hard for a visitor to find, such as religious ceremonies like cremations. Trips to remote areas or villages can also be a fine way to see aspects of rural life in Bali. Many come with local guides who take joy in describing customs, how crops such as rice are grown and other details of day-to-day life.

BOAT TOURS BETWEEN LOMBOK & FLORES

Travelling by sea between Lombok and Labuanbajo is a popular way to get to Flores, as you get to see far more of the region's spectacular coastline and dodge some seriously lengthy bus journeys and nonentity towns. Typical itineraries from Lombok take in snorkelling at Pulau Satonda off the coast of Sumbawa, a dragon-spotting hike in Komodo and other stops for swimming and partying along the way. From Labuanbajo it's a similar story, but usually with stops at Rinca and Pulau Moyo.

However, be aware that this kind of trip is no luxury cruise – a lot depends on the boat, the crew and your fellow travellers, who you are stuck with for the duration. Some shifty operators have reneged on 'all-inclusive' agreements en route, and others operate decrepit old tugs without life jackets or radio. Look things over and don't embark on any trip with those with dodgy set-ups.

Given these safety concerns, the well-organised tours on decent boats run by **Perama** (see Kuta, p118; Gili Trawangan, p304; Mataram, p288; Senggigi, p295 for contact details) are recommended. Current charges start at 1.4 million/2 million rupiah for cabin/deck for one-way multiday journeys.

A higher-end option is offered by **SeaTrek** (☎ 0361-283358; www.anasia-cruise.com), which has multi-day cruises aboard a luxury yacht to Flores and other eastern Indonesian islands.

Look to the following tour operators for more creative and inventive tours. Prices span the gamut but tend to be more expensive than the bog-standard tours aimed at tourists. See Bali & Lombok Outdoors (p86) for tours involving trekking, cycling and more; see p184 for details on the many tours around Ubud.

Bali Discovery Tours (☎ 0361-286283; www.balidiscovery.com) Offers numerous and customisable tours that differ from the norm. One visits a small rice-growing village in the west near Tabanan for hands-on demonstrations of cultivation.

JED (Village Ecotourism Network; ☎ 0361-735320; www.jed.or.id) Organises highly regarded tours of small villages, including coffee-growing Pelaga in the mountains, fruit-growing Sibetan in the east, seaweed farms on Nusa Ceningan and ancient Tenganan. You can make arrangements to stay with a family in the villages.

Suta Tours (☎ 0361-741 6665, 788 8865; www.sutatour.com) Arranges trips to cremation ceremonies and special temple festivals, market tours, and other custom plans.

Waka Land Cruise (☎ 0361-426972; www.waka experience.com) Luxurious tours deep into rice terraces and tiny villages.

Lombok

Some companies organise day tours around Lombok from Bali, which cost US$100 or more and involve round-trip flights and tearing through Senggigi and a few villages by minibus. A longer tour, with more time for sightseeing and relaxing, will be far more expensive but more satisfying.

Tours originating on Lombok are based in Senggigi. You can usually book market visits in Mataram, a jaunt out to the Gilis or a trip down the south coast.

Health Dr Trish Batchelor

CONTENTS

Before You Go	**363**
Insurance	363
Recommended Vaccinations	363
Required Vaccinations	364
Medical Checklist	364
Internet Resources	365
Further Reading	365
In Transit	**365**
Deep Vein Thrombosis (DVT)	365
Jet Lag & Motion Sickness	365
In Bali & Lombok	**365**
Availability & Cost of Health Care	365
Infectious Diseases	366
Traveller's Diarrhoea	369
Environmental Hazards	369
Women's Health	371

Treatment for minor injuries and common traveller's health problems is easily accessed in Bali and to a lesser degree on Lombok. But be aware that for serious conditions, you will need to leave the islands.

Travellers tend to worry about contracting infectious diseases when in the tropics, but infections are a rare cause of serious illness or death in travellers. Pre-existing medical conditions such as heart disease, and accidental injury (especially traffic accidents), account for most life-threatening problems. Becoming ill in some way, however, is relatively common. Fortunately most common illnesses can either be prevented with some common-sense behaviour or be treated easily with a well-stocked traveller's medical kit.

The following advice is a general guide only and does not replace the advice of a doctor trained in travel medicine.

BEFORE YOU GO

Make sure all medications are packed in their original, clearly labelled, containers. A signed and dated letter from your physician describing your medical conditions and medications (including generic names) is also a good idea. If you are carrying syringes or needles, be sure to have a physician's letter documenting their medical necessity. If you have a heart condition ensure you bring a copy of your electrocardiogram taken just prior to travelling.

If you happen to take any regular medication bring double your needs in case of loss or theft. In most Southeast Asian countries, excluding Singapore, you can buy many medications over the counter without a doctor's prescription, but it can be difficult to find some of the newer drugs, particularly the latest antidepressant drugs, blood pressure medications and contraceptive pills.

INSURANCE

Even if you are fit and healthy, don't travel without health insurance – accidents do happen. Declare any existing medical conditions you have – the insurance company will check if your problem is pre-existing and will not cover you if it is undeclared. You may require extra cover for adventure activities such as rock climbing. If your health insurance doesn't cover you for medical expenses abroad, consider getting extra insurance. If you're uninsured, emergency evacuation is expensive – bills of more than US$100,000 are not uncommon.

Find out in advance if your insurance plan will make payments directly to providers or reimburse you later for overseas health expenditures. (In many countries doctors expect payment in cash at the time of treatment.) Some policies offer lower and higher medical-expense options; the higher ones are chiefly for countries that have extremely high medical costs, such as the USA. You may prefer a policy that pays doctors or hospitals directly rather than you having to pay on the spot and claim later. If you have to claim later, make sure you keep all documentation. Some policies ask you to call back (reverse charges) to a centre in your home country where an immediate assessment of your problem is made.

RECOMMENDED VACCINATIONS

Specialised travel-medicine clinics are your best source of information; they stock all available vaccines and will be able to give specific recommendations for you and your trip. The doctors will take into account factors such as past vaccination history, the length of your trip, activities you may be undertaking and underlying medical conditions, such as pregnancy.

Most vaccines don't produce immunity until at least two weeks after they're given, so visit a doctor four to eight weeks before departure. Ask your doctor for an International Certificate of Vaccination (otherwise known as the yellow booklet), which will list all the vaccinations you've received.

The World Health Organization recommends the following vaccinations for travellers to Southeast Asia:

Adult diphtheria & tetanus Single booster recommended if none in the previous 10 years. Side effects include sore arm and fever.

Hepatitis A Provides almost 100% protection for up to a year, a booster after 12 months provides at least another 20 years protection. Mild side effects such as headache and sore arm occur in 5% to 10% of people.

Hepatitis B Now considered routine for most travellers. Given as three shots over six months. A rapid schedule is also available, as is a combined vaccination with Hepatitis A. Side effects are mild and uncommon, usually headache and sore arm. Lifetime protection occurs in 95% of people.

Measles, mumps & rubella (MMR) Two doses of MMR are required unless you have had the diseases. Occasionally a rash and flulike illness can develop a week after receiving the vaccine. Many young adults require a booster.

Polio In 2002, no countries in Southeast Asia reported cases of polio. Only one booster is required as an adult for lifetime protection. Inactivated polio vaccine is safe during pregnancy.

Typhoid Recommended unless your trip is less than a week and only to developed cities. The vaccine offers around 70% protection, lasts for two to three years and comes as a single shot. Tablets are also available, however the injection is usually recommended as it has fewer side effects. Sore arm and fever may occur.

Varicella If you haven't had chickenpox, discuss this vaccination with your doctor.

These immunisations are recommended for long-term travellers (more than one month) or those at special risk:

Japanese B Encephalitis Three injections in all. Booster recommended after two years. Sore arm and headache are the most common side effects. Rarely, an allergic reaction comprising hives and swelling can occur up to 10 days after any of the three doses.

Meningitis Single injection. There are two types of vaccination: the quadrivalent vaccine gives two to three years protection; meningitis group C vaccine gives around 10 years protection. Recommended for long-term backpackers aged under 25.

Rabies Three injections in all. A booster after one year will then provide 10 years protection. Side effects are rare – occasionally headache and sore arm.

Tuberculosis (TB) A complex issue. Adult long-term travellers are usually recommended to have a TB skin test before and after travel, rather than vaccination. Only one vaccine given in a lifetime.

REQUIRED VACCINATIONS

The only vaccine required by international regulations is yellow fever. Proof of vaccination will only be required if you have visited a country in the yellow-fever zone within the six days prior to entering Southeast Asia. If you are travelling to Southeast Asia from Africa or South America you should check to see if you require proof of vaccination.

MEDICAL CHECKLIST

Recommended items for a personal medical kit:

- antifungal cream (eg clotrimazole)
- antibacterial cream (eg muciprocin)
- antibiotic for skin infections (eg amoxicillin/clavulanate or cephalexin)
- antibiotics for diarrhoea including norfloxacin or ciprofloxacin; for bacterial diarrhoea azithromycin; for giardiasis or amoebic dysentery tinidazole
- antihistamine – there are many options (eg cetirizine for daytime and promethazine for night)
- antiseptic (eg Betadine)
- antispasmodic for stomach cramps (eg buscopan)
- contraceptives
- decongestant (eg pseudoephedrine)
- DEET-based insect repellent
- diarrhoea treatment – consider an oral rehydration solution (eg Gastrolyte), diarrhoea 'stopper' (eg loperamide) and antinausea medication (eg prochlorperazine)
- first-aid items such as scissors, Elastoplasts, bandages, gauze, thermometer (but not mercury), sterile needles and syringes, safety pins and tweezers
- ibuprofen or another anti-inflammatory
- indigestion medication (eg Quick Eze or Mylanta)
- laxative (eg Coloxyl)
- migraine medication – take your personal medicine

- paracetamol
- steroid cream for allergic/itchy rashes (eg 1% to 2% hydrocortisone)
- sunscreen and hat
- throat lozenges
- thrush (vaginal yeast infection) treatment (eg clotrimazole pessaries or diflucan tablet)
- Ural or equivalent if you're prone to urine infections

INTERNET RESOURCES

There is a wealth of travel health advice on the internet. The **World Health Organization** (WHO; www.who.int/ith/) publishes a superb book called *International Travel & Health,* which is revised annually and is available online at no cost. Another website of general interest is **MD Travel Health** (www.mdtravelhealth.com), which provides travel health recommendations for every country. The **Centers for Disease Control & Prevention** (CDC; www.cdc.gov) website also has good general information. For further information, **LonelyPlanet.com** (www.lonelyplanet.com) is a good place to start. You can also check the websites of various foreign embassies in Indonesia (see p335).

FURTHER READING

Lonely Planet's *Healthy Travel – Asia & India* is a handy pocket-sized book that is packed with useful information including pre-trip planning, emergency first aid, immunisation and disease information and what to do if you get sick on the road. Other recommended references include *Traveller's Health* by Dr Richard Dawood and *Travelling Well* by Dr Deborah Mills – check out the website (www.travellingwell.com.au).

IN TRANSIT

DEEP VEIN THROMBOSIS (DVT)

Deep vein thrombosis (DVT) occurs when blood clots form in the legs during plane flights, chiefly because of prolonged immobility. The longer the flight, the greater the risk. Although most blood clots are reabsorbed uneventfully, some may break off and travel through the blood vessels to the lungs, where they may cause life-threatening complications.

The chief symptom of DVT is swelling or pain of the foot, ankle or calf, usually but not always on just one side. When a blood clot travels to the lungs, it may cause chest pain and difficulty in breathing. Travellers with any of these symptoms should immediately seek medical attention.

To prevent the development of DVT on long flights you should walk about the cabin, perform isometric compressions of the leg muscles (ie contract the leg muscles while sitting), drink plenty of fluids, and avoid alcohol and tobacco.

JET LAG & MOTION SICKNESS

Jet lag is common when crossing more than five time zones; it results in insomnia, fatigue, malaise or nausea. To avoid jet lag try drinking plenty of fluids (nonalcoholic) and eating light meals. Upon arrival, seek exposure to natural sunlight and re-adjust your schedule (for meals, sleep etc) as soon as possible.

Antihistamines such as dimenhydrinate (Dramamine) and meclizine (Antivert, Bonine) are usually the first choice for treating motion sickness. Their main side effect is drowsiness. A herbal alternative is ginger, which works like a charm for some people.

IN BALI & LOMBOK

AVAILABILITY & COST OF HEALTH CARE

For serious conditions, foreigners would be best served in one of two private clinics that cater mainly to tourists and expats.

BIMC (Map p100; ☎ 0361-761263; www.bimcbali .com; Jl Ngurah Rai 100X, Kuta; ⊗24hr) is on the bypass road just east of Kuta near the Bali Galleria and easily accessible from most of southern Bali. It's a modern Australian-run clinic that can do tests, hotel visits and arrange medical evacuation. A basic consultation costs 600,000Rp.

International SOS Medical Clinic (Map p132; ☎ 0361-710505; www.sos-bali.com; Jl Ngurah Rai 505X, Kuta; ⊗24hr) is near BIMC and offers similar services at similar prices.

At both these places you should confirm that your health and/or travel insurance will cover you. In cases where your medical condition is considered serious you may well be evacuated by air ambulance to top-flight hospitals in Jakarta or Singapore. Here's where proper insurance is vital as these flights can cost more than US$10,000.

HEALTH

In South Bali and Ubud there are locally owned clinics catering to tourists and just about any hotel can put you in touch with an English-speaking doctor.

In more remote areas, facilities are basic; generally a small public hospital, doctor's surgery or *puskesmas* (community health centre). Specialist facilities for neurosurgery and heart surgery are nonexistent, and the range of available drugs (including painkillers) is limited. Travel insurance policies often have an emergency assistance phone number, which might be able to recommend a doctor or clinic, or use its contacts to find one in a remote area.

Health care is not free in Bali, and you will get more prompt attention if you can pay cash up-front for treatment, drugs, surgical equipment, drinking water, food and so on. Try to get receipts and paperwork so you can claim it all later on your travel insurance.

In government-run clinics and hospitals, services such as meals, washing and clean clothing are normally provided by the patient's family. If you are unfortunate enough to be on your own in a Bali hospital, contact your consulate – you need help. The best hospital on the island is Sanglah Hospital in Denpasar (p163).

The best hospital on Lombok is in Mataram, and there are more basic ones in Praya and Selong.

Self-treatment may be appropriate if your problem is minor (eg traveller's diarrhoea), you are carrying the appropriate medication and you cannot attend a recommended clinic. If you think you may have a serious disease, especially malaria, do not waste time – travel to the nearest quality facility to receive attention. It is always better to be assessed by a doctor than to rely on self-treatment.

In Bali, pharmacies are usually reliable. The Kimia Farma chain is good and has many locations, including one in Kuta (p105). Singapore's Guardian chain of pharmacies is also found in tourist areas. On Lombok you need to be more careful as fake medications and poorly stored or out-of-date drugs are common. Check with a large international hotel for a recommendation of a good local pharmacy.

INFECTIOUS DISEASES
Bird Flu
Otherwise known as Avian Influenza, the H5N1 virus has claimed more than 100 victims in Indonesia. Most of the cases have been in Java, west of Bali, although two people died in rural areas of Bali in 2007. Treatment is difficult, although the drug Tamiflu has some effect. Travellers to Bali and Lombok may wish to check the latest conditions before their journey. See Internet Resources (p365) and Health Advisories (left) for some good sources of current information.

Dengue Fever
This mosquito-borne disease is becomingly increasingly problematic throughout Southeast Asia, especially in the cities. As there is no vaccine available it can only be prevented by avoiding mosquito bites. The mosquito that carries dengue bites day and night, so use insect avoidance measures at all times. Symptoms include high fever, severe headache and body ache (dengue was previously known as 'breakbone fever'). Some people develop a rash and experience diarrhoea. There are regular outbreaks in Bali. There is no specific treatment, just rest and paracetamol – do not take aspirin as it increases the likelihood of haemorrhaging. See a doctor to be diagnosed and monitored.

Hepatitis A
A problem throughout the region, this food- and waterborne virus infects the liver, causing jaundice (yellow skin and eyes), nausea and lethargy. There is no specific treatment for hepatitis A, you just need to allow time for the liver to heal. All travellers to Southeast Asia should be vaccinated against hepatitis A.

Hepatitis B

The only sexually transmitted disease that can be prevented by vaccination, hepatitis B is spread by body fluids, including sexual contact. In some parts of Southeast Asia up to 20% of the population are carriers of hepatitis B, and usually are unaware of this. The long-term consequences can include liver cancer and cirrhosis.

Hepatitis E

Hepatitis E is transmitted through contaminated food and water and has similar symptoms to hepatitis A, but is far less common. It is a severe problem in pregnant women and can result in the death of both mother and baby. There is currently no vaccine, and prevention is by following safe eating and drinking guidelines.

HIV

HIV is a major problem in many Asian countries, and Bali has one of the highest rates of HIV infection in Indonesia. Official HIV figures in Indonesia are unrealistically low and it's believed the incidence of the disease will increase significantly unless hospital procedures are improved and safe sex is promoted. The main risk for most travellers is sexual contact with locals, prostitutes and other travellers – in Indonesia the spread of HIV is primarily through heterosexual activity.

The risk of sexual transmission of the HIV virus can be dramatically reduced by the use of a *kondom* (condom). These are available from supermarkets, street stalls and drugstores in tourist areas, and from the *apotik* (pharmacy) in almost any town (from about 1500Rp to 3000Rp each – it's worth getting the more expensive brands).

Japanese B Encephalitis

While a rare disease in travellers, at least 50,000 locals are infected each year. This viral disease is transmitted by mosquitoes. Most cases occur in rural areas and vaccination is recommended for travellers spending more than one month outside of cities. There is no treatment, and one-third of infected people will die while another third will suffer permanent brain damage. Highest risk areas include Vietnam, Thailand and Indonesia.

Malaria

The risk of contracting malaria in Bali is extremely low, but Lombok is viewed as a malaria risk area. During and just after the wet season (October to March), there is a very low risk of malaria in northern Bali, and a slightly higher risk in far western Bali, particularly in and around Gilimanuk. So, if you are staying in budget accommodation anywhere outside of southern Bali, or trekking in northern or western Bali during, or just after, the rainy season, you should consider taking antimalarial drugs and seek medical advice about this. However, it is not currently considered necessary to take antimalarial drugs if you are sticking to the tourist centres in southern Bali, regardless of the season – but confirm this with your doctor prior to departure.

If you are going away from the main tourist areas (Senggigi, the Gilis) of Lombok, or further afield in Indonesia, you should take preventative measures, even though significant progress has been made in reducing the number of mosquitoes on Lombok, and therefore the risk of malaria and other insect-borne diseases. The risk is greatest in the wet months and in remote areas. The very serious Plasmodium falciparum strain causes cerebral malaria and may be resistant to many drugs.

For such a serious and potentially deadly disease, there is an enormous amount of misinformation concerning malaria. You must get expert advice as to whether your trip actually puts you at risk. Many parts of Southeast Asia, particularly city and resort areas, have minimal to no risk of malaria, and the risk of side effects from the tablets may outweigh the risk of getting the disease. For most rural areas, however, the risk of contracting the disease far outweighs the risk of any tablet side effects. Remember that malaria can be fatal. Before you travel, seek medical advice on the right medication and dosage for you.

Malaria is caused by a parasite transmitted by the bite of an infected mosquito. The most important symptom of malaria is fever, but general symptoms such as headache, diarrhoea, cough or chills may also occur. Diagnosis can only be made by taking a blood sample.

Two strategies should be combined to prevent malaria – mosquito avoidance, and antimalarial medications. Most people who catch malaria are taking inadequate or no antimalarial medication.

HEALTH

Travellers are advised to prevent mosquito bites by taking these steps:

- Use a DEET-containing insect repellent on exposed skin. Wash this off at night, as long as you are sleeping under a mosquito net. Natural repellents such as Citronella can be effective, but must be applied more frequently than products containing DEET.
- Sleep under a mosquito net impregnated with Permethrin.
- Choose accommodation with screens and fans (if not air-conditioned).
- Impregnate clothing with Permethrin in high-risk areas.
- Wear long sleeves and trousers in light colours.
- Use mosquito coils.
- Spray your room with insect repellent before going out for your evening meal.

There are a variety of medications available:

Artesunate Derivatives of Artesunate are not suitable as a preventive medication. They are useful treatments under medical supervision.

Chloroquine & Paludrine The effectiveness of this combination is now limited in most of Southeast Asia. Common side effects include nausea (40% of people) and mouth ulcers. Generally not recommended.

Doxycycline This daily tablet is a broad-spectrum antibiotic that has the added benefit of helping to prevent a variety of tropical diseases, including leptospirosis, tickborne disease, typhus and melioidosis. The potential side effects include photosensitivity (a tendency to sunburn), thrush in women, indigestion, heartburn, nausea and interference with the contraceptive pill. More serious side effects include ulceration of the oesophagus – you can help prevent this by taking your tablet with a meal and a large glass of water, and never lying down within half an hour of taking it. Must be taken for four weeks after leaving the risk area.

Lariam (Mefloquine) Lariam has received much bad press, some of it justified, some not. This weekly tablet suits many people. Serious side effects are rare but include depression, anxiety, psychosis and having fits. Anyone with a history of depression, anxiety, other psychological disorder, or epilepsy should not take Lariam. It is considered safe in the second and third trimesters of pregnancy. It is around 90% effective in most parts of Southeast Asia, but there is significant resistance in parts of northern Thailand, Laos and Cambodia. Tablets must be taken for four weeks after leaving the risk area.

Malarone This new drug is a combination of Atovaquone and Proguanil. Side effects are uncommon and mild, most commonly nausea and headache. It is the best tablet for scuba divers and for those on short trips to high-risk areas. It must be taken for one week after leaving the risk area.

A final option is to take no preventive medication but to have a supply of emergency medication should you develop the symptoms of malaria. This is less than ideal, and you'll need to get to a good medical facility within 24 hours of developing a fever. If you choose this option the most effective and safest treatment is Malarone (four tablets once daily for three days). Other options include Mefloquine and Quinine but the side effects of these drugs at treatment doses make them less desirable. Fansidar is no longer recommended.

Rabies

Still a common problem in most parts of Southeast Asia (Bali had reported cases in 2008). Rabies is a uniformly fatal disease spread by the bite or lick of an infected animal – most commonly a dog or monkey. You should seek medical advice immediately after any animal bite and commence post-exposure treatment. Having the pre-travel vaccination means the post-bite treatment is greatly simplified. If an animal bites you, gently wash the wound with soap and water, and apply an iodine-based antiseptic. If you are not pre-vaccinated you will need to receive rabies immunoglobulin as soon as possible.

STDs

Sexually transmitted diseases most common in Southeast Asia include herpes, warts, syphilis, gonorrhoea and chlamydia. People carrying these diseases often have no signs of infection. Condoms will prevent gonorrhoea and chlamydia but not warts or herpes. If after a sexual encounter you develop any rash, lumps, discharge or pain when passing urine seek immediate medical attention. If you have been sexually active during your travels, have an STD check on your return home.

Tuberculosis

While rare in travellers, medical and aid workers and long-term travellers who have significant contact with the local population should take precautions. Vaccination is usually only given to children under the age of five, but adults at risk are recommended pre- and post-travel TB testing. The main symptoms are fever, cough, weight loss, night sweats and tiredness.

DRINKING WATER

- Never drink tap water.

- Bottled water is generally safe – check the seal is intact at purchase.

- Avoid ice.

- Avoid fresh juices – they may have been watered down.

- Boiling water is the most efficient method of purifying it.

- The best chemical purifier is iodine. It should not be used by pregnant women or those people who suffer from thyroid problems.

- Water filters should also filter out viruses. Ensure your filter has a chemical barrier such as iodine and a small pore size, eg less than four microns.

Typhoid

This serious bacterial infection is also spread via food and water. It gives a high and slowly progressive fever, headache and may be accompanied by a dry cough and stomach pain. It is diagnosed by blood tests and treated with antibiotics. Vaccination is recommended for all travellers spending more than a week in Southeast Asia, or travelling outside of the major cities. Be aware that vaccination is not 100% effective so you must still be careful with what you eat and drink.

Typhus

Murine typhus is spread by the bite of a flea whereas scrub typhus is spread via a mite. These diseases are rare in travellers. Symptoms include fever, muscle pains and a rash. You can avoid these diseases by following general insect-avoidance measures. Doxycycline will also prevent them.

TRAVELLER'S DIARRHOEA

Traveller's diarrhoea is by far the most common problem affecting travellers – between 30% and 50% of people will suffer from it within two weeks of starting their trip. In over 80% of cases, traveller's diarrhoea is caused by bacteria (there are numerous potential culprits), and therefore responds promptly to treatment with antibiotics. Treatment with antibiotics will depend on your situation – how sick you are, how quickly you need to get better, where you are etc.

Traveller's diarrhoea is defined as the passage of more than three watery bowel-actions within 24 hours, plus at least one other symptom such as fever, cramps, nausea, vomiting or feeling generally unwell.

Treatment consists of staying well hydrated; rehydration solutions such as Gastrolyte are the best for this. Antibiotics such as Norfloxacin, Ciprofloxacin or Azithromycin will kill the bacteria quickly.

Loperamide is just a 'stopper' and doesn't get to the cause of the problem. It can be helpful, for example if you have to go on a long bus ride. Don't take Loperamide if you have a fever, or blood in your stools. Seek medical attention quickly if you do not respond to an appropriate antibiotic.

Amoebic Dysentery

Amoebic dysentery is very rare in travellers but is often misdiagnosed by poor-quality labs in Southeast Asia. Symptoms are similar to bacterial diarrhoea, ie fever, bloody diarrhoea and generally feeling unwell. You should always seek reliable medical care if you have blood in your diarrhoea. Treatment involves two drugs; Tinidazole or Metroniadzole to kill the parasite in your gut and then a second drug to kill the cysts. If left untreated, complications such as liver or gut abscesses can occur.

Giardiasis

Giardia lamblia is a parasite that is relatively common in travellers. Symptoms include nausea, bloating, excess gas, fatigue and intermittent diarrhoea. 'Eggy' burps are often attributed solely to giardiasis, but work in Nepal has shown that they are not specific to this infection. The parasite will eventually go away if left untreated but this can take months. The treatment of choice is Tinidazole, with Metronidazole being a second-line option.

ENVIRONMENTAL HAZARDS
Diving

Divers and surfers should seek specialised advice before they travel to ensure their medical kit contains treatment for coral cuts and tropical ear infections, as well as the standard problems. Divers should ensure

HEALTH

their insurance covers them for decompression illness – get specialised dive insurance through an organisation such as **Divers Alert Network** (DAN; www.danseap.org). Have a dive medical before you leave your home country – there are certain medical conditions that are incompatible with diving and economic considerations may override health considerations for some dive operators in Southeast Asia.

Food

Eating in restaurants is the biggest risk factor for contracting traveller's diarrhoea. Ways to avoid it include eating only freshly cooked food, avoiding shellfish and food that has been sitting around in buffets. Peel all fruit, cook vegetables, and soak salads in iodine water for at least 20 minutes. Eat in busy restaurants with a high turnover of customers.

Heat

Many parts of Southeast Asia are hot and humid throughout the year. For most people it takes at least two weeks to adapt to the hot climate. Swelling of the feet and ankles is common, as are muscle cramps caused by excessive sweating. Prevent these by avoiding dehydration and excessive activity in the heat. Take it easy when you first arrive. Don't eat salt tablets (they aggravate the gut) but drinking rehydration solution or eating salty food helps. Treat cramps by stopping activity, resting, rehydrating with double-strength rehydration solution and gently stretching.

Dehydration is the main contributor to heat exhaustion. Symptoms include feeling weak, headache, irritability, nausea or vomiting, sweaty skin, a fast, weak pulse and a normal or slightly elevated body temperature. Treatment involves getting out of the heat and/or sun, fanning the victim and applying cool wet cloths to the skin, laying the victim flat with their legs raised and rehydrating with water containing one-quarter of a teaspoon of salt per litre. Recovery is usually rapid and it is common to feel weak for some days afterwards.

Heatstroke is a serious medical emergency. Symptoms come on suddenly and include weakness, nausea, a hot dry body with a body temperature of over 41°C, dizziness, confusion, loss of coordination, fits and eventually collapse and loss of consciousness. Seek urgent medical help and commence cooling by getting the person out of the heat, removing their clothes, fanning them and applying cool wet cloths or ice to their body, especially to hot spots such as the groin and armpits.

Prickly heat is a common skin rash in the tropics, caused by sweat being trapped under the skin. The result is an itchy rash of tiny lumps. Treat by moving out of the heat and into an air-conditioned area for a few hours and by having cool showers. Creams and ointments clog the skin so they should be avoided. Locally bought prickly-heat powder can be helpful.

Tropical fatigue is common in long-term expats based in the tropics. It's rarely due to disease and is caused by the climate, inadequate mental rest, excessive alcohol intake and the demands of daily work in a different culture.

Insect Bites & Stings

Bedbugs don't carry disease but their bites are very itchy. They live in the cracks of furniture and walls and then migrate to the bed at night to feed on you as you sleep. You can treat the itch with an antihistamine. Lice inhabit various parts of your body but most commonly your head and pubic area. Transmission is via close contact with an infected person. They can be difficult to treat and you may need numerous applications of an antilice shampoo such as Permethrin. Pubic lice are usually contracted from sexual contact.

Ticks are contracted after walking in rural areas. Ticks are commonly found behind the ears, on the belly and in armpits. If you have had a tick bite and experience symptoms such as a rash at the site of the bite or elsewhere, fever, or muscle aches you should see a doctor. Doxycycline prevents tick-borne diseases.

Leeches are found in humid rainforest areas. They do not transmit any disease but their bites are often intensely itchy for weeks afterwards and can easily become infected. Apply an iodine-based antiseptic to any leech bite to help prevent infection.

Bee and wasp stings mainly cause problems for people who are allergic to them. Anyone with a serious bee or wasp allergy should carry an injection of adrenaline (eg an Epipen) for emergency treatment. For others pain is the main problem – apply ice to the sting and take painkillers.

Most jellyfish in Southeast Asian waters are not dangerous, just irritating. Some jellyfish, including the Portuguese man-of-war, occur on the north coast of Bali, especially in July and August, and also between the Gili Islands and Lombok. The sting is extremely painful but rarely fatal. First aid for jellyfish stings involves pouring vinegar onto the affected area to neutralise the poison. Do not rub sand or water onto the stings. Take painkillers, and anyone who feels ill in any way after being stung should seek medical advice. Take local advice if there are dangerous jellyfish around and keep out of the water.

Parasites

Numerous parasites are common in local populations in Southeast Asia; however, most of these are rare in travellers. The two rules to follow if you wish to avoid parasitic infections are to wear shoes and to avoid eating raw food, especially fish, pork and vegetables. A number of parasites are transmitted via the skin by walking barefoot including strongyloides, hookworm and cutaneous *larva migrans*.

Skin Problems

Fungal rashes are common in humid climates. There are two common fungal rashes that affect travellers. The first occurs in moist areas that get less air such as the groin, armpits and between the toes. It starts as a red patch that slowly spreads and is usually itchy. Treatment involves keeping the skin dry, avoiding chafing and using an antifungal cream such as Clotrimazole or Lamisil. *Tinea versicolor* is also common – this fungus causes small, light-coloured patches, most commonly on the back, chest and shoulders. Consult a doctor.

Cuts and scratches become easily infected in humid climates. Take meticulous care of any cuts and scratches to prevent complications such as abscesses. Immediately wash all wounds in clean water and apply antiseptic. If you develop signs of infection (increasing pain and redness) see a doctor. Divers and surfers should be particularly careful with coral cuts as they become easily infected.

Snakes

Southeast Asia is home to many species of both poisonous and harmless snakes. Although you are unlikely to run into snakes in Bali or on Lombok (you may come across the black-and-white stripy sea snake on Lombok), assume all snakes are poisonous and never touch one.

Sunburn

Even on a cloudy day sunburn can occur rapidly. Always use a strong sunscreen (at least factor 30), making sure to reapply after a swim, and always wear a wide-brimmed hat and sunglasses outdoors. Avoid lying in the sun during the hottest part of the day (10am to 2pm). If you become sunburnt stay out of the sun until you have recovered, apply cool compresses and take painkillers for the discomfort. One per cent hydrocortisone cream applied twice daily is also helpful.

WOMEN'S HEALTH

Pregnant women should receive specialised advice before travelling. The ideal time to travel is in the second trimester (between 16 and 28 weeks), when the risk of pregnancy-related problems are at their lowest and pregnant women generally feel at their best. During the first trimester there is a risk of miscarriage and in the third trimester complications such as premature labour and high blood pressure are possible. It's wise to travel with a companion. Always carry a list of quality medical facilities available at your destination and ensure you continue your standard antenatal care at these facilities. Avoid rural travel in areas with poor transportation and medical facilities. Most of all, ensure travel insurance covers all pregnancy-related possibilities, including premature labour.

Malaria is a high-risk disease in pregnancy. The WHO recommends that pregnant women do *not* travel to areas with Chloroquine-resistant malaria. None of the more effective antimalarial drugs are completely safe in pregnancy.

Traveller's diarrhoea can quickly lead to dehydration and result in inadequate blood flow to the placenta. Many of the drugs used to treat various diarrhoea bugs are not recommended in pregnancy. Azithromycin is considered safe.

HEALTH

In the tourist areas of Bali, supplies of sanitary products and brands that are familiar are readily available. On Lombok the major-brand sanitary towels are not a problem to get hold of and are reasonably priced. Tampons, however, are like gold dust, they are hard to find and super-expensive! Try to bring your own from home or stock up on them in Hero supermarket in Mataram or in the supermarkets in Senggigi. Tampax and Lillets are available.

Birth-control options may be limited so bring adequate supplies of your own form of contraception.

Heat, humidity and antibiotics can all contribute to thrush. Treatments are antifungal creams and pessaries such as Clotrimazole. An alternative is a tablet of fluconazole (Diflucan). Urinary tract infections can be precipitated by dehydration or long journeys without toilet stops; bring suitable antibiotics.

Language

CONTENTS

Who Speaks What Where?	373
Bahasa Bali	373
Bahasa Indonesia	**374**
Pronunciation	375
Accommodation	375
Conversation & Essentials	376
Directions	376
Emergencies	377
Health	377
Language Difficulties	377
Numbers	377
Paperwork	377
Question Words	377
Shopping & Services	378
Time & Dates	378
Transport	378
Travel with Children	379

WHO SPEAKS WHAT WHERE?

Bali

The indigenous language, Bahasa Bali, has various forms based on traditional caste distinctions. The average traveller needn't worry about learning Balinese, but it can be fun to learn a few words. For practical purposes, it probably makes better sense to concentrate your efforts on learning Bahasa Indonesia.

Bahasa Indonesia is the national language, used in the education system and for all legal and administrative purposes. It's becoming more and more widely used, partly because of its official language status and partly because it serves as a lingua franca (a linking language), allowing the many non-Balinese now living and working in Bali to communicate – and avoid the intricacies of the caste system inherent in Bahasa Bali.

A good phrasebook is a wise investment. Lonely Planet's *Indonesian Phrasebook* is a handy, pocket-sized introduction to the language. The *Bali Pocket Dictionary* can be found at a few bookshops in Bali. It lists grammar and vocabulary in English, Indonesian, and low, polite and high Balinese.

English is common in the tourist areas, and is usually spoken very well. Many Balinese in the tourist industry also have a smattering (or more) of German, Japanese, French and/or Italian. A few older people speak Dutch and are often keen to practise it, but if you want to travel in remote areas, and communicate with people who aren't in the tourist business, it's a good idea to learn some Bahasa Indonesia.

Lombok

Most people on Lombok speak their own indigenous language (Sasak) and Bahasa Indonesia, which they are taught at school and use as their formal and official mode of communication. Apart from those working in the tourist industry, few people on Lombok speak English, and this includes police and other officials. English is becoming more widely spoken, but is still rare outside the main towns and tourist centres.

BAHASA BALI

The national language of Indonesia, Bahasa Indonesia, is widely used in Bali, but it isn't Balinese. Balinese, or Bahasa Bali, is another language entirely. It has a completely different vocabulary and grammar, and the rules governing its use are much more complex. It's a difficult language for a foreigner to come to grips with. Firstly, it isn't a written language, so there's no definitive guide to its grammar or vocabulary, and there is considerable variation in usage from one part of the island to another. Bahasa Bali isn't taught in schools either, and dictionaries and grammars that do exist are attempts to document current or historical usage, rather than set down rules for correct syntax or pronunciation.

Balinese is greatly complicated by its caste influences. In effect, different vocabularies and grammatical structures are used, depending on the relative social position of the speaker, the person being spoken to and the person being spoken about. Even traditional usage has always been somewhat arbitrary, because of the intricacies of the caste system.

The various forms of the language (or languages) and their respective uses are categorised as follows:

- Basa Alus is used among educated people, and is derived from the Hindu-Javanese court languages of the 10th century.
- Basa Lumrah (also called Biasa or Ketah) is used when talking to people of the same caste or level, and between friends and family. It is an old language of mixed origin, with words drawn from Malayan, Polynesian and Australasian sources.
- Basa Madia (also called Midah), a mixture of Basa Lumrah and Basa Alus, is used as a polite language for speaking to or about strangers, or people to whom one wishes to show respect.
- Basa Singgih, virtually a separate language, is used to address persons of high caste, particularly in formal and religious contexts. Even the Balinese are not always fluent in this language. It is based on the ancient Hindu Kawi language, and can be written using a script that resembles Sanskrit, as seen in the *lontar* (palm) books where it's inscribed on strips of leaf (see the boxed text on p260). Written Basa Singgih is also seen on the signs that welcome you to, and farewell you from, most villages in Bali.
- Basa Sor (also called Rendah) is used when talking with people of a lower caste, or to people who are noncaste.

The different vocabularies only exist for about 1000 basic words, mostly relating to people and their actions. Other words (in fact, an increasing proportion of the modern vocabulary) are the same regardless of relative caste levels.

Usage is also changing with the decline of the traditional caste system and modern tendencies towards democratisation and social equality. It is now common practice to describe the language in terms of only three forms:

- Low Balinese (Ia), equivalent to Basa Lumrah, is used between friends and family, and also when speaking with persons of equal or lower caste, or about oneself.
- Polite Balinese (Ipun), the equivalent of Basa Madia, is used for speaking to superiors or strangers, and is becoming more widespread as a sort of common language that isn't so closely linked to caste.
- High Balinese (Ida), a mixture of Basa Alus and Basa Singgih, is used to indicate respect for the person being addressed or the person being spoken about.

The polite and high forms of the language frequently use the same word, while the low form often uses the same word as Bahasa Indonesia. The polite form, Basa Madia or Midah, is being used as a more egalitarian language, often combined with Bahasa Indonesia to avoid the risk of embarrassment in case the correct caste distinctions aren't made.

So how does one Balinese know at which level to address another? Initially, a conversation between two strangers would commence in the high language. At some point the question of caste would be asked and then the level adjusted accordingly. Among friends, however, a conversation is likely to be carried on in low Balinese, no matter what the caste of the speakers may be.

Bahasa Bali uses very few greetings and civilities on an everyday basis. There are no equivalents for 'please' and 'thank you'. Nor is there a usage that translates as 'good morning' or 'good evening', although the low Balinese *kenken kebara?* (how are you?/ how's it going?) is sometimes used. More common is *lunga kija?,* which literally means 'where are you going?' (in low, polite and high Balinese).

BAHASA INDONESIA

Like most languages, Indonesian has a simplified colloquial form and a more developed literary form. It's among the easiest of all spoken languages to learn – there are no tenses, plurals or genders and, even better, it's easy to pronounce.

Apart from ease of learning, there's another very good reason for trying to pick up at least a handful of Indonesian words and phrases: few people are as delighted with visitors learning their language as Indonesians. They won't criticise you if you mangle your pronunciation or tangle your grammar and they make you feel like you're an expert even if you only know a dozen or so words. Bargaining also seems a whole lot easier and more natural when you do it in their language.

Written Indonesian can be idiosyncratic, however, and there are often inconsistent spellings of place names. Compound names are written as one word or two, eg Airsanih or Air Sanih, Padangbai or Padang Bai. Words starting with 'Ker' sometimes lose the 'e', as in Kerobokan/Krobokan.

In addition, some Dutch variant spellings remain in common use. These tend to occur in business names, with 'tj' instead of the modern **c** (as in Tjampuhan/Campuan), and 'oe' instead of the **u** (as in Soekarno/Sukarno).

PRONUNCIATION

Most letters have a pronunciation more or less the same as their English counterparts. Nearly all the syllables carry equal emphasis, but a good approximation is to stress the second-to-last syllable. The main exception to the rule is the unstressed **e** in words such as *besar* (big), pronounced 'be-sarr'.

a	as in 'father'
e	as in 'bet' when unstressed, although sometimes it's hardly pronounced at all, as in the greeting *selamat*, which sounds like 'slamat' if said quickly. When stressed, **e** is like the 'a' in 'may', as in *becak* (rickshaw), pronounced 'baycha'. There's no set rule as to when **e** is stressed or unstressed.
i	as in 'unique'
o	as in 'hot'
u	as in 'put'
ai	as in 'Thai'
au	as the 'ow' in 'cow'
ua	as 'w' when at the start of a word, eg *uang* (money), pronounced 'wong'
c	as the 'ch' in 'chair'
g	as in 'get'
ng	as the 'ng' in 'sing'
ngg	as the 'ng' in 'anger'
j	as in 'jet'
r	slightly rolled
h	a little stronger than the 'h' in 'her'; almost silent at the end of a word
k	like English 'k', except at the end of a word when it's like a closing of the throat with no sound released, eg *tidak* (no/not), pronounced 'tee-da'
ny	as the 'ny' in canyon

ACCOMMODATION

I'm looking for a ...	*Saya mencari ...*
campground	*tempat kemah*
guesthouse	*rumah yang disewakan*
hotel	*hotel*
youth hostel	*losmen pemuda*

MAKING A RESERVATION

(for written and phone inquiries)

I'd like to book ...	*Saya mau pesan ...*
in the name of ...	*atas nama ...*
date	*tanggal*
from ... (date)	*dari ...*
to ... (date)	*sampai ...*
credit card	*kartu kredit*
number	*nomor*
expiry date	*masa berlakunya sampai*
Please confirm availability and price.	*Tolong dikonfirmasi mengenai ketersediaan kamar dan harga.*

Where is a cheap hotel?
Hotel yang murah di mana?
What is the address?
Alamatnya di mana?
Could you write it down, please?
Anda bisa tolong tuliskan?
Do you have any rooms available?
Ada kamar kosong?

How much is it ... ?	*Berapa harganya ... ?*
per day	*sehari*
per person	*seorang*
one night	*satu malam*
one person	*satu orang*
room	*kamar*
bathroom	*kamar mandi*
I'd like a ...	*Saya cari ...*
bed	*tempat tidur*
single room	*kamar untuk seorang*
double bedroom	*tempat tidur besar satu kamar*
room with two beds	*kamar dengan dua tempat tidur*
room with a bathroom	*kamar dengan kamar mandi*
I'd like to share a dorm.	*Saya mau satu tempat tidur di asrama.*

Is breakfast included?	*Apakah harganya termasuk makan pagi/sarapan?*
May I see it?	*Boleh saya lihat?*
Where is the bathroom?	*Kamar mandi di mana?*
Where is the toilet?	*Kamar kecil di mana?*
I'm/we're leaving today.	*Saya/Kami berangkat hari ini.*

CONVERSATION & ESSENTIALS
Addressing People

Pronouns, particularly 'you', are rarely used in Indonesian. When speaking to an older man (or anyone old enough to be a father), it's common to call them *bapak* (father) or simply *pak*. Similarly, an older woman is *ibu* (mother) or simply *bu*. *Tuan* is a respectful term for a man, like 'sir'. *Nyonya* is the equivalent for a married woman, and *nona* for an unmarried woman. *Anda* is the egalitarian form designed to overcome the plethora of words for the second person.

To indicate negation, *tidak* is used with verbs, adjectives and adverbs; *bukan* with nouns and pronouns.

Welcome.	*Selamat datang.*
Good morning.	*Selamat pagi.* (before 11am)
Good day.	*Selamat siang.* (noon to 2pm)
Good day.	*Selamat sore.* (3pm to 6pm)
Good evening.	*Selamat malam.* (after dark)
Good night.	*Selamat tidur.* (to someone going to bed)
Goodbye.	*Selamat tinggal.* (to person staying)
Goodbye.	*Selamat jalan.* (to person leaving)
Yes.	*Ya.*
No. (not)	*Tidak.*
No. (negative)	*Bukan.*
Maybe.	*Mungkin.*
Please.	*Tolong.* (asking for help)
Please.	*Silahkan.* (giving permission)
Thank you (very much).	*Terima kasih (banyak).*
You're welcome.	*Kembali.*
Sorry.	*Maaf.*
Excuse me.	*Permisi.*
Just a minute.	*Tunggu sebentar*
How are you?	*Apa kabar?*
I'm fine.	*Kabar baik.*
What's your name?	*Siapa nama Anda?*
My name is ...	*Nama saya ...*
Are you married?	*Sudah kawin?*
Not yet.	*Belum.*

How old are you?	*Berapa umur Anda?*
I'm ... years old.	*Umur saya ... tahun.*
Where are you from?	*Anda dari mana?*
I'm from ...	*Saya dari ...*
I like ...	*Saya suka ...*
I don't like ...	*Saya tidak suka ...*
Good.	*Bagus.*
Good, fine, OK.	*Baik.*

DIRECTIONS

Where is ...?	*Di mana ...?*
How many kilometres?	*Berapa kilometer?*
Which way?	*Ke mana?*
Go straight ahead.	*Jalan terus.*
Turn left/right.	*Belok kiri/kanan.*
Stop!	*Berhenti!*
at the corner	*di sudut*
at the traffic lights	*di lampu merah*
here/there/over there	*di sini/situ/sana*
behind	*di belakang*
in front of	*di depan*
opposite	*di seberang*
far (from)	*jauh (dari)*
near (to)	*dekat (dengan)*
north	*utara*
south	*selatan*
east	*timur*
west	*barat*
beach	*pantai*
island	*pulau*
lake	*danau*
main square	*alun-alun*
market	*pasar*
sea	*laut*

SIGNS	
Masuk	Entrance
Keluar	Exit
Informasi	Information
Buka	Open
Tutup	Closed
Dilarang	Prohibited
Ada Kamar Kosong	Rooms Available
Penuh (Tidak Ada Kamar Kosong)	Full (No Vacancies)
Polisi	Police
Kamar Kecil/Toilet	Toilets/WC
Pria	Men
Wanitai	Women

LANGUAGE

EMERGENCIES

Help!	Tolong saya!
There's been an accident!	Ada kecelakaan!
I'm lost.	Saya tersesat.
Leave me alone!	Jangan ganggu saya!
Call ...!	Panggil ...!
a doctor	dokter
the police	polisi

HEALTH

I'm ill.	Saya sakit.
It hurts here.	Sakitnya di sini.
I'm ...	Saya sakit...
asthmatic	asma
diabetic	kencing manis
epileptic	epilepsi
I'm allergic to ...	Saya alergi...
antibiotics	antibiotik
aspirin	aspirin
penicillin	penisilin
bees	tawon/kumbang
nuts	kacang
antiseptic	penangkal infeksi/antiseptik
condoms	kondom
contraceptive	kontrasepsi
diarrhoea	mencret/diare
medicine	obat
nausea	mual
sunblock cream	sunscreen/tabir surya/sunblock
tampons	tampon

LANGUAGE DIFFICULTIES

I (don't) understand.
Saya (tidak) mengerti.
Do you speak English?
Bisa berbicara Bahasa Inggris?
Does anyone here speak English?
Ada yang bisa berbicara Bahasa Inggris di sini?
How do you say ... in Indonesian?
Bagaimana mengatakan ... dalam Bahasa Indonesia?
What does ... mean?
Apa artinya ...?
I can only speak a little (Indonesian).
Saya hanya bisa berbicara (Bahasa Indonesia) sedikit.
Please write that word down.
Tolong tuliskan kata itu.
Can you show me (on the map)?
Anda bisa tolong tunjukkan pada saya (di peta)?

NUMBERS

1	satu
2	dua
3	tiga
4	empat
5	lima
6	enam
7	tujuh
8	delapan
9	sembilan
10	sepuluh

A half is *setengah,* which is pronounced 'stenger', eg *stenger kilo* (half a kilo). 'Approximately' is *kira-kira.* After the numbers one to 10, the 'teens' are *belas,* the 'tens' are *puluh,* the 'hundreds' are *ratus,* the 'thousands' are *ribu* and 'millions' are *juta* – but as a prefix *satu* (one) becomes *se-,* eg *seratus* (one hundred). Thus:

11	sebelas
12	duabelas
13	tigabelas
20	dua puluh
21	dua puluh satu
25	dua puluh lima
30	tiga puluh
99	sembilan puluh sembilan
100	seratus
150	seratus limapuluh
200	dua ratus
888	delapan ratus delapan puluh delapan
1000	seribu

PAPERWORK

name	nama
nationality	kebangsaan
date of birth	tanggal kelahiran
place of birth	tempat kelahiran
sex/gender	jenis kelamin
passport	paspor
visa	visa

QUESTION WORDS

Who?	Siapa?
What?	Apa?
What is it?	Apa itu?
When?	Kapan?
Where?	Di mana?
Which?	Yang mana?
Why?	Kenapa?
How?	Bagaimana?

LANGUAGE

SHOPPING & SERVICES

What is this?	Apa ini?
How much is it?	Berapa (harganya)?
I'd like to buy ...	Saya mau beli ...
I don't like it.	Saya tidak suka.
May I look at it?	Boleh saya lihat?
I'm just looking.	Saya lihat-lihat saja.
I'll take it.	Saya beli.

this/that	ini/itu
big	besar
small	kecil
more	lebih
less	kurang
bigger	lebih besar
smaller	lebih keci
expensive	mahal
another/one more	satu lagi

Do you accept ...?	Bisa bayar pakai ...?
credit cards	kartu kredit
travellers cheques	cek perjalanan

What time does it open/close?	Jam berapa buka/tutup?
May I take photos?	Boleh saya potret?

I'm looking for a/the ...	Saya cari ...
bank	bank
church	gereja
city centre	pusat kota
embassy	kedutaan
food stall	warung
hospital	rumah sakit
market	pasar
museum	museum
police	kantor polisi
post office	kantor pos
public phone	telepon umum
public toilet	WC ('way say') umum
restaurant	rumah makan
telephone centre	wartel
tourist office	kantor pariwisata

TIME & DATES

What time is it?	Jam berapa sekarang?
When?	Kapan?
What time?	Jam berapa?
seven o'clock	jam tujuh
How many hours?	Berapa jam?
five hours	lima jam
in the morning	pagi
in the afternoon	siang

in the evening	malam
today	hari ini
tomorrow	besok
yesterday	kemarin
hour	jam
day	hari
week	minggu
month	bulan
year	tahun

Monday	hari Senin
Tuesday	hari Selasa
Wednesday	hari Rabu
Thursday	hari Kamis
Friday	hari Jumat
Saturday	hari Sabtu
Sunday	hari Minggu

January	Januari
February	Februari
March	Maret
April	April
May	Mei
June	Juni
July	Juli
August	Agustus
September	September
October	Oktober
November	Nopember
December	Desember

TRANSPORT
Public Transport

What time does the leave/arrive?	Jam berapa ... berangkat/datang?
boat/ship	kapal
bus	bis
plane	kapal terbang

I'd like a ... ticket.	Saya mau tiket ...
one-way	sekali jalan
return	pulang pergi
1st class	kelas satu
2nd class	kelas dua

I want to go to ...	Saya mau ke ...
The train has been delayed/cancelled.	Kereta terlambat/dibatalkan.

the first	pertama
the last	terakhir
ticket	karcis
ticket office	loket
timetable	jadwal

LANGUAGE

Private Transport

Where can I hire a ...?	*Di mana saya bisa sewa ...?*
I'd like to hire a ...	*Saya mau sewa ...*
bicycle	*sepeda*
car	*mobil*
4WD	*gardan ganda*
motorcycle	*sepeda motor*

ROAD SIGNS

Beri Jalan	Give Way
Bahaya	Danger
Dilarang Parkir	No Parking
Jalan Memutar	Detour
Masuk	Entry
Dilarang Mendahului	No Overtaking
Kurangi Kecepatan	Slow Down
Dilarang Masuk	No Entry
Satu Arah	One Way
Keluar	Exit
Kosongkan	Keep Clear

Is this the road to ...?	*Apakah jalan ini ke ... ?*
Where's a service station?	*Di mana pompa bensin?*
Please fill it up.	*Tolong isi sampai penuh.*
I'd like (20) litres.	*Saya mau (duapuluh) liter.*
diesel	*solar*
petrol	*bensin*
I need a mechanic.	*Saya perlu montir.*

The car has broken down at ...	*Mobil mogok di...*
The motorcycle won't start.	*Motor tidak bisa jalan.*
I have a flat tyre.	*Ban saya kempes.*
I've run out of petrol.	*Saya kehabisan bensin.*
I had an accident.	*Saya mengalami kecelakaan.*
(How long) Can I park here?	*(Berapa lama) Saya boleh parkir di sini?*
Where do I pay?	*Saya membayar di mana?*

TRAVEL WITH CHILDREN

Is there a/an ...?	*Ada .....?*
I need a ...	*Saya perlu....*
baby change room	*tempat ganti popok kamar*
car baby seat	*kursi anak untuk di mobil*
child-minding service	*tempat penitipan anak*
children's menu	*menu untuk anak-anak*
disposable nappies/diapers	*popok sekali pakai*
formula	*susu kaleng*
(English-speaking) babysitter	*suster yang bisa berbicara (Bahasa Inggris)*
highchair	*kursi anak*
potty	*pispot*
stroller	*kereta anak/dorongan anak*

Are children allowed?	*Boleh bawa anak-anak?*

LANGUAGE

Glossary

For food and drink terms, see p78.

adat – tradition, customs and manners
adharma – evil
aling aling – gateway backed by a small wall
alus – identifiable 'goodies' in an *arja* drama
anak-anak – children
angker – evil power
angklung – portable form of the *gamelan*
anjing – dogs
apotik – pharmacy
arja – refined operatic form of Balinese theatre; also a dance-drama, comparable to Western opera
Arjuna – a hero of the *Mahabharata* epic and a popular temple gate guardian image

bahasa – language; Bahasa Indonesia is the national language of Indonesia
bale – an open-sided pavilion with a steeply pitched thatched roof
bale banjar – communal meeting place of a *banjar;* a house for meetings and *gamelan* practice
bale gede – reception room or guesthouse in the home of a wealthy Balinese
bale kambang – floating pavilion; a building sur-rounded by a moat
bale tani – family house in Lombok; see also *serambi*
balian – faith healer and herbal doctor
banjar – local division of a village consisting of all the married adult males
banyan – a type of ficus tree, often considered holy; see also *waringin*
bapak – father; also a polite form of address to any older man; also *pak*
Barong – mythical lion-dog creature
Barong Tengkok – portable *gamelan* used for wed-ding processions and circumcision ceremonies on Lombok
baten tegeh – decorated pyramids of fruit, rice cakes and flowers
batik – process of colouring fabric by coating part of the cloth with wax, dyeing it and melting the wax out; the waxed part is not coloured, and repeated waxing and dyeing builds up a pattern
batu bolong – rock with a hole
belalu – quick-growing, light wood
bemo – popular local transport in Bali and Lombok; usually a small minibus but can be a small pick-up in rural areas
bensin – petrol (gasoline)

beruga – communal meeting hall in Bali; open-sided pavilion on Lombok
bhur – world of demons
bhwah – world of humans
bioskop – cinema
bokor – artisans; they produce the silver bowls used in traditional ceremonies
Brahma – the creator; one of the trinity of Hindu gods
Brahmana – the caste of priests and the highest of the Balinese castes; all priests are Brahmanas, but not all Brahmanas are priests
bu – mother; shortened form of *ibu*
bukit – hill; also the name of Bali's southern peninsula
bulau – month
buruga – thatched platforms on stilts

cabang – large tanks used to store water for the dry season
candi – shrine, originally of Javanese design; also known as *prasada*
candi bentar – entrance gates to a temple
cendrawasih – birds of paradise
cengceng – cymbals
cidomo – pony cart with car wheels (Lombok)
cili – representations of Dewi Sri, the rice goddess
cucuk – gold headpieces

dagang – mobile traders
dalang – puppet master and storyteller in a *wayang kulit* performance
Dalem Bedaulu – legendary last ruler of the Pejeng dynasty
danau – lake
dangdut – pop music
desa – village
dewa – deity or supernatural spirit
dewi – goddess
Dewi Sri – goddess of rice
dharma – good
dokar – pony cart; known as a *cidomo* on Lombok
Durga – goddess of death and destruction, and consort of *Shiva*
dusun –small village

endek – elegant fabric, like *songket,* with pre-dyed weft threads

Gajah Mada – famous *Majapahit* prime minister who defeated the last great king of Bali and extended *Majapahit* power over the island

Galungan – great Balinese festival; an annual event in the 210-day Balinese *wuku* calendar

gamelan – traditional Balinese orchestra, with mostly percussion instruments like large xylophones and gongs; also called a *gong*

Ganesha – elephant-headed son of *Shiva*

gang – alley or footpath

gangsa – xylophone-like instrument

Garuda – mythical man-bird creature, vehicle of *Vishnu*; modern symbol of Indonesia and the national airline

gedong – shrine

gendang beleq – a war dance; like the Oncer dance

gendong – street vendors who sell *jamu*, said to be a cure-all tonic

genggong – musical performance seen in Lombok

gili – small island (Lombok)

goa – cave; also spelt *gua*

gong – see *gamelan*

gong gede – large orchestra; traditional form of the *gamelan* with 35 to 40 musicians

gong kebyar – modern, popular form of a *gong gede*, with up to 25 instruments

gringsing – rare double ikat woven cloth; both warp and weft threads are pre-dyed

gua – cave; also spelt *goa*

gunung – mountain

gunung api – volcano

gusti – polite title for members of the *Wesia* caste

Hanuman – monkey god who plays a major part in the *Ramayana*

harga biasa – standard price

harga turis – inflated price for tourists

homestay – small, family-run accommodation; see also *losmen*

ibu – mother; also a polite form of address to any older woman

Ida Bagus – honourable title for a male *Brahmana*

iders-iders – long painted scrolls used as temple decorations

ikat – cloth where a pattern is produced by dyeing the individual threads before weaving; see also *gringsing*

Indra – king of the gods

jalak putih – local name for Bali starling

jalan – road or street; abbreviated to *Jl*

jalan jalan – to walk around

jamu – a cure-all tonic; see also *gendong*

jepun – frangipani or plumeria trees

jidur – large cylindrical drums played throughout Lombok

Jimny – small, jeeplike Suzuki vehicle; the usual type of rental car

Jl – *jalan*; road or street

kahyangan jagat – directional temples

kain – a length of material wrapped tightly around the hips and waist, over a sarong

kain poleng – black-and-white chequered cloth

kaja – in the direction of the mountains; see also *kelod*

kaja-kangin – corner of the courtyard

kaki lima – food carts

kala – demonic face often seen over temple gateways

Kalendar Cetakan – Balinese calendar used to plan myriad activities

kamben – a length of *songket* wrapped around the chest for formal occasions

kampung – village or neighbourhood

kangin – sunrise

kantor – office

kantor imigrasi – immigration office

kantor pos – post office

Kawi – classical Javanese; the language of poetry

kebyar – a type of dance

Kecak – traditional Balinese dance; tells a tale from the *Ramayana* about Prince Rama and Princess Sita

kedais – coffee house

kelod – in the direction away from the mountains and towards the sea; see also *kaja*

kelurahan – local government area

kemban – woman's breast-cloth

kempli – gong

kendang – drums

kepala desa – village head

kepeng – old Chinese coins with a hole in the centre

kori agung – gateway to the second courtyard in a temple

kota – city

kras – identifiable 'baddies' in an *arja* drama

kris – traditional dagger

Ksatriyasa – second Balinese caste

kuah – sunset side

kulkul – hollow tree-trunk drum used to sound a warning or call meetings

labuhan – harbour; also called *pelabuhan*

laki-laki – boy

lamak – long, woven palm-leaf strips used as decorations in festivals and celebrations

lambung – long black sarongs worn by *Sasak* women; see also *sabuk*

langse – rectangular decorative hangings used in palaces or temples

Legong – classic Balinese dance

legong – young girls who perform the *Legong*

leyak – evil spirit that can assume fantastic forms by the use of black magic

lontar – specially prepared palm leaves

losmen – small Balinese hotel, often family-run

lukisan antic – antique paintings

lulur – body mask
lumbung – rice barn with a round roof; an architectural symbol of Lombok

madia – the body
Mahabharata – one of the great Hindu holy books, the epic poem tells of the battle between the Pandavas and the Korawas
Majapahit – last great Hindu dynasty on Java
mandi – Indonesian 'bath' consisting of a large water tank from which you ladle cold water over yourself
manusa yadnya – ceremonies which mark the various stages of Balinese life from before birth to after cremation
mapadik – marriage by request, as opposed to *ngrorod*
mata air panas – natural hot springs
meditasi – swimming and sunbathing
mekepung – traditional water buffalo races
meru – multiroofed shrines in temples; the name comes from the Hindu holy mountain Mahameru
mobil – car
moksa – freedom from earthly desires
muncak – mouse deer

naga – mythical snakelike creature
ngrorod – marriage by elopement; see also *mapadik*
Ngrupuk – great procession where *ogoh-ogoh* figures are used to ward off evil spirits
ngulapin – cleansing, often used to describe a ritual
nista – the legs
nusa – island; also called *pulau*
Nusa Tenggara Barat (NTB) – West Nusa Tenggara; a province of Indonesia comprising the islands of Lombok and Sumbawa
nyale – wormlike fish caught off Kuta, Lombok
Nyepi – major annual festival in the Hindu *saka* calendar, this is a day of complete stillness after a night of chasing out evil spirits

odalan – Balinese 'temple birthday' festival; held in every temple annually, according to the *wuku* calendar, ie once every 210 days
ogoh-ogoh – huge monster dolls used in the *Nyepi* festival
ojek – motorcycle that carries paying passengers
oong – Bali's famed magic mushrooms

padi – growing rice plant
padmasana – temple shrine resembling a vacant chair
pak – father; shortened form of *bapak*
palinggihs – temple shrines consisting of a simple, little throne
panca dewata – centre and four cardinal points in a temple
pande – blacksmiths; they are treated somewhat like a caste in their own right

pantai – beach
paras – a soft, grey volcanic stone used in stone carving
pasar – market
pasar malam – night market
pecalang – village or *banjar* police
pedanda – high priest
pekelan – ceremony where gold trinkets and objects are thrown into the lake
pelabuhan – harbour; also called *labuhan*
Pelni – the national shipping line
pemangku – temple guardians and priests for temple rituals
penjor – long bamboo pole with decorated end, arched over the road or pathway during festivals or ceremonies
perbekel – government official in charge of a *desa*
perempuan – girl
pesmangku – priest for temple rituals
pitra yadna – cremation
plus plus – a combined tax and service charge of 21% added by midrange and top-end accommodation and restaurants
pondok – simple lodging or hut
prada – cloth highlighted with gold leaf, or gold or silver paint and thread
prahu – traditional Indonesian boat with outriggers
prasada – shrine; see also *candi*
prasasti – inscribed copper plates
pria – man; male
propinsi – province; Indonesia has 27 *propinsi* – Bali is a *propinsi*, Lombok and its neighbouring island of Sumbawa comprise *propinsi Nusa Tenggara Barat* (NTB)
puasa – to fast, or a fast
pulau – island; also called *nusa*
puputan – warrior's fight to the death; an honourable but suicidal option when faced with an unbeatable enemy
pura – temple
pura dalem – temple of the dead
pura desa – village temple for everyday functions
pura puseh – temple of the village founders or fathers, honouring the village's origins
pura subak – temple of the rice-growers' association
puri – palace
pusit kota – used on road signs to indicate the centre of town
puskesmas – community health centre

rajah – lord or prince
Ramadan – Muslim month of fasting
Ramayana – one of the great Hindu holy books; these stories form the keystone of many Balinese dances and tales
Rangda – widow-witch who represents evil in Balinese theatre and dance
raya – main road, eg Jl Raya Ubud means 'the main road of Ubud'

rebab – bowed lute
RRI – Radio Republik Indonesia; Indonesia's national radio broadcaster
RSU or RSUP – Rumah Sakit Umum or Rumah Sakit Umum Propinsi; a public hospital or provincial public hospital
rumah makan – restaurant; literally 'eating place'

sabuk – 4m-long scarf that holds the *lambung* in place
sadkahyangan – 'world sanctuaries'; most sacred temples
saiban – temple or shrine offering
saka – Balinese calendar based on the lunar cycle; see also *wuku*
sampian – palm-leaf decoration
Sasak – native of Lombok; also the language
sawah – rice field; see also *subak*
selandong – traditional scarf
selat – strait
sepeda – bicycle
sepeda motor – motorcycle
serambi – open verandah on a *bale tani,* the traditional Lombok family house
Shiva – the creator and destroyer; one of the three great Hindu gods
sinetron – soap operas
songket – silver- or gold-threaded cloth, handwoven using a floating weft technique
stupas – domes for housing Buddha relics
subak – village association that organises rice terraces and shares out water for irrigation
Sudra – common caste to which the majority of Balinese belong
sungai – river
swah – world of gods

tahun – year
taksu – divine interpreter for the gods
tambulilingan – bumblebees
tanjung – cape or point
tektekan – ceremonial procession
teluk – gulf or bay
tiing – bamboo
tika – piece of printed cloth or carved wood displaying the Pawukon cycle
tirta – water
toya – water

transmigrasi – government program of trans-migration
trimurti – Hindu trinity
triwangsa – caste divided into three parts *(Brahmana, Ksatriyasa* and *Wesia)*; means three people
trompong – drums
TU – Telepon Umum; a public telephone
tugu – lord of the ground
tukang prada – group of artisans who make temple umbrellas
tukang wadah – group of artisans who make cremation towers

undagi – designer of a building, usually an architect-priest
utama – the head

Vishnu – the preserver; one of the three great Hindu gods

wanita – woman; female
wantilan – large *bale* pavilion used for meetings, performances and cockfights; community hall
waria – female impersonator, transvestite or transgendered; combination of the words *wanita* and *pria*
waringin – large shady tree with drooping branches that root to produce new trees; see *banyan*
warnet – warung with internet access
wartel – public telephone office; contraction of *warung telekomunikasi*
warung – food stall
wayang kulit – leather puppet used in shadow puppet plays; see also *dalang*
wayang wong – masked drama playing scenes from the *Ramayana*
Wektu Telu – religion peculiar to Lombok; originated in Bayan and combines many tenets of Islam and aspects of other faiths
Wesia – military caste and most numerous of the Balinese noble castes
WIB – Waktu Indonesia Barat; West Indonesia Time
wihara – monastery
WIT – Waktu Indonesia Tengah; Central Indonesia Time
wuku – Balinese calendar made up of 10 different weeks, between one and 10 days long, all running concurrently; see also *saka*

yeh – water; also river
yoni – female symbol of the Hindu god *Shiva*

THE AUTHORS

The Authors

RYAN VER BERKMOES

Ryan Ver Berkmoes first visited Bali in 1993. On his visits since he has explored almost every corner of the island – along with side trips to Nusas Lembongan and Penida, and Lombok. Just when he thinks Bali holds no more surprises, he, for example, ducks behind Pura Luhur Batukau. Better yet, he simply never tires of the place. Four times in two years shows that; sometimes his Bali social calendar is busier than anywhere else. Off-island, Ryan lives in Portland, Oregon and writes about Bali and more at www.ryanverberkmoes.com.

MARIAN CARROLL

Marian first visited Bali at the age of six on a family holiday. Her earliest memories include horse-and-cart rides, crowded markets, heat rash and rocketing off diving boards into the hotel pool. It would be almost two decades before she returned and fell under the island's spell for good, as she stumbled across timeless rice-farming villages and the friendliest people you could ever meet. She now lives the dream, having moved to Bali as a freelance journalist in 2002. She previously co-authored Lonely Planet's *Best of Bali*. Home is an open-air house with her husband, their mongrel dog and more recently, their two (sometimes mongrel) children.

ADAM SKOLNICK

Adam Skolnick became travel-obsessed while working as an environmental activist in the mid '90s. He has since wandered six continents, and visited over 20 islands in his beloved Indonesia. A freelance journalist, he writes about travel, culture, health, sports and the environment for Lonely Planet, *Men's Health*, *Outside*, *Travel & Leisure*, and *Spa*. He has co-authored four previous Lonely Planet guidebooks, *Southeast Asia on a Shoestring*, *East Timor*, *Mexico*, and *The Carolinas, Georgia and the South Trips*, and he is the author of *Phuket Encounter*. You can read more of his work at www.adamskolnick.com.

LONELY PLANET AUTHORS

Why is our travel information the best in the world? It's simple: our authors are passionate, dedicated travellers. They don't take freebies in exchange for positive coverage so you can be sure the advice you're given is impartial. They travel widely to all the popular spots, and off the beaten track. They don't research using just the internet or phone. They discover new places not included in any other guidebook. They personally visit thousands of hotels, restaurants, palaces, trails, galleries, temples and more. They speak with dozens of locals every day to make sure you get the kind of insider knowledge only a local could tell you. They take pride in getting all the details right, and in telling it how it is. Think you can do it? Find out how at **lonelyplanet.com**.

Behind the Scenes

THIS BOOK

This is the 12th edition of Lonely Planet's *Bali & Lombok*. We first visited Bali, the island of the gods, way back in the early '70s, when a floral-shirted Tony Wheeler came through while researching the inaugural *Across Asia on the Cheap*. Since then an army of Lonely Planet authors has returned time and time again: following in Tony's sandalled footprints have been Mary Coverton (who worked with Tony on *Bali & Lombok* 1st edition, 1984), Alan Samagalski, James Lyon, Paul Greenway, Kate Daly, Ryan Ver Berkmoes, Lisa Steer-Guérard and Iain Stewart.

For this edition, Ryan Ver Berkmoes returned once again to Bali, while the intrepid, island-hopping Adam Skolnick researched and wrote the Lombok chapter. Bali local Marian Carroll wrote the Food & Drink, Architecture and Culture chapters, while expert medico Trish Batchelor wrote Health. This guidebook was commissioned in Lonely Planet's Melbourne office, and produced by the following:

Commissioning Editors Judith Bamber, Suzannah Shwer, Tashi Wheeler
Coordinating Editors Elizabeth Anglin, Carolyn Bain
Coordinating Layout Designer Paul Iacono
Managing Editors Helen Christinis, Katie Lynch

Managing Cartographer Dave Connolly
Managing Layout Designer Laura Jane
Assisting Editors Simon Williamson, Fionnuala Twomey
Cover Designer Mary Nelson Parker
Language Content Coordinator Quentin Frayne
Project Manager Chris Love

Thanks to Sasha Baskett, Sally Darmody, Nicole Hansen, James Hardy, Lisa Knights, Wayne Murphy, Carlos Solarte, Gerard Walker, Celia Wood

THANKS
RYAN VER BERKMOES

This list just seems to grow. Many thanks to friends like Jeremy Allan, Eliot Cohen, Jamie James, Hanafi, noted decorators Kerry and Milton Turner, Nicoline Dolman, Jack Daniels, Oka Wati, Marilyn, newlywed Wayan Suarnata, Heinz von Holzen, Arathorn (the warung God), Wayan Wiradnyana, Chrystine Hanley and many, many more (sometimes the menagerie even had a monkey or platypus).

At Lonely Planet, thanks to the entire publishing and production teams for guidance, understanding and the ability to fix a lot of bad spelling. Co-authors Marian Carroll and Adam Skolnick are the dream team.

THE LONELY PLANET STORY

Fresh from an epic journey across Europe, Asia and Australia in 1972, Tony and Maureen Wheeler sat at their kitchen table stapling together notes. The first Lonely Planet guidebook, *Across Asia on the Cheap,* was born.

Travellers snapped up the guides. Inspired by their success, the Wheelers began publishing books to Southeast Asia, India and beyond. Demand was prodigious, and the Wheelers expanded the business rapidly to keep up. Over the years, Lonely Planet extended its coverage to every country and into the virtual world via lonelyplanet.com and the Thorn Tree message board.

As Lonely Planet became a globally loved brand, Tony and Maureen received several offers for the company. But it wasn't until 2007 that they found a partner whom they trusted to remain true to the company's principles of travelling widely, treading lightly and giving sustainably. In October of that year, BBC Worldwide acquired a 75% share in the company, pledging to uphold Lonely Planet's commitment to independent travel, trustworthy advice and editorial independence.

Today, Lonely Planet has offices in Melbourne, London and Oakland, with over 500 staff members and 300 authors. Tony and Maureen are still actively involved with Lonely Planet. They're travelling more often than ever, and they're devoting their spare time to charitable projects. And the company is still driven by the philosophy of *Across Asia on the Cheap*: 'All you've got to do is decide to go and the hardest part is over. So go!'

Finally, there's Annah who always gives me a welcome 'merp', and Erin Corrigan, who discovered Bali for herself and proved that paradise begins at home.

MARIAN CARROLL

I'm grateful to I Nyoman Darma Putra, whose insights, anecdotes and encyclopaedic knowledge have fuelled my interest in Balinese culture since we first worked side-by-side in the press corp at Denpasar court. Big thanks to Ni Made Suardani and Ni Dewi Widiasari for tolerating constant questioning about all manner of things, with trademark Balinese patience and humour, and to Sugi Lunas and Made Wijaya for your invaluable input. Thanks to the Lonely Planet team – especially Ryan, Adam, Judith Bamber and Suzannah Shwer for guidance and support. Last but by no means least, thanks to Greg for simply everything!

ADAM SKOLNICK

Thanks to Brett Black, Jason Wolcott, Made, Yoni and Pak Madre in Bali, Helen and Gaz in Kuta, Simon, Will, and the Blue Marlin crew, Marcus, Anthony, and Jon at Manta Dive, Harriet and Miriam at Bale Sampan, Chris at Tir na Nog, Acok at Sama Sama, the Rinjani Master, Edy – the bizarro black-magic sex fiend, and to Heaven and all its angels. Thanks also to Suzannah Shwer and Judith Bamber in the Melbourne office, to the esteemed Ryan Ver Berkmoes, and to the forever sweet and lovely Georgiana Johnson.

OUR READERS

Many thanks to the travellers who used the last edition and wrote to us with helpful hints, useful advice and interesting anecdotes:

George Alexiou, Hans-Dieter Amstutz, Rachel Ashton, Chris Barnes, Yann Binot, Jean-Pierre Boudrias, Amanda Brown, James Bunning, John Coambs, Yvonne Duijst, Helen and David Duncan, Antoine Fleury, Timothy Fortlage, Tanja Gabler, Heloise and Julian Gornall-Thode, Dewi Handayani, Peter Hardy, Boby Eko Hariyanto, Bas Havekes, Don Hendry, Guenter Herrmann, Walter Jamieson, Mel Jason, Petra Grosskinsky Jeckelmann, Marla Johst, Linda Jones, Peter Jones, Matt Kasar, Jansen De Koning, Ed Kopkas, Shelley Laffin, Lynda Laushway, Garrick Law, David Lewis, Gisela Liebscher, Alan Maes, Sabrina Mariani, Christina Mattus, Dudley Mcfadden, Jody Merel, Amanda Miller, Petr Muller, Jessi Nabuurs, Chris Nelson, Linda Nicolai, Daryl Ong, Maurice Parker, Clifford Penn, Thomas Reichmann, Ben Ridder, Barry Rodgers-Smyth, Diah Sate, Lidwine Sauer, Steven Schiller, Felix Stockmann, Sarah Tibbatts, Jörg Tredup, Maarten van Buuren, Vicky van Wijck, Jolanda van den Brandt, Kim van den Broek, Wim vandenbussche, Matilde Visser, Reinier Vos, Rosemarie Vos, Rosy Waldron, Erin Westerhout-Hanna, Remco Wijnings, Alan Wilson, Zhengzhen Wu, Nancy Yu, Eric Zimmerman

ACKNOWLEDGMENTS

Many thanks to the following for the use of their content:

Globe on title page ©Mountain High Maps 1993 Digital Wisdom, Inc.

Internal photographs: p6 Eitan Simanor/Alamy; p9 E. Rowe/Axiom Photographic Agency/Getty Images. All other photographs by Lonely Planet Images, and by Andrew Brownbill p5, p9 (#2); John Banagan p6 (#1); Tim Rock p7 (#3); Paul Kennedy p7 (#4); Paul Beinssen p8 (#1), p10 (#1); Peter Ptschelinzew p10 (#2); Wibowo Rusli p11 (#3); Felix Hug p11 (#4); Gregory Adams p12 (#1).

All images are the copyright of the photographers unless otherwise indicated. Many of the images in this guide are available for licensing from Lonely Planet Images: www.lonelyplanetimages .com.

BEHIND THE SCENES

Index

A

Aas, *see* Amed
accommodation 21, 327-30, *see also individual locations*
activities 86-98, *see also* bungy jumping, canoeing, cycling, diving, golf courses, hiking, horse-riding, kayaking, rafting, snorkelling, surfing, water sports
Agung Rai Museum of Art 177
AIDS 367
Air Nyet 290
air pollution 85
air travel
    airlines 349-50
    airports 349-50
    to/from Bali & Lombok 349-52
    within Bali & Lombok 353
Amandari 34, 191, **34**
Amankila 223
Amed 232-6, **233**
Amlapura 228-30, **229**
amoebic dysentery 369
Ampenan, *see* Mataram
animals 80-3, *see also* Bali ponies, birds, dolphins, ducks, lizards, monkeys, sea turtles
Antosari 276
Anturan, *see* Lovina
architecture 29-36, 69
area codes 343, *see also inside front cover*
arja 61-2
art galleries, *see* museums & galleries
arts 58-69, *see also* crafts, dance, festivals & events, literature, music, painting, theatre
ARMA 177
ATMs 339
Awang 325

B

Bahasa Indonesia 374-9
Bajera 276
Balangan Beach 20, 94, 136

000 Map pages
000 Photograph pages

Bali Aga people 36, 48, 57, 67, 224, 237, 267
Bali Art Festival of Buleleng 257
Bali Arts Festival 20, 167
Bali belly 76
Bali Bird Park 203
Bali Botanical Gardens 247
Bali Orchid Garden 147
Bali ponies 93
Bali Safari & Marine Park 208
Bali starlings 81, 203, 280, 282
Bali Treetop Adventure Park 248
Balian Beach 94, 276
Bangli 209-10, **209**
Bangsal 296, 297, 310
banjar 18, 43
banyan trees 83
Banyumulek 290
bargaining 341
basket-weaving 69, 205
Bat Cave Temple 219
bathrooms 344
baths, *see also* hot springs
    Air Panas Banjar 9, 267, **8**
    Air Sanih 255
    Sawan 260
    Tejakula 237
    Tirta Empul 202, **31**
    Toya Devasya 246
    Yeh Sanih 255
batik 66-7, 183, 208, 209
Batu Koq 311-13
Batuan 204-5
Batubulan 203
Batur 244
Bawa, Geoffrey 34
Bayan 311
beaches 20
    Balangan Beach 20, 94, 136
    Balian Beach 94, 276
    Berewa 129
    Bias Tugal 219
    Bingin 136-7
    Blue Lagoon Beach 220
    Canggu 94, 129-30
    Coast Road 208
    Crystal Bay Beach 162
    Delod Berawan 278
    Dream Beach 155
    Echo Beach 130

Gerupak 325
Gili Air 297
Gili Islands 20
Gili Pentangan 326
Gili Sulat 326
Jungutbatu 154-5
Kalibukbuk 261
Kelating 275
Kuta (Bali) 20, 106-7, **6**
Kuta (Lombok) 321
Lebih 208
Lovina 9, 261, **9**
Mawan 325
Mawi 325
Medewi 276
Mushroom Bay 155
Nusa Dua 141
Nusa Lembongan 9, 20, 154-5, **9**
Nusa Penida 161-2
Padangbai 219-20
Pantai Beach 208
Pantai Segar 325
Pantai Selegimpak 155
Pantai Setangi 293
Pasir Putih 20, 228
Pererenan Beach 130
Pura Klotek Beach 208
Pura Masceti Beach 208
Saba Beach 208
Sanur 145, 146
Selong Blanak 325
Seminyak 120
Senggigi 9, 291, 293
Sira 310
Tegal Basar Beach 208
beauty salons, *see also* massage, spas
    Kuta & Legian 108
    Senggigi 293
    Ubud 180
Bebandem 218
Bedugul 247
Bedulu 198-200
begging 333
Belayu 272
Belega 205
Belimbingsari 278-9
bemo travel 353-4
Benoa Harbour 153
Berewa 129
Bertais, *see* Mataram

INDEX

Bickerton, Ashley 129
bicycle travel, *see* cycling
Bingin 94, 136-7
bird flu 366
birds 81, 179, 184, 203, 280, 282, 289, 300
black magic 52
Blanco, Antonio 177
boat travel, *see also* canoeing, cruises, kayaking, rafting
  to/from Bali & Lombok 352, 362
  within Bali & Lombok 354-5
bombings 44, 45, 106
Bona 205
Bonnet, Rudolf 63-4, 172, 176, 177
books
  architecture 33
  arts 58
  culture 46, 58, 59, 60, 61, 64, 71-9
  dance 59, 61
  environment 80, 84
  history 37, 41, 43, 44
  literature 65
  music 61
  painting 63
  surfing 96, 97
  travel literature 21-2, 50
  Ubud 173
  women 58
Botanic Garden Ubud 179
Brahma Vihara Arama 266-7
Buahan 245
Budakeling 232
Buddhist monastery 266-7
buffalo races 278, 321
Bugis people 267, 278, 290, 297
Bukit Demulih 210
Bukit Jambal 213-14
Bukit Kusambi 232
Bukit Peninsula 133-44, **132**
Bukit Sari 273
bull races 278
bungy jumping 108
Bunutan, *see* Amed
bus travel 355
bushwalking, *see* hiking
business hours 330
Butler, Kim 259

C

Cakra, I Nyoman 64
Cakranegara, *see* Mataram
calendars 66, 335-6
camping 327-8

Campuan Ridge
  walking tour 181-2, **182**
Candidasa 224-8, **226-7**
Candikuning 247-50
Canggu 94, 129-30
canoeing 92, 245
car travel 355-9
  driving licences 356-7
  insurance 358
  road distance chart 357, 360
  rules 359
caves
  Bat Cave Temple 219
  Elephant Cave 198-9, **199**
  Goa Gajah 198-9, **199**
  Goa Jepang 247
  Goa Karangsari 161
  Japanese Cave 247
  Pura Goa Lawah 219
Cekik 279
cell phones 343
Celuk 204
Celukanbawang 267
central Lombok 310, 318-19, **319**
Central Mountains 239-53, **240**
ceramics 68-9, 274-5, 290, 319, 320, 340-1
ceremonies 53-5, 65
  food 74
charitable organisations 184, 259, 346-7, *see also* volunteering
children, travel with 330-1
  activities 98, 331
  Bali Bird Park 203
  Bali Safari & Marine Park 208
  Bali Treetop Adventure Park 248
  Elephant Safari Park 202-3
  food 76, 331
  Kuta (Bali) 109
  Rimba Reptil Park 203
  Waterbom Park 107
child-sex tourism 56
Christianity 278
cidomo travel 359-60
climate 19-21, 331-2
climate change 350
clothes 341
Coast Road 207-8
cockfighting 82
coffee 249, 251
conservation, *see* environmental issues
consulates 335
cooking courses 77, 121, 143, 183
costs 21, *see also inside front cover*

courses 332
  arts & crafts 183, 332
  cooking 77, 121, 143, 183
  dance 183, 332
  diving 88-9
  language 183, 332
  meditation & spiritual interests 183, 332
  music 183, 332
  surfing 107
Coward, Noel 17
cows 82
crafts 65-9
credit cards 339
cremations 55
cruises 156, 158, 222-3, 268, 362
Crystal Bay Beach 162
culture 12, 46-69
  books 46, 58, 59, 60, 64, 71-9
customs 53-5, 77, 348
  Lombok 291
customs regulations 332-3
cycling 86-8, 354
  Bukit Peninsula 86-7
  Central Mountains 87
  East Bali 87
  Gili Air 298
  Gili Trawangan 306
  internet resources 86
  Lombok 87
  Lovina 261
  North Bali 87
  Nusa Lembongan 87, 156
  Nusa Penida 87, 160
  Senggigi 292
  Ubud 87, 180
  West Bali 87

D

Dalem Bedaulu 38, 198, 200
Danau Batur 245-6
Danau Bratan 247-51, **248**
Danau Buyan 250
Danau Tamblingan 250
dance 12, 58-60, 150, 196, 12
  Baris 60
  Barong & Rangda 59
  Batuan 205
  Batubulan 203
  Cupak 60
  Cupak Gerantang 60
  Kecak 59, 137
  Legong 59, 150
  Rudat 60
  Sanghyang 59-60

dance *continued*
  Tenganan 224
  Ubud 12, 195-6
Danes, Popo 30, 35
dangers 333-5
  Gili Islands 296, 297
  Gunung Batur 241
  Kuta & Legian 105-6
  South Lombok 325
de Neefe, Janet 73, 183, 192
deep-vein thrombosis (DVT) 365
dehydration 370
Delod Berawan 278
dengue fever 366
Denpasar 12, 162-70, **164-5**
  accommodation 167-8
  attractions 163-6
  emergencies 163
  food 168-9
  medical services 163
  shopping 169
  tourist information 163
  travel to/from 169-70
  travel within 170
  walking tour 166-7, **167**
Desa Bersih festival 290, 336
Desert Point 7, 97, 7
development 16-18, 35, 123, 136,
  152, 324, *see also* environmental
  issues
Dewi Sri 49, 65, 81, 290
diarrhoea 369, 371
directional temples 31, 51
disabilities, travellers with 344
diving 6-7, 88-91, 7
  Aas 232-3
  Amed 232-3
  Batu Aba 161
  Blue Lagoon Beach 220
  Candidasa 225
  courses 88-9
  far east coast 232-3
  Gili Pentangan 326
  Gili Sulat 326
  Gili Tepekong 225
  itineraries 27, **27**
  Jemeluk 232, 233
  Kuta (Lombok) 323
  Liberty wreck 236
  Lipah 233
  Lombok 90

  Lovina 261
  Nusa Lembongan 155-6, 159
  Nusa Penida 159, 160, 161
  Padangbai 220-1
  Pemuteran 268
  Pulau Menjangan 7, 280-1, 7
  safety 369-71
  Sanur 147-8
  Selang 233
  Senggigi 292
  Sira 310-11
  Taman Nasional Bali Barat 280-1
  Tanjung Benoa 143
  Tulamben 233, 236
dogs 82, 101, 184
dokar travel 359-60
Dolman, Nicoline 129
dolphins 81
  dolphin watching 261
Dreamland 94, 136
drinks 73-4
driving, *see* car travel
driving licences 356-7
drugs 333
ducks 83
Dutch colonialism 38-41, 162, 210,
  211, 250, 255, 257, 272
DVDs 328, 341
DVT 365

E
East Bali 206-38, **207**
east Lombok 326
Echo Beach 130
economy 43, 55-7
Ekas 326
electricity 328
Elephant Cave 198-9, **199**
Elephant Safari Park 202-3
embassies 335
emergencies, *see* medical services,
  inside front cover
Empu Kuturan 137, 219
environmental issues 16-18, 85
  air pollution 85
  climate change 350
  development 16-18, 35, 123, 136,
    152, 324
  reefs 268, 302
  responsible travel 84
  sea turtles 82, 153, 208, 268, 301
  sustainable travel 18, 397
  tourism 17
  water 17-18, 85, 106, 334, 369
ethnicity 57

etiquette 55, 77, 348
  Lombok 291
events, *see* festivals & events
exchange rates, *see inside front cover*
expats 129

F
fabrics, *see* textiles
far east coast (Bali) 232-6, **233**
ferry travel
  to/from Bali & Lombok 352, 362
  within Bali & Lombok 354-5
festivals & events 20, 321, 335-7
  Bali Art Festival of Buleleng 257
  Bali Arts Festival 20, 66, 167
  Bali Kite Festival 148
  Denpasar 167
  Desa Bersih festival 290, 336
  Kuningan 336
  Kuta Karnival 20, 109
  Lebaran Topat 321
  Lombok 336
  Malean Sampi 321
  Mandi Safar 309
  North Bali Festival 257
  Nyale Festival 323, 336
  Nyale Fishing Festival 20
  Nyepi 20, 62
  Perang Topat 336
  Sasak 321, 323
  temple festivals 336
  Ubud Writers & Readers Festival
    20, 184
  Usaba Sambah Festival 224
fish 81
Flores 362
flowers 83-5, 147, 179, 247
food 12, 70-9, 337
  books 71-9
  customs 77
  health 370
  hygiene 76
  internet resources 76
Friend, Donald 33-4, 69, 145
furniture 341

G
Gajah Mada 38, 39, 198, 205
galleries, *see* museums & galleries
Galungan 335-6
gardens
  Bali Botanical Gardens 247
  Bali Orchid Garden 147
  Botanic Garden Ubud 179
gay travellers 337

INDEX

Gelgel 38, 213
Gelgel dynasty 38, 211, 213
geography 80
geology 80
Gerupak 325
Gianyar 208-9
Gianyar dynasty 41, 208
giardiasis 369
Gilbert, Elizabeth 178
Gili Air 296, 297-300, **298**
Gili Islands 7, 20, 283, 295-310
Gili Meno 296, 300-3, **301**
Gili Pentangan 326
Gili Sulat 326
Gili Trawangan 296, 304-10, **305**
Gilimanuk 279-80, **279**
Gitgit 260
Goa Gajah 198-9, **199**
Goa Jepang (Japanese Cave) 247
Goa Karangsari 161
gold 204
golf courses 136, 141, 250, 311
Gondang 311
Goodman, Will 306
government 16, 41-5
GreenDex 397
Gunarsa, Nyoman 213
    Gunarsa Museum 213
Gunung Agung 42, 216-17, 237
Gunung Batukau 91, 252-3
Gunung Batur 91, 240-6, **242**
Gunung Kawi 11, 37, 201-2, 10
Gunung Pengsong 290
Gunung Rinjani 11, 85, 92, 283,
    314-18, **315**, 11

H
hawkers 333-4
health 363-72
    books 365
    insurance 363
    internet resources 365, 366
    services 365-6
    vaccinations 364
heatstroke 370
Helen Flavel Foundation 346
Helmi, Rio 178
    Rio Helmi Gallery 178
hepatitis 366-7
hiking 91-2
    Amed 233
    Bedugul 247
    Danau Buyan 250
    far east coast 233
    Gunung Agung 216-17

Gunung Batukau 252
Gunung Batur 241-4
Gunung Rinjani 11, 314-18, 11
Hutan Wisata Suranadi 289
Munduk 11, 250
Nusa Lembongan 156
Putung 218
Sembalun Valley 313
Senggigi 292
Seraya 233
Sidemen Road 11, 214, 10
Taman Nasional Bali Barat 281-2
Tirta Gangga 230-1
Hinduism 48, *see also* temples
    Ashram Gandhi Chandi 225
    culture 46, 48
    history 37-8, 39, 40
    Pura Besakih 215-16, **215**
    Pura Jagatnatha 166
history 37-45
    books 37, 41, 43, 44
    Dutch colonialism 38-41
    independence 41
    Japanese occupation 41
    WWII 41
hitching 359
HIV 367
holidays 19-20, 337-8
homestays 36
horse-riding 93, 128, 268, 275,
    306, 323
hot springs, *see also* baths
    Air Panas Banjar 9, 267, 8
    Gunung Rinjani 314, 316, 317
    Penatahan 275
    Sapit 313
    Toya Devasya 246
HPPGB 241
Hutan Wisata Suranadi 289

I
ikat, *see* textiles
immigration 57, 163, 349
Impossibles 94
Ingram, William 193
insect bites 370-1
insurance
    car 358
    health 363
    travel 338
internet access 338
internet resources 22
    accommodation 327, 329
    arts 67, 68
    cycling 86

food 76
health 365
surfing 94, 96, 97
travel 22
Islam 38, 39, 44, 45, 48, 291, 309,
    321
itineraries 23-8, **23**, **24**, **25**, **26**,
    27, **28**
    diving 27, **27**
    Lombok 27, **27**
    resorts 28, **28**
    spas 28, **28**
    temples 28, **28**

J
Jabrik, Tippi 107
Jagaraga 259-60
Japanese B encephalitis 367
Japanese occupation 41
Jatiluwih 11, 252, 11
Jayaprana 282
jellyfish 371
Jemaah Islamiyah 45
Jembrana 278
Jembrana Coast 276-7
Jemeluk, *see* Amed
Jero Gede Macaling 161
Jerowaru 326
jewellery 128, 197, 341
Jimbaran 133-5, **134**
Jungutan 218

K
Kaliasem, *see* Lovina
Kalibukbuk, *see* Lovina
Kamasan 213
Kapal 271
Karang, Anak Agung Made 287
Karangasem 219
Karangasem dynasty 41, 229, 230
kayaking 92, 306, *see also* canoeing
Kecak 59, 137
Kediri 274
Kedisan 245
Kelating 275
Kerambitan 275
Kerobokan 128-9
Keruak 326
Ketewel 94, 208
King Anak Agung Ngurah 289
King Sri Kesari Varma 145
Kintamani 244
kites 148, 183, 197
Klungkung 210-13, **211**
Klungkung dynasty 212

Koke, Robert & Louise 40, 42, 101, 107, 133, 177
Kotaraja 319
kris 68
Krotok 232
Kuban 245
Kubu Region 236
Kubutambahan 260
Kuningan 336
Kusamba 218-19
Kuta (Bali) 7, 20, 38, 99-118, **100**, **102-3**, 6
　accommodation 109-12
　activities 106-9
　emergencies 104
　entertainment 115
　festivals 109
　food 112, 113-14
　history 101
　internet access 104-5
　Kuta Karnival 20, 109
　medical services 105
　shopping 116-18
　surfing 94-5
　tourist information 105
　travel to/from 118
　travel within 118
Kuta (Lombok) 7, 321-5, **322**
Kutri 205

L

Labuhan Kayangan 326
Labuhan Lalang 282
Labuhan Lombok 326
Lalang-Linggah 276
Lange, Mads 41, 101, 211
language 373-9
　courses 183, 332
　food 77-9
Le Mayeur de Merpes, Adrien Jean 68, 139, 145, 146-7
Lebaran Topat 321
Lebih 94, 208
legal matters 338
Legian 99-118, **100**, **102-3**
　accommodation 110, 111, 112
　entertainment 116
　food 114-15
　medical services 105
　shopping 116, 117
Legong 59, 150

Lehan, *see* Amed
Lembar 290
Lembongan 155
Lempad, I Gusti Nyoman Lempad 36, 66, 176, 177, 179, 200
　Lempad's House 179
Lendang Nangka 319
lesbian travellers 337
Leyonsari 282
Liberty wreck 236
Liddiard, Simon 306
Ling Gwan Kiong 256
Lipah, *see* Amed
literature 64-5, *see also* books
Liyer, Ketut 178
lizards 80-1
Loloan Timur 278
Lombok 283-326, **284**
　activities 86, 87, 90, 92, 97
　architecture 69
　arts 60, 61, 65, 67, 68, 69
　culture 47, 53, 57
　economy 56-7
　festivals 309, 321, 323, 336
　food 72
　history 38-9, 41, 44
　itineraries 23, 24, 26, 27, **23, 24**, **26, 27**
　population 57
　tourism 56
lontar books 64-5, 260
Lovina 9, 260-6, **262**, 9
Loyok 319

M

magazines 58, 328
Majapahit dynasty 37-8, 48, 68, 198
Makam Jayaprana 282
malaria 367-8, 371
Mandala Wisata Wanara Wana 179
Mandi Safar 309
Manggis 223
Mangrove Information Centre 153
mangroves 85, 153, 280, 281
Mangsit 293, 294, 295
maps 338-9
Marga 272-3
Margarana 272
markets 70
　Bebandem 218
　Candikuning 247
　Denpasar 169
　Jimbaran 133
　Kintamani 244
　Padangbai 219

Pasar Hewan 274
　Semarapura 212
　Sukawati 204
　Ubud 196
Mas 205
Masbagik 319
Masjid Gelgel 213
Masjid Kuno 321
Masjid Kuno Bayan Beleq 311
masks 68, 204, 213, 295, 300
massage 9, 330, *see also* beauty salons, spas
　Denpasar 166
　Kuta & Legian 108
　Lovina 263
　Seminyak 120-1
　Senggigi 9, 292-3
　Ubud 180
Mataram 285-9, **286**
Mawan 325
Mawi 325
Mayura Water Palace 285-7
McPhee, Colin 22, 33, 60, 65, 172, 179, 182
measures 328, *see also* inside front cover
Medewi 95, 276-7
medical services 365-6
Meier, Theo 139, 214
Mendira 223
metric conversions, *see* inside front cover
mobile phones 343
money 21, 339-40, *see also* inside front cover
monkeys 137, 179, 228, 267, 273, 280, 290, 318
motorcycle travel 355-9
　driving licences 356-7
　insurance 358
　road distance chart 357, 360
　rules 359
Mt Batur Tour Guides Association 241
Muller, Peter 34
Muncan 218
Munduk 11, 250
museums & galleries
　Adi's Studio 178
　Agung Rai Gallery 178
　Agung Rai Museum of Art (ARMA) 177
　Art Zoo 255
　Blanco Renaissance Museum 177

INDEX

Gunarsa Museum 213
Komaneka Art Gallery 178
Lempad's House 179
Museum Buleleng 257
Museum Gunungapi Batur 244
Museum Le Mayeur 146-7
Museum Negeri Nusa Tenggara Barat 285
Museum Negeri Propinsi Bali 163-6
Museum of Fine Arts 176
Museum Pendet 179
Museum Purbakala 200
Museum Puri Lukisan 176
Museum Rudana 177
Museum Situs Purbakala Gilimanuk 279
Neka Art Museum 176
Neka Gallery 177
Pasifika Museum 139
Pho 178
Rio Helmi Gallery 178
Seniwati Gallery of Art by Women 177-8
Subak Museum 274
Symon Studio 178
Threads of Life Indonesian Textile Arts Center 177
music 60-1

N
national parks 85
Taman Nasional Bali Barat 85, 280-2, **281**
Taman Nasional Gunung Rinjani 11, 85, 92, 283, 314-18, **315**, 11
Negara 277-8
newspapers 328
Ngurah Rai, I Gusti 41, 42, 52, 272
Ni Polok 68, 146-7
Nirartha 38, 40, 51, 137, 205, 271, 277, 278
North Bali 254-69, **256-7**
North Bali Festival 257
north Lombok 310-19, **311**
Nuriasih, Wayan 178, 180
Nusa Ceningan 159
Nusa Dua 95, 139-42, **140**
Nusa Lembongan 9, 20, 96, 153-8, **154**, 9
Nusa Penida 159-62, **160**
Nyale Festival 323, 336
Nyale Fishing Festival 20
Nyepi 20, 62

O
ojek travel 360
orphanages 259

P
Padang Padang 96
Padangbai 219-22, **220**
painting 62-4, 204, 213, 342
palaces 32
Mayura Water Palace 285
Pura Agung Karangasem 229
Puri Anyar Kerambitan 275
Puri Gede 229
Puri Gianyar 208
Puri Kertasura 229
Taman Kertha Gosa 32, 41, 211-12, 33
Taman Tirta Gangga 230
Taman Ujung 230
Ubud Palace 176, 32
water palaces 230, 285
Palasari 278-9
Pancasari 250
Pancor 326
Pasir Putih 20, 228
passports 349
Pastika, Made 16
Pecatu Indah 136
Pejaten 274-5
Pejeng 200-1
Pejeng dynasty 37-8, 198, 200, 201, 202
Pelaga 249
Pemuteran 267-9
Penarukan 275
Penelokan 244
Penestanan 181, 182
walking tours 181, 182, **181**, **182**
Pengantap 325
Penujak 320
Penulisan 244-5
Perancak 278
Perang Topat 336
Pererenan Beach 130
Petulu 179-80
phonecards 343
photography 340
pigs 82
Pita Maha 63-4, 176
planning 19-22, *see also* itineraries
plants 83-5, 147, 179, 247
police 338
politics 16-18, 41-5
pollution 85, 106, 334

population 57
postal services 340, 342
pottery 68-9, 274-5, 290, 319, 320, 340-1
Praya 320
Puaya 204
Pulaki 267
Pulau Menjangan 7, 280-1, 7
Pulau Serangan 152-3
puppetry 61, 195-6, 204
Pupuan 253
puputan 39, 41, 42, 52, 162, 166, 212
Pura Agung Kerambitan 275
Pura Batu Bolong 260
Pura Batu Klotek 208
Pura Batur 244
Pura Beji 259
Pura Besakih 215-16, **215**
Pura Bukit Mentik 246
Pura Bukit Sari 273
Pura Bukit Tageh 214
Pura Dalem 209, 259
Pura Dalem Agung 179
Pura Dalem Balangan 136
Pura Dalem Penetaran Ped 161-2
Pura Dalem Penunggekan 210
Pura Dasar 204, 213
Pura Desa Ubud 176
Pura Gaduh 205
Pura Gamang Pass 228
Pura Gede Perancak 278
Pura Gili Kencana 281
Pura Goa Lawah 219
Pura Gunung Payung 139
Pura Jagat Natha 257
Pura Jagatnatha 166
Pura Kebo Edan 200-1
Pura Kedarman 205
Pura Kehen 210
Pura Krokoban 202
Pura Lempuyang 232
Pura Lingsar 289
Pura Luhur Batukau 12, 252
Pura Luhur Ulu Watu 28, 137, 30
Pura Maduwe Karang 260
Pura Marajan Agung 176
Pura Mas Suka 139
Pura Masceti 208
Pura Melanting 267
Pura Mengening 202
Pura Meru 287
Pura Pancering Jagat 245
Pura Penataran 277
Pura Penataran Agung 215, 216
Pura Penataran Sasih 201

Pura Petitenget 28, 119
Pura Ponjok Batu 255
Pura Pulaki 267
Pura Puncak Penulisan 245
Pura Puseh 204
Pura Puseh Batubulan 203
Pura Pusering Jagat 201
Pura Rambut Siwi 277
Pura Sadat 271
Pura Sakenan 152
Pura Sambu 216
Pura Samuan Tiga 200
Pura Segara (Lebih) 208
Pura Segara (Nusa Lembongan) 154
Pura Silayukti 219
Pura Suranadi 289
Pura Taman Ayun 271-2
Pura Taman Pule 205
Pura Taman Saraswati 176
Pura Taman Sari 212
Pura Tanah Lot 271, 29
Pura Tirta Empul 202, 31
Pura Ulun Danu Batur 246
Pura Ulun Danu Bratan 248-9
Pura Ulun Siwi 133
Puri Agung Karangasem 229
Puri Anyar Kerambitan 275
Puri Gede 229
Puri Gianyar 208
Puri Kertasura 229
Puri Saren Agung 176
Putung 218

R
rabies 368
radio 328
rafting 92-3, 180, 214, 217
Rai, Anak Agung 49, 177
Ramadan 21, 48, 291, 336
reef conservation 268, 302
religion 46, 48-49, 52, see also
    Christinaity, Hinduism, Islam,
    Wektu Telu
Rembitan 320-1
Rendang 217
responsible travel 84
restaurants 74, 75, see also individual
    locations
rice farming 49-50, 81, 11
Rimba Reptil Park 203
rituals 53-5, 65, 74

road distance charts
    Bali 357
    Lombok 360
Rudana, Nyoman 177
Rungkang 319

S
Sacred Monkey Forest Sanctuary 179
Sade 320-1
safe travel 105-6, 241, 296, 297, 325,
    332, 333-5, 366
Saleh, Raden 177
salt-making 218
Samaya 28
Sampalan 160
Sanda 253
Sangeh 273
Sanghyang 59
Sangsit 259
Sanur 145-52, **146**
    accommodation 148-9
    activities 147-8
    attractions 146-7
    emergencies 145
    food 149-51
    medical services 145
    shopping 151-2
    surfing 96
    travel to/from 152
    travel within 152
Sapit 313-14
Sasak people 37, 39, 47, 48, 57,
    310, 312
    architecture 69
    culture 53, 320
    festivals 321, 323
    food 72
    Sasak Village 321
Sawan 260
Sayan 182
scams 334
sea temples 38, 51
sea turtles 82, 153, 208, 268, 301
seaweed farming 155, 159
Sebatu 202
Selang, see Amed
Selong 326
Selong Blanak 325
Semarapura 210-13, **211**
Semaya 161
Sembalun Valley 313
Sembiran 237
Seminyak 99-100, 118-28, **100**, **120**
    accommodation 121-3
    activities 120-1

entertainment 125-6
    food 123-5
    medical services 119
    travel to/from 128
Senaru 311-13
Senggigi 9, 291-7, **292**
Sengkidu 223
Serangan 96
Seraya 230, 233
Seririt 267
Sesaot 290
sexually transmitted diseases 368
shadow puppetry 61, 195-6, 204
shipping 342
shopping 12, 340-2, see also
    bargaining, markets, textiles,
    see also individual locations
Sibetan 218
Sidan 209
Sidemen Road 11, 214-15, 10
silver 204, 255
Singapadu 203-4
Singaraja 255-9, **258**
Sira 310-11
Smit, Arie 139, 176, 179
snakes 371
Snel, Han 179
snorkelling 88-91, see also diving
    Gili Air 298, 302
    Gili Meno 301, 302
    Gili Trawangan 302, 304
Soeharto 42-3
Soekarno 41-2
solo travellers 342
Songan 246
songket 67, 166, 212, 214, 256, 272
South Bali 131-85, **132**
south coast (Bali) 96, 139
south Lombok 320-5
Southwestern Peninsula (Lombok)
    290-1
spas 330, see also beauty salons,
    massage
    Candidasa 225
    itineraries 28, **28**
    Kuta & Legian 108
    Lovina 9, 263, 9
    Nusa Dua 141
    Sanur 148
    Seminyak 120-1
    Senggigi 292-3
    Ubud 180
Spies, Walter 63-4, 163, 172, 177,
    179, 214
    Spies house 179

INDEX

sports 86-98
STDs 368
stick fighting 319, 321
stone carving 68, 203, 275
Suarnata, Made 275
Sucipta, Wayan Pasek 183, 187
Sudiarsa, Nyoman 177, 186
Sukaraja 326
Sukarara 320
Sukarnoputri, Megawati 44
Sukawati 204
Sukawati, Cokorda Gede Agung
   63, 172, 176
sunburn 371
sunfish 88, 158
Sungai Ayung 182
Sungai Telagawaja 214, 217
Sungai Unda 214
Supadmi, Nyoman 150
Suranadi 289
surfing 6-7, 93-7, **95**, 7
   Balangan 94
   Balian 94
   Bingin 94
   books 97
   Canggu 94, 129
   courses 107
   Desert Point 7, 97, 7
   Dreamland 94
   Ekas 326
   Gerupak 322, 325
   Gili Air 298
   Gili Islands 7
   Gili Trawangan 97, 306
   Impossibles 94
   internet resources 94, 96, 97
   Ketewel 94
   Kuta (Bali) 7, 94-5, 106, 107
   Kuta (Lombok) 7, 321, 322-3
   Lebih 94
   Lombok 97-8
   Mawi 97, 322
   Medewi 95, 276
   Nusa Ceningan 159
   Nusa Dua 95, 141
   Nusa Lembongan 96, 155
   Padang Padang 96
   Pulau Serangan 152
   safety 106
   Sanur 96, 147
   Serangan 96
   south coast (Bali) 96
   tours 94, 95
   Ulu Watu 7, 96-7, 137-8, 6
sustainable travel 18, *see also* Greendex

Sweta, *see* Mataram
swimming, *see* baths, beaches, hot
   springs
   dangers 334
Symon 178, 255
   Art Zoo 255

T
Tabanan 273-4, **274**
Taman Kertha Gosa 32, 41, 206,
   211-12, 33
Taman Nasional Bali Barat 85, 280-2,
   281
Taman Nasional Gunung Rinjani 11,
   85, 92, 283, 314-18, **315**, 11
Taman Rekreasi Bedugul 247-53
Taman Tirta Gangga 230
Taman Ujung 230
Taman Wedhi Budaya 166
Tampaksiring 201-2
Tanah Aron 232
Tandak Gerok 60
Tanglad 161
Tanjung Aan 325
Tanjung Benoa 142-5, **140**
Tanjung Luar 326
taxis 360-1
Tegalambengam 275
Tegalkuning 183
Tegallalang 202
Tejakula 237
telephone services 343
temples 31, 32, 51, 69, *see also*
   individual temples
   directional temples 51
   festivals 336
   itineraries 28, **28**
   sea temples 51
Tenganan 36, 60, 67, 224
terrorism 44, 45, 258
Tetebatu 318
textiles 66-7
   courses 183
   museums 163, 166, 177
   shopping 12, 117, 152, 196, 209,
      214, 224, 288, 295, 320, 341
theatre 61-2
theft 334
Tihingan 213
time 344
tipping 339
Tirta Empul 202, 31
Tirta Gangga 230-1
Tirta Telaga Tista 218
Tisna, Anak Agung Pandji 65

toilets 344
Topeng 60
tourism 56
tourist information 344, *see also*
   individual locations
tours 361-2
   cycling 88
touts 333-4
Toya Bungkah 245-6, **246**
Toya Mampeh 246
Toyapakeh 161
traffic 334-5
transport 21
travel to/from Bali & Lombok 349-52
travel within Bali & Lombok 353-62
travellers cheques 340
trees 83
trekking, *see* hiking
Trunyan 245
Tuban 101, 106, **100**, **108**
   accommodation 111-12
   entertainment 115
   food 112-13
tuberculosis 368
Tukad Mungga, *see* Lovina
Tulamben 236-7
Turtle Island 152-3
turtles, *see* sea turtles
typhoid 369
typhus 369

U
Ubud 12, 171-98, **174-5**, **186**
   accommodation 36, 184-91
   activities 180
   arts & crafts 183
   attractions 176-80
   courses 183
   drinking 194-5
   emergencies 173
   entertainment 12, 195
   festivals 184
   food 191-4
   history 172
   internet access 173
   medical services 173-6
   shopping 196-7
   tourist information 176
   tours 184
   travel to/from 197-8
   travel within 198
   walking tours 181-3, **181**, **182**
Ubud Palace 176, 32
Ubud Writers & Readers Festival
   20, 184

Ulu Watu 7, 96-7, 137-9, **138**, 6
Usaba Sambah Festival 224

V
vacations 19-20, 337-8
vegetarian travellers 75-6
video systems 328
villa accommodation 329
visas 344-6, *see also* passports
volcanoes 80
   Gunung Agung 42, 216-17, 237
   Gunung Batukau 91, 252-3
   Gunung Batur 91, 240-6, **242**
   Gunung Rinjani 11, 85, 92, 283,
      314-18, **315**, 11
volunteering 346-7
von Holzen, Heinz 71, 143

W
walking, *see* hiking
walking tours
   Denpasar 166-7, **167**
   Ubud 181-3, **181**, **182**
Wallace, Sir Alfred 83
Wallace Line 83
Warsa, Nyoman 183, 196
warung 12, 75

water parks
   Taman Rekreasi Bedugul 247
   Waterbom Park 107
water quality 17-18, 85, 106, 334,
   369
water sports 98
waterfalls
   Air Terjun Gangga 311
   Air Terjun Gitgit 260
   Air Terjun Joben 318
   Air Terjun Jukut 318
   Air Terjun Sindang Gila 312
   Air Terjun Singsing 266
   Air Terjun Tegenungan 205
   Air Terjun Tiu Kelep 312
   Air Terjun Tiu Pupas 311
   Air Terjun Yeh Mampeh 237
   Batukandik 161
   Munduk 251
   Pujungan 253
   Singsing Dua 266
   Tegenungan Waterfall 205
   Tetebatu 318
wayang kulit, see shadow puppetry
weather 20-1, 331-2
weaving 66-7, *see also*
   basket-weaving, textiles

websites, *see* internet resources
weights 328, *see also inside front
   cover*
Wektu Telu 48-9, 311, 312
West Bali 270-82, **272-3**
West Bali National Park, *see* Taman
   Nasional Bali Barat
western Lombok 285-95
white-water rafting 217
Wijaya, Made 22, 33, 35
wildlife, *see* animals, plants
women in Bali & Lombok 50-5
   artists 177-8
   books 58
women travellers 347
   health 371-2
woodcarving 67-8, 183, 205, 213,
   275, 326, 342
work 347-8, *see also* volunteering
WWII 41

Y
Yeh Gangga 275
Yeh Pulu 200
Yeh Sanih 255
yoga 180, 183, 224
Yudhoyono, Susilo Bambang 44-5

INDEX

GreenDex

The following activities, tours and accommodation choices have been selected by Lonely Planet authors because they meet our criteria for sustainable tourism. We've selected places that are run locally or by a community group with profits remaining in the community.

We've also included businesses such as hotels and tour companies that operate to green principles. Note that in Bali, many claim a green label, but few actually fulfil the promise. The places we list are actually making a difference.

We want to keep developing our sustainable-travel content. If you think we've omitted somewhere that should be listed here, or if you disagree with our choices, contact us at www.lonelyplanet .com/contact and set us straight for next time. For more information about sustainable tourism and Lonely Planet, see www.lonelyplanet.com/responsibletravel.

CENTRAL MOUNTAINS
accommodation
  JED 249
  Puri Lumbung Cottages 251
  Sarinbuana Eco-Lodge 253
activities
  Bali Sunrise Trekking &
    Tours 92
  C.Bali 245
  JED 249

EAST BALI
accommodation
  Aiona Garden of Health 234
  Bloo Lagoon Village 221
  Blue Moon Villas 235
  Hotel Uyah Amed 234
  Meditasi 235

KUTA, LEGIAN & SEMINYAK
accommodation
  Desa Seni 129
food
  Depot Organic 128
  Earth Cafe 124

LOMBOK
accommodation
  Desa Dunia Beda 308
  Heaven on the Planet 326

entertainment
  Coco Beach 295
food
  Astari 324

NORTH BALI
accommodation
  Damai Lovina Villas 264
  Taman Sari Bali Cottages 268
food
  Akar 265

SOUTH BALI
accommodation
  Udayana Eco Lodge 134
food
  Sanur's organic market 149
  Warung Beras Bali 168

UBUD
accommodation
  Alam Sari 202
  Bambu Indah 191
  Homestay Rumah Roda 187
  Matahari Cottages 189
  Ubud Sari Health Resort 189
activities
  Archipelago Adventure 88
  Bali Bintang 88
  Bali Bird Walks 184
  Bali Culture Tours 92

Bali Eco & Educational Cycling
    Tours 88
  Bali Fun & Action 88
  Bali Nature Walk 92
  Banyan Tree Cycling 184
  Bike-Baik Bali Countryside Tours 88
  Herb Walks 184
  Nomad's Organic Farming 184
  Sacred Monkey Forest
    Sanctuary 179
  Ubud Sari Health Resort 180
  Wayan Nuriasih 180
  Yoga Barn 180
food
  Bali Buddha 193
  Dragonfly 192
  Juice Ja Café 192
  Kafe 193
  Nomad 191
  Pizza Bagus 194
  Ubud's organic farmers
    markets 191
shopping
  Bali Cares 196
  Kou 197
  Truth 197

WEST BALI
accommodation
  Bali Homestay Program 274
  Waka Shorea 282

400

MAP LEGEND

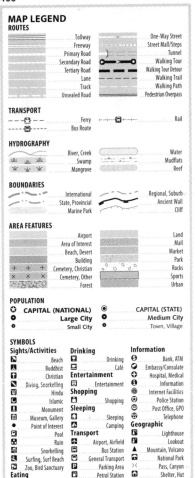

ROUTES
............Tollway
............Freeway
............Primary Road
............Secondary Road
............Tertiary Road
............Lane
............Track
............Unsealed Road
............One-Way Street
............Street Mall/Steps
............Tunnel
............Walking Tour
............Walking Tour Detour
............Walking Trail
............Walking Path
............Pedestrian Overpass

TRANSPORT
............Ferry
............Bus Route
............Rail

HYDROGRAPHY
............River, Creek
............Swamp
............Mangrove
............Water
............Mudflats
............Reef

BOUNDARIES
............International
............State, Provincial
............Marine Park
............Regional, Suburb
............Ancient Wall
............Cliff

AREA FEATURES
............Airport
............Area of Interest
............Beach, Desert
............Building
............Cemetery, Christian
............Cemetery, Other
............Forest
............Land
............Mall
............Market
............Park
............Rocks
............Sports
............Urban

POPULATION
⊙ **CAPITAL (NATIONAL)**
● **Large City**
● **Small City**
◉ CAPITAL (STATE)
● Medium City
○ Town, Village

SYMBOLS
Sights/Activities
............Beach
............Buddhist
............Christian
............Diving, Snorkelling
............Hindu
............Islamic
............Monument
............Museum, Gallery
............Point of Interest
............Pool
............Ruin
............Snorkelling
............Surfing, Surf Beach
............Zoo, Bird Sanctuary
Eating
............Eating

Drinking
............Drinking
............Café
Entertainment
............Entertainment
Shopping
............Shopping
Sleeping
............Sleeping
............Camping
Transport
............Airport, Airfield
............Bus Station
............General Transport
............Parking Area
............Petrol Station
............Taxi Rank

Information
............Bank, ATM
............Embassy/Consulate
............Hospital, Medical
............Information
............Internet Facilities
............Police Station
............Post Office, GPO
............Telephone
Geographic
............Lighthouse
............Lookout
............Mountain, Volcano
............National Park
............Pass, Canyon
............Shelter, Hut
............Waterfall

LONELY PLANET OFFICES

Australia
Head Office
Locked Bag 1, Footscray, Victoria 3011
☎ 03 8379 8000, fax 03 8379 8111
talk2us@lonelyplanet.com.au

USA
150 Linden St, Oakland, CA 94607
☎ 510 250 6400, toll free 800 275 8555
fax 510 893 8572
info@lonelyplanet.com

UK
2nd fl, 186 City Rd,
London EC1V 2NT
☎ 020 7106 2100, fax 020 7106 2101
go@lonelyplanet.co.uk

Published by Lonely Planet Publications Pty Ltd
ABN 36 005 607 983

© Lonely Planet Publications Pty Ltd 2009

© photographers as indicated 2009

Cover photograph: Rice field, central Bali, Jon Arnold Images Ltd/ Alamy. Many of the images in this guide are available for licensing from Lonely Planet Images: www.lonelyplanetimages.com.

Printed by Toppan Security Printing Pte. Ltd.
Printed in Singapore.